The Complete Works of John Owen

The Complete Works of John Owen

The Trinity
Vol. 1   *Communion with God*
Vol. 2   *The Trinity Defended: Part 1*
Vol. 3   *The Trinity Defended: Part 2*
Vol. 4   *The Person of Christ*
Vol. 5   *The Holy Spirit—His Person and Work: Part 1*
Vol. 6   *The Holy Spirit—His Person and Work: Part 2*
Vol. 7   *The Holy Spirit—The Helper*
Vol. 8   *The Holy Spirit—The Comforter*

The Gospel
Vol. 9   *The Death of Christ*
Vol. 10 *Sovereign Grace and Justice*
Vol. 11 *Justification by Faith Alone*
Vol. 12 *The Saints' Perseverance: Part 1*
Vol. 13 *The Saints' Perseverance: Part 2*
Vol. 14 *Apostasy from the Gospel*

The Christian Life
Vol. 15 *Sin and Temptation*
Vol. 16 *An Exposition of Psalm 130*
Vol. 17 *Heavenly-Mindedness*
Vol. 18 *Sermons and Tracts from the Civil Wars (1646–1649)*
Vol. 19 *Sermons from the Commonwealth and Protectorate (1650–1659)*
Vol. 20 *Sermons from the Early Restoration Years (1669–1675)*
Vol. 21 *Sermons from the Later Restoration Years (1676–1682)*
Vol. 22 *Miscellaneous Sermons and Lectures*

The Church
Vol. 23 *The Nature of the Church: Part 1*
Vol. 24 *The Nature of the Church: Part 2*
Vol. 25 *The Church Defended: Part 1*
Vol. 26 *The Church Defended: Part 2*
Vol. 27 *The Church's Worship*
Vol. 28 *The Church, the Scriptures, and the Sacraments*

Hebrews
Vol. 29 *An Exposition of Hebrews: Part 1, Introduction to Hebrews*
Vol. 30 *An Exposition of Hebrews: Part 2, Christ's Priesthood and the Sabbath*
Vol. 31 *An Exposition of Hebrews: Part 3, Jesus the Messiah*
Vol. 32 *An Exposition of Hebrews: Part 4, Hebrews 1–2*
Vol. 33 *An Exposition of Hebrews: Part 5, Hebrews 3–4*
Vol. 34 *An Exposition of Hebrews: Part 6, Hebrews 5–6*
Vol. 35 *An Exposition of Hebrews: Part 7, Hebrews 7–8*
Vol. 36 *An Exposition of Hebrews: Part 8, Hebrews 9–10*
Vol. 37 *An Exposition of Hebrews: Part 9, Hebrews 11–13*

Latin Works
Vol. 38 *The Study of True Theology*

Shorter Works
Vol. 39 *The Shorter Works of John Owen*

Indexes
Vol. 40 *Indexes*

The Complete Works of John Owen

THE CHRISTIAN LIFE

VOLUME 18

Sermons and Tracts from the Civil Wars (1646–1649)

John Owen

INTRODUCED AND EDITED BY
Martyn C. Cowan

GENERAL EDITORS
Lee Gatiss and Shawn D. Wright

WHEATON, ILLINOIS

Sermons and Tracts from the Civil Wars (1646–1649)
© 2025 by Crossway
Published by Crossway
      1300 Crescent Street
      Wheaton, Illinois 60187

All rights reserved. No part of this publication may be reproduced, stored in a retrieval system, or transmitted in any form by any means, electronic, mechanical, photocopy, recording, or otherwise, without the prior permission of the publisher, except as provided for by USA copyright law. Crossway® is a registered trademark in the United States of America.

Scripture quotations marked ESV are from the ESV® Bible (The Holy Bible, English Standard Version®), © 2001 by Crossway, a publishing ministry of Good News Publishers. Used by permission. All rights reserved. The ESV text may not be quoted in any publication made available to the public by a Creative Commons license. The ESV may not be translated in whole or in part into any other language.

Scripture quotations marked GNV are from the 1599 Geneva Bible. Public domain.

Scripture quotations marked KJV are from the King James Version of the Bible. Public domain.

Cover design: Jordan Singer

Cover image: Marble Paper Artist: Vanessa Reynoso, Marbled Paper Studio

First printing 2025

Printed in China

Hardcover ISBN: 978-1-4335-6047-7
ePub ISBN: 978-1-4335-8609-5
PDF ISBN: 978-1-4335-8607-1

Library of Congress Cataloging-in-Publication Data

Names: Owen, John, 1616–1683 author. | Cowan, Martyn C., editor.
Title: Sermons and tracts from the Civil Wars (1646–1649) / John Owen ; introduced and edited by Martyn C. Cowan ; general editors, Lee Gatiss and Shawn D. Wright.
Description: Wheaton, Illinois : Crossway, [2024] | Series: The complete works of John Owen ; volume 18 | Includes bibliographical references and index.
Identifiers: LCCN 2024007310 (print) | LCCN 2024007311 (ebook) | ISBN 9781433560477 (hardcover) | ISBN 9781433586071 (pdf) | ISBN 9781433586095 (epub)
Subjects: LCSH: Sermons, English—17th century.
Classification: LCC BX5201 .O795 2024 (print) | LCC BX5201 (ebook) | DDC 252/.059—dc23/eng/20240812
LC record available at https://lccn.loc.gov/2024007310
LC ebook record available at https://lccn.loc.gov/2024007311

Crossway is a publishing ministry of Good News Publishers.

RRD		34	33	32	31	30	29	28	27	26	25
15	14	13	12	11	10	9	8	7	6	5	4	3	2	1

Volume 18
Contents

Works Preface   vii
Editor's Introduction   1
Outlines   91

A Vision of Unchangeable Free Mercy, in Sending the Means of Grace to Undeserved Sinners   103
   Appended Tracts:
   A Short Defensative about Church Government, Toleration and Petitions about These Things   169
   A Country Essay for the Practice of Church Government There   185

Ebenezer: A Memorial for the Deliverance of Essex, County, and Committee   217

A Sermon Preached to the Honorable House of Commons, in Parliament Assembled: On January 31   293
   Appended Tract:
   Of Toleration: And the Duty of the Magistrate, about Religion   339

Οὐρανῶν Οὐρανία: The Shaking and Translating of Heaven and Earth   411

Human Power Defeated   463

General Index   489
Scripture Index   502

Works Preface

JOHN OWEN (1616–1683) is one of the most significant, influential, and prolific theologians that England has ever produced. His work is of such a high caliber that it is no surprise to find it still in demand more than four centuries after his birth. As a son of the Church of England, a Puritan preacher, a statesman, a Reformed theologian and Bible commentator, and later a prominent Nonconformist and advocate of toleration, he is widely read and appreciated by Christians of different types all over the globe, not only for the profundity of his thinking but also for the depth of his spiritual insight.

Owen was born in the year that William Shakespeare died, and in terms of his public influence, he was a rising star in the 1640s and at the height of his power in the 1650s. As chaplain to Oliver Cromwell, dean of Christ Church, and vice-chancellor of Oxford University, he wielded a substantial degree of power and influence within the short-lived English republic. Yet he eventually found himself on the losing side of the epic struggles of the seventeenth century and was ousted from his position of national preeminence. The Act of Uniformity in 1662 effectively barred him from any role in the established church, yet it was in the wilderness of those turbulent post-Restoration years that he wrote many of his most momentous contributions to the world of theological literature, despite being burdened by opposition, persecution, family tragedies, and illness.

There was an abortive endeavor to publish a uniform edition of Owen's works in the early eighteenth century, but this progressed no further than a single folio volume in 1721. A century later (1826), Thomas Russell met with much more success when he produced a collection in twenty-one volumes. The appetite for Owen only grew; more than three hundred people had subscribed to the 1721 and 1826 editions of his works, but almost three thousand subscribed to the twenty-four-volume set produced by William H. Goold from 1850 onward. That collection, with Goold's learned introductions and notes, became the standard edition. It was given a new lease on life when the Banner of Truth Trust reprinted it several times beginning in 1965, though without some of Owen's Latin works, which had appeared in Goold's edition, or his massive Hebrews commentary, which Banner did eventually reprint in 1991. Goold corrected various errors in the original seventeenth- and eighteenth-century publications, some of which Owen himself had complained of, as well as certain grammatical errors. He thoroughly revised the punctuation, numeration of points, and Scripture references in Owen and presented him in a way acceptable to nineteenth-century readers without taking liberties with the text.

Since the mid-nineteenth century, and especially since the reprinting of Goold's edition in the mid-twentieth century, there has been a great flowering of interest in seventeenth-century Puritanism and Reformed theology. The recent profusion of scholarship in this area has resulted in a huge increase of attention given to Owen and his contribution to these movements. The time has therefore come to attempt another presentation of Owen's body of work for a new century. This new edition is more than a reprint of earlier collections of Owen's writings. As useful as those have been to us and many others, they fail to meet the needs of modern readers who are often familiar with neither the theological context nor the syntax and rhetorical style of seventeenth-century English divinity.

For that reason, we have returned again to the original editions of Owen's texts to ensure the accuracy of their presentation here but have conformed the spelling to modern American standards, modernized older verb endings, reduced the use of italics where they do not clarify meaning, updated some hyphenation forms, modernized capitalization both for select terms in the text and for titles of Owen's works, refreshed the typesetting, set lengthy quotations in block format, and both checked and added Scripture references in a consistent format where necessary. Owen's quotations of others, however, including the various editions of the Bible he used or translated, are kept as they appear in his original. His marginal notes and footnotes have been clearly marked in footnotes as his (with "—Owen" appearing at the end of his content) to distinguish them from editorial comments. Foreign languages such as Greek, Hebrew, and Latin (which Owen knew and used extensively) have been translated into modern English, with the original languages retained in footnotes for scholarly reference (also followed by "—Owen"). If Goold omitted parts of the original text in his edition, we have restored them to their rightful place. Additionally, we have attempted to regularize the numbering system Owen employed, which was often imprecise and inconsistent; our order is 1, (1), [1], {1}, and 1st. We have also included various features to aid readers' comprehension of Owen's writings, including extensive introductions and outlines by established scholars in the field today, new paragraph breaks marked by a pilcrow (¶), chapter titles and appropriate headings (either entirely new or adapted from Goold), and explanatory footnotes that define archaic or obscure words and point out scriptural and other allusions in the text. When a contents page was not included in the original publication, we have provided one. On the rare occasions when we have added words to the text for readability, we have clearly marked them using square brackets. Having a team of experts involved, along with the benefit of modern online database technology, has also enabled us to make the prodigious effort to identify sources and citations in Owen that Russell and Goold deliberately avoided or were unable to locate for their editions.

Owen did not use only one English translation of the Bible. At various times, he employed the Great Bible, the Geneva Bible, or the Authorized Version (KJV), as well as his own paraphrases or translations from the original languages. We have not sought to harmonize his biblical quotations to any single version. Similarly, we have left his Hebrew and Greek quotations exactly as he recorded them, including the unpointed Hebrew text. When it appears that he has misspelled the Hebrew or Greek, we have acknowledged that in a footnote with reference to either *Biblia Hebraica Stuttgartensia* or *Novum Testamentum Graece*.

This new edition presents fresh translations of Owen's works that were originally published in Latin, such as his *Θεολογούμενα Παντοδαπά* (1661) and *A Dissertation on Divine Justice* (which Goold published in an amended eighteenth-century translation). It also includes certain shorter works that have never before been collected in one place, such as Owen's prefaces to other people's works and many of his letters, with an extensive index to the whole set.

Our hope and prayer in presenting this new edition of John Owen's complete works is that it will equip and enable new generations of readers to appreciate the spiritual insights he accumulated over the course of his remarkable life. Those with a merely historical interest will find here a testimony to the exceptional labors of one extraordinary figure from a tumultuous age, in a modern and usable critical edition. Those who seek to learn from Owen about the God he worshiped and served will, we trust, find even greater riches in his doctrine of salvation, his passion for evangelism and missions, his Christ-centered vision of all reality, his realistic pursuit of holiness, his belief that theology matters, his concern for right worship and religious freedom, and his careful exegetical engagement with the text of God's word. We echo the words of the apostle Paul that Owen inscribed on the title page of his book Χριστολογία (1679), "I count all things but loss for the excellency of the knowledge of Christ Jesus my Lord, for whom I have suffered the loss of all things, and do count them but dung that I may win Christ" (Phil. 3:8).

Lee Gatiss
CAMBRIDGE, ENGLAND

Shawn D. Wright
LOUISVILLE, KENTUCKY, UNITED STATES

Editor's Introduction

Martyn C. Cowan

OWEN THE PREACHER

John Owen had the high view of preaching that was typical of the later English Puritans, and his sermon style involved the threefold method of doctrine, reason, and use.¹ We generally find him "opening" the text by carefully exegeting its context, grammar, and vocabulary. He then "divides" the text, a process whereby he identifies key words and phrases and from which he derives or "raises" the doctrine(s) to be expounded. Owen then concisely states a doctrinal proposition in what he often terms an "observation" before establishing it by recourse to multiple scriptural proof texts and supporting argumentative heads he terms "reasons." In this part of his exposition, Owen frequently resolves possible objections to the doctrine by way of confirmation. The third and final element of this expository method involves him applying the doctrine under consideration according to certain observations of its use(s). This can produce highly complex sermons with multiple points and subpoints.

Even in his day, Owen's methodology was ridiculed by some detractors. For example, Samuel Parker scathingly criticized the second sermon in this volume, originally published in 1648 as *Ebenezer*. The theme of the sermon was on a particular type of song from the book of Psalms, and Owen managed to raise over twenty doctrinal observations from the text and applied them in some twenty-five different uses. Parker mocked Owen's ability "to raise Edification out of a pair of Bagpipes."² The eighteenth-century Dissenter

---

1 Mary Morrissey, "Scripture, Style and Persuasion in Seventeenth-Century English Theories of Preaching," *Journal of Ecclesiastical History* 53, no. 4 (2000): 687, 693.
2 Samuel Parker, *A Defence and Continuation of the Ecclesiastical Politie* [...] (London, 1671), 604.

Robert Robinson also condemned the method employed in that sermon as "abstruse" since Owen resorted to "almost one hundred and fifty observations, uses, reasons, &c."[3] Despite such criticisms, the formal structure of Owen's sermons provided both him and his hearers a shared set of expectations. Even those who differed from him on many matters recognized the power of his pulpit ministry. For example, Anthony Wood recalled the impact of Owen's preaching on many of his hearers:

> He had a very graceful behaviour in the Pulpit, an eloquent Elocution, a winning and insinuating deportment, and could by the persuasion of his oratory, in conjunction with some other outward advantages, move and wind the affections of his admiring Auditory almost as he pleased.[4]

Owen provided a sophisticated rationale of his underlying theology of preaching in Πνευματολογια: Or, A Discourse concerning the Holy Spirit (1674) and called on all preachers to familiarize themselves with how the Holy Spirit made the preaching of the word of God "instrumental for the effecting of this new birth and life."[5] This was, of course, something that he himself had experienced when sermon gadding in London in 1642. On one such occasion, he received assurance of salvation through the "plain familiar discourse" of an otherwise unknown country preacher.[6] He articulated his high view of preaching in a sermon preached at an ordination service in September 1682: "And I will give you pastors according to my heart, which shall feed you with knowledge and understanding" (Jer. 3:15). He contended that the "first duty" of a pastor was to feed the flock by means of diligent preaching. Pastors were to preach with a powerful "unction" that came from prayerful dependence on the Spirit of God.[7] It was essential that the preacher placed himself under the authority of God's word: "I think, truly, that no man preaches that sermon well to others that doth not first preach it to his own heart"; and "it is an easier thing to bring our heads to preach than our hearts to preach."[8] True

---

3 Robert Robinson, *An Essay on the Composition of a Sermon: Translated from the Original French of the Revd. John Claude*, vol. 2 (London: Scollick, 1788), 458.
4 Anthony à Wood, *Athenae Oxonienses* [. . .], vol. 2 (London, 1692), 741.
5 John Owen, *Πνευματολογια: Or, a Discourse concerning the Holy Spirit* (London, 1674), 177, 188, 189.
6 John Asty, "Memoirs of the Life of John Owen," in *A Complete Collection of the Sermons of the Reverend and Learned John Owen* [. . .], ed. John Asty (London: John Clark, 1721), 5.
7 John Owen, *Thirteen Sermons Preached on Various Occasions. By the Reverend and Learned John Owen, D.D. Of the Last Age. Never Before Printed* (London, 1756), 106.
8 Owen, *Thirteen Sermons Preached on Various Occasions*, 104.

preaching of the gospel would, he believed, be "accompanied by a powerful persuasive efficacy."[9]

All this is, in many ways, unsurprising to those who have some familiarity with Owen. However, any careful reader of Owen's sermons will quickly come to see that much of his preaching is best described as "prophetic" because, adopting the posture of a prophet, he explains how the unique and undeserved blessings that his hearers have experienced place on them the obligation to respond in faith and obedience, individually, corporately, and nationally.[10] Often there is lamentation because such a response is not forthcoming, and this led him to issue serious warnings of judgment to come. Many of the sermons in these volumes sought to bring a prophetic word to bear on contemporary religiopolitical events and consequently employ oblique discourse in which commentary on contemporary political events is couched in the language of the stories, tropes, and metaphors of the Bible.[11] This allowed for the "oblique discourse" in which criticism of contemporary political events was voiced by couching it in scriptural metaphor. As Kevin Killeen explains, in the early modern sermon, "the biblical idiom was its own and sufficient political comment: a measured, subtle, and precise medium of criticism and a vocabulary of political exordium."[12]

The corpus of Owen's sermonic material is diverse. It includes a number of stand-alone public sermons that Owen prepared for publication, usually in response to an invitation to publish. Most of the sermon-genre works that Owen prepared for the press were delivered between 1646 and 1659, with one notable exception being *An Humble Testimony* (1681). However, there is also extensive sermonic material that emerged in other forms. Many of the works contained in the other volumes in this project emerged from Owen's pulpit ministry. From the early days of his ministry in Essex, he was adapting his preaching for publication in the form of tracts: for example, *The Duty of Pastors and People Distinguished* (1644) was "resolved from the ordinary pulpit

---

[9] Henk Van den Belt, "*Vocatio* as Regeneration: John Owen's Concept of Effectual Calling," in *John Owen: Between Orthodoxy and Modernity*, ed. Willem van Vlastuin and Kelly M. Kapic (Leiden: Brill, 2019), 153.

[10] Martyn C. Cowan, *John Owen and the Civil War Apocalypse: Preaching, Prophecy, and Politics* (London: Routledge, 2017).

[11] Kevin Killeen, "Chastising with Scorpions: Reading the Old Testament in Early Modern England," *Huntington Library Quarterly* 73, no. 3 (2010): 493.

[12] Kevin Killeen, "Veiled Speech: Preaching, Politics and Scriptural Typology," in *The Oxford Handbook of the Early Modern Sermon*, ed. Peter McCullough, Hugh Adlington, and Emma Rhatigan (Oxford: Oxford University Press, 2011), 387–88.

method into its own principles."[13] This was a habit that he would continue throughout his life. For example, well-known works such as *Communion with God* (1657) and *Mortification of Sin in Believers* (1656) found their origin in Owen's pulpit ministry in Oxford. The former took a number of years, and some persuasion from others, to find its way into print. The latter came about because Owen's preaching on mortification had enjoyed "some comfortable success," and he published the material "with such additions and alterations as I should judge necessary."[14] In it, Gribben has detected "the strategies of the pulpit" in Owen's "pithy soundbites."[15] His *Practical Exposition of the 130th Psalm* (1669) has obvious links to his preaching from the later part of the decade, but so too does his monumental commentary on Hebrews since during its composition Owen was engaged in some extended sermon series on the book. Even at the end of his life, we see numerous connections between his sermons on death from the autumn of 1680 and his preface to *Meditations and Discourses on the Glory of Christ* (1684).[16] Consequently, it is important to recognize that the genesis of much of Owen's work lies in a pastoral context in which he was engaged in the time-consuming labor of preaching.

Many of Owen's sermons have come down to us from notes taken by auditors.[17] From the mid-1660s, Sir John Hartopp (ca. 1637–1722) took shorthand notes that he later wrote out in notebooks, producing a record that Gribben describes as often being "detailed and compelling."[18] The extant corpus of sermons contains well over one hundred sermon texts.[19] Many of the posthumously published sermons appeared in the 1721 collection edited by the Independent minister John Asty (1675–1730).[20] These were augmented by

13 John Owen, *The Duty of Pastors and People Distinguished* [...] (London, 1644), sig. A2r; Owen, *The Works of John Owen*, ed. William H. Goold, 24 vols. (Edinburgh: Johnstone and Hunter, 1850–1855), 13:3.
14 John Owen, *Of the Mortification of Sinne in Believers* (London, 1656), sig. A3r; Owen, *Works*, 6:3.
15 Crawford Gribben, *John Owen and English Puritanism: Experiences of Defeat* (New York: Oxford University Press, 2016), 165.
16 Kelly MacPhail, "'This Peculiar Constitution of Our Nature': John Owen's Perception of Death, Ontology, and the *Isangeloi*," *The Seventeenth Century* 36, no. 2 (2021): 271–86.
17 John Owen, *A Complete Collection of the Sermons of the Reverend and Learned John Owen, D.D.* (London, 1721), preface.
18 Gribben, *John Owen and English Puritanism*, 239.
19 The fullest record has been cataloged by Mark Burden as "John Owen, Learned Puritan" on the University of Oxford Centre for Early Modern Studies website, accessed October 18, 2023, https://earlymodern.web.ox.ac.uk/john-owen-learned-puritan.
20 The *Complete Collection of the Sermons* was printed for the London bookseller John Clark, one of "the most important sermon publishers in the early eighteenth century." See Jennifer Farooq, *Preaching in Eighteenth-Century London* (Woodbridge, UK: Boydell, 2013), 82. John Asty was the son of Robert, an associate of Owen. Clark was one of "the principal London booksellers of

Thirteen Sermons Preached on Various Occasions (1756).[21] The Scottish Presbyterian minister William Goold (1815–1897) added further unpublished sermons to his nineteenth-century edition of Owen's works (1850–1855).

This volume covers Owen's preaching to the Long Parliament and its Rump—including his most (in)famous sermon delivered the day after the regicide—as well as a thanksgiving sermon held in London on the occasion of the defeat of the Levellers. Two of these sermons were first published with appended tracts dealing with matters pertaining to the debates about the nature of the postwar church settlement, and these are also included. By the end of the time frame covered in this volume, Owen's role as a spokesman for the new revolutionary regime is evident, something confirmed by his appointment as preacher to the new executive arm of government, the Council of State. He also delivered a further parliamentary sermon in June 1649, but this is not extant.[22] What is included in this volume is, of course, only a very limited selection of Owen's preaching between 1646 and 1649, and one that is restricted to sermons delivered on the national stage. During this time, Owen was also engaged in parish ministry in rural Essex. In the parish of Coggeshall, Owen was preaching to, perhaps, some two thousand people at public worship.[23]

Some of these sermons have an obvious timeless quality and edifying character to them. Others are very much of a historical moment that has now passed. The utility of the former is clear, and the reader may derive immediate benefit from many of the sermons, especially those from his ministry to dissenting congregations seeking to be faithful in hard and challenging days. The latter might have less obvious relevance, but actually, as we strain to hear Owen preach, in a way so unfamiliar to the modern ear, these sermons have much to teach the contemporary church.

---

works by Presbyterians and Congregationalists" at that time. See Isabel Rivers, *Vanity Fair and the Celestial City: Dissenting, Methodist, and Evangelical Literary Culture in England, 1720–1800* (Oxford: Oxford University Press, 2018), 10.

21 *Thirteen Sermons Preached on Various Occasions* was printed for James Buckland (1710–1790) at "The Buck," 57 Paternoster Row, in partnership with the particularly talkative bookseller Edward Dilly (1732–1779), who had premises at the Rose and Crown in the Poultry. See *Literary Anecdotes of the Eighteenth Century: Comprizing Biographical Memoirs of William Boywer, Printer, FSA, and Many of His Learned Friends*, vol. 3, ed. John Nichols (London, 1812), 191. In the second half of the eighteenth century, the Dilly brothers sold "a very large number of religious works by seventeenth-century puritans" such as Baxter, Bunyan, Flavel, Owen, and Sibbes. See Rivers, *Vanity Fair and the Celestial City*, 24.

22 Gribben, *John Owen and English Puritanism*, 115.

23 Tim Cooper, *John Owen, Richard Baxter, and the Formation of Nonconformity* (Farnham, UK: Ashgate, 2011), 40.

Three lessons stand out. First, the corporate application of Owen's preaching markedly contrasts the individualism of much modern preaching. These sermons remind us of how a preacher may address his auditors, not simply as members of the congregation but also as citizens of the nation. Second, there is an ever-present providentialism in the sermons. Undoubtedly, for many seventeenth-century preachers, there was, it appears, an overconfidence in the ability to interpret and apply the lessons of providence. That said, if contemporary preaching makes no careful, humble, and judicious attempt to interpret providence, then the people of God will be impoverished. There are still national and congregational, familial and individual blessings that ought to be, in Owen's language, improved, and there are similar types of warnings whose call should be heeded. Finally, in Owen's sermons we see what a pervasive influence one's eschatology can exercise over every aspect of thought and practice. It is a mistake to think that eschatology may be treated as a discrete isolated area of doctrine of, perhaps, only secondary importance. In Owen, we see how a preacher may be enthused and emboldened by his end-times convictions and consequently persevere even in the face of opposition and government-sponsored hostility. In light of this, we should endeavor to have a proper eschatological perspective permeate the preaching ministry of the church. If our preaching was less individualistic, recovered the application of providence, and declared more of the end-times realities of the gospel, then it would surely speak with greater prophetic clarity in our own days.

A VISION OF UNCHANGEABLE FREE MERCY

The Context of Owen's First Parliamentary Fast Sermon

As the newly appointed "minister of the gospel" at Coggeshall, Essex, Owen was invited to preach before the Long Parliament at its monthly fast on Wednesday, April 29, 1646. The other preacher chosen for that day was to be the London Presbyterian minister James Nalton (1600–1662). Owen had been nominated by the member of Parliament for Tamworth, Sir Peter Wentworth (1593–1675), and the member of Parliament for Hythe, the soldier Thomas Westrowe (1616–1653).[24] Wentworth was "keenly interested in religious matters" and was regarded as an Erastian because of his commitment to the state's role in controlling and regulating the church.[25] He was active in

---

24 John F. Wilson, *Pulpit in Parliament: Puritanism During the English Civil Wars, 1640–1648* (Princeton, NJ: Princeton University Press, 1969), 62.

25 *The History of Parliament: The House of Commons, 1640–1660*, ed. Stephen K. Roberts, 9 vols. (Woodbridge, UK: Boydell and Brewer, 2023), s.v. "Wentworth, Sir Peter (1593–1675)."

nominating preachers and, as such, may not necessarily have known Owen personally.²⁶ The other nominator, Westrowe, had, like Owen, been a student at Queen's College, Oxford, and Gribben suggests that in bringing the nomination "he may have been doing his old college friend a special favor."²⁷ Westrowe was a "middle group" politician and a religious Independent who favored a "broadly irenic" tolerationist church settlement and had been part of a parliamentary committee tasked with considering the remonstrance of the "Dissenting Brethren."²⁸

The venue for the sermon was St Margaret's Church, Westminster, where the Commons usually held its fast. It played host to more than two hundred fifty parliamentary sermons in the period of 1640–1653 and consequently witnessed some of the most important religiopolitical events of the day. This setting aside of the last Wednesday of every month for "public humiliation" began as England was edging closer to war in February 1642 and lasted until February 1649. Members of Parliament were obliged to attend and could face a ten-shilling fine if they were absent.²⁹ As a preaching venue, St Margaret's was preferred over Westminster Abbey because the remodeling that had taken place in the late fifteenth century provided a large, unified nave and

---

Erastianism is the idea, often associated with the thought of Thomas Erastus (1524–1583), that ecclesiastical power is subordinate to the state and that the state may exercise jurisdiction over the church.

26 Sarah Barber, "Wentworth, Sir Peter (1592–1675), Politician," in *Oxford Dictionary of National Biography* (Oxford: Oxford University Press, 2004), accessed October 18, 2023, https://doi.org/10.1093/ref:odnb/29052. Como describes him as one of the "more extreme" members of Parliament. See David R. Como, *Radical Parliamentarians and the English Civil War* (Oxford: Oxford University Press, 2018), 133. The following year, 1647, Wentworth would be numbered among the minority of members who were prepared to countenance a political settlement that did not include the king. In the autumn of 1648, he supported that Army Remonstrance, but he retired to the country in the days leading up to the Regicide.

27 Gribben, *John Owen and English Puritanism*, 73. See also David Underdown, *Pride's Purge: Politics in the Puritan Revolution* (Oxford: Clarendon, 1971), 126, 219, 291; Blair Worden, *The Rump Parliament, 1648–1653* (Cambridge: Cambridge University Press, 1977), 277.

28 *History of Parliament*, s.v. "Westrowe, Thomas (1616–53)."

29 For the background to these fasts, see H. R. Trevor-Roper, "The Fast Sermons of the Long Parliament," in *The Crisis of the Seventeenth Century: Religion, the Reformation, and Social Change*, ed. H. R. Trevor-Roper (London: Macmillan, 1967), 294–344; Christopher Durston, "'For the Better Humiliation of the People': Public Days of Fasting and Thanksgiving during the English Revolution," *Seventeenth Century* 7, no. 2 (1992): 129–49; Tom Webster, "Preaching and Parliament, 1640–1659," in McCullough, Adlington, Rhatigan, *Oxford Handbook of the Early Modern Sermon*, 404–20; Ann Hughes, "Preachers and Hearers in Revolutionary London: Contextualising Parliamentary Fast Sermons," *Transactions of the Royal Historical Society* 24 (2014): 57–77; Ann Hughes, "Preaching the 'Long Reformation' in the English Revolution," *Reformation* 24, no. 2 (2019): 151–64.

chancel deemed more appropriate for godly preaching.[30] In terms of Owen's auditors, the makeup of the membership of the Long Parliament that heard these fast sermons was changing because of the presence of newly elected "recruiter" members of Parliament who were filling seats left vacant by deaths or by absent royalists.[31]

As members of the Commons gathered for the fast, the war that had broken out between King Charles I and his opponents was all but over after the parliamentary coalition enjoyed a string of successes in March and April. Parliament had duly appointed thanksgiving days, one earlier in the month and another for April 28 (further days of thanksgiving were also set aside for May).[32] Now, however, an increasingly intense battle would rage at Westminster about the nature of the impending post–Civil War settlement as the parliamentary cause divided into two dominant and competing factions that sought to shape the peace: "political Presbyterians" and "political Independents." These somewhat fluid groupings represented political and religious differences as well as differing attitudes regarding how the war should be concluded. Despite their names, they were often united more in what they opposed than on their positive visions for one particular form of church government. There are a number of important factors to consider in order to contextualize Owen's sermon and the tracts that accompanied the published version of it: the failure to find an accommodation over different views on church government; the resulting debates about any toleration that might be granted; the English Parliament's piecemeal establishment of a modified Presbyterian settlement; the ongoing petitioning campaigns, particularly by those in favor of a strict Presbyterian settlement; and the "tacit cooperation" that existed between Congregationalists and the parliamentary Erastians.

These various factors had led to polarizing opinions among the godly over matters of church government and liberty, so much so that this related network of issues could be described by one contemporary as "the great controversie of these times."[33] On the one hand, the Congregationalists at the Westminster Assembly (the so-called Dissenting Brethren) and the gathered churches advocated that all the godly (a term that could be defined in a broad

---

30 J. F. Merritt, *Westminster, 1640–60: A Royal City in a Time of Revolution* (Manchester: Manchester University Press, 2013), 112.

31 David Underdown, "Party Management in the Recruiter Elections, 1645–1648," *English Historical Review* 83 (1968): 235–64.

32 Natalie Mears et al., eds., *National Prayers: Special Worship Since the Reformation*, vol. 1, *Special Prayers, Fasts and Thanksgivings in the British Isles, 1533–1688* (Woodbridge, UK: Boydell, 2013), 460–63.

33 J[asper] M[ayne], *The Difference about Church Government Ended* (London, [May 30,] 1646), 1.

or narrow way) ought to be either included in the national church or allowed the freedom to practice and worship alongside it. These Independents had managed to build quite significant support from the "political Independents" in the Commons, and they were backed by an increasingly powerful and confident army. Often associated with this grouping was a concern about authoritarian clergy wielding too much control, thereby leaving the church free from appropriate state influence. On the other hand, there were those who remained insistent on a thoroughgoing Presbyterian reformation, on the basis of the Solemn League and Covenant (the alliance between the English Parliament and the Scottish Covenanters sealed in 1643). Often associated with this was anxiety about religious heterodoxy and a conviction that deviant views and practices could be countered only by an effective and compulsory national Presbyterian church. This position was that of many of the London Presbyterian ministers, influential activists within the City of London government, the majority within the Westminster Assembly, the "political Presbyterians" in Parliament, and the Scottish Covenanter regime. Therefore, in this controversy, zeal for orthodoxy "jostled for position" with zeal for liberty of conscience for the godly: "Whilst many feared heresy, others feared a new persecution of the godly."[34]

In this context in which the godly were divided, an Accommodation Order had been pushed through the Commons by the Independents in September 1644, directing a parliamentary committee

> to take into Consideration the Differences in Opinion of the Members of the Assembly [of Divines] in point of Church-Government, and to endeavour an Union, if it be possible; and, in case that cannot be done, to endeavour the finding out some way, How far tender Consciences, who cannot in all Things submit to the common Rule which shall be established, may be borne with according to the Word, and as may stand with the publick Peace.[35]

The goal of this committee had been to find a means whereby the godly and orthodox could be comprehended within Parliament's national Presbyterian church. The committee met for two sessions: the autumn of 1644 and the

---

34 John Coffey, "A Ticklish Business: Defining Heresy and Orthodoxy in the Puritan Revolution," in *Heresy, Literature and Politics in Early Modern English Culture*, ed. David Loewenstein and John Marshall (Cambridge: Cambridge University Press, 2006), 122.
35 *Journals of the House of Commons*, 13 vols. (London: HMSO, 1802–1803), 4:314. See Youngkwon Chung, "Parliament and the Committee for Accommodation, 1644–46," *Parliamentary History* 30, no. 3 (2011): 289–308.

winter of 1645–1646.³⁶ The idea that such a compromise would be written into the postwar church settlement horrified many of the high Presbyterians.³⁷ The attempts to broker such an accommodation ended at an impasse in the month before Owen delivered this sermon. Owen is very likely referring to this when he speaks about the failure of accommodation between "dissenting parties about church government."

A range of voices was now calling for some kind of toleration, and Owen himself was well aware that "much discourse about toleration has been of late days among men." By now, gathered and separatist churches were meeting much more openly, and the sects were also growing in number and visibility. All of these groups sought some form of toleration, and the loose Independent coalition within Parliament was sympathetic to granting toleration. However, it should be recognized that there was a wide range of opinion over the nature of this toleration, and Owen pointed out that clarity in this matter was important because many "ambiguous words" had recently been spoken and written about the subject.³⁸

The Congregationalists wanted to clear the ambiguity by insisting that they advocated only a limited toleration of orthodox Protestants and were committed to upholding the magistrate's role in religion. For example, in 1645 Thomas Goodwin (1600–1680) made it clear that he was not calling for a universal toleration: "If any man think I am pleading for liberty of all opinions," he wrote, "I humbly desire them to remember that I only plead for the saints."³⁹ Preaching before the Lords in November 1645, Jeremiah Burroughes (1599–1646) said that he joined the "great outcry against the toleration of all religions."⁴⁰ In the summer of 1646, he would answer the accusations made about the content of that sermon, asserting that he

> did not preach for a universall, an unlimited toleration of all Religions, of all things, as both my selfe and others are very sinfully reported to doe . . .

---

36 Murray Tolmie, *Triumph of the Saints: The Separate Churches of London, 1616-1649* (Cambridge: Cambridge University Press, 1977), 128; Robert Baillie, *The Letters and Journals of Robert Baillie 1637-1662*, ed. David Laing, 3 vols. (Edinburgh: Robert Ogle, 1841–1842), 2:326, 343.
37 Baillie, *Letters and Journals*, 2:344.
38 John Coffey, "The Toleration Controversy during the English Revolution," in *Religion in Revolutionary England*, ed. Christopher Durston and Judith Maltby (Manchester: Manchester University Press, 2006), 44–45; Avihu Zakai, "Religious Toleration and its Enemies: The Independent Divines and the Issue of Toleration during the English Civil War," *Albion* 21, no. 1 (1989): 1–33.
39 Thomas Goodwin, *The Great Interest of States and Kingdomes* [. . .] (London, 1645), 53.
40 Jeremiah Burroughes, *A Sermon Preached before the* [. . .] *House of Peers* (London, 1645), 45.

> For my part, as I never was, so I am now not for a toleration of all things, nay I should be loth to live in *England* if ever it should be here.⁴¹

Nevertheless, Congregationalists like Goodwin and Burroughes were willing to tolerate a wider diversity among the godly than what was deemed acceptable by many Presbyterians.

At the other end of the toleration spectrum were radical voices who questioned the magistrate's coercive power in matters of religion and who were calling for a much more far-reaching toleration that would extend to include the toleration of heresy and even false religions. Roger Williams (1603–1683), the tolerationist who had founded Rhode Island, published his manifesto for liberty of conscience in London in 1644. In *The Bloudy Tenent of Persecution*, he called for a broad liberty that would be extended to not only all the godly but also Roman Catholics, Muslims, and even pagans.⁴² That same year, the future Leveller leader William Walwyn (d. 1681) argued that "the tyrannie over conscience that was exercised by the Bishops, is like to bee continued by the Presbyter: . . . [T]he oppressors are only changed."⁴³ The following year, Richard Overton (d. 1664) produced his *Arraignment of Mr. Persecution* (1645), which presented arguments for liberty of conscience and called for a similarly broad toleration. In his *Sacred Decretal* (1645), he warned that the clergy were becoming new Babylonian taskmasters threatening to enslave both Parliament and the people. In late January 1646, religious Nonconformity was defended in Walwyn's *Tolleration Justified, and Persecution Condemn'd* and Overton's *Divine Observations upon the London-Ministers Letter against Toleration*. Such appeals for a more radical form of liberty of conscience increased in the month before Owen preached this sermon: John Saltmarsh (d. 1647) produced his *Groanes for Liberty* (1646), and Overton was involved in the production of the anti-Presbyterian pamphlet *The Last Warning to all the Inhabitants of London* (1646), which declared that "no opinion is so dangerous, or heretical, as that of compulsion in things of Religion."⁴⁴

---

41 Jeremiah Burroughes, *A Vindication of Mr Burroughes, against Mr Edwards His Foule Aspersions, in his Spreading Gangraena, and His Angry Antiapologia. Concluding with a Briefe Declaration What the Independents Would Have* (London, 1646), 23–24 (italics original).

42 [Roger Williams,] *The Bloudy Tenent, of Persecution, for Cause of Conscience Discussed in a Conference betweene Truth and Peace* [. . .] (London, 1644), 18; John Coffey, "Puritanism and Liberty Revisited: The Case for Toleration in the English Revolution," *Historical Journal* 41, no. 4 (1998): 965–68.

43 William Walwyn, *The Compassionate Samaritane: Unbinding the Conscience* [. . .] (London, 1644), 17.

44 [Richard Overton], *Last Warning to all the Inhabitants of London* (London, [March] 1646), 8.

On April 20, the Commons dealt with a "scandalous paper" that graphically identified Presbyterian uniformity with both Roman Catholicism and Laudian episcopacy by an illustration that showed pope, prelate, and presbyter standing together. Owen would have had some sympathies for the point being made: it seemed as if the persecuted were preparing to become persecutors.

Thus, in 1646 support for some kind of toleration was gaining pace as many feared a return to religious persecution. Those making such appeals often envisaged fundamentally different postwar ecclesiastical settlements. Congregationalists rejected unbridled religious liberty and supported a ministry maintained through tithes with Parliament exercising authority in matters of religion. Others hoped for something much more radical. For example, Overton's Mar-Priest tract *The Ordinance for Tythes Dismounted* (1645) was a fierce polemic against an educated ministry supported by the collection of tithes.[45] Nonetheless, despite these differences among the tolerationists, there appeared to be a providential mandate for such an approach: in the now victorious New Model Army, Congregationalists had served alongside Baptists, Arminians, and other sectaries, and the army's cause had prospered under such de facto toleration. Oliver Cromwell had been pressing this very point. After victory at the battle of Naseby in June 1645, he wrote to the Speaker of the House of Commons about the God-given liberty of conscience enjoyed by his troops. Again, after the surrender of Bristol to the New Model Army, in September 1645, Cromwell once again appealed to the tolerance exercised in his own ranks as an example for the nation:

> Presbyterians Independentes all had here the same spiritt of faith & prayer; the same pretence & answer, they agree here, know no names of difference; pitty it is, it should be otherwise, anywhere . . . as for being united in formes, Commonly called uniformity, every Christian will for peace take studdy and doe as far as Conscience will permitt, and from brethren in things of the minde, we looke for no Compulsion, but that of Light and reaason.[46]

Many within Parliament were concerned about such religious sentiments, so they omitted them from the published version of the report of the successful storming of Bristol.[47] However, Cromwell's postscript on liberty of conscience was circulated in an unauthorized version. Across London,

---

45 Como, *Radical Parliamentarians*, 360.
46 Oliver Cromwell, *The Letters, Writings, and Speeches of Oliver Cromwell*, ed. John Morrill, 3 vols. (Oxford: Oxford University Press, 2022), 1:314–15.
47 Ronald Hutton, *The Making of Oliver Cromwell* (New Haven, CT: Yale University Press, 2021), 290.

people were "highly sensitised" to the implications of the triumph of the New Model Army.[48] The Presbyterian book collector, George Thomason (d. 1666), scribbled on his version that it had been "printed by the Independent partie and scattrd up and downe the streets Last night but expresly omitted by order of the howse."[49] For many religious or political Presbyterians, the idea of allowing for Nonconformity threatened to overturn an essential part of English Protestantism. Earlier in the decade, these Presbyterians had shown some willingness to allow a degree of toleration, but now many of them were coming to believe that there could be no true settlement if Congregationalism was allowed. This was particularly the case because of the delaying tactics and outright resistance of the Independents to a Presbyterian settlement. Such concerns were one of the factors that led to an antitoleration campaign in 1646.

This was ostensibly a crusade against tolerating the alarmingly heterodox ideas that had become widespread by the mid-1640s. What was viewed as alarming heresy had arisen for a variety of reasons: the removal of the structures of ecclesiastical discipline; the breakdown of press censorship that allowed controversial religious ideas to be promoted; the New Model Army had allowed radical ideas to ferment, and these had widespread reach through the preaching of soldiers and officers while on campaign; finally, an apocalyptic view of the mid-century crisis led some to believe that new spiritual truths would emerge after the destruction of the antichrist. In December 1645, the London Presbyterian ministers from Sion College wrote to the Assembly decrying "that great *Diana* of Independents, and all the Sectaries . . . viz. *A Toleration*." For these Presbyterians, their concern was that the lack of proper discipline and uniformity was causing the disease of heresy and schism. They believed that various sects and promoters of heresy sought "safeguard and shelter . . . under the wings of *Independency*."[50] The years in which Owen delivered his sermon and published the appended treaties witnessed a number of high-profile sermons preached against toleration: these included James Cranford's *Haereseo-machia: or, The Mischiefe Which Heresies Doe* (1646), delivered before the Lord Mayor on February 1, and Matthew Newcomen's *The Duty of Such as Would Walke Worthy of the Gospel To Endeavour Union Not Division nor Toleration* (1646), preached at St Paul's on February 8. In January, Presbyterian mobilization in London

---

48 Ian Gentles, *The New Model Army: Agent of Revolution* (New Haven, CT: Yale University Press, 2022), 43.
49 Como, *Radical Parliamentarians*, 342–43.
50 *A Letter of the Ministers of the City of London, Presented the First of Jan. to the Reverend Assembly of Divines* [. . .] (London, 1645), 4, 6.

led to the city submitting an antitoleration petition to both houses of Parliament, calling for a strict church settlement "according to our most Solemne Covenant" and demanding that "no Toleration be granted."[51] There were also provincial petitions. That February, in the county where Owen's own rural parish lay, "Divers Ministers about Colchester in the County of Essex" had written to the Westminster Assembly desiring that "a blessed Reformation may be endeavoured against an intolerable Toleration."[52]

Perhaps the voice that best represents this antitoleration crusade was Thomas Edwards (d. 1647). He played an infamous role in stoking fears about the dangers of Independency, Dissent, and the sects. At the beginning of the year he published the first installment of his "heresiographical blockbuster," *Gangraena* (1646).[53] He portrayed heresy as something that needed to be cut off and cauterized like a gangrenous limb before it proved fatal. The work presented a specter of religious anarchy by cataloging 176 errors, heresies, and blasphemies; 28 pernicious practices; and 16 types of sectaries. In *Gangraena*, error was "out of control . . . found all over the place, never subject to final definition or full description."[54] For Edwards, heresies had erupted because of the delay in establishing a church settlement, and he saw only two options: sectarian anarchy or Presbyterian polity. In doing so, Edwards was seeking to discredit mainstream Congregationalists by lumping them together with the radical sects and equating toleration with religious and political anarchy. For Edwards, their campaign for liberty of conscience for themselves would, inevitably, offer protection for heretical voices. Coffey describes how this polemical approach worked by creating the following dichotomy: "orthodoxy-Presbyterianism-coercion versus heresy-Independency-toleration."[55] Edwards's aim was to build support for a thoroughgoing Presbyterian settlement by portraying gathered churches as a source of heresy and therefore as something that should not be tolerated. This approach had some plausibility because although the Congregationalists were not separatists, they had found a degree of common cause with some of the more radical groups in a broad Independent alliance since late 1644. This alliance of convenience was designed to counter the attempts to establish Presbyterian uniformity. Nevertheless, the Congregationalists in-

51 *The Humble Petition of the Lord Mayor, Aldermen, and Commons of the City of London in Common Councell Assembled, concerning Church-Government* [. . .] (London, 1646), 1–3.
52 *A True Copy of a Letter from Divers Ministers about Colchester in the County of Essex, to the Assembly of Divines, against a Toleration* (London, 1646).
53 Como, *Radical Parliamentarians*, 411.
54 Ann Hughes, *Gangraena and the Struggle for the English Revolution* (Oxford: Oxford University Press, 2004), 106.
55 Coffey, "Ticklish Business," 112.

tended to extend toleration only to include the orthodox godly. By the time of this April fast, Edwards's work had already proved to be phenomenally popular. The initial part had already been reprinted twice, and the second part would be published in May before a final installment in December.[56]

This offensive against toleration coincided with one infamous case of heresy being brought before Parliament, that of the anti-Trinitarian Paul Best (1590–1657). Best had been influenced by radical religious ideas while serving as a solider on the continent during the Thirty Years War. In June 1645, he found himself imprisoned in the Gatehouse for promoting Socinian ideas.[57] The members of the Westminster Assembly had appeared en masse before the House of Commons to denounce Best's "blasphemies" and to demand "condign Punishment upon an Offender of so High a Nature."[58] As the Westminster divines continued pressing for action to be taken against Best, intense debate in Parliament ensued over how his case ought to be handled, and in the spring of 1646 members of Parliament became divided over whether to impose the death penalty on Best.[59] One of the challenges was that Parliament lacked the appropriate mechanisms to deal with such a case because the laws and judicial bodies that had been used in the past to deal with heretics were now obsolete. The case was deeply divisive because what was at stake was the wider issue of how orthodoxy was best defended. For some, Best's activities demonstrated the urgent need for a church settlement in which the civil magistrate had coercive power to administer corporal punishments to heretics and blasphemers. For others, the fear was that Best's case would be used to establish a legal precedent for the suppression of those who dissented from the Presbyterian settlement.

Despite the high-profile case of Best and the Presbyterian propaganda campaign, a significant number were unpersuaded that the problem of heresy was quite as widespread as many conjectured and that the antitoleration campaign was alarmist at best, if not outright untruthful at worst. For example, Joseph Caryl (1602–1673), preacher at Lincoln's Inn and pastor of Magnus Church, preached before members of both houses of Parliament, the London city authorities, and members of the Westminster Assembly on April 20, 1646. The occasion was a thanksgiving to mark the ending of royalist

56 Hughes, *Gangraena*, 2–4, 22–49.
57 Nigel Smith, "Paul Best, John Biddle, and Anti-Trinitarian Heresy in Seventeenth-Century England," in Loewenstein and Marshall, *Heresy, Literature and Politics in Early Modern English Culture*, 160–84; Sarah Mortimer, *Reason and Religion in the English Revolution: The Challenge of Socinianism* (Cambridge: Cambridge University Press, 2010), 158–60.
58 Baillie, *Letters and Journals*, 2:280.
59 *Journals of the House of Commons*, 4:444, 447, 460, 469, 514–15, 518, 524, 540, 556, 563, 586; 5:4.

resistance in the West. Caryl acknowledged that undoubtedly "no fore-head can deny" that "dangerous destructive and damnable" errors are among us, "perverting souls, and wasting the vitals of religion."[60] Nevertheless, Caryl claimed that there are fewer errors than people think, and, furthermore, "All is not errour which every one thinks to be errour." He cautioned against taking the heresiographers like Edwards at their word, suggesting that "there may be an errour in taxing some with errours."[61] What errors and heresies there were ought, Caryl argued, to be countered with gospel weapons rather than carnal weapons. He contended that God

> hath given a *compleat Armour* to his Church, wherewith to fight against all the errours and unsound doctrines of seducers. Therefore search the *Magazines of the Gospel*, bring out all the artillery, ammunition and weapons stored up there, look out all the chains and fetters, the whips and rods, which either the letter of the Gospel, or the everlasting equity of the Law hath provided to binde errour with, or for the back of heresie: let them all be imployed, and spare not. *I hope we shall never use* (I am perswaded we ought not) *Antichrists broom to Sweep Christs house with, or his weapons to fight against errours with.*[62]

On the same occasion, Hugh Peter (1598–1660), who had played a prominent role as a preacher to the parliamentary army, said that he did not need to tell his hearers that "every where the greater party is the Orthodoxall, and the lesser the Hereticks."[63] In this sermon and its tracts, Owen shared the perspective of both Caryl and Peter, particularly in regarding the heresiographers as somewhat alarmist and in emphasizing the need to counter heresy with spiritual weapons.

Against the backdrop of these calls for action against heresy and the ongoing debates about the limits and dangers of toleration, faltering steps were nonetheless being taken toward a moderate Presbyterian settlement for the English church. Parliament was attempting to achieve Presbyterian-Independent unity by a toleration of Congregationalists within the national

---

60 Joseph Caryl, *Englands Plus Ultra, Both of Hoped Mercies, and of Required Duties: Shewed in a Sermon Preached to the Honourable Houses of Parliament, the Lord Major, Court of Aldermen, and Common-Councell of London; Together with the Assembly of Divines, at Christ-Church, April 20, 1646* [. . .] (London, 1646), 23.
61 Caryl, *Englands Plus Ultra*, 24.
62 Caryl, *Englands Plus Ultra*, 24–25 (italics original).
63 Hugh Peter, *Gods Doings and Mans Duty* [. . .] (London, 1646), 43.

church. An anticlerical majority in the Commons was intent on revising the Westminster Assembly's proposals for a Presbyterian settlement based on the model of the Church of Scotland. Many in Parliament rejected the divine right theory of the clericalist Presbyterians, fearing that it would lead to the church exercising arbitrary power. For example, on June 13, 1645, Parliament rejected the Assembly's claim that the church possessed the final authority in matters of church discipline. A majority in the Commons did not believe that this was the prerogative of the church. Consequently, as Parliament's Presbyterian settlement developed in a rather haphazard and piecemeal fashion, it fell far short of the aspiration of most Presbyterians.[64]

The first ordinance, of August 19, 1645, provided for the election of parish elders and for the organization of churches "under the Government of Congregational, Classical, Provincial, and National Assemblies."[65] In this four-tier structure, congregations were grouped into classes comprising ten to twenty parishes. Classes were grouped into provinces, one for each English county and the City of London. The ordinance outlined the classical makeup in London but left the organization of the classes in the rest of the country in the hands of Parliament. Furthermore, the national assembly of the church was also under the ultimate authority of Parliament and would meet only when Parliament chose. Many of the zealous Presbyterians in the Westminster Assembly and the city of London viewed the August ordinance as inadequate. Those who sought a Presbyterian settlement based on the Scottish model considered this "Presbyterian" system to be a merely nominal one because elders had the authority to exercise sacramental discipline over only a small number of specified "scandalous" offenses. A parliamentary judicial committee would be the final court of appeal that would adjudicate in all other cases that might be brought by any of the classes. Thus, the disciplinary power of a parish eldership was severely restricted.

Consequently, from the second half of 1645, the English Presbyterians in the Westminster Assembly and the City of London along with their Scottish allies were involved in a petitioning campaign for a strict enforcement of Presbyterian uniformity.[66] This is something that Owen explicitly refers

---

64 Elliot Vernon, "A Ministry of the Gospel: The Presbyterians during the English Revolution," in Durston and Maltby, *Religion in Revolutionary England*, 116–17.

65 "August 1645: Ordinance regulating the Election of Elders," in *Acts and Ordinances of the Interregnum, 1642–1660*, ed. C. H. Firth and R. S. Rait, 3 vols. (London: HMSO, 1911), 1:749–54.

66 The petitions from the London Presbyterian ministers were part of a broader campaign. See Michael Mahony, "Presbyterianism in the City of London, 1645–1647," *The Historical Journal* 22, no. 1 (1979): 93–103; Keith Lindley, *Popular Politics and Religion in Civil War London* (Aldershot, UK: Scholar Press, 1997), 356–70. For a more general introduction to the role of

to in his sermon. In a period of eight months, the assembly petitioned and wrote to Parliament sixteen times regarding the question of suspension from the Lord's Table.[67] Alongside this, the London Presbyterian ministers stepped up their campaign in favor of the recommendation of the Westminster Assembly by orchestrating a campaign of intense petitioning about matters pertaining to the independent authority of the church in any proposed settlement.[68] This was designed to increase pressure for Parliament to establish a more rigorously Presbyterian church. For example, in August they petitioned Parliament, calling for the power to exclude from the Supper to be given to the church.[69] In September, Parliament voted a petition on church government that was circulating in London scandalous and ordered that it be suppressed.[70] Undeterred, the London Presbyterian ministers then petitioned the City's Common Council, protesting about how Parliament's proposed ordinance for the election of elders failed to recognize the "Intrinsicall" power that church courts received directly from Christ. In November, the Council in turn petitioned Parliament about these matters and was rebuffed by the Commons, which was still seeking accommodation with the Independents.[71] Then, in the new year, the fears of "a Toleration of such Doctrines as are against our Covenant, under the Notion of Liberty of Conscience" prompted the City of London government to petition both houses of Parliament on January 15–16, 1646, for the settling of the Presbyterian government.[72]

On March 14, revised legislation was passed, which, according to Parliament, laid "the foundation of a Presbyterial Government in every Congregation with Subordination to Classical, Provincial, and National Assembly, and

---

petitioning at this time, see David Dean, "Public Space, Private Affairs: Committees, Petitions and Lobbies in the Early Modern English Parliament," in *Parliament at Work: Parliamentary Committees, Political Power and Public Access in Early Modern England*, ed. Chris R. Kyle and Jason Peacey (Woodbridge, UK: Boydell, 2002), 169–78; and David Zaret, "Petitions and the 'Invention' of Public Opinion in the English Revolution," *American Journal of Sociology* 101, no. 6 (May 1996): 1497–555.

67 *Minutes and Papers of the Westminster Assembly, 1643–1652*, ed. Chad Van Dixhoorn, 5 vols. (Oxford: Oxford University Press, 2012), 1:32.

68 Elliot Vernon, *The London Presbyterians and the British Revolutions, 1638–64* (Manchester: Manchester University Press, 2021), 118, 130.

69 *Journals of the House of Commons*, 4:253; *Journals of the House of Lords*, 42 vols. (London: HMSO, 1767–1830), 7:557–59.

70 *Journals of the House of Commons*, 4:280.

71 Vernon, "Presbyterians during the English Revolution," 118; Mark A. Kishlansky, *Rise of the New Model Army* (Cambridge: Cambridge University Press, 1979), 79–80.

72 *Journals of the House of Lords*, 5:8.

of them all to the Parliament."[73] However, for high Presbyterians, what was now proposed remained insufficient to establish a properly reformed ecclesiastical settlement because, according to this ordinance, although ministers and elders were given a significant role in church discipline, it was Parliament that determined the grounds of excommunication and appointed commissioners to supervise matters of excommunication. The English Parliament was not prepared to give up its control of the reformation of the church by agreeing to the type of synodical autonomy the Presbyterians demanded.

The petitioning that Owen identified continued in the lead up to this fast sermon with both the London Presbyterians and the Westminster Assembly petitioning Parliament against this proposed church settlement. In March, after intense debate, the City government petitioned Parliament against a revised program of lay commissioners in each of the ecclesiastical provinces, arguing that such power to regulate church discipline belonged to presbyteries.[74] This was presented to the House of Lords but was voted a breach of parliamentary privilege, and this forced the London government to give up its demands for a fully fledged Presbyterian settlement.[75] (The thanksgiving on April 2 at which Caryl and Peter preached was aimed at reconciling Parliament and the City after the controversial March petition.) Alongside the City's petition, the Westminster Assembly protested that what was being proposed was "so contrary to that Way of Government which Christ hath appointed in His Church, in that it giveth a Power to judge of the Fitness of Persons to come to the Sacrament unto such as our Lord Christ hath not given that power."[76] The assembly's petition was also rebuffed as a breach of privilege, and Parliament established a committee to appoint the commissioners. Robert Baillie (1602–1662), a Scottish Representative to the Assembly, castigated what was on offer as nothing more than "a lame Erastian Presbyterie" that lacked the power to effect true reformation.[77] This form of Presbyterian settlement was dubbed "Erastian" because the judicial and disciplinary powers of the

---

73 "March 1646: An Ordinance for Keeping of Scandalous Persons from the Sacrament of the Lord's Supper, the Enabling of Congregations for the Choice of Elders and Supplying of Defects in Former Ordinances and Directions of Parliament concerning Church Government," in *Acts and Ordinances of the Interregnum*, 1:833–38.

74 Thomas Juxon, *The Journal of Thomas Juxon, 1644–1647*, ed. Keith Lindley and David Scott (Cambridge: Cambridge University Press, 1999), 107–11.

75 Baillie, *Letters and Journals*, 2:366.

76 For the text, see "104. Protest to Both Houses of Parliament against Its Ordinance for Suspension from the Lord's Supper 20 March 1646," in *Minutes and Papers of the Westminster Assembly*, 5:301–2. See also *Journals of the House of Commons*, 4:485; and *Journals of the House of Lords*, 8:227.

77 Baillie, *Letters and Journals*, 2:361–62.

church were effectively subordinate to the authority of the English Parliament. As John Coffey explains, "a coalition of Erastians and Independents" in Parliament was now "calling the shots."[78] Owen was an ideal preacher for those in the Commons who shared these concerns because he was prepared to enter into such a working alliance in order to limit the influence of assertive Scottish-style Presbyterianism on the proposals for the settlement of the national church.[79] By 1644, Baillie was persuaded that the Congregationalists and Erastians were working together, and he and the other Scottish Presbyterians in London played a key role in labeling them and anyone else who advocated the supremacy of the civil magistrate in spiritual matters as "Erastian."[80] This was not without reason: by the mid-1640s, the magisterial Congregationalists were arguing that the Congregational Way was the form of church government that best recognized the magistrate's religious prerogatives over against centralized, hierarchical, clerical power.[81] The term is potentially misleading because English "Erastianism" predated the writings of Thomas Erastus (1524–1582). It had been the formal position on the relationship of church and state since the Henrician Reformation, which saw the spiritual and temporal realms united under one head. It was captured in Parliament declaring Queen Elizabeth to be the Supreme Governor of the Church and developed at length in the writings of Richard Hooker (1554–1600).[82] During the Laudian era, the church sought to assert divine-right episcopacy in such a way as to undermine this concept. This was believed to have resulted in what many regarded as an ecclesiastical tyranny that threatened the very nature of England's Reformation church settlement.[83] An "Erastian" impulse for religious reform was fundamental to the Long Parliament's political program and had been one of the factors that brought the country to civil war. Parliamentary Erastians were concerned that same *jure divio* claims made

---

[78] John Coffey, *John Goodwin and the Puritan Revolution: Religion and Intellectual Change in Seventeenth-Century England* (Woodbridge, UK: Boydell, 2006), 136.

[79] Jeffrey R. Collins, *The Allegiance of Thomas Hobbes* (Oxford: Oxford University Press, 2005), 101, 109.

[80] William M. Lamont, *Godly Rule: Politics and Religion, 1603–60* (London: Palgrave Macmillan, 1969), 114–16; Johann Sommerville, *Royalists and Patriots: Politics and Ideology in England, 1603–1640*, 2nd ed. (London: Longman, 1999), 120–21; Baillie, *Letters and Journals*, 2:129, 197–99.

[81] Collins, *The Allegiance of Thomas Hobbes*, 109; Jacqueline Rose, *Godly Kingship in Restoration England: The Politics of the Royal Supremacy, 1660–1688* (Cambridge: Cambridge University Press, 2011), 79.

[82] Charles D. Gunnoe Jr., *Thomas Erastus and the Palatinate: A Renaissance Physician in the Second Reformation* (Leiden: Brill, 2010), 398.

[83] Ofir Haivry, *John Selden and the Western Political Tradition* (Cambridge: Cambridge University Press, 2017), 378.

by the Laudian bishops were now being made by the high Presbyterians. It was thought that this was a threat to the supremacy of Parliament because it created an independent sphere of ecclesiastical jurisdiction. Owen's dedication to the members of the House of Commons in the printed version of his sermon reveals his deferential attitude to the civil magistrate, and in the sermon itself he urged members of Parliament to continue to exercise their authority in the reform of the English church. When he describes himself as pleading for "presbyterial government," it is Parliament's "lame Erastian Presbyterie" that he has in view. Owen is perhaps signaling his commitment to some of the priorities of the parliamentary Erastians by referencing the work of William Prynne (1600–1669).

On April 17, just over a week before the fast day on which Owen delivered this first parliamentary sermon, the Commons issued a wide-ranging declaration that promised a settlement in line with the Solemn League and Covenant but with two important qualifications: first, the church would not be allowed to exercise "arbitrary and unlimited Power and Jurisdiction"; second, there was an insistence on "due regard" for "tender consciences which differ not in fundamentals of religion."[84] (Tellingly, it did not specify how such a complex resolution might be achieved, and it is highly plausible to see the published version of this sermon as a proposed solution.) Several days later, the Commons told the Westminster Assembly, in no uncertain terms, that it was an advisory committee and that it should cease to submit petitions that asserted divine-right Presbyterianism and claimed full jurisdiction over matters of parish discipline and censure. Parliament would determine heresies and oversee the ordination of ministers and matters of excommunication.[85] Those Presbyterians intent on securing an uncompromising Presbyterian settlement were deeply frustrated by this and refused to comply. Consequently, the day after Owen preached this fast sermon, a belligerent House of Commons censured the assembly for its clericalist ambitions, charging it with a breach of privilege and threatening it with *praemunire*.[86] A delegation from the Commons presented Nine Queries to the Assembly, demanding evidence that the assembly's proposed government was that set down in Scripture as having divine warrant "by the will and appointment of Jesus Christ."[87]

---

84 *Journals of the House of Commons*, 4:512–13.
85 John Harrington, *The Diary of John Harrington, M.P., 1646–53*, ed., Margaret F. Stieg (Taunton, UK: Somerset Record Society, 1977), 15–21.
86 *Minutes and Papers of the Westminster Assembly*, 4:82–97; *Journals of the House of Commons*, 4:514–21.
87 *Minutes and Papers of the Westminster Assembly*, 4:97; cf. 1:33.

At the same time, the counterrevolutionary City Remonstrance was being promoted in London.[88] This is essential context for Owen's sermon, and on the day that he preached it, Juxon recorded in his journal that "the City remonstrance . . . finds great cause of debate."[89] Presented to both houses of Parliament at the end of May, it argued for a rapid settlement with the king, on Presbyterian lines, in accord with the terms of the Solemn League and Covenant. It expressed outrage at "the daily invectives against us from the Pulpit, . . . the scurrilous and seditious Pamphlets daily broached against, and in the City: And the great contempt of . . . the Ministers of the Gospel, who adhere to the Presbyteriall Government." It also demanded the suppression of London's "separate congregations" and called for the exclusion of Separatists from public office.[90] It regretted that because of Parliament's declaration on April 17, many now expected some form of toleration. Owen's published sermon should be understood as part of a broader campaign in opposition to the Presbyterian Remonstrance. Like those who were petitioning against the Remonstrance, Owen was prepared to work around Parliament's Presbyterian settlement as laid out in the April declaration.[91]

It was into this complex and febrile context, one in which the parliamentary coalition was fracturing, that Owen delivered his sermon at St Margaret's, Westminster. Owen's participation marked a new phase of "more radical preachers" being invited to address the Parliament.[92] Nevertheless, as Tim Cooper notes, Owen addressed Parliament "as an insider" with references to the success of "our armies" and "our councils."[93] And while Trevor-Roper noted that these new preachers had to be "discreet," Owen's concerns were very clear, and they come into striking focus when set alongside the vision presented in the first sermon delivered on the day of the April humiliation. Nalton had called for the further reformation of the English church according to "that solemn sacred league"—that is, the Solemn League and Covenant that had been taken by members of Parliament in St Margaret's Church on September 25, 1643. In particular, Nalton emphasized how a covenanted nation must deal with the "canker or gangrene" of error and

---

88 Ian Gentles, "The Struggle for London in the Second Civil War," *Historical Journal* 26, no. 2 (1983): 280.
89 Juxon, *Journal of Thomas Juxon*, 119.
90 Robert Brenner, *Merchants and Revolution: Commercial Change, Political Conflict, and London's Overseas Traders, 1550–1653* (Princeton, NJ: Princeton University Press, 1993), 469–77, 499–505; Coffey, *John Goodwin and the Puritan Revolution*, 137–38.
91 For details of petitioning against the City Remonstrance, see Hughes, *Gangraena*, 357.
92 Trevor-Roper, "Fast Sermons," 299.
93 Cooper, *John Owen, Richard Baxter*, 40.

idolatry.⁹⁴ The Presbyterian minister cautioned members of Parliament: "Beware, lest out of cowardice or carnal fears, out of sinful compliance or conformity to the wills of men, you tolerate what God would not have tolerated."⁹⁵ For Nalton, it was imperative that Parliament act against heretical teaching: "Take some speedy course to stop this flood-gate lest we be drowned."⁹⁶ Those magistrates who failed to suppress error and heresies would be "charged with them."⁹⁷ Nalton would have been pleased that later that day the Commons voted to form a committee to draft a bill for "the Prevention of the Growth and spreading of Heresies and Blasphemies and for the Punishment of Divulgers and Assertors of them."⁹⁸ It was also ordered that a list be prepared of all members of Parliament who had not taken the Solemn League and Covenant, "and that those Members be injoined to take the Covenant the next Fast-Day."⁹⁹

After these sermons were preached, both preachers were thanked by Sir Peter Wentworth and the member of Parliament for Cricklade, the religious conservative Robert Jenner (ca. 1584–1651), and, as was customary, they were invited to publish their sermons.¹⁰⁰ The majority of fast day sermons were printed, and this helped to disseminate the ideas to a wider audience where they were read and discussed. Owen's sermon was published for Philemon Stephens, a London bookseller with a forty-year career who had already sold all three of Owen's earlier works: *A Display of Arminianism* (1643), *The Duty of Pastors and People Distinguished* (1644), and *Two Short Catechisms* (1645). With his premises at Paul's Cross Churchyard, he was "a mainstay in Dissenting publishing," and his list of publications is illustrative of "business acumen informing godly fervor."¹⁰¹ At this time, "virtually every frontage in the Cross Yard either was, or had been, a bookshop."¹⁰² The different bookshops were known by their devices, in this case a gilded lion. Stephens remained at

---

94 James Nalton, *Delay of Reformation Provoking Gods Further Indignation* [...] (London, 1646), 33.
95 Nalton, *Delay of Reformation Provoking Gods Further Indignation*, 38.
96 Nalton, *Delay of Reformation Provoking Gods Further Indignation*, 41.
97 Nalton, *Delay of Reformation Provoking Gods Further Indignation*, 3.
98 *Journals of the House of Commons*, 4:513, 526. A draft of this bill came to the house on September 2, 1646, and the ordinance was eventually passed on May 2, 1648.
99 *Journals of the House of Commons*, 4:526.
100 *Journals of the House of Commons*, 4:526.
101 Sharon Achinstein, *Literature and Dissent in Milton's England* (Cambridge: Cambridge University Press, 2003), 201; Kathleen Lynch, "Devotion Bound: A Social History of *The Temple*," in *Books and Readers in Early Modern England: Material Studies*, ed. Jennifer Anderson and Elizabeth Sauer (Philadelphia: University of Pennsylvania Press, 2002), 191.
102 Peter W. M. Blayney, *The Bookshops of Paul's Cross Churchyard* (London: Bibliographical Society, 1990), 5.

these premises "until at least 1665."[103] The printer "G.M." was responsible for a number of high-profile sermons that were published in 1646, producing those by the likes of John Dury, Richard Vines, Joseph Caryl, Samuel Bolton, Francis Woodcock, and William Jenkyn. This is almost certainly a reference to George Miller's printshop in Blackfriars.[104]

Owen's preaching had not been universally well received, particularly his defense of a limited toleration and his call for parliamentary support for all "godly, orthodox, peace-loving pastors." In response, when publishing his sermon, Owen took the opportunity to add two additional pieces: The first was *A Short Defensative*, in which he particularly explained his own reluctance to subscribe to recent petitions calling for the implementation of a strict Presbyterian settlement. This was followed by a *Country Essay*, at the request of a "worthy friend," in which he laid out his vision for a form of church government that might find acceptance by all the godly. It was a proposal for how Parliament's Presbyterian settlement might have due regard for "tender consciences."

Summary and Analysis of the Sermon

In this sermon, Owen presents his own Macedonian call to the English Parliament to extend the work of gospel proclamation. Articulating a vision of England as a land recently visited by the Lord, he calls on Parliament to provide the necessary assistance to ensure that gospel preachers are sent out. In the dedicatory epistle, Owen makes very clear his understanding of the supremacy of the English Parliament and the central importance of religious reform to its work. He likens the task of the ongoing reformation of the English church at the end of the First Civil War to that of the workers in the days of Nehemiah, building the walls of Jerusalem with one hand while holding weapons of war in the other. As the political conflict at Westminster increased, he likened the experience of the mid-century turmoil to trying to find a way through a "maze or labyrinth," something only complicated by kings with "their flattering counselors" and the conspiracy of "malignant nations about them." Readers could draw the relevant analogies for themselves. Changing the illustration, the Parliament was seeking to direct the ship of the nation to port through a storm that had "quite puzzled the pilots and mariners" to an unexpected place, somewhere "on which their thoughts were

---

103 Blayney, *Bookshops of Paul's Cross Churchyard*, 40.
104 Peter McCullough, "Print, Publication, and Religious Politics in Caroline England," *The Historical Journal* 51, no. 2 (2008): 285–313, esp. 296. See also Sara J. van den Berg and W. Scott Howard, "G. M. Revealed: Printer of the First Attacks on 'The Doctrine and Discipline of Divorce,'" *Milton Quarterly* 38, no. 4 (2004): 242–52.

not all fixed." Nonetheless, Owen was confident that the divine artist was at work and the finished masterpiece would be glorious.

As the title suggests, this strongly anti-Arminian sermon insists that God, in his "free mercy," uses various outward means to propagate the gospel among "undeserved sinners." This had been the case since the first announcement of the gospel promise to Adam, down through redemptive history, and on into the subsequent history of the church. The text of the published sermon is replete with references to anti-Pelagian authors such as Augustine of Hippo (354–430) and Prosper of Aquitaine (ca. 390–post 455) as it seeks to exalt "God's uncontrollable eternal purpose." This pertained to the propagation of the gospel at both an individual and a national level. As was borne out by recent and more distant British history, the coming of the gospel to a nation, and its continuance there, was all due to divine mercy. However, England was to "beware" because a nation's rejection of the gospel could lead to God withdrawing the gospel, leaving the people with only a nominal form of religion. At that moment in time, Owen explained that the nation had, by divine mercy, been saved from that fate by deliverance from the Laudian regime. The Laudians had been attempting to reverse the English Reformation with a corruption of doctrine, superstitious worship, and ecclesiastical tyranny, and Owen believed that the English church would have been led back to Rome if the Laudians had had their way. Wishing to press home the need for thankful acknowledgment of these mercies, he claimed that England was, at present, largely unthankful, despite its peculiar state of being the recipient of "as full a dispensation of mercy and grace, as ever nation in the world enjoyed."[105]

Those jeopardizing the cause of the English Reformation were not restricted to Laudians. Owen singled out two aspects of the Presbyterian campaign of 1646 for sharp criticism. First, he identified heresiographers, with their "catalogs of errors still among us," as being representative of those who failed to recognize God's mercy to the nation. Although they were not seeking to return to Roman Catholicism, Owen did believe that they were seriously misguided in their assessment of God's providential dealings with the English church. He was skeptical of their accounts, presenting them as having a distorted vision of the mercy that God had shown to the nation. They were "disturbed in their optics," as if they had "gotten false

---

[105] In the Restoration, Samuel Parker mocked Owen for this "Vision (seen by himself) of Gods unchangeable Free Mercy, and uncontroulable Eternal Purpose in sending and continuing the Gospel unto this Nation, maugre all the Opposition of King and Bishops." See Parker, *Defence and Continuation*, 114.

glasses"; so instead of seeing God's unchangeable free mercy, all they saw was "nothing but errors, errors of all sizes, sorts, sects, and sexes." Second, in a point that was surely implicitly directed against the high Presbyterians, he argued that the cause of gospel reformation was threatened by those "pretending to power and jurisdiction over others." Despite the alarmist claims of those involved in the antitoleration campaign, he believed this abuse of power to be a much more significant threat than the "heedless and headless" errors and heresies of what he termed over five hundred "scattered individuals." The parliamentary Erastians in the congregation would have concurred with his warning against any form of church polity that fell victim to the Roman Catholic error of mixing and confusing civil and ecclesiastical power.

The form of toleration that Owen advocated was not the great enemy of the church and certainly did not threaten Reformed orthodoxy. Throughout the sermon, he displayed his Reformed credentials and argued that the need of the hour was not for imposed uniformity but, rather, was for gospel preachers to be sent out to those in darkness. The preaching of the gospel would bring salvation from a lost eternity, communion with God in this life through the administration of gospel ordinances, and the hope of heaven. This was the one great thing that mattered above all else, and in this regard the English nation was blessed in a peculiar manner at that moment. However, there was no place for presumption because the English "cities" and those "other places" that had enjoyed gospel ordinances in new and significant ways in the past few years were not responding appropriately. If they rejected the gospel, judgment would come on them and the mercies that they had experienced would be only "fuel for hell." Those in the nation who took confidence in their prosperity and "the catalog of their titles" would be called to account, and their palaces would be destroyed and left desolate.

Throughout the published sermon, the Exodus trope is significant.[106] As John Coffey explains, "no story captured the imagination of the godly" quite like that Exodus narrative because it explained that the parliamentary cause was akin to leading the children of Israel out of the bondage to arbitrary government and prelatical slavery toward the freedom of a promised land. Owen presented "Egypt" as the place of darkness and idolatry, and he quoted Juvenal's *Satires*, ridiculing the Egyptians for their superstition on two

---

[106] For the wider context of how the Exodus account was deployed politically at the time, see John Coffey, "'The Only Parallel': The Puritan Revolution as England's Exodus," in his *Exodus and Liberation: Deliverance Politics from John Calvin to Martin Luther King Jr.* (Oxford: Oxford University Press, 2014), 25–55.

occasions in the published work. The nation had been led out on its exodus during the Henrician Reformation only to backslide and heed Laudian calls for "a captain to return to Egypt." Despite the national deliverance experienced in the 1640s, "the bulk of the people are as yet in the wilderness," and there were still those who would "rather be again in Egypt" than take the hazardous "pilgrimage" toward their place of "rest." They were "inhabitants of Goshen," a place of light, but were preoccupied with questions about "the bounds of their pasture." This trope enabled Owen to handle the contentious issue of the bounds of parishes, classes, and provinces within the national church in a somewhat oblique manner ("I shall not touch this wound, lest it bleed"). The "fierce contentions" that were ongoing about such "unprofitable questions" resulted in a neglect of "the weightier things of the gospel"—in particular, the fact that so many were still living in darkness. In a Macedonian-like call, he pressed home his point: "Does not Wales cry, and the north cry, yea and the west cry, 'Come and help us?'"[107] Owen relativized what he regarded as differences in circumstantial matters about church government, confident that the preaching of the "doctrine of the gospel" was what would "make way for the discipline of the gospel." He therefore implored the members of the "honorable assembly" of the House of Commons to explore all options available to them for bringing the gospel to the "poor Macedonians" of the land. His emphasis on the "wonderful variety" of external means that God employs would seem to suggest an implied criticism of attempts to enforce uniformity before gospel preaching has been able to produce its fruit. Owen was calling members of Parliament to "inhabit" these biblical narratives by not shrinking back from their calling.[108]

107 Parliament had described Wales as one of the darkest of the many "dark corners of the land," and a number of itinerant preachers were sent to Wales in 1646. In June, Vavasor Powell (1617–1670) was called to preach the gospel in Wales by commissioners from Parliament's Committee for Plundered Ministers. Then in July, Walter Cradock (ca. 1606–1659) stood in the pulpit of St Margaret's and echoed Owen's call to the members of Parliament: "Oh let not poore Wales continue sighing, famishing, mourning and bleeding . . . in thirteene Counties there should not be above thirteene conscientious Ministers who in these times expressed themselves firmly and constantly faithfull to the Parliament, and formerly preached profitably in the Welch Language." Walter Cradock, *The Saints' Fullnesse of Joy* [. . .] (London, 1646), 34. Parliament sent Cradock to Wales in October 1646. See *Journals of the House of Commons*, 4:242. See also Christopher Hill, "Puritans and the 'Dark Corners of the Land,'" *Transaction of the Royal Historical Society* 13 (1963): 77. Another work from the time that highlighted the plight of the Welsh and called on Parliament to propagate the gospel in Wales was John Lewis's *Contemplations upon the Times, or The Parliament Explained to Wales* [. . .] (London, 1646). Sir Peter Wentworth, who had nominated Owen to preach this sermon, would be part of the Commission for the Propagation of the Gospel in Wales established in 1650.

108 Coffey, *Exodus and Liberation*, 26.

Summary and Analysis of the Appended Tracts

The Short Defensative[109]

This short piece deals with three highly contentious matters: church government, toleration, and petitioning. Owen, somewhat reluctantly, felt compelled to address these because he believed that his message had been misrepresented by those preoccupied with bringing about conformity to the implementation and enforcement of a high Presbyterian settlement. This "defensative" sought to defend the contours of Parliament's proposed settlement by offering some proposals for how it could be implemented in a satisfactory manner. It was also a personal defense. After he delivered the sermon, some high-ranking individuals had accused him of undermining church government and opening the gate for the "Trojan horse" of toleration. Owen was well aware that in addressing these issues he might stir up a nest of hornets in "these quarrelsome days." Nonetheless, after the sermon itself had been "printed to the last sheet," he spent "a few hours" clarifying his position on both church polity, liberty of conscience, and ongoing campaigns about such things.

Owen believed he had been wrongly accused by those who were too quick to impose the label of "heretic" on those who expressed legitimate differences of opinions. Such people ought to be more charitable in their judgments or, failing that, at least be more imaginative in adopting a less counterproductive approach. Too many went into the pulpit and turned what he regarded as the "little" or "small" differences that existed among "godly and peaceable" men into something "horrid"—namely, calling all whom they disagreed with "sectaries." Such people were, he believed, preoccupied with asserting Presbyterian polity as "the only way" and claimed that all problems in the church could be explained by a failure to implement such a church settlement and almost immediately solved by the implementation of high Presbyterianism: "Conformity is grown the touchstone. . . . Dissent is the only crime." Owen objected to the warlike language used by those who exaggerated the differences between the "two great parties" at "variance about government" (Independents and Presbyterians) and turned fellow believers into "mortal adversaries," effectively implying that the kingdom of Jesus Christ consisted "in forms, outward order, positive rules, and external government." Owen believed that such an approach would do little to propagate the gospel and was unlikely to make any real progress in resolving "disputable questions."

In terms of petitioning about church government, Owen thought that many of those who put their names to petitions did so without understanding what

---

[109] A defensative is an argument or plea made in defense of something.

exactly was at stake and that some of those who refused to did so for valid reasons. At the time when the *Short Defensative* was being prepared for the press, a petition was circulating among the ministers of Essex, calling for the establishment of a Presbyterian system. This petition from three hundred ministers in Essex and neighboring Suffolk was presented to the House of Lords at the end of May, calling for "Church Government to be established"; the delays in doing so had resulted in "the Name of the Most High God [being] blasphemed, His precious Truths corrupted, His word despised, His Ministers discouraged, His Ordinances vilified." The petitioners demanded action against "Scismaticks, hereticks, seducing teachers, and soul-subverting Books."[110] Owen joined his fellow ministers in signing this particular petition but explained that he could not subscribe to a petition, even if he agreed with many of the "general words," if it stated that "the cause of all the evils" was the lack of one particular form of church government. To him it was obvious that many of the exact same errors of his day had also existed at times when church discipline had been "most severely executed." He believed that the heresies that often were "enumerated" in pro-Presbyterian petitions were best countered by "spiritual weapons." He also challenged one of the assumptions underlying such petitions—namely, that the House of Commons had not already established the essentials of a Presbyterian form of government. He reminded his readers that, rightly in his mind, such petitioning had "not long since" been voted a breach of privilege because it undermined "the honor of our noble Parliament." Furthermore, Owen believed that there were adequate grounds to believe that some of the petitions were masterminded by those "distant and unseen," perhaps implying the hand of the Scots. Owen was unpersuaded that the Solemn League and Covenant required the implementation of one particular form of polity.

Owen then presented his own proposal in the hope that they would "give some light into a way for the profitable and comfortable practice of church government" and prevent further unnecessary division and separation among the godly. This was an exercise in formulating a workable ecclesiology, which avoided some of the most contentious theological questions, that he had "long since" drawn up at the request of a "worthy friend" and had been circulating in manuscript form. He made much of the fact that he did not have time to revise the document because its inclusion was done in "extreme haste," with the printer looking over his shoulder.

[110] *Journals of the House of Lords*, 8:338; *The Humble Petition of the Ministers of the Counties of Suffolke and Essex, Concerning Church-Government* [. . .] (London, 1646). This was presented to the Lords on May 29 and printed on June 1.

The Country Essay

In this piece, Owen advocated a mediating position that incorporated elements of Presbyterianism and the Congregational Way. As Ethan Shagan points out, one noteworthy feature of the English revolution was "the desire of virtually all participants to claim the mantle of moderation."[111] It was a proposal for a way forward in which the Parliament's recently established national church would be flexible enough in its structure to accommodate congregational government and discipline. Hardline advocates of Presbyterian Uniformity would have been troubled by Owen's comments about the "paucity of positive rules in the Scripture for church government" and his proposals for gathered churches to have greater autonomy alongside parochial structures. The essay began by praising the work of Parliament, through its Committee for Plundered Minsters, for playing an active role in placing deserving ministers, approved by the Westminster Assembly, in vacant parishes so that there were now "in many parishes godly, orthodox, peace-loving pastors." However, when it came to the people of these parishes, Owen acknowledged that "very many" were "extremely ignorant, worldly, profane [and] scandalously vicious." While in most parishes there were at least some visible saints, their number included "very few, gifted, fitted, or qualified" to serve in the government of the church. The need to find a pragmatic solution was pressing because many of the godly were now "inclined" to become separatists. Owen's proposals were designed to find a way to achieve "comfortable communion" alongside the parish system.

First, with due deference to parliamentary authority, Owen asked that the mapping out of parishes into classes be left to the discretion of the churches themselves rather than parliamentary committees simply grouping them into the existing parish grouping traditionally used for keeping peace and gathering taxation. In matters that he termed "purely ecclesiastical," he thought the civil magistrate ought not to claim any privilege. Owen was anxious about an overly rigid parochial system that would inhibit the work of the gospel.

Second, he offered a reassurance that godly "clergy" would continue to minister in their parishes across the land. There they would be assisted in matters of rule and discipline by those chosen according to the August 1645 ordinance for the election of elders.

Crucially, alongside this, gathered churches of visible saints would be established on the basis of something like a church covenant with the congregation

---

[111] Ethan Shagan, "Rethinking Moderation in the English Revolution: The Case of *An Apologeticall Narration*," in *The Nature of the English Revolution Revisited: Essays in Honor of John Morrill*, ed. Stephen Taylor and Grant Tapsell (Woodbridge, UK: Boydell, 2013), 27.

having the power to determine the membership and to elect any suitably godly parish ministers to the office of teaching elder. These ministers would exercise the ecclesiastical authority that belonged to a regional church court with the help of any elders that the gathered church chose to elect: it would be "one church, with one presbytery." Since Parliament claimed to possess the final authority in matters of excommunication, Owen's proposal was that special care should be taken in preparing potential candidates for membership to ensure that congregations were comprised of visible saints. He recognized that assistance may be required from the civil magistrates if the "stubbornly obstinate, or openly wicked" desired admission to the congregation.

These proposals were ones that Owen thought could gain broad acceptance, satisfying the concerns of both Presbyterians and Independents. He then turned to address an issue from his fast sermon that had generated some controversy—namely, the perplexing question of the possibility of some form of toleration. He was aware that there was strong opposition to any form of toleration from some clergy who claimed that it would disturb the peace of the civil state. He expressed strong Erastian-style sentiments as he reasoned that such divines lacked the skill and competence in the "secular affairs" of a commonwealth in order to make such a judgment. He then raised the question of whether the hypocrisy that would be produced by enforced uniformity was better or worse than the existence of heresy.[112]

In terms of his own thoughts on the nature of toleration, he clarified that he was not seeking an "unbounded," "universal toleration." That was something that he believed would not be conducive to the peace of the church but would, he feared, lead to sectarian violence. This was a rejection of the radical form of toleration being argued for by people like Roger Williams. As Coffey points out, here Owen's remarks are "very brief" because "the main thrust of the essay lay elsewhere"—namely, against advocates of thoroughgoing Presbyterianism that would preclude any form of toleration.[113] Owen made it very clear that the uniformity brought about by coercion was not the same thing as true Christian unity. In fact, claims about the importance of unity could be used as "a cloak for tyranny," as was the case with the Papacy. It was all too easy for the persecuted to become persecutors once they had the backing of those in authority. Owen reasoned that if, as it was being argued, the magistrate ought to suppress all error, then ultimately those in error could be put

---

[112] Westrowe, one of those required to ask Owen to preach, was known for believing that religious coercion made more hypocrites than true converts and that hypocrisy was worse than error. See *History of Parliament*, s.v. "Westrowe, Thomas (1616–53)."

[113] Coffey, "John Owen and the Puritan Toleration Controversy," 232.

to death; although those who advocated religious coercion made what Owen judged to be "fair pretenses" to the contrary, nevertheless he reasoned this was the logical consequence of their position. If universal toleration and religious coercion were the only two options, then it would be possible "to oppose both toleration and nontoleration, without any contradiction." The crucial question was where the bounds of toleration lay, and this involved distinguishing some potentially "ambiguous words." Owen highlighted one significant distinction that existed in the various discussions about the extent and boundaries of toleration. Some advocated toleration "in communion" with the established church, despite "great differences in opinion," such as was the case with the Remonstrants in the Dutch Reformed Church in the years prior to the Synod of Dordt (1618–1619).[114] Others proposed toleration of gathered churches that were "out of communion" with the national church, provided such Dissenters were peaceable and typically agreed "in all substantials of doctrine."

Owen went on to state his position on toleration by way of nine assertions:

1. Heresy and error ought not to be tolerated, especially in "fundamentals of the common faith," and should be dealt with by all means that "the gospel holds forth."
2. The civil magistrate may act against false doctrine that disturbs the peace of the commonwealth or undermines "lawful government." (Here the examples that Owen gives are Roman Catholicism and Anabaptism.)
3. Those whose teaching is associated with either "notorious" immorality or "abominable idolatry" should be punished "more severely."
4. Dissenters should not seek to undermine the established church and its ministers, for example by preaching against ministerial maintenance by way of tithes.
5. There ought to be a "charitable" posture to those in error because of the difficulty in distinguishing between error and heresy, especially if "stubbornness" is to be judged as a defining mark. Although some things are so clearly laid down in Scripture that the denial of them leaves a person self-condemned, there are many other errors that pertain to things that are less clear and harder to understand.
6. One great consideration to bear in mind is the "sovereign dictate of nature" expressed in a negative rendering of the Golden Rule: "Do not

---

114 Jonathan Israel, "The Intellectual Debate about Toleration," in *The Emergence of Tolerance in the Dutch Republic*, ed. C. Berkvens-Stevelinck, J. Israel, and G. H. M. Posthumus Meyjes (Leiden: Brill, 1997), 11–14.

do unto others what you do not want done to yourself." This would ensure appropriate "Christian forbearance" in "disputable things" and great care being exercised in the restraint and punishment of those who advocate "grosser errors," especially when they are outwardly "disorderly."

7. The "burning, hanging, or killing" of heretics "for simple heresy" was indefensible. Heresy ought to be distinguished from blasphemy, and in charging people with respect to the latter of these one "cannot be too cautious." The spreading of destructive error did not in itself constitute an act of blasphemy punishable by death.

8. A historical consideration of punishment of those deemed heretics by means of "death, imprisonment, banishment, and the like" revealed that, more often than not, those who suffered were actually martyrs for the truth. The idea of punishing heretics was virtually unheard of in the early church and only began to emerge as the papacy usurped civil power in order "to suppress error and heresies." Then, "for a thousand years," the "martyrs of Jesus" were slain as heretics. Owen mentioned those whom he regarded as forerunners of the Reformation who had been persecuted by the Roman Church: sects such as the Waldenses of the Piedmontese Alps, the Albigenses of southern France, and the Hussites of Bohemia.

9. Finally, it is a logical fallacy to mistake correlation for causation in the simultaneous occurrence of heterodoxy and "tumults and troubles" in the commonwealth, thereby accusing those with whom you disagree with "sedition." For Owen, down through the centuries, and especially in the sixteenth-century Reformations, the godly were falsely accused of seeking to destroy lawful authority.

In any consideration of toleration, Owen thought that the attitude and action of erring individuals should be taken into consideration. He had firsthand experience of some whom he thought were humble, sincere, and peaceable, while others could be proud and wicked. It seems reasonable to assume that Owen would have supported the decision one month beforehand to send representatives from the Westminster Assembly to confer with Paul Best in the hope of talking Best into a recantation.[115] He closed his essay with two final words of caution. First, church discipline should be preserved "as pure and unmixed from secular power as possible." Second, he warned against

---

[115] *Journals of the House of Commons*, 4:500.

even setting out on a trajectory that could in time lead to "new persecution upon new pretenses."

For Owen, the Presbyterian propaganda campaign against toleration that sought to present "the least allowance of Dissent" as "the mother of abominations" was simply absurd. A degree of "hesitancy" was required because of the complex and interrelated questions involved in making judgments about "errors and erroneous persons." The following were among the most important considerations that still needed to be addressed: the magistrate's power in matters of religion, the different "restraints" that were under consideration, what distinguished "dangerous fundamental" error from things in which some latitude was permissible, and separating out the various "interests" and agendas in debates about toleration. These were all things that would concern Owen in the coming years and that he dealt with, to one degree or another, in subsequent parliamentary sermons.

He closed with three pertinent questions to those engaged in the antitoleration campaign. The first asked how religious coercion would be exercised. The second was about what particular errors they had in mind. The final question concerned the degree to which there had been actual serious engagement with some of those calling for a degree of toleration. Once those questions had been answered, Owen was willing to respond.

EBENEZER: A MEMORIAL OF THE DELIVERANCE OF ESSEX, COUNTY, AND COMMITTEE

The Context of Owen's Preaching after the Relief of the Siege of Colchester

At the beginning of 1648, the parliamentary cause was under threat. In terms of a church settlement, efforts to include all the godly seemed unworkable, and with the proliferation of the sects, many were coming to believe that an uncompromising approach to uniformity was the only way forward. The London Presbyterians campaigned for this and succeeded in gaining widespread support. Their pamphlet titled *A Testimony to the Truth of Jesus Christ* called for the proper implementation of a covenanted Presbyterian settlement and for action to be taken against heresies.[116] Over 900 ministers from 13 English counties signed similar printed "testimonies" or "attestations" supporting a Presbyterian settlement according to the Solemn League and Covenant and

---

116 *A Testimony to the Truth of Jesus Christ and Our Solemn League and Covenant* [. . .] (London, 1647).

often denouncing toleration.[117] In Owen's county, the Essex testimony was very well supported with 132 signatures, but it is of note that it expressed a more moderate sentiment, hoping for the accommodation of "tender consciences" and reserving its strongest criticism for popery, Arminianism, and Socinianism.[118] There were other important reasons why the parliamentary cause was under pressure. The New Model Army, now a significant political force, was increasingly distrusted and disliked, especially by many in Parliament and the City of London. There were growing complaints about Parliament's County Committees, bodies that had replaced the traditional local government and were charged with carrying out the orders of Parliament, particularly in the collection of the high taxes needed to support the army.[119] On top of this, the king had signed an engagement with the Hamiltonian faction of the Scottish Covenanters to invade England in support of his cause. Against this backdrop, the Presbyterian cause was somewhat emboldened, and there were early indications that Parliament might give its backing to a covenanted Presbyterian settlement. At the beginning of May, a Blasphemy Ordinance was passed by Parliament, marking the culmination of a long campaign to deal with heterodoxy.[120] This legislation provided for the death penalty for anti-Trinitarianism and imprisonment for the promotion of certain heterodox ideas.[121]

Alongside this, things were coming to a head militarily. By the spring, with the threat of Scottish invasion looming, there was a series of armed insurrections in south Wales and the north of England. Essex, the county where Owen ministered, had been a stronghold for the parliamentary cause during the First Civil War, but now there were signs of the beginning of a turn away from the cause. The Chelmsford grand jury petitioned for a peace treaty with the king that would see the New Model Army disbanded. This country petition attracted some twenty thousand signatures, and at the beginning

[117] Hughes, *Gangraena*, 373–78.
[118] *A Testimony of the Ministers in the Province of Essex, to the Trueth of Jesus Christ, and to the Solemn League and Covenant; As Also Against the Errors, Heresies, and Blasphemies of These Times, and the Toleration of Them. Sent up to the Ministers within the Province of London, Subscribers of the First Testimony* (London, 1648). Ann Hughes, "Thomas Edwards's Essex: Evaluating Gangraena," *Transaction of the Essex Society for Archaeology and History* 34 (2004): 186.
[119] John Morrill, *The Revolt of the Provinces: Conservatives and Radicals in the English Civil War, 1630–1650* (London: Longman, 1980), 122–23, 204–5.
[120] *Journals of the House of Commons*, 5:549; *Journals of the House of Lords*, 10:240–41.
[121] See *An Ordinance of the Lords and Commons Assembled in Parliament, for the Punishing of Blasphemies and Heresies* (London, 1648). Although introduced in 1646, the ordinance was only passed on May 2, 1648. It is reprinted in *Acts and Ordinances of the Interregnum*, 1:1133–36. Coffey, "The Toleration Controversy during the English Revolution," 48.

of May, some two thousand men brought this petition to Westminster.[122] When this was rebuffed, the grand jury declared for the king.[123] Meanwhile in Kent, rebellion broke out toward the end of May after the County Committee attempted to suppress a petition calling for a treaty with the king and the disbandment of the New Model Army. George Goring, Earl of Norwich, attempted to lead this armed insurrection of perhaps around eleven thousand men in order to take London. The army sent forces to suppress these various rebellions: Lieutenant General Oliver Cromwell laid siege to the medieval fortress of Pembroke Castle in Wales; John Lambert went north to defend against any Scottish invasion; and Lord Thomas Fairfax, commander-in-chief of Parliament's land forces, advanced to the most immediate threat, taking Maidstone on June 1 and pacified Kent within a fortnight.[124]

In Essex, Lieutenant-Colonel Henry Farr, an officer in the earl of Warwick's local regiment of militia, led one thousand of his men to declare for the king in a "spectacular" mass defection.[125] On June 4, Farr arrested members of Parliament's County Committee who were meeting in emergency session at Chelmsford in order to respond to the local crisis. Farr's militia combined with a larger royalist force assembled under a number of experienced leaders such as Lord Capel, the commander of royalist forces in Essex; Sir Charles Lucas, a talented solider who, as a native of Colchester, had invaluable local expertise; and a soldier of fortune named Sir George Lisle. They were joined with the Earl of Norwich, who had crossed the Thames with what was left of the defeated royalist force from Kent. On June 10, the insurgents moved to Braintree and en route plundered the house of Robert Rich, Earl of Warwick, at Leighs. Owen may have alluded to this as he envisages the enemy kitted out with "rich booty from their enemies." Sir Thomas Honywood, one of the men to whom Owen dedicated the published version of the sermon, was one of the country commissioners who had not been taken hostage, and he managed to assemble what remained of the Essex-trained bands in order to

---

[122] Robert Ashton, *Counter-Revolution: The Second Civil War and Its Origins, 1646–8* (New Haven, CT: Yale University Press, 1994), 142–43.

[123] Brian Lyndon, "Essex and the King's Cause in 1648," *The Historical Journal* 29, no. 1 (1986): 21–24.

[124] Gentles, *New Model Army*, 114–15. General Sir Thomas Fairfax, Commander in Chief of the New Model Army, had succeeded as Lord Fairfax of Cameron upon the death of his father in March 1648. See Ian Gentles, "Fairfax, Thomas, third Lord Fairfax of Cameron (1612–1671)," in *Oxford Dictionary of National Biography*, accessed October 18, 2023, https://doi.org/10.1093/ref:odnb/9092.

[125] Ashton, *Counter-Revolution*, 465–66; Andrew Hopper, *Turncoats and Renegadoes: Changing Sides during the English Civil Wars* (Oxford: Oxford University Press, 2012), 96.

secure the county's arsenal. The insurgents arrived at Colchester on June 12 in the hope of recruiting more men before advancing toward Norfolk and Suffolk, where they expected to secure further support and supplies from the continent. Fairfax was determined to thwart this design and, moving at astonishing speed, rendezvoused with Honywood's forces and Colonel Edward Whalley's cavalry brigade. Fairfax had hoped to confront the enemy in a swift attack, like what he had executed so successfully at Maidstone, but the royalists retreated inside Colchester, and a protracted eleven-week siege ensued. The parliamentarians built "the most sophisticated set of siege lines of either civil war," which functioned as a "noose around the Essex town."[126] It was an unusually cold and wet English summer, and the conditions both in and around the town were appalling: the royalist cavalry's horses were slaughtered for food; there was large-scale intentional burning of property; allegations were made that the royalists were using poisoned bullets; and there was a refusal to relieve the suffering of noncombatants.[127] As Gribben writes, "Even by the standards of early modern warfare, the city's residents witnessed and were subject to spectacular suffering."[128] It seemed almost apocalyptic: one observer wrote that a "terrible red duskie bloody Cloud seemed to hang over the Towne all night."[129] The town was left devastated:

> The town hath suffered as well as the men, being ruined in its buildings, provisions, people, and trade; what fair streets are here of stately houses now laid in ashes? . . . [T]hey who had houses to live in now live desolate for want of habitation.[130]

Elsewhere the parliamentary army's cause prospered. Pembroke Castle fell in mid-July after a six-week-long siege, and this allowed Cromwell to join Lambert to confront the Scottish Engagers and English royalists at the Battle of Preston on August 17–19. The New Model Army routed the Scottish-royalist army, taking some ten thousand prisoners in a victory that signaled the end of the Second Civil War. News of the humiliating defeat of their allies reached Colchester at the end of August, whereupon all hope

---

126 Barbara Donagan, *War in England, 1642–1649* (Oxford: Oxford University Press, 2010), 323; Mark Kishlansky, *A Monarchy Transformed: Britain, 1603–1714* (London: Penguin, 1997), 180.
127 Brian Lyndon, "The Parliament's Army in Essex, 1648," *Journal of the Society for Army Historical Research* 59, no. 239 (1981): 233.
128 Gribben, *John Owen and English Puritanism*, 92.
129 *Colchesters Teares: Affecting and Afflicting City and Country* [. . .] (London, 1648), 13–14.
130 *A True and Exact Relation of the Taking of Colchester* (London, 1648), 4.

of relief for those holed up in the town vanished. Threatened by mutiny, the royalists in the town surrendered on August 28. Lord Capel and the Earl of Norwich were sent to be judged by the House of Lords.[131] Fairfax convened a council of war at the King's Head tavern, and afterward Henry Ireton led two of the royalist commanders, Lucas and Lisle, out to where they were summarily executed by firing squad to "avenge for the innocent blood they have caused to be spilt, and the trouble, damage, and mischief they have brought upon the town."[132] All this was in accord with the laws of war at the time.[133]

Colchester was only a few miles from Coggeshall, and over the summer of 1648, Owen became acquainted with Fairfax and other senior members of the New Model Army. After the siege, he preached two thanksgiving sermons. The first was preached before Fairfax at a thanksgiving on August 31, and the second before members of the recently liberated County Committee on September 28.[134] The two sermons appeared under the title *Ebenezer: A Memorial for the Deliverance of Essex, County, and Committee*. The work is part of a wider body of printed works designed to represent and interpret the events in Colchester, such as the illustrated broadsheet *The Siege of Colchester By the Lord Fairfax As It Was With the Line and Outworks* (1648).[135] Gribben suggests that Owen's decision to self-publish the work is evidence that Philemon Stephens "was no longer prepared to take financial risk on a relatively unknown writer in the increasingly crowded world of print."[136] Evidence from ornaments and decorative initials reveal the printer that he used to be William Wilson (d. 1665) of Little St Bartholomew's Hospital.[137] The annotation on the copy acquired by the book collector George Thomason indicated that the work was available in December 1648.

---

131 Proceedings against them opened on February 10, 1649, in the newly convened High Court of Justice. They were sentenced to death on March 6. Norwich's life was spared, but Capel was executed on March 9 outside Westminster Hall.
132 Donagan, *War in England*, 364.
133 Ashton, *Counter-Revolution*, 438; Gentles, *New Model Army*, 120–21.
134 Parliament ordered that the victory should be celebrated on September 7. See Mears et al., *Special Prayers, Fasts and Thanksgivings*, 490–91.
135 For a discussion of this piece of print propaganda, see Anke Fischer-Kattner, "Colchester's Plight in European Perspective: Printed Representations of Seventeenth-Century Siege Warfare," in *The World of the Siege: Representations of Early Modern Positional Warfare*, ed. Anke Fischer-Kattner and Jamel Ostwald (Leiden: Brill, 2019), 44–84.
136 Crawford Gribben, "Becoming John Owen: The Making of an Evangelical Reputation," *Westminster Theological Journal* 79, no. 2 (2017): 313.
137 C. William Miller, "A London Ornament Stock, 1598–1683," *Studies in Bibliography* 7 (1955): 125–51.

The title of the published work evokes the name of the stone that the prophet Samuel set up to memorialize a great victory (1 Sam. 7:10–14). The parallels to the events of the summer of 1648 would not have been lost on the biblically literate: captured cities were recovered, resulting in peace from both external invaders (either the Philistines or the Scots) and internal enemies (either the Amorites or the royalists).[138] The first preface was addressed to Lord Fairfax and portrayed the general in a light very different from the royalist propagandists who, in the immediate aftermath of Colchester, had vilified him as dishonorable and barbaric.[139] The second preface was addressed to four men: Sir William Masham,[140] Sir William Rowe (who had been imprisoned in the town), Sir Henry Mildmay of Wanstead,[141] and Sir Thomas Honywood (who had been with Fairfax's troops).[142] Through the experience, Owen was getting to know some important figures on the national stage, and Masham and Mildmay would provide Owen with opportunities to once again preach to Parliament in the coming years.[143]

---

138 In *Steadfastness of the Promises* [. . .] (London, 1650), Owen spoke of raising an Ebenezer for the victories in the Cromwellian conquest of Ireland.

139 Andrew Hopper, *"Black Tom": Sir Thomas Fairfax and the English Revolution* (Manchester: Manchester University Press, 2007), 87.

140 Sir William Masham (1591–1656) of Otes, High Laver, was a well-established member of the Essex gentry, member of Parliament, and the most prominent prisoner during the siege of Colchester. He was described as "a very factious Puritan" and sought a strong and reformed state church. Masham was "clearly suspicious of the moves towards greater religious freedom." Recently appointed to the Derby House Committee, he was also active in arranging fast preachers for Parliament. Masham was released in a prisoner exchange early in August 1648. See Donagan, *War in England*, 349; Underdown, *Pride's Purge*, 188, 313; *History of Parliament*, s.v. "Masham, Sir William, 1st bt. (1591–1656)."

141 Sir Henry Mildmay (ca. 1594–1664) was the member of Parliament for Maldon and had a grand estate in Wanstead, Essex. Lyndon describes him as "one of the Parliamentary zealots of the county." He was a political ally of the Earl of Warwick and his wife was a member of the gathered church in Stepney. A war party member of Parliament, Mildmay had been instrumental in raising troops to support Fairfax at the siege of Colchester and had been one of those tasked with offering Parliament's thanks to Fairfax after the rebels surrendered. See Lyndon, "Essex and the King's Cause in 1648," 22–23; Brenner, *Merchants and Revolution*, 533; Underdown, *Pride's Purge*, 93, 100, 127, 138.

142 Sir Thomas Honywood of Marks Hall, Essex, was a parliamentary colonel who led a body of militia that played a prominent role in the siege of Colchester. With most of the other members of the parliamentary standing committee held captive, and despite some from his own regiment having defected, Honywood succeeded in securing the county magazine before it could be seized by the royalist forces. He led the delegation that accepted the surrender of Colchester on August 27 and went on to act as the governor of the town. Underdown, *Pride's Purge*, 312; *History of Parliament*, s.v. "Honywood, Sir Thomas (1587–1666)."

143 *Journals of the House of Commons*, 6:107, 152, 217, 374, 544; 7:13.

Summary and Analysis of the Sermon

Owen opens the first sermon with a reflection on the "mixed" nature of providence in contemporary events: "an evil time" of "fearful judgments," not only in war but also in poor weather and failed harvests, while simultaneously a time of mercy in "unexpected deliverance." As Gribben notes, the Second Civil War was "a crisis of existential propositions, in which providence itself seemed fickle."[144] Owen appealed to a text to which he would often return in the years ahead to describe "a dispensation that seems almost as much against us, as for us": "the light shall not be clear nor dark: but it shall be one day which shall be known to the Lord: not day nor night" (Zech. 14:6–7). In such a season, the "well-tuned" response of the godly (God's "secret ones") to the "speaking providence of God" will be "to rejoice with thankful obedience for mercy received, and to be humbled with soul-searching, amending repentance, for judgments inflicted." "Special mercies," such as the deliverance of Colchester, "must have special observation" by "remembrance with thanksgiving." Owen made particular reference to the need to remember the events of Marston Moor and Naseby and to add to this list the parliamentary victories of 1648. The preacher rhapsodized on the words of Habakkuk 3:3, drawing the strongest of parallels between the acts of salvation that Habakkuk remembered in his prayer and the contemporary parliamentary victories:

> God came from Naseby, and the holy one from the West [Pembroke]: Selah: his glory covered the Heavens, and the earth was full of his praise. He went forth in the North [Lancashire], and in the East [Colchester] he did not withhold his hand.

The "manifestation" of such great works of God would be an encouragement to press on and "serve providence" in "great works." The published work was dedicated to Fairfax and other leading members of the parliamentary cause and it called them to persevere in "great undertakings" and in "great and high" matters, not turning back in "the heat of the day." From Owen's point of view, he had seen too many "drop off" in apostasy, not least the "backslidings of our days" by those "acted upon by engagements." This is likely a reference to the Scots who supported the Treaty of Engagement with King Charles. The Scottish Covenanters had played a vital role in the victory of Marston Moor, but Owen believed that those among them who had supported the Engagement had actually apostatized from God's work. To avoid

---

[144] Gribben, *John Owen and English Puritanism*, 94.

such a danger and in order to "serve the will of God in this generation" it was necessary to conduct "a diligent inquiry" into "the designs of God." The implication was that those in leadership needed "new light" to face the challenges ahead. This would require "applications of providences, with wise consideration of times and seasons."

Owen insisted that the judgments that had been experienced in the "visitations of the last years" ought to be taken as a warning to "the enemies of this nation," those "that hate us," that their "total destruction" lay ahead. Contrary to the expectations of many, the day of those "factious Independents" did not come because God was on their side. God's people would have their "portion and inheritance," and all of those, including "kings and others," who might attempt to take away "their liberties, ordinances, privileges, [and] lives" would be guilty of touching "forbidden things." Aware that the language of sacrilege had gained currency in recent debates, he referred to the fable of the eagle that stole sacrificial flesh from an altar, not realizing that a coal was still attached that consequently set her nest on fire. Owen distinguished his understanding of sacrilege from those who had "abused" the notion to argue against the sale of episcopal and church lands—for example, in recent days, the authors of *The Humble Petitions* [. . .] *of the Eastern Association* (April 1648). Owen cautioned those in power to remember how in war God had broken those who would encroach upon the privileges of the saints. Now that peace had come, he cautioned against any attempt to take away the "liberties, privileges, ordinances or ways of worship" from the godly. Owen was familiar with the arguments that claimed that religious uniformity was essential for "peace and truth" but regarded them as "arguments for persecution . . . dyed in the blood" of the martyrs from "1,200 years" of persecution under the antichrist. In the preface addressed to members of the parliamentary County Committee, some of whom were members of Parliament, Owen urged that serious consideration needed to be given to the danger of "encroaching" upon the "portion, lot, privileges or inheritance" of the saints, particularly by any form of persecution of the godly. Owen stated that all who did so would fall under divine judgment, which he illustrated by referring to the divine punishment that fell on King Uzziah when he attempted to offer incense in the temple. In his pride, Uzziah had ignored warnings from the priests, attempted to take to himself their ministerial privilege, and was consequently smitten with leprosy (2 Chron. 26:18).[145] This proof text was also used in the New England *Cambridge Platform* (1648)(the preface of which expressed the

---

145 Lyndon, "Essex and the King's Cause," 19.

desire that "the example of such poor outcasts as ourselves, might prevail if not with all . . . yet with some other of our brethren in England"):

> As it is unlawful for church officers to meddle with the sword of the magistrate, so it is unlawful for the magistrate to meddle with the work proper to church officers. The acts of Moses and David, who were not only princes, but prophets, were extraordinary, therefore not imitable. Against such usurpation, the Lord witnesses, by smiting Uzziah with leprosy, for presuming to offer incense.[146]

Owen's point contrasted sharply with that offered by the other preacher at the public thanksgiving in Romford, Essex, the rector of Kedington in Suffolk, Samuel Fairclough (1594–1677). His sermon, later published as *The Prisoners Praises*,[147] was from Psalm 149:

> Let the high Praises of God be in their mouths, and a two edged sword in their hands; to execute vengeance upon the heathen; and punishment upon the people. To bind their Kings with Chains, and their Nobles with Fetters of Iron (Ps. 149:6–8).

Fairclough told his hearers, "Raise the actual expression of your praise with the two-edged Sword of God in your hand, by improving your liberty by way of Vindication in executing vengeance upon the Heathen, punishments upon the People; by binding their Kings in chains, and Princes in fetters of iron." The chains with which Fairclough wished the king to be bound were none other than "our solemn League and Covenant" and the principal cause of the Second Civil War was Parliament's failure to implement a covenanted settlement.[148] In complete contrast, Owen went so far as to claim relief of the siege to be a providential warning to those who were endeavoring to impose such a Presbyterian settlement. Owen believed that the saints were being liberated from their Babylonian captivity, and that any who continued to hinder or oppose them would face this "vengeance of the temple."

---

[146] *The Cambridge Platform* (1648), XVII.v: "Of the Civil Magistrate's Powr in Matters Ecclesiastical." For text, see *A Platform of Church Discipline Gathered Out of the Word of God: And Agreed Upon by the Elders: And Messengers of the Churches Assembled in the Synod at Cambridge in New England* (Cambridge, MA, 1649), 28.

[147] Samuel Clarke, *The Lives of Sundry Eminent Persons in This Later Age* [. . .] (London, 1683), 172–73.

[148] Samuel Fairclough, *The Prisoners Praises for Their Deliverance from the Long Imprisonment in Colchester* [. . .] (London, 1650), 37–40.

Owen's sermon sounded a note of strong support for the soldiers of the New Model Army, whom he regarded as "worthy instruments" carrying out the divine purpose as they went about "the work of the Lord." The point was clear: Fairfax and Cromwell had been led by God, who had "marched before them, and traced out their way from Kent to Essex, [and] from Wales to the North." "Round about" were "oppressing nations" who were either "gross idolaters" or "envious apostates" (probably an implied reference to the Irish and the Scots). Now that the "season of the church's deliverance" had come, the remaining opposers would be "subdued." For Owen this could be seen written with the finger of God in recent events in "the workings of God's providences" during the Second Civil War: "crafty counsels" being brought to nothing, armies destroyed, and strongholds demolished. In Essex, Owen portrayed the enemy as outnumbering those loyal to Parliament with "very many old experienced soldiers" among their number. There is some dispute about the size of the military forces involved at Colchester, but Donagan supposes that Fairfax's troops were indeed outnumbered.[149] Owen's suggestion that those loyal to Parliament were outnumbered ten to one ("near as many thousands, as we had hundreds") may not necessarily be hyperbolic, especially if taken as a description of the situation prior to the arrival of Fairfax. Ireton's account would concur with Owen's likening Colchester and its defenders to "a great beehive, and our army to a small swarm of bees sticking on one side of it."[150] Despite such opposition, the army had prevailed.

In the second sermon, Owen considered the recent surrender of Colchester as "a mercy of first magnitude" and a significant demonstration of "God's power and the efficacy of his providence." Essex had largely been spared from conflict during the first civil war, and, in Owen's mind, the saints had abused the peace. However, the conflict of the summer of 1648 had seen the people of God united and "set in a hopeful way." Owen identified the hand of providence at work in what he believed to be the "innumerable" foolish choices made by the enemy. He took this to be evidence of God thwarting and confusing the plans of those who had plotted and schemed for rebellion in at least three ways. First, in Owen's estimation, had the royalists not taken up arms in rebellion, such were the "divisions" in the parliamentary cause that within six months "I think we should suddenly have chosen them, and theirs, to be umpires of our

---

149 Donagan, *War in England*, 318. See also Austin Woolrych, *Britain in Revolution, 1625–1660* (Oxford: Oxford University Press, 2002), 413.
150 Edmund Ludlow, *The Memoirs of Edmund Ludlow, Lietenant-General of the Horse in the Army of the Commonwealth of England, 1625–1672*, ed. C. H. Firth, 2 vols. (Oxford: Clarendon, 1894), 1:197.

quarrels." Second, Owen placed great emphasis on the uncoordinated nature of the various risings. Had the rebellions been coordinated to coincide with the invasion of the Engager army, the whole nation would have been "swallowed up in that deluge." The Lord had thwarted their plans, and so the "homebred eruptions" were suppressed in turn, and the "discontented soldiery and divided nation" were roused and united, "ready to resist the Scottish invasion." The Essex rebellion was allowed to grow in strength only after Fairfax had "broken" the royalists in Kent and after the surrender of Pembroke castle, the last rebel stronghold in south Wales, on June 11. This providential ordering of events meant that Cromwell was able to march north to bolster the parliamentary forces set to confront the Duke of Hamilton's Scottish Engagers. This Scottish invasion was doomed from the start because of lack of resources and being several weeks too late to coincide with the risings in England and Wales. After the battle of Preston and the subsequent rout of the Duke of Hamilton's forces at Winwick Pass, several thousand of the Engager army had been slaughtered and almost ten thousand captured.[151] The third way in which the folly of the enemy was seen occurred just prior to the siege of Colchester, on the night of June 11, when the trained bands from Owen's own "little Village" of Coggeshall succeeded in blocking the road ahead of the advancing royalists. Compared to their enemy, these Coggeshall men were inexperienced (Owen said there were "not three men, that had ever seen any fighting"), and yet they forced the royalists to make a detour in order to reach their destination.[152] Fourth, the Colchester royalists refused Fairfax's offer of peace on the basis of a number of false hopes. For example, unaware that the parliamentary navy had blockaded the mouth of the River Colne, they had been expecting seaborne relief. Similarly, they had misplaced optimism that there might be a treaty between the king and Parliament.[153]

Owen recounted that many had doubted that Fairfax's army would prevail—"Greater armies than this, have been buried under lesser walls"—especially since they were originally outnumbered by seasoned veterans "famous and renowned" for their "skill in war." Nonetheless, in an extraordinary providence, they had prevailed in a deliverance that was "beyond the ken of sense and reason" or any explanation by means of "secondary causes."[154]

[151] Gentles, *New Model Army*, 121–27.
[152] See Ian Gentles, *The English Revolution and the Wars of the Three Kingdoms, 1638–1652* (Harlow, UK: Pearson, 2007), 338–40.
[153] Donagan, *War in England*, 324–25.
[154] In marked contrast to Owen's providentialist account of the siege of Colchester in *Ebenezer*, the royalist poet Henry King attributed the deaths of Sir Charles Lucas and Sir George Lisle

Owen recognized the gravity of the situation, alluding to the main theaters of the conflict: "The north invaded, the south full of insurrections, Wales unsubdued, the great city at least suffering men to lift up their hands against us." He is referring to how the City of London had been "a powder keg" that was in danger of revolting as it had done the previous year.[155]

In a particularly apt turn of phrase, given the martial context, Owen spoke of how the deliverance being celebrated that day at the thanksgiving in Romford came not from outward fortifications but from the "main fort" of God's "all-sufficiency." Such obvious manifestations of "the finger of God" had the power to convince even kings of old like Nebuchadnezzar and Darius (and, by implication, the contemporary crown) that God fights for his people.

Ominously, in a provocative adaption of his earlier treatment of miraculous water being brought "out of the flint," he called his audience to recollect "the stream from the flint"—that is, the stream of smoke rising from the firing squad of flintlock muskets at the execution of Lisle and Lucas. Some of those with local knowledge may have remembered that this sentence took place outside the King's Head tavern.

As for the five thousand "hard-bitten men" in Colchester, they were dangerous and unpredictable.[156] Owen portrayed them as "an enraged, headless, lawless, godless multitude, gathered out of inns, taverns, alehouses, stables, highways, and the like nurseries of piety and pity." It was no small thing to be rescued from their clutches because they had been reticent to even enter into negotiations for a prisoner exchange and, as the Parliamentarians alleged, their captors had deliberately housed the hostages in a dangerous position where they might succumb to friendly fire.[157] Having been delivered from them, the appropriate response was both thankfulness and a commitment to avoid all "animosities, strife, contention, and violence" among the godly.

Owen warned those who were magistrates against "sinful compliances with wicked men" and urged them to conquer their fears, reject hypocrisy, and trust the promises of God as they committed themselves to serving the kingdom of Christ in "justice" and "equity." Owen's call was prescient, at least to some degree. For example, Sir Henry Mildmay, one of those to whom the published work was dedicated, became one of the "pivotal figures" in the move toward

---

to chance and contingency: "Through Warr's stern chance in heat of Battle Dy'd." See James Loxley, *Royalism and Poetry in the English Civil Wars: The Drawn Sword* (Basingstoke, UK: Macmillan, 1997), 194.

155 Gentles, "The Struggle for London in the Second Civil War," 298–99.
156 Gentles, *New Model Army*, 117.
157 Donagan, *War in England*, 348.

revolution.[158] In the coming months, he would oppose all attempts to negotiate with the king and became an instrumental figure in the revolutionary turn. Mildmay was nominated as a commissioner to try the king in January 1649, and in his role as Master of the Jewel House he provided a sword of state to be placed in Westminster Hall.[159] His attendance at the trial was sporadic, but he was listed as a regicide, even though he refused to sign the king's death warrant. Two of the others named in the dedication (Sir William Masham and Sir Thomas Honywood) were also named as commissioners for the trial of the king, but neither of them took part.

As Owen prepared the sermons for publication at the beginning of October, the army and Parliament were on a collision course. Even before the first of these sermons was preached, on August 24 the parliamentary majority saw the balance of power shifting toward the army and acted to repeal the Vote of No Addresses in order to reopen negotiations with the king at Newport.[160] On August 29, the Commons passed the Ordinance for Presbyterian Church Government, which brought together the earlier ordinances but made no provision for toleration.[161] The army was more confident than ever in the justice of its cause, especially since providence had now witnessed on its behalf in the victories of two civil wars. The ongoing negotiations for a Presbyterian-royalist settlement that had begun in Newport on the Isle of Wight in the middle of September seemed like a betrayal. The army's providential mandate (so forcefully laid out by Owen in his preaching) was being rejected, and the moderate majority in the Commons was intent on negotiations with the one who was ultimately to blame for the suffering of the past months. Furthermore, there was little sign of the negotiations leading to any form of toleration.

Although Fairfax was said to have been "radicalised" by his experiences in the summer of 1648, by the end of September there were some who were frustrated by his refusal to intervene in order to terminate the negotiations

---

158 Brenner, *Merchants and Revolutions*, 533.
159 Sean Kelsey, "Staging the Trial of Charles I," in *The Regicides and the Execution of Charles I*, ed. Jason Peacey (Basingstoke, UK: Palgrave, 2001), 82.
160 In June 1649, Owen claimed that he could offer an example, "as yet not much above half a year old," of those who "having followed God for a season in their enjoyment of success and protection, they turn aside to pursue their own ends." This is likely an allusion to the moderate majority in Parliament reopening negotiations with the kind. See Owen's sermon *Human Power Defeated*.
161 "August 1648: An Ordinance for The Form of Church Government to Be Used in the Church of England and Ireland, Agreed Upon by the Lords and Commons Assembled in Parliament, after Advice, Had with the Assembly of Divines," in *Acts and Ordinances of the Interregnum*, 1:1188–215.

with the king.¹⁶² Edmund Ludlow feared that Fairfax was going to betray the cause and took the matter to Ireton, who himself attempted to resign over Fairfax's failure to move against the negotiation.¹⁶³ As Owen drafted the dedication on October 5, Fairfax was about to be inundated with petitions from the army condemning the ongoing talks with the king. Owen had gotten to know Fairfax during the siege and perhaps knew that he needed some encouragement to capitalize on the victory. By dedicating the work to the general, Owen might well have been hoping to remind him of what he had witnessed and to make good on this providential deliverance, especially in the issue that he highlighted—namely, refusing to countenance illegitimate persecution of the saints.

One of the "uses" of Owen's sermon was that in "every distress," the godly were to "learn to wait with patience for this appointed time." That is what the army grandees did on November 26 during an eight-hour prayer meeting, whose purpose was "only to wait upon God for his direction." Days later, Fairfax wrote to Speaker Lenthall, explaining how he believed he was "attending and acting the providence of God for the gaining of such ends as we have proposed in our . . . *Remonstrance*."¹⁶⁴ This *Remonstrance*, which articulated a program for revolutionary political intervention, had been drafted by Ireton, who had come to believe that any accommodation with the king would repudiate all that the army had fought for.¹⁶⁵ In Parliament, Mildmay—who argued against ongoing negotiations with the king at Newport, saying that he was "no more to be trusted than a lion that had been caged, and let loose again"¹⁶⁶—became an important figure in the moves toward the revolution.¹⁶⁷ Owen's sermon contained an ominous note about what might lie ahead in the coming months, describing how God would "break nations, kings and kingdoms" because of his love for the saints. He reiterated this point by arguing that not even the opposition of "kings and princes" would stand. The "great tumultuating" of the day should not trouble the godly because all the oppressors would fall, and therefore those who had been used as instruments in the fulfillment of God's purposes should persevere. As Owen exhorted his audience, "Up and be doing, you that are about the work of the Lord."

---

162 Hopper, *Black Tom*, 94.
163 *The Memoirs of Edmund Ludlow*, 1:203–4; Underdown, *Pride's Purge*, 191.
164 Cited in Gentles, *New Model Army*, 132–33.
165 Underdown, *Pride's Purge*, 116–27.
166 *Old Parliamentary History, or The Parliamentary or Constitutional History of England* [. . .], 24 vols. (London, 1751–1762), 18:301–2.
167 Underdown, *Pride's Purge*, 93, 100, 127, 138.

A SERMON PREACHED [. . .] *JANUARY 31*

The Context of Owen's Postregicide Fast Sermon

This sermon was preached in the immediate wake of the revolutionary turn of events that began in early December 1648. In the negotiations with the king after the Second Civil War, Charles played for time in the hope that the Duke of Ormond would enlist military support from the Irish Catholic Confederacy.[168] At the beginning of December, a majority in the Commons voted to accept the concessions that the king had made, and this forced the army to act, seizing control of the English Parliament and purging it of those members of Parliament who sought a negotiated settlement with the king and leaving behind what was came to be derisively referred to as the "Rump" Parliament. According to Underdown, 45 members of Parliament were arrested, 186 members were prevented from taking their seats, and 86 more moderate members stayed away from the house, often as an act of protest. Those members whom Owen would address "shared few common objectives."[169]

In order to contextualize Owen's sermon and its appended tract, it is necessary to rehearse the situation with respect to the debates that were ongoing about the nature of the postrevolutionary religious settlement. Parliament's Presbyterian settlement from the end of August was now more or less dead in the water, and the Blasphemy Ordinance of May 1648 was not put into effect.[170] The shift in the balance of power meant that a new political and religious settlement was required, and discussions about this were held at Whitehall in December 1648 to January 1649. Among those present to debate relevant matters of religion were Henry Ireton and other officers; clergy, such as John Goodwin, Philip Nye, and Hugh Peter; and representative of the Levellers: the Presbyterian clergy refused to participate.[171] There was a significant divergence of views among the participants: some contended for freedom of conscience for all, while others argued for limits to religious freedom.[172] In regard to the question about the civil magistrate's role in matters of religion, the radicals argued that the magistrate had no coercive power in this area,

---

[168] Ashton, *Counter-Revolution*, 295–97.

[169] Underdown, *Pride's Purge*, 173, 212.

[170] This notorious ordinance deemed blasphemies such as anti-Trinitarianism worthy of death and outlined a second tier of errors worthy of imprisonment. See "August 1648: An Ordinance for The Form of Church Government to be used in the Church of England and Ireland, Agreed upon by the Lords and Commons Assembled in Parliament," *Acts and Ordinances of the Interregnum*, 1:1133–36.

[171] Vernon, *London Presbyterians and the British Revolutions*, 211.

[172] William Clarke, *The Clarke Papers* [. . .], ed. C. H. Firth, 4 vols. (London: Camden Society, 1891–1901), 2:81.

with John Goodwin stating the matter very bluntly: "God hath nott invested any power in a Civill magistrate in matters of religion."[173] Others held that the magistrate had a negative power to restrain and to act against heresy and blasphemy. Still others advocated that the magistrate also had a positive role in encouraging the true religion. For example, Ireton argued that the magistrate's authority comprehended "spiritual" as well as "civil" matters, and that while the magistrate could not exercise "compulsive" power in matters of religion, he could exercise "restrictive" power.[174] The Leveller leader John Lilburne quickly withdrew from the debate and published his own views in *Foundations of Freedom*, in which he sought to argue that the magistrate had no power either to "compell" or to "restraine" in matters of religion.[175] The result of the Whitehall debate was the compromise *Officers' Agreement of the People*: according to the ninth head, Christianity was to be "held forth and recommended, as the public profession in this nation"; ministers would be maintained by the public purse rather than by tithes; religious compulsion was renounced and instead people were to be won by sound teaching and good example; there would be limited liberty of conscience for those "differing in judgment," but this excluded "popery and prelacy" and any who would disturb "the public peace"; finally, all existing legislation to the contrary would be repealed and nullified.[176]

At the end of December, Owen was given notice that he would be the preacher at the next monthly parliamentary fast by one of the Essex County Committee, Sir Henry Mildmay (ca. 1594–1668).[177] Mildmay had been instrumental in raising troops to support Fairfax at the siege of Colchester and had been one of those tasked with offering Parliament's thanks to Fairfax after the rebels surrendered. In the wake of the Second Civil War, he opposed all attempts to negotiate with the king.[178] Owen's neighboring clergyman, Ralph Josselin, believed that this would be the final monthly fast since "people doe so exceedingly neglect the same."[179]

---

173 Clarke, *Clarke Papers*, 2:115–18.
174 Carolyn Polizzotto, "Liberty of Conscience and the Whitehall Debates of 1648-9," *Journal of Ecclesiastical History* 26, no. 1 (1975): 69–82.
175 John Lilburne, *Foundations of Freedom* [. . .] (London, 1648), 11. The book collector George Thomason dated his copy December 15.
176 *A Petition from His Excellency Thomas Lord Fairfax and the General Council of Officers* [. . .] (London, 1649), 26–27.
177 *Journals of the House of Commons*, 6:107.
178 *The History of Parliament*, s.v. Mildmay, Sir Henry (ca. 1594–1668).
179 Ralph Josselin, *The Diary of Ralph Josselin, 1616–1683*, ed. Alan Macfarlane, Records of Social and Economic History (Oxford: Oxford University Press, 1976), 155.

The new republican regime was facing a crisis of legitimacy on two significant fronts. There were counterrevolutionaries who wished to reverse what had taken place in the past number of weeks. The Presbyterian pulpits of London denounced the army's revolutionary activities as covenant breaking.[180] There were also social revolutionaries, like the Levellers, who believed that the revolution had already been betrayed. As Underdown explains, the regime at the time was seeking to advance "two incompatible aims": the first, "revolution"; the second, "conciliation."[181]

Both of these aims are discernible in Owen's sermon. First, he sets out to justify the basis on which the government rested. Second, the sermon is an exercise in broadening the support base of the regime. He is seeking to engage with those who refused to actively support the army coup but who now might be persuaded to adopt a pragmatic approach and return to Parliament, given that the revolution was now a *fait accompli*. Owen had already been engaged in this task with the lawyer and moderate member of Parliament Bulstrode Whitelocke (1605–1675) as part of a wider endeavor to restore relationships with some of the secluded members, thus broadening the base of the new regime.[182] Owen was sent (Blair Worden believes by Oliver Cromwell) to Whitelocke at his country seat of Henley-on-Thames in order to persuade him to return to Westminster. There, in a bitterly cold winter in which the Thames had frozen over, Owen preached what the lawyer-politician described as "two excellent sermons" on December 31. Whitelocke noted that "upon discourse concerning the present affairs of the army he seemed much to favour them, and spoke in dislike of those members who voluntarily absented themselves from the House, having no particular force upon their persons."[183] It appears that those involved in this conciliation had some success. The day after Owen preached, a newspaper reported that "Divers members [have] since the death of the King, intimated a desire to come in."[184] That February, around eighty members were readmitted to the Commons—for example, Sir Henry Vane the Younger (1613–1662) and Sir William Masham (one of those to whom Owen dedicated *Ebenezer* [1648]).[185]

---

[180] Eliot Vernon, "The Quarrel of the Covenant: The London Presbyterians and the Regicide," in Peacey, *The Regicides and the Execution of Charles I*, 203–4.

[181] Underdown, *Pride's Purge*, 200.

[182] Underdown, *Pride's Purge*, 68, 173.

[183] Bulstrode Whitelocke, *Memorials of the English Affairs from the beginning of the reign of Charles the First to the Happy Restoration of King Charles the Second*, 4 vols. (Oxford: University Press, 1853), 2:486.

[184] *Moderate Intelligencer*, 203 (February 1–8, 1649), cited in Underdown, *Pride's Purge*, 215.

[185] Worden, *The Rump Parliament*, 69; *History of Parliament*, s.v. "Sir William Masham (1591–1656)."

As Owen would have been preparing to preach, the High Court of Justice was conducting the trial of the king between January 18 and 27. (It would also try the Duke of Hamilton and Lord Capel who had been responsible for the siege in Colchester.) The king would be sentenced to death on Saturday, January 27, condemned as a "tyrant, traitor and murderer," and executed on January 30.

The following day, Owen came to preach before the Parliament. The nature of this sermon, and particularly what may be gleaned from it about Owen's view of the regicide, has been contentious. For example, an early biography suggested that Owen turned down the opportunity for easy promotion by ignoring the subject altogether.[186] Appleby says that Owen deployed texts from the Old Testament to justify the regicide without referring to it directly."[187] Gribben describes Owen's sermon as "ambiguous," one that "pulled its punches," especially in comparison to the sermon preached by John Cardell.[188] Cardell "tiptoed warily around" the subject of the regicide while making it explicitly clear that victory in the Second Civil War was the work of God rather than of men:[189]

> Remember but the *wonders* (I had almost said, the *miracles*) of this last *Summer* . . . when the *Malignant* party in both *Kingdoms* were *desperately* inraged against you; And I know not how many *thousands* of them, a second time up in *arms* against you, and nothing to *stand, between* you and all this *danger, but a poor despised, unpaid Army*; and yet, what a *wonderful*, what a *sudden*, what an *unexpected*, what an *unparalleld deliverance*, did the Lord *work* out for you.[190]

Cardell condemned those who were "vexing, and fretting, and *fuming* at present *Providential* Administrations, and consequently *flying* in the *very face*

---

186 Asty, "Memoirs of the Life of John Owen," vii; William Orme, *Memoirs of the Life, Writings and Religious Connections of John Owen* (London, 1820), 89–90.
187 David J. Appleby, "Sermons and Preaching," in *The Oxford History of Protestant Dissenting Traditions*, vol. 1, *The Post-Reformation Era, c.1559–1689*, ed. John Coffey (Oxford: Oxford University Press, 2020), 446.
188 Gribben, *John Owen and English Puritanism*, 98.
189 Appleby, "Sermons and Preaching," 446.
190 John Cardell, *Gods Wisdom Justified, and Mans Folly Condemned, Touching All Maner of Outward Providential Administrations, in a Sermon* (London, 1649), 37 (italics original). Cardell, minister of All Hallows, Lombard Street, became known as an independent in 1648, and at this time he was moving toward a strict Congregationalist position. See Vernon, *London Presbyterians and the British Revolutions*, 183; Tai Liu, *Puritan London: A Study of Religion and Society in the City Parishes* (Newark, DE: University of Delaware Press, 1986), 112.

of *God* himself, for not *ordering* things just as they *would* have him."[191] In the immediate aftermath of the king's trial and execution, Cardell was clear that a commitment to justice required "*courage* to *execute*, and to *carry* on the work *vigorously*."[192] Tom Webster describes the sermons delivered by both preachers as "fairly celebratory sermons, but moderate nonetheless," and comments that the preacher to the soon-to-be-abolished House of Lords, Stephen Marshall, was addressing "probably the smallest congregation of his career" (this sermon was not printed).[193] Nevertheless, Gribben points out that the fact that Owen preached at all indicates his "willingness, however hesitant, to be identified with a revolutionary, regicidal regime" and how he was fast becoming "the favorite preacher of the army elite ... a principal spokesperson for the new regime, its prophet of a new world order."[194]

Owen's sermon was published by Matthew Simmons (1608–1654), one of the most important progovernment printers of 1649.[195] Simmons was a liveryman of the Stationers' Company since 1647 and as a "diehard independent" was a supporter of antiepiscopal and proparliamentary works. His premises were located near the Gilded Lion. He had been "notorious for unlicensed printing" in the 1640s and printed a number of prose works by John Milton, including *Doctrine and Discipline of Divorce* (1643) and, in February 1649, *The Tenure of Kings and Magistrates*. Simmons also printed works by John Goodwin, including, in January 1649, his defense of Pride's Purge, *Right and Might Well Met*.[196]

As Gribben notes, Owen enjoyed "his first literary success" with the sermon, and this encouraged Philemon Stephens to reissue some of Owen's earlier works in a single volume.[197] Simmons printed a second edition later that year for the bookseller Henry Cripps (1620–ca. 1658).[198]

There is no doubt that Owen condoned the regicide, despite the attempts of some to dissociate him from it. Samuel Parker mocked Owen for seeking to defend the "Equity of Gods Judgments" in the trial and execution of the king on the basis of the people's "retained Soveraignty" and the need to "restrain" the king from continuing in "his provoking ways."[199] Something

---

191 Cardell, *Gods Wisdom*, 19 (italics original).
192 Cardell, *Gods Wisdom*, 35 (italics original).
193 Webster, "Preaching and Parliament, 1640–1659," 409.
194 Gribben, *John Owen and English Puritanism*, 98–99, 104.
195 Amos Tubb, "Printing the Regicide of Charles I," *History* 89, no. 4 (2004): 502, 509, 521.
196 Como, *Radical Parliamentarians*, 38, 183, 320; Coffey, *John Goodwin and the Puritan Revolution*, 179.
197 Gribben, "Becoming John Owen," 313.
198 See English Short Title Catalogue.
199 See Parker, *Defence and Continuation*, 114.

of how the sermon was received can be deduced from the fact that it was burned in Oxford in 1683. Zachary Grey, in his writings against the Nonconformists, was able to include passages from the sermon that, he alleged, supported the regicide.[200] Owen's support of the regicide was not because he espoused republicanism as a political theory—that is, he did not believe that "the common good of a community can never be satisfactorily assured under a monarchical form of government."[201] Pocock's argument that republicanism was "far more the effect than the cause of the execution of the King" holds true for Owen.[202]

Summary and Analysis of the Sermon

The dedicatory epistle of the published sermon revealed Owen's awareness that there was no lack of opposition to the Rump Parliament, whose members he styled as "visible instruments" of God's great work in that generation, those serving "in the high places of Armageddon" and engaged in "rolling up" the nation's "heavens." Indeed, writing from his parish in Coggeshall at the end of February, he anticipated that there would be further opposition on a number of fronts. Nonetheless, now that the die had been cast and the Rubicon had been crossed, Parliament was set to work in "the unraveling of the whole web of iniquity, interwoven of civil and ecclesiastical tyranny, in opposition to the kingdom of the Lord Jesus." As suggested in the title of the sermon in the 1721 edition, this was Owen's call for Parliament to continue to exercise righteous zeal. Owen took the following as his text: "Let them return to thee, but return not thou unto them. And I will make thee unto this people a fenced brazen wall, and they shall fight against thee, but they shall not prevail against thee: for I am with thee to save thee, and to deliver thee, saith the Lord" (Jer. 15:19–20). Two months later, Oliver Cromwell would employ the same trope that Owen developed from this text at the meeting of the Army General Council at Whitehall on March 23, 1649, to express his confidence in the Parliament enjoying divine protection for as long as it continued to do God's work: "wee shall finde hee will bee as a wall of brasse round about us till wee have finished that worke that hee has for us to doe."[203]

---

200 Zachary Grey, *An Impartial Examination of the Third Volume of Mr. Daniel Neal's History of the Puritans* [. . .] (London, 1737), 358.
201 Quentin Skinner, "The State," in *Political Innovation and Conceptual Change*, ed. Terrence Ball, James Farr, and Russell L. Hanson (Cambridge: Cambridge University Press, 1989), 114.
202 J. G. A. Pocock and G. J. Schochet, "Interregnum and Restoration," in *The Varieties of British Political Thought, 1500–1800*, ed. J. G. A. Pocock et al. (Cambridge: Cambridge University Press, 1993), 148.
203 Cromwell, *Letters, Writings, and Speeches of Oliver Cromwell*, 1:27.

Owen begins the sermon with a consideration of a sinful people and the various judgments that God brings against them, including God taking a king away in his wrath (Hos. 13:11). He highlights how in the "civil politic body" "the sins of the king" bring divine judgments on a nation. He employed the example of Manasseh, the wicked king of Judah, who had turned his back on Hezekiah's reformation by introducing false worship and persecuting those who refused to participate (2 Kings 20-21; 2 Chron. 33). As Kevin Killeen has shown, biblical figures could be used to prefigure a number of contemporary figures.[204] However, Owen's concerns extend beyond the late king, and he is "careful in balancing responsibility for the sins of the realm."[205] The people were complicit in this in a number of ways. First, they had "set him up" by way of "plenary consent" and so "may justly be called to answer for his miscarriage." Second, for various reasons the majority of people allowed themselves to be seduced into apostasy. Third, the bulk of the people had failed to "restrain" the king. Here he quoted Bishop Thomas Bilson's *True Difference between Christian Subjection and Unchristian Rebellion* (1585), which argued that subjects should not consent to the wickedness of a tyrannical king but instead had a responsibility to call kings to account. According to Anthony Wood's recollections, Bilson "did contribute much to the ruin" of Charles, and the historian William Lamont claims that *True Difference* "was probably more quoted on the parliamentary side in the English Civil War than any other source."[206] Manasseh's two great sins were idolatry and tyranny, and Owen claimed that providence had made clear that there was "a parallel" between Manasseh's day and current events in England. In so doing, Owen was provocatively likening King Charles to the very worst of the Judean kings. First, like Manasseh, Charles had been guilty of shedding "innocent blood." This followed the line of the army's *Remonstrance* from December, which held the king to be "guilty of all the innocent blood" spilt in the Second Civil War.[207] Second, like Manasseh, Charles had led the people into various forms of idolatry. For Owen, this included the recent observance of advent and Christmas, what Owen termed "the late solemn superstition." In the appended tract,

---

[204] Killeen, "Chastising with Scorpions: Reading the Old Testament in Early Modern England," 491–506; Killeen, "Hanging up Kings: The Political Bible in Early Modern England," *Journal of the History of Ideas* 72, no. 4 (2011): 549–70.

[205] Margaret Aston, *Broken Idols of the English Reformation* (Cambridge: Cambridge University Press, 2016), 73.

[206] Richard Baxter, *A Holy Commonwealth*, ed. William M. Lamont (Cambridge: Cambridge University Press, 1994), xxvi; Anthony à Wood, *Athenae Oxonienses* [. . .], vol. 1 (London, 1691), 334.

[207] *Old Parliamentary History*, 18:183–84.

Owen described the magistrate's responsibility to deal with the nation's idolatry: for example, the potent symbol of Roman Catholic worship in the center of London at Somerset House. Owen believed these two sins of oppression and idolatry were "inseparable concomitants" (a "close-woven web of destruction"), and when the state committed these evils, with the people's consent, then the nation was doomed to "remediless ruin," except there be an "unprecedented" deliverance.

Owen believed that his exposition of the major themes of Jeremiah 15 enabled him to address "the very state and condition of this nation at this time." His analysis was stark: the very future of "poor England" was in jeopardy because, "under several administrations of civil government," it had now fallen on three occasions into "nation-destroying sins." He highlighted how in his days "God's choicest servants," who could be instrumental in delivering the people from this judgment, often had to endure the burden of being cursed by the people.[208] This was, of course, nothing new because it was the experience of Moses as he led the people out of Egypt in a "wonderful and unparalleled deliverance." Owen suggested that one of the reasons behind this opposition was that the nature of the deliverance did not conform to the expectations or satisfy the desires of many of the people. As for "the saints of God," the path of providence was indeed dark and perplexing, and he therefore urged his audience to be "tender toward fainters in difficult seasons." Owen sounded a conciliatory note toward those who had been slow to support the revolution and regicide, recalling how even Martin Luther had initially been "bewildered" at the idea that the "inferior magistrate may in some case resist the superior."[209]

As Owen offered "God's direction" for the future, he was realistic in his assessment that "the bulk of the people" did not support the new regime. Nevertheless, as the members of the Rump Parliament sought "to swim against the stream of an unreformable multitude," they should be undeterred. If some of those who had backslidden from the cause were to return, they ought to be embraced; indeed, hard work was to be done in order "to recover others." As for the rest, Owen insisted that there should be no dealings with those who had acted treacherously in "the late workings of things among us." In the first instance, this meant any who refused to bring justice and retribution against the enemies of the nation. Given that Owen emphasized that

---

208 Samuel Parker's hostile account of Owen's words claimed that the enmity came about because "the People of *England* [were] enraged against them for murthering their Sovereign." See his *Defence and Continuation*, 503.

209 Owen cited bk. 8 of John Dawes, *A Famouse Cronicle of Oure Time* [. . .] (London, 1560).

this was justice against "the mighty," this was an oblique reference to those secluded members of Parliament who refused to bring the king to justice. The second area in which there could be no compromise was with those who were willing to countenance the persecution of the saints: some of these would-be persecutors had themselves been persecuted but now were willing to countenance persecution because of their commitment to coerced uniformity. Owen's explanation of such "deviation" into the "crooked walking" of injustice and persecution was twofold: either "carnal fear" or a "covetousness and ambition" for "perishing things." With respect to the first, "most men in authority" were too taken up with pragmatic considerations about their own safety. This was similar to that of Captain George Joyce when, on January 13, he accused Fairfax—who withdrew from sitting as a commissioner for the king's trial—of having "a spirit of feare" on him, "studying to please men" rather than engaging in "the greatest work of righteousness that ever was amongst men."[210] The second cause, that of desiring perishing things, was what led Saul to spare king Agag and his cattle (1 Sam. 15). John Cardell also appealed to this text because it illustrated how the unwillingness to execute a tyrannical king incurred God's displeasure and necessitated another—in this case, Samuel—to intervene, enacting justice by means of the sword. Since the end of the First Civil War in 1646, Owen thought that many had succumbed to "backsliding" brought about by either fear or ambition and had now reached the point that they derided those with whom they once had common cause as a "parliament of saints" and an "army of saints."

In order to restore backsliders to the "paths of righteousness," Owen's primary exhortation was to avoid the ways that "the Lord has blasted under your eyes": oppression, self-seeking, and persecution. With regard to the first, there were many poor and oppressed people after three poor harvests and two civil wars. Earlier that month, one of Owen's neighboring clergy, Ralph Josselin, recorded in his diary "the great dearness of everything," noting that "men expect it will be dearer and dearer."[211] Owen warned, "Oh let it be considered by you, that it be not considered upon you!" This would resonate with an ominous warning from the Leveller weekly newspaper, *The Moderate*, that March: "Either take some care to ease, or relieve" the poor, it warned, "else their necessities will enforce them to be rich and level what they never intended." The *Kingdomes Faithful and Impartiall Scout* concurred, "If the Lord puts it not into the hearts of the Parliament to take some speedy course

[210] Cited in Underdown, *Pride's Purge*, 182.
[211] Josselin, *Diary of Ralph Josselin*, 154–6, 162–63, 167; Steve Hindle, "Dearth and the English Revolution: The Harvest Crisis of 1647–50," *Economic History Review*, new series 61 (2008): 64–98.

for the care of the people," "we shall then fear nothing but confusion, and many will turn Levellers upon necessity."[212] Owen's practical recommendation was that "a committee of your honourable house might sit once a week" to deal with the issue. Three months after Owen preached, the Rump passed its *Act for the Relief and Employment of the Poor, and Punishment of Vagrants and Other Disorderly Persons within the City of London*.[213] This was perceived to be a new beginning in "reformation of and provision for the necessitous poor."[214] Second, he warned of the fate awaiting those "self-seeking" persons who endeavored to "build their honors, greatness, and preferments" on the "tottering foundation" of the "heaps and ruins" of what God had pulled down. The final way "blasted" by God were those "pretenses" and "contrivances" that would have resulted in persecution, something Owen would return to at length in the tract on toleration published with the sermon.

Even if some might be restored and reconciled to the cause, Owen did accept that he was calling members of Parliament to "the greatest undertakings" in a time of the most significant "difficulty and opposition." He therefore promised them that as "instruments of [God's] glory," they would, like Moses, be strengthened for the task of leading the people out from under the bondage of a tyrannical and angry king because he had been deprived of his sovereignty. Furthermore, in England's exodus the very people being liberated were, again, so accustomed to slavery that they initially opposed their liberation. In fact, as had happened under Moses, many appealed to God against their God-given liberators: the heavy rain and a further poor harvest of 1648 was "laid on the shoulders of the present government."[215] The opposition was certainly great, but Moses provided an example of how God gave his chosen liberators "unconquerable" support. The new regime—"parliament, people, [and] army"—ought to be confident because all opposition would ultimately turn out to be either futile or self-destructive. Of those who at present opposed them, some would simply be destroyed while others would be transformed. Here Owen offered the example of what had happened to some of the ministers in Scotland after the defeat of the Engager

---

212 *The Moderate* (March 20–27, 1649), 375; *The Kingdomes Faithful and Impartiall Scout* (August 17–24, 1649).

213 *Journals of the House of Commons*, 6:202; *Acts and Ordinances of the Interregnum*, 2:104–10; Valerie Pearl, "Puritans and Poor Relief: The London Workhouse, 1649–1660," in *Puritans and Revolutionaries: Essays in Seventeenth-Century History Presented to Christopher Hill*, ed. D. Pennington and K. Thomas (Oxford: Clarendon, 1978), 206–32.

214 [Rice Bush], *The Poor Mans Friend, or A Narrative of What Progresse Many Worthy Citi[zens] of London Have Made in That Godly Work of Providing for the Poor* [. . .] (London, 1649).

215 Hindle, "Dearth and the English Revolution," 64–98.

army at Preston some months beforehand. He also expressed optimism that something similar would happen to the ministers in Ireland. This promise was conditional, however. Too many of those who had gone before (presumably including those now secluded from Parliament) had been preoccupied with public opinion, particularly a desire to preserve the support of "the city."

This was significant, given what had taken place in London in 1648 when the city leadership, dominated by political Presbyterians, sought a parliamentary settlement with the king that would bring about a return to pre–civil war normality.[216] Owen contended that the preoccupation of those in power ought instead to ensure that God would not be provoked by their actions. At its heart, this required Parliament to "assert, maintain, [and] uphold the order of the gospel, and administration of the ordinances of Christ." Owen was aware of "novel fancies" such as contempt for divine ordinances, and he indicated that he would address this in the appended tract, *Toleration*. By "ordinances," Owen is referring to the outward means of grace within the church—that is, such things as preaching, the administration of the sacraments, and the exercise of church discipline. Radical antiformalism had been growing through the 1640s, particularly among those, often described as "Seekers," who claimed that all outward church "forms" and "ordinances" had ceased.[217] In the spring, the Leveller William Walwyn anonymously published *The Vanity of the Present Churches*, arguing that the Independent clergy were really no different from the Laudians and Presbyterians in their "hankering after persecution," and he called his readers to "disentangle" themselves "from all religious forms."[218] Similarly, the two leaders of the Digger movement who came to prominence in April, Gerrard Winstanley and William Everard, both rejected outward ordinances and forms.[219] This antiformalist "contempt" for ordinances would continue to grow. Abiezer Coppe, one of those who came to be known as Ranters, rejected water baptism, claiming that he was "above ordinances."[220]

This prognosis led Owen into an extended theological discussion about the nature of divine sovereignty and human responsibility. Through this he

---

216 Vernon, *London Presbyterians and the British Revolutions*, 208.
217 Alec Ryrie, "Seeking the Seekers," *Studies in Church History* 57 (2021): 185–209; J. C. Davis, "Against Formality: One Aspect of the English Revolution," *Transactions of the Royal Historical Society*, 6th series, 3 (1993): 265–88.
218 [William Walwyn], *The Vanity of the Present Churches* [. . .] (London, 1649).
219 Ariel Hessayon, "Early Modern Communism: The Diggers and the Community of Goods," *Journal for the Study of Radicalism* 3 (2009): 18–22.
220 Ariel Hessayon, "The Making of Abiezer Coppe," *Journal of Ecclesiastical History* 62, no. 1 (2011): 55–56.

sought to explain how even though the furious opposition of a "hardened multitude" was ultimately futile, it nonetheless served the divine purpose: this was something he believed to be evident down through the history of the people of God. Such opposition served to seal up the destruction of a "provoking people" and to reveal God's glory in keeping his remnant. Owen was seeking to reassure a regime without a significant support base that God had worked through a godly remnant in the past and that he could do so again. He believed that this would prepare members of Parliament for whatever storm might come and should also cause those opposed to the Parliament to engage in self-examination in order to consider whether they were undergoing judicial hardening. Owen's final note in the sermon was one of optimism. In all the ongoing "sinful advisings and undertakings," all the "reasonings, debates, [and] consultations," God in his sovereignty was able "to bring light out of darkness."

Summary and Analysis of the Appended Tract

As Owen had done with his first parliamentary sermon, when the work came to print, he appended an additional tract—in this case *Of Toleration: And the Duty of the Magistrate, about Religion*.[221] This important work should be understood as a plea for a workable middle way rather than a call for a toleration from which he would eventually distance himself. He explained how the ongoing toleration debate had taken on "sinful and dangerous extremes" and hoped that he might reach some agreement from both sides, thus "pouring a little cold water upon the common flames." He intended to remove the arguments that were advanced for "nontoleration," or what he insisted was actually more accurately described as the civil "punishment of erring persons." In doing so, he was directly challenging the approach adopted that month by the Commissioners of the General Assembly of the Church of Scotland, who had issued *A Solemn Testimony against Toleration, and the Present Proceedings of Sectaries and Their Abettors in England, in Reference to Religion and Government* (Edinburgh, 1649). This tract was circulating in London in the middle of January and was intended to be a public rebuke of the Rump Parliament by the Scots. It declared that "we have searched

---

221 A number of scholars have examined Owen's views on religious toleration: e.g., John Coffey, "John Owen and the Puritan Toleration Controversy, 1646–1659," in *The Ashgate Research Companion to John Owen's Theology*, ed. Kelly M. Kapic and Mark Jones (Farnham, UK: Ashgate, 2012), 227–48; and Paul Lim, "The Trinity, Adiaphora, Ecclesiology, and Reformation: John Owen's Theory of Religious Toleration in Context," *Westminster Theological Journal* 67, no. 2 (2005): 281–300.

after the minde of Christ . . . and no where can we finde in the Scriptures of truth, either precept or precedent allowed of God for Toleration of any Errour, much lesse did it ever come into his minde, or did he speak to any of his servants concerning a Toleration of all Errour."[222] For the Scots, what the English Army and Parliament had done threatened the very idea of a covenanted reformation. Before he set out to address the arguments like these that were being advanced in favor of enforced uniformity, Owen clarified his own position on a number of points. First, he distinguished the approach that might be taken to those who simply maintained "errors" from that required toward those engaged in "peace-disturbing enormities." Owen also denied the claim (one made by the Commissioners of the Kirk) that those like him who "plead for toleration" hold that the magistrate cannot punish sins against both tables of the Law.[223] He was clear that the magistrate could punish sins against the first table of the Law that "tend to the disturbance of the public peace." Here he differed from more radical tolerationists like John Goodwin, who believed that the magistrate's power was restricted to the second table of the Decalogue.[224] Thus, at the outset, Owen offered a reassurance that the Congregationalists' strong line on the role of the magistrate in religion was coupled with strong opposition to the persecution of the godly. Second, it allowed him to distinguish his position from that of the more radical tolerationists, something that would be very important for one of the great needs of the hour—namely, building alliances.[225]

In the first major section of the tract, Owen devoted considerable attention to rejecting the arguments that were used in an attempt to justify the capital punishment of heretics. First, that the penal sanctions of the Old Testament (the "Judaical polity") against idolatry and blasphemy warranted the punishment of those who hold "any error whatsoever": For Owen, there was no straightforward equivalence between simply maintaining an error and engaging in acts of idolatry and blasphemy. This was significant because, according to Coffey, at this time "the Israel model remained central to the case for persecution."[226] Owen then dealt with three specific key texts that

---

[222] *A Solemn Testimony against Toleration, and the Present Proceedings of Sectaries and Their Abettors in England, in Reference to Religion and Government* [. . .] (Edinburgh, 1649), 3, 8.
[223] *Solemn Testimony against Toleration*, 3.
[224] Coffey, *John Goodwin and the Puritan Revolution*, 143.
[225] Clarke, *Clarke Papers*, 2:74; Coffey, "Puritanism and Liberty Revisited," 961–85; G. E. Aylmer, *The Levellers in the English Revolution* (London: Thames and Hudson, 1975), 41; Polizzotto, "Liberty of Conscience and the Whitehall Debates," 69–82.
[226] John Coffey, *Persecution and Toleration in Protestant England, 1558–1689* (London: Longman, 2000), 31.

were commonly used to establish the doctrine of coercion. First, he rejected the argument from Zechariah 13:6, advanced by the likes of Samuel Rutherford and William Prynne, that the punishment by death of a false prophet warranted the punishment of those in doctrinal error. In terms of the New Testament, Owen also dismissed the claim that according to Romans 13 it was the duty of the magistrate to suppress error by external force. Finally, he gave more sustained attention to the argument for coercion based on the punishment of the seducer in Deuteronomy 13 because it had "more show of reason" than any of the other arguments that were advanced. This text was utilized by the commissioners of the Kirk—George Gillespie and Samuel Rutherford—and by William Prynne in their various works in support of the state's role in punishing those who publicly promoted or practiced certain forms of heterodoxy.[227] Once again, Owen argued that there was no straightforward parallel between what was in view with the case of the seducer and that of the obstinate heretic.

Owen then turned to premise some "general observations." The first was that error was to be opposed "by gospel mediums, and spiritual weapons," in particular by "the sword of the Spirit," that "hammer of the word," and also by "the sword of discipline" in the form of church "censures." He claimed that if those "despised instruments" of proclamation of the word and administration of discipline were employed as they had been by the primitive churches from the first to the third centuries, then they would "quickly make the proudest heretic to tremble." His second observation was to state what he believed to be the crux of the acrimonious debate that was taking place—namely, whether the lawful magistrate had authority "to coerce, restrain, punish, confine, imprison, banish, hang, or burn" those who did not "embrace, profess, believe, and practice, that truth and way of worship" that was held out by the state. His answer was that there was no scriptural warrant for the magistrate to punish those who would not "forsake their own convictions" in matters of belief and worship. He laid down a number of arguments in support of this.

He began by tracing the lineage of the idea of "force and violence" in matters of religion, arguing that the cruelty of the pagan Babylonians and Romans against Dissenters had simply been "inserted into the church's orthodoxies" by anti-Christian Rome under the name of "*Haereticidium*." This was done by legislating against any worship that was not established by law that was typically justified on two grounds: the first being that toleration would disturb

---

[227] See, e.g., Samuel Rutherford, *A Free Disputation against Pretended Liberty of Conscience* [. . .] (London, 1649), 70–71.

the peace and prosperity of the commonwealth; the second that Dissent should be regarded as a dangerous plague that would cause untold troubles. This resulted in "the most orthodox" being charged with all sorts of "foolish, absurd, detestable, pernicious, sinful, wicked" things. For Owen, this applied not only to the primitive Christians but also to the Waldensians, Lollards, Reformers, Brownists, and Puritans. Owen warned that "the old Roman way" was to seek to destroy the truth under the name of destroying error.

Owen then considered the utility of coercion, arguing that the punishment of so-called heretics had rarely been "serviceable" to "the maintenance of the truth" but had instead resulted in the blood of countless martyrs. He offered a number of examples of significant violence against those who were orthodox: the tyrannical rule of Fernando Álvarez de Toledo (1507–1582), the third Duke of Alva, in the Netherlands (1567–1573); the persecution of the adherents of Nicene orthodoxy in the fifth century by the Arian Vandals in North Africa; the persecution of the followers of Athanasius in Alexandria by Emperor Valens; and the iconoclasm controversy of the eighth and ninth centuries, particularly the violence of the image-worshiping *Iconodules*. Owen claimed that in the seven-hundred-year period at the height of the reign of Satan and the antichrist (850–1550) there had been "millions of martyrs." Those put to death as "heretics" included the Albigensians in southern France in the twelfth and thirteenth centuries and, at the end of the period, the Waldensians in the village of Mérindol (1545). Owen appears to cite the words of Joseph Caryl by way of caution, telling his readers to beware using "the broom of Antichrist" to "sweep the church of Christ."[228] Persecution, he reasoned, simply did not work. It frequently turned those who really were heretics into martyrs, resulting in their ideas being "confirmed and propagated" rather than suppressed. It also proved counterproductive to those who employed it in an attempt to suppress the spread of the reformations in Bohemia, Germany, the Netherlands, Scotland, and France. In all those places, religious persecution led to wearying cycles of violence and war. Peace and prosperity came about when magistrates offered toleration, whether under the brief reign of emperor Jovian (363–364) or with the Edict of Nantes (1598) that brought to an end the French Wars of Religion. Owen pressed this point home by calling for a serious consideration of the Dutch model of tolerance.[229] The founding charter of the confederation of

---

[228] Caryl, *Englands Plus Ultra*, 24.
[229] For the often-neglected continental context of Owen's vision for reformation, see Adam Quibell, "The Grounds, Method, Scope, and Impact of Independentism's Efforts for Union, 1654–1659" (PhD diss., Queen's University Belfast, 2024).

Dutch provinces that became the independent Dutch Republic in 1581 was the Union of Utrecht (1579). Article 13 had stipulated that "nobody shall be persecuted or examined for religious reasons." This had evolved into the magistrate keeping the peace between the official Reformed Church (*publicke kerk*) and other religious communities. This tacit toleration had clear limits since some confessional groups were condemned to clandestine worship (e.g., Roman Catholics were not allowed to publicly practice their religion), and no toleration was extended to anti-Trinitarians and atheists.[230] A number of the exiled future leaders of English Congregationalism had found a safe haven in the Netherlands during the drive against Nonconformity during the Laudian era.[231] There in exile they had firsthand experience of the limited toleration that was practiced in the Low Countries. For example, William Bridge, Jeremiah Burroughes, and Sidrach Simpson had been in the English church in Rotterdam, and Thomas Goodwin and Philip Nye had gathered a church at Arnhem.[232] The proposals of the Dissenting Brethren in the *Apologeticall Narration* (1644) recalled the authors' experience of exile in the Netherlands, where they had enjoyed "a latitude" with respect to "some lesser differences" and their ongoing "brotherly correspondency" with members of the Dutch Reformed Church.[233] Owen's call for this Dutch model to be "seriously considered" was an appeal to find a middle way through the acrimonious debates that were taking place. His approach would probably have done little for those at loggerheads with one another. Many Presbyterians believed that the Dutch went too far. For example, the heresiographer Thomas Edwards thought if England embraced toleration, it would become "a chaos, a Babel, another Amsterdam."[234] On the other hand, some of the more radical tolerationists thought that the Dutch did not go far enough. Thus, Owen is appealing for something of a middle way, one with the viability of being akin to the policy and practice

---

230 M. E. H. N. Mout, "A Comparative View of Dutch Toleration in the Sixteenth and Seventeenth Centuries," in *The Emergence of Toleration in the Dutch Republic*, ed. C. Berkvens-Stevelinck, J. Israel, and G. H. M Posthumus Meyjes (Leiden: Brill, 1997), 41; and Benjamin J. Kaplan, "Fictions of Privacy: House Chapels and the Spatial Accommodation of Religious Dissent in Early Modern Europe," *American Historical Review* 107, no. 4 (2002): 1034, 1048.

231 John Marshall, *John Locke, Toleration and Early Enlightenment Culture* (Cambridge: Cambridge University Press, 2006), 138–93, 335–70.

232 Keith L. Sprunger, *Dutch Puritanism: A History of the English and Scottish Churches of the Netherlands in the Sixteenth and Seventeenth Centuries* (Leiden: Brill, 1982), 162–72, 227–32.

233 Thomas Goodwin et al., *An Apologeticall Narration* [...] (London, 1644), 8, 24, 31.

234 Thomas Edward, *Gangraena: or a Catalogue and Discovery of Many of the Errours, Heresies, Blasphemies and Pernicious Practices of the Sectaries of This Time, Vented and Acted in England in These Last Four Years* (London, 1646), pt. 1, p. 120.

of another nearby Protestant state.[235] It is important to note Owen's appeal because the Cromwellian church settlement that he would help forge in the 1650s "bore more than a passing resemblance to the religious settlement of the early Dutch Republic."[236]

Owen recognized that it was on occasion necessary to act "against erroneous persons" in order to defend the gospel and preserve the peace of the church, although he did not believe that such action was "so urgent as is pretended." He pointed out that for the first three centuries, the church had no assistance from the Christian magistrate, and during that period "there was not one long-lived, or far-spreading heresy." Ante-Nicene fathers such as Polycarp, Ignatius of Antioch, Irenaeus, Tertullian, and Cyprian contended for the faith by spiritual means such as "church censures" and "communion among the churches" but said nothing at all about the corporal punishment of heretics, a doctrine Owen believed to have a "poor footing in antiquity." It was only when those in civil power "began to interpose in the things of religion" that heresies such as Arianism became widespread. Furthermore, although initially the magistrate acted to defend catholic orthodoxy, this was a Satanic ruse through which "the Roman pontiffs . . . advanced their own supremacy." In all this, Owen pinned the blame on those "who called themselves bishops," "aspiring prelates" and their "associates," and "turbulent priests." They persuaded Constantine to reverse his initial policy of toleration by means of "lies, flatteries, [and] equivocations." The way in which Owen presented these fourth-century developments resonated with contemporary debates about the role of the magistrate in matters of religion because this retrograde step toward religious persecution came about when those in power had been "wearied by the importunity of the orthodox," not least with their "petitions." There was also an implicit warning from history in Owen's explanation of how these developments led to all sorts of troubles with religion becoming more and more a matter of "external pomp and dominion" and a servant of the antichrist.

Owen concluded his critique of the arguments advanced in favor of the civil magistrate "proceeding against erring persons" with a survey of the providential judgments that came on persecutors. Employing ancient histories—such as

---

235 For a discussion of how different groups appealed to the example of the Dutch during the seventeenth-century controversy, see John Coffey, "European Multiconfessionalism and the English Toleration Controversy, 1640–1660," in *A Companion to Multiconfessionalism in the Early Modern World*, ed. Thomas Max Safley (Leiden: Brill, 2011), 340–64.

236 Hugh Dunthorne, *Britain and the Dutch Revolt, 1560–1700* (Cambridge: Cambridge University Press, 2013), 170.

those by Eusebius and Theodoret, and *De mortibus persecutorum* by Lactantius—he described in somewhat gruesome detail the downfall and deaths of the persecuting Roman emperors. Owen believed that similar judgments had occurred in more recent English and European history, and he argued that this should serve as a caution to any who might be tempted to fight against God by persecuting the faithful.

For the final part of the tract, Owen turned to consider "what positively the civil magistrate, may, nay, ought to do, in the whole business of religion." This had been a matter of considerable dispute in the Whitehall debates, and Owen handled it in a threefold manner. He began with what he thought was the most important consideration—namely, the magistrate's duty toward the truth and those who professed it, "the settling and establishing of the profession of the gospel." He laid out five position statements. First, the supreme magistrate was to ensure that the truth of the gospel be preached and declared to the nation. Second, it was incumbent upon the magistrate to act against any "unruly men" who employed "force or violence" against the progress of the gospel. Third, the magistrate was to ensure the provision of places of public worship. Fourth, worshipers were to be protected from any who would disturb their gatherings, which included acting against those who had been excommunicated who might try to disrupt a church gathering. Finally, when necessary, it was the duty of the magistrate to provide ministerial maintenance until churches were "settled" and able to provide for their ministers in the "ordinary way." Owen clarified that those who were in error should not expect any support from the magistrate beyond protection from violence, and in so doing the magistrate was not exercising a duty in matters of religion but was simply preserving the public peace. Additionally, the "minute differences" that existed between "Presbyterians and Independents" were not a matter for the civil magistrate, and therefore both those groups should expect the magistrate to support them.

As Owen laid out his vision for the role of the magistrate in matters of religion, he considered how the magistrate should respond to those who opposed the truth that was officially embraced by those in power, not least by way of "disturbances" and blasphemy. In the first instance, the government was to ensure that no public places were used for false worship. This required the removal of altars, crosses, religious images, and prayer books so that those buildings "commonly called churches" could be properly used. For Owen, it also would logically imply the demolition of mosques. This all was straightforward, but he conceded that the question of how to deal with those in error was altogether more difficult.

Nonetheless, he believed that there were "certain clear rules," the first of which was that those who disturbed the peace ought to be restrained. Here he offered the example of the rebellion of radical Anabaptists in the German city of Münster in 1534–1535. The second rule was to apply the negative version of the Golden Rule: "Do not that to another that you would not have done unto yourself." Owen had made this same point in the *Country Essay* of 1646. Third, he dealt with those who endeavored to propagate error with respect to "matters of great weight and importance." Here he referenced the notorious anti-Trinitarian phrase "*Tricipitem Cerberum.*"[237] Such rhetoric had been used by Miguel Servet and, in recent days, had been employed by another anti-Trinitarian, Paul Best.[238] For Owen, the issue here was not "disbelieving" the truth but rather the resultant public blasphemy of "reviling opprobrious speeches." In such cases, Owen was inclined to support some degree of "corporal restraint." He was much more convinced about the need for judicial action to be taken against certain itinerant preachers whom he portrayed as lazy vagrants.[239] This was a call for the magistrate to act against such itinerants by utilizing the legal means for dealing with vagabonds. In May, shortly after this tract was written, the Rump Parliament's Poor Act would include additional legislation to deal with "rogues, vagabonds, and beggars."[240] Well aware of the antitolerationist propaganda that was designed to stoke fear, Owen expressed a measure of skepticism about many of the salacious stories that were circulating regarding the "vice and sin" of the sects (presumably about those who would generically come to be referred to as "Ranters" in the 1650s), likening it to the anti-Separatist and anti-Puritan propaganda he remembered from his childhood. Nonetheless, the magistrate was justified in exercising restraining power to "set hedges of thorns" around those who "[broke] forth into disturbance of common order" with "enormities against the light of nature."

Finally, Owen turned to what the magistrate ought to do with the various kinds of "Dissenters." Once again, he did this by setting forth a number

---

237 In Greek and Latin mythology, Cerberus was the three-headed hound guarding the gates to the underworld.

238 Bruce Gordon, *The Swiss Reformation* (Manchester: Manchester University Press, 2002), 219; Mortimer, *Reason and Religion*, 195.

239 David Underdown, *Revel, Riot, and Rebellion: Popular Politics and Culture in England, 1603–1660* (Oxford: Oxford University Press, 1985), 250; David Hitchcock, *Vagrancy in English Culture and Society, 1650–1750* (London: Bloomsbury, 2016), 21–26.

240 See "May 1649: An Act for the Relief and Imployment of the Poor, and the Punishment of Vagrants, and other disorderly Persons, within the City of London, and the Liberties thereof," in *Acts and Ordinances of the Interregnum*, 2:104–10.

of position statements. First, given the present "confusion" and "the great disorder of the churches," he thought the question was in some ways premature, and his proposals were more provisional than what he had laid out in the earlier part of the tract. Next, he suggested that the state might utilize the Apostles' Creed, "that ancient symbol commonly esteemed apostolical," as an initial summary of the "chief heads of religion" for the churches that would be "owned and protected" to consent to. He thought that this would be a necessary precursor to resolving the recent disputes about "the nature and use of confessions." Third, he recognized that Dissent from the doctrine and worship that would be established could be either in "less matters of small consequence" or in fundamentals. With respect to the former, Owen was clear that if the peace of the church and society was not disturbed, then the magistrate should not attempt to force conscientious Dissenters, "sound in so many fundamentals," to submit or deploy "the laws against idolatry and blasphemy." This can be taken as Owen's dismissal of Parliament's Blasphemy Ordinance of May 1648, which would have punished with imprisonment a multitude of Dissenters, including those who claimed Presbyterianism and paedobaptism to be unlawful.[241] When it came to those who dissented in more fundamental matters, Owen contended that spiritual means should be employed, and if these proved ineffectual, the magistrate ought to act against only Dissenters who disturbed the peace. He acknowledged that there would, undoubtedly, be controversy and disagreement, but this was better than any "compelled peace" because only the Holy Spirit had the power to quiet the conscience.

Owen concluded by suggesting that Parliament might find it necessary to facilitate further debate among those "who are differently minded as to this business of toleration." He sought to define the boundaries of that debate with two corollaries: it was wrong to claim that the magistrate had no powers in matters of religion; second, "corporal punishments for simple error" were anti-Christian. In other words, as Coffey explains, Owen adopted a "measured and judicious approach" that rejected coerced uniformity while leaving a significant role in matters of religion for the civil magistrate.[242]

Owen's tract *Toleration* supported the essence of the religious settlement laid out in *Officers' Agreement*. What was in view in both documents would find later expression in the religious clauses of the Instrument of Government that established the Protectorate in 1653 and that served as the basis for the

---

241 *Journals of the House of Commons*, 5:549; *Acts and Ordinances of the Interregnum*, 1:1133–36.
242 Coffey, "John Owen and the Puritan Toleration Controversy," 235.

Cromwellian church settlement. The instrument stated that "the Christian religion, as contained in the Scriptures, be held forth and recommended as the public profession of these nations."[243] However, this state-sponsored national church, united by fundamentals, privileged in so many ways, would be noncompulsory; there would be toleration for anyone outside it who did not disturb the peace, provided they were not advocating popery or prelacy. Similarly, the ideas in this tract found expression in the religious settlement in the Protectorate's second constitution, the *Humble Petition and Advice* (1657).[244] The same view would be present in the Congregationalists' *Savoy Confession* of 1658. Magistrates were "bound to encourage, promote and protect the Professors and Profession of the Gospel" and "to take care that men of corrupt minds and conversations do not licentiously publish and divulge Blasphemy and Errors in their own nature subverting the faith, and inevitably destroying the souls of them that receive them." However, when it came to secondary differences among the godly, those "holding the foundation" and not disturbing the peace were to be protected even when they did not accept the "public profession" in "the Doctrines of the Gospel, or ways of the worship of God."[245] At that time, ten years after the writing of the tract, Owen still regarded the position on toleration set out in *Toleration* as in line with his "Present Judgment" on the matter and was directing readers to it.[246]

ΟΥΡΑΝΩΝ ΟΥΡΑΝΙΑ: THE SHAKING AND TRANSLATING OF HEAVEN AND EARTH

The Context of the Sermon

Οὐρανῶν Οὐρανία: *The Shaking and Translating of Heaven and Earth* was the second sermon that Owen preached to the purged Parliament at St Margaret's Westminster. In the past three months, the revolution had continued with

---

[243] David L. Smith, "The *Agreements of the People* and the Constitutions of the Interregnum Governments," in *The Agreements of the People, the Levellers and the Constitutional Crisis of the English Revolution*, ed. Philip Baker and Elliot Vernon (Basingstoke, UK: Macmillan, 2012), 247–48.

[244] *Acts and Ordinances of the Interregnum*, 2:1048–56.

[245] *A Declaration of the Faith and Order Owned and Practised by the Congregational Churches in England* [...] (London, 1659), 17–18.

[246] John Owen, *An Answer to a Late Treatise of the Said Mr. Cawdrey about the Nature of Schism* (Oxford, 1658), 67. See also Owen's letter to Du Moulin in which he mentioned how he had written on the subject and that "the general opinion of most theologians in England is for a civil toleration of those who do not err in fundamental matters." See Adam Quibell, "John Owen's Lost Huguenot Letters: French Reformed Protestants and the Reception of Congregational English Puritan Ecclesiology and Politics," *Journal of Ecclesiastical History* (2023), 12.

acts abolishing the office of the king and the House of Lords. The sermon was delivered on the occasion of a national fast, one that had been postponed several times (previous proposed dates were March 22 and April 5) before it finally took place on Thursday, April 19, 1649.[247] According to the parliamentary order, the purpose of the national day of fasting and humiliation was "to implore Gods forgiveness for the ingratitude of the people," particularly "unthankfulness and unfruitfulness under unparalled mercies and deliverances."[248] The idea being "to set the godly tone for the newly established Commonwealth."[249]

The Rump's membership had broadened since Owen's postregicide sermon, and as a preacher he had significant work to do in order to persuade some of the more moderate members of Parliament that the revolutionary events they had witnessed in some horror were indeed providential mercies to be celebrated. According to a hostile royalist newspaper, across the rest of London, the national fast "was not observed in any Church of note," something that it reported caused the government "great grief and vexation."[250] Days afterward, on April 23, the Rump abolished the regular monthly fasts, established in 1642, and replaced them by days of fasting called on a more occasional basis.[251] One of the reasons why they came to an end was the fear that they had become a matter of mere "formal observance."[252] Other reasons included the widespread unpopularity and neglect of the fasts and (perhaps the thing most concerning for the new regime) the fact that on such occasions some pulpits were being used to undermine the government.[253] For example, John Clopton recorded in his diary that the fast "was not kept" in and around his parish on the Essex-Suffolk border.[254] That month, there were serious concerns about the messages that some were communicating from their pulpits: on April 3, the Rump formed a committee to consider "an Act prohibiting Ministers and

---

[247] *Journals of the House of Commons*, 6:152, 158, 166, 175.

[248] *An Act of the Commons of England Assembled in Parliament, for the Keeping a Day of Humiliation upon Thursday the 19 Day of April, 1649* (1649); *The Kingdomes Faithfull and Impartiall Scout* (April 13–20, 1649), 96; *A Perfect Summary of Exact Passages of Parliament* (April 17–23, 1649), 130.

[249] Mears et al., *National Prayers*, 1:497.

[250] *Mercurius Pragmaticus* (for King Charles II) (April 17–24, 1649), sig. A3v.

[251] "April 1649: An Act For setting apart A Day of Solemn Fasting and Humiliation, and Repealing the Former Monethly Fast," in *Acts and Ordinances of the Interregnum*, 2:79–81.

[252] Hughes, "Preachers and Hearers in Revolutionary London," 59; Milton, *England's Second Reformation*, 304.

[253] *Perfect Occurrences* 120 (April 13–19, 1649), 944; *Perfect Occurrences* 122 (April 27–May 4, 1649), 1006. See Durston, ' "For the Better Humiliation of the People," ' 142.

[254] Mears et al., *Special Prayers, Fasts and Thanksgivings*, 497.

Preachers, in Praying or Preaching, to intermeddle with Matters of State";[255] it returned to the matter of disaffected preaching within a fortnight, establishing a committee to discuss the problem of hostile preaching designed "to stir up and disaffect the people."[256] The new regime was under siege and needed preachers like Owen to serve as apologists for the revolution.

Two of the parliamentarians to whom Owen had dedicated *Ebenezer* (1648) issued the invitations to the preachers who were to participate: Owen was invited by Sir William Masham, and Sir Henry Mildmay extended the invitation to John Warren (1621–1696), minister of Hatfield, Broad Oak, Essex.[257] Afterward, the House ordered that the sermons be printed, and Owen's was duly published by John Cleaver, who was also now selling copies of the published version of Owen's preaching on the occasion of the victory at Colchester.[258] Warren's sermon, *The Potent Potter* (1649), emphasized divine sovereignty in the "breaking down, and building up of Nations." He insisted that "God can deal with any people or Nation, as the potter dealeth with his clay." Well aware of the "blustring storms that rage amongst us at these present alterations," Warren argued that in matters of government, God had authority "when he hath removed one forme, to introduce another." His sermon was very much in line with Owen's; echoing the title of his fellow preacher's published sermon, Warren likened the change of government that had taken place to "an old house translated into a new form."[259]

Owen's sermon appears to have had an immediate impact on at least one of his auditors. According to the memoirs of Asty, Oliver Cromwell heard Owen preach this sermon and a few days later encountered him at the home of Thomas Fairfax. Cromwell informed Owen that he was "the person I must be acquainted with." Owen is said to have responded, "That will be much more to my advantage than yours," to which Cromwell replied, "We shall see."[260] Cromwell's experience was far from unique because this sermon continued to resonate with those living in times of political crisis. In 1655, the Fifth Monarchist John Spittlehouse quoted extensively from this sermon to accuse Owen of abandoning his earlier convictions.[261] Similarly, in the turmoil of 1659, a Fifth Monarchist pamphlet

---

[255] *Journals of the House of Commons*, 6:178.
[256] *Journals of the House of Commons*, 6:183, 186–87.
[257] *Journals of the House of Commons*, 6:152.
[258] Wilson, *Pulpit in Parliament*, 96; Gribben, *John Owen and English Puritanism*, 107.
[259] John Warren, *The Potent Potter* (London, 1649), 6, 9–10,12–13.
[260] Asty, "Memoirs of the Life of John Owen," 9.
[261] John Spittlehouse, *The Royall Advocate. Or, An Introduction to the Magnificent and Honourable Laws of Jehovah the Lord Christ, Now Contaminated and Despised by the Present Army-Men of this Nation* (London, 1655), 50–59.

reminded readers of exactly what had been said by "Dr. Owen in his Sermon [on] Heb. 12.27."[262] Some years later, in the revolutionary fervor of the late eighteenth century, this sermon was reissued in London in 1793, Edinburgh in 1774, Belfast and Monaghan in 1795, and again in Belfast in 1797.[263]

The subject matter was apt, given that the new republic no doubt felt as if it were being shaken to its very foundations by a range of domestic and international threats. At home, the new regime was widely unpopular and faced a very difficult economic situation, particularly with the rising costs of food and fuel. Politically, it was encountering opposition from both conservatives wishing to restore the monarchy and disgruntled radicals alike.[264] Two days after Owen delivered the sermon, the London women's petition was presented to the Commons, expressing concerns about a nation "laid waste" and the day-to-day reality of "poverty, misery and famine."[265] Within the rank-and-file soldiers of the New Model Army, there was also mounting dissatisfaction due to arrears of pay and the prospect of the being shipped to Ireland. There was also the very real prospect of a Leveller rising among the soldiers. The Leveller leader, John Lilburne, had published *Englands New Chains Discovered*, attacking the Independents and the army for betraying the cause and adopting the character of the old tyrannical regime.[266] Some in the army believed that there should be no Irish expedition until the English liberties were protected in An Agreement of the People.[267] The Commons voted *The Second Part of Englands New-Chaines* "highly seditious," and Lilburne along with three others Leveller leaders were sent to the Tower to await trial, from where they did all that they could to stir up sedition in the army.[268] A week after Owen preached, there was a minor mutiny in one of the regiments in London, which saw trooper Robert Lockyer executed by way of exemplary punishment.[269] On the day Owen penned his preface (May 1), the four imprisoned leaders orchestrated the publication of the most radical Leveller constitution, *An Agreement of the Free People of England*.[270]

---

262 *The Fifth Monarchy, or Kingdom of Christ, in Opposition to the Beasts, Asserted, by the Solemn League and Covenant, Several Learned Divines, the Late General and Army, (viz.) in their Declaration at Muslebrough, August 1650* (London, 1659), 7–8.
263 Gribben, "Becoming John Owen," 319.
264 Underdown, *Pride's Purge*, 281.
265 Gary S. De Krey, *Following the Levellers*, vol. 1, *Political and Religious Radicals in the English Civil War and Revolution, 1645–1649* (London: Palgrave Macmillan, 2017), 239.
266 *Englands New Chains Discovered* (London, [February 26,] 1649).
267 See, for example, *The English Souldiers Standard* (London, [April 5,] 1649), 9.
268 John Lilburne, *The Second Part of Englands New-Chaines Discovered* (London, [March 24,] 1648).
269 Gentles, *New Model Army*, 164–65.
270 De Krey, *Following the Levellers*, 244–47.

In the wider context, the covenanted Scots were horrified at the death of the king and had immediately recognized his son as Charles II. On top of this, a significant part of the navy had revolted during the second Civil War and was now under the control of Prince Rupert.[271] In Ireland, the regicide had united the main rival factions in support of a Stuart restoration: in January, James Butler, Marquess of Ormond, had negotiated an alliance between royalist and Irish Roman Catholic forces termed the Second Ormond Peace.[272] For a time, the Scottish Presbyterians in Ulster allied with them. It is no wonder that as Owen surveyed the nations of the world, he lamented how so many were "wasted, destroyed, [and] spoiled," and concluded that "God has taken quietness and peace from the earth."

Despite these domestic and foreign threats, this sermon gives voice to what Worden describes as "an exultant mood in and about [Owen's] circle in the period around the regicide."[273] Coffey captures the essence of this sermon by describing it as "apocalyptic."[274] In his postregicide sermon from January, Owen had already spoken of how "the shaking of heaven and earth" would result in further political turmoil. This sermon anticipates the prospect of the reconstruction of the political and religious structures of England as Owen boldly proclaimed that the "season of the accomplishment of [God's] great intendments for the good of his church" was "nigh at hand, even at the doors." Owen was fully persuaded that God was at work to "refashion the governments of the world."[275] Despite some opposition, plans were advancing for the conquest of Ireland, and the day before Owen preached lots were cast to select the four New Model regiments that would be sent to give "timely relief to that distressed Country."[276] Such widescale millenarian optimism was, no doubt, bolstered by news that France was experiencing its own internal crisis, the Fronde (1648–1653), a series of civil wars and disturbances during the minority of Louis XIV. Like the conflict in England, this revolt came about through a desire to curb royal authority in support of the ancient liberties of the people. In London at the end of February, news reports circulated about how the French king had been forced "to yield" by calling a

---

271 Bernard Capp, "Naval Operations," in John P. Kenyon and Jane Ohlmeyer (eds.), *The Civil Wars: A Military History of England, Scotland and Ireland, 1638–1660* (Oxford: Oxford University Press, 1998), 184–87.

272 Micheál Ó Siochrú, *Confederate Ireland 1642–1649: A Constitutional and Political Analysis* (Dublin: Four Courts Press, 1999), 185–204.

273 Worden, *God's Instruments*, 335.

274 Coffey, *John Goodwin and the Puritan Revolution*, 193.

275 Gribben, *John Owen and English Puritanism*, 107.

276 *Perfect Weekly Account* (April 11–April 18, 1649), 445; *Perfect Weekly Account* (April 18–April 25, 1649), 453.

"generall Parliament of the Estates."[277] The Spanish branch of the Habsburg Empire was having to deal with the secessionist revolts in Naples (1647), Catalonia (1640–1653), and Portugal (1640–1668). It is therefore unsurprising that Owen felt that he "need not speak one word" about the "shaking of civil constitutions" that had taken place "under our eyes." He believed that this would usher in a whole new era: "the prosperous estate of the kingdom of Christ."

The sermon was printed by Matthew Simmons, who had published Owen's postregicide parliamentary sermon from January 1649. It was to be sold by John Cleaver. This is Cleaver's "only recorded publication."[278] His bookshop was located close St Paul's School, founded in 1509 by the Dean of the Cathedral, John Colet.[279] A deed in the London Metropolitan Archives reveals that by 1653 Cleaver's shop at St Paul's Churchyard was in the hands of another stationer by the name of George Greene.[280]

Summary and Analysis of the Sermon

Owen's aim in this sermon was "the confirming and establishing [of] his countrymen in the faith of this glorious gospel" so that he would "persuade professors to constancy in the paths of the gospel." His text from Hebrews enabled him to address those who because of "opposition or persecution" had succumbed to "apostasy" and "backsliding." John Tweeddale describes how in Owen's careful exegesis of the text, he can be seen at the opening of the sermon in "noting linguistic nuances, expounding the wider biblical context of the letter, and interacting with differing commentators on the passage."[281] The central trope he chose to focus on was the shaking of the heavens and earth. He rejects what he regarded as three inappropriate interpretations of what it meant for heaven and earth to be shaken.[282] First, the view of Rollock and Piscator and "sundry other famous divines," that it is humanity and the angels

---

277 *Perfect Weekly Account* (February 21–February 28, 1649), 403.
278 Blayney, *The Bookshops of Paul's Cross Churchyard*, 51, 77. A stationer of the name John Cleaver is referenced in *A Transcript of the Registers of the Company of Stationers of London, 1554–1640*, ed. Edward Arber, 5 vols. (London, 1875–1894), 2:736.
279 For the print culture associated with this area, see Benjamin King-Cox and Daniel Starza Smith, "Buying and Selling Books Around St Paul's Cathedral: 'Be Dishonest, and Tell Lies,'" in *Old St Paul's and Culture*, ed. Shanyn Altman and Jonathan Buckner (London: Palgrave Macmillan, 2021), 269–92.
280 City of London Corporation, *Miscellaneous Deeds at the London Metropolitan Archives* (CLC/522), Add. Mss. 0924, 326.
281 John W. Tweeddale, *John Owen and Hebrews: The Foundation of Biblical Interpretation* (London: T&T Clark, 2019), 33.
282 See John H. Duff, *"A Knot Worth Unloosing": The Interpretation of the New Heavens and Earth in Seventeenth-Century England* (Göttingen: Vandenhoeck & Ruprecht, 2019), 49–64.

who are shaken through the incarnation of the Son. Owen dismisses this on a twofold basis: at the time when the epistle to the Hebrews was being written, the shaking was presented as a future event yet to take place; and Hebrews states that what is shaken is removed, which makes no sense if human beings and the angelic company are in view. Second, Owen rejected the interpretation of Junius and "most" English commentators that the shaking is that of the creation by way of the events that accompanied Christ's birth, death, and resurrection—for example, the star, the darkness, and the earthquake. Owen denied this interpretation on the same basis as the first. The third interpretation denied by Owen is that the shaking in view is that which takes place at the consummation of all things. Owen rejects this because he believed that although the kingdom of Christ had not yet been revealed in its full glory, it nonetheless had been established by Jesus Christ. Owen's interpretation is based on the meaning of "heaven and earth" in the passage from Haggai from which the quotation is drawn (Hag. 2:6–7). He argues that the author has employed more words than is strictly necessary ("pleonasm") in order to emphasize that the heavens and earth of all nations will be shaken. According to his interpretation, as is typical in prophetic literature, the idiom refers to the shaking of a nation's government (its "heaven") and the people of the nations (the "earth").

The trope of shaking from Hebrews 12:27 was also employed by others close to Owen to explain how the kingdom of Christ would be ushered in.[283] In the posthumously published *Supereminence of Christ above Moses*, Thomas Goodwin spoke of the "unparalleled changes, alterations, and abolitions of things which were already begun . . . and are to go on till they are to be consummated in the latter day." Like Owen, Goodwin contended that "States and kingdoms, and the governments, and powers, and ranks in them, are as ordinarily set forth by this metaphor of heaven and earth." For Goodwin, the scope of this shaking was comprehensive and included the establishment of the "ordinances, institutions, and administrations . . . of gospel worship"; "all other alterations of religions, false and suppositious"; and "all the alterations, shakings and removals civil that have been in states."[284]

---

[283] William Strong, *The Vengeance of the Temple: Discovered in a Sermon Preached Before the Right Honourable the Lord Major [. . .] May 17 1648. Being the Day of Publique Thanksgiving for a Victory Obtayned by the Forces Under the Command of Colonell Horton, at St. Faggons, Neere Cardiffe in Wales* (London, 1648), 44; M. Barker, *A Christian Standing & Moving upon the True Foundation* (London, 1648), 47; John Cotton, *The Powring Out of the Seven Vials* (London, 1642), "The Seventh Vial," 7; Thomas Goodwin's treatise *Supereminence of Christ Above Moses* is an exposition of these two texts, in *The Works of Thomas Goodwin, D.D. Sometime President of Magdalen Colledg in Oxford*, 5 vols. (London, 1681–1704), 5:439–62.

[284] Goodwin, *Supereminence of Christ*, in *Works of Thomas Goodwin*, 5:439–40, 457–59.

This exposition enabled him to play his part in helping justify the new and unpopular regime by explaining that what was taking place was a "civil shaking" of "the political heights, the splendor and strength of the nations of the earth." Owen sought to persuade members of Parliament that in contemporary events, "heaven and earth" were being shaken to make way for the things that were unshakeable—namely, the prosperous estate of the kingdom of Christ. He believed that this prophetic idiom included the transformation of a nation's "political heights and glory" (its heavens) and "the nation's earth," which he understood to be "the multitudes of their people, their strength and power, whereby their heavens, or political heights, are supported."[285] This would bring down "the pillars" and "props" that upheld the spiritual city of Babylon—namely, the governing powers of the world in their present form.[286] In the process, God was planting new heavens and laying the foundations of a new earth (Isa. 51)—that is, establishing governments that would allow "the Nations, as Nations," to serve the kingdom of Christ (Rev. 11:15).

In the past, God had shaken to pieces the heavens and earth of the Roman Empire ("the pagan-Roman state"; Owen points to Rev. 6:12–15). This began in the plagues that came on the persecuting Roman emperors and ended "in the ruin of the empire itself." Subsequently, from the "crumbled" remains of the Roman Empire, Satan "molded" the heaven and earth of "papal anti-Christian Rome," which was spread "through all the nations of the West." Owen contended that this era of "anti-Christian tyranny" would soon be brought to an end by those Western nations and their "political heights," "governments," and constitutions being shaken. From the "confusion," these nations would emerge "translated [and] new-molded" and be instrumental in both the destruction of the antichrist as the bringing in of Christ's "peaceable kingdom." There were, he said, "innumerable promises" about the "visible glorious appearance" of the Christ's kingdom in the last days. It would be an era marked by the blessings of "the special presence of Christ," such as "multitudes of the elect being . . . born," the callings of the Jews, and the renewal of the worship of the church. Owen did not subscribe to what he thought to be fanciful ideas of "a terrene kingly state" associated with "the personal reign of the Lord Jesus on earth," viewing the "curiosities" of some as undermining authority in both church and state. Owen was also concerned that the Fifth Monarchists were undermining the legitimate

---

[285] Samuel Parker drew attention to Owen's use of this language. See Parker, *Defence and Continuation*, 114.

[286] In 1655, Cromwell utilized the same trope to describe Spain as "the great underproper" of "Romain Babilon." See Cromwell, *Letters, Writings, and Speeches of Oliver Cromwell*, 2:231.

civil power. According to him, they too mistakenly thought that the political heights would be removed rather than translated. He clearly distanced himself from those who "for sinister ends pretend . . . to fancy to themselves a terrene kingly state, unto each private particular saint," thinking that this would lead to "the disturbance of all order and authority, civil and spiritual," and that Christ would "exceedingly abhor" such "confusion and disorder." For Owen, the visible appearance of Christ on earth was something that would take place only at his future glorious appearance as Judge (Rev. 19:13). Rather, he expected that by "the special presence of Christ" the church would enjoy in the near future a golden era characterized by freedom from persecution and purity of worship.

Owen turned to confirm what he had said by way of appeal to the timeline of events outlined in Daniel 2 and Revelation 17. This prophetic chronology, one that would help bolster the new regime, was employed by a number of republican polemicists at this time.[287]

According to this scheme, in the fifth century, when the Germanic peoples settled the territory of the former Western Roman Empire, ten nations emerged as "distinct dominions." This was also the time when the Papacy emerged. This "Roman harlot" gained the support and allegiance of these nations that promised to undertake the defense of the "holy church." Having "submitted to the usurpation of the man of sin," these nations effectively came into papal servitude. Owen claimed that in the period from approximately 750 to 1066, "the pope had a hand" in every alteration of government that took place across Europe, and this brought "all these nations into subjection to his Babylonish usurpations." This resulted in the "false worship" and the "witnesses of the Lamb" being persecuted "with fire and sword" as "heretics." Owen referenced the work of the martyrologist John Foxe as he outlined how the persecution of the true church began in earnest in the tenth century and continued with the persecution of groups such as the Lollards, Waldensians, Cathars, and the Hussites. Owen's assessment of the government of most of the European kingdoms was that they were "purely framed for the interest of Antichrist" and thus stood "in direct opposition to the bringing in of the kingdom of Christ." Adopting a decidedly antimonarchical tone, Owen claimed that all the Western kings were united in this "implacable enmity" toward the godly and that "the papal interest" lay at the bottom of all or the most ruling lines in Christendom. The "Western nations" had

---

[287] Nicole Greenspan, *Selling Cromwell's Wars: Media, Empire and Godly Warfare, 1650–1658* (London: Routledge, 2016), 20.

been tricked and deceived by the papacy, the whore of Babylon, and brought into "spiritual and civil slavery" while their rulers were "drunk with the cup of her abominations." Owen's point that many kings were in the service of popery would have gained plausibility from Charles II being allied with Irish Roman Catholics and seeking assistance from other Roman Catholic kings to secure his restoration. The articles of Second Ormond Peace of January 1649, well-publicized in London, offered a number of concessions to Irish Roman Catholics, including freedom of worship, a discharge of all indictments since 1641, and the possibility of holding public office.[288] Uncovering these links between the institutions of monarchy and popery was part of how Owen sought to build support for the new godly regime and to explain the nature of the opposition that it faced.

Owen believed that the European nations that evolved out of the old Roman Empire were in the process of being thoroughly shaken so that they would no longer support the Papacy. After this shaking of the nations, the Papacy would be dethroned, and the church would enjoy peace and prosperity. No amount of "digging or mining" would be able to change the present constitutions that were "directly framed to the interest of Antichrist" ("dig you never so deep, build you never so high"). Rather, what was required was for Christ to "so far open their whole frame to the roots, as to pluck out all the cursed seeds of the mystery of Iniquity, which by the craft of Satan and exigencies of State, or methods of advancing the pride and power of some sons of blood, have been sown among them." Contextually, it is plausible to see oblique references here to two groups of which members of Parliament were well aware of: first, the Diggers (or True Levellers) sowing seed and, second, the Derbyshire miners of the Peak District.

Three weeks before Owen preached this sermon, Gerrard Winstanley and around thirty others established a settlement on St George's Hill, Walton-on-Thames, Surrey. They began to cultivate the commons, "casting in Seed, that we may eat our Bread together in righteousness."[289] These "Diggers" declared the earth a common treasury and called for an end to private property as the source of all bondage and violence. This was a highly provocative assault on the existing social structures because Winstanley and his small group of followers had no legal right to the land. On April 16, the Council of State

---

[288] *Perfect Diurnall* [...] (March 26–April 2, 1649), 2388–89.
[289] Gerrard Winstanley, *The True Levellers Standard Advanced* (April 1649), in *The Complete Works of Gerrard Winstanley*, ed. T. N. Corns et al. (Oxford: Oxford University Press, 2010), 252; John Gurney, "Gerrard Winstanley and the Digger Movement in Walton and Cobham," *Historical Journal* 37, no. 4 (1994): 775–802.

ordered Fairfax to disperse them, and on the day of Owen's sermon, Captain Gladman was in Surrey investigating. The following day, April 20, Winstanley and William Everard were brought to Whitehall to explain themselves (both refused to remove their hats).[290]

Regarding the second group with levelling tendencies, for several years the Earl of Rutland had been involved in a dispute with lead miners who claimed the right to mine on his Derbyshire estate. On March 28, Rutland had petitioned the Commons to declare against the miners who had recently won the support of the Levellers.[291] Countering such levelling ideas, Owen explained that the change of government that was to be expected would be a "translation," not "a destruction and total amotion, of the great things of the Nations" (the legal term *amotion* means either "removal of a person from office" or "removal of property from its owner"). He believed that the magistracy would be "new molded for the interest of the Lord Jesus," rather than be levelled. Anthony Ascham expressed similar sentiments that year when he wrote against those who "by a new Art of levelling, thinke nothing can be rightly mended or reformed, unlesse the whole piece ravell out to the very end, and that all intermediate greatnesse betwixt Kings and them, should be crumbled even to dust, where all lying levell together as in the first Chaos."[292]

In a context in which there was intense debate about the nature and legitimacy of government, Owen argued that turning to other "carnal" forms of government was, likewise, no solution. He described those for whom "no sooner is one carnal form shaken out, but they are ready to cleave to another: yea to warm themselves in the feathered nests of unclean birds." In the Bible, the unclean birds are listed in Leviticus 11:13–19 and Deuteronomy 14:11–18, and in Revelation, fallen Babylon (i.e., Rome) becomes "a cage of every unclean and hateful bird" (Rev. 18:2). It would appear that by these "feathered nests," Owen may have been alluding to the ideas of the political thought of classical antiquity. At that time, some were attempting to legitimize the new regime by appealing to the ideas of classical republicanism and the Renaissance humanism of the city-states of the Italian peninsula.[293] The journalist Marchamont Nedham would be responsible

---

290 William Clarke, *The Clarke Papers*, vols. 1–4, ed. C. H. Firth (London: Camden Society, 1891–1901), 2:210–12.
291 *Journals of the House of Commons*, 6:175; Andy Wood, *The Politics of Social Conflict: The Peak Country, 1520–1770* (Cambridge: Cambridge University Press, 1999), 279–85.
292 Anthony Ascham, *Of the Confusions and Revolutions of Governments* (London, 1649), 18.
293 Blair Worden, "Classical Republicanism and the Puritan Revolution," in *History and Imagination: Essays in Honour of H. R. Trevor-Roper*, ed. Hugh Lloyd-Jones, Valerie Pearl, and Blair Worden (London: Duckworth, 1981), 184–93; J. G. A. Pocock, "Political Thought in the Cromwellian

for widely disseminating these neoclassical ideas, first in *The Case of the Commonwealth of England, Stated* (1650) and then in the government newspaper *Mercurius Politicus* (1651–1652).[294] Just over a month before Owen made these comments, the godly in England's second city, Norwich, voiced similar concerns about those who looked to the ideas of "heathen Rome and Athens."[295] His assessment was that "the whole present constitution of the government of the nations, is so cemented with anti-Christian mortar, from the very top to the bottom," that the only solution was the "thorough shaking" that Owen was expounding. Similarly, the "invented idolatrous worship" of the nations was likewise "riveted and cemented" into the European nations. Owen believed that the idolatry of the Roman Catholic Church was the most significant obstacle to Jewish conversion. An apocalyptic shaking and metamorphosis of the nations would be required if it was to be removed. This would shake out all idolatrous practices such as "iconolatry, artolatry, hagiolatry, staurolatry, and mass abominations." These tropes of "riveting" and "cementing" were used across the spectrum to refer to strong coupling of episcopacy into the old constitution. On the one hand, for example, the radical army chaplain John Saltmarsh described how prelacy "remained rivetted into our Laws and usages" and on the other, Bishop John Bramhall, spoke of episcopacy as "woven and riveted into the body of our law" and "cemented into our laws."[296] Thus, according to Owen, constitutional reformation would require the separation of powers that had been strongly intertwined. This would involve them being "translated in mind, interest, and perhaps government" so that they would become "instrumental in the hand of Christ for the ruin of that anti-Christian state which before they served."

Owen applied this by way of six "uses." He devoted significant material to the first point of application as he called his hearers to understand the "times

---

Interregnum," in *W. P. Morrell: A Tribute*, ed. G. A. Wood and P. S. O'Connor (Dunedin: University of Otago, 1973), 21–36.

294 Blair Worden, "Marchamont Nedham and the Beginnings of English Republicanism, 1649–1656," in *Republicanism, Liberty, and Commercial Society, 1649–1776*, ed. David Wootton (Stanford, CA: Stanford University Press, 1994), 45–81.

295 *Certain Quaeres Humbly Presented in Way of Petition* (London, [February 1649]), 3; Sarah Barber, *Regicides and Republicanism: Politics and Ethics in the English Revolution, 1646–1659* (Edinburgh: Edinburgh University Press, 1998), 192.

296 John Saltmarsh, *A Solemn Discourse upon the Grand Covenant* (London, 1643), 50; John Bramhall, *The Serpent Salve* (1643), in *Works*, 5 vols. (Oxford, 1842–1845), 3:468–69; David L. Smith, *Constitutional Royalism and the Search for a Settlement, c.1640–1649* (Cambridge: Cambridge University Press, 1994), 220–23.

and seasons" and to familiarize themselves with "the mind and will of God" in their "generation"—in particular, "the season of the accomplishment of his great intendments for the good of his church." The results of such a diligent inquiry would deliver them being preoccupied with attempts to establish a uniform liturgy or polity within the church. It was folly to work "night and day to set up what God will pull down." It would also dispel "sinful cares" about "the force and power of this or that growing monarchy," perhaps a reference to fears that William II was seeking to become the absolute monarch of the United Provinces and might seek to intervene in English affairs on behalf of his brother-in-law, Charles II. Such understanding of the prophetic chronology would remove anxiety about "wars, and rumors of wars, appearances of famine, invasions, conspiracies, revolts, treacheries, sword, blood." In order to "follow hard after God," it was necessary to have insight into the work that God was accomplishing at that time. Owen explained that the "peculiar light of this generation" lay in "the great discovery" "of the mystery of civil and ecclesiastical tyranny"—that is, the "anti-Christian interest" that saw "civil and spiritual" things being "interwoven, and coupled together." Months later, Milton would employ similar language to "discover more of Mysterie and combination between Tyranny and fals Religion," those "twisted Scorpions" of "temporal and spiritual Tyranny" whose "very dark roots" "twine and interweave."[297] For Owen, civil and ecclesiastical powers had to be unraveled, and this would require an "earthquake," an entirely new constitutional settlement.

Owen believed that Scripture was silent on exactly how, or for how long, the shaking would proceed: the new Babylon had taken over "a thousand years" to build and so it was unlikely to fall in under "a thousand days." This apocalyptic shaking would continue until "the interest of anti-Christianity be wholly separated from the power of those nations." Owen thought that it was significant that the shaking of the "heavens" of the nations had already reached the point where the political controversy was now about "the interest of the many" rather than being taken up with "the power and splendor of single persons." As well as events in England, Owen may have had in mind the secessionist revolts in Portugal, Catalonia, and Naples against the absolutism of the Spanish Habsburgs, the Fronde rebellion designed to curb royal authority, and opposition to the monarchical tendencies of William II, Orange stadtholder in the Netherlands.[298] The saints were expecting the liberty that would come as both civil and ecclesiastical tyranny came to an end.

297 John Milton, *Eikonoklestes in Answer to a Book Intitl'd Eikon Basilike* (London, 1650), 148, 200.
298 Donald H. Pennington, *Europe in the Seventeenth Century*, 2nd ed. (Abingdon, UK: Routledge, 2014), 326–31, 388–97, 469–75.

Owen's second use was to call his hearers to "embrace the Lord Jesus in his kingly power" by enthroning Christ in their hearts. For those serving in government, this required serious consideration of how the Lord was shaking the heavens and earth of the nations, bringing the "potentates" of this world to justice for their sins and a realization that his aim was "to frame and form" them as "kingdoms of the Lord Jesus." Owen referred his readers to the tract *Toleration*, which he had appended to the published version of his fast sermon from January, explaining how it set out what the true interest of the nation involved.

The final four uses were covered is less detail. The realization that the heavens of the nation were being shaken would help explain how "some who pretended to be church stars" and who sought a place in the "political heavens" of the nation were shaken to the ground. For Owen, this served as a warning to those who were vacillating, unsure of which way to turn, that if they failed to serve the interests of Christ they too would be shaken from their places. This resulted in a call to self-examination because the nation was "entering the most purging trying furnace, that ever the Lord set up on the earth." Consequently, Owen called his hearers to be "loose from all shaken things" and to keep their eyes, hearts, and hands focused on the things that would not be shaken. Well aware that "some are angry, some troubled, some in the dark, [and] some full of revenge," Owen closed with the uncompromising assertion that "Babylon shall fall" and the kingdoms of the earth would become "the kingdoms of our Lord Jesus Christ" (Rev. 11:5).

HUMAN POWER DEFEATED

The Context of Owen's Sermon Celebrating the Defeat of the Levellers at Burford

In the spring of 1649, the army was "seething with unrest": Parliament had not acted to settle arrears in pay, there was reluctance to embark on the impending expedition to Ireland, and the government was slow to implement hoped-for reform. This discontent was further stirred up by the Levellers.[299] This group was associated with John Lilburne, Richard Overton, and William Walwyn, and its political agenda was to extend the electoral franchise and safeguard the political and religious liberties of the English people under a new written constitution. The Leveller movement had emerged during the civil wars as the parliamentarian side became increasingly divided over

[299] Gentles, *The English Revolution*, 386.

questions about the religious settlement, the role of the ancient institutions, and the nature and legitimacy of government. The first known political use of the term *Leveller* was in 1607, when it was used to name a group in Northamptonshire who protested the enclosure of commons by filling in the ditches and levelling the fences that marked the new boundaries. The first use of the term for the movement in question may quite possibly have been by Oliver Cromwell at the Putney Debates of 1647.[300] The leaders of the movement objected to the term because it suggested that they wished to obliterate distinctions in rank and to challenge traditional property rights. A draft constitution termed *An Agreement of the People* went through several editions between 1647 and 1649, and during this time Leveller ideas took hold in the army. There had been a rapprochement between the senior army officers and the Leveller leaders late in 1648, but this had broken down. In the negotiations that took place in November 1648 to January 1649, no consensus was reached, and there were fundamental differences between the Levellers' second *Agreement* and the *Officers' Agreement*. The Levellers felt betrayed and viewed the events of the revolution as simply the exchange of one tyranny for another. On March 28, four days after the appearance of *The Second Part of Englands New-Chaines Discovered*, a blistering attack on the new military regime, the government arrested Lilburne, Overton, Walwyn, and Thomas Prince. This tract was viewed as seditious and as a threat to the reconquest of Ireland by fomenting further war at home.[301] The prisoners were taken before the Council of State and, after refusing to answer any questions, committed to the Tower of London on suspicion of high treason. On May 14, Parliament passed a new Treason Act that made "Writing, Printing, or openly Declaring, that the ... government is Tyrannical, Usurped or Unlawful" a capital offence.[302]

There was a small mutiny in Colonel Edward Whalley's cavalry regiment on April 24, which saw one of the ringleaders, Robert Lockyer, court-martialed and executed. Significant defiance against the regime was demonstrated at his funeral.[303] The following month, there was a much more serious mutiny.

---

300 Blair Worden, "Appendix—'The Levellers': The Emergence of the Term," in *The Putney Debates of 1647: The Army, the Levellers and the English State*, ed. Michael Mendel (Cambridge: Cambridge University Press, 2001), 280–82.

301 Michael Braddick, *The Common Freedom of the People: John Lilburne and the English Revolution* (Oxford: Oxford University Press, 2018), 168.

302 "July 1649: An Act Declaring What Offences shall be adjudged Treason," in *Acts and Ordinances of the Interregnum*, 2:120–21.

303 Ian Gentles, "Political Funerals During the English Revolution," in *London and the Civil War*, ed. Stephen Porter (Basingstoke, UK: Macmillan, 1996), 218–21.

On May 1 at Salisbury in Wiltshire, a significant number of the troops in Colonel Scroop's regiment of horse, en route for embarkation at Bristol, revolted, refusing to go to Ireland until their grievances were met. The mutineers outlined their grievances in *The Resolutions of the Private Souldiery of Col. Scroops Regiment of Horse* (1649). They called for "Freedom, Peace, and Happiness [to be] Setled in the Nation, and that the Souldiery should have Satisfaction" prior to the Irish expedition, and they also sought the restoration of the elected army council of 1647. They were joined by elements from Ireton's regiment at Old Sarum from where they issued a declaration on May 11.[304] They refused to participate in the "Relief of Ireland" until their "Native Liberties" were restored, and they called for the return of the General Council with representatives from each regiment.[305]

They were joined by other mutineers, including a troop from Harrison's regiment, making a total force of around nine hundred men.[306] William Thompson, a Leveller who had been a corporal in Whalley's regiment, led another group of several hundred mutineers who made for Banbury on May 6 and issued *England's Standard Advanced*. It articulated the demands of the soldiers and included the text of the latest Leveller manifesto, *The Agreement of the People*. Thompson's aim was to rally with the main group of mutineers from Wiltshire at Burford, but this came to nothing because of the intervention of Colonel Reynolds. There was also the suggestion of a mutiny in Buckinghamshire, but this failed to materialize.[307]

Fairfax and Cromwell mustered forces loyal to them in Hyde Park on May 9 and set out along the Thames Valley to the Cotswolds. The main body of mutineers converged on the Oxfordshire village of Burford. Fairfax decided that decisive action was required before the mutiny spread. Cromwell led a surprise assault in the early hours of May 15 with his cavalry and a detachment of Colonel Okey's dragoons. Major Francis White was negotiating with the mutineers when Cromwell attacked.[308] Despite some initial resistance, in the dazed confusion many of the Levellers immediately surrendered and the loss of life was minimal.[309] Cromwell held around three hundred forty

---

304 *The Levellers (Falsly So Called) Vindicated* (London, 1649), 3–5.
305 *The Unanimous Declaration of Colonel Scroope's and Commissary Gen. Ireton's Regiments* (London, 1649); *The Moderate* (May 1–8, 1649).
306 Gentles, *New Model Army*, 166–70.
307 Braddick, *Common Freedom of the People*, 171.
308 Francis White, *A True Relation of the Proceedings in the Businesse of Burford* (London, 1649), 7.
309 *Moderate Intelligencer* (May 10–17, 1649), 2048; William Eyre, *Serious Representation of Col. William Eyre* (London, 1649), 5; Richard L. Greaves and Robert Zaller, *Biographical Dictionary of British Radicals in the Seventeenth Century* (Brighton: Harvester, 1984), s.v. "Eyre, William."

men captive in Burford parish church.[310] The Council of War had determined that all mutineers were liable to death, but, since the majority confessed to "the odious wickedness" of what they had done, the punishment was limited to those deemed to be the four main leaders. Four of the ringleaders were court-martialed and sentenced to death. On the morning of May 17, Cornet James Thompson (William's brother) and Corporals Church and Perkins were executed in the churchyard. A second cornet from Scrope's regiment, Henry Denne, was appropriately penitent and was pardoned.[311] Denne was a General Baptist preacher who preached a sermon of repentance to the other mutineers in the parish church. Denne wrote a tract designed to persuade others that the Levellers were a "dangerous and destructive Faction."[312] Denne thanked "the great providence of God" for stopping the Levellers "from turning all things upside down."[313] The mutineers who fled were hunted down, with William Thompson being killed in Wellingborough, Northamptonshire, on May 17 and William Eyre being imprisoned in Oxford.

Gentles describes the event as "the most serious internal challenge faced by the republican regime until 1659."[314] With the suppression of the mutineers, army discipline was restored, and with the Leveller leaders in the Tower, any thought of further Leveller mobilization disappeared. Cromwell reported to the Commons that the victory was like waking from a bad dream. If the rebellion had not been crushed, the mutineers would soon have been joined by "discontented persons, Servants, Reformadoes, beggars &c." He claimed that their plan was to "cast off all Government, and chose some among themselves to have made new Lawes." It would have led to the murder of all "Ministers and Lawyers,"[315] (including Episcopalians and Presbyterians), and an eradication of private property.

On May 26, a public thanksgiving was appointed for Thursday, June 7, and Thomas Goodwin and Owen were called to preach.[316] The order was passed on June 1, and on June 5 it was decided that the day should also be used to give thanks for recent naval successes. Christ Church, Newgate Street, was

---

310 *Full Narrative of All the Proceedings between His Excellency the Lord Fairfax and the Mutineers* (London, [May 18,] 1649), 3.
311 *A Declaration of the Proceedings of His Excellency the Lord General Fairfax in the Reducing of the Revolting Troops* (London, [May 23,] 1649), 10–11.
312 Henry Denne, *The Levellers Designe Discovered: Or the Anatomie of the Late Unhappie Mutinie* (London, 1649), 3. The book collector Thomason acquired his copy on May 24.
313 Denne, *Levellers Designe Discovered*, 5.
314 Gentles, *New Model Army*, 172.
315 *Perfect Occurrences* 126 (May 25–June 1, 1649), 1054.
316 *Journals of the House of Commons*, 6:218, 220–21; *Perfect Occurrences* 126, 1054.

appointed as the place where the thanksgiving service would take place.[317] Reviving an earlier practice, the London Common Council resolved on May 29 to invite members of Parliament, the Council of State, and senior army officers to dinner at the Grocers' Hall to demonstrate "the city's good affections towards them."[318] The regime hoped that the occasion would help reconcile the City of London to the new government, and the consensus of the news reports was that Goodwin and Owen both preached of "the great blessing of peace and unity."[319] Once again, Christ Church was "a focal point for the enactment of parliamentarianism as ideology and alliance."[320] For example, one report described how "Mr. Thomas Goodwin and Mr Owen of Coxhall in Essex preacht before them, and applyed themselves notably to the time and occasion incouraging all men to Love and Unity: Of which, here is a rare and reall example of the happy Union betwixt the Parliament, City and Army."[321] Not everyone in London was rejoicing, according to *The Moderate*: "the Ministers of the City were very much blamed, for their great neglect, in not observing thereof." Some of the Presbyterian clergy used the day to pray openly for the new king.[322] In Essex, John Clopton reported that the day of thanksgiving was "kept of very few."[323] After the thanksgiving service there was a lavish feast. According the Bulstrode Whitelocke, a member of the new Council of State, "The Music was only drums and trumpets."[324] The events were widely mocked: for example, *Hosanna: or, A Song of Thanksgiving* (1649) published spoof speeches supposedly delivered at the event.[325]

---

[317] At the time, this was one of the largest church buildings in the City of London. The thirteenth-century Gothic style building had originally been established as a monastic church but became a parish church after the Dissolution of the Monasteries. Rather poignantly, Owen's old opponent, the heresiographer Thomas Edwards, had held a weekly lectureship from its pulpit in the 1640s. It would be destroyed in the Great Fire of London (1666) and subsequently rebuilt by Sir Christopher Wren. See Hughes, *Gangraena*, 31–31, 135–36; Derek Pearsall, *Gothic Europe 1200–1450* (London: Pearson, 2001), 96.

[318] Christ Church had hosted the thanksgiving services for victory at the battle of Naseby (June 1645) and for the suppression of royalist resistance in the west (April 1646). For the practice of feastings at the Grocers' Hall, see Juxon, *Journal of Thomas Juxon*, 113.

[319] *A Modest Narrative of Intelligence* 10 (June 2–9, 1649), 80. See also *Perfect Occurrences* 127 (June 1–8, 1649), 1096; *A Perfect Summary of an Exact Dyarie of Some Passages of Parliament* 21 (June 4–11, 1649), 165.

[320] Hughes, *Gangraena*, 134.

[321] *The Kingdomes Faithfull and Impartiall Scout* 19 (June 1–8, 1649), 142.

[322] *The Moderate* 48 (June 5–12, 1649), 551.

[323] Mears et al., *Special Prayers, Fasts and Thanksgivings*, 503.

[324] Whitelocke, *Memorials of the English Affair*, 3:47.

[325] See also *The Man in the Moon* 8 (May 28–June 5, 1649), 73; *Mercurius Elenctius* 12 (July 9–16, 1649), 89.

The establishment regarded Owen's sermon as very satisfactory, with the *Commons Journal* recording,

> That the Thanks of this House be returned unto Mr. *Owen*, for his great Pains taken in his Sermon, preached before this House Yesterday, in *Christ Church, London*, being the Day appointed for Publick Thanksgiving: And that he be desired to print his Sermon: And that he have the like Privilege in printing the same, as others in like case have usually had.
>
> *Ordered*, That Mr. *Allen* do give Thanks to Mr. *Owen* accordingly.[326]

Whitelocke recorded that "hearty thanks" was to be given to Owen and Goodwin for their sermons.[327] As had been the case after his postregicide sermon, Owen was thanked by Francis Allein and invited to publish the sermon.[328] He chose not to do so, and the sermon was published posthumously under the title "Humane Power Defeated."[329]

Summary and Analysis of the Sermon

Owen conjectures that Psalm 76 describes the deliverance of Jerusalem from the vast army of Sennacherib, and from this he makes the observation that the "whole course of affairs in the world, is steered by providence in reference to the good of Salem"—that is, the church. The mistake of those who had mutinied was to assume "that their right hand had accomplished the work of the Lord, and that the end of it must be the satisfaction of their lusts." In their pride, these soldiers had not realized they were of "no account in the eyes of the Lord in all he is accomplishing." They failed to recognize that all the great providential shakings had been for the sake of the church, in particular so that the ordinances of worship of the church might be purified and vindicated. Instead, out of a desire for "preeminence," these murmuring "rebels" challenged the regime, those whom the Lord had "chosen" to deliver his people. For Owen,

---

[326] *Journals of the House of Commons*, 6:226.
[327] Whitelocke, *Memorials of the English Affair*, 3:47.
[328] Alderman Francis Allein (1605–1658), a recruiter member of Parliament for Cockermouth in Cumberland, was a wealthy goldsmith and member of the London Common Council. Although he did not sign the king's death warrant, he did take a hard line in the High Court of Justice and broadly supported the revolution as an active member of the Rump Parliament. See Underdown, *Pride's Purge*, 214, 242. Allein also had the responsibility for thanking Owen for *A Sermon Preached to the Honourable House of Commons, in Parliament Assembled: On January 31* [. . .] (London,1649).
[329] Owen, *Complete Collection of the Sermons*, 79–91.

this was little different from how the "thankless" Israelites had complained against Moses. Down through the centuries, there were numerous "monuments and trophies" of victories against the enemies of the church. Owen included in his list crowns and clerical vestments, spoils belonging to enemies and oppressors who occupied the civil and ecclesiastical spheres respectively.

The mutineers were a "formidable" enemy: strong, courageous, powerful, and puffed up with pride because of "former success" (a phrase Owen repeats six times in the sermon). Full of "fury and folly," they mistakenly thought that "the God of the Parliament could not help." The enemy was no "poor, effeminate Sardanapalus, a poor, sensual, hypocritical wretch, as some have been" (surely a jibe at the late king).[330] Rather, the mutineers were experienced soldiers, with historians believing that at least twenty-five hundred men were in active mutiny or on the brink of it.[331] However, in a work in which the *digitus Dei* was revealed as "their strength departed," they cast themselves "to the mercy of those against whom they rose and opposed themselves." These Leveller-inspired troops thought that they would achieve "their hearts' lusts, and cobweb fancies"—"throwing up all bounds and fences" and "laying all common to their lusts"—but all they were left with was "shame and disappointment." God had broken the mutiny just as he was breaking "the old monarchies" and "papal power." Its suppression was to be regarded as a providential sign of "the Lord's continuing presence." With all the millenarian optimism of his parliamentary sermon from April 1649, Owen insisted that the morning star of the promised latter-day glory had appeared.

Owen applied these observations in a twofold manner. First, he believed this ought to inspire courage in the face of "strong combinations" that might arise. This word of application was apt as thoughts turned toward the reconquest of Ireland. Second, he thought it stood as a warning to others that "great endowments are ofttimes great temptations."

Owen moved on to explain how providential deliverances were tailored according to "the qualifications of the opposers." In other words, the proud are brought low, the strong are made weak, and the wise become foolish. Here the mutineers had provoked God by engaging against the authority that God had owned and established—that is, the new Commonwealth regime. Owen thought that the legitimacy of the new regime could be defended by recourse to "the rule of reason, law, and common established principles

---

330 Sardanapalus was the legendary last emperor of the Assyrian monarchy in the seventh century BC. For a contemporary description, see Thomas Beard, *Theatre of Gods Judgments* [. . .] (London, 1642), 280.
331 Gentles, *New Model Army*, 166–74.

among men" but instead chose to offer six a posteriori evidences.[332] First, despite opposition, the Lord had "honored" it "with success and protection in great, hazardous, and difficult undertakings for himself." Second, those in power acted for God rather than pursuing selfish ambition. Here Owen said that he could offer an example "yet not much above half a year old," which presumably is a reference to those in Parliament who wished to continue to negotiate for a Presbyterian-royalist settlement at Newport. Third, the government that would be owned and protected by God would be comprised of those who "rule according to the interest of Christ and his gospel," which he summarized in terms reminiscent of his parliamentary sermon delivered eight weeks beforehand: "ordering, framing, carrying on of affairs, as is most conducible to the unraveling and destruction of the mystery of iniquity." Fourth, such rulers would seek the peace and prosperity of the godly and enjoy their prayerful support. Fifth, such powers would administer the rule of law, "especially in those great and unusual acts of justice" (presumably a reference to the trial of the king). Finally, such government would be untainted by idolatry and tyranny (two things with which Owen charged the late king in his postregicide sermon). Owen reminded his hearers of how he had "not long since" demonstrated that governments that gave their support to false worship and persecuted the godly would be shaken, broken, and destroyed.

Acknowledging that his claim would be contested by "thousands," Owen stated that "the Lord has borne witness" that these six marks were "for the main" to be found "in your assemblies" (both the Rump Parliament and the London Common Council). He therefore assured members of Parliament and members of the London government that the opposition they faced would be unsuccessful. He marshaled two reasons why this was the case from his text. First, the "stout hearts" of their opponents would be taken away. This could happen in a variety of ways. As their hearts "rage for revenge," they could be stirred up in a self-destructive "untamable fury." Alternatively, they could be given over to folly, unable to take counsel. Owen believed that "never did any providence speak plain in any latter age" about this than in "the late dispensation," when God added folly to the fury of the mutineers and consumed them with fear. Another way in which "stout hearts" could be taken away was by "changing them," giving them "contrition and humility." This offered an explanation of the surrender of the majority of the mutineers. The second reason why opposition to the new regime would be unsuccessful

---

[332] Owen may be alluding to defenses of the new republican regime on the basis of natural law principles such as *salus populi suprema lex* ("the good of the people is the highest law") and that of self-preservation.

would be because God would take away the power and strength of the hands of those who opposed it.

Owen applied this by means of four uses. The first was to explain how the Leveller-inspired mutiny was ultimately an "undertaking against the Lord." This was, first of all, because of its "declared enmity to the ministry of the gospel," particularly in the administration of ordinances, and against "the spiritual ordinances of God." Owen placed Coverdale's translation of the "levelling" words of the Edomites in their mouths: "Down with it! Down with it even to the ground!" (Ps. 137:7). The mutineers had been unwilling to go to Ireland until their desires had been met. Owen reasoned that in opposing the cause of Christ they endured more losses in one week than they would have suffered in seven years of fighting the antichrist in Ireland. He believed that God would impress on the members of the Irish expeditionary force that Zion was able to withstand the strongest enemies (Ps. 48:12–14). The mutiny was also an undertaking against the Lord because it was against those magistrates "whom the Lord has owned in the darkest day that ever this nation saw."[333] The Levellers had insisted on implementing the *Agreement of the People* before the king would be brought to trial. Owen suggested that this would have dangerously "wrapped us in confusion for a few months." In opposing "Parliament, and their own commander," the mutiny opened the door to either anarchy or tyranny.

Second, Owen urged those in power to "be in the ways of God, and do the things of God." Having received another sign of divine protection and deliverance, he "trembled" as he asked, "Where shall we have hearts large enough to receive all these mercies?" Owen told his hearers that "peace and safety" were to be found in upholding those things that their enemies sought to destroy: in other words, the ordinances of the gospel and the administration of judgment.

Third, Owen warned his hearers to a watchful examination of themselves to ensure that they were not "engaged against the Lord." As he had done in his April 1649 sermon, he invoked Samson as an illustration, telling them that just as Samson's strength lay in the locks of his hair, so the secret to their strength lay in walking in the ways of the Lord.[334]

---

333 Owen's neighboring clergyman wrote of "the black providence of putting the King to death." See Josselin, *Diary of Ralph Josselin*, 155.

334 As Gribben notes, Samson became "increasingly popular among radical voices in and after the revolutionary decade, most famously in Milton's *Samson Agonistes* (London, 1671)." Gribben, *John Owen and English Puritanism*, 107. Harvey comments on how "many revolutionaries cited Samson as the illustrious example of one who destroyed the idolaters in his time." See Elizabeth D. Harvey, "Samson Agonistes and Milton's Sensible Ethics," in *The Oxford Handbook of Milton*, ed. Nicholas McDowell and Nigel Smith (Oxford: Oxford University Press, 2009), 647.

Owen's final use was a call to see what God can do and to trust and bless him for it. This deliverance ought to encourage them to value the gospel and its ordinances, which had been recovered from Babylonian corruption. Furthermore, they should rejoice that the civil wars had led to the establishment of the peace and liberty of the nation and that they had been preserved from anarchy and tyranny. He implied that the army, one of the "instruments of our deliverance," should not be "the scorned object of men's revengeful violence" and held out the hope that the Cromwellian expedition to Ireland would lead to the relief of the "distressed handful" in that country. Thus, this rather "fiery" sermon ends with Owen constructing an ideological justification of the forthcoming Cromwellian reconquest of Ireland.[335] All was now in place for this long-deferred expedition, and as the recently appointed Lord Lieutenant of Ireland, Lieutenant General Oliver Cromwell would leave London early in July.

---

[335] Gribben, *John Owen and English Puritanism*, 104.

Outlines

A VISION OF UNCHANGEABLE FREE MERCY

    I. Introduction
        A. The ground and foundation of the growth of the kingdom
        B. The purpose of this fast-day sermon
        C. Initial exegesis of the vision
            1. The manner of the vision
            2. The time of the vision and its messenger
            3. The message of the vision
    II. Three observations based on the sovereign will of God and the propagation of the gospel
        A. The sovereign will of God regulates the great variety that is seen in the propagation of the gospel
            1. The outward means of grace have been dispensed in a variety of ways
            2. God works effectually in various ways in different individuals
            3. The rules that govern this variety
            4. Uses arising from the first observation
                a. God's glorious purposes in the ongoing reformation of the English church
                b. God uses a wide variety of means to accomplish his purposes
        B. The sovereign good pleasure of God accounts for why the gospel is sent to any nation or person
            1. Three initial premises regarding God's distinguishing mercy
            2. Proof of this second observation

3. Three further points relating to the second observation
4. Four uses arising from the second observation
   a. Humbling an unworthy and undeserving nation
   b. Warning the nation about despising newfound gospel light and liberty
   c. Revealing the wonder of divine sovereignty in salvation
   d. Warning the nation about the danger of losing the gospel
C. There is no distress comparable to being without the gospel
   1. Four lessons that arise from this observation
      a. Without the gospel there is darkness and distress
      b. Without the gospel there is no communion with God in this life or in eternity
      c. Without the gospel there is ignorance of the greatest need
      d. Without the gospel national mercies are worse than of no value
   2. Three uses arising from the third observation
      a. The nation was enjoying unique privileges
      b. The nation was now obligated to respond
      c. The particular obligation upon ministers and magistrates

Appended Tracts: *Short Defensative* and *Country Essay*

I. The *Short Defensative about Church Government, Toleration and Petitions* about These Things
   A. Four equitable demands made in the context of the anti-toleration campaign
      1. Exercise charity rather than seeking to create guilt by association
      2. Do not exaggerate differences unnecessarily
      3. Understand legitimate concerns about the current petitioning campaigns
      4. Recognize that labeling other godly Protestants as sectaries is unhelpful
   B. Introduction to the proposals set down in the *Country Essay*
II. The *Country Essay for the Practice of Church Government There*
   A. Introduction

B. Eighteen requests to those in government for a moderate church settlement
   C. Answers to three possible objections
   D. Response to the accusation that this tolerates error
   E. Unresolved issues in current debates about toleration
   F. Clarification of the nature of toleration
   G. Nine assertions regarding toleration
      1. Heresy ought not to be tolerated, especially in fundamentals, but should be dealt with by appropriate means
      2. The magistrate may act against heresy that disturbs the peace or undermines lawful government
      3. False teaching associated with immorality or idolatry ought to be punished more severely
      4. Dissenters should not seek to undermine the established church and its ministry
      5. Charity toward those who err in nonfundamentals
      6. The Golden Rule should guide all undertakings
      7. Heresy does not necessarily amount to blasphemy
      8. Many who were punished as heretics were actually martyrs for the truth
      9. Take care not to equate heresy with sedition
   H. Two concluding words of caution
   I. Three questions to be answered by those who favor religious coercion

EBENEZER: A MEMORIAL OF THE DELIVERANCE OF ESSEX, COUNTY, AND COMMITTEE

   I. Part 1: The title and preface to Habakkuk's prayer (3:1)
      A. Exposition of the title of the prayer (3:1a)
         1. Believers are called to fervent prayer in a season of divine judgment
      B. Exposition of what it is for a prayer to be "upon Shigionoth" (3:1b)
         1. God's people are often called to sing a song mixed of both joy and sorrow
            a. Two reasons why the saints are called to sing songs "upon Shigionoth"
            b. The saints should therefore learn to sing such songs

II. Part 2: Habakkuk's fear and the main request of his prayer (3:2)
   A. Exposition of Habakkuk's fearful condition (3:2a)
      1. The saints should fear God in the season of his appearance
   B. Exposition of Habakkuk's request (3:2b)
      1. God will revive his work by remembering mercy
      2. God will act in mercy in his appointed season
         a. Two reasons why God will act in his appointed season
         b. Since deliverance will come in God's time, the godly should wait in faith
III. Part 3: The arguments in Habakkuk's prayer that support faith (3:3–17)
   A. Exposition of Habakkuk remembering the former works of God (3:3)
      1. The saints anticipate future blessing by remembering former mercies
         a. Two reasons why the saints should anticipate future blessing by remembering former mercies
         b. Remember the great recent works of God in the First Civil War
   B. Exposition of the glory manifest in God's former works (3:4)
      1. God reveals his great purposes to the saints
         a. Two reasons why God makes such revelations
         b. Seriously consider the new light that had been revealed
   C. Exposition of the fearful harbingers of a great work of God (3:5)
      1. God has all means at his disposal to bring judgment on his enemies
         a. Two uses arising from this observation
            i. Fear such a mighty God
            ii. Be confident that no enemy can stand against him
   D. Exposition of God surveying the land before driving out the nations (3:6)
      1. God carefully surveys the promised inheritance of his people
         a. Be content knowing that God has carefully measured out his people's lot and inheritance

2. Do not attempt to rob the saints of their liberties and privileges
    a. Two uses arising from this observation
        i. Understand the relevant lessons of history
        ii. Understand God's purposes in recent events
3. God does the work of driving out the nations
    a. Continue to play your part in God's work

E. Exposition of the state of the surrounding oppressive nations (3:7)
    1. Faith makes both past and future mercies present to the soul
        a. Two reasons for this observation
        b. Two uses from this observation
            i. Use the past to transform the present
            ii. Use the future to transform the present
    2. Special consideration should be given to how God treats his enemies in the season of the church's deliverance
        a. Two reasons to engage in such serious consideration
        b. Seriously consider how God dealt with his enemies in the Second Civil War
    3. The enemies of the saints are motivated by envy and fear
        a. Two reasons for this observation
        b. The church's deliverance provokes both oppressors and the superstitious
    4. The enemies of the church rise only to be destroyed
        a. Three reasons for this observation
        b. Faith makes the promises of future deliverance present to the soul

F. Exposition of the mighty works of God for his people (3:8)
    1. In his mighty works, God shakes the heaven and the earth
        a. Proud hearts should tremble
    2. No people or nation can thwart the deliverance of the saints
        a. The reason for this observation
        b. The events of the Second Civil War show that nothing can hinder God's purposes
    3. God has all means at his disposal to deliver his people

IV. Second part of the sermon expounding 3:9
   A. Exposition of God manifesting his almighty power according to his promise (3:9a)
      1. In his mighty power, God will keep all his promises
         a. Two reasons for this observation
         b. Four uses of this observation
            i. In the events of the siege, God manifested his power to keep his promises
            ii. Such deliverances are gracious and undeserved
            iii. Thankful obedience is the appropriate response
            iv. Learn the lessons taught by this providential judgment
   B. Exposition of God's mighty work (3:9b)
      1. Bringing great rivers from flinty rocks
      2. This is a type of God's unexpected deliverance of his church
      3. God continues to bring about unexpected deliverances
      4. The divine deliverance of Colchester
      5. God's promise to bring about such unexpected deliverances
         a. Two reasons why God delivers weak saints in such seemingly dire straits
         b. Four uses
            i. Consider Colchester to be such an unexpected deliverance
            ii. Learn to live by faith
            iii. Respond with gratitude to such a mighty deliverance
            iv. Learn spiritual lessons from this temporal deliverance

A SERMON PREACHED [. . .] JANUARY 31

I. Part 1: God threatens a range of judgments against a sinful people (Jer. 15:3–10)
II. Part 2: Divine judgment comes against idolatrous and tyrannical nations (15:4, 6)
   A. God justly punishes the nation for the sins of the king
   B. The people are "wrapped up" in the sins of their king

III. Part 3: Ruin is inevitable unless there is spiritual renewal (15:1)
IV. Part 4: God's instruments often endure such hard providences and opposition that they feel ready to give up (15:10, 15–18)
   A. God's instruments often face severe opposition from the people
   B. God's instruments often feel at a loss and ready to abandon the cause
   C. A call for patience and tenderness toward those who are faltering
V. Part 5: God's word to the nation in such a condition (15:11–14, 19–21)
   A. Direction to those engaged in God's work about the dangers of compromise and backsliding
      1. Compromise and backsliding are often caused by fear and a desire for perishing things
      2. Several specific applications to those in government
         a. Many have backslidden in recent years
         b. Backsliders restored by a commitment to righteous zeal
   B. The promise of divine guidance and protection to God's chosen instruments
      1. Three applications of this principle to those in government
         a. The folly of opposition to God's chosen instruments
         b. The wisdom of recognizing that Parliament's victories come from God
         c. God will be with Parliament so long as it does God's work in God's way
   C. Judicial hardening stands behind the self-defeating opposition to God's instruments
      1. Four reasons why God remains both just and good in giving up his enemies
         a. The nature of God's sovereignty
         b. The distinction between primary and secondary causation
         c. God's use of means
         d. The difference between divine and human purposes
      2. Three applications to those in government and those who oppose them

           a. Those who follow God in difficult days should expect opposition
           b. Those opposed to the cause should engage in self-examination
           c. All should see the sovereign hand of God at work

Appended Tract: *Of Toleration*
- I. Part 1: Consideration of the grounds for nontoleration
  - A. Eight problems with the arguments used to support religious coercion
    1. Those opposed to toleration have yet to provide a compelling case for the civil punishment of those in error
    2. Those opposed to toleration should recognize that not all things fall under human cognizance
    3. It is wrong to say that those in favor of toleration do not allow for the punishment of those in error who disturb the peace
    4. It is problematic to apply the law against idolatry to those in error
    5. Similar challenges in applying the law against blasphemy
    6. Further problems in applying the punishment of false prophets
    7. Take more care in the interpretation of Romans 13
    8. The law concerning the death of the seducer is difficult to apply
- II. Part 2: Assertion of the truth about toleration
  - A. General presuppositions
    1. The church should oppose error with gospel means
    2. The main question in the toleration debate
       - a. Defining the question
       - b. The manner in which the debate has been carried out
  - B. No warrant for the magistrate to punish those simply in error
  - C. Relevant considerations
    1. Religious coercion has frequently been used to suppress the truth
    2. Religious coercion has either harmed the church or done little for truth
    3. Grounds and reasons offered in favor of lawful coercion resemble those employed by unjust persecutors

4. The pre-Constantinian church received no support from the magistrate, and yet there were no long-lasting heresies
5. Providential judgments have frequently fallen on persecutors
III. Part 3: The role of the magistrate in matters of religion
   A. First head: The duty of the magistrate in settling and establishing the profession of the gospel set out in five propositions
      1. Ensure that the gospel is declared to the nation
      2. Protect the propagation of the gospel from those who oppose it
         a. Introduction to further responsibilities
         b. Four proofs that the magistrate has such responsibilities
      3. Provide places for gospel worship
      4. Protect the church from violent disturbances
      5. Maintain and support as required
   B. Implications arising from these five position statements on the duty of the magistrate
      1. Three consequences
         a. These positive responsibilities do not extend to those in error
         b. All people, including those who err, are to be protected from violence
         c. Minor differences do not fall under the magistrate's purview
      2. Two corollaries concerning Dissent
   C. Second head: The duty of the magistrate to support, maintain, and defend the profession of the gospel from opposition, disturbance, and blasphemy
      1. Ensure that no public places are used for false worship
      2. Five rules regarding the more difficult issue of restraining people who publicly oppose the truth
         a. Those who disturb the peace should be restrained
         b. The Golden Rule should always be applied
         c. With blasphemy there is a case for a degree of corporal restraint

            d. Problematic itinerant preachers can be dealt with by existing legislation
            e. The magistrate should act against the worst excesses of the sects
        3. The remaining issue of how to respond to peaceable error
            a. Three things that cannot be assumed
            b. Legal arguments against corporal restraint and punishment of those in peaceable error
            c. Arguments from the nature of the gospel against corporal restraint and punishment in such cases
            d. Examples of the other arguments that could be advanced against corporal restraint and punishment in such cases
    D. Third head: how the magistrate might deal with various sorts of Dissent
        1. The provisional nature of this response
        2. The Apostles' Creed as a starting point for defining fundamentals, given the controversy over confessions
        3. The importance of distinguishing Dissent in lesser matters from Dissent in fundamentals
        4. Spiritual means should be employed, and the magistrate should act against only those Dissenters who disturb the peace
        5. True uniformity requires a work of the Spirit
        6. Two assumptions for any further debate about toleration

ΟΥΡΑΝΩΝ ΟΥΡΑΝΙΑ: THE SHAKING AND TRANSLATING OF HEAVEN AND EARTH

    I. Introduction: The grace and duty of perseverance
    II. Opening of the text
        A. The assertion: "The things that are shaken shall be removed"
            1. Defining the things that are shaken
            2. The shaking of these things involves a shaking of governments
            3. This shaking will take place prior to this new era
            4. The removal involves a transformation

B. The proof of this assertion: "This word, once more, signifies no less"
C. The inference from the assertion: "The things that cannot be shaken must remain"
   1. The dawn of a new golden era for the church
   2. These things will remain and be firmly established
III. Doctrine arising from the opening of the text
   A. Proof of the doctrine
      1. Confirmation from Daniel 2:44
      2. Confirmation from other Old Testament texts
   B. Four reasons for the doctrine
      1. To bring justice against the persecutors of the saints
      2. To establish government that will advance the kingdom of Christ
      3. To fulfill God's promise for an ingathering of the Jews
      4. To stir up the saints to lay hold of the kingdom of Christ
   C. Six uses of the doctrine
      1. Be acquainted with the special work that God is doing in these days in order to be able to follow hard after God
         a. Four sins that would hinder gaining such wise understanding
         b. Four ways to gain this understanding of the work of God
      2. Enthrone Christ as King
         a. The priority of a personal commitment to Christ as King
         b. Two particular responsibilities of the magistrate in these days
      3. Expect this shaking to continue
      4. Prepare for a time of purging and purification
      5. Look to heavenly things
      6. Be confident that all opposition will end

HUMAN POWER DEFEATED

I. The occasion and structure of Psalm 76
   A. The exordium (76:1–2)
   B. A narrative of the great work that God did for his people (76:3, 5–6)

1. Remembering the place where God did this great work
2. Remembering the great work that God did in this day of distress

II. Three main doctrinal observations
   A. Strong and courageous men often oppose the ways of God
      1. Two uses of the first observation
         a. Faith delivers the saints from fear
         b. The strong and mighty must be watchful
   B. In God's works of providence, the nature of divine deliverance is fittingly tailored
   C. God turns the courage and strength of those who engage against him into weakness and folly
      1. Six ways that those in power can know they are truly engaged in God's cause and therefore be confident of divine protection
      2. Two reasons why even the strongest opposition will not succeed
         a. God has a host of ways to take away the courage of his enemies
         b. God can simply take away the strength of his enemies
      3. Four uses of this doctrine
         a. At Burford God defeated the Levellers, turning their strength into weakness and thwarting their evil designs against church and state
         b. Providence reassures those in power of divine protection, so long as they are walking in God's ways
         c. Providence calls those who are strong and mighty to watchful self-examination
         d. Providence calls for trust in God, especially in the context of the forthcoming Irish expedition

A VISION OF UNCHANGEABLE FREE MERCY, IN SENDING THE MEANS OF GRACE TO UNDESERVED SINNERS

Wherein God's Uncontrollable Eternal Purpose, in Sending and Continuing the Gospel unto This Nation, in the Midst of Oppositions and Contingencies, Is Discovered; His Distinguishing Mercy in This Great Work Exalted, Asserted against Opposers, Repiners. Whereunto Is Annexed, a Short Defensative about Church Government, (With a Country Essay for The Practice of Church Government There) Toleration and Petitions about These Things.

By John Owen, minister of the gospel at Coggeshall in Essex

London,
printed by G. M. for Philemon Stephens at the sign of the gilded lion in Paul's Churchyard. 1646.

[Parliamentary Order]

Die Mercurii, 29 Aprilis, 1646.[1]

Ordered, by the Commons assembled in Parliament, that M[r]. Jenner[2] and Sir Peter Wentworth[3] do from this House give thanks to M[r]. Nalton[4] and M[r]. Owen for the great pains they took in the sermons they preached this day, at the entreaty of this House (it being a day of public humiliation), at Margaret's,[5] Westminster. And to desire them to print their sermons: and it is ordered that none shall presume to print their sermons without license under their handwriting.

H. Elsynge, Cler. Parl. D. Com.[6]

I do appoint Philemon Stephens, and none else, to Print my Sermon.

John Owen.

---

1 Lat. "Wednesday, 29 April, 1646."
2 Robert Jenner (ca. 1584–1651), a religious conservative and the member of Parliament for Cricklade, Wiltshire.
3 Sir Peter Wentworth (1593–1675), the member of Parliament for Tamworth, Staffordshire.
4 James Nalton (1600–1662), who was a leading London Presbyterian minister at St Leonard's, Foster Lane. This was Jenner's London parish. See *The History of Parliament: The House of Commons, 1640–1660*, ed. Stephen K. Roberts, 9 vols. (Woodbridge, UK: Boydell and Brewer, 2023), s.v. "Jenner, Robert (c. 1584–1651)."
5 St Margaret's Church, Westminster.
6 This is a reference to Henry Elsynge (1598–1654), who would officiate as clerk of the House of Commons until 1648.

[Dedication]

TO THE MOST HONORABLE SENATE, the most renowned convention of the people of England, on account of the laws of the energetic and faithful defense of the ancient rights of the Anglo-Britons:[1] the recovery of our ancestral freedom (almost wholly sunk into oblivion by the villainous exertions of certain men);[2] the courageous, equitable, moderate, and impartial administration of justice; the abolition of an unholy, tyrannical authority in ecclesiastical matters, as well as of Popish rites, innovations, and antichrists;[3] the newly restored privileges of common Christians; and especially the protection of Almighty God graciously granted to all these and countless others in counsel, in war, at home, and abroad—to this most deserving body, highly and justly renowned in all the world, which ought to be enshrined in everlasting memory by this whole island, to the most noble, preeminent, and outstanding men assembled from the ranks of the Commons in the august House of Parliament, John Owen dedicated this

---

1 The Parliament of England defended an ancient legal tradition that rejected political absolutism. The Commons had responded to petitioning from the Westminster Assembly on April 18 with *A Declaration of the Commons of England Assembled in Parliament, of Their True Intentions concerning the Ancient and Fundamental Government of the Kingdom, the Government of the Church, the Present Peace; Securing the People against All Arbitrary Government, and Maintaining a Right Understanding Between the Two Kingdoms of England and Scotland, according to the Covenant and Treaties* (London, 1646).

2 The arbitrary power exercised by the monarchy in the pre–Civil War period, especially during Charles's personal rule.

3 The arbitrary power, exercised by bishops claiming to govern by divine right, in pursuit of liturgical uniformity according to the ceremonial style of the Laudian church. Parliament's religious reform program had now dismantled the Laudian church. As Owen made this dedication, many in Parliament feared Presbyterians were attempting to secure such divine right power.

oration in divinity (to be sure, a very modest one on that occasion), delivered originally in private at the desire and bidding of those very gentlemen, and now presented publicly.[4]

Dedicated by John Owen.[5]

---

[4] In the text: *AMPLISSIMO SENATUI, Inclytissimo populi Anglicani conventui, (ob) Prisca Anglo-Britannorum* jura *strenue & fideliter asserta: Libertatem Patriam (nefariis quorundam molitionibus paene pessundatam) recuperatam: Justitiam fortiter,* ἴσως, ἐπιεικῶς ἀπροσωπολή- πτως *administratam,* Ἀρχὴν *in Ecclesiasticis* Ἀνιερο τυραννικὴν *dissolutam, Ritus Pontificios, novitios, Antichristianos abolitos, Privilegia plebis Christianae postliminio restituta, Potissimum Protectionem Dei O.M. his omnibus, aliisque innumeris, consilio, Bello, Domi, foras gratiose potitam,) Toto orbe jure meritissimo Celeberrimo, Toti huic Insulae aeternâ memoriâ recolendo, Viris illustribus Clarissimis, selectissimis, ex Ordine Communium in suprema curia Parliam. congregatis, Concionem hanc sacram, humilem illam quidem, ipsorum tamen voto jussuque prius coram ipsis habitam, nunc luce donatam.*—Owen. The "O.M." is a abbreviation of *optimus maximus* (best and greatest), a title appended to God's name in some early modern Latin texts in imitation of the classical epithet "Jupiter Optimus Maximus." I wish to thank Tyler Flatt for his assistance with the Latin here and in other places in this volume.

[5] In the text: DDC *Ioannes Owen.*—Owen. "DDC" is an abbreviated form of *Dedicaverunt.*

A Sermon Preached before the Honorable House of Commons, on the Day of Their Public Fast, April 29, 1646

And a vision appeared to Paul in the night, there stood a man of Macedonia, and prayed him, saying, Come over into Macedonia, and help us.

ACTS 16:11[1]

INTRODUCTION

The Ground and Foundation of the Growth of the Kingdom

The kingdom of Jesus Christ is frequently in the Scripture compared to growing things; small in the beginning and first appearance, but increasing by degrees unto glory and perfection.[2] The shapeless stone cut out without hands, having neither form nor desirable beauty given unto it,[3] becomes a great mountain, filling the whole earth (Dan. 2:35). The small vine brought out

---

1   The reference should be corrected to Acts 16:9.
2   In the margin: *Ecclesia sicut luna defectus habet, et ortus frequentes; sed defectibus suis crevit, etc. Haec est vera Luna, quae de fratris sui luce perpetua, lumen sibi immortalitatis et gratiae mutuatur* Amb. Hex *lib* 4. *Cap* 8.—Owen. This is a citation from Ambrose's *Hexameron* 4.8, which says, "Looking down, then, the Church has, like the moon, her frequent risings and settings. She has grown, however, by her settings and has by their means merited expansion.... This is the real moon which from the perpetual light of her own brother [Christ, the sun] has acquired the light of immortality and grace." For the Latin text, see Ambrose, *Hexameron*, in *Opera omnia*, ed. J.-P. Migne, Patrologia Latina 14 (Paris: Migne, 1845), 204. For the English translation, see Ambrose, *Hexameron, Paradise, and Cain and Abel*, trans. John J. Savage, Fathers of the Church 42 (Washington, DC: Catholic University of America Press, 1961), 156.
3   Isa. 53:2.

of Egypt quickly covers the hills with her shadow, her boughs reach unto the sea, and her branches unto the rivers (Ps. 80:8). The "tender plant"[4] becomes as the cedars of God;[5] and the grain of mustard seed to be a tree for the fowls of the air, to make their nests in the branches thereof.[6] Mountains are made plains before it,[7] every valley is filled, and the crooked paths made straight,[8] that it may have a passage to its appointed period;[9] and all this, not only, not supported by outward advantages, but in direct opposition to the combined power of this whole creation,[10] as fallen, and in subjection to the "god of this world," the head thereof.[11] As Christ was "a tender plant," seemingly easy to be broken; and "a root out of a dry ground,"[12] not easily flourishing, yet "lives for ever":[13] so his people and kingdom, though as a "lily among thorns,"[14] as "sheep among wolves,"[15] as a "turtledove" among a multitude of devourers, yet stands unshaken,[16] at least unshivered.[17]

The main ground and foundation of all this is laid out, [in] verses 6–9 of this chapter, containing a rich discovery how all things here below, especially such as concern the gospel and church of Christ, are carried along through innumerable varieties and a world of contingencies, according to the regular motions and goings forth of a free, eternal, unchangeable decree: as all inferior orbs, notwithstanding the eccentrics and irregularities of their own inhabitants, are orderly carried about by the first mover.

In verse 6, the planters of the gospel are "forbid to preach the word in Asia" (that part of it peculiarly so called), and verse 7, assaying[18] to go with the same message into Bithynia,[19] they are crossed by the Spirit, in their attempts; but in my text, are called to a place, on which their thoughts were not at all fixed: which calling, and which forbidding, were both subservient

---

4   Isa. 53:2.
5   Cf. Vulgate of Ps. 80:10.
6   Luke 13:19.
7   Zech. 4:7.
8   Luke 3:5.
9   In the margin: Psal. 108:13; Isa. 54:11; Zech. 4:7; Isa. 53:3–5.—Owen.
10 In the margin: 1 Joh. 3:13; Rev. 2:10.—Owen.
11 In the margin: 2 Cor. 4:4.—Owen.
12 In the margin: Isa. 53:2.—Owen.
13 In the margin: Heb. 7:25.—Owen.
14 In the margin: Cant. 2:2.—Owen. This is an abbreviation for Canticles—i.e., Song 2:2.
15 In the margin: Mat. 10:16.—Owen.
16 In the margin: Ps. 74:19.—Owen.
17 I.e., unbroken, intact.
18 I.e., attempting.
19 I.e., a region in northwest Asia Minor.

to his free determination "who worketh all things according to the counsel of his own will" (Eph. 1:11).[20]

And no doubt but in the dispensation of the gospel, throughout the world, unto this day, there is the like conformity to be found, to the pattern of God's eternal decrees: though to the messengers not made known aforehand by revelation, but discovered in the effects, by the mighty working of providence.

Among other nations, this is the day of England's visitation, "the day-spring from on high" having visited this people, and "the Sun of righteousness" arising upon us "with healing in his wings,"[21] a man of England has prevailed for assistance, and the free grace of God, has wrought us help by the gospel.

The Purpose of This Fast-Day Sermon

Now in this day three things are to be done, to keep up our spirits unto this duty, of bringing down our souls by humiliation.

First, to take us off the pride of our own performances, endeavors, or any adherent worth of our own: "Not for your sakes do I this, saith the Lord; be it known unto you, be you ashamed and confounded for your own ways, O house of Israel," (O house of England) (Ezek. 36:32).

Secondly, to root out that atheistical corruption, which depresses the thoughts of men, not permitting them in the highest products of providence, to look above contingencies, and secondary causes, though God "hath wrought all our works for us" (Isa. 26:12), and "known unto him are all his works from the beginning of the world" (Acts 15:18).

Thirdly, to show that the bulk of this people are as yet in the wilderness, far from their resting place, like sheep upon the mountains, as once Israel (Jer. 50:6), as yet wanting help by the gospel.

---

20 In the margin: *Eo ipso tempore, quo ad omnes gentes praedicatio Evangelii mittebatur, quaedam loca Apostolis adire prohibebatur ab eo, qui vult omnes homines salvos fieri.* Prosp. *Ep ad Rufin.* Διὸς δ' ἐτελείετο βουλή Hom.—Owen. This Latin quotation is from Prosper of Aquitaine's defense of the Augustinian view of grace in his Letter to Rufinus (a person otherwise unidentified). This letter was a significant text in the so-called semi-Pelagian controversy. For the Latin text, see Prosper, *Epistola ad Rufinum*, in *Opera omnia*, ed. J.-P. Migne, Patrologia Latina 51 (Paris: Migne, 1846), 85. "At the very moment that the preachers of the gospel were sent out to all the nations, the apostles were forbidden to go to certain regions by Him who will have all men to be saved" [1 Tim. 2:4]. For the English translation, see Prosper of Aquitaine, *Defense of St. Augustine*, trans. P. de Letter, Ancient Christian Writers 32 (New York: Newman, 1963), 32. The Greek quotation that follows in the marginal note is from the opening lines of Homer's *Iliad* 1.5, which may be translated "The will of Zeus was brought to fulfillment." For the text and translation, see Homer, *Iliad*, vol. 1, *Books 1–12*, trans. A. T. Murray, rev. William F. Wyatt, Loeb Classical Library 170 (Cambridge, MA: Harvard University Press, 1924), 12–13.

21 In the margin: Mal. 4:2.—Owen.

The two first of these will be cleared, by discovering, how that all revolutions here below, especially everything that concerns the dispensation of the gospel and kingdom of the Lord Jesus, are carried along, according to the eternally fixed purpose of God, free in itself, taking neither rise, growth, cause nor occasion, from anything among the sons of men.

The third, by laying open the helpless condition of gospel-wanting souls, with some particular application, to all which my text directly leads me.

The words in general are the relation of a message from heaven unto Paul, to direct him in the publishing of the gospel, as to the place, and persons wherein, and to whom he was to preach.[22] And in them you have these four things:

1. The manner of it, it was by vision, "A vision appeared."
2. The time of it, "In the night."
3. The bringer of it, "A man of Macedonia."
4. The matter of it, help for the Macedonians, interpreted, verse 10, to be by preaching of the gospel.[23]

Initial Exegesis of the Vision

A little clearing of the words will make way for observations.

The Manner of the Vision

1. For the manner of the delivery of this message, it was by vision: of all the ways that God used of old, to reveal himself unto any in an extraordinary manner, which were sundry and various (Heb. 1:1), there was no one so frequent, as this of vision: wherein this did properly consist, and whereby it was distinguished from other ways, of the discovery of the secrets of the Lord, I shall not now discuss: in general, visions are revelations of the mind of the Lord, concerning some hidden things present or future, and not otherwise to be known: and they were of two sorts;

(1) Revelations merely by word, or some other more internal species, without any outward sensible appearance, which, for the most part, was the Lord's way of proceeding with the prophets; which transient light or discovery of things before unknown, they called a vision.[24]

---

22 In the margin: *1. A quo. 2. Ad quem.*—Owen. Owen is distinguishing the *terminus a quo* ("the point from which") and the *terminus ad quem* ("the point to which") of this message. In other words, it has come from heaven, and it will be sent to the Macedonians.

23 In the margin: *Modus. Tempus. Instrumentum. Materia.*—Owen. Owen links these four points to the classical *elementa narrationis* (components of the story): means, time, instrument, and matter.

24 In the margin: Isa. 1:1; Amos 1:1; Nah. 1:1; Obad. 1.—Owen.

(2) Revelations, accompanied with some sensible apparitions, and that either:

[1] Of things, as usually among the prophets, rods and pots, wheels and trees, lamps, axes, vessels, rams, goats and the like, were presented unto them.[25]

[2] Of persons, and those according to the variety of them, of three sorts;

{1} of the second person of the Trinity; and this either;

1st, in respect of some glorious beams of his deity, as to Isaiah, chapter 6:1, with John 12:41, to Daniel 10:5-6, as afterward to John (Rev. 1:13-15), to which you may add the apparitions of the glory of God, not immediately designing the second person, as Ezekiel 1.

2nd, with reference to his humanity to be assumed, as to Abraham (Gen. 18:1-2) to Joshua (5:13-15), etc.

{2} of angels, as unto Peter (Acts 12:7), to the women (Matt. 28:2), to John (Rev. 22:8), etc.

{3} of men, as in my text.[26]

Now the several advancements of all these ways in dignity and preeminence, according as they clearly make out, intellectual verity, or according to the honor and exaltation of that whereof apparition is made, is too fruitless a speculation for this day's exercise.[27]

Our vision is of the latter sort, accompanied with a sensible appearance, and is called ὅραμα; there be two words in the New Testament signifying vision, ὅραμα and ὀπτασία, coming from different verbs, but both signifying "to see." Some distinguish them, and say, that ὀπτασία is a vision, χαθ' ὕπαρ, an appearance to a man awake; ὅραμα χαθ' ὄναρ, an appearance to a man asleep: called sometimes a dream (Job 33:15), like that which was made to Joseph (Matt. 2:19). But this distinction will not hold: our Savior calling that vision, which his disciples had at his transfiguration, when doubtless they were waking, ὅραμα (Matt. 17:9). So that I conceive Paul had his vision waking; and the night, is specified, as the time thereof, not to intimate his being asleep, but rather his watchfulness, seeking counsel of God in the night which way he should apply himself, in the preaching, of the gospel: and such I suppose was that of later days, whereby God revealed to Zuinglius a strong

---

25 In the margin: Jer. 1:11; Jer. 1:13; Ezek. 1:5-7; Zech. 1:8; 3:9-10 etc.; Dan. 7:8-9.—Owen.
26 In the margin: Zech. 2:1.—Owen.
27 In the margin: Vid. Aquin. 2.2 q. 174. Art. 3, 4. Scot in dist. Tert.—Owen. The first part of this reference is to Aquinas's *Summa theologiae* 2a2ae.174, dealing with a. 3, "Whether grades of prophecy can be distinguished in terms of imaginative vision?," and a. 4, "Was Moses greater than all the prophets?" For the text and translation, see Thomas Aquinas, *Summa theologiae*, vol. 45, *Prophecy and Other Charisms (2a2ae. 171-178)*, trans. Roland Potter (Cambridge: Cambridge University Press, 2006), 76-85.

confirmation of the doctrine of the Lord's Supper (from Ex. 12:11), against the factors for that monstrous figment of transubstantiation.[28]

The Time of the Vision and Its Messenger

2. For the second or time of this vision, I need say no more, than what before I intimated.

3. The bringer of the message, ἀνήρ τις ἦν Μακεδὼν ἑστὼς, he was a man of Macedonia in a vision: the Lord made an appearance unto him, as of a man of Macedonia; discovering even to his bodily eyes a man, and to his mind, that he was to be conceived as a man of Macedonia. This was, say some, an angel,[29] the tutelar[30] angel of the place, say the Popish expositors, or the genius of the place,[31] according to the phrase of the heathens, of whom they learned their demonology, perhaps him, or his antagonist, that not long before appeared to Brutus [at] Philippi.[32] But these are pleasing dreams: us it may suffice, that it was the appearance of "a man," the mind of Paul being enlightened to

---

28 Huldrych Zwingli (1484–1531), the principal Reformer of Zürich, wrote about a dream that he had on the night before the first celebration of the Reformed rite of the Lord's Supper in the Grossmünster in April 1525. For the text, see "*Subsidium sive coronis de eucharistia*," in *Huldreich Zwinglis sämtliche werke*, vol. 4 (Leipzig: Heinsius, 1927), 458–504, esp. 483–84. For the English translation, see "Subsidiary Essay or Crown of the Work on the Eucharist," in *Huldrych Zwingli Writings*, vol. 2, *In Search of True Religion: Reformation, Pastoral and Eucharistic Writings*, ed. and trans. H. W. Pipkin (Allison Park, PA: Pickwick, 1984), 194–231, esp. 199. For an account of this episode, see Bruce Gordon, "Huldrych Zwingli's Dream of the Lord's Supper," in *Crossing Traditions: Essays on the Reformation and Intellectual History in Honour of Irena Backus*, ed. Maria-Cristina Pitassi and Daniela Solfaroli Camillocci (Leiden: Brill, 2018), 296–310. For Zwingli's rejection of the Roman Catholic doctrine of transubstantiation, see "Explanation of the Sixty-Seven Articles," in *Huldrych Zwingli Writings*, vol. 1, *The Defense of the Reformed Faith*, ed. and trans. E. J. Furcha (Allison Park, PA: Pickwick, 1984), 92–124.
29 For example, the Lutheran commentator Georg Major (1502–1574). See Georg Major, *Auslegung der epistel S. Pauli an die Philipper* (Wittenberg, 1555), sig. 18r–19r.
30 I.e., having guardianship of a person or a thing.
31 The *genius loci* was thought to be the protective or presiding spirit of a particular place.
32 In the margin: A Lapide, Sanctius in locum, etc. Mede. Apost. Of later times. Plutarch, in vit. Bruti.—Owen. The first two references represent the writings of those to whom Owen referred as "Popish expositors"—namely, the Flemish Jesuit Cornelius à Lapide (1542–1613) and his *Commentaria in Acta Apostolorum* (Antwerp, 1627), and then, by way of the Latinized form of his name, the Spanish Jesuit Gaspar Sánchez (1554–1628) and his *Commentarii in Actus Apostolorum* (Lyon, 1616). The third reference is to Joseph Mede's *Apostasy of the Latter Times* [. . .] (London, 1641), which is cited in support of his claim that Roman Catholic demonology was of pagan origin. The final reference is to an example of pagan demonology taken from Plutarch's account of an apparition that Brutus received in his tent prior to the Battle of Philippi (42 BC). For the text and translation, see Plutarch, *Lives*, vol. 6, *Dion and Brutus. Timoleon and Aemilius Paulus*, trans. Bernadotte Perrin, Loeb Classical Library 98 (Cambridge, MA: Harvard University Press 1918), 206–7.

apprehend him as "a man of Macedonia": and that with infallible assurance, such as usually accompanies divine revelations in them to whom they are made, as Jeremiah 23:28, for upon it, Luke affirms, verse 10, they assuredly concluded, that the Lord called them into Macedonia.[33]

The Message of the Vision

4. The message itself is a discovery of the want of the Macedonians, and the assistance they required, which the Lord was willing should be imparted unto them: their want is not expressed, but included in the assistance desired, and the person unto whom for it they were directed. Had it been to help them in their estates, they should scarcely have been sent to Paul, who I believe, might for the most part say with Peter, "Silver and gold have I none."[34] Or had it been with a complaint, that they, who from a province of Greece, in a corner of Europe, had on a sudden been exalted into the empire of the Eastern world, were now enslaved to the Roman power and oppression, they might better have gone to the Parthians, then the only state in the world, formidable to the Romans.[35] Paul, though a military man, yet fought not with Nero's legions, the then-visible devil of the upper world, but with legions of hell, of whom the earth was now to be cleared.[36] It must be a soul want, if he be entrusted with the supplying of it.

[33] In the margin: Calvin, in locum, *Dicebat se discernere (nescio quo sapore, quem verbis explicare non poterat) quid interesset inter Deum revelantem*, etc. Aug. confes.—Owen. The first reference is, presumably, to Calvin's Commentary on Acts 16, which makes the point that there are different modes of revelation and some "are better suited for confirmation." See John Calvin, *The Acts of the Apostles 14–28*, trans. John W. Fraser, ed. David W. Torrance and Thomas F. Torrance (Edinburgh: Oliver and Boyd, 1966), 69. The second reference is to Augustine's *Confessions* 6.13.23, which recounts his mother Monica's claim to be able to discern "by a certain small indescribable in words, the difference between [God's] revelation and her own soul dreaming." For the Latin text, see Augustine, *Confessions*, vol. 1, *Introduction and Text*, ed. James J. O'Donnell (Oxford: Clarendon, 1992), 70. For an English translation, see Saint Augustine, *Confessions*, trans. Henry Chadwick (Oxford: Oxford University Press, 1992), 108.

[34] In the margin: Acts 3:6.—Owen.

[35] Originally a province of the Persian and Seleucid empires, the Parthian kingdom was a dominant power in the ancient East.

[36] In the margin: Plutarch, de *defectu oracu*. Ἑβραῖος κέλεταί με παῖς μακάρεσσιν ἀνάσσων, Τὸν δὲ δόμον προλιπεῖν καὶ ὁδὸν πάλιν αὖθις ἱκέσθαι. Respons. Apoll. Apud Euseb. Niceph.—Owen. The first reference is to Plutarch's *De defectu oraculorum*, 5. For the Greek text and English translation, see Plutarch, *Moralia*, vol. 5, *Isis and Osiris. The E at Delphi. The Oracles at Delphi No Longer Given in Verse. The Obsolescence of Oracles*, trans. Frank Cole Babbitt, Loeb Classical Library 306 (Cambridge, MA: Harvard, 1936), 350–51. Owen's second reference is to the Byzantine ecclesiastical historian Nicephorus Callistus (ca. 1256–ca. 1335), who, relying on Eusebius, gave an account of an oracle, attributed to the Delphic Apollo, that foresaw the birth of Christ and the eventual decline of oracles: "A Hebrew boy, who rules [over] the blessed ones, commands me to leave this house and to return again [to Hades]" (editor's translation).

And such this was, help from death, hell, Satan, from the jaws of that devouring lion:[37] of this the Lord makes them here to speak, what everyone in that condition ought to speak, help for the Lord's sake, it was a call to preach the gospel.

THREE OBSERVATIONS BASED ON THE SOVEREIGN WILL OF GOD AND THE PROPAGATION OF THE GOSPEL

The words being opened, we must remember what was said before of their connection with the verses foregoing; wherein the preachers of the gospel, are expressly hindered from above, from going to other places, and called hither. Whereof no reason is assigned, but only the will of him that did employ them: and that no other can be rendered, I am farther convinced, by considering the empty conjectures of attempters.[38]

God foresaw that they would oppose the gospel, says our Beda:[39] so say I might he of all nations in the world, had not he determined to send his effectual grace for the removal of that opposition: besides, he grants the means of grace to despisers (Matt. 11:21).

They were not prepared for the gospel, says Oecumenius:[40] as well say I as the Corinthians, whose preparations you may see (1 Cor. 6:9–11), or any other nation, as we shall afterward declare; yet to this foolish conjecture adhere the Papists and Arminians.[41] God would have those places left for to

---

For the Greek text and Latin translation, see Nicephorus Callistus Xanthopolus, *Ecclesiasticae historiae libri i–vii*, ed. J.-P. Migne, Patrologia Graeca 145 (Paris: Migne-Garnier, 1857), 683–84.

37 See 1 Pet. 5:8.
38 In the margin: . . . a nullo duro corde resistitur, quia cor ipsum emollit. Aug. Ezek. 36 26. Deut. 30.6.—Owen. It is unclear what Owen is referring to with this quotation attributed to Augustine. There is a similarity to Augustine's *De praedestinatione sanctorum* 8.13. For the Latin text, see Augustine, *Liber de preadestinatione sanctorum*, in *Opera Omnia*, ed. J.-P. Migne, Patrologia Latina 44 (Paris: Migne, 1865), 971. For an English translation, see Augustine, *Selected Writings on Grace and Pelagianism*, ed. Boniface Ramsey, trans. Roland Teske (Hyde Park, NY: New City Press, 2011), 434. The Old Testament texts that Owen cites appeal to the promise that the Lord will circumcise the hearts of his people (Deut. 30:6), taking away the heart of stone and replacing it with a heart of flesh (Ezek. 36:26).
39 The Venerable Bede (ca. 673/4–735) was an English monk, historian, and theologian. For the English text and translation, see Bede, *Commentary on the Acts of the Apostles*, trans. Lawrence T. Martin (Kalamazoo, MI: Cistercian Publications, 1989), 136.
40 Pseudo-Oecumenius, *Commentaria*, in *Opera Omnia*, ed. J.-P. Migne, Patrologia Graeca 118 (Paris: Migne-Garnier, 1857), 226–28.
41 In the margin: *Lapide. Sanctius*. In loc. Rom Script. Synd ar. 1.—Owen. Owen again contrasts his exegesis to that of the Jesuit commentators Cornelius à Lapide and Gaspar Sánchez. The next reference is possibly to the Remonstrant records of the Synod of Dordt, *Acta et scripta synodalia Dordracena ministrorum Remonstrantium* (Harderwijk, 1620).

be converted by John, says Sedulius,[42] yet the church at Ephesus the chief city of those parts was planted by Paul, says Ignatius,[43] and Irenaeus.[44]

He foresaw a famine to come upon those places, says Origen;[45] from which he would deliver his own, and therefore, it seems, left them to the power of the devil.

More such fancies might we recount, of men, unwilling to submit to the will of God; but upon that as the sole discriminating cause of these things we rest, and draw these three observations.

1. The rule whereby all things are dispensed here below, especially in the making out of the means of grace, is the determinate will and counsel of God: stay not in Asia, go not into Bithynia, but come to Macedonia. "Even so, O Father; for so" etc.[46]

---

42 Sedulius Scottus, a ninth-century Irish poet and scholar, was an important figure in the Carolingian Renaissance who was well-known for his Scriptural commentaries.

43 In the margin: Ὑμεῖς μὲν οὖν ἐστε τοιοῦτοι, ὑπὸ τοιῶνδε παιδευτῶν στοιχειωθέντες. Ignat. Epist. Ad Ep.—Owen. In order to support his claim that the church in Ephesus was planted by Paul, Owen provides a quotation, in Greek, attributed to Ignatius of Antioch from his *Epistle to the Ephesians* 6.4. This is not found in the authentic short recension of Ignatius's letter but comes from the end of the longer version. "Such, then are you, having been taught by such instructors, Paul the Christ-bearer." For the Greek text, see Ignatius, *Epistolae*, ed. J.-P. Migne, Patrologia Graeca 5 (Paris: Migne-Garnier, 1857), 757–58. For the English text and translation, see Ignatius, *Epistle of Ignatius to the Ephesians*, in *Ante-Nicene Fathers: The Writings of the Fathers Down to A.D. 325*, 10 vols., ed. Alexander Roberts and James Donaldson (1886; repr., Peabody, MA: Hendrickson, 1995), 1:52.

44 In the margin: Irae lib. 3. Cap. 3. *Qui causam quae sit volun-tatis divinae, a-liquid majus co quaerit*, Aug. *Voluntas Dei nullo modo cau-sam habet*. Aquin. P. q [text is unclear] a 5.—Owen. The first part of this reference is an appeal to Irenaeus, *Against Heresies* 3.3.4, in which he claimed that the Ephesian church was founded by Paul and preserved by John. For an English translation, see Irenaeus, *Against Heresies*, in *Ante-Nicene Fathers*, 1:416. Owen then invoked Augustine, by way of Peter Lombard, "*Qui causum quaerit voluntatis divinae, aliquid majus ea quaerit*" ("He that seeks a cause of the divine will, seeks something greater that it, whilst there is nothing greater"). See Lombard, *Sententiarum* 1, Dist. 45.4. For the Latin text, see Peter Lombard, *Sententiarum libri quatuor*, in *Opera omnia*, ed. J.-P. Migne, Patrologia Latina 192 (Paris: Migne, 1855), 642. This is drawn from Augustine, *On Eighty-Three Diverse Questions*, Q. 28. For the Latin text, see Augustine, *De diversis quaestionibus lxxxiii*, in *Opera omnia*, ed. J.-P. Migne, Patrologia Latina 40 (Paris: Migne, 1865), 18. For the English translation, see Augustine, *Eighty-Three Different Questions*, trans. David L. Mosher, The Fathers of the Church 70 (Washington, DC: Catholic University of America Press, 1982), 54. The final reference is to Aquinas's *Summa theologiae* 1a, q. 19, a. 5. "*Dicendum quod nullo modo voluntas Dei causam habet*" ("God's willing is not in any way caused"). For the Latin text and English translation, see Thomas Aquinas, *Summa theologiae*, vol. 5, *God's Will and Providence (1a. 19–26)*, trans. T. Gilby and I. Hislop (Cambridge: Cambridge University Press, 2006), 22–23.

45 Origen of Alexandria (ca. 184–ca. 253). Origen discusses the shepherd-angel of Macedonia in his homily on Luke 2:2–3. For the text, see Origen, *Homilies on Luke*, trans. Joseph T. Lienhard, Fathers of the Church 94 (Washington, DC: Catholic University of America Press, 1996), 49.

46 Matt. 11:26, which reads "for so it seemed good in thy sight" (KJV).

2. The sending of the gospel to any nation, place or persons rather than others, as the means of life and salvation, is of the mere free grace and good pleasure of God. "Stay not in Asia," etc.

3. No men in the world want help, like them that want the gospel. "Come and help us."

The Sovereign Will of God Regulates the Great Variety That Is Seen in the Propagation of the Gospel

[Observation] 1. Begin we with the first of these, the rule whereby, etc. or all events and effects, especially concerning the propagation of the gospel, and the church of Christ, are in their greatest variety, regulated by the eternal purpose and counsel of God.[47] All things below in their events, are but the wax, whereon the eternal seal of God's purpose, has left its own impression, and they every way answer unto it.¶[48]

It is not my mind to extend this to the generality of things in the world, nor to show how the creature, can by no means deviate from that eternal rule of providence whereby it is guided, no more than an arrow can avoid the mark, after it has received the impression of an unerring hand, or well-ordered wheels not turn, according to the motion given them by the master spring, or the wheels in Ezekiel's vision move irregularly to the spirit of life that was in them.[49]

Nor yet secondly, how that, on the other side, does no way prejudice the liberty of second causes, in their actions agreeable to the natures they are endued withal. He who made and preserves the fire, and yet hinders not, but that it should burn, or act necessarily agreeable to its nature; by his making, preserving and guiding of men, hinders not, yea, effectually causes, that they work freely, agreeable to their nature.[50]

---

47 In the margin: Θεία πάντων ἀρχὴ, δι᾽ ἧς ἅπαντα καὶ ἔστι, καὶ διαμένει. Theo. Phrast. *Apud Picum, de prov. Providentia est ratio ordinis rerum ad finem.* Th. p.q. 22. a1.6.—Owen. The first part of the reference is to Aristotle's successor, the Greek philosopher, Theophrastus, and his *Metaphysics* 4b. 15–16: "For the principle of all things, by virtue of which all things both are and endure, is divine." For the text and translation, see Theophrastus *Metaphysics*, trans. M. van Raalte (Leiden: Brill, 1993), 38–39. Owen has drawn the quotation from a work by the Italian renaissance philosopher Giovanni Pico della Mirandola (1463–1494), presumably his treatment of Seneca, *De providentia* [*On Providence*]. Owen then cites Aquinas, *Summa theologiae* 1a, q. 22, a. 1. "Providence is the ordaining of things to their end." For the text and translation, see Aquinas, *Summa theologiae*, 5:88–89.
48 The ¶ symbol indicates that a paragraph break has been added to Owen's original text.
49 In the margin: Ezek. 1.—Owen.
50 In the margin: *Non tantum res sed rerum modos*—Owen. Lat. "Not only the matter but also the manner of things."

Nor yet thirdly, to clear up what a straight line runs through all the darkness, confusion and disorder in the world, how absolutely, in respect of the first fountain, and last tendency of things, there is neither deformity, fault, nor deviation, everything that is amiss, consisting in the transgression of a moral rule, which is the sin of the creature, the first cause being free:[51] as he that causes a lame man to go, is the cause of his going, but not of his going lame: or the sun exhaling a smell from the kennel, is the cause of the smell, but not of its noisomeness, for from a garden his beams raise a sweet savor: nothing is amiss but what goes off from its own rule, which he cannot do who will do all his pleasure, and knows no other rule (Isa. 46:10).[52] But omitting these things, I shall tie my discourse to that which I chiefly aimed at in my proposition, viz. to discover how the great variety which we see in the dispensation of the means of grace, proceeds from, and is regulated by, some eternal purpose of God, unfolded in his word. To make out this, we must lay down three things.

(1) The wonderful variety in dispensing of the outward means of salvation, in respect of them, unto whom they were granted, used by the Lord since the fall: I say, since the fall, for the grace of preserving from sin, and continuing

---

51 In the margin: *Videtur ergo, quod non sit aliqua inordinatio, deformitas, aut peccatum simpliciter in toto universo, sed tantumuodo respectu inferiorum causarum, ordinationem superioris causae volentium, licet non valentium, perturbare.* Brad. De caus. Dei, lib. i. cap. 34. Ἡ ἁμαρτία ἐστὶν ἀνομία.—Owen. The Latin text is a citation from Thomas Bradwardine, *In Defense of God against the Pelagians and on the Power of Causes* (1344). Bradwardine (ca. 1300–ca.1349), often referred to as *Doctor Profundus*, was an Augustinian theologian and Archbishop of Canterbury. For the Latin text, see Bradwardine, *Summa de causa Dei contra Pelagium et de virtute causarum ad suos Mertonenses*, ed. Henry Savile (London, 1618), 301. "Therefore it seems—since no disorder, disfigurement, or sin can exist, strictly speaking, in the whole universe, except with regard to lower causes—to disturb the relative position of the higher cause of those who are willing, though not able." The Greek text in this marginal note is translated "Sin is lawlessness" (1 John 3:4).

52 In the margin: *Adeo summa iustitiae regula est Dei voluntas, ut quicquid vult, eo ipso quod vult, iustum habendum sit.* Aug. de gen. con man. Lib. 1. Isa. 46:10.—Owen. The first reference is a quotation from Calvin's *Institutes*, 3.23.2: "The will of God is so much the highest rule of righteousness that whatever he wills, by the very fact that he will it, must be considered righteous." For the Latin text, see Calvin, *Institutio Christianae religionis* [. . .] (Geneva, 1559), 346. For the English translation, see *The Institutes of the Christian Religion*, ed. John T. McNeill and trans. Ford Lewis Battles, 2 vols. (Philadelphia: Westminster Press, 1960). The next reference is to Augustine's *On Genesis: A Refutation of the Manichees* 1.2.4, which is found in the marginal note of the *Institutes*. It refers to Augustine's claim that "anyone . . . who goes on to say, 'Why did he wish to make heaven and earth?' is looking for something greater than God's will is; but nothing greater can be found." For the Latin text, see Augustine, *De genesi contra Manichaeos*, in *Opera omnia*, ed. J.-P. Migne, Patrologia Latina 34 (Paris: Migne, 1865), 175. For the English translation, see Augustine, *On Genesis: A Refutation of the Manichees*, trans. Edmund Hill, *The Works of Saint Augustine: A Translation for the 21st Century* I/13 (Hyde Park, NY: New City Press, 1990), 42.

with God, had been general, universally extended to every creature; but [as] for the grace of rising from sin, and coming again unto God, that is made exceeding various, by some distinguishing purpose.

(2) That this outward dispensation being presupposed, yet in effectual working upon particular persons, there is no less variety, for "he hath mercy on whom he will have mercy."[53]

(3) Discover the rules of this whole administration.

The Outward Means of Grace Have Been Dispensed in a Variety of Ways

[1] For the first, the promise was at first made unto Adam,[54] and by him doubtless conveyed to his issue, and preached to the several generations which his eyes beheld proceeding from his own loins;[55] but yet by the wickedness of the old world, all flesh corrupting their ways,[56] we may easily collect, that the knowledge of it quickly departed from the most: sin banishing the love of God from their hearts, hindered the knowledge of God from continuing in their minds.[57]

[2] After many revivings,[58] by visions, revelations, and covenants,[59] it was at length called in from the wide world, and wholly restrained to the house, family, and seed of Abraham:[60] with whom alone, all the means of grace continued,[61] for thrice fourteen generations;[62] they alone were in Goshen, and all the world besides in thick darkness:[63] the dew of heaven was on them as the fleece, when else all the earth was dry.[64] God "shewed his word unto Jacob, his statutes and judgments unto Israel, he hath not dealt so with any nation" (Ps. 147:19–20). The prerogative of the Jews was chiefly in this, that to them "were committed the oracles of God" (Rom. 3).[65] To them pertained "the adoption, and the glory, the covenants and the giving of the law, and the service of God, and the promises" (Rom. 9:4).

---

[53] Rom. 9:18.
[54] In the margin: Gen. 3:15.—Owen.
[55] In the margin: Chap. 4:26.—Owen. I.e., Gen. 4:26.
[56] Gen. 6:12.
[57] In the margin: Gen. 6:5.—Owen.
[58] In the margin: Gen. 5:25.—Owen. This should probably be corrected to Gen. 5:24.
[59] In the margin: Gen. 6:18.—Owen.
[60] In the margin: Gen. 12:1; 18:1–2; Ps. 76:1–2.—Owen.
[61] In the margin: John 4:22.—Owen.
[62] Matt. 1:17.
[63] Ex. 10:23.
[64] Judg. 6:37.
[65] Rom. 3:2.

[3] But when the "fulness" of time came,⁶⁶ the Son of God being sent "in the likeness of sinful flesh,"⁶⁷ drew "all men" unto him;⁶⁸ and God, who had before "winked" at the time of their "ignorance," then called them "every where to repent,"⁶⁹ commanding the gospel to be preached to the universality of reasonable creatures, and the way of salvation to be proclaimed unto all;⁷⁰ upon which, in few years the sound of the gospel went out into all nations,⁷¹ and "the Sun of righteousness"⁷² displayed his beams upon the "habitable" parts of the earth.⁷³

[4] But yet once more this light, by Satan and his agents, persecutors and seducers, is almost extinguished, as was foretold (2 Thess. 2), remaining but in few places, and burning dim where it was, the kingdom of the beast being full of darkness (Rev. 16:10). Yet God again raises up reformers, and by them kindles a light, we hope, never to be put out.⁷⁴ But alas, what a spot of ground does this shine on, in comparison of the former vast extents and bounds of the Christian world. Now is all this variety, think you, to be ascribed unto chance, as the philosopher thought the world was made by a casual concurrence of atoms?⁷⁵ Or has the idol free will, with the new goddess contingency, ruled in these dispensations?⁷⁶ Truly neither the one nor the other, no more than the fly raised the dust by sitting

---

66 In the margin: Gal. 4:4.—Owen.
67 Rom. 8:3.
68 In the margin: John 12:32.—Owen.
69 In the margin: Acts 17:30.—Owen.
70 In the margin: Mark 16:15.—Owen.
71 In the margin: Tertullian, Lib. Ad. Jud. Reckoning almost all the known Nations of the world, and affirming that they all, that is, some in them, in his days, submitted to the scepter of Christ: he lived in the end of the second century.—Owen. Owen here cites Tertullian's *Adversus Judaeos*, in which the North African apologist sought to argue that the universal spread of the gospel is proof that God's promises are being fulfilled. Owen may have in mind chapter 12.1–2, "Further Proofs of the Calling of the Gentiles." For the English text, see Tertullian, *An Answer to the Jews*, in *Ante-Nicene Fathers*, 3:168–72.
72 In the margin: Mal. 3:4.—Owen. The quotation is a reference to Mal. 4:2.
73 In the margin: Prov. 8:31.—Owen.
74 This is an allusion to the dying exhortation of Bishop Hugh Latimer to Nicholas Ridley, as reported by John Foxe in *Acts and Monuments* [...] (London, 1570), 1976. Echoing the words of Polycarp, Latimer is given these words: "Be of good comfort M[r]. Ridley, and play the man: we shall this day lyght such a candle by Gods grace in England, as (I trust) shall never be put out."
75 This is the Epicurean hypothesis. See Reid Barbour, *English Epicures and Stoics: Ancient Legacies in Early Stuart Culture* (Amherst, MA: University of Massachusetts, 1998).
76 Here Owen is paraphrasing the title of *A Display of Arminianism* (1643) and, as Gribben notes, "Given his record of self-promotion, and his publisher's later attempt to offload surplus copies of the text, one could be forgiven for imagining that Owen, in the most important sermon of his life to date, was waving around a copy of his first book." Crawford Gribben, *John Owen and English Puritanism: Experiences of Defeat* (New York: Oxford University Press, 2016), 77.

on the chariot wheel;[77] but all these things have come to pass, according to a certain unerring rule, given them by God's determinate purpose and counsel.

God Works Effectually in Various Ways in Different Individuals

(2) Presupposing this variety in the outward means, how is it that thereupon, one is taken, another left?[78] The promise is made known to Cain and Abel; one the first murderer, the other the first martyr.[79] Jacob and Esau had the same outward advantages, but the one becomes Israel, the other Edom, the one inherits the promises, the other sells his right for a "mess of pottage."[80] At the preaching of our Savior, some believed, some blasphemed; "some said he was a good man, others said, nay, but he deceiveth the people":[81] have we not the word in its power this day, and do we not see the like various effects, some continuing in impenitency, others in sincerity closing with Jesus Christ? Now what shall we say to these things? What guides these wheels? Who thus steers his word for the good of souls? Why this also, as I said before, is from some peculiarly distinguishing purpose of the will of God.

The Rules That Govern This Variety

(3) To open the third thing proposed, I shall show, first, that all this variety is according to God's determinate purpose, and answers thereunto; secondly, the particular purposes from whence this variety proceeds.

[1] "He worketh all things according to the counsel of his own will" (Eph. 1:11): as a man may be said to erect a fabric,[82] according to the counsel of his will, when he frames it before in his mind, and makes all things in event, answer his preconceived platform; all things (especially τὰ πάντα, all those things, of which the apostle there treats, gospel things) have their futurition, and manner of being, from his eternal purpose:[83] whence also is the idea in the

---

77 This fable of the fly on the chariot wheel appeared in the *Hecatomythium* (1490) of the Italian writer Laurentius Abstemius (Lorenzo Astemio). Francis Bacon included it at the start of Essay 54, titled "Of Vaine-Glory." For the text, see Francis Bacon, *Bacon's Essays*, ed. Alfred S. West (Cambridge: Cambridge University Press, 1931), 159. This illustration is also used in Owen's 1649 sermon *Human Power Defeated*, which is included in this volume.
78 Matt. 24:40.
79 Gen. 4:8.
80 The "mess of pottage" refers to the meal for which Esau sold his birth right to his younger brother Jacob (Gen. 25:29–34; cf. Heb. 12:16). The phrase itself appeared as a chapter heading in several sixteenth-century English Bibles.
81 In the margin: Joh. 7:12.—Owen.
82 I.e., an edifice, building.
83 In the margin: Piscat. *In loc.* Πάντα δὲ λέγω τὰ οὐκ ἐφ᾽ ἡμῖν, τὰ γὰρ ἐφ᾽ ἡμῖν, οὐ τῆς προνοίας, ἀλλὰ τοῦ ἡμετέρου αὐτεξουσίου. Damascen. *Satis impie.*—Owen. The first reference is to the

mind of God, of all things with their circumstances,[84] that shall be: that is, the first mover, continuing itself immovable: giving to everything a regular motion, according to the impression which from that it does receive: "For known unto him are all his works from the beginning of the world" (Acts 15:18).[85]

If any attendants of actions, might free and exempt them, from the regular dependence we insist upon, they must be either contingency or sin; but yet for both these, we have, besides general rules, clear particular instances: what seems more contingent and casual than the unadvised slaying of a man, with the fall of the head of an axe from the helve,[86] as a man was cutting wood by the way side? (Deut. 19:5). Yet God assumes this as his own work (Ex. 21:13). The same may be said of free agents, and their actions: and for the other, see Acts 4:27–28, in the crucifying of the Son of God's love, all things came to pass according as his counsel had before determined that it should be done. Now how in the one of these liberty is not abridged, the nature of things not changed in the other, sin is not countenanced, belongs not to this discourse. "The counsel of the Lord," then, "standeth for ever, the thoughts of his heart unto all generations" (Ps. 33:11). "His counsel standeth, and he will do all his pleasure" (Isa. 46:10). For he is the Lord, and he changes not (Mal. 3:6). With him is neither "variableness nor shadow of turning" (James 1:17). All things that are, come to pass in that unchangeable method in which he has laid them down from all eternity.[87]

German theologian Johannes Piscator (1546–1625) and his *Analysis logica sex epistolarum Pauli: videlicet ad Galatas. Ephesios. Philippenses. Colossenses. Utriusq; ad Thessalonicenses* [...] (Herborn, 1589), 81. The second reference is to John of Damascus (d. 749), one of the fathers of the Eastern church, and his *An Exact Exposition of the Orthodox Faith* 2.29, "On Providence." For the Greek text, see John of Damascus, *Expositio fidei orthoxae*, ed. J.-P. Migne, Patrologia Graeca 94 (Paris: Migne-Garnier, 1857), 964. Owen is contrasting his view with that of the Damascene: "When I say 'all', I am referring to those things which do not depend upon us, because those which do depend upon us do not belong to providence, but to our own free will." For this English translation, see *Saint John of Damascus: Writings*, trans. Frederic H. Chase Jr., Fathers of the Church 37 (Washington, DC: Catholic University of America Press, 1958), 261.

84 In the margin: Mat. 10:29. Iob 14:5. Prov. 16:33. Prov. 21:1, 30 & 19:21. *Nihil fit nisi omnipotens fieri velit, vel ipse faciendo, vel sinendo ut fiat. Augustine.*—Owen. This is a reference to Augustine's *Enchiridion* 95. For the Latin text, see *Enchiridion*, in *Opera omnia*, 40:275–76. "So nothing happens unless the Almighty wills it, either by allowing it to happen or by doing it himself." For the translation, see *The Augustine Catechism: The Enchiridion on Faith and Hope*, ed. Boniface Ramsey, trans. Bruce Harbert, in *Works of Saint Augustine*, 1:118.

85 In the margin: Gen. 45:4–7; 1 Kings 22:19–21; 2 Kings 5:18–19; Psal. 76:10; Eccles. 7:26; Isa. 6:9–11 etc.—Owen.

86 I.e., handle.

87 In the margin: *Deus non operatur in malis, quod ei displicet, sed operatur per eos quod ei placet, recipientur vero, non pro eo quod Deus bene usus est ipsorum operibus malis, sed pro eo, quod ipsi male abusi sunt Dei operibus bonis*: Fulgent. *Ad Monim.*—Owen. "[God] does not work in

[2] Let us look peculiarly upon the purposes according to which the dispensations of the gospel, both in sending, and withholding it do proceed.

{1} For the not sending of the means of grace unto any people, whereby they hear not the joyful sound of the gospel, but have in all ages followed dumb idols,[88] as many do unto this day. In this chapter of which we treat, the gospel is forbidden to be preached in Asia and Bithynia, which restraint the Lord by his providence, as yet continues to many parts of the world: now the purpose from whence this proceeds, and whereby it is regulated, you have, [in] Romans 9:22, "What if God willing to show his wrath, and to make his power known, endured with much long-suffering the vessels of wrath fitted to destruction," compared with Matthew 11:25–26, "Thou hast hid these things from the prudent and wise, even so, O Father, for so it seemed good before thee": and with Acts 14:16, he "suffered all nations to walk in their own ways." Now God's not sending the truth, has the same design and aim with his sending, the efficacy of error, viz. "that they all may be damned,"[89] who have it not: there being "no other name under heaven, whereby they may be saved,"[90] but only that which is not revealed unto them. God in the meantime, being no more the cause of their sins,[91] for which they incur damnation, than the sun is the cause of cold and darkness, which

---

them what displeases him but works through them what pleases him. Afterwards, he is going to give them what they deserve from his justice. They will receive it not because God has made good use of their evil works but because they have badly used the good work of God." This is a quotation from the *Letter to Monimus* 1.27.1 by Fulgentius (ca. 467–532), bishop of Ruspe (North Africa). Fulgentius was born into a noble family from Carthage and was moved by the preaching of Augustine to become a monk. This work contains his response to a number of doctrinal questions from Monimus, an otherwise unknown correspondent, in which Fulgentius expounds an Augustinian view of predestination. For the Latin text, see Fulgentius, *Libri tres ad Monimum*, in *Opera Omnia*, ed. J.-P. Migne, Patrologia Latina 65 (Paris: Migne, 1847), 174. For the English translation, see Fulgentius, *Selected Works*, trans. Robert B. Eno, Fathers of the Church 95 (Washington, DC: Catholic University of America Press, 1997), 225.

88 See 1 Cor. 12:2.
89 In the margin: 2 Thes. 2.—Owen. In particular, 2:12.
90 In the margin: Acts 4.—Owen. In particular, 4:12.
91 In the margin: *Liberatur pars hominum, parte pereunte; sed cur horum misertus sit Deus, illorum non misertus, quae scientia comprehendere potest? Latet discretions ratio, sed non latet ipsa discretio.* Prosp. De Vocat. Gen.—Owen. This is a reference to Prosper of Aquitaine, *De vocatione omnium gentium* 1.15: "One section of mankind attains salvation.... But who is so learned as to understand ... why God did not have mercy on the former, but was merciful towards the latter? The reason of this discrimination escapes us; the difference itself we see." For the Latin text, see Prosper, *De vocatione omnium gentium*, in *Opera omnia*, ed. J.-P. Migne, Patrologia Latina 51 (Paris: Migne-Garnier, 1861), 663. For the English translation, see Prosper, *The Call of All Nations*, trans. P. de Letter, Ancient Christian Writers 14 (Westminster, MD: Newman, 1952), 58–59.

follow the absence thereof: or he is the cause of a man's imprisonment for debt, who will not pay his debt for him, though he be no way obliged so to do. So then the not sending of the gospel to any people, is an act regulated by that eternal purpose of God, whereby he determines to advance the glory of his justice, by permitting some men to sin, to continue in their sin, and for sin to send them to their own place; as a king's not sending a pardon to condemned malefactors, is an issue of his purpose, that they shall die for their faults. When you see the gospel strangely, and through wonderful varieties, and unexpected providences, carried away from a people, know, that the spirit which moves in those wheels,[92] is that purpose of God which we have recounted.

{2} To some people, to some nations, the gospel is sent. God calls them to repentance and acknowledgment of the truth, as in my text, Macedonia: and England the day wherein we breathe. Now there is in this a twofold aim: (1) peculiar, toward some in their conversion; (2) general toward all for conviction, and therefore it is acted according to a twofold purpose, which carries it along, and is fulfilled thereby.

First, his purpose of saving some in and by Jesus Christ, effectually to bring them unto himself, for the praise of his glorious grace:[93] upon whomsoever the seal of the Lord is stamped, that God knows them, and owns them as his,[94] to them he will cause his gospel to be revealed.[95] Paul is commanded to abide at Corinth, and to preach there, because God had "much people" in that city (Acts 18:10): though the devil had them in present possession, yet they were God's in his eternal counsel. And such as these they were, for whose sake the man of Macedonia is sent on his message.[96] Have you never

---

92 Ezek. 1:20–21.
93 In the margin: Rom. 8:28–29; Eph. 1:4.—Owen.
94 In the margin: 2 Tim. 2:19.—Owen.
95 In the margin: Ephes. 2:1, 11.—Owen.
96 In the margin: *Non ob aliud dicit, non vos me elegistis, sed ego vos elegi, nisi quia non elegerunt eum, ut eligeret eos; sed ut eligerent eum, elegit eos. Non quia praescivit eos credituros, sed quia facturus ipse fuerit credentes. Electi sunt itaque ante mundi constitutionem, ea praedestinatione, qua Deus ipse sua futura facta praevidit: electi sunt autem de mundo ea vocatione, qua Deus id quod praedestinavit implevit.* August. De bon. Persev. Cap. 16, 17.—Owen. Although Owen references *De bono perseverantiae* (The good of perseverance), this quotation is from *De praedestinatione sanctum* (Predestination of the Saints), 17 (34). From the ninth century, *De bono perseverantiae* was the more common title for *De dono perseverantiae* (*The Gift of Perseverance*), the title of the second part of this anti-Pelagian work (ca. 428). "Whence, for no other reason does he say, 'You have not chosen me, but I have chosen you,' than because they did not choose him so that he could choose them, but he chose them in order that they might choose him.... God foreknew that they would believe, not because he himself was going to make them believers.... [T]hey were chosen before the foundation of the world by that predestination by which God foreknew

seen the gospel hover about a nation, now and then about to settle, and anon feared and upon wing again, yet working through difficulties, making plains of mountains, and filling valleys, overthrowing armies, putting aliens to flight,[97] and at length taking firm root like the cedars of God?[98] Truly if you have not, you are strangers to the place wherein you live. Now, what is all this but the working of the purpose of God to attain its proposed end, of gathering his saints to himself? In the effectual working of grace also, for conversion and salvation, whence do you think it takes its rule and determination, in respect of particular objects, that it should be directed to John, not Judas; Simon Peter, not Simon Magus?[99] Why, only from this discriminating counsel of God from eternity, to bring the one, and not the other to himself by Christ. "The Lord added to the church such as should be saved" (Acts 2:47). The purpose of saving is the rule of adding to the church of believers. And, "As many believed as were ordained to eternal life" (Acts 13:48). Their foreordaining to life eternal gives them right to faith and belief. The purpose of God's election is the rule of dispensing saving grace.

Secondly, his purpose of leaving some inexcusable in their sins, for the farther manifestation of his glorious justice, is the rule of dispensing the word unto them.[100] Did you never see the gospel sent or continued to an unthankful people, bringing forth no fruits meet for it?[101] Wherefore it is so sent, see Isaiah 6:9–10, which prophecy you have fulfilled, [in] John 12:41–42,[102] in men described [in] Jude 4 and 1 Peter 2:8. But here we must strike sail, the waves swell, and it is no easy task to sail in this gulf, the righteousness of God is a great mountain (easy to be seen) but his judgments are like the great deep, (who can search into the bottom thereof?) (Ps. 36:6). And so I hope I have discovered, how all things here below, concerning the promulgation of the gospel, are, in their greatest variety, straightly regulated by the eternal purposes and counsel of God.

---

his future actions, but they were chosen out of the world by that calling, by which God fulfilled that which he predestined." For the Latin text, see Augustine, *De praedestinatione sanctorum*, in *Opera omnia*, ed. J.-P. Migne, Patrologia Latina 44 (Paris: Migne-Garnier, 1865), 986. For English translation see Augustine, *Predestination of the Saints*, in *Four Anti-Pelagian Writings*, trans. John A. Mourant and William J. Collinge, Fathers of the Church 86 (Washington, DC: Catholic University of America Press, 1992), 260.

97 Heb. 11:34.
98 Ezek. 31:8.
99 Simon the magician (Acts 8:9–24).
100 In the margin: Mat. 11:21; Acts 13:46.—Owen.
101 In the margin: Luk. 2:34; 1 Pet. 2:7; Ezek. 2:5; Matth. 24:15; Rom. 9:23.—Owen.
102 Following Goold, the reference should be expanded to John 12:37–42.

Uses Arising from the First Observation
The uses of it follow.

God's Glorious Purposes in the Ongoing Reformation of the English Church

Use 1. To discover whence it is, that the work of reforming the worship of God, and settling the almost departing gospel, has so powerfully been carried along in this nation: that a beautiful fabric is seen to arise in the midst of all oppositions, with the confusion of axes and hammers sounding about it:[103] though the builders have been forced oftentimes, not only with one hand, but with both to hold the weapons of war:[104] that although the wheels of our chariots have been knocked off, and they driven heavily,[105] yet the regular motions of the superior wheels of providence, have carried on the design, toward the resting place aimed at; that the ship has been directed to the port, though the storm had quite puzzled the pilots and mariners; even from hence, that all this great variety, was but to work out one certain foreappointed end, proceeding in the tracts and paths, which were traced out for it from eternity; which though they have seemed to us a maze or labyrinth, such a world of contingencies and various chances has the work passed through; yet indeed all the passages thereof have been regular and straight, answering the platform laid down for the whole in the counsel of God. Daniel, chapter 9, makes his supplication for the restoration of Jerusalem; an angel is sent to tell him, that "at the beginning of his supplication the commandment came forth," verse 23, viz. that it should be accomplished; it was before determined, and is now set on work: but yet what mountains of opposition, what hinderances lay in the way?[106] Cyrus must come to the crown by the death or slaughter of Darius; his heart be moved to send some to the work; in a short time Cyrus is cut off.[107] Now difficulties arise from the following kings: what their flattering counselors, what the malignant nations about them conspired,[108] the books of Nehemiah and Ezra sufficiently declare. Whence, verse 25, the angel tells Daniel, that

---

[103] See 1 Kings 6:7.
[104] In the margin: Neh. 4:17.—Owen.
[105] Ex. 14:25.
[106] In the margin: Zech. 4:7.—Owen.
[107] In the margin: Scal. De Emend. Temp.—Owen. This is a reference to the Huguenot scholar Joseph Justus Scaliger (1540–1609) and his work *De emendatione temporum* [...] (Paris, 1583), which proposed a chronology for Cyrus that was fed into debates about the interpretation of the seventy weeks of Daniel 9.
[108] At this time, there were concerns about King Charles's discussions with the Irish rebels and the Scots.

from "the commandment, to restore and build Jerusalem, unto Messiah the Prince, shall be seven weeks, and sixty-two weeks; the street shall be built again, and the wall, in troublesome times":[109] that is, it shall be seven weeks to the finishing of Jerusalem, and thence to Messiah the Prince sixty-two weeks; seven weeks, that is, forty-nine years, for so much it was,[110] from the decree of Cyrus, to the finishing of the wall by Nehemiah: of which time the temple, as the Jews affirmed, was all but three years in building (John 2:20), during which space, how often did the hearts of the people of God faint in their troubles, as though they should never have seen an end, and therefore ever and anon they were ready to give over, as Haggai 1:2, but yet we see the decree was fixed, and all those varieties, did but orderly work in an exact method, for the glorious accomplishment of it.

England's troubles have not yet endured above half the odd years[111] of those reformers' task,[112] yet, good God, how short-breathed are men! What fainting is there! What repining, what grudging against the ways of the Lord? But, let me tell you, that as the water in the stream will not go higher than the head of the fountain, no more will the work in hand be carried

---

[109] Dan. 9:25.

[110] In the margin: I follow in this the vulgar or common account, otherwise there is no part of Scripture chronologie so contended about, as these weeks of Daniel: most concluding, that they are terminated in the death of Christ, happening about the middest of the last week: but about their original or rise there is no small debate, of the four decrees made by the Persian Kings about the building of Jerusalem, viz. 1. By Cyrus (2 Chron. 3:6). 2. By Darius (Ezek. 6:3). 3. By Artaxerxes (Ezek. 7), of the same to Nehemiah (Neh. 2). Following the account of their reign set down in profane stories, the last only holds exactly. Tertullian *ad Judae*. Begins it from Darius, when this vision appeared to Daniel, whom it seems he conceived to be Darius Hyslaspes, that followed the Magi, and not Medus, that was before Cyrus: and so with a singular kind of Chronologie makes up his account. Vid: Euseb. *Demon. Evan lib.* 8. Cap. 2. Funck. *Com. In Chron.* Beroald. *Chron.* Lib. 3. Cap. 7, 8 Montacu. *Apparat.*—Owen. In this very lengthy marginal note, Owen acknowledges the contested chronology, referencing the following works: Tertullian, *Adversus Judaeos*; Eusebius of Caesarea, *Demonstratio evangelica*; Johann Funck (1516–1566), *Chronologia cum commentariis chronologiis ab initio mundi ad resurrectionem Christi* (Nuremberg, 1545); Matthieu Béroalde (1520–1576), *Chronicum, Scripturae sacrae autoritate constitutum* (Geneva, 1575); and Bishop Richard Montagu (1577–1641), *Apparatus ad origens ecclesiasticas* (Oxford, 1635). For a discussion of the contested nature of biblical chronology at this time, see Scott Mandelbrote, "'The Doors Shall Fly Open': Chronology and Biblical Interpretation in England, c. 1630–c. 1730," in *The Oxford Handbook of the Bible in Early Modern England, c. 1530–1700*, ed. Kevin Killeen, Helen Smith, and Rachel Willie (Oxford: Oxford University Press, 2015), 176–95.

[111] I.e., approximate number of years.

[112] According to Owen, England's troubles have not yet gone on for half of forty-nine years. This implies that he dates the beginning of these troubles to no earlier than the 1620s. See Anthony Milton, *England's Second Reformation: The Battle for the Church of England, 1625–1662* (Cambridge: Cambridge University Press, 2021), 34–67.

one step higher, or beyond the aim of its fountain, the counsel of God, from whence it has its rise: and yet as a river will break through all oppositions, and swell to the height of mountains, to go to the sea, from whence it came; so will the stream of the gospel, when it comes out from God, break down all mountains of opposition, and not be hindered from resting in its appointed place. It were an easy thing to recall your minds, to some trembling periods of time, when there was trembling in our armies, and trembling in our councils, trembling to be ashamed, to be repented of, trembling in the city and in the country, and men were almost at their wits' end for the sorrows and fears of those days: and yet we see how the unchangeable purpose of God has wrought strongly through all these straits, from one end to another, that nothing might fall to the ground, of what he had determined. If a man in those days had gone about to persuade us that all our pressures were good omens, that they all wrought together for our good, we could have been ready to cry with the woman, who when she had recounted her griefs to the physician, and he still replied they were good signs, οἴ μοι ἀγαθῶν ἀπόλλυμαι, "Good signs have undone me,"[113] these good signs will be our ruin; yet behold (we hope) the contrary. Our day has been like that mentioned [in] Zechariah 14:6–7, a day whose light is neither clear nor dark, a day known only to the Lord, seeming to us to be neither day nor night: but God knew all this while that it was a day, he saw how it all wrought for the appointed end: and in the evening, in the close, it will be light, so light as to be to us discernible. In the meantime, we are like unskillful men, going to the house of some curious artist, so long as he is about his work, despise it as confused; but when it is finished, admire it as excellent: while the passages of providence are on us, all is confusion, but when the fabric is reared, glorious.

God Uses a Wide Variety of Means to Accomplish His Purposes

Use 2. Learn to look upon the wisdom of God, in carrying all things, through this wonderful variety, exactly to answer his own eternal purpose: suffering so many mountains to lie in the way of reforming his churches, and settling the

---

113 Owen is referring to Aesop's fable of the doctor and his dying patient, the moral of which is that "death-bed flattery is the worst of treacheries." See "A Doctor and his Patient" in Roger L'Estrange, *Fables of Aesop and Other Eminent Mythologists: With Morals and Reflexions* (London, 1694), 89. During the 1630s, Aesop's *Fables* began to be used for increasingly political purposes. See Mark Kishlansky, "Turning Frogs into Princes: Aesop's *Fables* and the Political Culture of Early Modern England," in *Political Culture and Cultural Politics in Early Modern England*, ed. Susan D. Amussen and Mark A. Kishlansky (Manchester: Manchester University Press, 1995), 338–60.

gospel, that his Spirit may have the glory, and his people the comfort in their removal. It is a high and noble contemplation, to consider the purposes of God, so far as by the event revealed, and to see what impressions his wisdom and power do leave upon things accomplished here below, to read in them a temporary history of his eternal counsels. Some men may deem it strange, that his determinate will, which gives rule to these things, and could in a word have reached its own appointment, should carry his people so many journeys in the wilderness, and keep us thus long in so low estate. I say, not to speak of his own glory, which has sparkled forth of this flinty opposition, there be divers[114] things, things of light, for our good, which he has brought forth out of all that darkness, wherewith we have been overclouded: take a few instances.

(1) If there had been no difficulties, there had been no deliverances: and did we never find our hearts so enlarged toward God upon such advantages, as to say, "Well, this day's temper of spirit, was cheaply purchased by yesterday's anguish and fear? That was but a being sick at sea."

(2) Had there been no tempests and storms, we had not made out for shelter: did you never run to a tree for shelter in a storm, and find fruit which you expected not? Did you never go to God for safeguard in these times,[115] driven by outward storms, and there find unexpected fruit, the "peaceable fruit of righteousness,"[116] that made you say, "Happy tempest, which cast me into such a harbor"? It was a storm that occasioned the discovery of the golden mines of India:[117] has not a storm driven some to the discovery of the richer mines of the love of God in Christ?

(3) Had not Esau come against him, with four hundred men, Jacob had not been called Israel; he had not been put to it, to try his strength with God, and so to prevail.[118] Who would not purchase with the greatest distress that heavenly comfort, which is in the return of prayers? The strength of God's Jacobs in this kingdom, had not been known, if the Esaus had not

---

114 I.e., of varying types.
115 In the margin: Prov. 18:10.—Owen.
116 In the margin: Heb. 12:11.—Owen.
117 In the margin: Pet. Mart. De Relig. Jud. Decad. i. lib. 1.—Owen. This is a reference to the Italian scholar Pietro Martire d'Anghiera (1457–1526), who collected the writings of European travelers to the New World in *De orbe novo decades octo* (1511–1525). In the first of his decades, he describes Columbus enduring great storms before chancing upon what he thought was Solomon's abandoned gold mine of Ophir (1 Kings 9:28) on the island of Hispaniola (Haiti) in 1495. For the English translation of Martire's chronicle, see Richard Eden, *The Decades of the Newe Worlde or West India* (London, 1555), sig. A2r–v.
118 Gen. 32–33.

come against them. Some say, this war has made a discovery of England's strength,[119] what it is able to do. I think so also, not what armies it can raise against men, but with what armies of prayers and tears it is able to deal with God. Had not the brethren strove in the womb, Rebekah had not asked, "Why am I thus?" nor received that answer, "The elder shall serve the younger":[120] had not two sorts of people struggled in the womb of this kingdom, we had not sought, nor received, such gracious answers.[121] Thus do all the various motions of the lower wheels, serve for our good, and exactly answer the impression they receive from the master spring, the eternal purpose of God. Of this hitherto.

The Sovereign Good Pleasure of God Accounts for Why the Gospel Is Sent to Any Nation or Person

Observ[ation] 2. The sending of the gospel to any one nation, rather than another, as the means of life and salvation, is of the mere free grace and good pleasure of God.[122]

Now before I come to make out the absolute independency and freedom of this distinguishing mercy, I shall premise three things.

Three Initial Premises Regarding God's Distinguishing Mercy

(1) That the not sending of the gospel to any person or people, is of God's mere good pleasure, and not of any peculiar distinguishing demerit in that person or people.[123] No man or nation does *majorem ponere obicem*, lay more or greater

---

119 The First English Civil War (1642–1646).
120 Gen. 25:23.
121 This trope of the twins was used to describe the religious and political struggles of the 1640s that divided the nation by identifying an enemy within. See Rosemary D. Bradley, "'Jacob and Esau Struggling in the Wombe': A Study of Presbyterian and Independent Religious Conflicts, 1640–48" (PhD Thesis, University of Kent, 1975). For example, Francis Cheynell: "Two Nations, two manner of people struggling in the bowels of this Text and Kingdome, *Jacob* and *Esau*." See his *Sions Memento, and Gods Alarum. In a Sermon at Westminster, before the Honourable House of Commons, on the 31 of May, 1643* [. . .] (London, 1643), 1, 20.
122 In the margin: *Qui liberatur, gratiam diligat, qui non liberatur, debitum agnoscat*. Aug. de bon. Persev., cap. 8.—Owen. This a quotation from Augustine's *De bono perseverantiae* (The good of perseverance) 8.16. "So let him who is delivered love his grace, and him who is not delivered acknowledge his desert." For the Latin text, see Augustine, *De dono perseverantiae*, in *Opera omnia*, ed. J.-P. Migne, Patrologia Latina 45 (Paris: Migne-Garnier, 1865), 1002. For the English translation see Augustine, *Predestination of the Saints*, in *Four Anti-Pelagian Writings*, 283.
123 In the margin: *Ex nequissimis in ipso vitae exitu gratia invenit quos adoptet, cum tamen multi, etiam qui minus nocentes videantur, doni hujus alieni sunt*. Prosp. De voc. Gen. lib. 1. Cap. 17.—Owen. This is a reference to Prosper, *De vocatione omnium gentium* 1.17. "Grace seeks its adopted sons even among the worst sinners in their very last moments, and that many who

obstacles against the gospel than another.[124] There is nothing imaginable to lay a block in the passage thereof, but only sin. Now these sins are, or may be, of two sorts; either first, against the gospel itself, which may possibly hinder the receiving of the gospel, but not the sending of it, which it presupposes. Secondly, against the covenant they are under, and the light they are guided by, before the beams of the gospel shine upon them: now in these generally all are equal, all having sinned and come short of the glory of God. And in particular sins against the law and light of nature, no nations have gone farther than they which were soonest enlightened with the word, as afterward will appear: so that the sole cause of this is the good pleasure of God, as our Savior affirms (Matt. 11:25–26).

(2) That sins against the covenant of works, which men are under before the gospel comes unto them, cannot have any general demerit, that the means of life and salvation by free grace should not be imparted to them.[125] It is true, all nations have deserved to be turned into hell, and a people that have had the truth, and detained it in ungodliness, deserve to be deprived of it. The first, by virtue of the sanction of the first broken covenant: the other, by sinning against that, which they had of the second; but that men in a fallen condition, and not able to rise, should hereby deserve not to be helped up, needs some distinction to clear it.

There is then a twofold demerit and indignity: one merely negative, or a not deserving to have good done unto us: the other positive, deserving that good should not be done unto us. The first of these, is found in all the world, in respect of the dispensation of the gospel: if the Lord should bestow it only on those who do deserve it, he must forever keep it closed up in the eternal treasure of his own bosom. The second is found directly in none, in respect of that peculiar way which is discovered in the gospel, because they had not sinned against it: which, rightly considered, gives no small luster to the freedom of grace.

(3) That there is a right in the gospel, and a fitness in that gracious dispensation, to be made known to all people in the world; that no singular portion of the earth should be any longer a holy land, or any mountain of the world lift up its head above its fellows. And this right has a double foundation.

[1] The infinite value and worth of the blood of Christ, giving fullness and fitness to the promises founded thereon to be propounded to all mankind,[126]

---

looked less wicked are denied this gift." For the Latin text, see Prosper, *De vocatione omnium gentium*, 670. For the English translation see Prosper, *Call of All Nations*, 61.

124 In the margin: 1 Cor. 1:25–26.—Owen.

125 In the margin: Acts 14:16–17; Ch. 17:30–31.—Owen.

126 In the margin: Rom. 8:32; Joel 2:28; Joh. 17:32; Rom. 1:5; 16:26.—Owen. The John 17:32 reference should be connected to John 12:32.

for through his blood "remission of sins" is preached to whosoever believes on him (Acts 10:43), "to every creature" (Mark 16:15). God would have a price of that infinite value for sin, laid down, as might justly give advantage, to proclaim a pardon infinitely to all that will come in, and accept of it, there being in it no defect at all (though intentionally only a ransom for some) but that by it, the world might know that he had done whatsoever the Father commanded him (John 14:31).

(2) In that economy and dispensation of the grace of the new covenant, breaking forth in these latter days, whereby all external distinction, of places and persons, people and nations, being removed,[127] Jesus Christ takes all nations to be his inheritance,[128] dispensing to all men the grace of the gospel,[129] bringing salvation, as seems best to him (Titus 2:11–12). For being lifted up, he drew all unto him,[130] having redeemed us with his blood, "out of every kindred and tongue, people and nation" (Apoc. 5:9).[131] And on these two grounds it is, that the gospel has in itself a right and fitness, to be preached to all, even as many as the Lord our God shall call.

Proof of This Second Observation

These things being premised, I come to the proof of the assertion.

Moses is very careful in sundry places to get this to take an impression upon their spirits, that it was mere free grace that exalted them into that condition and dignity wherein they stood, by their approach unto God, in the enjoyment of his ordinances (Deut. 7:7–8): in this most clearly rendering the cause of God's love in choosing them, mentioned, verse 7 to be only his love, verse 8 his love toward them is the cause of his love, his free love eternally determining, of his free love actually conferring those distinguishing mercies upon them: it was not for their righteousness, for they were "a stiff-necked people" (Deut. 6:6).[132]

Our Savior laying both these things together, the hiding of the mysteries of salvation from some, and revealing them to others, renders the same reason and supreme cause of both, of which no account can be rendered, only the good pleasure of God: "I thank thee, Father" (Matt. 11:25–26). And if any will proceed higher, and say, "Where is the justice of this, that men

---

127 In the margin: Rom. 9:13.—Owen.
128 In the margin: Ephes. 2:14–15.—Owen.
129 In the margin: Mat. 28:19.—Owen.
130 John 12:32.
131 Rev. 5:9.
132 The correct reference is Deut. 9:6.

equally obnoxious, should be thus unequally accepted?" we say with Paul, "That he will have mercy on whom he will have mercy, and whom he will he hardeneth, and who art thou, O man, that disputest against God?"[133] "But if you are human and I am human, let us both listen to him saying, O man, who are you":[134] to send a pardon to some that are condemned, suffering the rest to suffer, has no injustice. If this will not satisfy, let us say with the same apostle, Ὦ βάθος, "O the depth of the" etc. (Rom. 11:33).

Yea so far is it from truth, that God should dispense, and grant his word and means of grace, by any other rule, or upon any other motive, than his own will and good pleasure, that we find in Scripture the direct contrary to what we would suppose, even, mercy showed to the more unworthy, and the more worthy passed by, reckoning worthiness and unworthiness by less or greater sin, with less or more endeavors.[135] Christ preaches to Chorazin and Bethsaida which would not repent; and at the same time denies the word to Tyre and Sidon, which would have gotten on sackcloth and ashes, when the other continued delicate despisers (Matt. 11:21). Ezekiel is sent to them that would not hear him, passing by them that would have hearkened (Ezek. 3:5); which is most clear, "The Gentiles which followed not after righteousness, have attained to righteousness, even the righteousness which is of faith; but Israel which followed after the law of righteousness, have not attained to it" (Rom. 9:30–31). If in the dispensation of the gospel, the Lord had had any respect to the desert of people, Corinth that famous place of sinning, had not so soon enjoyed it, the people whereof, for worship, were led away with dumb idols ([1] Cor. 12:2); and for their lives, you have them drawn to the life, "Fornicators,

---

133 Rom. 9:18, 20.
134 In the text: *Si tu es homo, et ego homo, audiamus dicentem, O homo, Tu quis.*—Owen. In the margin: August.—Owen. Owen is repeating a phrase used by Augustine in *Sermon 26, 14*. For the Latin text, see Augustine, *Sermo xxvi*, in *Opera omnia*, ed. J.-P. Migne, Patrologia Latina 38 (Paris: Migne-Garnier, 1865), 178. For the English translation, see Augustine, *Sermons II (20–50) on the Old Testament*, trans. Edmund Hill, ed. John Rotelle, in *The Works of Saint Augustine: A Translation for the 21st Century* III/2 (Hyde Park, NY: New City Press, 2001), 101.
135 In the margin: *Si hoc voluntatum meritis voluerimus ascribere, ut malos neglexisse gratia, bonos autem elegisse videatur; resistet nobis innumerabilium causa populorum, quibus per tot saecula nulla coelestis doctrinae annuntiatio coruscavit. Nec meliores fuisse eorum posteros possumus dicere, de quibus scriptum est, Gentium populus, qui sedebat in tenebris, lucem vidit magnam,* Prosp. *De voc. Gen.* lib.1. cap. 15.—Owen. This is a quotation from Prosper's *De vocatione omnium gentium* 1.15. "Were we to ascribe this to individual merits and say that grace left off the wicked and chose the good, then we would be faced with the case of countless peoples to whom for so many ages no messenger of the heavenly doctrine has appeared. And we should not say that their posterity were better than they, for it is written of them: *The nation of the Gentiles that was sitting in darkness has seen a great light* [Isa. 9:2]." For the Latin text, see *De vocatione omnium gentium*, 668. For the English translation, see Prosper, *Call of All Nations*, 58.

idolaters, adulterers, effeminate, abusers of themselves with mankind, thieves, covetous, drunkards, revilers, extortioners" (1 Cor. 6:9–11), καὶ ταῦτά τινες ἦτε,[136] which is to be repeated, ἀπὸ τοῦ κοινοῦ,[137] "Some of you were fornicators, some idolaters; 'but ye are sanctified:' " seem not these to the eye of flesh goodly qualifications for the gospel of Jesus Christ? Had these men been dealt withal according as they had disposed themselves, not fitter fuel for hell could the justice of God require: but yet you see, to these the gospel comes, with the first, a light shines "to them that sit in darkness and in the shadow of death."[138]

Reason 1.[139] If God send or grant the gospel, which is the means of grace, upon any other ground, but his mere good pleasure, then it must be an act of remunerative justice. Now there is no such justice in God toward the creature, but what is founded upon some preceding covenant, or promise of God to the creature, which is the only foundation of all relation between God and man, but only those that attend creation and sovereignty. Now what promise do you find made to, or covenant with a people as yet without the gospel: I mean conditional promises, inferring any good to be bestowed on any required performance on their part? Free, absolute promises there are innumerable, that light should shine to them that were in darkness, and those be called God's people which were not his people; but such as depend on any condition on their part to be fulfilled, we find none. God bargains not with the creature about the gospel,[140] knowing how unable he is to be merchant for such

---

136 Gk. "And such were some of you."
137 Gk., lit., "from the common." This refers to an *apo koinou* construction in which the clause "and such were some of you" links 6:9–10 with 6:11.
138 Luke 1:79.
139 In the margin: *Si de debito quaeratur respectu creaturae, in Deum cadere non potest, nisi ex aliqua suppositione ipsi Deo voluntaria [ac libera], quae non potest esse nisi promissio, aut pacto aliqua, ex quibus fidelitatis aut justitiae debitum oriri solet.*—Owen. This is a quotation from Franciscus Suárez, *De libertate divinae voluntatis, disputatio* (On the freedom of the divine will) 2.2.5. Suárez (1548–1617) was a Spanish Jesuit. For the Latin text see Suárez, *Opera omnia*, ed. Vivès, vol. 11 (Paris, 1858), 414. "If the question concerns an obligation with respect to the creature, nothing can be laid upon God, unless it derives from some free and voluntary undertaking initiated by God himself, which necessarily takes the form of a promise or covenant of the sort from which obligations of fidelity or justice generally arise."
140 In the margin: *Deus nulla obligatione tenetur, antequam ipse fidem suam astringat, ergo ante promissionem nulla justitia distributiva in Deo reperitur.* Vasq. In q. 21, a. 1, disp. 86.—Owen. This is a reference to the Spanish Jesuit Gabriel Vásquez (1549–1604), who was Suárez's successor to the chair of theology at Rome (ca. 1550–1604). The reference summarizes material from his most famous work, a commentary on Aquinas' *Summa*, titled *Disputations on Thomas*, q. 21, art. 1, disput. 86. For the Latin text, see Vásquez, *Commentariorum ac disputationum in primam partem & in primam secundae Sancti Thomae* (Venice, 1608), 429. "God is bound by no constraint before he himself pledges his binding word; thus, before the promise, no principle of distributive justice is found in God."

pearls. If a man had all that goodness which may be found in man, without Jesus Christ, they would not in the least measure procure a discovery of him.

I deny not but God may, and perhaps sometimes does, reveal himself to some in a peculiar and extraordinary manner. Whereunto tends that story in Aquinas,[141] of a corpse taken up in the days of Constantine and Irene,[142] with a plate of gold, and this inscription on it, "Christ shall be born of a virgin, and in Him, I believe. O sun, during the lifetime of Irene and Constantine, thou shalt see me again."[143] But that this should be regular unto men living, μετὰ λόγου, in Justin Martyr's phrase,[144] or using their naturals aright (which is impossible they should, the right use of naturals depending on supernaturals), is wide from the word.

If there be any outward motive of granting the gospel unto any, it is some acceptable performances of theirs, holding up to the rule and will of God: now this will and rule having no saving revelation but by the gospel, which should thus be procured by acts agreeable unto it, makes up a flat contradiction, supposing the revelation of the gospel, before it be revealed; doubtless according to all rules of justice to us made known, it is an easier thing, to

---

141 In the margin: Aquin. 2, 2, q. 2, art. 7.—Owen. This is a reference is to Aquinas, "Whether explicit faith in the mystery of Christ is a matter of salvation for all people?" See Thomas Aquinas, *Summa theologiae*, vol. 31, *Faith (2a2ae. 1–7)*, trans. T.C. O'Brien (Cambridge: Cambridge University Press, 2006), 87.

142 The story of the discovery of the Thracian coffin in the eighth century that, allegedly, contained the remains of an unknown pagan with an inscription predicting both the birth of Christ and the joint rule of the young Byzantine emperor, Constantine VI, alongside his mother, Irene, as regent. This is recounted by Theophanes in *Chronographia* AM 6273 [AD 780/1]. See *The Chronicle of Theophanes Confessor: Byzantine and New Eastern History, AD 284–813*, trans. Cyril Mango and Roger Scott, with Geoffrey Greatrex (Oxford: Clarendon, 1997), 627. Aquinas made use of this supposed prophecy in his discussion of how pagans received revelations concerning the coming of Christ (see the section quoted in the marginal note referenced in the previous footnote). This is part of Thomas's response to the third objection in the seventh article in which he argues that "many of the gentiles received revelations of Christ, as is clear from their predictions."

143 In the text: *Christus nascetur ex virgine, ego credo in illum. O sol sub Irenae & Constantini temporibus iterum me videbis.*—Owen. A comparison with the Latin text of Theophanes reveals that Owen cites this example from Aquinas. For the text and translation, see Aquinas, *Summa theologiae*, 31:92–93; cf. *Chronographia*, ed. B. G. Niebuhr, 2 vols., Corpus Scriptorum Historiae Byzantinae (Bonn: Weber, 1839–1841), 2:249.

144 In the margin: Justin. Apol.—Owen. In his *First Apology* 46.3, Justin Martyr speaks of how those who lived "with reason" (μετὰ λόγου) before the coming of Christ—e.g., the Philosophers Heraclitus and Socrates—are to be regarded as Christian even though they had been considered atheists. This is the view that Owen believes to be "wide from the word." For the text and translation, see Denis Minns and Paul Purvis, *Justin, Philosopher and Martyr: Apologies*, Oxford Early Christian Texts (Oxford: Oxford University Press, 2009), 200–01.

deserve heaven by obedience, now under the covenant of works, than being under that covenant, to do anything that might cause a new way of salvation, such as the gospel is, to be revealed.

With some observations I descend to application.

Three Further Points Relating to the Second Observation

Obs[ervation] 1. First, there is the same reason of continuing the gospel unto a people, as of sending it; especially if oppositions rise high, apt and able in themselves for its removal:[145] never nation as yet enjoyed the word, that deserved the continuance of the word. God has always something against a people, to make the continuing of his grace, to be of grace, the not removing of his love, to be merely of love, and the preaching of the gospel, to be a mercy of the gospel, free and undeserved. Though there be work, and labor, and patience for Christ's sake at Ephesus, yet there is somewhat against Ephesus (Rev. 2:4–5), for which he might justly remove his candlestick; and if he does it not, it is of the same mercy that first set it there. As God lays out goodness and grace in the entrance, so patience, long-suffering and forbearance in the continuance; he bears with our manners, while we grieve his Spirit. Look upon the face of this kingdom, and view the body of the people, think of the profaneness, villainy, trampling upon the blood of Jesus,[146] ignorance, contempt of God and his ways, despising his ordinances, reviling his servants, branding and defaming the power of godliness,[147] persecuting and tearing one another, and yet hear the joyful sound of the word in every corner; and you will quickly conclude, that you see a great fight of God's love against our sins, and not of our goodness for his love.

[Observation 2]. Secondly, there is the same reason of the reformation of the doctrine of the gospel corrupted with error, and of the worship of God collapsed with superstition, as of the first implantation of the gospel: God in his just judgment of late ages, had sent upon the Western world the efficacy of error, that they should believe lies, because they received not the love of the truth; as he foretold (2 Thess. 2).[148] Now whence is it, that we see some of

---

145 In the margin: Hos. 11:8–9.—Owen.
146 Heb. 10:29.
147 During the 1630s opposition to the policies of the Laudian regime was often dealt with harshly. For example, in 1637 William Prynne, John Bastwick, and Henry Burton were punished and imprisoned for their criticism of the Laudian church. Owen's words may have reminded some of how Prynne was branded with the initials "S. L." for "Seditious Libeler." See William Lamont, "Prynne, William (1600–1669)," in *Oxford Dictionary of National Biography* (Oxford: Oxford University Press, 2004), accessed October 18, 2023, https://doi.org/10.1093/ref:odnb/22854.
148 Esp. 2 Thess. 2:11.

the nations thereof as yet suffered to walk in their own ways,[149] others called to repentance, some wildernesses turned into green pastures for the flock of God, and some places made barren wildernesses for the wickedness of them that dwell therein?[150] How comes it that this island glories in a reformation, and Spain sits still in darkness? Is it because we were better than they? Or less engaged in anti-Christian delusions? Doubtless no: no nation in the world drank deeper of that cup of abomination; it was a proverbial speech among all, "England was our good ass" (a beast of burden) for (Antichrist whom they called) the pope.[151] Nothing but the good pleasure of God and Christ, freely coming to refine us (Mal. 3:1–4), caused this distinction.

Obser[vation] 3. Though men can do nothing toward the procuring of the gospel, yet men may do much for the expulsion of the gospel: if the husband-men[152] prove idle or self-seekers, the vineyard will be let to others;[153] and if the people love darkness more than light,[154] the candlestick will be removed;[155] let England beware. Now this men may do, either upon the first entrance of the gospel, or after some continuance of it: the gospel spreading itself over the earth, finds entertainment, like that of men's seeking plantations among barbarous nations, sometimes kept out with hideous outcries, at the shore, sometimes suffered to enter with admiration, and a little after violently assaulted.[156]

In the first way, how do we find the Jews, putting far from them the word of life, and rejecting the counsel of God at its first entrance, calling for night at the rising of the sun? Hence, Paul concludes his sermon to them, with,

---

149 Acts 14:16.

150 Ps. 107:34.

151 The chronicler Adam Murimuth (ca. 1274/5–1347) recorded the proverb that "the English are good asses, ready to carry all the intolerable burdens" placed on them by the Papacy. See *Adae Murimuth continuatio chronicarum*, ed. E. M. Thompson, Rolls Series 93 (London, 1889), 175. John Foxe's *Acts and Monuments* noted that England "played still the ass ... under the pope's thraldom." See *The Acts and Monuments of John Foxe: A New and Complete Edition* [. . .], ed. Stephen Reed Cattley, 8 vols. (London: Seeley and Burnside, 1837–1841), 2:438.

152 I.e., those that plow and cultivate the land.

153 Matt. 21:41.

154 John 3:19.

155 Rev. 2:5.

156 The English Parliament would have been mindful of the fate of Protestant planters in Ulster after the wake of the 1641 Irish Rebellion, particularly in light of the publication, days beforehand on April 27, of Sir John Temple's *The Irish Rebellion: or, An History of the Attempts of the Irish Papists to Extirpate the Protestants in the Kingdom of Ireland* [. . .] (London, 1646). This book, with its description of "the barbarous cruelties and bloody massacres" of 1641, had a significant impact on English policy in Ireland. See John Adamson, "Strafford's Ghost: The British Context of Viscount Lisle's Lieutenancy of Ireland," in *Ireland from Independence to Occupation, 1641–1660*, ed. Jane H. Ohlmeyer (Cambridge: Cambridge University Press, 1995), 131–41.

"Hear, ye despisers, wonder and perish" (Acts 13:41), and, verse 46, "it was necessary the word should be preached to them," but seeing they judged themselves "unworthy," they were forsaken: and, verse 51, they shake off the dust of their feet against them, a common symbol in those days, of the highest indignation and deepest curse: the like stubbornness we find in them, whereupon the apostle wholly turned himself to the Gentiles (Acts 28:28). How many nations of Europe, at the beginning of the Reformation, rejected the gospel of God, and procured Christ, with the Gadarenes,[157] to depart as soon as he was entered, will be found at the last day written with the blood of the martyrs of Jesus, that suffered among them?

Secondly, after some continuance; so the church of Laodicea, having for a while enjoyed the word, fell into such a tepid condition, so little moved with that fire that Christ came to send upon the earth (Rev. 3:15–16),[158] that the Lord was even sick and weary with hearing them. The Church of Rome, famous at the first, yet quickly, by the advantage of outward supportments and glorious fancies, became head of that fatal rebellion against Jesus Christ, which spread itself over most of the churches in the world;[159] God hereupon sending upon them the "efficacy of error to believe a lie, that they all might be damned that believed not the truth, but had pleasure in unrighteousness" (2 Thess. 2)[160] suffering them to retain the empty names of Church and Gospel, which because they usurp, only for their advantage here, to appear glorious, the Lord will use for the advancing of his justice hereafter, to show them inexcusable. O Lord, how was England of late by your mercy delivered from this snare? A captain being chosen for the return of this people into Egypt: oh how has your grace fought against our backsliding? And let none seek to extenuate this mercy, by catalogs of errors still among us,[161] there is more danger of apostasy against Christ, and rebellion against the truth, in one Babylonish error, owned by men, pretending to power

---

157 Luke 8:37.
158 Luke 12:49.
159 In the margin: Νῦν δέ ἐστιν ἀποστασία, ἀπέστησαν γὰρ οἱ ἄνθρωποι τῆς ὀρθῆς πίστεως. Cyrillus Hieros, Κατήχησις.—Owen. Owen is referencing Cyril of Jerusalem's *Catechesis* 15.9: "The apostasy has come, for men have forsaken the true faith." Cyril (315–86) saw the reign of the pagan Roman emperor Flavius Claudius Julianus (331–363), better known as Julian "the Apostate," and heresies such as Arianism, as part of the coming apostasy spoken of by the apostle Paul (2 Thess. 2). For the English translation, see *The Works of Saint Cyril of Jerusalem*, vol. 2, trans. Leo P. McCauley and A. A. Stephenson, Fathers of the Church 64 (Washington, DC: Catholic University of America Press, 1970), 59.
160 2 Thess. 2:10–11.
161 Here Owen is referring to the work of the Presbyterian heresiographers. For example, the first part of Thomas Edwards's infamous *Gangraena: or a Catalogue and Discovery of Many of the Errours, Heresies, Blasphemies and Pernicious Practices of the Sectaries of This Time, Vented and*

and jurisdiction over others, than in five hundred scattered among inconsiderable disunited individuals: I would to God, we could all speak, and think the same things, that we were all of one mind, even in the most minute differences that are now among us; but yet the truth is, the kingdom of Jesus Christ never shakes among a people,[162] until men pretending to act, with a combined mixed power of heaven and earth, unto which all sheaves must bow or be thrashed, do by virtue of this trust, set up and impose things or opinions deviating from the rule, as it was in the Papacy, errors owned by mixed associations.[163]

Civil and ecclesiastical [mixtures], are for the most part incurable, be they never so absurd and foolish; of which the Lutheran ubiquities and consubstantiation are a tremendous example:[164] these things being presupposed.

Four Uses Arising from The Second Observation
Humbling an Unworthy and Undeserving Nation
Use 1. Let no flesh glory in themselves,[165] but let every mouth be stopped;[166] for we have all sinned and come short of the glory of God.[167] Who has made the possessors of the gospel to differ from others? Or what have they that they have not received? (1 Cor. 4:7). Why are these things hidden from the great and wise of the world, and revealed to babes and children, but because, O Father, so it pleased you? (Matt. 11:26). "He hath mercy on whom he will have mercy, and whom he will he hardeneth" (Rom. 9).[168] Ah Lord, if the glory and pomp of the world might prevail with you to send your gospel, it would supply the room of the cursed Alkoran,[169] and spread itself in the palaces of that strong lion of the east, who sets his throne upon the necks of kings;[170]

Acted in England in These Last Four Years (London, 1646). The second part of *Gangraena* would be published in the month after Owen preached this sermon.
162 This is a trope from Heb. 12:27, to which Owen gave particular attention in his parliamentary fast sermon from April 1649. See Martyn C. Cowan, *John Owen and the Civil War Apocalypse: Preaching, Prophecy, and Politics* (London: Routledge, 2017), 55–56.
163 In the margin: Revel. 13:17.—Owen.
164 Owen is referring to what he takes as the irrationality of the Lutheran understanding of the communication of properties (*communicatio idiomatum*) that leads to the doctrine of a real presence of Christ's body and blood in the elements of the Lord's Supper on the basis of a claim to the ubiquity of Christ's human nature.
165 1 Cor. 1:29.
166 Rom. 3:19.
167 Rom. 3:23.
168 Rom. 9:18.
169 I.e., Qur'an.
170 This is probably a reference to the Sultan of the Ottoman Empire, at this time Ibrahim I (r. 1640–1648).

but alas, Jesus Christ is not there. If wisdom, learning, pretended gravity, counterfeit holiness, real policy were of any value in your eyes to procure the word of life, it would be as free and glorious at Rome as ever; but alas, Antichrist has his throne there, Jesus Christ is not there. If will worship and humilities, neglect of the body, macerations,[171] superstitions, beads,[172] and vainly repeated prayers, had any efficacy before the Lord, the gospel, perhaps, might be in the cells of some recluses and monks; but alas, Jesus Christ is not there. If moral virtues, to an amazement, exact civil honesty and justice, that soul of human society, could have prevailed aught,[173] the heathen worthies in the days of old, had had the promises; but alas, Jesus Christ was far away. Now if all these be passed by, to whom is the "report" of the Lord made known? To "whom is his arm revealed?"[174] Why! to a handful of poor sinners among the nations formerly counted fierce and barbarous.[175] And what shall we say to these things? Ὦ βάθος, "O the depth," etc.[176]

Warning the Nation about Despising Newfound Gospel Light and Liberty

Use 2. Let England consider with fear and trembling the dispensation that it is now under, I say, with fear and trembling: for this day is the Lord's Day, wherein he will purge us or burn us,[177] according as we shall be found silver or dross: it is our day, wherein we must mend or end: let us look to the rock from whence we were hewed, and the hole of the pit from whence we were digged.[178] Was not our father an Amorite, and our mother a Hittite?[179] Are we not the posterity of idolatrous progenitors?[180] Of those who worshiped

---

171 I.e., the causing of the body to waste away by fasting.
172 I.e., rosary beads.
173 I.e., anything at all.
174 Isa. 53:1.
175 In the margin: *Britannorum inaccessa Romanis loca Christo vero subdita*. Tertul.—Owen. This is a citation from Tertullian's *Adversus Iudaeos* (Against the Jews) 7.4: "The region of the Britons that is inaccessible to the Romans but subject to Christ." For the Latin text, see Tertullian, *Adversus Judaeos*, in *Opera omnia*, ed. J.-P. Migne, Patrologia Latina 2 (Paris: Migne-Garnier, 1844), 610. For the English translation, see Geoffrey D. Dunn, *Tertullian* (London: Routledge, 2004), 55. For a treatment of the early modern view of England as an elect nation, see Patrick Collinson, "John Foxe and National Consciousness," in *John Foxe and His World*, ed. Christopher Highley and John N. King (Aldershot, UK: Ashgate, 2002), 10–36.
176 Owen again cites Rom. 11:33.
177 See Isa. 4:4.
178 Isa. 51:1.
179 Ezek. 16:3.
180 In the margin: *Britanniam in Christianam consentire religionem*, Origin Hom. 4. In Ezek.—Owen. Owen cites Origin of Alexandria's *Homily 4 on Ezekiel*: "When [before the coming of Christ] did the land of Brittany agree with the religion of the one God?" For Latin text, see Origen,

them who by nature were no gods? How often also has this land forfeited the gospel? God having taken it twice away, who is not forward to seize upon the forfeiture. In the very morning of the gospel, the Sun of Righteousness shone upon this land, and they say the first potentate on the earth, that owned it, was in Britain:[181] but as it was here soon professed, so it was here soon abused. That part of this isle which is called England, being the first place, I read of, which was totally bereaved of the gospel; the sword of the then pagan Saxons fattening the land with the blood of the Christian inhabitants; and in the close wholly subverting the worship of God. Long it was not ere this cloud was blown over, and those men who had been instruments to root out others, submitted their own necks to the yoke of the Lord, and under exceeding variety in civil affairs, enjoyed the word of grace: until by insensible degrees, like summer unto winter, or light unto darkness, it gives place to anti-Christian superstition, and left the land in little less than a paganish darkness, drinking deep of the cup of abominations mingled for it by the Roman harlot.[182] And is there mercy yet in God to recover a twice over lost backsliding people? Might not the Lord have said unto us, "What shall I do unto you, O island? "How shall I make you as Admah? How shall I set you as Zeboim?"[183] But his heart is turned within him, his repentings are kindled together: the dry

---

Translatio homiliarum Origenis in Ezechielem, in *Opera omnia*, ed. J.-P. Migne, Patrologia Latina 25 (Paris: Migne-Garnier, 1845), 723. For the English translation, see *Origen: Homilies 1–14 on Ezekiel*, trans. Thomas P. Scheck, Ancient Christian Writers 62 (Mahwah, NJ: Paulist, 2010), 68.

181 In the margin: Niceph. *Lib. 2 cap.* 40. *Epist.* Eleuth. *Ad Lucium*, an. 169. Apud Bar. Anno 469. The Saxons entered.—Owen. Here Owen references the Byzantine historian Nicephorus Callistus's *Historia ecclesiastica* 2.40. For the Greek text, see Nicephorus, *Ecclesiasticae historiae*, 863–64. He claimed that Simon the Zealot brought the gospel to the western ocean and Britain. Owen then appeals to the account of King Lucius writing to Eleutherius, bishop of Rome, asking him to send preachers to Britain. Owen references the letter from the works of the sixteenth-century ecclesiastical historian Cardinal Cesare Baronio's *Annales ecclesiastici* (Rome, 1588–1607). Godly English Protestants thought that this demonstrated that the British church existed long before the papal missionary Augustine (d. 604) set foot in England at the end of the sixth century and thereby provided the basis for an independent British church. For a discussion of the supposed King Lucius of the late second century, see Felicity Heal, "What Can King Lucius Do for You? The Reformation and the Early British Church," *English Historical Review* 120 (2005): 593–614. Owen's final marginal note concerns the arrival of Saxon invaders in the year 469. Gildas (a sixth-century British monk) and Bede explained the Saxon invasion of the fifth century as a divine judgment. See Bede, *History of the English Church and People*, trans. Leo Sherley-Prince, rev. R. E. Latham (Harmondsworth, UK: Penguin 1968), 56–57; Gildas, *The Ruin of Britain and Other Works*, ed. and trans. Michael Winterbottom (London: Phillimore, 1978), 24–26.

182 In Owen's view of history, the conversion of the Saxon invaders was not actually a true conversion at all, and the English church degenerated through the sixth century. See Cowan, *John Owen and the Civil War Apocalypse*, 10–11.

183 Hos. 11:8.

bones shall live,[184] and the fleece shall be wet, though all the earth be dry.[185] God will again water his garden,[186] once more purge his vineyard, once more of his own accord he will take England upon liking, though he had twice deservedly turned it out of his service; so that coming as a refiner's fire, and as fuller's soap to purify the sons of Levi, to purge them as gold and silver, to offer to the Lord an offering in righteousness,[187] to reform his churches, England, as soon as any, has the benefit and comfort thereof. Nay, the reformation of England shall be more glorious than of any nation in the world, being carried on, neither by might nor power, but only by the Spirit of the Lord of hosts.[188] But is this the utmost period of England's sinning, and God's showing mercy, in continuing and restoring of the gospel? No truly: we again in our days have made forfeiture of the purity of his worship, by an almost universal treacherous apostasy: from which the free grace, and good pleasure of God has made a great progress again toward a recovery.

There are two sorts of men that I find exceedingly ready to extenuate and lessen the superstition and Popish tyranny of the former days, into which we were falling.

First, such as were industriously instrumental in it,[189] whose suffrages had been loud for the choice of a captain to return into Egypt:[190] men tainted with the errors, and loaded with the preferments of the times:[191] with all those who blindly adhere to that faction of men, who as yet covertly drive on that design. To such as these, all was nothing, and to them it is no mercy to be delivered. And the truth is, it is a favor to the lamb and not the wolf, to have him taken out of his mouth: but these men have interest by those things which have no ears, against which there is no contending.

Secondly, such as are disturbed in their optics, or have gotten false glasses, representing all things unto them in dubious colors: which way soever they look, they can see nothing but errors, errors of all sizes, sorts, sects, and sexes.[192]

---

184 Ezek. 37:5.
185 Judg. 6:36–40.
186 Isa. 58:11.
187 Mal. 3:3.
188 Zech. 4:6.
189 This is a reference to the Laudians of the English church.
190 Num. 14.4.
191 The godly believed that under the ecclesiastical patronage of Archbishop William Laud, preferment was more likely to be given to clergy with Arminian beliefs. See Kenneth Fincham, "William Laud and the Exercise of Caroline Ecclesiastical Patronage," *Journal of Ecclesiastical History* 51, no. 1 (2000): 69–93.
192 A reference to the Presbyterian heresiographers such as Thomas Edwards.

Errors and heresies from the beginning to the end, which have deceived some men, not of the worst, and made them think, that all before was nothing, in comparison of the present confusion.[193] A great sign they felt it not, or were not troubled at it; as if men should come into a field, and seeing some red weeds and cockle[194] among the corn, should instantly affirm there is no corn there, but all weeds, and that it were much better the hedges were down, and the whole field laid open to the boar of the forest;[195] but the harvest will one day show the truth of these things. But that these apprehensions may not too much prevail, to the vilifying and extenuating of God's mercy, in restoring to us the purity and liberty of the gospel: give me leave in a few words, to set out the danger of that apostasy, from which the good pleasure of God has given us a deliverance. I shall instance only in a few things: observe then that.

First, the darling errors of late years were all of them stones of the old Babel, closing and coupling with that tremendous fabric which the man of sin had erected to dethrone Jesus Christ: came out of the belly of that Trojan horse, that fatal engine,[196] which was framed to betray the city of God. They were Popish errors, such as whereof that apostasy did consist, which only is to be looked upon, as the great adverse state of the kingdom of the Lord Christ. For a man to be disorderly in a civil state, yea oftentimes through turbulency to break the peace, is nothing to an underhand combination with some formidable enemy, for the utter subversion of it. Heedless and headless errors may breed disturbance enough, in scattered individuals, unto the people of God: but such as tend to a peace and association, *cum ecclesia*

---

193 In the margin: *Nunc igitur, si nominis odium est, quis nominum reatus, quae accusatio vocabulorum, nisi si aut barbarum sonat aliqua vox nominis aut infaustum aut maledicum aut impudicum.* Tertul. Apol. Ad Gen. cap. 3.—Owen. This is quotation from Tertullian's *Apologeticus adversus gentes* 3.5: "Tell me, then, if it is hatred of a name, how can you indict names? What charge can lie against words, unless the pronunciation of some name has a barbarous sound about it—something unlucky or scurrilous or lewd?" For the Latin text and the English translation, see Tertullian, *Apology*, in Tertullian, Minucius Felix, *Apology. De Spectaculis. Minucius Felix: Octavius*, trans. T. R. Glover and Gerald H. Rendall, Loeb Classical Library 250 (Cambridge, MA: Harvard University Press, 1931), 20–21. In this chapter titled "Concerning the Odious Title of Christian," Tertullian argues that at times Christians were persecuted for the name only and not because of any substantial reason.

194 The term *cockle* appears in Job 31:40, and in the Authorized Version (KJV) a marginal note provides the alternative rendering "noisome weeds." It refers to those weeds that particularly infest a grain field.

195 See Isa. 5:5.

196 I.e., ingenious scheme. In the first part of *Gangraena*, Thomas Edwards described toleration as "the grand designe of the Devil, his Masterpeece and chiefe Engine he works by at this time to uphold his tottering Kingdome." Edwards, *Gangraena*, 153.

malignantium,[197] tending to a total subversion of the sacred state, are far more dangerous. Now such were the innovations of the late hierarchists;[198] in worship, their paintings, crossings, crucifixes, bowings, cringings,[199] altars, tapers,[200] wafers, organs, anthems,[201] litany,[202] rails,[203] images, copes,[204] vestments; what were they but Roman varnish, an Italian dress for our devotion, to draw on conformity with that enemy of the Lord Jesus;[205] in doctrine, the divinity of episcopacy,[206] auricular confession,[207] free will, predestination on faith, yea, works foreseen,[208] *limbus patrum*,[209] justification by works, falling from grace, authority of a church, which none knew what it was,[210] canonical obedience,[211] holiness of churches,[212] and the like innumerable, what were they

197 Owen is speaking of English Protestants who sought peace with what he believed to be "the church of the wicked"—that is, the Roman Catholic Church.
198 I.e., a derogatory term for those individuals associated with the Laudian agenda.
199 I.e., a derogatory term for bowing in a manner judged to be servile or obsequious.
200 I.e., long waxed candles used for devotional or penitential purposes.
201 I.e., a liturgical piece to be chanted or sung.
202 I.e., an appointed form of public prayer.
203 I.e., altar rails.
204 I.e., vestments that resembled cloaks, often worn in in processions.
205 For these ceremonialist trends in the English Church, see Bryan Spinks, *Sacraments, Ceremonies and the Stuart Divines: Sacramental Theology and Liturgy in England and Scotland, 1603–1662* (Aldershot, UK: Ashgate, 2002), 47; and Kenneth Fincham and Nicholas Tyacke, *Altars Restored: The Changing Face of English Religious Worship, 1547–c. 1700* (Oxford: Oxford University Press, 2007). The Laudian regime sought to beautify parish churches, chapels, and cathedrals so that orderly worship would be conducted in the "beauty of holiness." Laudian policy included the following: reviving the use of organs; singing elaborate choral anthems; placing communion tables as altars, set behind rails, and adorned with candles; instructing a number of cathedrals to purchase copes for the celebrants officiating at holy communion; and bowing at the name of Jesus (opponents described the bowing of ceremonialist clergy as "cringing").
206 For the conflict over between those who advocated divine right episcopacy and those who called for the abolition of episcopacy "root and branch," see Tom Webster, *Godly Clergy in Early Stuart England: The Caroline Puritan Movement, c.1620–1643* (Cambridge: Cambridge University Press, 1997), 319–26.
207 For the Laudian practice of encouraging private confession to a priest, see Anthony Milton, *Catholic and Reformed: The Roman and Protestant Churches in English Protestant Thought, 1600–1640* (Cambridge: Cambridge University Press, 1995), 473.
208 Descriptions of the anti-Calvinism of the Laudian Arminians.
209 Lat. "the borderland of the patriarchs," where the saints of the Old Testament were said to wait for their redemption to be accomplished by Christ.
210 Perhaps a reference to the so-called et cetera oath from the Laudian Canons of 1640, which required a commitment never to consent "to alter the government of this church by archbishops, bishops, dean and archdeacons *et cetera*, as it stands now established and as by right it ought to stand." A minister was to swear not to alter unspecified institutions. Kevin Sharpe, *The Personal Rule of Charles I* (New Haven, CT: Yale University Press, 1995), 877–78.
211 I.e., an oath of obedience to the diocesan bishop.
212 I.e., the beautifying of the interior of church buildings.

but helps to Sancta Clara,²¹³ to make all our articles of religion speak good Roman Catholic?²¹⁴ How did their old father of Rome refresh his spirit,²¹⁵ to see such chariots as those provided, to bring England again unto him? This closing with popery, was the sting in the errors of those days, which cause pining, if not death, in the episcopal pot.²¹⁶

Secondly, they were such as raked up the ashes of the ancient worthies, whose spirits God stirred up to reform his church, and rendered them contemptible before all, especially those of England, the most whereof died in giving their witness against the blind figment of the real presence, and that abominable blasphemy of the cursed mass;²¹⁷ in especial, how did England, heretofore termed ass, turn ape to the pope, having set up a stage, and furnished it with all things necessary for an unbloody sacrifice, ready to set up

---

213 The Franciscan "Sancta Clara"—i.e., Christopher Davenport (ca. 1595–1680—had sought to demonstrate the compatibility of the Church of England's Thirty-Nine Articles with the decrees of the Council of Trent in *Deus, natura, gratia* [...] (Lyon, 1634). See Anne Ashley Davenport, *Suspicious Moderate: The Life and Writings of Francis à Sancta Clara (1598–1680)* (Notre Dame, IN: University of Notre Dame Press, 2017).

214 In the margin: See Canterburian self-conviction, See Ld dee. Coll. Etc.—Owen. The first reference is to Robert Baillie, *Ladensium autokatakrisis, the Canterburians Self-Conviction, or, An Evident Demonstration of the Avowed Arminianisme, Poperie, and Tyrannie of That Faction* (London, 1640). In Baillie's analysis of the "Canterburians" (followers of Archbishop Laud), he believed that crypto-popery was discernible in the some of the following beliefs and practices mentioned by Owen: cringing (p. 52), rails (pp. 17, 105), tapers (pp. 60, 85), canonical obedience (p. 87), auricular confession (pp. 63, 75), and *limbus partum* (pp. 79–80). The second part of the marginal note is probably a reference to the Laudian bishop of Peterborough, Francis Dee (d. 1638), and the third part is possibly a reference to Samuel Collins (1576–1651), provost of King's College and regius professor of divinity at the University of Cambridge, whom Baillie includes among the Canterburians (p. 22). There is very similar material in William Prynne's *Canterburies Doome, or, The First Part of a Compleat History of the Commitment, Charge, Tryall, Condemnation, Execution of William Laud* (London, 1646). In Prynne's official history of the trial of Laud, he outlined how the following were well-known advocates of the "innovations" Owen had referred to: Peter Heylyn for a "domineering" divine right episcopacy (p. 227); John Pocklington for auricular confession (p. 189); Robert Shelford for free will and justification by works (p. 209); Bishop Richard Montague for the existence of purgatory and *limbus patrum* (p. 207) as well as "total and final apostasy from grace" (p. 219); Christopher Dow for canonical obedience (p. 197); and Richard Tedder for the view that the consecration of churches makes them holy (p. 218).

215 A reference to the pope.

216 Isa. 38:12; 2 Kings 4:40.

217 In the margin: Coal from the Altar.—Owen. This is a reference to *A Coale from the Altar* [...] (London, 1636), a publication by the royal chaplain Peter Heylyn (1599–1662) that helped ignite the altar controversy. This was one of the most controversial of the Laudian reforms and involved placing the Communion table as an altar at the east end behind rails. See Anthony Milton, *Laudian and Royalist Polemic in Seventeenth-Century England: The Career and Writings of Peter Heylyn* (Manchester: Manchester University Press, 2007), 56.

the abomination of desolation,[218] and close with the god Maozim,[219] who has all their peculiar devotion at Rome?[220]

Thirdly, they were in the management of men which had divers dangerous and pernicious qualifications; as—

First, a false repute of learning, I say, a false repute for the greater part, especially of the greatest: and yet taking advantage of vulgar esteem, they bare out as though they had engrossed a monopoly of it: though I presume the world was never deceived by more empty pretenders; especially in respect of any solid knowledge in divinity or antiquity:[221] but yet their great preferments, had got them a great repute of great deservings, enough to blind the eyes of poor mortals adoring them at a distance, and to persuade them, that all was not only law, but gospel too, which they broached: and this rendered the infection dangerous.

Secondly, a great hatred of godliness in the power thereof, or anything beyond a form, in whomsoever it was found;[222] yea, how many odious appellations[223] were invented for bare profession, to render it contemptible?[224]

Especially in the exercise of their jurisdiction, thundering their censures against all appearance of zeal, and closing with all profane impieties; for were a man a drunkard, a swearer, a Sabbath breaker,[225] an unclean person, so he

---

218 Matt. 24:15; cf. Dan. 11:31.
219 This reference to the Vulgate rendering of *eloah ma'umzzin* ("god of fortresses") as Maozim (Dan. 11:31, 38). Some Protestants had called the mass Maozim in an allusion to this idol. See Cowan, *John Owen and the Civil War Apocalypse*, 23.
220 In the margin: *Altare Christianum. Antidotum Lincoln. Case of Greg.*—Owen. The first is a reference to John Pocklington's work *Altare Christianum, or, The Dead Vicars Plea* [. . .] (London, 1637). The second is to Peter Heylyn's *Antidotum Lincolniense* [. . .] (London, 1637). The final reference was to a legal case from 1633 over the placement of the Communion table that had been used as precedent for the Laudian altar policy. See Cowan, *John Owen and the Civil War Apocalypse*, 22.
221 In an age when theological controversies were often thought to be intricately tied to questions of historical fact, here Owen seeks to discredit the historical basis for the antiquity of the position of his opponents. See Milton, *Laudian and Royalist Polemic*, 119–20.
222 2 Tim. 3:5.
223 I.e., names, titles or designations such as *puritan*, *precisionist*, or *sectary*.
224 In the margin: *Sapientior sis Socrate; doctior Augustino, &c. Calvinianus si modo dicare clam vel pro palam, mox Tartaris, Moscis, Afris, Turcisque saevientibus & jacebis exsecratior, &c.*—Owen. "Though you are wiser than Socrates, more learned than Augustine, etc., if you should be called a Calvinist, privately or publicly, you will soon be more accursed than a raging Tartar, Russian, African, or Turk (and so forth)." All these named groups were proverbial in early modern England for their cruelty and barbarity.
225 The reissuing of the King's *Book of Sports* in 1633, which encouraged dancing and games after church, made Sabbatarianism a highly contentious issue. Laud insisted that it be read from pulpits and exercised his jurisdiction by censuring ministers who refused to do so. See Ken-

were no Puritan, and had money, "The door of gloomy Dis stands open,"[226] the episcopal heaven was open for them all. Now, this was a dangerous and destructive qualification, which I believe, is not professedly found in any party among us.

Thirdly, which was worst of all, they had centered in their bosoms an unfathomable depth of power civil and ecclesiastical, to stamp their apostatical errors with authority, giving them not only the countenance of greatness, but the strength of power, violently urging obedience; and to me, the sword of error, never cuts dangerously, but when it is managed with such a hand. This I am sure, that errors in such are not recoverable without the utmost danger of the civil state.[227]

Let now, I beseech you, these and the like things be considered, especially the strong combination that was throughout the papal world for the seducing of this poor nation: that I say nothing how this vial was poured out upon the very throne,[228] and then, let us all be ashamed and confounded in ourselves, that we should so undervalue and slight the free mercy of God, in breaking such a snare, and setting the gospel at liberty in England. My intent was, having before asserted this restoration of Jerusalem,[229] to the good pleasure of God, to have stirred you up to thankfulness unto him, and self-humiliation

---

neth L. Parker, *The English Sabbath: A Study of Doctrine and Discipline from the Reformation to the Civil War* (Cambridge: Cambridge University Press, 1988), 180–216.

226 In the text: *patet atri janua ditis*. This is a quotation from epic poet Virgil's *Aeneid*, 6.126. It records Sibyl's words to Aeneas before his descent to the underworld of which Dis was the god. For the text and translation, see Virgil, *Aeneid: Books 1–6*, trans. H. Rushton Fairclough, Loeb Classical Library 63 (Cambridge, MA: Harvard University Press, 1999), 540–41.

227 In the margin: *Romes Masterpiece. Royall favourite.*—Owen. Owen directs the reader to two texts by William Prynne, *Romes Master-Peece. Or, I Grand Conspiracy of the Pope and His Jesuited Instruments to Extirpate the Protestant Religion, Re-Establish Popery, Subvert Lawes, Liberties, Peace, Parliaments, by Kindling a Civill War in Scotland, and All His Majesties Realmes, and to Poyson the King Himselfe in Case Hee Comply Not with Them in These Their Execrable Designes* (London, 1643); and *The Popish Royall Favourite: or, A Full Discovery of His Majesties Extraordinary Favours to, and Protections of Notorious Papists, Priestes, Jesuites, Against All Prosecutions and Penalties of the Laws Enacted against Them Notwithstanding His Many Royall Proclamations, Declarations, and Protestations to the Contrary: As Likewise of a Most Desperate Long Prosecuted Designe to Set It Up? Popery, and Extirpate the Protestant Religion by Degrees* [. . .] (London, 1643). For a discussion of these texts, see Jason Peacey, *Politicians and Pamphleteers: Propaganda During the English Civil Wars and Interregnum* (Aldershot, UK: Ashgate, 2004), 262.

228 For a discussion of how Congregationalists such as John Cotton and Thomas Goodwin linked the pouring out of the fifth vial of divine wrath on "the throne of the beast" (Rev. 16:10) to the destruction of episcopacy in its various forms, see Cowan, *John Owen and the Civil War Apocalypse*, 14.

229 The restoration of the true worship of God based on Owen's interpretation of Dan. 9:2, 25.

in consideration of our great undeserving of such mercy; but alas; as far as I can see, it will scarce pass for a mercy: and unless every man's persuasion may be a Joseph's sheaf,[230] the goodness of God shall scarce be acknowledged; but yet let all the world know, and let the house of England know this day, that we lie unthankfully under as full a dispensation of mercy and grace, as ever nation in the world enjoyed, and that without a lively acknowledgment thereof, with our own unworthiness of it, we shall one day know what it is (being taught with briers and thorns)[231] to undervalue the glorious gospel of the Lord Jesus. Good Lord! What would helpless Macedonians give for one enjoyment? O that Wales, O that Ireland, O that France, where shall I stop? I would offend none, but give me leave to say, O that every, I had almost said, O that any part of the world, had such helps and means of grace, as these parts of England have, which will scarce acknowledge any mercy in it: the Lord break the pride of our spirits, before it break the staff of our bread,[232] and the help of our salvation. O that the bread of heaven, and the blood of Christ might be accounted good nourishment, though everyone has not the sauce he desires. I am persuaded that if every Absalom in the land, that would be a judge for the ending of our differences, were enthroned (he spoke the people's good, though he intended his own power)[233] the case would not be much better than it is. Well, the Lord make England, make this honorable audience, make us all to know these three things.

First, that we have received such a blessing, in setting at liberty the truths of the gospel, as is the crown of all other mercies, yea, without which they were not valuable, yea, were to be despised: for success without the gospel, is nothing but a prosperous conspiracy against Jesus Christ.

Secondly, that this mercy is of mercy, this love of free love, and the grace that appears, of the eternal hidden, free grace of God. He has showed his love unto us because he loved us, and for no other reason in the world, this people being guilty of blood and murder, of soul and body, adultery, and idolatry, and oppression, with a long catalog of sins and iniquities.

Thirdly, that the height of rebellion against God, is the despising of spiritual gospel mercies; should Mordecai have trodden the robes under his feet, that were brought him from the king, would it not have been severely revenged?[234] Does the King of heaven lay open the treasures of his wisdom, knowledge

[230] Gen. 37:7.
[231] Judg. 8:16.
[232] Ezek. 4:16.
[233] 2 Sam. 15:3–6.
[234] Est. 6:10.

and goodness for us, and we despise them? What shall I say, I had almost said, hell punishes no greater sin: the Lord lay it not to our charge: O that we might be solemnly humbled for it this day, before it be too late.

Revealing the Wonder of Divine Sovereignty in Salvation

Use 3. To discover unto us the freedom of that effectual grace, which is dispensed toward the elect, under and with the preaching of the word: for if the sending of the outward means be of free undeserved love, surely the working of the Spirit under that dispensation, for the saving of souls, is no less free:[235] for, "who hath made us differ from others, and what have we that we have not received?"[236] O that God should say unto us in our blood, "live";[237] that he should breathe upon us when we were as dry bones,[238] dead in trespasses and sins;[239] let us remember, I beseech you, the frame of our hearts, and the temper of our spirits, in the days wherein we knew not God and his goodness, but went on in a swift course of rebellion;[240] can none of you look back upon any particular days or nights, and say, "Ah Lord, that you should be so patient and so full of forbearance, as not to send me to hell at such an instant; but O Lord, that you should go farther, and blot out mine iniquities for thine own sake,[241] when I made thee serve with my sins;[242] Lord, what shall I say it is? It is the free grace of my God: what expression transcends that, I know not.

Warning the Nation about the Danger of Losing the Gospel

Use 4. Of caution: England received the gospel of mere mercy, let it take heed, lest it lose it by justice; the placer of the candlestick can remove it;[243] the truth

---

235 In the margin: *Non libertate gratiam sed gratia libertatem, consequimur.* Aug. *de Correp.* etc. Gil. Cap. 8.—Owen. This is a quotation from Augustine's anti-Pelagian work *De correptione et gratia* 8.17 (ca. 424–428). For the Latin text, see Augustine, *De correptione et gratia*, in *Opera omnia*, ed. J.-P. Migne, Patrologia Latina 44 (Paris: Migne-Garnier, 1865), 926. "Not obtaining grace through its freedom, but its freedom through grace." For the English translation, see Augustine, *Admonition and Grace*, trans. John C. Murray, in *Christian Instruction; Admonition and Grace; the Christian Combat; Faith, Hope and Charity*, trans. John G. Gavigan, John C. Murray, Robert P. Russell, and Bernard Peebles, Fathers of the Church 2 (Washington DC: Catholic University of America Press, 1947), 265–66.
236 1 Cor. 4:7.
237 Ezek. 16:6.
238 Ezek. 37:5.
239 Eph. 2:1.
240 In the margin: Ezek. 36:26; Acts 16:14; Phil. 1:29; 2:13.—Owen.
241 Isa. 43:25.
242 Isa. 43:24.
243 Rev. 2:5.

is, it will not be removed unless it be abused, and woe to them, from whom mercies are taken for being abused; from whom the gospel is removed for being despised; it had been better for the husbandmen never to have had the vineyard, than to be slain for their ill using of it;[244] there is nothing left to do them good, who are forsaken for forsaking the gospel.

The glory of God was of late by many degrees departing from the temple in our land. That was gone to the threshold, yea to the mount:[245] if now at the return thereof, it find again cause to depart, it will not go by steps, but all at once; this island, or at least the greatest part thereof, as I formerly intimated, has twice lost the gospel; once, when the Saxons wrested it from the Britons, when, if we may believe their own doleful moaning historian, they were given over to all wickedness, oppression, and villainy of life:[246] which doubtless was accompanied with contempt of the word, though for faith and persuasion we do not find that they were corrupted, and do find that they were tenacious enough of antique discipline, as appeared in their following oppositions to the Roman tyranny, as in Beda.[247]

Secondly, it was lost in regard of the purity and power thereof, by blind superstition and anti-Christian impiety, accompanied also with abominable lewdness, oppression, and all manner of sin, in the face of the sun, so that first profaneness, working a despising of the gospel, then superstition ushering in profaneness, have in this land showed their power for the extirpation[248] of the gospel; Oh, that we could remember the days of old, that we could "consider the goodness and severity of God,"[249] on them which fell severity, but toward us goodness, if we continue in that goodness; for otherwise even we also shall be cut off: yet here we may observe, that though both these times there was a forsaking in the midst of the land, yet there was in it a tenth for

---

244 Matt. 21:41.
245 Ezek. 10:18.
246 In the margin: Gildas, *de Excid. Britanniae, Omnia que Deo placebant et displicebant aequali lance, pendebantur,* [...] *non igitur admirandum est degeneres tales patriam illam amittere, quam praedicto modo maculabant. Hist. M. S. apud Foxum.*—Owen. Owen has already mentioned the sixth-century monk Gildas (ca. 504–570) and his *De excidio et conquestu Britanniae* 21-22. In this reference, John Foxe described Gildas as preaching to the "old Britains" urging them to repent and warning of plagues of divine judgment: "All things whether they pleased or displeased God, they regarded alike. Therefore it is not to be marvelled, that such people so degenerating and going out of kind should lose that country, which they had after this manner defiled." For Latin text and English translation, see Foxe, *Acts and Monuments*, 1:98, 324.
247 Bede also explained the Saxon invasion as a divine punishment. See his *History of the English Church and People*, 56–57.
248 I.e., the act of destroying completely.
249 Rom. 11:22.

to return "as a teil-tree, and as an oak, whose substance is in them when they cast their leaves, so was the holy seed the substance thereof" (Isa. 6:13). As in the dereliction of the Jews,[250] so of this nation, there was a remnant that quickly took root, and brought forth fruit, both in the one devastation and the other, though the "watcher and the holy one" from heaven had called to cut down the tree of this nation, and to scatter its branches from flourishing before him; yet the stump and root was to be left in the earth "with a band of iron," that it might spring again.[251] Thus twice did the Lord come seeking fruit of this vine, doing little more than pruning and dressing it, although it brought forth wild grapes:[252] but if he come the third time and find no fruit, the sentence will be, "Cut it down, why cumbereth it the ground?"[253] Now to prevent this I shall not follow all those gospel-supplanting sins we find in Holy Writ, only I desire to cautionate you and us all in three things.

1. First, take heed of pretending or holding out the gospel for a covert or shadow for other things. God will not have his gospel made a stalking horse[254] for carnal designs: put not in that glorious name, where the thing itself is not clearly intended; if in anything it be, let it have no compeer;[255] if not, let it not be named; if that you aim at be just, it needs no varnish; if it be not, it is the worse for it. Gilded pills lose not their bitterness, and painted faces are thought to have no native beauty; all things in the world should serve the gospel; and if that be made to serve other things, God will quickly vindicate it into liberty.

From the beginning of these troubles,[256] right honorable, you have held forth religion and the gospel, as whose preservation and restoration was principally in your aims, and I presume malice itself is not able to discover any insincerity in this, the fruits we behold proclaim to all the conformity of your words and hearts. Now the God of heaven grant that the same mind be in you still, in every particular member of this honorable assembly, in the whole nation, especially in the magistracy and ministry of it, that we be not like the boatmen, look one way, and row another; cry "Gospel," and mean the other thing; "Lord, Lord,"[257] and advance our own ends, that the Lord may not stir up the staff of his anger and the rod of his indignation against us, as a hypocritical people.[258]

---

250 I.e., the intentional abandonment of Jerusalem to her enemies.
251 Dan. 4:13–15.
252 Isa. 5:2–4.
253 Luke 13:7.
254 I.e., something made use of as a pretext to hide something sinister or underhand.
255 I.e., companion.
256 The British Civil Wars.
257 Matt. 7:21–22.
258 Isa. 10:5–6.

2. Secondly, take heed of resting upon, and trusting to the privilege, however excellent and glorious, of the outward enjoyment of the gospel. When the Jews cried, "The temple of the Lord, the temple of the Lord," the time was at hand that they should be destroyed.²⁵⁹ Look only upon the grace that did bestow, and the mercy that does continue it; God will have none of his blessings rob him of his glory, and if we rest at the cistern, he will stop at the fountain.²⁶⁰

3. Thirdly, let us all take heed of barrenness under it, "For the earth that drinks in the rain that cometh upon it, and beareth thorns and briers, is rejected, and nigh unto cursing, whose end is to be burned" (Heb. 6:7–8). Now what fruits does it require? Even those reckoned, "The fruit of the Spirit is love, joy, peace, long-suffering, gentleness, goodness, faith, meekness, temperance" (Gal. 5:22–23); O that we had not cause to grieve for a scarcity of these fruits, and the abundant plenty of those works of the flesh recounted (Gal. 5:19–21). O that that wisdom which is an eminent fruit of the gospel might flourish among us, it "is first pure, then peaceable, gentle, easy to be entreated" (James 3:17), that we might have less writing and more praying, less envy and more charity; that all evil surmisings, which are works of the flesh, might have no toleration in our hearts, but be banished for nonconformity to the Golden Rule of love and peace, but ἀπέχω.²⁶¹ Come we now to the last proposition.

There Is No Distress Comparable to Being without the Gospel

Obs[ervation] 3. No men in the world want help, like them that want the gospel. Or, of all distresses want of the gospel cries loudest for relief.

Rachel wanted children, and she cries, "Give me children, or I die";²⁶² but that was her impatience, she might have lived, and have had no children, yea, see the justice of God, she dies so soon as ever she has children:²⁶³ Hagar wants water for Ishmael, and she will go far from him, that she may not see him die;²⁶⁴ an heavy distress, and yet if he had died, it had been but an early paying of that debt, which in a few years was to be satisfied. But they that want the gospel may truly cry, "Give us the gospel, or we die," and that not temporally with Ishmael, for want of water, but eternally in flames of fire.

---

259 Jer. 7:4.
260 Jer. 2:13.
261 Gk. "it is enough."
262 In the margin: Gen. 30:1.—Owen.
263 In the margin: Gen. 35:18.—Owen.
264 In the margin: Gen. 21:16.—Owen.

A man may want liberty, and yet be happy, as Joseph was:[265] a man may want peace, and yet be happy, as David was: a man may want children, and yet be blessed, as Job was:[266] a man may want plenty, and yet be full of comfort, as Micaiah was:[267] but he that wants the gospel, wants everything that should do him good. A throne without the gospel is but the devil's dungeon. Wealth without the gospel, is fuel for hell. Advancement without the gospel, is but a going high to have the greater fall.

Abraham wanting a child, complains, "What will the Lord do for me, seeing I go childless, and this Eliezer of Damascus must be my heir?"[268] Much more may a man without the means of grace complain, what shall be done unto me, seeing I go gospelless? And all that I have is but a short inheritance for this lump of clay, my body?

When Elisha was minded to do something for the Shunammite who had so kindly entertained him, he asks her whether he should speak for her to the king or the captain of the host?[269] She replies, she dwelt in the midst of her own people, she needs not those things: but when he finds her to want a child, and tells her of that, she is almost transported. Ah how many poor souls are there, who need not our word to the king or the captain of the host;[270] but yet being gospelless, if you could tell them of that, would be even ravished with joy?

Think of Adam after his fall, before the promise, hiding himself from God: and you have a perfect portraiture of a poor creature without the gospel:[271] now this appears.

Four Lessons That Arise from This Observation

Without the Gospel There Is Darkness and Distress

1. From the description we have of the people that are in this state and condition without the gospel;[272] they are a people that sit in darkness, yea in the region and shadow of death (Matt. 4:16–17). They are even darkness itself

---

265 Gen. 39:20–22.
266 Job 1:18–21.
267 1 Kings 22:27–28.
268 In the margin: Gen. 15:2.—Owen.
269 In the margin: 2 King 4:13–14.—Owen.
270 Owen here prioritizes the need for an effective gospel ministry over peace negotiations. The previous month, King Charles had written of his desire "to draw either the Presbyterians or the Independents to side with me, for extirpating the one or the other, that I shall be really King again." See Charles's letter to Lord Digby from Oxford on March 26, 1646, in Thomas Carte, *History of the Life of James, Duke of Ormonde* [. . .], 3 vols. (London, 1735–1736), 3:452.
271 In the margin: Gen. 3:8.—Owen.
272 In the margin: Matth. 6:23; Luk. 1:79; Act. 26:18; Rom. 2:19; Ephes. 5:8; Col. 1:13.—Owen.

(John 1:5) within the dominion and dreadful darkness of death; darkness was one of Egypt's plagues,[273] but yet that was a darkness of the body, a darkness wherein men lived: but this is a darkness of the soul, a darkness of death, for these men though they live, yet are they dead; they are fully described, "Without Christ, aliens from the commonwealth of Israel, strangers from the covenants of promise, having no hope, and without God in the world" (Eph. 2:12). Christless men, and godless men, and hopeless men, and what greater distress in the world? Yea, they are called dogs, and unclean beasts,[274] the wrath of God is upon them,[275] they are the people of his curse and indignation. In the extreme north, one day and one night divide the year; but with a people without the gospel, it is all night, the Sun of Righteousness shines not upon them, it is night while they are here, and they go to eternal night hereafter. What the men of China say concerning themselves and others, that they have two eyes, the men of Europe one, and all the world besides is blind, may be inverted too.[276] The Jews had one eye, sufficient to guide them, they who enjoy the gospel have two eyes, but the men of China, with the rest of the nations that want it, are stark blind, and reserved for the chains of everlasting darkness.[277]

Without the Gospel There Is No Communion with God in This Life or in Eternity

2. By laying forth what the men that want the gospel, do want with it.

(1) They want Jesus Christ: for he is revealed only by the gospel. Austin refused to delight in Cicero's *Hortensius*, because there was not in it the name of Jesus Christ.[278] Jesus Christ is all, and in all, and where he is wanting, there can be no good. Hunger cannot truly be satisfied without manna, the bread of life, which is Jesus Christ: and what shall a hungry man do that has no bread?[279] Thirst cannot be quenched, without that water or living spring, which

---

[273] Ex. 10:21–23.

[274] Matt. 15:26–27; Rev. 22:15.

[275] 1 Thess. 2:16.

[276] This Chinese proverb was copied by Sir John Mandeville in the fourteenth century. See *The Book of John Mandeville, with Related Texts*, trans. Ian Macleod Higgins (Indianapolis, IN: Hackett, 2011), 217.

[277] Jude 6.

[278] In the margin: *Nomē Iesu non erat ibi*.—Owen. "The name of Jesus was not there." This is Augustine's lament while reading Cicero's *Hortensius* during his studies at Carthage (only fragments of this work survive). The text, which Augustine otherwise considered praiseworthy, awakened his interest in philosophy and played an important role in his conversion. Augustine, *Confessions* 3.4.8. For the Latin text, see Augustine, *Confessions*, vol. 1, *Introduction and Text*, ed. James J. O'Donnell (Oxford: Clarendon, 1992), 26. For the English translation, see Augustine, *Confessions*, 40.

[279] In the margin: Joh. 6:50; Revel. 2:17.—Owen.

is Jesus Christ: and what shall a thirsty soul do without water?[280] A captive, as we are all, cannot be delivered without redemption, which is Jesus Christ:[281] and what shall the prisoner do without his ransom? Fools as we are, all cannot be instructed without wisdom, which is Jesus Christ, without him we perish in our folly. All building without him is on the sand, which will surely fall:[282] all working without him is in the fire, where it will be consumed:[283] all riches without him have wings, and will away:[284] "*Mallem ruere cum Christo, quam regnare cum Caesare,*"[285] said Luther,[286] a dungeon with Christ, is a throne; and a throne without Christ, a hell. Nothing so ill, but Christ will compensate: the greatest evil in the world is sin, and the greatest sin was the first; and yet Gregory feared not to cry, "*O felix culpa quae talem meruit redemptorem,*" "O happy fault, which found such a Redeemer";[287] all mercies without Christ are bitter; and every cup is sweet that is seasoned but with a drop of his blood, he truly is "*amor et deliciae humani generis,*"[288] the love and delight of the sons of men, without whom they must perish eternally: "for there is no other name given unto them, whereby they may be saved" (Acts 4).[289] He is the way,[290] men without him are Cains, wanderers, vagabonds:[291] he is the truth, men without him are liars, devils, who was so of old:[292] he is the life,

---

280 In the margin: Joh. 4:14; Cant. 4:12; Joh. 7:37–38.—Owen.
281 In the margin: 1 Cor. 1:30.—Owen.
282 Matt. 7:26–27.
283 1 Cor. 3:12–15.
284 Prov. 23:5.
285 In a letter dated June 30, 1530, Martin Luther reprimanded Philip Melanchthon for attempting to reform the church by human wisdom rather than the bold proclamation of the gospel, stating, "I would rather fall with Christ than stand with the Emperor." For the text, see "Luther and Melanchthon, Coburg, 30.6.1530," *D. Martin Luthers Werke: Kritische Gesamtausgabe*, 127 vols. (Weimar: Hermann Böhlaus Nachfolger, 1883–2009), 5:412, Nr. 1611. For the English translation see "§123 Luther at the Coburg," in Philip Schaff, *History of the Christian Church*, vol. 7, *The German Reformation: The Beginning of the Protestant Reformation up to the Diet of Augsburg, 1517–1530* (Grand Rapids, MI: Eerdmans, 1910), 727.
286 In the margin: *Pauca igitur de Christo*. Tertul.—Owen. This is a reference to Tertullian's *Apology* 21.3, which reads, "*Necesse et igitur pauca de Christo ut deo*" ("We must then say a few words about Christ as God"). This comes immediately after a comment about the "delight" of being condemned under the name of Christ. For the text and translation, see Tertullian, *Apology*, 102–3.
287 Words from the *Exultet*, or the Paschal Proclamation, of the Easter Vigil service.
288 Suetonius, in *Lives of the Caesars* 8.2, spoke of Titus as "the darling and delight of the human race." For the text and translation, see Suetonius, *Lives of the Caesars*, vol. 2, trans. J. C. Rolfe, Loeb Classical Library 38 (Cambridge, MA: Harvard University Press, 1914), 306–7.
289 Acts 4:12.
290 In the margin: Joh. 14:5.—Owen.
291 Gen. 4:12.
292 John 8:44.

without him men are dead, dead in trespasses and sins:[293] he is the light,[294] without him men are in darkness, and go they know not whither:[295] he is the vine, those that are not grafted in him, are withered branches, prepared for the fire:[296] he is the rock, men not built on him are carried away with a flood:[297] he is α and ω,[298] the first and the last, the author and the ender, the founder and the finisher of our salvation;[299] he that has not him, has neither beginning of good, nor shall have end of misery. O blessed Jesus, how much better were it, not to be, than to be without you? Never to be born, than not to die in you? A thousand hells come short of this, eternally to want Jesus Christ, as men do, that want the gospel.

(2) They want all holy communion with God, wherein the only happiness of the soul does consist. He is the life, light, joy, and blessedness of the soul: without him, the soul in the body is but a dead soul, in a living sepulcher. It is true, "There be many that say, Who will show us any good?", but unless the Lord "lift up the light of his countenance upon us," we perish for evermore.[300] "Thou hast made us for thyself, O Lord; and our heart is unquiet until it come to thee."[301] You who have tasted how gracious the Lord is, who have had any converse and communion with him, in the issues and goings forth of his grace, those delights of his soul with the children of men,[302] would you live? Would not life itself, with a confluence of all earthly endearments, be a very hell without him? Is it not the daily language of your hearts, "Whom have we in heaven but thee? And on earth there is nothing in comparison of thee?"[303] The soul of man is of a vast boundless comprehension, so that if all created good were centered into one enjoyment, and that bestowed upon one soul, because it must needs be finite and limited, as created, it would give no solid contentment to his affections, nor satisfaction to his desires. In the presence and fruition of God alone there is joy for evermore: at his right hand are rivers of pleasure, the wellsprings of life and blessedness.[304]

---

293 Eph. 2:1.
294 In the margin: Joh. 1:3–5; Ephes. 4:18.—Owen.
295 1 John 2:11.
296 John 15:6.
297 In the margin: Mat. 7:25–26 Mat. ch. 16:18.—Owen.
298 Gk. "alpha and the omega" (Rev. 1:8).
299 Heb. 12:2.
300 In the margin: Psal. 4:6.—Owen.
301 Augustine, *Confessions*, 1.1.1. For an English translation, see Augustine, *Confessions*, 3.
302 Prov. 8:31.
303 Ps. 73:25.
304 Ps. 16:11.

Now if to be without communion with God in this life, wherein the soul has so many avocations[305] from the contemplation of its own misery (for earthly things are nothing else), is so unsupportable a calamity, ah what shall that poor soul do, that must want him for eternity? As all they must do, who want the gospel.

(3) They want all the ordinances of God, the joy of our hearts and comfort of our souls.[306] Oh the sweetness of a Sabbath! The heavenly raptures of prayer! Oh the glorious communion of saints, which such men are deprived of! If they knew the value of the hidden pearl, and these things were to be purchased, what would such poor souls not part with for them?[307]

(4) They will at last want heaven and salvation; they shall never come to the presence of God in glory: never inhabit a glorious mansion: they shall never behold Jesus Christ, but when they shall call for rocks and mountains to fall upon them, to hide them from his presence:[308] they shall want light, in utter darkness,[309] want life, under the second death, want refreshment, in the midst of flames,[310] want healing, under gnawing of conscience, want grace, continuing to blaspheme, want glory, in full misery: and, which is the sum of all this, they shall want an end of all this, for "their worm dieth not, neither is their fire quenched."[311]

Without the Gospel There Is Ignorance of the Greatest Need

3. Because being in all this want, they know not that they want anything, and so never make out for any supply. Laodicea knew much, but yet because she knew not her wants, she had almost as good have known nothing.[312] Gospelless men know not that they are blind, and seek not for eyesalve;[313] they know not that they are dead, and seek not for life; whatever they call for, not knowing their wants, is but like a man's crying for more weight to press him to death: and therefore, when the Lord comes to any with the gospel, he is "found of them that sought him not, and made manifest to them that asked not after him" (Rom. 10:20). This is a seal upon their misery, without God's free mercy, like the stone laid upon the mouth of the cave by Joshua, to keep

---

305 I.e., diversions of thought and distractions.
306 In the margin: Psal. 42:1–2; Psal. 84:1–4 etc.—Owen.
307 Matt. 13:46.
308 In the margin: Revel. 6:16.—Owen.
309 In the margin: Matth. 22:13.—Owen.
310 In the margin: Luk. 16:24.—Owen.
311 In the margin: Mark 9:43–44; Isa. 66:24.—Owen.
312 In the margin: Revel. 3:17.—Owen.
313 Rev. 3:18.

in the five kings, until they might be brought out to be hanged.[314] All that men do in the world, is but seeking to supply their wants; either their natural wants, that nature may be supplied, or their sinful wants, that their lusts may be satisfied, or their spiritual wants, that their souls may be saved. For the two first, men without the gospel, lay out all their strength; but of the last, there is among them a deep silence.[315] Now this is all one, as for men to cry out that their finger bleeds, while a sword is run through their hearts, and they perceive it not: to desire a wart to be cured, while they have a plague sore upon them; and hence perhaps it is, that they are said to go to hell "like sheep" (Ps. 49:14),[316] very quietly, without dread, "as a bird hasting to the snare, and not knowing that it is for his life" (Prov. 7:23) and there lie down in utter disappointment and sorrow for evermore.

Without the Gospel National Mercies Are Worse Than of No Value

4. Because all mercies are bitter judgments to men that want the gospel; all fuel for hell; aggravations of condemnation; all cold drink to a man in a fever: pleasant at the entrance, but increasing its torments in the close: like the book in the Revelation, sweet in the mouth, but bitter in the belly.[317] When God shall come to require his bread and wine, his flax and oil,[318] peace and prosperity, liberty and victories, of gospelless men, they will curse the day that ever they enjoyed them; so unspiritual are many men's minds, and so unsavory their judgments, that they reckon men's happiness, by their possessions, and suppose the catalog of their titles, to be a roll of their felicities: calling "the proud happy," and advancing in our conceits them "that work wickedness" (Mal. 3:15). But God will one day come in with another reckoning, and make them know that all things without Christ are but as ciphers[319] without a figure, of no value. In all their banquets where Christ is not a guest, "their vine is of the vine of Sodom, and of the field of Gomorrah, their grapes are

---

314 In the margin: Josh. 10:18.—Owen.
315 In the margin: *Ego propero ad inferos, nec est ut aliquid pro me agas: advocatus quidam moriens apud Bel. de Arte Mor. Lib. ii. Cap. 10.*—Owen. This is a reference to Cardinal Bellarmine's *De arte bene moriendi libri duo* [*The Art of Dying Well*, book two] 11 (Paris, 1620), 305. Bellarmine described a visit to a dying lawyer who told him "I am on my way to hell, and there is nothing that you can do for me." For the English translation, see *Robert Bellarmine: Spiritual Writings*, ed. and trans. John Patrick Donnelly and Roland J. Teske (New York: Paulist, 1989), 358.
316 In the margin: לשׁאל.—Owen. Owen inserts the Hebrew for "to Sheol" (presented defectively without the vav) from Ps. 49:14.
317 Rev. 10:9.
318 Hos. 2:5–9.
319 I.e., arithmetical symbols of no value without a corresponding figure of significance.

grapes of gall, their clusters are bitter" (Deut. 32:32–33), their palaces, where Christ is not, are but habitations of ziim and ochim, dragons and unclean beasts.[320] Their prosperity is putting them into full pasture, that they may be fatted for the day of slaughter,[321] the day of consumption decreed for all the bulls of Bashan:[322] the gospel bringing Christ, is the salt that makes all other things savory.[323]

Three Uses Arising from the Third Observation
The Nation Was Enjoying Unique Privileges
Use 1. To show us the great privilege and preeminence, which, by the free grace of God, many parts of this island do enjoy. To us that sat in darkness and in the shadow of death a great light is risen, to guide us into the ways of peace.[324] Let others recount, the glories, benefits, profits, outward blessings of this nation, let us look only upon that which alone is valuable in itself, and makes other things so to be, the gospel of Christ. It is reported of the heralds of our neighbor monarchs, that when one of them had repeated the numerous titles of his master of Spain, the other often repeated, France, France, France; intimating that the dominion which came under that one denomination would counterpoise the long catalog of kingdoms and dukedoms, wherewith the other flourished.[325] Were we to contend with the *grand seignior*[326] of the east, about our enjoyments, we might easily bear down his windy, pompous train of titles with this one, which *millies repetitum placebit*,[327] the gospel, the gospel: upon all the other things you may put the inscription in Daniel,

---

320 These terms describe the strange creatures that haunt the desolated ruins after the judgment of God on a sinful nation (Isa. 13:21–22; cf. 34:13–14). The Hebrew transliterations "Ziim" and "Ochim" are found in the marginal notes of the Authorized Version, and in the text these terms are translated as "wild beasts of the desert" and "doleful creatures" (13:21 KJV). The transliterations were, perhaps, better known because the Geneva Bible had included the transliterated terms "Ziim" and "Ohim" in the text itself (13:21 and 34:14 GNV). Owen may have chosen to use the Hebrew terms to give due recognition to the danger and strangeness of this desolation. See Karen L. Edwards, "The King James Bible and Biblical Images of Desolation," in Killeen, Smith, and Willie, *Oxford Handbook of the Bible in Early Modern England*, 71–82.
321 James 5:5.
322 Ezek. 39:17–19.
323 Matt. 5:13.
324 Luke 1:79.
325 This is a reference to the rivalry of Francis I, king of France (1494–1547), and the Habsburg emperor of the Holy Roman Empire, Charles V (1500–1558). Charles held the following dukedoms: Burgundy, Brabant, Limburg, Lothier, Luxemburg, and Guelders. He was also king of Castile and León, Aragon and Sicily, Naples and the Romans.
326 A designation for the Ottoman sultan who was known for his many titles.
327 Lat. "it bears repeating a thousand times."

"*mene, mene, tekel*,"[328] they are "weighed in the balances, and found wanting," but proclaim before those that enjoy the gospel, as Haman before Mordecai, "Lo, thus shall it be done to them whom the Lord will honour."[329] The fox in the fable had a thousand wiles to save himself from the hunters; but the cat knew "*unum magnum*," "one great thing" that would surely do it.[330] Earthly supports and contentments, are but a thousand failing wiles, which will all vanish in the time of need: the gospel and Christ in the gospel, is that "*unum magnum*," that "*unum necessarium*,"[331] which alone will stand us in any stead. In this, this island is as the mountain of the Lord, exalted above the mountains of the earth,[332] it is true, many other nations partake with us in the same blessing: not to advance our own enjoyments, in some particulars wherein perhaps we might justly do it: but take all these nations with us, and what a molehill are we to the whole earth, overspread with Paganism, Mohammedanism, anti-Christianism, [with] innumerable foolish heresies? And what is England, that it should be among the choice branches of the vineyard, the top boughs of the cedars of God?

The Nation Was Now Obligated to Respond

Use 2. Shows that such great mercies, if not esteemed, if not improved, if abused, will end in great judgments; woe be to that nation, that city, that person, that shall be called to an account for despising the gospel, "You only have I known of all the families of the earth" (Amos [3]:2). What then? Surely some great blessing is coming to that people, whom God thus knows, and so owns, as to make himself known unto them. No: but, "Therefore will I visit upon you all your iniquities."[333] However others may have some ease or mitigation in their punishments, do you expect the utmost of my wrath. Luther said, he thought hell was paved with the bald skulls of friars;[334] I know nothing of that; yet of this sure I am, that none shall have their portion so low in the nethermost hell,

---

[328] An Aramaic phrase interpreted by Daniel to mean "God hath numbered thy kingdom, and finished it. . . . Thou art weighed in the balances, and art found wanting (Dan. 5:25–27 KJV).

[329] Est. 6:11.

[330] In Aesop's *Fables* the fox knows many tricks, while the cat knows "only one great one"—i.e., to run up a tree. That one thing was worth all when the hounds came. See John Ogilby, *The Fables of Aesop Paraphras'd in Verse* (London, 1651), 45.

[331] Lat. "the one or only necessity" (cf. Luke 10:42).

[332] Isa. 2:2.

[333] Amos 3:2.

[334] Commenting on Matthew 7:21, Luther wrote, "Hell is paved with nothing but tonsures." See *Luther's Works*, vol. 21, *The Sermon on the Mount (Sermons) and the Magnificat*, ed. Jaroslav Pelikan (Saint Louis, MO: Concordia, 1956), 268. This proverbial saying is said to date from at least the time of John Chrysostom (ca. 347–407).

none shall drink so deep of the cup of God's indignation, as they, who have refused Christ in the gospel. Men will curse the day to all eternity, wherein the blessed name of Jesus Christ was made known unto them, if they continue to despise it. He that abuses the choicest of mercies, shall have judgment without mercy; what can help them, who reject the counsel of God for their good?[335] If now England has received more culture from God than other nations, there is more fruit expected from England, than other nations. A barren tree in the Lord's vineyard, must be cut down for cumbering the ground,[336] the sheep of God must "every one bear twins, and none be barren amongst them" (Cant. 4:2). If after all God's care and husbandry, his vineyard brings forth wild grapes, he will take away the hedge, break down the wall, and lay it waste.[337] For the present the vineyard of the Lord of hosts is the house of England, and if it be as earth, which when the rain falls upon it, brings forth nothing but thorns and briars, it is nigh unto cursing, and the end thereof is to be burned (Heb. 6).[338] Men utterly and forever neglect that ground, which they have tried their skill about, and laid out much cost upon, if it bring not forth answerable fruits. Now here give me leave to say, (and the Lord avert the evil deserved by it) that England (I mean these cities, and those other places, which since the beginning of our troubles, have enjoyed the gospel, in a more free and plentiful manner than heretofore) has showed itself not much to value it.

(1) In the time of straits, though the sound of the gospel passed through all our streets, our villages enjoying them who preached peace, and brought glad tidings of good things,[339] so that neither we, nor our fathers, nor our fathers' fathers, ever saw the like before us; though manna fell round about our tents every day: yet as though all were lost, and we had nothing, manna was loathed as light bread,[340] the presence of Christ made not recompense for the loss of our swine:[341] men had rather be again in Egypt, than hazard a pilgrimage in the wilderness. If there be any here that ever entertained thoughts, to give up the worship of God to superstition, his churches to tyranny, and the doctrine of the gospel to episcopal corruptions, in the pressing of any troubles, let them now give God the glory, and be ashamed of their own hearts, lest it be bitterness in the end.

335 Luke 7:30.
336 Luke 13:7–9.
337 Isa. 5:2–6.
338 Heb. 6:7–8.
339 Isa. 52:7; Rom. 10:15.
340 Num. 11:6–10; 21:5.
341 Matt. 8:34.

(2) In the time of prosperity, by our fierce contentions about mint and cumin, while the weightier things of the gospel have been undervalued,[342] languishing about unprofitable questions, etc.[343] but I shall not touch this wound, lest it bleed.

The Particular Obligation upon Ministers and Magistrates

Use 3. For exhortation, that every one of us, in whose hand there is anything, would set in, for the help of those parts of this island, that as yet sit in darkness, yea, in the shadow of death,[344] and have none to hold out the bread of life to their fainting souls.[345] Does not Wales cry, and the North cry, yea and the West cry, "Come and help us?" "We are yet in a worse bondage than any by your means we have been delivered from: if you leave us thus, all your protection will but yield us a more free and jovial passage to the chambers of death."[346] Ah, little do the inhabitants of Goshen[347] know, while they are contending about the bounds of their pasture, what darkness there is in other places of the land;[348] how their poor starved souls would be glad of the crumbs that fall from our tables:[349] O that God would stir up the hearts.

---

[342] Matt. 23:23.

[343] Titus 3:9.

[344] Ps. 23:4.

[345] John 6:35.

[346] Worden described the principality of Wales as "a land notoriously resistant to Puritan understandings of God's word." See Blair Worden, *The Civil Wars: 1640–1660* (London: Orion, 2009), 115. Parliament had a narrow support base in Wales, and there were significant challenges to implementing its reformation on the Welsh church in an area that was overwhelmingly royalist in its sympathies.

[347] I.e., a place of light rather than darkness (Ex. 10:23).

[348] Questions regarding the boundaries of presbyteries and who would determine them were particularly contentious in the 1640s. In May 1645, the Westminster Assembly offered "Advice for a committee of the House of Commons about the boundaries of presbyteries and selection of elders." See *Minutes and Papers of the Westminster Assembly, 1643–1652*, ed. Chad Van Dixhoorn, 5 vols. (Oxford: Oxford University Press, 2012), 5:193–94. Then, in August 1645, Parliament issued an ordinance for the establishment of a Presbyterian polity laying out the "extent and bounds of the Province of London" and the various classes into which it was divided. See "August 1645: Ordinance Regulating the Election of Elders," in *Acts and Ordinances of the Interregnum, 1642–1660*, ed. C. H. Firth and R. S. Rait, 3 vols. (London: HMSO, 1911), 1:749–54; and Tai Liu, "The Founding of the London Provincial Assembly, 1645–47," *Guildhall Studies in London History* 3 (1978): 112. The issue of the bounds of presbyteries continued to be an issue. In August 1646, the Lords and Commons would publish *An Ordinance of the Lords and Commons for the Ordination of Ministers by the Classical Presbyters within Their Respective Bounds* (London, 1646).

[349] Matt. 15:27.

(1) Of ministers, to cast off all by-respects,[350] and to flee to those places, where in all probability, the harvest would be great, and the laborers are few or none at all.[351] I have read of a heretic that swam over a great river in a frost, to scatter his errors:[352] the old Jewish, and now Popish Pharisees, compass sea and land to make proselytes;[353] the merchants trade not into more countries, than the factors[354] of Rome do, to gain souls to his holiness:[355] East and West, far and wide, do these locusts spread themselves,[356] not without hazard of their lives, as well as the loss of their souls, to scatter their superstitions: only the preachers of the everlasting gospel seem to have lost their zeal. O that there were the same mind in us that was in Jesus Christ,[357] who counted it his meat and drink, to do his Father's will, in gaining souls.[358]

(2) Of the magistrates,[359] I mean, of this honorable assembly, to turn themselves every lawful way, for the help of poor Macedonians: the truth is, in this I could speak more than I intend, for perhaps my zeal, and some men's judgments, would scarce make good harmony. This only I shall say, that if Jesus Christ might be preached, though with some defects in some circumstances, I should rejoice therein.[360] O that you would labor, to let all the parts of the kingdom, taste of the sweetness of your successes, in carrying to them the gospel of the Lord Jesus: that the doctrine of the gospel might make way for the discipline of the gospel, without which, it will be a very skeleton. When manna fell in the wilderness from the hand of the Lord, everyone had an equal share:[361] I would there were not now too great an inequality in the scattering of manna, when secondarily in the hand of men; whereby some have all, and others none, some sheep daily picking the choice flowers of every pasture, others wandering upon the barren mountains, without guide or food: I make no doubt, but the best ways for the furtherance of this, are known full well

---

350 I.e., a side aim or motivation.
351 Matt. 9:37. Gribben notes that Owen may be "less persuasive" here given his complaints about the people of the parish of Fordham and the fact that he had chosen to leave them only months beforehand. See Gribben, *John Owen and English Puritanism*, 77.
352 This is possibly a reference to the endeavors of Jesuit missionaries in the area of North America colonized by the French.
353 Matt. 23:15.
354 I.e., agents or representatives.
355 I.e., a title of the pope.
356 Perhaps a reference to Rev. 9:3–11.
357 Phil. 2:5.
358 John 4:34.
359 I.e., any officer charged with the administration of law or government.
360 Phil. 1:18.
361 Ex. 16:18.

unto you, and you therefore have as little need to be petitioned in this as other things.[362] What then remains? But that for this, and all other necessary blessings, we all set our hearts and hands to petition the throne of grace.

Soli Deo gloria.

---

[362] Owen is dismissive of the sustained petitioning campaign in 1645–1646 in which the London Presbyterian leaders attacked the sects and called for a purer form of Presbyterian government. See Valerie Pearl, "London's Counter-Revolution," in *The Interregnum: The Quest for Settlement*, ed. G. E. Aylmer (London: Macmillan, 1978), 29–56, esp. 32–34. Robert Ashton, *Counter-Revolution: The Second Civil War and Its Origins, 1646-8* (New Haven, CT: Yale University Press, 1994), 133–34.

[THE TRACTS APPENDED TO THE PUBLISHED VERSION OF THE SERMON]

A Short Defensative about Church Government, Toleration and Petitions about These Things

READER, THIS, be it what it will, you have no cause to thank or blame me for.[1] Had I been mine own, it had not been thine. My submission unto others' judgments, being the only cause of submitting this unto your censure. The substance of it, is concerning things now adoing: in some whereof, I heretofore thought it my wisdom, modestly *haesitare*,[2] (or at least, not with the most, peremptorily to dictate to others my apprehensions), as wiser men have done in weightier things:[3] and yet this, not so much for want of persuasion in my own mind, as out of opinion that we have already had too many needless and fruitless discourses about these matters. Would we could agree to spare perishing paper,[4]

---

1 In the margin: *Laudatur ab his, culpatur ab illis.*—Owen. This is a reference to Horace's *Satires* 1, 2.11: "He is praised by some, blamed by others." For the Latin text and English translation, see Horace, *Satires. Epistles. The Art of Poetry*, trans. H. Rushton Fairclough, Loeb Classical Library 194 (Cambridge, MA: Harvard University Press, 1926), 18–19.
2 Lat. "hesitating."
3 In the margin: August. Ep. 7. 28. 157, *de orig. anim.*—Owen. These refer to the following works by Augustine and are examples of what "wiser men have done in weightier things": the first reference is to Epistle 7, a letter from Augustine to his friend Nebridius, about the nature of memory; the second is to Epistle 28, a letter from Augustine to Jerome about lying; and the third is to Epistle 157, Augustine's reply to Hilary about a series of questions concerning various Pelagian teachings. The final reference is to Epistle 166 from Augustine to Jerome (415), which was also known as *De origine animae* (On the origin of the soul). For the text, see Augustine, *Part II—Letters*, vol. 1, *Letters 1–99*, ed. John E. Rotelle, trans. Roland Teske, *The Works of Saint Augustine: A Translation for the 21st Century* (Hyde Park, NY: New City Press, 2001), 26–29, 91–94; *Part II—Letters*, vol. 3, *Letters 156–210*, ed. Boniface Ramsey, trans. Roland Teske, *The Works of Saint Augustine: A Translation for the 21st Century* (Hyde Park, NY: New City Press, 2004), 16–39, 77–93.
4 In the margin: *Deferri in vicum vendentem thus et odores, et piper, et quicquid chartis amicitur ineptis. Occidit miseros crambe repetita magistros. Semper ego auditor tantum?*—Owen.

and for my own part had not the opportunity of a few lines in the close of this sermon, and the importunity of not a few friends urged, I could have slighted all occasions, and accusations, provoking to publish those thoughts which I shall now impart: the truth is, in things concerning the church (I mean things purely external, of form, order, and the like), so many ways have I been spoken, that I often resolved to speak myself, desiring rather to appear (though conscious to myself of innumerable failings) what indeed I am, than what others incuriously[5] suppose. But yet the many, I ever thought unworthy of an apology, and some of satisfaction; especially those, who would make their own judgments a rule for themselves and others: impatient that any should know, what they do not, or conceive otherwise than they, of what they do; in the meantime, placing almost all religion in that, which may be perhaps a hindrance of it, and being so valued, or rather overvalued, is certainly the greatest. Nay, would they would make their judgments, only so far as they are convinced, and are able to make out their conceptions to others, and not also their impotent desires, to be the rule: that so they might condemn only that, which complies not with their minds, and not all that also, which they find to thwart their aims and designs. But so it must be.[6] Once more conformity is grown the touchstone (and that not in practice, but opinion), among the greatest part of men, however otherwise of different persuasions. Dissent is the only crime, and where that is all, that is culpable, it shall be made, all that is so.[7] From such as these, who

---

The first quotation is from Horace, *Epistulae* (*Epistles*) 2.1.269: "Be carried into the street where they sell frankincense and perfumes and pepper and everything else that is wrapped in sheets of useless paper." For the Latin text and English translation, see Horace, *Satires. Epistles. The Art of Poetry*, 418–19. The second reference is to the Roman satirist Juvenal, *Satire* 7.154: "All that rehashed cabbage kills the poor teachers." The final reference is, again, from Juvenal, and is from the opening line of *Satire* 1: "Shall I always be stuck in the audience?" For the Latin text and English translation, see *Juvenal and Persius*, ed. and trans. Susanna Morton Braund, Loeb Classical Library 91 (Cambridge, MA: Harvard University Press, 2004), 130–31, 310–11.

5 I.e., carelessly and without due attention to detail.

6 In the margin: *Immortale odium et nunquam sanabile bellum, ardet adhuc, Combos et Tentyra, summus utrinque inde furor volgo, quod numina vicinorum odit uterque locus.* Juven.—Owen. This is a reference to Juvenal, *Satires* 15.34–37: "Between the neighbours Cambos and Tentyra there still blazes a lasting and ancient feud, an undying hatred, a wound that can never be healed. On each side, the height of mob fury arises because each place detests the deities of their neighbours." The text and quotation are slightly adapted from that provided in *Juvenal and Persius*, 490–91. The satirist is referring to a religious disagreement in Upper Egypt in which the people of Combos participated in the cult of the crocodile while the people of Tentyra hunted crocodiles.

7 In the margin: *Graece scire, aut polite loqui, apud illos haeresis est:* Eras, de Scholiast.—Owen. This is a paraphrase of Erasmus's letter 1033 to Albert of Brandenburg of October 19, 1519: "To know Greek or to speak like one who is educated is heresy among them." For the Latin

almost has not suffered? But toward such, the best defense is silence. Besides, my judgment commands me, to make no known quarrel my own. But rather if it be possible, and as much as in me lies, live peaceably with all men,[8] Ἱερὸν πόλεμον,[9] I proclaim to none, but men whose bowels are full of gall. In this spring of humors, lenitives[10] for our own spirits, may perhaps be as necessary, as purges for others' brains. Further, I desire to provoke none; more stings than combs are got at a nest of wasps:[11] even cold stones, smitten together, sparkle out fire:[12] "The wringing of the nose bringeth forth blood."[13] Neither do I conceive it wisdom in these quarrelsome days, to entrust more of a man's self with others, than is very necessary. The heart of man is deceitful;[14] some that have smooth tongues have sharp teeth: such can give titles on the one side,[15] and wounds on the other.[16] Any of these considerations, would easily have prevailed with me, *stultitiâ hac caruisse*,[17] had not mine ears been filled, presently after the preaching of the precedent sermon, with sad complaints of some, and false reports of others, neither of the lowest rank of men, as though I had helped to open a gate, for that which is now called a Trojan horse,[18] though heretofore counted

---

text, see *Opus epistolarum Des. Erasmi Roterdami*, ed. P. S. and H. M. Allen, 12 vols. (Oxford: Clarendon, 1906–1958) 4:106. For the English version of the letter, see *The Correspondence of Erasmus. Letters 993–1121; 1519–1520*, trans. R. A. B. Mynors, *Collected Works of Erasmus* 7 (Toronto: University of Toronto Press, 1987), 115.

8   Rom. 12:18.
9   Gk. "a holy war." The notion of a "holy war" was used to justify Parliament's use of force. Edward Vallance, *Revolutionary England and the National Covenant: State Oaths, Protestantism and the Political Nation, 1553–1682* (Woodbridge, UK: Boydell, 2005), 75.
10 I.e., soothing medicines.
11 In the margin: *Noli irritare crabrones.*—Owen. This quotation from Plautus, *Amphitryon*, act 2, sc. 2, l. 707, is translated as "Do not stir up hornets." For the text on which this is based, see Plautus, *Amphitryon. The Comedy of Asses. The Pot of Gold. The Two Bacchises. The Captives*, ed. and trans. Wolfgang de Melo, Loeb Classical Library 60 (Cambridge MA: Harvard University Press, 2011), 80–81.
12 In the margin: *Si lapides teras nonne ignis erumpit?* Ambros. *Lib*. 1. Cap. 21.—Owen. This is a reference to Ambrose's *De officiis* (On the offices of ministry) 1.93: "If you rub stones together, is it not inevitable that fire breaks out?" Owen's own translation is in the text. For the Latin text and this translation, see Ivor J. Davidson, *Ambrose De Officiis*, vol. 1, *Introduction, Text and Translation* (New York: Oxford University Press, 2001), 172–73.
13 In the margin: Prov. 30:33.—Owen.
14 Jer. 17:9.
15 In the margin: Job 32:21.—Owen.
16 In the margin: Prov. 25:18.—Owen.
17 Horace, *Epistulae* (*Epistles*) 1.1.42: "By this way to have got rid of folly." For the text and translation from which this is adapted, see Horace, *Satires. Epistles. The Art of Poetry*, 254–55.
18 Presbyterians spoke of toleration as a Trojan horse that allowed a horde of heresies to enter the city. Lim explains that "Obadiah Sedgwick, Richard Vines, Thomas Edwards, Robert Baillie, and Samuel Rutherford regarded the allowance of liberty of conscience as Satan's Trojan

an engine likelier to batter the walls of Babylon,[19] than to betray the towers of Zion.[20] This urged some, to be urgent with me, for a word or two, about church government, according to the former suggestions undermined, and a toleration of different persuasions, as they said asserted.[21] Now truly to put the accusers to prove the crimination (for so it was, and held forth a grievous crime in their apprehensions), (what is really so, God will judge) had been sufficient.[22] But I could not so evade: and therefore, after my sermon was printed to the last sheet, I was forced to set apart a few hours, to give an account, of what has passed from me in both these things, which have been so variously reported;[23]

---

horse to destroy the basis of trinitarian orthodoxy and order." See Paul C. H. Lim, *Mystery Unveiled: The Crisis of the Trinity in Early Modern England* (New York: Oxford University Press, 2012), 78.

19 In the margin: *Vid. Remed. contra Gravam. Nationis Germanicae Luther praefatio.* ad lib. de Conciliis. Protest. 34 *ministrorum.*—Owen. In this note, Owen is referring to a number of voices raised in protest against abuses of ecclesiastical power. The first reference is to *Remedium contra gravamina nationis Germaniae* (1519). This *Redress of the Grievances of the German Nation* contained a long list of complaints about the supposed greed of the Papacy and its failings with respect to the church in Germany and was submitted with the intent of gaining redress. At the time of the Diet of Worms, this list numbered some 102 grievances. See C. Scott Dixon, *The Reformation in Germany* (2002; repr., Oxford: Wiley, 2008), 17–19. The second reference is to the "*Praefatio*," of Martin Luther's most extensive ecclesiological work, *On Councils and Churches* (1539). In this preface, the Saxon Reformer described how "desperate tyrants" used Church councils to "buttress their tyranny, and to oppress Christendom with far greater burdens than ever before" and to "coerce . . . poor Christians with the sword." See *Luther's Works*, vol. 41, *Church and Ministry III*, ed. Eric W. Gritsch (Philadelphia: Fortress, 1966), 10–11.

20 Thomas Case (1598–1682), a member of the Westminster Assembly, preached before the House of Lords at the monthly fast of February 1646, cautioning peers to "take heed" of toleration, and likening it to "a *Gunpowder-Treason* to blowe up Religion." According to Case, the unity of the church would be best achieved by the purity of the church, and so he also warned against a form of toleration that he termed "connivence." Thomas Case, *Deliverance-Obstruction: Or, The Set-backs of Reformation. Discovered in a Sermon Before the Right Honourable the House of Peers, in Parliament Now Assembled. Upon the Monthly Fast, March 25. 1646.* (London, 1646), 36–37.

21 For attitudes to toleration, see John Coffey, "The Toleration Controversy during the English Revolution," in *Religion in Revolutionary England*, ed. Christopher Durston and Judith Maltby (Manchester: Manchester University Press, 2006), 42–68; and J. Sears McGee, "Francis Rous and 'Scabby or Itchy Children': The Problem of Toleration in 1645," *Huntingdon Library Quarterly* 67, no. 3 (September 2004): 401–22.

22 In the margin: 4. Conclus. That generally all writers at the beginning of the Reformation. *Si accusasse sufficiet, quis erit innocens?*—Owen. This is a quotation from the Roman soldier and historian Ammianus Marcellinus (ca. 325–ca. 395), *History* 18.14: "If the mere accusation be sufficient, who then will be innocent?" For the Latin text and English translation from which this is adapted, see Ammianus Marcellinus, *History*, vol. 1, *Books 14–19*, trans. J. C. Rolfe, Loeb Classical Library 300 (Cambridge, MA: Harvard University Press, 1950), 404–5.

23 In the margin: *Nec nos obniti contra, nec tendere tantum sufficimus.*—Owen. This is a quotation from Virgil's *Aeneid* 5.21: "We cannot resist or stem the gale." It is drawn from a section in

hoping that the reading may not be unuseful to some, as the writing was very necessary to me. And here at the entrance, I shall desire at the hands of men, that shall cast an eye on this heap of good meaning, these few, as I suppose, equitable demands.

FOUR EQUITABLE DEMANDS MADE IN THE CONTEXT OF THE ANTITOLERATION CAMPAIGN

Exercise Charity Rather Than Seeking to Create Guilt by Association

First, not to prosecute men into odious appellations; and then themselves, who feigned the crime, pronounce the sentence. Like him, who said of one brought before him, "If he be not guilty, it is fit he should be": involving themselves in a double guilt, of falsehood and malice, and the aspersed parties, in a double misery, of being belied, in what they are, and hated for what they are not: if a man be not, what such men would have him, it is odds, but they will make him what he is not: if what he really is, do not please, and that be not enough to render him odious, he shall sure enough be more. Ithacius will make all Priscillianists who are anything more devout than himself"[24] if men do but desire to see with their own eyes, presently they are enrolled of this, or that sect: every mispersuasion, being beforehand, in petitions, sermons, etc. rendered odious and intolerable: in such a course, innocency itself cannot go long free. Christians deal with one another in earnest, as children in their plays, clap another's coat upon their fellow's shoulder, and pretending to beat that, cudgel him they have clothed with it. "What shall be given unto thee, thou false tongue?"[25] If we cannot be more charitable, let us be more ingenuous; many a man has been brought to a more favorable opinion of such as are called by dreadful names, than formerly, by the experience of false impositions on himself.

---

which a dark storm threatens the passage of Aeneas and his fleet to Italy. For the Latin text and English translation, see Virgil, *Aeneid: Books 1–6*, trans. H. Rushton Fairclough, Loeb Classical Library 63 (Cambridge, MA: Harvard University Press, 1999), 472–73.

24 In the margin: Sulp. Sever. Epist. Hist. Eccles.—Owen. This is a reference to Sulpicius Severus and his early fifth-century *Chronicle*. Priscillian was a fourth-century Spanish convert who taught doctrines that were said to be Gnostic or Manichaean. Ithacius, bishop of Ossonoba (Faro), anathematized Priscillian, and after trial before the emperor, Priscillian was tortured and executed. According to Severus, Ithacius was not a "holy man" and even accused Bishop Martin of Tours of being a Priscillian heretic simply because he fasted and was studious. For an account, see "The Execution of Priscillian and His Friends, 385: Sulpicius Severus," in *Creeds, Councils and Controversies: Documents Illustrating the History of the Church, AD 337–461*, ed. J. Stevenson (London: SPCK, 1989), 160–62.

25 Ps. 120:3.

Do Not Exaggerate Differences Unnecessarily

Secondly, not to clothe our differences with expressions, fitting them no better than Saul's armor did David;[26] nor make them like a little man in a bumbast[27] coat upon stilts, walking about like a giant: our little differences may be met at every stall, and in too many pulpits, swelled by unbefitting expressions, into such a formidable bulk, as poor creatures are even startled at their horrid looks and appearance: while our own persuasions are set out ῥήμασι βυσσίνοις,[28] with silken words, and gorgeous apparel, as if we sent them into the world a wooing. Hence, whatever it is, it must be temple building,[29] God's government, Christ's scepter, throne, kingdom, the only way,[30] that, for want of which, errors, heresies, sins, spring among us, plagues, judgments, punishments come upon us.[31] To such things as these, all pretend, who are

---

26 1 Sam. 17:39.

27 I.e., stuffed with wool padding.

28 In the margin: Plut. Apoth.—Owen. This is a reference to Plutarch's *Apophthegmata* (Apothegms) 174. Parysatis advised those who wish to speak frankly to the king to use words of the "softest texture." For the Greek text and English translation, see Plutarch, *Moralia. Sayings of Kings and Commanders. Sayings of Romans. Sayings of Spartans. The Ancient Customs of the Spartans. Sayings of Spartan Women. Bravery of Women.*, trans. Frank Cole Babbitt, Loeb Classical Library 245 (Cambridge, MA: Harvard University Press, 1931), 20–21.

29 According to Guibbory, in the parliamentary fast sermons "the most interesting and most frequently invoked analogy was to the rebuilding of the temple." See Achsah Guibbory, "Israel and English Protestant Nationalism: 'Fast Sermons' during the English Revolution," in *Early Modern Nationalism and Milton's England*, ed. David Loewenstein and Paul Stevens (Toronto: University of Toronto Press, 2008), 120. In February 1644, Robert Baillie preached against those in church or state who "oppose the building of the Temple." See Robert Baillie, *Satan the Leader in Chief to All Who Resist the Reparation of Sion. As It Was Cleared in a Sermon* [. . .] *Febr. 28. 1643* (London, 1644), 36–37. In his fast sermon from February 25, William Jenkyn (1613–1685) had argued that the rebuilding of the temple required Parliament to "demolish that *Babel* of a confused toleration of all practices," something that was "lamentably undermining the building of Gods house amongst us." See William Jenkyn, *Reformations Remora: or, Temporizing the Stop of Building the Temple* (London, 1646), 35. At the previous monthly fast, Thomas Case had told members of the House of Lords that they were "in the work of Temple-Reformation." See Case, *Deliverance-Obstruction*, "Epistle Dedicatory."

30 These various terms were used to describe Presbyterian polity. For example, in another of the fast sermons from February 25, the Presbyterian Anthony Burgess called for reformation by putting all things "into a submission unto the Scepter of Christ Jesus" that would "set up Christs order and government." See Burgess, *Publick Affections, Pressed in a Sermon Before the Honourable House of Commons* [. . .] (London, 1646), "Epistle Dedicatory," 14–15. In June, the Moderator of the Scottish Kirk wrote to the Westminster Assembly, calling on it to defend a polity that persevered "the prerogative of the Crowne, and extent of the Scepter of Jesus Christ." See *Several Letters from the Parliament and General Assembly of the Kirk of Scotland, to the Houses of Parliament of England, the Lord Mayor, Aldermen, and Common Council of the City of London, and the Assembly of Divines at Westminster* (London, 1646), 22.

31 Thomas Edwards spoke of the "a great plague and judgement of God" in which the "Sword of Heresie, and Plague of Error like a Gangrene" that had "over-run the Kingdome." See Edwards,

very confident they have found out the only way. Such big words as these, have made us believe, that we are mortal adversaries (I speak of the parties at variance about government); that one kingdom, communion, heaven, cannot hold us. Now truly if this course be followed, so to heighten our differences, by adorning the truth we own, with such titles as it does not merit, and branding the errors we oppose, with such marks, as in cold blood we cannot think they themselves, but only in their (by us supposed) tendence, do deserve, I doubt not but that it will be bitterness unto us all in the end. And *Quaere*[32] whether by this means, many have not been brought to conceive the kingdom of Jesus Christ, which himself affirms to be within us,[33] to consist in forms, outward order, positive rules, and external government.[34] I design none, but earnestly desire, that the two great parties, at this day litigant in this kingdom,[35] would seriously consider, what is like to be the issue of such proceedings; and whether the mystery of godliness in the power thereof,[36] be like to be propagated by it. Let not truth be weighed in the balance of our interest; will not a dram[37] of that, turn the scale with some against many arguments? Power is powerful to persuade.

Understand Legitimate Concerns about the Current Petitioning Campaigns

Thirdly, not to measure men's judgments, by their subscribing or refusing to subscribe petitions in these days about church government; for subscribers, would that everyone could not see, with what a zealous nescience[38] and

---

The Third Part of Gangraena [. . .] (London, 1646), 265–66. According to Robert Baillie, "blasphemous heresies are now spread here more than ever in any part of the world." See Robert Baillie to David Dickson (March 17, 1646) in Baillie, *The Letters and Journals of Robert Baillie, 1637–1662*, ed. David Laing, 3 vols. (Edinburgh: Robert Ogle, 1841), 2:361. See also James Cranford (who both licensed and wrote a preface to Edwards's *Gangraena*), *Haereseo-machia: or, The Mischiefe Which Heresies Doe, and the Means to Prevent It* [. . .] (London, 1646). This work was based on a sermon preached to the city of London authorities and spoke of how Toleration "so frequent in the mouthes of Sectaries" as "the mother of peace" would only lead to "disorder and confusion." See Cranford, *Haereso-machia*, 12, 14.

32 I.e., one may ask.
33 Luke 17:21.
34 Here Owen appeals to what Como refers to as a "loose anti-formal impulse" that was shared by "many of the most powerful political actors in England" and was the "adhesive" that held together the Independency as a religiopolitical force. See David R. Como, *Radical Parliamentarians and the English Civil War* (Oxford: Oxford University Press, 2018), 406.
35 Presbyterians and Independents.
36 1 Tim. 3:16; cf. 2 Tim. 3:5.
37 I.e., a small fluid measure.
38 I.e., ignorance or lack of knowledge.

implicit judgment many are led. And for refusers, though perhaps they could close with the general words, wherewith usually they are expressed, yet there are so many known circumstances, restraining those words to particular significations, directing them to by, and secondary tendencies, as must needs make some abstain: for mine own part, from subscribing late petitions, about church government, I have been withheld by such reasons as these.

1. I dare not absolutely assert, maintain, and abide by it (as rational men ought to do every clause, in anything owned by their subscription), that the cause of all the evils, usually enumerated in such petitions, is, the want of church government, taking it for any government, that ever yet was established among men, or in notion otherwise made known unto me. Yea, I am confident that more probable causes in this juncture of time might be assigned of them; neither can any be ignorant, how plentifully such evils abounded, when church discipline was most severely executed;[39] and lastly, I am confident, that whoever lives to see them suppressed by any outward means (when spiritual weapons shall be judged insufficient) will find it to be, not anything, either included in, or necessarily annexed unto, church discipline, that must do it, but some other thing, not unlike that, which in days of yore, when all the world wondered after the beast,[40] suppressed all truth and error, but only what the archenemy of Jesus Christ, was pleased to hold out to be believed; but of this afterward.[41]

---

39 In the margin: *Vid. catal. Haeret. Apud* Tertul. *De praescript.* Epiphan. Aug. Vincent.—Owen. Owen is providing four examples of how multiple heresies existed even at times when church discipline was "most severely executed." The first reference is to a catalog of thirty-two heresies by Pseudo-Tertullian, sometimes appended to Tertullian's *De praescriptione haereticorum* (On the prescription against heretics) but more usually known under the title *Adversus omnes haereses* (*Against All Heresies*). For an English translation, see *Against All Heresies*, in *Ante-Nicene Fathers: The Writings of the Fathers Down to A.D. 325*, 10 vols., ed. Alexander Roberts and James Donaldson (1886; repr., Peabody, MA: Hendrickson, 1995), 3:649–54. The second reference is to Epiphanius, the late fourth-century bishop of Salamis, known as the "hammer of heretics," who cataloged eighty heresies in his *Panarion omnium haeresium* (*Medicine Chest against All Heresies*). See *The Panarion of Epiphanius of Salamis*, 2nd ed., trans. Frank Williams, 2 vols. (Leiden: Brill, 2009–2012). The next reference is to Augustine, who, for example, provided a detailed explanation of heresies, past and present, in his *De haeresibus* (*On Heresies*) (ca. 428). For the text, see *The De Haeresibus of Saint Augustine*, trans. Liguori G. Müller, Patristic Studies 90 (Washington, DC: The Catholic University of America, 1956), 54–129. The final reference is to the fifth-century work compiled by Vincent of Lérins, the *Commonitorium*, which enumerated the many heresies that were besetting the church. For an English translation, see *A Commonitory of Vincent of Lérins*, in *A Select Library of Nicene and Post-Nicene Fathers of the Christian Church, Second Series*, ed. Philip Schaff, and Henry Wace, 14 vols. (1890–1900; repr., Peabody: Hendrickson, 2004), 11:131–56.

40 Rev. 13:3.

41 In the margin: *Ego ancillae tuae fidem habui, nonne tu impudens, qui nec mihi ipsi credis? Philos. Apud* Plut. *Apoth.*—Owen. Although Owen references Plutarch's *Apophthegmata*, this appears

2. I dare not affirm that the Parliament has not established a government already, for the essentials of it, themselves affirming that they have, and their ordinances about rulers, rules, and persons to be ruled (the *requisita*[42] and materials of government), being long since extant.[43] Now to require a thing to be done, by them, who affirm that they have already done it, argues, either much weakness or supine negligence in ourselves, not to understand what is effected, or a strong imputation, on those that have done it, either fraudulently, to pretend that which is false, or foolishly to averse, what they do not understand; yet though I have learned to obey as far as lawfully I may, my judgment is exceedingly far from being enslaved, and according to that, by God's assistance, shall be my practice; which if it run cross to the prescriptions of authority, it shall cheerfully submit to the censure thereof; in the meantime, all petitioning of any party about this business, seems to thwart some declarations of the House of Commons, whereunto I doubt not, but they intend for the main, inviolably and unalterably to adhere. Add hereunto, that petitioning in this kind, was not long since voted breach of privilege, in them, who might justly expect, as much favor and liberty in petitioning, as any of their brethren in the kingdom, and I have more than one reason to suppose, that the purpose and design of theirs and others, was one, and the same.[44]

3. There are no small grounds of supposal, that some petitions have not their rise from among them by whom they are subscribed, but that the spring

---

to be a reference to a humorous incident from Cicero's *De oratore*. 2.276. Scipio Nasica called at Ennius's home and overheard the poet telling his servant to report that he was not at home. When Ennius visited Nasica shortly afterward, Nasica shouted out that he was not at home. Ennius recognized his voice and challenged being turned away, to which Nasica replied, "You are a shameless fellow; when I asked for you, I believed your maid when she said you were not at home; do you not believe me when I tell you the same thing at first hand?" For the Latin text and English translation, see Cicero, *On the Orator: Books 1–2*, trans. E.W. Sutton and H. Rackham, Loeb Classical Library 348 (Cambridge, MA: Harvard University Press, 1942), 408–9. The implication is clear: Owen is indicating that he thinks he is no fool in not taking the Presbyterians at their word.

42 Lat. "requirements."

43 The English Parliament began to implement a Presbyterian form of government in a somewhat piecemeal way with the ordinance for the election of elders (August 19, 1645). See "August 1645: Ordinance Regulating the Election of Elders," in *Acts and Ordinances of the Interregnum, 1642–1660*, ed. C. H. Firth and R. S. Rait, 3 vols. (London: HMSO, 1911), 1:749–54. The Congregationalists were hoping to achieve relative autonomy for individual congregations within a national church settlement.

44 In March 1646, the high Presbyterians of Sion College had organized a petitioning campaign against Parliament's moves to define the scandalous sins that would result in suspension from the Lord's Supper. The Westminster Assembly supported this because it believed that the right to judgment over admission to the sacrament belonged to the church rather than the state. On April 11, the Commons voted that in so doing the Assembly was in breach of the privilege of Parliament. See *Journals of the House of Commons*, 13 vols. (London: HMSO, 1802–1803), 4:505–6.

and master wheels giving the first motion to them, are distant and unseen;[45] myself having been lately urged to subscription, upon this ground, that directions were had for it from above (as we used to speak in the country), yea in this, I could say more then I intend, aiming at nothing but the quieting of men's spirits, needlessly exasperated, only I cannot but say, that honest men ought to be very cautious, how they put themselves upon any engagement, that might make any party or faction in the kingdom; suppose that their interest in the least measure, does run cross to that of the great Council thereof, thereby to strengthen the hands or designs of any, by occasioning an opinion that, upon fresh or new divisions (which God of his mercy prevent), we would not adhere constantly to our old principles, walking according to which, we have hitherto found protection and safety. And I cannot but be jealous for the honor of our noble Parliament, whose authority is every day undermined, and their regard in the affections of the people shaken, by such dangerous insinuations, as though they could in an hour put an end to all our disturbances, but refuse it. This season also for such petitions, seems to be very unseasonable, the greatest appearing danger impendent to this kingdom, being from the contest about church government, which by such means as this, is exceedingly heightened, and animosity added to the parties at variance.

4. A particular form of church discipline is usually in such petitions, either directly expressed, or evidently pointed at, and directed unto, as that alone which our covenant[46] engages us to embrace; yea, as though it had long since designed that particular way, and distinguished it from all others; the embracing of it, is pressed under the pain of breach of covenant, a crime abhorred of God and man. Now truly to suppose that our covenant did tie us up absolutely to any one formerly known way of church discipline, the words formally engaging us into a disquisition out of the word, of that which is agreeable to the mind and will of God, is to me, such a childish, ridiculous, selfish conceit, as I believe no knowing men will once entertain, unless prejudice begotten by their peculiar interest, has disturbed their intellectuals: for my part I know no church government in the world already established among any sort of

---

45 The reference to "those distant and unseen" is most likely an allusion to the Scottish influence. For example, Robert Baillie had become something of a mentor to the London Presbyterians. See "Petitions and Politics," in Robert Ashton, *Counter-Revolution: The Second Civil War and Its Origins, 1646–8* (New Haven, CT: Yale University Press, 1994), 132–34.

46 I.e., The Solemn League and Covenant (1643). The commitments entailed by the Covenant would have been issues of dispute in this context. As outlined in the editor's introduction above, the other preacher that day had called for the further reformation of the English church according to "that solemn sacred league." Preaching at the previous monthly fast in the House of Lords, Thomas Case told his hearers "to minde your Covenant." Case, *Deliverance-Obstruction*, 38.

men of the truth, and necessity whereof, I am convinced in all particulars, especially if I may take their practice to be the best interpreter of their maxims.

Recognize That Labeling Other Godly Protestants as Sectaries Is Unhelpful

Fourthly, another *postulatum*[47] is, that men would not use an overzealous speed, upon every small difference, to characterize men (otherwise godly and peaceable) as sectaries, knowing the odiousness of the name, among the vulgar, deservedly or otherwise imposed, and the evil of the thing itself, rightly apprehended, whereunto lighter differences do not amount;[48] such names as this, I know are arbitrary, and generally serve the wills of the greater number. They are commonly sectaries, who (*jure aut injuria*)[49] are oppressed. Nothing was ever persecuted under an esteemed name. Names are in the power of many things, and their causes are known to few. There is none in the world can give an ill title to others, which from some he does not receive: the same right which in this kind I have toward another, he has toward me: unless I affirm myself to be infallible, not so him: those names which men are known by, when they are oppressed, they commonly use against others whom they seek to oppress. I would therefore that all horrid appellations, as "increasers of strife," "kindlers of wrath," "enemies of charity," "food for animosity," were forever banished from among us. Let a spade be called a spade, so we take heed Christ be not called Beelzebub.[50] I know my profession to the greatest part of the world is sectarism, as Christianity:[51] among those who profess the name of Christ, to

---

47 I.e., a postulated proposition.
48 In the margin: *Nunc vero si nominis odium est, quis nominum reatus? quaaccusatio vocabulorum? nisi aut Barbarum sonat aliqua vox nominis, aut maledicum, aut impudicum?* Tertul Apol.—Owen. This is a reference to Tertullian, *Apologeticus* 3.5: "Tell me, then, if it is hatred of a name, how can you indict names? What charge can lie against words, unless the pronunciation of some name has a barbarous sound about it—something unlucky or scurrilous or lewd?" For the Latin text and English translation, see Tertullian, *Apology*, in Tertullian, Minucius Felix, *Apology. De Spectaculis. Minucius Felix: Octavius*, trans. T. R. Glover and Gerald H. Rendall, Loeb Classical Library 250 (Cambridge, MA: Harvard University Press, 1931), 20–21.
49 Lat. "rightly or wrongly."
50 Matt. 10:25; 12:24–27. Gribben describes this as Owen's "longest passage of self-categorization." See Crawford Gribben, *John Owen and English Puritanism: Experiences of Defeat* (New York: Oxford University Press, 2016), 78.
51 In the margin: Act. 24:14; 28:22. *Haeresis christianorum*. Tertul *secta Christ*. Id. *Haeresis catholice, & haeresis sanctissima*, Constant. *Epist. Chr. Syrac.*—Owen. In the first references from Acts, Paul speaks of Christianity as a "heresy." The Latin term *secta* retained a more neutral sense for some time, and this is captured in the reference to Tertullian, who, in his *Apologeticus* 27.3, spoke of the second-century Christians as a *secta*. For the text and translation, see Tertullian, *Apology*, 168–69. Even in the fourth century, Constantine lamented those who left the "catholic" (general)

the greatest number I am a sectary, because a Protestant: among Protestants, at least the one half, account all men of my persuasion,[52] Calvinistical sacramentarian sectaries;[53] among these again, to some I have been a puritanical sectary, an Arian heretic,[54] because antiprelatical:[55] yea and among these last, not a few account me a sectary, because I plead for presbyterial government in churches: and to all these am I thus esteemed, as I am fully convinced,

---

"heresy" and the "most holy heresy." See "Copy of an Imperial Letter Commanding a Second Synod to Be Held with a View to the Healing of All Divisions between the Bishops" addressed to "Chrestus, bishop of Syracusans" in Eusebius, *Ecclesiastical History* 10.5.21–22. For the Greek text and English translation, see Eusebius, *Ecclesiastical History*, vol. 2, *Books 6–10*, trans. J. E. L. Oulton, Loeb Classical Library 265 (Cambridge, MA: Harvard University Press, 1932), 456–59.

52 In the margin: *mislenta systema: quo probare conatur Calvinianos esse haeretices*. Hun. Calv. Tur.—Owen. The opening reference is to the uncompromising Polish Lutheran polemicist Coelestin Myslenta (1588–1653), of Königsberg, who attacked the East Prussian court for its willingness to tolerate the Reformed, whom he tried to argue were heretics. The next reference appears to be to the Lutheran professor of theology Aegidius Hunnius (1550–1603), author of *Calvinus Judaizans* [. . .] (Wittenberg, 1593). Hunnius claimed that Calvin was a "Judaizer" who had undermined Trinitarian orthodoxy. The final reference would seem to be to the thousand-page work by the exiled Roman Catholic Englishmen William Rainolds and William Giffard, titled *Calvino-Turcismus, id est, Calvinisticae perfidiae, cum mahumetana collatio, et dilucida utriusque sectae confutation* [. . .] (Antwerp, 1597), which sought to discredit Calvinism by means of associating it with Islam.

53 In response to the agreement reached between Bullinger and Calvin in the *Consensus Tigerinus* (1549), the Lutheran pastor from Hamburg, Joachim Westphal (1510–1574), published *Farrago confusanearum et inter se dissidentium opinionum de Coena Domini ex Sacramentariorum* (Magdeburg, 1552), in which he described "sacramentarians" like Zwingli and Calvin, who denied the corporal presence of Christ in the Lord's Supper, as heretics. See Esther Chung-Kim, *Inventing Authority: The Use of the Church Fathers in Reformation Debates over the Eucharist* (Waco, TX: Baylor University Press, 2011), 59–98.

54 From Elizabethan times, English Puritans had been likened to Arians (and therefore beyond the bounds of orthodoxy). See Patrick Collinson, *Richard Bancroft and Elizabethan Puritanism* (Cambridge: Cambridge University Press, 2013), 4. In the seventeenth century, the Laudian polemicist Peter Heylyn categorized Puritans as Arians because of their "oppositions to monarchical and episcopal government." See Paul C. H. Lim, "Puritans and the Church of England: Historiography and Ecclesiology," in *The Cambridge Companion to Puritanism*, ed. John Coffey and Paul C. H. Lim (Cambridge: Cambridge University Press, 2008), 225.

55 In the margin: Andrews *Epist ad Molinae*.—Owen. This is a reference to the bishop of Winchester, Lancelot Andrewes (1555–1626), and his correspondence in 1618–1619 with Pierre du Moulin (1568–1658), a prominent minister in the French Reformed church, known for his irenicism. Du Moulin had written three epistles on the nature of the ministry to which Andrewes responded by insisting on the divine right nature of episcopacy. Andrewes' letters were printed in his *Opuscula quaedam posthuma* (London, 1629), 161–200. Du Moulin responded by saying that Andrewes was effectively "unchurching" the French Reformed Church. Andrewes' work would, shortly, be translated into English and published as *Of Episcopacy. Three Epistles of Peter Moulin* [. . .] *Answered by* [. . .] *Lancelot Andrews* (London, 1647). For further details of this debate, see Anthony Milton, *Catholic and Reformed: The Roman and Protestant Churches in English Protestant Thought, 1600–1640* (Cambridge: Cambridge University Press, 1995), 468, 475.

causelessly and erroneously, what they call sectarism, I am persuaded is *ipsissima veritas*, the "very truth itself," to which they also ought to submit, that others also though upon false grounds, are convinced of the truth of their own persuasion, I cannot but believe; and therefore as I find by experience, that the horrid names of heretic, schismatic, sectary, and the like, have never had any influence or force upon my judgment, nor otherwise moved me, unless it were unto retaliation; so I am persuaded it is also with others, for *homines sumus*;[56] forcing them abroad in such liveries,[57] does not at all convince them, that they are servants to the master of sects indeed, but only makes them wait an opportunity, to cast the like mantle on their traducers.[58] And this usually is the beginning of arming the more against the few, with violence: impatient of bearing the burdens, which they impose on others' shoulders:[59] by means whereof, Christendom has been made a theatre of blood: and one among all, after that by cruelty and villainy, he had prevailed above the rest, took upon him to be the only dictator in Christian religion: but of this afterward.

Now by the concession of these, as I hope not unequitable demands, thus much at least I conceive will be attained, viz., that a peaceable dissent in some smaller things, disputable questions, not absolutely necessary assertions, deserves not any rigid censure, distance of affections, or breach of Christian communion and amity: in such things as these, "This privilege we expect and we give it in return":[60] if otherwise, I profess I can hardly bring my mind to comply and close in with them, among whom almost anything is lawful but to dissent.

INTRODUCTION TO THE PROPOSALS SET DOWN IN THE COUNTRY ESSAY

These things being premised, I shall now set down and make public, that proposal, which heretofore I have tendered, as a means to give some light into a way for the profitable and comfortable practice of church government;

---

56 Lat. "we are all but men."
57 During the Laudian era, hundreds had gone into exile in the Low Countries or New England. David Cressy, *Coming Over: Migration and Communication between England and New England in the Seventeenth Century* (Cambridge: Cambridge University Press, 1987); Tom Webster, *Godly Clergy in Early Stuart England: The Caroline Puritan Movement, c.1620–1643* (Cambridge: Cambridge University Press, 1997), 41, 155–57, 270–85.
58 I.e., those who speak in such a manner as to damage the reputation of someone else. Owen is arguing that persecution is self-perpetuating because too often the persecuted turn persecutors.
59 Matt. 23:4.
60 In the text: *veniam petimusque damusque vicissim.*—Owen. This is a quotation from Horace, *Ars poetica*, 11. For the Latin text, see Horace, *Satires. Epistles. The Art of Poetry*, 450–51.

drawing out of general notions what is practically applicable, so circumstantiated, as of necessity it must be: and herein I shall not alter anything, or in the least expression go off from that which long since I drew up at the request of a worthy friend, after a discourse about it: and this, not only because it has already been in the hands of many, but also because my intent is not, either to assert, dispute, or make out anything farther of my judgment in these things, than I have already done (hoping for more leisure so to do, than the few hours assigned to the product of this short appendix will permit), but only by way of a defensative, to evince, that the rumors which have been spread by some, and entertained by others, too greedily about this matter, have been exceeding causeless and groundless; so that though my second thoughts have, if I mistake not, much improved some particulars in this essay, yet I cannot be induced, because of the reason before recounted (the only cause of the publication thereof), to make any alteration in it, only I shall present the reader with some few things, which gave occasion and rise to this proposal. As—

1. A fervent desire to prevent all farther division and separation, disunion of minds among godly men, suspicions and jealousies in the people toward their ministers, as aiming at power and unjust domination over them, fruitless disputes, languishings about unprofitable questions, breaches of charity for trifles, exasperating the minds of men one against another: all which growing evils, tending to the subversion of Christian love, and the power of godliness, with the disturbance of the state, are too much fomented[61] by that sad breach and division, which is here attempted to be made up.

2. A desire to work and draw the minds of all my brethren (the most I hope need it not) to set in, for a thorough reformation, and for the obtaining of Holy Communion, to keep off indifferently the unworthy from church privileges, and profaning of holy things.[62] Whereunto, I presumed the discovery of a way whereby this might be effected, without their disturbance in their former station, would be a considerable motive.

3. A consideration of the paucity of positive rules in the Scripture for church government with the great difficulty of reducing them to practice in these present times (both sufficiently evidenced by the endless disputes, and

---

61 I.e., roused, incited.
62 There was an ongoing controversy between the Commons and the Westminster Assembly over who was worthy and unworthy to participate in the Lord's Supper and who had responsibility for these decisions of admission and suspension from the Table. See Chad Van Dixhoorn, "Politics and Religion in the Westminster Assembly and the 'Grand Debate,'" in *Insular Christianity: Alternative Models of the Church in Britain and Ireland, c. 1570–c. 1700*, ed. Robert Armstrong and Tadhg Ó hAnnracháin (Manchester: Manchester University Press, 2013), 132–36.

irreconcilable differences of godly, precious, and learned men about them), made me conceive, that the practice of the apostolical churches, (doubtless for a time observed in those immediately succeeding), would be the best external help for the right interpretation of those rules we have, and pattern to draw out a church way by. Now truly after my best search, and inquiry, into the first churches and their constitution, framing an idea and exemplar of them, this poor heap following, seems to me, as like one of them, as anything that yet I have seen: nothing at all doubting, but that if a more skillful hand had the limning[63] of it, the proportions, features and lines, would be very exact, equal and parallel:[64] yea, did not extreme haste, now call it from me, so that I have no leisure, so much as to transcribe the first draft, I doubt not but, by God's assistance, it might be so set forth, as not to be thought altogether undesirable; if men would but a little lay aside beloved preconceptions: but the printer stays for every line: only I must entreat every one that shall cast a candid eye, on this unwillingly exposed embryo, and rude abortion, that he would assume in his mind, any particular church mentioned in the Scripture, as of Jerusalem, Corinth, Ephesus, or the like, consider the way and state they were then, and some ages after, in respect of outward immunities and enjoyments, and tell me, whether any rational man can suppose, that either there were in those places, sundry particular churches, with their distinct peculiar officers, acting in most pastoral duties severally in them, as distinguished and divided into entire societies, but ruling them in respect of some particulars loyally in combination, considered as distinct bodies; or else, that they were such single congregations, as that all that power and authority which was in them, may seem fitly and conveniently to be entrusted, with a small handful of men, combined under one single pastor, with one, two, or perhaps no associated elders. More than this, I shall only ask, whether all ordinary power, may not without danger, be asserted to reside in such a church as is here described, reserving all due right and authority, to councils and magistrates. Now for the fountain, seat, and rise of this power, for the just distribution of it, between pastors and people, this is no place to dispute; these following lines were intended merely to sedate and bury such contests, and to be what they are entitled, viz.

---

63 I.e., depiction in painting or words.
64 In the margin: Ἀμέραι δ᾽ ἐπίλοιποι μάρτυρες σοφώτατοι. Pind., Od. i. Olym.—Owen. This is a quotation from the Greek lyric poet Pindar and his *Olympian Odes*, 1.33–34: "Days to come are the wisest witnesses." For the Greek text and English translation, see Pindar, *Olympian Odes. Pythian Odes*, trans. William H. Race, Loeb Classical Library 56 (Cambridge, MA: Harvard University Press, 1997), 50–51.

A Country Essay for the Practice of Church Government There

INTRODUCTION

Our long expectation of some accommodation, between the dissenting parties about church government, being now almost totally frustrate:[1] being also persuaded, partly through the apparent fruitlessness of all such undertakings, partly by other reasons, not at this time seasonable to be expressed, that all national disputes tending that way, will prove birthless tympanies,[2] we deem it no ungrateful endeavor, waiving all speculative ideas, to give an essay in such expressions, as all our country friends, concerned in it, may easily apprehend, of what we conceive, among us may really be reduced to comfortable and useful practice: concealing for a while all arguments for, motives and inducements unto this way, with all those rocks and shelves,[3] appearing very hideous in former proposals, which we strive to avoid; until we perceive whether any of our giants in this controversy, will not come, and look, and so overcome it, that at first dash the whole frame be irrecoverably ruined.[4]

Neither would we have any expect our full sense to each particular imaginable in this business: it being only a heap of materials, most what,[5] unhewed[6]

1 The Committee of Accommodation, created by Parliament in the autumn of 1644, met until March 1646 in the hope of finding a means to include the Reformed who could not agree on matters of polity within the national Presbyterian church. See Youngkwon Chung, "Parliament and the Committee for Accommodation, 1644–6," *Parliamentary History* 30, no. 3 (2011): 289–308.
2 I.e., distensions of the abdomen, especially in relation to pregnancy.
3 Figurative of how submerged layers of rock render the waters both shallow and dangerous.
4 In the margin: The form being given to this Essay at the first, I thought not good to alter any things about it.—Owen.
5 I.e., for the most part.
6 I.e., not cut or fashioned into shape.

that we intend, and not a well-compacted fabric;[7] and if the main be not condemned, we are confident no difference will ensue, about particulars, which must have their latitude. However, if it be received as candidly, as it is offered, no inconvenience will ensue: now that the whole may be better apprehended, and the reasons, if not the necessity of this undertaking intimated, we shall premise some things concerning the place and persons for whose use is this proposal.

First, for ministers: the place having all this while, through the goodness of God, been preserved in peace and quietness, and by the rich supply of able men sent hither by Parliament, there are in many parishes godly, orthodox, peace-loving pastors.[8]

Secondly, for the people.

1. Very many, as in most other places, extremely ignorant, worldly, profane, scandalously vicious.

2. Scarcely any parish where there are not some visibly appearing, of all ages, sexes, and conditions, fearing God, and walking unblameably with a right foot, as beseems the gospel: though in some places, they are but like the berries after the shaking of an olive tree.[9]

3. Among these, very few, gifted, fitted, or qualified for government.

4. Many knowing professors, and such of a long standing, inclined to separation, unless some expedient may be found for comfortable communions, and in this resolution seem to be settled to a contempt of allurements, and threatenings.

5. Seducers everywhere lying in wait to catch and deceive well-meaning souls, anything discontented with the present administration of church affairs.

6. Upon all which it appears, that comfortable communion is not to be attained, within the bounds of respective parishes.

EIGHTEEN REQUESTS TO THOSE IN GOVERNMENT FOR A MODERATE CHURCH SETTLEMENT

Farther to carry on our intentions, we would desire of authority,

---

7 I.e., a densely packed edifice.

8 Parliament's Committee for Plundered Ministers, successor to the Committee for Scandalous Ministers, had been active in finding vacancies for deserving ministers who had been approved by the Westminster Assembly. In mid-1646, it was meeting several times a week. See Joel Halcomb, "The Examination of Ministers," in *Minutes and Papers of the Westminster Assembly*, 1:217–26; and *The History of Parliament: The House of Commons, 1640–1660*, ed. Stephen K. Roberts, 9 vols. (Woodbridge, UK: Boydell and Brewer, 2023), s.v. "Religion, Committees for."

9 Isa. 17:6. A reference to a godly remnant within the parochial congregations of England.

1. That our divisions may not be allotted out by our committees,[10] who without other consideration, have bounded us with the precincts of high constables,[11] but be left to the prudence of ministers, and other Christians, willingly associating themselves in the work.

2. That men placed in civil authority, may not by virtue of their authority, claim any privilege in things purely ecclesiastical.

In the several parishes let things be thus ordered.

1. Let every minister continue in his station, taking especial care of all them that live within the precincts of his parish: preaching, exhorting, rebuking, publicly, and from house to house;[12] warning all, using all appointed means, to draw them to Jesus Christ, and the faith of the gospel, waiting with all patience on them that oppose themselves,[13] until God give them repentance to the acknowledging of the truth:[14] and in so doing, rest upon the calling he has already received.

2. Let the respective elders of the several parishes, to be chosen according to the ordinance of Parliament (annually, or otherwise),[15] join with the ministers, in all acts of rule and admonition, with those other parts of their charge, which the parochial[16] administration does require.

3. Let all criminal things, tending to the disturbance of that church administration which is among them, be by the officers orderly delated[17] to such as the civil magistrate shall appoint, to take cognizance, and determine of such things.

---

10 Parliamentary County Committees had been charged with mapping out parishes into classes within in a reorganized national church. See John Morrill, *The Nature of the English Revolution* (London: Longman, 1993), 156. For the background to these groups that were established by Parliament to coordinate the local war effort and to provide a means of local government, see Morrill, *The Revolt of the Provinces: Conservatives and Radicals in the English Civil War, 1630–1650* (London: Longman, 1980), 58–60, 64–76.

11 I.e., officers responsible for keeping the peace and gathering taxation with a group of parishes within a county known as a hundred or a wapentake.

12 Acts 20:20.

13 2 Tim. 4:2.

14 2 Tim. 2:25.

15 "August 1645: Ordinance regulating the Election of Elders," in *Acts and Ordinances of the Interregnum, 1642–1660*, ed. C. H. Firth and R. S. Rait, 3 vols. (London: HMSO, 1911), 1:749–54. In this ordinance there was a "considerable lack of detail" regarding ruling elders, especially in comparison to the detail presented for ministers. See William M. Abbott, "Ruling Eldership in Civil War England, the Scottish Kirk, and Early New England: A Comparative Study of Secular and Spiritual Aspects," *Church History* 75, no. 1 (2006): 53. More broadly, the legislation was "generally unsatisfactory." See Elliot Vernon, "Presbyterians in the English Revolution," in *The Oxford History of Protestant Dissenting Traditions*, vol. 1, *The Post-Reformation Era, c.1559–c.1689*, ed. John Coffey (Oxford: Oxford University Press, 2020), 65.

16 I.e., of or relating to a church parish.

17 I.e., handed over.

And thus far have we proposed nothing new, nothing not common: neither in that which follows, is there anything so indeed, may it be but rightly apprehended.

For the several combinations of ministers and people.

1. Let the extremes of the division not be above eight or ten miles distant, and so the middle or center not more than four or five miles from any part of it, which is no more than some usually go to the preaching of the word, and in which space, Christians are generally as well known to one another in the country, as almost at the next door in cities; but yet this may be regulated according to the number of professors, fit for the society intended, which would not be above five hundred, nor under one hundred.[18]

2. In this division let there be, in the name of Christ, and the fear of God, a gathering of professors (visible saints, men and women of good knowledge, and upright conversation, so holding forth their communion with Christ), by their own desire, and voluntary consent,[19] into one body, uniting themselves, by virtue of some promissory engagement, or otherwise, to perform all mutual duties, to walk in love and peace, spiritual and church communion, as beseems the gospel.[20]

3. Let everyone so assembling have liberty, at some of the first meetings, to except against another, whether minister or others, so it be done with a spirit of meekness and submission of judgment: or to demand such questions, for satisfaction, as shall be thought fit to be propounded.

4. When some convenient number are thus assembled, let the ministers, if men of approved integrity and abilities, be acknowledged as elders respectively, called to teach and rule in the church, by virtue of their former mission, and be assumed to be so, to this society, by virtue of their voluntary consent and election.

5. Let the ministers engage themselves in a special manner, to watch over this flock, everyone according to his abilities, both in teaching, exhorting, and ruling, so often as occasion shall be administered, for things

---

[18] Ryan Shelton suggests that these "idiosyncratic proposals" should be understood in the specific context of Owen's ministry to "regional conventicles of the godly in Essex," which may have included ministry in St Botolph's Colchester. See Ryan Shelton, "A Social History and Genealogy of Congregationalist New Covenant Theology in Milton's Paradise Lost (1667)" (PhD diss., Queen's University Belfast, 2023), 117.

[19] John Coffey describes the principle of voluntary consent as "one of the foundation stones of congregationalism." See John Coffey, *John Goodwin and the Puritan Revolution: Religion and Intellectual Change in Seventeenth-Century England* (Woodbridge, UK: Boydell, 2006), 118.

[20] Members of Congregationalist churches subscribed to church covenants in which they bound themselves to certain behaviors.

that contain ecclesiastical rule and church order: acting jointly, and as in a classical[21] combination, and putting forth all authority that such classes are entrusted with.

6. If it be judged necessary, that any officers[22] be added to them for the purpose before named, let them be chosen by the consent of the multitude.

7. If not: let the ministers have the whole, distributed among themselves, respectively, according to the difference of their gifts, reserving to the people their due and just privileges.

8. Let this congregation assemble at the least once in a month, for the celebration of the communion, and other things, them concerning, the meeting of the ministers may be appointed by authority, for those of a classis.[23]

9. If anyone after his admission be found to walk unworthily, let him after solemn repeated admonition, be by joint consent, left to his former station.

10. Let any person, in any of the parishes combined as before, that is desirous to be admitted into this society, as is thought fit, be received, at any time.

11. If the number in process of time, appear to be too great, let it be divided and subdivided, according to conveniency.

12. Any one of the ministers, may administer the sacrament, either to some, or all of these, in their several parishes, or at the common meeting, as opportunity shall serve.

13. Let the rules of admission into this society and fellowship be scriptural, and the things required in the members, only such, as all godly men affirm to be necessary for everyone, that will partake of the ordinances, with profit and comfort, special care being taken, that none be excluded, who have the least breathings of soul in sincerity, after Jesus Christ.

Now beyond these generals for the present, we judge it needless to express ourselves, or otherwise to confirm what we have proposed, each assertion almost directly pointing out unto what in that particular we do adhere, which being sufficiently confirmed by others, were but a superfluous labor to undertake: neither shall we trouble you with a catalog of conveniences, whereof men are put upon an express annumeration, when otherwise they do not appear, but commit the consideration of the tendence of the whole, to everyone's judgment: and conclude with the removal of a few obvious objections, being resolved hereafter, by God's assistance, to endeavor satisfaction about this way unto all, unless to such as shall be so simple or malicious, as to ask, whether this way be that of the Presbyterians or Independents.

---

[21] I.e., of, or relating to, a church assembly at a regional level.
[22] E.g., ruling elders.
[23] I.e., an ecclesiastical assembly consisting of pastors and elders from within a regional area.

ANSWERS TO THREE POSSIBLE OBJECTIONS

Ob[jection] 1. By this means parishes will be unchurched.

Ans[wer] 1. If by churches, you understand such entire societies of Christians, as have all church power, both according to right and exercise, in, and among themselves, as Independents speak of congregations, then they were never churched by any.

2. If only civil divisions of men, that may conveniently be taught by one pastor, and ruled by elders, whereof some may be fit to partake of all the ordinances, some not, as Presbyterians esteem them, then by this way they receive no injury, nor are abridged of any of their privileges.

Obj[ection] 2. This is to erect churches among churches, and against churches.

Ans[wer] No such thing, but a mere forming of one church, with one presbytery.

Obj[ection] 3. It is against the Parliament's ordinance,[24] to assume a power, of admitting and excluding of church members, not exactly according to their rule, nor subordinate to the supervising of such as are appointed by them.

Ans[wer] 1. For the rules set out by ordinance, we conceive that the church officers are to be interpreters of them, until appeal be made from them, unto which we shall submit; and if it be so determined against us, that any be put on our communion *ipsi viderint*,[25] we shall labor to deliver our own souls.[26]

2. Though the Parliament forbid any but such, authoritatively to be excluded, yet it does not command that any be admitted but such as desire it: and we shall pray for such a blessing upon the work of our ministry, as will either prepare a man for it, or persuade them *pro tempore*[27] from it: unless they be stubbornly obstinate, or openly wicked, against whom we hope for assistance: unto objections arising from trouble and inconvenience, we answer, it cost more to redeem their souls.

The God of peace and unity give the increase.

If you know something better than these precepts, pass it on, my good fellow. If not, follow them.[28]

---

24 "March 1646: An Ordinance for Keeping of Scandalous persons from the Sacrament of the Lord's Supper, the Enabling of Congregations for the Choice of Elders and Supplying of Defects in Former Ordinances and Directions of Parliament concerning Church Government," in *Acts and Ordinances of the Interregnum* 1:833–38.
25 Lat. "let them see it themselves."
26 See Ezek. 14:14, 20.
27 Lat. "for the time being."
28 In the text: *Si quid novisti rectius istis, Candidus imperti, si non, his utere.*—Owen. This quotation is from Horace, *Epistulae* (*Epistles*) 1.6.67–68. For the Latin text and English translation,

And this is all which for the present I shall assert in this business, and this also is my own vindication: time and leisure may give me advantage hereafter (if God permit) to deal seriously in this cause; in the meantime, it is not unknown to many, that so much as this, was necessary for me to do, and I will not add now anything that is not necessary.

RESPONSE TO THE ACCUSATION THAT THIS TOLERATES ERROR

Now for the other head of the accusation about toleration of errors; "I want to philosophize, but only in a few words,"[29] something I shall add of my own present judgment in this matter, but with willing express submission unto those, whom the use and experience of things, with knowledge of foreign parts, skill in the rules of commonwealths, acquaintedness with the affections and spirits of men, have enabled to look practically into the issues and tendencies of such a toleration. The main prejudice against it, arises from the disturbances which it naturally (they say) produces in civil states: I conceive no sort of men, more unfit to judge of this, than those, whose abilities of learning, do properly put them upon the discussing of this, and other controversies, as far as they are purely ecclesiastical: no men more frequently betraying narrowness of apprehension, and weakness in secular affairs: for other consequences, I shall not be much moved with them, until it be clearly determined, whether be worse, heretics, or hypocrites, to maintain an error, or counterfeit the truth, and whether profession upon compulsion be acceptable to God or man: laying those aside, let the thing itself be a little considered.[30]

Peace ecclesiastical, quiet among the churches (which without doubt would be shaken by a universal toleration), is that which most men aim at, and

---

see Horace, *Satires. Epistles. The Art of Poetry*, trans. H. Rushton Fairclough, Loeb Classical Library 194 (Cambridge, MA: Harvard University Press, 1926), 290–91.

29 In the text: *philosophare volo, sed paucis.*—Owen. This quotation is adapted from the words placed on the lips of Neoptlolemus by Ennius as transmitted by Cicero in his *Tusculan Disputations* 2.1.1–4. For the Latin text and English translation, see Cicero, *Tusculan Disputations*, trans. J. E. King, Loeb Classical Library 141 (Cambridge, MA: Harvard University Press, 1927), 146–47.

30 In the margin: *Hostiae ab animo libenti accipiuntur*, Tertul.—Owen. This is a reference to Tertullian, *Ad Scapulam* 2.2: "Sacrifices are accepted of a willing mind." Tertullian, writing in the early third century, is arguing that religion cannot be compelled. For the Latin text from which this is adapted, see Tertullian, *Ad Scapula*, in *Opera omnia*, ed. J.-P. Migne, Patrologia Latina 1 (Paris: Migne, 1844), 699. For the English text, which has been modified to match Owen's adaptation of the Latin text, see Tertullian, *To Scapula*, in *Ante-Nicene Fathers: The Writings of the Fathers Down to A.D. 325*, 10 vols., ed. Alexander Roberts and James Donaldson (1886; repr., Peabody, MA: Hendrickson, 1995), 3:105.

desire; and truly he that does not, scarcely deserves the name and privilege of a Christian: unity in the Scripture, is so pressed, so commanded, and commended, that not to breathe after it, argues a heart acted by another spirit, than that, which moved the holy penmen thereof. But yet every agreement and consent among men, professing the name of Christ, is not the unity and peace commended in the Scripture, that which some think to be Christ's order, may perhaps be anti-Christian confusion: the specious name of unity may be a cloak for tyranny. Learned men have reckoned up a sevenfold unity in the Papacy,[31] all which, notwithstanding, are far enough from that true evangelical unity, which we are bound to labor for. Again, that which is good must be sought in a right manner, or it will not be so to us: peace and quiet is desirable; but there must be good causes and very urgent, to make us build our habitations out of others' ruins, and roll our pillows in their blood: I speak of things ecclesiastical; the historian makes it a part of the oration spoken by Galgacus,[32] the chieftain of the British forces, to stir them up against the Roman insolency, that when they had finished their depopulations, then they said they had peace:[33] the same men have set up bishoprics in the Indies, as their forefathers did colonies here and elsewhere, with fire, and sword.[34] I know not how it comes to pass, but so it is, this proceeding with violence in matters of religion, has pleased and displeased all sorts of men, however distinguished by a true or false persuasion, who have enjoyed a vicissitude of the supreme power in any place, in supporting or suppressing of them: *Ure,*

31 In the margin: 1. Satanica; 2. Ethnica; 3. Belluina; 4. Iscariotica; 5. Tyrannica; 6. Herodiana; 7. Ventris causa." Illyricus, de Variis Sectis ap. Papistas.—Owen. This is a reference to the Lutheran controversialist Matthias Flacius Illyricus (1520–1575) and his anti–Roman Catholic polemic *On the Sects, Dissensions, Contradictions and Confessions of the Doctrine of Papal Religion, Papal Authors and Doctors of the Church*. For the Latin text see *De sectis, dissensionibus, contradictionibus et confusionibus doctrinae, religionis, scriptorium et doctorum Pontificiorum* (Basel, 1565), 236. Editor's translation: "Satanic, pagan, bestial, of [Judas] Iscariot, tyrannical, of Herod, of the belly."
32 Calgacus was a Caledonian chieftain who fought against the Roman army of Julius Agricola at the battle of Mons Graupius (ca. AD 83).
33 In the margin: *Solitudinem ubi faciunt, pacem appellant.* Tacitus Vita Agr. cap. 30.—Owen. This is a reference to Tacitus, *De et vita moribus Iulii Agricolae* (*On the Life and Character of Julius Agricola*) 30.5. It records an incident from the life of the Roman governor of Britain in which Calgacus speaks to his troops about how the Romans extend their empire by plunder, butchery, and theft. "They make a desolation and they call it peace." For text and translation, see Tacitus, *Agricola. Germania. Dialogue on Oratory*, trans. M. Hutton and W. Peterson, rev. R. M. Ogilvie, E. H. Warmington, Michael Winterbottom, Loeb Classical Library 35 (Cambridge, MA: Harvard University Press, 1914), 80–81.
34 A reference to the establishment of bishoprics in the wake of the Spanish conquest of the Americas.

seca, occide,³⁵ is the language of men backed with authority: "Do not do unto others what you do not want done to yourself,"³⁶ say the same men under oppression: to give particular instances, were to lay open that nakedness, which I suppose it my duty rather to cover.³⁷ What then you will say, shall everyone be suffered to do what he pleases? (You mean, think or believe what he pleases, or that which he is convinced to be a truth.) Must all sorts of men and their opinions be tolerated? These questions are not in one word to be resolved; many proposals are to be confirmed, many notions distinguished and retained, before a positive answer can be given: take them in their whole latitude, and they may serve all men's turns. A negative universal resolution, may tantamount unto; the many, entrusted with authority, or having that, to back them, ought not to tolerate any of different persuasions from them, if they suppose them erroneous. Now truly for my part, were I in Spain or Italy, a native of those places, and God should be pleased there, to reveal that truth of his gospel unto me, which he has done in England, I believe those states ought to tolerate me, though they were persuaded that I were the most odious heretic under heaven; and what punishment soever they should impose on me for my profession, would be required at their hands: unless they can convince me, that God allows men to slay his servants for professing the gospel, if they believe them to be heretics: and so also excuse the Jews in crucifying his dear Son, because they esteemed him as an impostor. Christ was once crucified among thieves: he may be again, in them that are so supposed. I shall

---

35 Lat. "Burn, cut, and kill." This phrase is reminiscent of Justus Lipsius (1547–1606) and his use of language drawn from Cicero in support of the call for religious dissidents to be suppressed because it promoted disorder, sedition, and war. See Justus Lipsius, *Politica: Six Books of Politics or Political Instruction*, ed. and trans. Jan Waszink (Assen: Van Gordum, 2004), 144.

36 In the text: *Quod tibi fieri non vis, alteri ne feceris*.—Owen. This is a negative version of the Golden Rule, often associated with Augustine. For text and translation, see Augustine, *De doctrina Christiana*, ed. and trans. R. P. H. Green (Oxford: Oxford University Press, 1995), 3.14.22.

37 In the margin: *Humani juris et naturalis potestatis est unicuique quod putaverit, colere*. Tertul. *Quis imponet mihi necessitatem aut credendi quod nolim, aut quod velim non credendi*. Lactan.—Owen. The first is a further reference to Tertullian's letter to Scapula: "It is the law of mankind and the natural right of each individual to worship what he thinks proper." For the Latin text, see *Ad Scapula*, 699. For the English translation, see Tertullian, *Apologetical Works*, trans. Rudolph Arbesmann, Emily Joseph Daly, Edwin A. Quain, Fathers of the Church 10 (Washington, DC: Catholic University of America, 1950), 152. The second is an adapted form of the question asked by Lactantius (ca. 250–ca. 325) in his early fourth-century work *Divine Institutes* 5.13: "Who can force me to believe what I will not, or not to believe what I will?" For the Latin text, see Lactantius, *Divinarum institutionum*, in *Opera omnia*, ed. J.-P. Migne, Patrologia Latina 6 (Paris: Migne, 1844), 594. For the English text, see Lactantius, *The Divine Institutes, Books I–VII*, trans. Mary Francis McDonald, Fathers of the Church 49 (Washington, DC: Catholic University of America Press, 1964), 361.

therefore summarily set down, what I conceive in answer to these questions, premising a few things, if I mistake not, universally granted.

UNRESOLVED ISSUES IN CURRENT DEBATES ABOUT TOLERATION

And yet a word or two concerning toleration itself, that some guess may be given at what we aim and intend, must interpose. Much discourse about toleration has been of late days among men. Some pleading for it, more against it: as it always must be; toleration is the alms of authority, yet men that beg for it, think so much at least their due: some say it is a sin to grant it, others that it is no less to deny it: generally the pleaders of each side, have their interest in the cause. I never knew one contend earnestly for a toleration of Dissenters, but was so himself: nor any for their suppression, but were themselves of the persuasion which prevails: for if otherwise, this latter would argue a Circumcellion fury,[38] willfully to seek their own ruin: the former so much charity, and commiseration of the condition of mortality, as in these days would procure of the most, no other livery[39] but a fool's coat. Who almost would not admire at such new-discovered antipodes,[40] as should offer to assert, an equal regiment of Trojans and Tyrians, a like regard and allowance from authority, for other sects, as for that, whereof themselves are a share?[41] Now among these contesters, few (nay not any) have I found, either on the one side or the other, clearly and distinctly to desire what they mean by toleration, or what is the direct purpose, signification, and tendence of nontoleration (a word in its whole extent, written only in the forehead of the man of sin),[42]

---

38 The Circumcellions were a group of zealots on the fringe of the Donatist movement, active in North Africa from 340. Its more extreme adherents committed acts of violence and sought death by martyrdom.

39 I.e., a ceremonial uniform worn by servants or officials.

40 I.e., inhabitants from the opposite side of the earth; direct opposites.

41 In the margin: *Tros, Tyriusque mihi nullo discrimine agetur.*—Owen. This is a quotation from Virgil's *Aeneid* 1.574: "Trojan and Tyrian I shall treat alike." Dido, Queen of Carthage, welcomes the shipwrecked Trojan hero Aeneas and proclaims that she will not discriminate between Trojans and Tyrians. This harmony does not last, as soon Aeneas turns out to be a treacherous guest, and this leads to the tragic death of Dido. For text and translation, see Virgil, *Aeneid: Books 1–6*, trans. H. Rushton Fairclough, Loeb Classical Library 63 (Cambridge, MA: Harvard University Press, 1999), 302–3.

42 In the margin: *Late sibi summovet omnes, [Volgus et] in vacua regnet Basiliscus arena.*—Owen. This is a quotation from the Roman poet Lucan's *Pharsalia* 9.725–26. The poet speaks of a poisonous snake that "compels all the inferior serpents to keep their distance, and lords it over the empty desert." For the Latin text and English translation, see Lucan, *The Civil War (Pharsalia)*, trans. J. D. Duff, Loeb Classical Library 220 (Cambridge, MA: Harvard University Press, 1928), 558–59.

what bounds, what terriers are to be assigned,[43] to the one, or to the other? Unto what degrees of longitude, or latitude their pole is to be elevated? Some perhaps by a toleration, understand a universal uncontrolled license, *vivendi ut velis*,[44] in things concerning religion: that everyone may be let alone, and not so much as discountenanced,[45] in doing, speaking, acting, how, what, where or when he pleases, in (*agendis et credendis fidei*)[46] all such things, as concern the worship of God, articles of belief, or generally anything, commanded in religion. And in the meantime the parties at variance, and litigant about differences, freely to revile, reject, and despise one another, according as their provoked genius shall dispose their minds thereunto.

Now truly though every one of this mind, pretend to cry for mercy to be extended unto poor afflicted truth, yet I cannot but be persuaded that such a toleration would prove exceeding pernicious to all sorts of men, and in the end, end in a dispute, like that recounted by Juvenal, between two cities in Egypt, about their differences between their garden and river deities;[47] or like the contest related by Vertomannus in his travels,[48] among the Mohammedans, about Haly and Homar,[49] the pretended successors to their grand impostor,[50] where everyone plied his adversary, "with lances, shield,

---

43 The assignment of terriers is recorded in the register of the lands belonging to a landowner. It included details of the tenant, the boundaries of the holding, and the rents that were due.
44 Cicero's reply that liberty is the power to "live as you want to." See *Paradoxa Stoicorum* 5.1.34. For the Latin text and English translation, see Cicero, *Stoic Paradoxes*, in *On the Orator: Book 3. On Fate. Stoic Paradoxes. Divisions of Oratory*, trans. H. Rackham, Loeb Classical Library 349 (Cambridge, MA: Harvard University Press, 1942), 284–85. Owen distances himself from those calling for the toleration of all religions.
45 I.e., to look on with disfavor.
46 Lat. "matters of faith to be practiced and believed."
47 In the margin: *Sanctas gentes, quibus haec nascantur in hortis numina.*—Owen. This is a quotation from Juvenal's *Satires* 15.10–11 ridiculing the superstitious character of the Egyptian worship of cats, dogs, fish, and onions: "Such holy peoples, to have these gods growing in their gardens!" For the Latin text and English translation, see *Juvenal and Persius*, ed. and trans. Susanna Morton Braund, Loeb Classical Library 91 (Cambridge, MA: Harvard University Press, 2004), 488–89. Juvenal thought it preposterous that the Egyptians would abstain from vegetables while practicing cannibalism. See Tom T. Tashiro, "English Poets, Egyptians Onions, and the Protestant View of the Eucharist," *Journal of the History of Ideas* 30, no. 4 (1969): 563–78.
48 The Bolognese explorer Ludovico di Varthema (ca. 14470–1517) was one of the first Europeans to visit Medina and Mecca.
49 Owen is referring to di Varthema's account of the origins of the Shi'a-Sunni "split" in Islam. "Haly" is Muhammad's son-in-law, Ali ibn Abi Talib (599–661), whom Shi'a Muslims regard as the first rightful caliph who was wrongly usurped by "Homar"—i.e., the companion of Muhammad, Umar ibn al-Khattab (ca. 584–644).
50 A reference to Muhammed. See Matthew Dimmock, *Mythologies of the Prophet Muhammad in Early Modern English Culture* (Cambridge: Cambridge University Press, 2013), 170.

and weighty stones":[51] cleaving their skulls, and making entrance for their arguments by dint of sword; and I wish experience did not sufficiently convince us, that the profession of Christianity, where the power of godliness is away, will not prevent these evils, "So potent was Superstition in persuading to evil deeds."[52] Others there are that press for a nontoleration, of anything that opposes or contradicts the truth in any part, themselves being in their own judgments fully possessed of all; their tenets being unto them the only form of wholesome words:[53] moreover (for these things recounted make not the difference, for it is so with all sects of men), the magistrates, or those who are entrusted with all the power over men, which for the preservation of human society, God has been pleased to make out from himself, are also of the same persuasion with them: these they supplicate that an effectual course may be taken (asserting, not only that they are entrusted with power from above so to do, but also that it is their great sin if they do it not), whereby all sectaries and erroneous persons may not only, not be countenanced, or kept within bounds, and not be forborne in any disturbing insolent miscarriage, but also that all that doctrine which is not publicly owned, may be sure to be supplanted, by the restraint and punishment of the Dissenters, whether unto imprisonment, confiscation of goods, or death itself,[54] for they must not cease, nay (if the thing is to be effected) they cannot rationally assign where to stay in punishing, before they come to the period of all, death itself, that is the point and center wherein all the lines of this sentence meet: wherein, to me truly there is nothing but "everywhere was cruel grief, everywhere panic, and full many a shape of death."[55] I know it is colored with fair pretenses, but "Why am I to listen to words, seeing that I have the deeds before my

---

51 In the text: *Hastisque, clipeisque, et saxis grandibus.*—Owen. This is adapted from Homer's *Iliad* 13.324. For the Greek text and English translation, see Homer, *Iliad*, vol. 2, *Books 13–24*, trans. A. T. Murray, rev. William F. Wyatt, Loeb Classical Library 171 (Cambridge, MA: Harvard University Press, 1925), 26–27.

52 In the text: *Tantum religio potuit suadere malorum.*—Owen. Owen cites Lucretius's didactic poem *De rerum natura* 1.101. For the English translation, see Lucretius, *On the Nature of Things*, trans. W. H. D. Rouse, rev. Martin F. Smith, Loeb Classical Library 181 (Cambridge, MA: Harvard University Press, 1924), 10–11.

53 1 Tim. 6:3.

54 In the margin: *Inventus, Chrysippe, tui finitor acervi.*—Owen. Owen is citing Persius's *Satire* 6.80: "Chrysippus, the man to put a limit to your heap is found!" Chrysippus was a stoic philosopher famous for his "sorites" paradox: how many grains may be removed from a heap before it ceases to be a heap? For the Latin text and English translation, see *Juvenal and Persius*, 124–25.

55 In the text: *luctus ubique, pavor, et plurima mortis imago.*—Owen. Owen is referencing Virgil's *Aeneid* 2.368–69 and Aeneas's recollection of the bloodshed at Troy. For the Latin text and English translation, see Virgil, *Aeneid: Books 1–6*, 340–41.

eyes?"[56] It is written with red letters, and the pens of its abettors[57] are dipped in the blood of Christians. Doubtless between these extremes lies the way.[58]

Again, some by a toleration, understand a mutual forbearance in communion, though there be great differences in opinion; and this the generality of the clergy (as heretofore they were called), did usually incline unto, viz. that any men almost might be tolerated, while they did not separate: and these lay down this for a ground, that there is a latitude in judgment to be allowed: so that the communion may be held by men of several persuasions, in all things, with an allowance of withdrawing in those particulars, wherein there is Dissent among them: and this the Belgic Remonstrants pressed hard for, before they were cast out by the Synod of Dort.[59]

Others plead for a toleration out of communion, that is, that men renouncing the communion of those, whose religion is owned and established by authority, may yet peaceably be suffered to enjoy the ordinances in separation. Moreover by communion, some understand one thing, some another; some think that is preserved sufficiently, if the Dissenters do acknowledge those from whom they do dissent, to be true churches, to enjoy the ordinances of Christ, to have the means of life and salvation in them, closing with them in all substantials of doctrine, but yet because of some disorders, in, and among them, they dare not be as of them, but yet only separate from those disorders.

Others again think that communion is utterly dissolved, if any distinctions of persons be made, more than all acknowledge ought to be, any differences in the administration of the ordinances, any divisions in government at all.

Now all these things, and many more that might be added, must clearly be distinguished and determined by him that would handle his matter, at large

---

56 In the text: *quid ego verba audiam, facta cum video?*—Owen. Owen is referencing Cicero, *Tusculan Disputations* 3.20. For the Latin text and English translation, see Cicero, *Tusculan Disputations*, 282–83.
57 I.e., those who aid others in committing a crime.
58 In the margin: Ἐχθρὸς γάρ' 'οἱ' κεῖνος ὁμῶς ἀΐδαο πύλῃσιν, Ὅς χ' ἕτερον μὲν κεύθει ἐνὶ φρεσὶν, ἄλλο δὲ βάζει.—Owen. This is a quotation from Homer's *Iliad* 9.312–13: "For hateful in my eyes as the gates of Hades is that man who hides one thing in his mind and says another." For the Greek text and English translation, see Homer, *Iliad*, vol. 1, *Books 1–12*, trans. A. T. Murray, rev. William F. Wyatt, Loeb Classical Library 170 (Cambridge, MA: Harvard University Press, 1924), 416–17.
59 In years before the Synod of Dordrecht (1618–1619), Dutch Arminians, like Hugo Grotius (1583–1645), argued for the limited toleration of differences in nonfundamental points of doctrine within the state church. After the Synod, the Remonstrants were declared to be "heretics" and "disturbers of the peace," and the leading Arminian, Simon Episcopius (1583–1643), was one of those "cast out" into exile. Jonathan Israel, "The Intellectual Debate about Toleration," in *The Emergence of Tolerance in the Dutch Republic*, ed. C. Berkvens-Stevelinck, J. Israel, and G. H. M. Posthumus Meyjes (Leiden: Brill, 1997), 11–14.

and exactly, that we may know what he means by those ambiguous words, and in what acceptation he owns them. Until this be done a man may profess to oppose both toleration and nontoleration, without any contradiction at all, because in their several senses they do not always intend the same.

CLARIFICATION OF THE NATURE OF TOLERATION

For my part, as on the one side, if by toleration you mean *potestatem vivendi ut velis*,[60] (as the Stoics defined liberty), a universal concession of an unbounded liberty, or rather, bold unbridled licentiousness, for everyone to vent what he pleases, and to take what course seems good in his own eyes, in things concerning religion and the worship of God, I cannot give my vote for it; so if by nontoleration, you mean that which the gloss upon that place, *Haereticum hominem devita*,[61] intended by adding *supple tolle*,[62] to make up the sense,[63] as if they were not to be endured in any place who dissent only in not-fundamentals, from that which is established, but to be hated, *ad furcas et leones*,[64] as the Christians of old, or to have their new derided lights, extinguished in that light, "where men stand burning with their throats fastened tight":[65] in a Nero's bonfire:[66] into the secrets of them that are thus minded, let not my soul descend. "In their anger they will slay a man, and in their self-will they dig down a wall; cursed be their anger for it is fierce, and their wrath for it is cruel":[67] these things then being so ambiguous, doubtful and uncertain, we dare not be too peremptorily dogmatical, nor positively assert but only what is certainly true: as are these following.

60 In the margin: Ἐξουσία αὐτοπραγίας Cicer. Parad.—Owen. This is a quotation from Cicero, *Paradoxa Stoicorum* 5.1. For the Greek text and English translation, see Cicero, *Stoic Paradoxes*, 284–85. Once again, Owen distances himself from Cicero's reply that liberty is the power to "live as you want to."
61 Words from the Latin Vulgate text of Titus 3:10: "A man that is a heretic . . . reject."
62 Lat. "supply the word *take*."
63 In the margin: *Tolle de vita.*—Owen. "Take out of life." Owen is referring to an incident, also reported by Erasmus, in which an elderly Roman Catholic priest spoke at the English convocation in support of the burning of heretics. His view was said to have been based on a misreading of the Vulgate text of Titus 3:10, in which *devita* was confused with *de vita*. Thus, the imperative to "avoid" a heretic was taken as a command to "take out of life" (i.e., execute) a heretic. See Erasmus, *The Praise of Folly*, ed. P. S. Allen, trans. John Wilson (Oxford: Clarendon, 1913), 169.
64 Lat. "to the gallows and the lions."
65 In the text: *qua stantes ardent, qui fixo gutture fumant.*—Owen. Juvenal, *Satires* 1.156. For the Latin text and English translation, see *Juvenal and Persius*, 144–45.
66 Perhaps a reference to the Neronian persecution. See Tacitus, *Annals of Imperial Rome* 15.44. For the Latin text and an English translation, see Tacitus, *Annals: Books 13–16*, trans. John Jackson, Loeb Classical Library 322 (Cambridge, MA: Harvard University Press, 1937), 280–83.
67 Gen. 49:6–7. This recalls Jacob's rebuke to Levi and Simeon for their actions in Shechem.

NINE ASSERTIONS REGARDING TOLERATION

Heresy Ought Not to Be Tolerated, Especially in Fundamentals, but Should Be Dealt with by Appropriate Means

1. That heresies and errors ought not to be tolerated: that is, men ought not to connive at, or comply with those ways and opinions, which they are convinced, to be false, erroneous, contrary to sound doctrine, and that form of wholesome words which is delivered unto us,[68] as (next unto Christ) the greatest treasure of our souls: especially if credibly supposed to shake any fundamentals of the common faith: but with all their strength and abilities, in all lawful ways, upon every just call, to oppose, suppress and overthrow them, to root them up, and cast them out, that they may not as noxious weeds and tares overgrow and choke the good corn, among which, they are covertly scattered:[69] all predictions of false Christs, false prophets, false teachers to come, and to be avoided,[70] all cautions to try spirits,[71] avoid heretics, beware of seducers, keep close to the truth received, to hate the doctrine of Nicolaitanes,[72] to avoid endless disputes, strife of words, old fables, languishing about unprofitable questions:[73] the epithets given to, and descriptions made of heresies, that they are pernicious, damnable,[74] cankers,[75] works of the flesh,[76] and the like, are all incitations and encouragements, for the applying of all expedient means, for the taking out of the way these stumbling blocks. Let then the Scriptures be searched, and all ways embraced, which the gospel holds forth, for the discovering, convincing, silencing, reproving, confuting of errors, and persons erring, by admonitions, reproofs, mighty Scripture convictions, evidencing of the truth, with fervent prayers, to Almighty God, the God of truth, that he would give us one heart and one way.[77] And if these weapons of our warfare[78] do not prevail, we must let them know, that one day their disobedience will be revenged with being cut off, and cast out, as unprofitable branches, fit to be cast into the fire.[79]

---

68 1 Tim. 6:3.
69 Owen appears to be conflating language from the parable of the sower and the parable of the wheat and the weeds (Matt. 13: 7, 22, 27–28).
70 Matt. 24:24; 2 Pet. 2:1.
71 1 John 4:1.
72 1 John 2:26; 4:1; Rev. 2:6, 15. *Nicolaitanes* is a term used to describe groups of libertines from Ephesus and Pergamum (Rev. 2:5–6, 15–16).
73 1 Tim. 4:7; 6:4; Titus 3:9.
74 2 Pet. 2:1–2.
75 I.e., cancer (2 Tim. 2:17).
76 Gal. 5:19.
77 Jer. 32:39.
78 2 Cor. 10:4.
79 John 15:6.

The Magistrate May Act against Heresy That Disturbs the Peace or Undermines Lawful Government

2. That any doctrine tending undeniably in its own nature (and not by strained consequences), to the disturbance of the civil state, may be suppressed, by all such means, as are lawfully to be used for the conservation of the peace and safety of the state. Jesus Christ, though accused of sedition, taught none, practiced none, his gospel gives not control to magistracy, righteous laws, or any sort of lawful government established among men: and therefore they whose faith is faction, and whose religion is rebellion,[80] I mean Jesuits and Jesuitical Papists,[81] some of the articles of whose creeds are directly repugnant to the safety, yea, being of any commonwealths, wherein themselves and men of their own persuasion, do not domineer and rule,[82] may be proceeded against by them who bear not the sword in vain.[83] The like may be said of men, seditious under any pretenses whatsoever, like the Anabaptists at Munster.[84]

False Teaching Associated with Immorality or Idolatry Ought to Be Punished More Severely

3. That such heresies or mispersuasions as are attended with any notorious sin in practice (I mean, not in consequences, but owned by their abettors, and practiced accordingly), (beyond Epicurus, whose honest life was not corrupted by his foul dishonest opinion), like the Nicolaitanes, teaching, as most suppose, promiscuous lust, and the Papists', express abominable idolatry,

---

80 This line is from the prayer for November 5 in the prayer book. Henry Burton and William Prynne noted that Archbishop Laud had modified the Powder Plot prayer in the 1635 edition of the prayer book to imply that the Puritans were the enemies of religion and the state. See Henry Burton, *For God, and the King. The Summe of Two Sermons Preached on the Fifth of November* [. . .] (London, 1636), 131; and William Prynne, *A Quench-Coale* [. . .] (London, 1637), 13. See Milton, *Catholic and Reformed*, 91.

81 Jesuits were those associated with the Society of Jesus, founded by Ignatius of Loyola (1491–1556) in 1540.

82 According to Jesuit political theory, the pope, as the spiritual sovereign, had an indirect power that allowed him, when necessary, to intervene in temporal affairs—e.g., in abolishing laws and deposing kings. For a treatment of Bellarmine's view of indirect power as articulated in his *De potestate summi pontificis in rebus temporalibus* [Concerning the power of the supreme pontiff in temporal matters] (Rome, 1610), see Stefania Tutino, *Empire of Souls: Robert Bellarmine and the Christian Commonwealth* (Oxford: Oxford University Press, 2010).

83 Rom. 13:4.

84 The Melchiorite uprising led by the Dutch prophet Jan Matthijs (d. 1534) in the Westphalian city of Münster in 1534–1535. Matthijs believed himself to be one of the witnesses from Revelation 11 and declared Münster to be the New Jerusalem. The fanatical actions practiced by him and his successor, Jan Bockelson (1509–1536) of Leiden, became a byword for religious anarchy.

may be in their authors, more severely punished, than such crimes not owned and maintained do singly deserve.

To pretend conscience in such a case will not avail; "the works of the flesh are manifest,"[85] easy to be discerned, known to all; *Apologies* for such, argue searedness, not tenderness:[86] such "evil communication" as "corrupteth good manners,"[87] is not to be tolerated.

Dissenters Should Not Seek to Undermine the Established Church and Its Ministry

4. No pretenses whatsoever, nor seeming color, should countenance men, dissenting from what is established, to revile, traduce,[88] deride, or otherwise expose to vulgar contempt, by words, or actions, the way owned by authority (if not evidently fallen off from Jehovah to Baal), or fasten bitter uncharitable appellations, on those who act according to that way; that is, the public ministers, and ministry, acknowledged, owned, and maintained by the supreme magistrate, where they both are. Where by the way, I cannot but complain, of want of ingenuity and candid charity in those men, who having a comfortable maintenance arising another way, do yet (*ad faciendum populum*)[89] continually in pulpits, and other public places, inveigh against that way of maintenance, which is allowed by the magistrate,[90] and set apart for those "that labor in the word and doctrine";[91] unto whom I wish no farther evil, but only forced patience, when their neighboring tradesmen, shall have persuaded the people about him, that preachers of the gospel, ought to live by the work of their hands,[92] and so the contribution for their maintenance be subducted.

Such men as these, do show of what spirit they are, and what they would do, if they were lions, seeing they bark so much, being but snarling dogs: and therefore truly, if some severe course were used for the restraint of those, who

---

85 Gal. 5:19.
86 1 Tim. 4:2.
87 1 Cor. 15:33.
88 I.e., to speak badly or falsely about so as to damage the reputation.
89 Lat. "to please the people."
90 Those who opposed the forced maintenance of ministers by payment of tithes included the anonymous *Christs Order, and the Disciples Practice concerning the Ministers Maintenance, and Releeving of the Poore* (1644) and Richard Overton's *The Ordinance of Tythes Dismounted* [. . .] (London, 1645). See Margaret James, "The Political Importance of the Tithes Controversy in the English Revolution, 1640–1660," *History* 26 (1941): 1–8.
91 1 Tim. 5:17.
92 1 Cor. 4:12.

in our days, strive to get themselves a name, and to build up their repute, by slighting, undervaluing, and by all uncharitable malicious ways, rendering odious those from whom they dissent, I should not much intercede for them: these are evil works, fruits of the flesh, evident to all.[93] Now these and such things as these, are acknowledged by all even-spirited men: some few I shall now add; I hope not unlike them. As—

Charity toward Those Who Err in Nonfundamentals

5. That it is a most difficult undertaking, to judge of heresies and heretics, no easy thing, to show what heresy is in general; whether this, or that particular error be a heresy or no, whether it be a heresy in this, or that man: especially if such things, as stubbornness, and pertinacy upon conviction, with the like, be required to make a man a heretic; for such things cannot be evidenced, or made out, but only (for the most part) by most obscure conjectures, and such as will scarcely satisfy a charitable judgment. Papists indeed, who have laid it down for a principle, that a contradiction of the doctrine of the church, known to be so, and continued in after admonition, does infallibly make a man a heretic, are very clear, uniform, and settled in that, which they have made the ground, warrant, and foundation of slaying millions of men, professing the name of Christ: but for all other Christians who acknowledge an infallibility in the rule, but no infallibility in any, for the discovery of the truth of that rule (though exceeding clear and perspicuous in things necessary) for them I say, understanding and keeping close to their own principles, it is a most difficult thing to determine of heresy; with an assurance, that they are so out of danger of erring, in that determination, as to make it a ground of rigorous proceedings, against those, of whom they have so concluded. Some things indeed, are so clearly in the Scripture laid down and determined, that to question or deny them bespeaks a spirit self-condemned in that which he does profess:[94] that twice two, makes four; that he that runs, moves, are not things more evident to reason, than many things in the Scripture are to every captivated understanding: a willful deviation in such, merits no charity. But generally, errors are about things hard to be understood, not so clearly appearing, and concerning which it is very difficult to pass the sentence of heresy. No judge of heresy, since the apostles' days, but has been obnoxious to[95] error in that judgment; and those, who have been forwardest,[96] to assume

93 Gal. 5.
94 Titus 3:11.
95 I.e., liable to.
96 I.e., most extreme.

a judicature, and power of discerning, between truth and error, so as to have others regulated thereby, have erred most foully. Of old, it was generally conceived to be in councils. Now I should acknowledge myself obliged to any man that would direct me to a council, since that, Acts 15, which I may not be forced from the word to assert, that it (in some thing or other) went astray.

Luther feared not to affirm, of the first and best of general synods, that he understood not the Holy Ghost to speak in it: and that the canons thereof, were but plain hay and stubble.[97] Yea and Beza, that such was the folly, ignorance, ambition, wickedness, of many bishops in the best times, that you would suppose the devil to have been president in their assemblies:[98] insomuch as Nazianzen complained that he never saw a good end of any, and affirmed that he was resolved never to come at them more:[99] and in truth, the fightings and brawls, diabolical arts of defamation, and accusing one another, abominable pride, ambition, and affectation of preeminence, which appeared in most of them, did so far prevail, that in the issue they became (as one was entitled)[100] dens of thieves,[101] rather than conventions of humble and meek disciples of Jesus Christ; until at length, the holy dove being departed, an ominous owl overlooked the Lateran fathers; and though with much clamor, they destroyed the appearing fowl, yet the foul spirit of darkness and error,

---

97 In the margin: *Hic prorsus non intelligo Sanctum Spiritum in hoc concilio: hi omnes articuli fœnum stramen, ligna, stipulae fuerunt.* Luth *de conc.*—Owen. Owen once again references Martin Luther's *De conciliis et ecclesia liber* (1539), 91, 122. Luther regarded Council of Nicaea as "the best" after the time of the apostles; nevertheless, when speaking of some of its decision, he said that "here I do not understand the Holy Spirit in this council at all," and he said of many of the articles produced that "they were hay, straw, and wood." For the English translation, see "On the Councils and the Church, 1539," in *Luther's Works*, vol. 41, *Church and Ministry III*, ed. Eric W. Gritsch (Philadelphia: Fortress, 1966), 33, 41–42, 61.

98 In the margin: *In optimis illis temporibus, ea fuit nonnullorum episcoporum, partim ambitio, partim futilitae et ignorantis, etc.* Beza, preefat, ad no. Testa.—Owen. This is drawn from Theodore Beza's "Epistola" to his Latin New Testament, which was first published in 1556 as *Jesu Christi Domini nostri Novum Testamentum sive novum foedus*.

99 In the margin: *Ego, si vera scribere oportet, ita animo affectus sum, ut omnia episcoporum concilia fugia, quoniam nullius concilii finem lactum fastumque vidi: nec quod depulsionem malorum potius quam accessionem et incrementum habuerit.* Greg. Naz. Ep. Ad Procop.—Owen. Owen is citing a letter by Gregory Nazianzus replying to the high official Procopius in order to decline an invitation to participate in another church council. "For my part, if I am to write the truth, my inclination is to avoid all assemblies of bishops, because I have never seen any council come to a good end, nor turn out to be a solution of evils." For the English translation, see "Gregory of Nazianzus: The Futility of Councils, 382," in *Creeds, Councils, and Controversies: Documents Illustrating the History of the Church, AD 337–461*, ed. J. Stevenson (Cambridge: SPCK, 1991), 118.

100 The Second Council of Ephesus (449) was known as the Robber Council (*Latrocinium*). Its decisions were reversed by the Council of Chalcedon (451).

101 See Matt. 21:13.

wrought as effectually in them as ever.¹⁰² But to close this discourse; ignorance of men's invincible prejudices, of their convictions, strong persuasions, desires, aims, hopes, fears, inducements, sensibleness of our own infirmities, failings, misapprehensions, darkness, knowing but in part, should work in us a charitable opinion of poor erring creatures, that do it perhaps with as upright sincere hearts and affections, as some enjoy truth. Austin tells the Manichees,¹⁰³ the most paganish heretics that ever were, that they only raged and were high against them, who knew not what it was, to seek the truth and escape error; with what ardent prayers the knowledge of truth is obtained? And how tender is Salvian in his judgment of the Arians?¹⁰⁴ They are, saith he, "heretics, but know it not: heretics to us, but not to themselves."¹⁰⁵ Nay, they think themselves so catholic, that they judge us to be heretics; what they are to us, that are we to them: they err, but with a good mind, and for this cause God shows patience toward them:¹⁰⁶ Now if any should dissent from what I have before asserted concerning this particular, I would entreat him

---

102 John Foxe records how a "monstrous owl" appeared at a church council in Rome called by the Antipope John XXIII (1410–1415). The appearance of this supposedly Satanic omen was depicted in "The Description of the Pope's Council" woodcut in *Acts and Monuments* [. . .] (London, 1570), 760.

103 In the margin: *Illi in vos saeviunt, qui nesciunt cum quo labore verum inveniatur, et quam difficile caveantur errores*, &c. Aug.—Owen. This is a reference to Augustine's *Contra epistolam Manichaei quam vocant Fundamenti* (397): "Let those rage against you who do not know the labor by which the truth is found and how difficult it is to avoid error." Manichaeism was a movement that was widespread in antiquity. It derived its name from Mani (ca. 216–274), a Persian prophet, and was known for combining different elements from various religions and for a strong dualism between light and darkness. For the Latin text, see Augustine, *Contra epistolam Manichaei quam vocant Fundamenti liber unus*, in *Opera omnia*, ed. J.-P. Migne, Patrologia Latina 42 (Paris: Migne-Garnier, 1865), 174. For the English translation, see "Answer to the Letter of Mani Known as *The Foundation*," in *The Manichean Debate*, ed. Boniface Ramsey, trans. Roland Teske, *The Works of Saint Augustine: A Translation for the 21st Century* (Hyde Park, NY: New City Press, 2006), 234.

104 In fifth-century Roman Gaul, Salvian, the presbyter of Marseilles, urged toleration toward the Arians because they were unwitting heretics.

105 This is a quotation from Salvian, *De gubernatione Dei* (On the government of God) 5.2. For the Latin text, see Salvian, *De gubernatione Dei*, in *Opera omnia*, ed. J.-P. Migne, Patrologia Latina 53 (Paris: Migne-Garnier, 1865), 95. The English translation in the text is Owen's. For the English text, see *The Governance of God*, in *The Writings of Salvian, the Presbyter*, trans. Jeremiah F. O'Sullivan, Fathers of the Church 3 (Washington, DC: Catholic University of America Press, 1962), 130.

106 In the margin: *Apud nos sunt haeretici, apud se non sunt,—quod ergo illi nobis sunt, hoc nos illis*, &c. Salv. de Prov. &c.—Owen. Owen is continuing to quote from Salvian: "With us they are heretics, but in their own opinion they are not. . . . What they are to us, therefore, we are to them." For the Latin text, see *De gubernatione Dei*, 95. For the English translation, see *Governance of God*, 130.

to lay down some notes, whereby heresies may infallibly be discerned to be such, and he shall not find me repugning.

The Golden Rule Should Guide All Undertakings

6. That great consideration ought to be had, of that sovereign dictate of nature, the sum of all moral duties, *Quod tibi fieri non vis, alteri ne feceris*;[107] "Do not that unto others, which you would not have done to you, were you in the same condition with them," in the business in hand, we are supposed by others, to be in that estate, wherein we suppose those to be, of whom we speak: those others being to us, what we are to them: now truly if none of the former inconveniences, and iniquities, which we recounted (assertion 2, 3, 4) or the like, do accompany erring persons, it will be something difficult to make it appear, how we may, if enjoying authority over them, impose any coercion, restraint or punishment on them, which we would not acknowledge to be justly laid on us by others (supposing it should be laid), having authority over us, convinced that our persuasion differing from them, is false and erroneous. No sort of Christians but are heretics and schismatics to some Christians in authority; and it may be their lot, to live under the power and jurisdiction of men so persuaded of them; where they ought to expect, that the same measure will be given unto them, which in other places, they have consented to mete out to others.¶[108]

Yea, but men will say, and all men pleading the cause of nontoleration in its full extent, do say, that they are heretics, and erroneous persons, whom we do oppose: we ourselves are orthodox, and no law of nature, no dictate of the Scripture requires, that we should think it just, to render unto them that are orthodox, as unto them that are heretics, seducers, and false teachers; because thieves are punished, shall honest men fear, that they shall be so too?¶

But a thief is a thief in all the world, unto all men: in opinions it is not so: he is a heretic, that is to be punished: but to whom? In whose judgment? In his own? No more than we are in ours: but he is so to them that judge him: true! Put [the] case, a Protestant were to be judged by a Papist, as a thousand saints have been; is he not the worst of heretics to his judge? These things turn in a circle: what we are to ourselves, that he is to himself: what he is to us, that we are unto others that may be our judges.¶

But however, you will say, we are in the truth, and therefore ought to go free; now truly this is the same paralogism:[109] who says we are in the truth?

---

107 A negative version of the Golden Rule.
108 The ¶ symbol indicates that a paragraph break has been added to Owen's original text.
109 I.e., a piece of illogical or fallacious reasoning.

Others? No: ourselves? Who says erroneous persons (as so supposed), are heretics, or the like? They themselves? No, but we: and those that are to us, as we are to them, say no less of us. Let us not suppose that all the world will stoop to us, because we have the truth, as we affirm, but they do not believe: if we make the rule of our proceedings against others, to be our conviction that they are erroneous; others will, or may make theirs of us, to be their rule of proceeding against us. We do thus to them, because we so judge of them: will not others, who have the same judgment of us, as we of them, do the like unto us? ¶

Now here I profess that I do not desire to extend anything in this discourse, to the patronizing of any error whatsoever, I mean anything, so commonly esteemed in the Reformed churches, as myself owning any such: much less, to the procuring of a licentious immunity, for everyone in his way: and least of all, to countenance men walking disorderly in any regard, especially in the particulars before recounted; but only to show how warily, and upon what sure principles, that cannot be retorted on us, we ought to proceed, when any severity is necessarily required, in case of great danger: and how in lesser things, if the unity of faith may in some comfortable measure be kept, then to assert the proposition, in its full latitude, urging and pleading for Christian forbearance, even in such manner to be granted, as we would desire it from them, whom we do forbear; for truly in those disputable things, we must acknowledge ourselves in the same series with other men, unless we can produce express patents for our exemptions; but some perhaps will say, that even in such things as these, Gamaliel's counsel is not good;[110] better all go on with punishing that can; truth will not be suppressed, but error will; Good God! Was not truth oppressed by anti-Christian tyranny? Was not outward force the engine that for many generations kept truth in corners? But of this afterward.

Now I am mistaken, if this principle, that the civil magistrate ought to condemn, suppress, and persecute, everyone that he is convinced to err, though in smaller things, do not at length, in things of greater importance, make Christendom a very theatre of bloody murders, killing, slaying, imprisoning men round in a compass; until the strongest becomes dictator to the rest, and he alone be supposed to have infallible guidance, all the rest to be heretics, because overcome and subdued (when I speak of death and killing in this discourse, I understand not only forcible death itself, but that also which is equivalent thereunto, as banishment, or perpetual imprisonment),

---

110 Acts 5:38–39.

I had almost said, that it is the interest of mortality, to consent generally to the persecution of a man, maintaining such a destructive opinion.

Heresy Does Not Necessarily Amount to Blasphemy

7. That whatsoever restraint, or other punishment may be allowed in case of grosser errors, yet slaying of heretics for simple heresy, as they call it, for my part, I cannot close withal: nor shall ever give my vote to the burning, hanging, or killing of a man, otherwise upright, honest, and peaceable in the state, merely because he misbelieves any point of Christian faith. Let what pretenses you please, be produced, or colors flourished, I should be very unwilling, to pronounce the sentence of blood, in the case of heresy. I do not intend here to dispute: but if anyone will, upon Protestant principles, and Scripture grounds, undertake to assert it, I promise (if God grant me life) he shall not want a convert, or an antagonist. I know the usual pretenses; such a thing is blasphemy: but search the Scripture; look upon the definitions of divines, and by all men's consent, you will find heresy, in what head of religion soever it be, and blasphemy properly so called, to be exceedingly distant. Let a blasphemer, undergo the law of blasphemy: but yet I think we cannot be too cautious, how we place men in that damnable series, calling heaven and earth to witness the contrary: but again, to spread such, errors will be destructive to souls: so are many things, which yet are not punishable with forcible death; let him that thinks so, go kill Pagans and Mohammedans: as such heresy is a canker, but a spiritual one; let it be prevented by spiritual means: cutting off men's heads is no proper remedy for it: if state physicians think otherwise, I say no more, but that I am not of the college, and what I have already said, I submit to better judgments.

Many Who Were Punished as Heretics Were Actually Martyrs for the Truth

8. It may be seriously considered upon a view of the state and condition of Christians, since their name was known in the world, whether this doctrine of punishing erring persons with death, imprisonment, banishment, and the like, under the name of heretics, has not been as useful and advantageous for error, as truth; nay, whether it has not appeared the most pernicious invention that ever was broached: in the first, second, and third ages, we hear little of it; nothing for it; something against it:[111] much afterward against it, in Austin and

---

111 In the margin: Τοὺς μισοῦντας τὸν Θεὸν, μισεῖν χρὴ καὶ ὑμᾶς, καὶ ἐπὶ τοῖς ἐχθροῖς αὐτοῦ ἐκτήκεσθαι· οὐ μὴν καὶ τύπτειν αὐτοὺς ἢ διώκειν, καθὼς τὰ ἔθνη τὰ μὴ εἰδότα τὸν Κύριον καὶ Θεὸν, ἀλλ' ἐχθροὺς μὲν ἡγεῖσθαι καὶ χωρίζεσθαι ἀπ' αὐτῶν. Ignat. Epist. ad Philad.—Owen.

others. Marlinus, the famous French bishop,[112] rejected the communion of a company of his associate bishops, because they had consented, with Maximus the emperor,[113] unto the death of the Priscillianists, as vile heretics as ever breathed.[114] At the end of the fourth and beginning of the fifth century, when the Arians and orthodox had successively procured the supreme magistrate to join with them, men were killed and dismembered like beasts: banishments, imprisonments, plunderings, especially by the Arians were as frequent, as in new subdued kingdoms:[115] but never was this tragedy so acted to the life, as by the worshipers of images on the one side, and their adversaries on the other:[116] which difference rose about the year 130,[117] and was carried on with that barbarous outrage on both sides, especially by the *Iconolatrae*[118] (as the

---

This is quotation from Ignatius of Antioch's *Epistolae ad Philadelphenses* 3. "You ought therefore to 'hate those that hate God, and to waste away [with grief] on account of His enemies.' I do not mean that you should beat them or persecute them, as do the Gentiles 'that know not the Lord and God;' but you should regard them as your enemies, and separate yourselves from them." This is from the longer version of the epistle that is not regarded as part of the authentic text. For the Greek text, see Ignatius, *Epistolae*, ed. J.-P. Migne, Patrologia Graeca 5 (Paris: Migne-Garnier, 1857), 821. For the English translation, see *The Epistle of Ignatius to the Philadelphians: Shorter and Longer Versions*, in *Ante-Nicene Fathers*, 1:80.

112 Martin, bishop of Tours (316–397).

113 Maximus was Roman emperor in the western portion of the empire from 383 to 388.

114 Priscillian was burned at the stake in 385. Although opposed to the doctrinal errors of the Priscillian sect, Martin of Tours did not support the principle of putting heretics to death.

115 Owen is referring to events in North Africa when the anti-Nicene Vandals persecuted the catholic Christians. King Huneric (r. 477–484) removed many orthodox bishops, giving them a choice between conversion to Arianism or exile. During this persecution, thousands of Nicene Christians were exiled, and some were tortured. With the Byzantine conquest, Justinian established catholicism as the imperial church, and the Vandals were expelled. The Byzantine emperors also vigorously persecuted the Monophysites.

116 In the margin: Theophanes. *Histor. Miscel.* lib. 22. cap. 30.—Owen. This is a reference to the *Chronographia* of Theophanes the Confessor (d. 818), a Byzantine abbot and iconodule who fell victim to the iconoclastic persecution. Owen cites Theophanes, *Chronicle* AM 6253 [AD 760/61] as it is found in Book 22 of *Historia Romana*, the compilation of Paul the Deacon, continued by Landolfus Sagax, which itself was often known as *Historia Miscella* (the title of the Basel edition of 1569). For a modern English translation of Theophanes, see *The Chronicle of Theophanes Confessor: Byzantine and New Eastern History, AD 284–813*, trans. Cyril Mango and Roger Scott, with Geoffrey Greatrex (Oxford: Clarendon, 1997), 597–98. This example had been employed by Joseph Mede, who provided a short summary of how the iconoclast emperor Constantine V (718–775) ordered that Andrew Kalybites be scourged to death in the Hippodrome of St. Mamas (761/762). See Mede, *The Apostasy of the Latter Times* [. . .] (London, 1644), 149–50.

117 The correct year is 730.

118 I.e., image worshipers (also known as *iconodules* or *image servants*). Sometime between 726 and 730, the Byzantine Emperor Leo III issued an edict forbidding the making or venerating of religious images. This led to the destruction of icons and the persecution of iconodules with Leo's son, Constantine V, executing a number of iconodule martyrs (the first of whom is thought to be

worst, were ever best at such proceedings), as is wonderful to consider. Now excepting only those idolatrous heretics in the last, who were paid home in their own coin, for a thousand years together this doctrine was put in practice, against none almost, but the martyrs of Jesus. The Roman stories of the killing of heretics, are all martyrologies, thousands slain for heretics, now lie under the altar, crying for vengeance,[119] and shall one day sit upon thrones, judging their judges:[120] so that where one man has suffered for an error, under the name of a heretic, five hundred under the same notion, have suffered for truth (a principle would seem more befitting Christians, to spare five hundred for the saving of one guiltless person). Truth has felt more of the teeth of this scorpion than error.[121] And clearly it grew up by degrees with the whole mystery of iniquity,[122] in the gospel we have nothing like it; the acts of Christ purging the temple, Peter pronouncing the fate of Ananias,[123] and Paul smiting Elymas with blindness,[124] seem to me heterogeneous. The first laws of Constantine speak liberty and freedom.[125] Pecuniary mulcts[126] afterward were added, and general edicts against all sects, and so it is put over into the hands of the Arians, who exceedingly cherished it:[127] yet for a good while

---

Andrew Kalybites). Owen's view of the particular persecuting zeal manifest by the iconodules is representative of the English Protestant understanding articulated in the homily "Against Peril of Idolatrie" from the *Second Tome of Homilies* (1563). The three-part homily describes Empress Irene's reintroduction of images and her posthumous public condemnation of her iconoclast father-in-law, Constantine V, whose remains she had exhumed, burned, and thrown into the sea. In this version of the history, elements of which are contested by modern historians, Irene is presented as an infamously wicked and unnaturally cruel ruler who betrayed the Eastern Church's laudable iconoclasm. During her son's minority, she orchestrated the Second Council of Nicaea (787), which affirmed the use of images and ordered the confiscation of iconoclastic writings. Eventually she was said to have had her own son executed and so became sole ruler until she herself was deposed. See Gerald Bray ed., *The Book of Homilies: A Critical Edition* (Cambridge: James Clarke., 2015), 242–44; Margaret Aston, *England's Iconoclasts* (Oxford: Clarendon, 1988), 52, 56.

119 Rev. 6:9–10.
120 Rev. 20:4.
121 Rev. 9:10–19.
122 2 Thess. 2:7.
123 Acts 5:5.
124 Acts 13:11.
125 In the margin: Eusebius, vit. Const. l. 2. c. 27.—Owen. Owen appears to be referring to Eusebius, *Vita Constantini* 2.20. For the text, see Eusebius, *Life of Constantine*, trans. Averil Cameron and Stuart G. Hall (Oxford: Clarendon, 1999), 102–3.
126 A mulct was a punishment which could be monetary (pecuniary, as it is here) or corporal. For Constantine's suppression of the sects after the Council of Nicaea, see the discussion by Cameron and Hall in *Life of Constantine*, 306–7.
127 Owen probably has in mind Emperor Valens (364–378), who engaged in persecution of Nicene Christians (371–373).

pretenses must be sought out.[128] Eustathius of Antioch,[129] must be accused of adultery, Athanasius of sedition, magic, and I know not what,[130] that a color might be had for their persecution. The Arian kings in Africa, were the first that owned it, γυμνῇ κεφαλῇ,[131] and acted according to their persuasions:[132] methinks I hear the cries of poor dismembered, mangled creatures, for the faith of the Holy Trinity.[133] Next to these through a few civil constitutions of some weak emperors, it wholly comes to reside in the hands of the pope, kings and princes are made his executioners, and he plays his game to the purpose. Single persons serve not this Bel and dragon,[134] whole nations must be slaughtered, that he may be drunk with blood.[135] He sends whole armies

128 In the margin: Socrat. Evang. Rufinus. Zozom.—Owen. Owen is referring to the works of three fifth-century historians and their accounts of the persecution of the orthodox by Valens: Socrates of Constantinople "Scholasticus," Rufinus of Aquileia, and Sozomen (Salamanes Hermias Sozomenos). See Socrates, *Ecclesiastical History* 4.16–21 in *Nicene and Post-Nicene Fathers*, Second Series, ed. Philip Schaff and Henry Wace, 14 vols. (1890–1900; repr. Peabody: Hendrickson, 2004), 2:104–5; Sozomen, *Ecclesiastical History* 6.10–20 in *Nicene and Post-Nicene Fathers*, Second Series, 2:352–57; Rufinus, *Church History* 11.2–5 in his *History of the Church*, trans. Philip R. Amidon, Fathers of the Church 133 (Washington, DC: Catholic University of America, 2016), 435–40.

129 The deposition of Eustathius, bishop of Antioch, marked the beginning of moves against supporters of Nicaea. Eusebius of Nicomedia had him condemned as an adulterer based on the uncorroborated claims of a woman that Eustathius had fathered her child. See Socrates, *Ecclesiastical History* 1.24; Sozomen, *Ecclesiastical History* 2.19; and Rufinus, *Church History* 10.31. For the texts by Socrates and Sozomen, see their respective histories in *Nicene and Post-Nicene Fathers*, Second Series, 2:27–28, 270–71. For the treatment by Rufinus, see *History of the Church*, 424–46.

130 Having removed Eustathius, the Arians brought wide-ranging charges against Athanasius before the Emperor. See Socrates, *Ecclesiastical History* 1.27; Sozomen, *Ecclesiastical History* 2.28; and Rufinus, *History of the Church* 10.16. For texts by Socrates and Sozomen, see their respective histories in *Nicene and Post-Nicene Fathers*, Second Series, 2:29–30, 278–79. For the treatment by Rufinus, see *History of the Church*, 407–8.

131 Gk. lit. "bareheaded," meaning "without shame."

132 The Vandal kings of North Africa, particularly Huneric and the persecution of 484.

133 John Coffey suggests that this may echo John Milton's *Areopagitica* (1644). See John Coffey, "John Owen and the Puritan Toleration Controversy, 1646–1659," in *The Ashgate Research Companion to John Owen's Theology*, ed. Kelly M. Kapic and Mark Jones (Farnham, UK: Ashgate, 2012), 232.

134 The story of Bel and the Dragon is found in the apocryphal additions to the book of Daniel. It told of thieving priests, a false idol, and the worship of a dragon who would soon be destroyed.

135 In the margin: Albigenses. Waldenses. Bohemians.—Owen. Through the works of John Bale and John Foxe, many English Protestants came to view the Waldensians (named after the founder, Pierre Vaudès, or Peter Waldo, of Lyons), the Albigenses of southern France (named after the town of Albi), and the Hussites of Bohemia (followers of Jan Hus, condemned to death at the Council of Constance in 1415) as forerunners of the Reformation, not least because of the persecution that these sects endured after being driven into separation by the Roman Church in the same way that Protestants believed they had been. See Euan Cameron, "Medieval Heretics as Protestant Martyrs," *Studies in Church History* 30 (1993): 185–207.

to crucify Christ afresh,[136] he gives every one of his soldiers a cross:[137] hence followed cruel sights, bloody battles, wasting of kingdoms, raging against the names, ashes, sepulchers of the dead, with more than heathenish cruelty,[138] such evil fruits have this bitter root sent forth, the streams of this fountain have all been blood: so that it cannot be denied, but that a judicature[139] of truth, and the contrary assumed, with a forcible backing of the sentence, was the bottom stone in the foundation, and highest in the corner of the tower of Babel; and I believe that upon search it will appear, that error has not been advanced by anything in the world so much, as by usurping a power for its suppression. In divers contests that the pope had with others, the truth was on his side (as in the business of Athanasius, and others in the East deposed by the Arians)[140] now who would not have thought, that his standing up with all earnestness for the truth, would not have been the ruin of the devil's kingdom of darkness, and almost have spoiled the plot of the mystery of iniquity, when the truth is, the largest steps that ever the man of sin took toward his throne,[141] was by usurping of power to suppress errors and heresies. It would be a great encouragement to use that way for the extirpation of errors (if any such be, besides the preaching of the gospel, and convictions from thence), which anyone could produce and give assurance, that it has not been tried, or been tried and proved ineffectual for the supplantation of truth, and if such a way be not produced, what if both should grow together until harvest?[142]

Take Care Not to Equate Heresy with Sedition

9. Let us not be too hasty in pressing any opinion arising and divulged with odious consequences, of sedition, turbulency, and the like, because tumults and troubles happen in the commonwealth, where it is asserted; a coincidence

---

136 Heb. 6:6.
137 E.g., those who vowed to go on crusade were given a cross from the pope and pronounced soldiers of the cross. Jonathan Riley-Smith, "The State of Mind of Crusaders to the East, 1095–1300," in *The Oxford History of the Crusades*, ed. Jonathan Riley-Smith (Oxford: Oxford University Press, 1999), 69–72.
138 For example, Owen may have been thinking of the exhumation of the iconoclast emperor Constantine V, the grave of John Wyclif (d. 1384) being opened and his ashes thrown on the river Swift (1427), or how, in Cambridge, the bones of Martin Bucer (1491–1551) and Paul Fagius (ca. 1504–1549) were disinterred and burned at the stake in an act of posthumous humiliation (1557).
139 I.e., the action of judging.
140 In the margin: Soc. L. 2. c. 11.—Owen. This is a reference to Socrates, *Ecclesiastical History* 2.11. It records how Athanasius, having been forced to flee Alexandria, found refuge in Rome. See *Ecclesiastical History*, in *Nicene and Post-Nicene Fathers*, Second Series, 2:40.
141 2 Thess. 2:3–4, 7.
142 Matt. 13:30.

of events, is one of the principal causes of error and misjudgings in the world, because errors and tumults arise together, therefore one is the cause of the other, may be an argument, *a baculo ad angulum*.[143] It is a hard thing to charge them with sedition who protest against it: and none can make it appear that it is *contraria factis*,[144] by any of their actions, but only because it is fit they should bear the blame of what happens evilly in their days: upon every disaster in the empire, the noise of old was,[145] *Christianos ad leones*;[146] for our part, we ought to remember that we were strangers in Egypt,[147] it is but little more than a hundred years since all mouths were opened and filled with reproaches against that glorious Reformation, wherein we rejoice. Was it not the unanimous voice of all the adversaries thereof, that a new religion was brought in, tending to the immediate ruin of all states and commonwealths, attended with rebellion, the mother of sedition?[148] Have we not frequent apologies of our divines, for the confutation of such false, malicious and putid criminations?[149] It is true indeed, the light of the gospel breaking out, was accompanied with war and not peace (according to the prediction of our Savior) whereof the gospel was no more the cause, than John Diazius was

---

143 Lat. "from the staff to the corner." This phrase is used to describe the type of logical fallacy exemplified by the claim that because a stick stands in the corner today, therefore tomorrow it will rain.

144 Lat. "contrary to the facts."

145 In the margin: Arnob.—Owen. This is a reference to Arnobius of Sicca (d. ca. 330), an apologist during the reign of Diocletian (284–305), who explained how the Christians were blamed for natural catastrophes in *Against the Pagans* 1.1, 7. For the English text, see *Arnobius: The Case Against the Pagans*, trans. George E. McCracken, Ancient Christian Writers 6 (Westminster, MD: Newman, 1949), 58–59, 65.

146 Lat. "the Christians to the lions." This is a quotation from Tertullian's *Apologeticus* 39.2. For the Latin text and English translation, see Tertullian, *Apology*, in Tertullian, Minucius Felix, *Apology. De Spectaculis. Minucius Felix: Octavius*, trans. T. R. Glover and Gerald H. Rendall, Loeb Classical Library 250 (Cambridge, MA: Harvard University Press, 1931), 182–83.

147 Ex. 22:21; Lev. 19:34; Deut. 10:19.

148 A reference to anti-Protestant rhetoric that began during the Henrician Reformation of the 1530s. During the Marian Counter Reformation (1553–1558), Protestants were classed as adherents of a "new religion," and their doctrine was spoken of as "the readiest way to stir up sedition, and trouble the quiet of the Commonwealth." See the record of the "Conference" between Nicholas Ridley (ca. 1502–1555) and Hugh Latimer (ca. 1485–1555), in which they prepared to face interrogation by Stephen Gardiner (ca. 1495–1555), Bishop of Winchester and Lord Chancellor, in *The Works of Nicholas Ridley*, ed. Henry Christmas (Cambridge: University Press, 1841), 143.

149 See, e.g., the Marian exile John Jewel (1522–1571), who was appointed bishop of Salisbury on his return and then penned his *Apologia pro ecclesiae Anglicanae* [Apology for the church of England] (London, 1562). It was followed by *A Defence of the "Apologie of the Churche of England"* (London, 1567). One of the charges which Jewel sought to answer was that Protestantism destroyed civil authority and obedience to the magistrate.

of that horrible murder, when his brains were chopped out with an axe by his brother Alphonsus, because he professed the gospel.¹⁵⁰ Hence Luther, the vehemency of whose spirit gave no way to glosses and temporizing excuses, plainly affirms those tumults to be such necessary appendixes of the preaching of the gospel, that he should not believe the word of God to be abroad in the world, if he saw it not accompanied with tumults, which he had rather partake in, than perish under the wrath of God in an eternal tumult:¹⁵¹ the truth must go on, though thereby the world should be reduced to its primitive chaos and confusion. Were it not a perpetual course, for men of every persuasion to charge sedition and the like, upon that which they would have suppressed, knowing that no name is more odious unto them who have power to effect their desire; and did I not find that some, who have had much ado, while they were sheep, to keep off that imputation from themselves, within a few years, becoming lions, have laid it home upon others, as peaceable as they, I might perhaps be more rigid than now these discoveries will suffer me to be: far be it from me to apologize for truth itself, if seditious; only I abhor those false, malicious criminations, whereby God's people in these days wherein we live, have exceedingly suffered. It has pleased God, so to order things in this kingdom, that the work of recovering his worship to its purity, and restoring the civil state to its liberty, should be both carried on at the same time by the same persons; are there none now in this kingdom, to whom this reforming is an almost everting of God's worship? And are there none that have asserted that our new religion has caused all those tumults and bloodshed? And does not every unprejudiced man see, that these are hellish lies and malicious accusations, having indeed neither ground nor color, but only their coincidence in respect of time? Is any wise man moved

---

150 In the margin: Sleid. Com.—Owen. This is a reference to the Lutheran historian Johannes Sleidanus (1506–1556) and his *De statu religionis et reipublicae, Carolo Quinto, Caesare, commentarii* [*Commentaries on the State of Religion and the Empire under Charles V*] (Strasbourg, 1555), 1.17. Juan Díaz converted to Protestantism, and when his brother, Alfonso, a lawyer for the papal curia, was unable to persuade him to abandon Protestantism, he had him murdered by one of his servants in Neuburg-on-Danube (1546). For the account of the incident, see the translation by John Dawes, *A Famous Cronicle of Oure Time* [. . .] (London, 1560), 235.

151 In the margin: *Ego nisi istos tumultus viderem, verbum Dei in mundo non esse dicerem* [. . .] *Praeligimus temporali tumultu collidi . . . quam aeterno tumultu sub ira Dei* [. . .] *conteri. Luth. de Ser. Ar c. 32, 33, 34.*—Owen. This is a reference to Martin Luther, *De servo arbitrio* (1525). For the Latin text, see *D. Martin Luthers Werke, kritische Gesamtausgabe* (Weimar: Hermann Böhlau und Nachfolger, 1883–2009), 18:625–26. For an English translation of the wider context, see *The Bondage of the Will: A New Translation of "De servo arbitrio" (1525); Martin Luther's Reply to Erasmus of Rotterdam*, trans. J. I. Packer and O. R. Johnston (Cambridge: James Clarke, 1957), 90–92.

with their clamors? Are their aspersions considerable? Are we the only men that have been thus injuriously traduced? Remember the difference between Elijah and Ahab:[152] what was laid to the charge of Paul;[153] see the apologies of the old Christians, and speak what you find.

Much might here be added concerning the qualifications, carriages, humility, peaceableness, of erring persons: all which ought to be considered, and our proceedings toward them to be, if not regulated, yet much swayed by such considerations. Some I have known myself, that I daresay the most curious inquirer into their ways, that sees with eyes of flesh, would not be able to discover anything, but mere conviction and tenderness of conscience, that causes them to own the opinions, which different from others they do embrace. Others again so exceeding supercilious, scorning, proud, selfish, so given to contemning[154] of all others, reviling and undervaluing of their adversaries, that the blindest pity cannot but see much carnalness and iniquity in their ways. These things then deserve to be weighed, all passion and particular interest being set aside. And then, if the die be cast, and we must forward, let us take along with us these two cautions.

TWO CONCLUDING WORDS OF CAUTION

1. So to carry ourselves in all our censures, everyone in his sphere (ecclesiastical discipline being preserved as pure and unmixed from secular power as possible), that it may appear to all, that it is the error which men maintain, which is so odious unto us, and not the consequent or their Dissent from us, whether by subducting themselves from our power, or withdrawing from communion; for if this latter be made the cause of our proceeding against any, there must be one law for them all, all that will not bow to the fiery furnace:[155] recusancy[156] is the fault, and that being the same in all, must have the same punishment: which would be such an unrighteous inequality, as is fit for none, but Antichrist to own.

2. That nothing be done to any, but that the bound and farthest end of it be seen at the beginning, and not leave way and room for new persecution

---

152 Ahab accused Elijah of being a troubler of Israel (1 Kings 18:17).
153 Paul was accused of being "a mover of sedition" (Acts 24:5 KJV).
154 I.e., treating with contempt.
155 Dan. 3:11.
156 I.e., the act of recusing oneself from the worship services of the national church. The recusancy laws dated from the Elizabethan Act of Settlement and were a set of civil laws used against Roman Catholics and other Dissenters. The penalties included stiff fines and imprisonment.

upon new pretenses: "Give me another and another,"[157] one stripe sometimes makes way for another, and how know I that men will stay at thirty-nine?[158] "Resist beginnings."[159]

THREE QUESTIONS TO BE ANSWERED BY THOSE WHO FAVOR RELIGIOUS COERCION

All these things being considered, I cannot so well close with them, who make the least allowance of Dissent, to be the mother of abominations; words and hated phrases, may easily be heaped up to a great number, to render anything odious, which we have a mind to oppose: but the proving of an imposed evil or absurdity, is sometimes a labor too difficult for every undertaker. And so I hope I have said enough to warrant my own hesitancy in this particular. Some might now expect, that I should here positively set down what is my judgment concerning errors and erroneous persons, dissenting from the truth, received and acknowledged by authority, with respect unto their toleration: unto whom I answer, that to consider the power of the magistrate about things of religion, and over consciences; the several restraints that have been used in this case, or are pleaded for; the difference between dangerous fundamental errors, and others; the several interests of men, and ways of disengaging; the extent of communion, and the absolute necessity of a latitude to be allowed in some things; with such other things as would be requisite for a full handling of the matter in hand, ask a longer discourse, and more exactness, than the few hours allotted to this appendix can afford: only for the present I ask, if any will take the pains to inform me.

1. What they mean by a nontoleration; whether only a not countenancing nor holding communion with them; or if crushing and punishing them, then how? To what degree? By what means? Where they will undoubtedly bound?

---

[157] In the text: *cedo alteram et alteram.*—Owen. This is a quotation from Tacitus, *Annals* 1.23. This is an account of a centurion named Lucilius, who was infamous for calling out for another vine staff when he had broken one while beating one of his soldiers. For the Latin text and an English translation, see Tacitus, *Histories: Books 4–5. Annals: Books 1–3*, trans. Clifford H. Moore, Loeb Classical Library 249 (Cambridge, MA: Harvard University Press, 1931), 284–85.

[158] The law had forbidden more than forty lashes (Deut. 25:1–3), but the later Jews, for fear of transgressing this limit, opted to administer thirty-nine lashes (2 Cor. 11:24).

[159] In the text: *Principiis obsta.*—Owen. This is a quotation from Ovid's *Remedia amoris* (*The Remedies for Love*) 91. For the Latin text and English translation, see Ovid, *Art of Love. Cosmetics. Remedies for Love. Ibis. Walnut-tree. Sea Fishing. Consolation*, trans. J. H. Mozley, rev. G. P. Goold, Loeb Classical Library 232 (Cambridge, MA: Harvard University Press, 1929), 184–85.

2. What the error is concerning which the inquiry is made? The clear opposition thereof to the word of God, the danger of it, the repugnancy that is in it to peace, quietness, and the power of godliness?

3. What, or who are the erring persons? How they walk? In what manner of conversation? What is their behavior toward others, not of their own persuasion? What gospel means have been used for their conviction? What may be supposed to be their prejudices, motives, interests, and the like?

And then, if it be worth asking, I shall not be backward to declare my opinion. And truly without the consideration of these things, and other such circumstances, how a right judgment can be passed in this case I see not. And so hoping the courteous reader will look with a candid eye upon these hasty lines, rather poured out than written, and consider that a day's pains in these times may serve for that, which is but for a day's use, the whole is submitted to his judgment, by him, who professes his all in this kind, to be, the love of truth and peace.

FINIS.[160]

---

[160] Lat. "The End."

EBENEZER

*A Memorial of the Deliverance of
Essex, County, and Committee,
Being an Exposition of the First Ten Verses
of the Third Chapter of the Prophecy of
Habakkuk in Two Sermons. The First Preached
at Colchester before His Excellency on a Day
of Thanksgiving for the Surrender Thereof.
The Other at Rumford unto the Committee
Who Were Imprisoned by the Enemy Sep. 28.
A Day Set Apart unto Thanksgiving
for Their Deliverance.*

———

The righteous man is delivered out of trouble,
and the wicked cometh in his stead.

PROV. 11. 18

———

By John Owen pastor of the church
of God which is at Coggeshall

———

London, printed by W. Wilson,
for the author, 1648.
To his excellency Thomas Lord Fairfax, &c.

[Dedications]

SIR,[1]

Almighty God having made you the instrument, of that deliverance and peace, which in the county of Essex, we do enjoy, next to his own goodness, the remembrance thereof is due unto your name. "Those who honour him, he will honour, and those who despise him shall be lightly esteemed" (1 Sam. 2:30). Part of these ensuing sermons, being preached before your excellency, and now by providence called forth to public view, I am emboldened to dedicate them unto your name, as a small mite of that abundant thankfulness, wherein all peace-loving men of this county stand obliged unto you.

It was the custom of former days, in the provinces of the Roman Empire, to erect statues and monuments of grateful remembrance, to those presidents and governors, who in the administration of their authority, behaved themselves with wisdom, courage, and fidelity.[2] Yea instruments of great deliverances and blessings, through corrupted nature's folly, became the pagans' deities.

There is scarce a county in this kingdom wherein and not one from which, your excellency has not deserved a more lasting monument, than ever was erected of Corinthian brass:[3] but if the Lord be pleased, that your worth shall dwell only in the praises of his people, it will be your greater glory, that being the place, which himself has chosen to inhabit.[4] Now for a testification of this, is this only intended; beyond this, toward men, God pleading for you, you need nothing but our silence. The issue of the last engagements, whereunto you were called,

---

1 The correct reference for the Scripture quotation on the title page is Prov. 11:8.
2 In the margin: *Lubens meritoque*.—Owen. I.e., an inscription formula, often abbreviated as *l.m.* used in paying a vow "with pleasure and deservedly."
3 I.e., a highly valued metal alloy in classical antiquity, said to be composed of gold, silver, and copper.
4 Ps. 22:3.

and enforced, answering, yea outgoing your former undertakings, giving ample testimony of the continuance of God's presence, with you, in your army, having stopped the mouths of many gainsayers,[5] and called to the residue in the language of the dumb-speaking Egyptian hieroglyphic, Ὦ γενόμενοι καὶ ἀπογινόμενοι, Θεὸς μισεῖ ἀναίδειαν,[6] "Men of all sorts know, that God hateth impudence."[7]

It was said of the Romans in the raising of their empire, that they were "often overcome in battles but never in war";[8] so naked has the bow of God been made for your assistance,[9] that you have failed neither in battle nor war.

Truly had not our eyes beheld the rise, and fall, of this latter storm, we could not have been persuaded that the former achievements of the army under your conduct, could have been paralleled.[10] But he who always enabled them to outdo not only others, but themselves, has in this carried them out, to outdo, whatever before himself had done by them, that they might show more kindness and faithfulness, in the latter end, than in the beginning. The weary ox, treads hard.[11] Dying bites, are often desperate. Half-ruined Carthage, did more perplex Rome, than when it was entire.[12] Hydra's heads (in the fable) were increased by their loss; and every new stroke begat a new opposition.[13] Such seemed the late tumultuating of the exasperated party in this nation.

5   I.e., disagreeable persons who contradict or deny what is said.
6   In the margin: Plut. De Iside et Osir.—Owen. This is a reference to Plutarch's *Isis and Osiris* 32. For the text, see Plutarch, *Moralia*, vol. 5, *Isis and Osiris. The E at Delphi. The Oracles at Delphi No Longer Given in Verse. The Obsolescence of Oracles*, trans. Frank Cole Babbitt, Loeb Classical Library 306 (Cambridge, MA: Harvard, 1936), 78–81.
7   Samuel Parker made a sarcastic reference to this in *A Defence and Continuation of the Ecclesiastical Politie* [. . .] (London, 1671), 628.
8   In the text: *saepe praelio victi, bello nunquam.*—Owen. According to Lucilius of Suessa Aurunca, *Satires* 26.708–9, this is what Florus had said of Rome. For text and translation, see *Remains of Old Latin*, vol. 3 *Lucilius. The Twelve Tables*, trans. E. H. Warmington, Loeb Classical Library 329 (Cambridge, MA: Harvard University Press, 1938), 228–29.
9   Hab. 3:9.
10 Perhaps especially the New Model Army's decisive triumph at Naseby (June 1645), which Owen refers to later in the sermon.
11 A proverb frequently attributed to Jerome from a letter to the young Augustine. See "Letter 68," in *Letters 1–99 II/I*, ed. John E. Rotelle, trans. Roland Teske, *The Works of Saint Augustine: A Translation for the 21st Century* (Hyde Park, NY: New City Press, 2001), 261.
12 Carthage, on the coast of North Africa, was the chief rival of Rome during the Punic Wars. This is a reference to Florus's account of the Third Punic War (149–146 BC), which describes how the city, as the last remaining stronghold, held out longer than was expected. "But, just as the bite of a dying animal is always most deadly, even so Carthage, half destroyed, caused more trouble than when it was whole." Florus, *Epitome of Roman History* 1.31. For the text, see Florus, *Epitome of Roman History*, trans. E. S. Forster, Loeb Classical Library 231 (Cambridge, MA: Harvard University Press, 1929), 138–39.
13 In Greek mythology, Hercules, a hero with unrivaled strength, killed the many-headed Hydra. Milton addresses a sonnet to Fairfax at the siege of Colchester, in which he also employed this

In the many undertakings of the enemy, all which themselves thought secure, and others esteemed probable, if they had prevailed in anyone, too many reasons present themselves, to persuade, they would have done so in all. But to none of those worthies, which went out under your command, to several places in the kingdom, can you say with Augustus to Varus, upon the slaughter of his legions by Harminius in Germany, "Quintilius Varus, give me back my legions!"[14] God having carried them all on with success and victory.

One especially in his northern expedition,[15] I cannot pass over with silence, who although he will not, dare not, say of his undertakings, as Caesar of his Asian war, *Veni, vidi, vici*,[16] knowing who works all his works for him, nor shall we say of the enemy's multitude, what Captain Gam, did of the French, being sent to spy out their numbers before the battle of Agincourt, that there were of them enough to kill, and enough to take, and enough to run away,[17] yet of him, and them, both he, and we, may freely say, "It is nothing with the Lord to help, either with many, or with them that have no power."[18]

The war being divided, and it being impossible your excellency should be in every place of danger; according to your desire, the Lord was pleased to call you out personally unto two, of the most hazardous, dangerous, and difficult undertakings:[19] where besides the travail, labor, watching, heat and cold, by day and night, whereunto you were exposed, even the life of the meanest soldier in your army was not in more imminent danger, than oftentimes was your own. And indeed during your abode at the league[20] among us, in this only were our thoughts burdened with you, that self-preservation was of no more weight in your

---

    trope, speaking of his victory over the "Hydra heads" of multiple enemies during the Second Civil War. See John Milton, "Sonnet XV: To the Lord General Fairfax, at the Siege of Colchester," in *Milton: Poetical Works*, ed. Douglas Bush (Oxford: Oxford University Press, 1966), 188.

14 In the text: *Quintile Vare redde legiones*.—Owen. The despairing words spoken by Emperor Augustus upon receiving news that General Publius Quinctilius Varus (d. AD 9) had lost the three Roman legions under his command in the Battle of Teutoburg Forest (AD 9). The Germanic tribes were led to victory by Arminius, chieftain of the Cherusci (d. AD 21). For the text, see Suetonius, *Vita divi Augustus* 23.2. For the Latin text and the English translation, see Suetonius, *The Lives of the Caesars*, vol. 1, *Julius. Augustus. Tiberius. Gaius. Caligula*, trans. J. C. Rolfe, Loeb Classical Library 31 (London: Heinemann, 1914), 182–83.

15 Presumably a reference to Oliver Cromwell, who had led the parliamentary army which defeated the Scottish Engagers at Preston.

16 Lat. "I came. I Saw. I conquered." These words are attributed to Julius Caesar. Suetonius, *Vita divi Julii* 37.2. For the Latin text and English translation, see *Lives of the Caesars*, 82–83.

17 The report given to King Henry V about the French army by Dafydd Gambe before the Battle of Agincourt (1415). See Sir Walter Raleigh's *The Historie of the World* (London, 1614), 619.

18 2 Chron. 14:11.

19 In the margin: Kent. Essex.—Owen. Fairfax defeated the forces of the Earl of Norwich at Maidstone in Kent before crossing the Thames to put down the rebellion in Essex.

20 I.e., the military siege camp at Colchester, from the Dutch *leger* ("army").

counsels and undertakings. And I beseech you pardon my boldness, in laying before you this expostulation[21] of many thousands (if we may say to him, who has saved a kingdom, what was sometime said unto a king), "Know you not that 'you are worth ten thousands of us,'[22] why should you 'quench such a light in Israel?'"[23]

Sir, I account it among those blessings of providence, wherewith the days of my pilgrimage have been seasoned, that I had the happiness for a short season, to attend your excellency, in the service of my master Jesus Christ.[24] As also that I have this opportunity, in the name of many, to cast in my χαῖρε[25] into the kingdom's congratulations of your late successes. What thoughts concerning your person, my breast is possessed withal, as in their storehouse they yield me delightful refreshment, so they shall not be drawn out, to the disturbance of your self-denial. The goings forth of my heart, in reference to your excellency, shall be chiefly to the Most High, that being "more than conqueror"[26] in your spiritual and temporal warfare, you may be long continued for a blessing, to this nation, and all the people of God.

Sir,
Your excellency's most humble and devoted servant,
John Owen.

Coggeshall, Essex
October 5, 1648.[27]

To the worthy and honored Sir William Masham,[28] Sir William Rowe,[29] with the rest of the Gentlemen of the Committee lately under imprisonment by the enemy in Colchester, as also to the honored Sir Henry Mildmay of

---

21 I.e., exclamation.
22 2 Sam. 18:3.
23 2 Sam. 21.17. Owen is claiming that the parliamentary general has as great a care of "self-protection" as that due the king.
24 Owen appears to have served as a temporary army chaplain to Fairfax.
25 Gk. "hail" (lit. "rejoice").
26 Rom. 8:37.
27 In the text: Octo. 5. 1648.—Owen.
28 Sir William Masham (1591–1656) of Otes, High Laver, was member of Parliament for Essex and the most important prisoner held hostage by the royalists in Colchester.
29 Sir William Rowe (1585–1667) of Higham Hall, Walthamstow, Essex, had also been imprisoned in Colchester.

Wansted,[30] Col. Sr. Thomas Honywood[31] with the rest of the gentlemen and officers, lately acting and engaged against the same enemy.

Sirs,

The righteous judgments of God, having brought a disturbance, and noise of war, for our security, unthankfulness, murmuring, and devouring one another, upon our country, those who were entrusted with the power thereof, turned their streams into several channels. Troublous times are times of trial.

"Many shall be purified, and made white, and tried, but the wicked shall do wickedly, and none of the wicked shall understand, but the wise shall understand" (Dan. 11:10).[32] Some God called out to suffer, some to do, leaving "treacherous dealers to deal treacherously."[33]

Of the two first sorts are you. This honor have you received from God either with patience and constancy to undergo involuntarily a dangerous restraint, or with resolution and courage, voluntarily to undertake, a hazardous engagement, to give an example, that faith and truth, so shamefully despised in these evil days, have not altogether forsaken the sons of men.

It is not in my thoughts to relate unto yourselves, what some of you suffered, and what some of you did: what difficulties and perplexities you wrestled withal, within, and without the walls of your enemies (the birds in the cage, and the field, having small cause of mutual emulation), for that which remains of these things, is only a returnal of praise to him, by whom all your works are wrought.

It cannot be denied, but that providence was eminently exalted, in the work of your protection and delivery: yet truly, for my part, I cannot but conceive that it vails to the efficacy of grace, in preventing you, from putting forth your hands unto iniquity,[34] in any sinful compliance with the enemies of our peace. The times wherein we live, have found the latter more rare than the former. What God wrought in you, has the preeminence of what he wrought for you: as much as to be given up to the sword, is a lesser evil, than to be given up to a treacherous spirit.

What God has done for you all, all men know; what I desire you should do for God, I know no reason why I should make alike public. The general and particular

---

30 Sir Henry Mildmay (ca. 1594–1664) was the member of Parliament for Maldon and had a large estate in Wanstead, Essex.
31 Sir Thomas Honywood (1587–1666) of Marks Hall, Essex, was a parliamentary colonel who led a body of militia that played a prominent role in the siege of Colchester.
32 The correct reference is Dan. 12:10.
33 Isa. 24:16.
34 Ps. 125:3.

civilities I have received, from all and every one of you, advantaging me to make it out in another way. I shall add nothing then to what you will meet withal, in the following discourse, but only my desire, that you would seriously ponder the eleventh observation, with the deductions from thence.[35] For the rest, I no way fear, but that that God, who has so appeared with you, and for you, will so indulge to your spirits, the presence and guidance of his grace, in these shaking times,[36] that if any "speak evil of you as of evil-doers, they may be ashamed that falsely accuse your good conversation in Christ,"[37] and "glorify God in the day of visitation."[38]

For these following sermons, one of them was preached at your desire, and is now published upon your request. The first part of the labor, I willingly and cheerfully underwent, the latter merely in obedience to your commands: being acted in it, more by your judgments, than mine own; you were persuaded (mean as is was), it might be for the glory of God, to have it made public, whereupon my answer was, and is, that, for that, not only it, but myself also, should by his assistance be ready for the press. The failings and infirmities, attending the preaching and publishing of it (which the Lord knows to be very many), are mine. The inconveniences of publishing such a tractate[39] from so weak a hand, whereof the world is full, must be yours; the fruit and benefit, both of the one, and other, is his, for whose pardon of infirmities and removal of inconveniences, shall be, as for you, and all the church of God, the prayer of,

Sirs,
Your most humble and obliged servant in the work of the Lord,

Coggeshall October 5.[40]
1648.

John Owen.

Some few literal faults have escaped, viz. wrath for wroth, reveled for levelled; which the ingenious reader will amend as well as discern.

---

[35] The eleventh observation concerns the danger of "encroaching" upon the "portion, lot, privileges or inheritance" of the saints, particularly by any form of persecution of the godly.
[36] Heb. 12:26–27.
[37] 1 Pet. 3:16.
[38] 1 Pet. 2:12.
[39] I.e., tract.
[40] In the text: Coggesh: Octob. 5.—Owen.

A Memorial of the Deliverance of Essex, County, and Committee, in Two Sermons

Habakkuk 3:1–9.[1]

1. A prayer of Habakkuk the prophet upon Shigionoth.
2. O Lord, I have heard thy speech, and was afraid: O Lord, revive thy work in the midst of the years, in the midst of the years make known; in wrath remember mercy.
3. God came from Teman, and the holy One from mount Paran. Selah. His glory covered the heavens, and the earth was full of his praise.
4. And his brightness was as the light: he had horns coming out of his hand, and there was the hiding of his power.
5. Before him went the pestilence, and burning coals went forth at his feet.
6. He stood and measured the earth: he beheld, and drove asunder the nations; and the everlasting mountains were scattered, the perpetual hills did bow: his ways are everlasting.
7. I saw the tents of Cushan in affliction: and the curtains of the land of Midian did tremble.
8. Was the Lord displeased against the rivers? Was thine anger against the rivers? Was thy wrath against the sea, that thou didst ride upon thine horses, and thy chariots of salvation?
9. Thy bow was made quite naked, according to the oaths of the tribes, even thy word. Selah. Thou didst cleave the earth with rivers.

---

[1] In the text: Habakkuk Chap. 3. Vers. 1, 2, 3, 4, 5, 6, 7, 8, 9.—Owen.

Sermon 1 (Exposition of 3:6–8)[1]

INTRODUCTION AND OUTLINE OF THE CHAPTER

Of this chapter there are four parts.

First, the title and preface of it, verse 1.

Secondly, the prophet's main request in it, verse 2.

Thirdly, arguments to sustain his faith in that request, from verse 3 unto the 17.

Fourthly, a resignation of himself, and the whole issue of his desires unto God: from thence to the end. We shall treat of them in order.

PART 1: THE TITLE AND PREFACE TO HABAKKUK'S PRAYER (3:1)

Exposition of the Title of the Prayer (3:1a)

The prophet having had visions from God, and prediscoveries of many approaching judgments,[2] in the first and second chapters, in this, by faithful prayer, sets himself to obtain a sure footing, and quiet abode in those nation-destroying storms. "A prayer of Habakkuk the prophet," that is the title of it. And an excellent prayer it is, full of arguments to strengthen faith, acknowledgment of God's sovereignty, power, and righteous judgments, with resolutions to a contented, joyful rolling him upon him under all dispensations.

---

1 In the margin: SERM. I.—Owen.
2 In the margin: The time of his prophecy is conceived to be about the end of Josiah's reign, not long before the first Chaldean invasion.—Owen. In other words, shortly before the Judean king Josiah was killed at the battle of Megiddo in 609 BC and prior to the Babylonian invasion of 604 BC.

Believers Are Called to Fervent Prayer in a Season of Divine Judgment

Observation 1. *Prayer is the believer's constant, sure retreat in an evil time, in a time of trouble.* It is the righteous man's wings to the "name of the Lord," which is his "strong tower."[3] A Christian soldier's sure reserve in the day of battle:[4] if all other forces be overthrown, here he will abide by it: no power under heaven can prevail upon him, to give one step backward. Hence that title of Psalm 102, "A prayer of the afflicted, when he is overwhelmed." Tis the overwhelmed man's refuge, and employment: when "he swooneth with anguish" (as in the original),[5] this fetches him to life again. So for it Psalm 61:2–3. In our greatest distresses, let neither unbelief, nor self-contrivances, jostle us out of this way to the rock of our salvation.

Observation 2. *Prophets' discoveries of fearful judgments must be attended with fervent prayers.* That messenger has done but half his business, who delivers his errand, but returns not an answer. He that brings God's message of threats unto his people, must return his people's message of entreaties, unto him. Some think they have fairly discharged their duty, when they have revealed the will of God to man: without laboring to reveal the condition and desires of men unto God. He that is more frequent in the pulpit to his people, than he is in his closet for his people, is but a sorry watchman. Moses did not so (Ex. 32:31), neither did Samuel so (1 Sam. 12:23), neither was it the guise of Jeremiah in his days (Jer. 14:17). If the beginning of the prophecy be (as it is), "The burden of Habakkuk," the close will be (as it is) "The prayer of Habakkuk." Where there is a burden upon the people, there must be a prayer for the people. Woe to them who have denounced desolations, and not poured out supplications: such men delight in the evil, which the prophet puts far from him: "I have not desired the woful day, (O Lord), thou knowest" (Jer. 17:16).

---

3   In the margin: Prov. 18:10.—Owen.
4   In the margin: *Preces et lachrimae sunt arma Ecclesiae*. Tertul.—Owen. "Prayers and tears are the weapons of the church." This quotation is attributed to Ambrose and his response to the Arian bishop Auxentius over the surrender of basilicas in Milan in 386 in his *Sermo contra Auxentius* 2, 16. For the Latin text, see Ambrose, *Epistolae*, in *Opera omnia*, ed. J.-P. Migne, Patrologia Latina 16 (Paris: Migne-Garnier, 1845), 1007, 1017. For the English translation, see Ambrose, *Sermon against Auxentius*, in *Nicene and Post-Nicene Fathers*, Second Series, ed. Philip Schaff, and Henry Wace, 14 vols. (1890–1900; repr., Peabody: Hendrickson, 2004), 10:430, 432. A similar thought is found in Tertullian who described prayer as the church's "armour defensive and offensive." See Tertullian, *De oratione* 29.3. For the Latin text, see Tertullian, *De oratione*, in *Opera omnia*, ed. J.-P. Migne, Patrologia Latina 1 (Paris: Migne, 1844), 1196. For the English translation, see Tertullian, *On Prayer*, in *Ante-Nicene Fathers: The Writings of the Fathers Down to A.D. 325*, 10 vols., ed. Alexander Roberts and James Donaldson (1886; repr., Peabody, MA: Hendrickson, 1995), 3:691.
5   From the superscription of Ps. 102.

Exposition of What It Is for a Prayer to Be "Upon Shigionoth" (3:1b)

Verse 1. Now this prayer is "upon Shigionoth": that is, 1. It is turned to a song: 2. Such a song. For the first, that it is a song, penned in meter, and how done so: (1) to take the deeper impression; (2) to be the better retained in memory; (3) to work more upon the affections; (4) to receive the ingredients of poetical loftiness for adorning the majesty of God; with (5) the use of songs in the old church; (6) and for the present; (7) their times and seasons, as among the people of God, so all nations of old. Of all, or any of these, being besides my present purpose, I shall not treat. Of the second, that it is "upon Shigionoth," a little may be spoken.

The word is once in another place (and no more) used in the title of a song: and that is Psalm 7, "Shiggaion of David": and it is variously rendered. It seems to be taken from the word שָׁגָה, *erravit*, to err, or wander variously. [In] Proverbs 5:20 the word is used for delight,[6] to stray with delight: "In her love תִּשְׁגֶּה thou shalt err with delight," we have translated it, "be ravished," noting affections out of order. The word then holds out a delightful wandering and variety: and this literally, because those two songs, Psalm 7 and Habakkuk 3, are not tied to any one certain kind of meter, but have various verses for the more delight: which, though it be not proper to them alone, yet in them the Holy Ghost, would have it especially noted:

But now surely the kernel of this shell, is sweeter than so. Is not this written also for their instruction, who have no skill in Hebrew songs? The true reason of their meter, is lost to the most learned. Are not then God's variable dispensations toward his, held out under these variable tunes, not all fitted to one string: not all alike pleasant and easy? Are not the several tunes, of mercy and judgment in these songs? Is not here affliction and deliverance, desertion and recovery, darkness and light, in this variously? Doubtless it is so.

God's People Are Often Called to Sing a Song Mixed of Both Joy and Sorrow

Observation 3. *God often calls his people unto songs upon Shigionoth:*[7] keeps them under various dispensations, that so drawing out all their affections,

---

6 The same Hebrew word is used in both Prov. 5:19 and 5:20, and here Owen quotes from the former.

7 In the margin: *Graviter in eum decernitur cui etiam ipsa. Conectio denegatur.* Prosp: Sent.—Owen. This is a citation from Prosper of Aquitaine's *Liber sententiarum Sancti Augustini* (*Sentences Derived from Saint Augustine*) 87. For the Latin text, see Prosper, *Sententiarum*, in *Opera omnia*, ed. J.-P. Migne, Patrologia Latina 51 (Paris: Migne, 1846), 439. This is translated "He is judged severely indeed from whom even communion itself is withheld."

their hearts may make the sweeter melody unto him. They shall not have all honey, nor all gall: all judgment, lest they be broken, nor all mercy, lest they be proud. "Thou answeredst them, O Lord our God, thou was a God that forgavest them, though thou tookest vengeance of their inventions" (Ps. 99:8). Here is a song "upon Shigionoth." They are heard in their prayers and forgiven, there is the sweetest of mercies: vengeance is taken of their inventions, there's a tune of judgment. "By terrible things in righteousness wilt thou answer us O God of our salvation," Psalm 65:5 is a song of the same tune. To be answered in righteousness, what sweeter mercy in the world? Nothing more refreshes the panting soul, than an answer of its desires: but to have this answer by terrible things! That string strikes a humbling, a mournful note. Israel hears of deliverance by Moses,[8] and at the same time have their bondage doubled by Pharaoh. There's a song upon Shigionoth. Is it not so in our days?[9] Precious mercies, and dreadful judgments, jointly poured out upon the land! We are clothed by our Father, like Joseph by his, in a party-colored coat:[10] here a piece of unexpected deliverance, and there a piece of deserved correction: at the same hour, we may rejoice at the conquest of our enemies, and mourn at the loss of our harvest.[11] Victories for his own name's sake, and showers for our sins' sake, both from the same hand, at the same time. The cry of every soul, is like the cry of the multitude of old and young at the laying the foundation of the second temple: "Many shouted aloud for joy," and many "wept with a loud voice," so that it was a mixed noise, and the several noises could not be distinguished (Ezra 3:12–13). A mixed cry is in our spirits, and we know not which is loudest in the day of our visitation. I could instance in sundry particulars, but that everyone's observation, will save me that easy labor. And this the Lord does—

8   In the margin: *Duplicantur lateres quando venit Moses.*—Owen. This is a medieval proverb that is translated "When the tale of bricks is doubled, Moses comes." This proverb about deliverance coming in the very worst of times had been used by Anthony Burgess in his fast sermon to the House of Commons in February 1646. Burgess, *Publick Affections, Pressed in a Sermon before the Honourable House of Commons Assembled in Parliament* [. . .] (London, 1646), 2.

9   In the Restoration, Samuel Parker mocked Owen for this interpretation of providence by recourse to the notion of a song on Shigionoth. See Parker, *A Defence and Continuation of the Ecclesiastical Politie* [. . .] (London, 1671), 114.

10 In the margin: Gen. 37:3.—Owen.

11 The heavy rain over the summer and the storms that came in August led to a poor harvest in 1648 with resultant high grain prices. See *Kingdomes Weekly Intelligencer* 272 (August 8–15, 1648). The diarist John Evelyn wrote in December 1648 that "this was a most exceeding wet year." See John Evelyn, *The Diary of John Evelyn*, ed. E. S. De Beer, 6 vols. (Oxford: Clarendon, 1955), 2:546–47.

Two Reasons Why the Saints Are Called to Sing Songs "upon Shigionoth"

Reason 1. To fill all our sails toward himself at once: to exercise all our affections.[12] I have heard that a full wind behind the ship, drives her not so fast forward, as a side wind, that seems almost so much against her as with her: and the reason they say is, because a full wind, fills but some of her sails, which keep it from the rest, that they are empty: when a side wind fills all her sails, and sets her speedily forward.[13] Which way ever we go in this world, our affections are our sails: and according as they are spread and filled, so we pass on, swifter and slower, whither we are steering. Now if the Lord should give us a full wind, and continual gale of mercies, it would fill but some of our sails, some of our affections, joy, delight, and the like: but when he comes with a side wind, a dispensation that seems almost as much against us, as for us, then he fills all our sails, takes up all our affections, making his works, wide, and broad enough, to entertain them every one, then are we carried freely and fully, toward the haven where we would be.[14] A song upon Shigionoth, leaves not one string of our affections untuned. It is a song that reaches every line of our hearts, to be framed by the grace and Spirit of God. Therein, hope, fear, reverence with humility and repentance have a share, as well as joy, delight, and love, with thankfulness. Interchangeable dispensations, take up all our affections, with all our graces: for they are gracious affections, exercised and seasoned with grace, of which we speak. The stirring of natural affections as merely such, is but the moving of a dunghill to draw out a stinking steam, a thing the Lord neither aims at, nor delights in: their joys are his provocation, and he laughs in the day of their calamity, when their fear comes (Prov. 1:26–27).

Reason 2. Secondly, to keep them in continual dependence upon himself.[15] He has promised his own daily bread, not goods laid up for many years. Many

---

12 In the margin: *Namque bonos non blanda inflant, non aspera frangunt, sed fidei invictae gaudia vera juvant.* Prosp. Epig in Sent. August.—Owen. This is a reference to Prosper of Aquitaine, *Epigrammata ex sententiis* (Versified sentences from Augustine) 49. For the Latin text, see Prosper, *Epigrammatum ex sententiis S. Augustini*, in *Opera omnia*, ed. J.-P. Migne, Patrologia Latina 51 (Paris: Migne, 1846), 513. This is translated, "For indeed, the good are neither puffed up by prosperity nor broken by adversity, but the true joy of an unconquerable faith comes to their aid."

13 A description of this maritime phenomenon may be found in the first part of Francis Bacon's work of natural history, *Historia ventorum* (London, 1622). For a translation, see the "History of the Wind," in *The Works of Francis Bacon*, vol. 5, *Translations of the Philosophical Works 2*, ed. James Spedding, Robert Leslie Ellis and Douglas Denon Heath (Cambridge: Cambridge University Press, 1858), 182.

14 In the margin: Psal. 119:67; Hos. 5:15; Heb. 12:10–11; 1 Pet. 1:6.—Owen.

15 In the margin: *In caelo non in terra mercedem promisit esse reddendam: quid alibi poscis quod alibi debetur?* Ambros. Offic, Lib. 1. Cap 16.—Owen. This is a quotation from Ambrose, *De officiis* (*On*

children have been undone by their parents giving them too large a stock to trade for themselves: it has made them spendthrifts, careless, and wanton.[16] Should the Lord entrust his people with a continued stock of mercy, perhaps they would "be full and deny him, and say who is the Lord?" (Prov. 30:9). Jeshurun did so (Deut. 32:14–15). Ephraim was filled according to their pasture, and forgot the Lord (Hos. 13:6).

Neither, on the other side, will he be always chiding: his anger shall not burn forever very sore. It is our infirmity (at the least) if we say, "God has 'forgotten to be gracious,' and 'shut up his tender mercies' in displeasure" (Ps. 77:9). But laying one thing against another, he keeps the heart of his, in an even balance, in a continual dependence upon himself: that they may neither be wanton through mercy, nor discouraged by too much oppression. Our tender Father is therefore, neither always feeding, nor always correcting. "And it shall come to pass in that day, that the light shall not be clear nor dark: but it shall be one day which shall be known to the Lord: not day nor night, but it shall come to pass that at evening time it shall be light": says the prophet Zechariah (14:6–7), seeking out God's dispensations toward his, ending in joy and light in the evening.

The Saints Should Therefore Learn to Sing Such Songs

Use 1. Labor to have your hearts right tuned for songs on Shigionoth, sweetly to answer all God's dispensations in their choice variety. That instrument will make no music, that has but some strings in tune. If when God strikes with mercy upon the string of joy and gladness, we answer pleasantly, but when he touches upon that of sorrow and humiliation, we suit it not, we are broken instruments that make no melody unto God.[17] We must know how to receive good and evil at his hand. "He hath made every thing beautiful in its time" (Eccl. 3:11), everything in that whole variety which his wisdom has

---

the *Duties of Office*) 1.59. "It was in heaven, not on earth. Why are you demanding something in one place that is due in another?" For the Latin text and English translation, see *De Officiis*, vol. 1, *Introduction, Text and Translation* (New York: Oxford University Press, 2001), 152–53.

16 I.e., undisciplined; unruly.

17 In the margin: *cum vexamur ac premimur, tum maxime gratias agimus indulgentissimo patri; quod corruptelam nostram non patitur longius procedure* [...] *hinc intelligimus nos esse Deo curae.* Lactan.—Owen. "When we are troubled and oppressed, then especially do we give thanks to our most indulgent Father because He does not allow our corruption to proceed too far.... From this we know that we are in God's care." This is a reference to Lactantius and his *Divinarum Institutionum Divinarum institutionum* 5.22. For the Latin text, see Lactantius, *Divinarum Institutionum*, in *Opera omnia*, ed. J.-P. Migne, Patrologia Latina 6 (Paris: Migne, 1844), 627. For English translation, see Lactantius, *The Divine Institutes: Books I–VIII*, trans. Mary Francis McDonald, Fathers of the Church 49 (Washington, DC: Catholic University of America Press, 1964), 388.

produced. A well-tuned heart must have all its strings, all its affections, ready to answer every touch of God's finger: to improve judgments and mercies both at the same time. Sweet harmony arises out of some discords. When a soul is in a frame to rejoice with thankful obedience for mercy received, and to be humbled with soul-searching, amending repentance, for judgments inflicted at the same time, then it sings a song on Shigionoth, then it is fit for the days wherein we live. Indeed both mercies and judgments aim at the same end, and should be received with the same equal temper of mind. A flint is broken between a hammer and a pillow: an offender is humbled between a prison and a pardon: a hard heart may be mollified, and a proud spirit humbled between those two.[18] In such a season the several rivulets of our affections flow naturally in the same stream. When has a gracious soul the soundest joys, but when it has the deepest sorrows! "They have great joy in wounds."[19] When has it the humblest meltings but when it has the most ravishing joys! Our afflictions, which are naturally at the widest distance, may all swim in the same spiritual channel—rivulets rising from several heads are carried in one stream to the ocean. As a mixture of several colors make a beautiful complexion for the body, so a mixture of divers affections under God's various dispensations, gives a comely frame unto the soul. Labor then to answer every call, every speaking providence of God, in its right kind, according to the intention thereof: and the Lord reveal his mind unto us that so we may do.

PART 2: HABAKKUK'S FEAR AND THE MAIN REQUEST OF HIS PRAYER (3:2)

Verse 2. Having passed the title, let us look a little on those parts of the prayer itself that follow.

---

[18] The trope of the flint being broken on a pillow was very popular with preachers at the time. See, e.g., Edwards Reynolds, *A Sermon Touching the Peace and Edification of the Church* (London, 1638), 24; Richard Vines, *Calebs Integrity [. . .] A Sermon Preached at St Margarets Westminster, Before the Honourable House of Commons* (London, 1642), 28; Lazarus Seaman, *The Head of the Church, The Judge of the World [. . .] A Sermon Preached before [. . .] the House of Peers* (London, 1647), 6; Ralph Cudworth, *A Sermon Preached before the Honourable House of Commons at Westminster* (Cambridge, 1647), 62. Here Owen's language shows marked similarity to a passage of Reynolds that appears to have been included in Samuel Clarke's collection of memorable sayings. "The heart of man is broken as a flint, with a hard and a soft together: A Hammer and A Pillow is the best way to breake a flint; A Prison and a Pardon, A Scourge and a Salve." See Reynolds, *Three Treatises of the Vanity of the Creature, The Sinfulnesse of Sinne, and the Life of Christ* (London, 1631), 391; Clarke, *The Saints Nose-Gay, or a Posie of 741 Spiritual Flowers* (London, 1642), 15.

[19] In the text: *Habent et gaudia vulnus.*—Owen. This is a quotation from Prosper, *Epigrammatum* 110. For the Latin text, see Prosper, *Epigrammata*, 526.

Exposition of Habakkuk's Fearful Condition (3:2a)

The beginning of it in verse 2 has two parts:

First, the frame of the prophet's spirit in his address to God: "O Jehovah I have heard thy speech, and was afraid."

Secondly, his request in this his condition: "O Lord revive thy work in the midst of the years, in the midst of the years make known, in wrath remember mercy."

1. In the first you have particularly his frame, he was afraid, or trembled; which he wonderfully sets out, verse 16, "When I heard, my belly trembled, my lips quivered at the voice: rottenness entered into my bones, and I trembled in myself."

2.[20] Secondly, the cause of this fear and trembling: he "heard the speech of God." If you will ask what speech or report this was, that made the prophet himself so exceedingly quake and tremble! I answer it is particularly that which you have [in] chapter 1:5–12 containing a dreadful denunciation of the judgments of God against the people of Israel, to be executed by the proud cruel insulting Chaldeans. This voice, this report of God makes the prophet tremble.

The Saints Should Fear God in the Season of His Appearance

Observation 4. *An appearance of God in anger and threats against a people, should make his choicest secret ones among them to fear, to quake, and tremble.* Trembling of man's heart, must answer the shaking of God's hand. At the delivery of the law with all its attending threats, so terrible was the sight, that Moses himself (though a mediator then), did "exceedingly fear and quake" (Heb. 12:21). God will be acknowledged in all his goings. If men will not bow before him, he will break them. They who fear not his threatenings, shall feel his inflictings. If his word be esteemed light, his hand will be found heavy. For—

1. In point of deserving, who can say, I have purged my heart, I am clean from sin![21] None ought to be fearless, unless they be senseless. God's people are so far from being always clear of procuring national judgments, that sometimes judgments have come upon nations for the sins of some of God's people among them: as the plague in the days of David.[22]

2. In point of suffering who knows but they may have a deep share![23] The prophet's book is written within, as well as without, with lamentation,

---

20 The numbering is added for clarity and consistency.
21 In the margin: Iob 14:4; Ch. 15:15–16; Prov. 16:2; Chap. 20:9.—Owen.
22 In the margin: 2 Sam. 24:15; 2 Chron. 32:25.—Owen.
23 In the margin: *Omnes seculi plagae nobis in admonitionem, vobis in castigationem à Deo veniunt.* Tertul. Apol. cap. 42.—Owen. This is a quotation from Tertullian, *Apologeticus*

mourning, and woe (Ezek. 2 ult.).[24] If the lion roars, who can but fear? (Amos 3:8) Fear to the rooting out of security not the shaking of faith. Fear to the pulling down of carnal presidence, not Christian confidence. Fear to draw out our souls in prayer, not to swallow them up in despair. Fear, to break the arm of flesh, but not to weaken the staff of the promise. Fear, that we may draw nigh to God, with reverence, not to run from him with diffidence: in a word, to overthrow faithless presumption, and to increase gracious submission.

Exposition of Habakkuk's Request (3:2b)

2. Secondly, here is the prophet's request: and in this there are these two things,

    (1) The thing he desires: "the reviving God's work," "the remembering mercy."
    (2) The season he desires it in, "In the midst of the years."

God Will Revive His Work by Remembering Mercy

(1) For the first, that which in the beginning of the verse, he calls God's "work," in the close of it, he terms "mercy": and the reviving of his work, is interpreted to be a remembering mercy. These two expressions then are parallel. The reviving of God's work toward his people, is a re-acting of mercy: a bringing forth the fruits thereof, and that in the midst of the execution of wrath, as a man in the midst of another, remembering a business of more importance, instantly turns away, and applies himself thereunto.

    Observation 5. *Acts of mercy are God's proper work toward his people, which he will certainly awake, and keep alive in the saddest times.* Mercy you see is his work, his proper work, as he calls judgment "his strange act" (Isa. 28:21): "He retaineth not his anger for ever, because he delighteth in mercy" (Mic. 7:18). This is his proper work; though it seem to sleep, he will awake it, though it seem to die, he will revive it. "Can a woman forget her child, that she should not have compassion on the son of her womb? Yea they may forget, yet will I not forget thee: behold, I have graven thee upon the palms of my hands, thy walls are continually before me" (Isa. 49:16–17).[25]

41.4: "All the plagues of the world . . . come on us for admonition, on you for chastisement, from God." For the Latin text and English translation, see Tertullian, *Apology*, in Tertullian, Minucius Felix, *Apology. De Spectaculis. Minucius Felix: Octavius*, trans. T. R. Glover and Gerald H. Rendall, Loeb Classical Library 250 (Cambridge, MA: Harvard University Press, 1931), 188–89.

24 *Ult* from *ultimo*, meaning "last." Owen is referencing Ezek. 2:10.
25 Following Goold, this should be corrected to Isa. 49:15–16.

God Will Act in Mercy in His Appointed Season

(2)[26] Secondly, for the season of this work, he prays that it may be accomplished, "in the midst of the years": upon which you may see what weight he lays by his repetition of it in the same verse. It is something doubtful what may be the peculiar sense of these words: whether "the midst of the years," do not denote the whole time of the people's bondage under the Chaldeans (whence Junius renders the words *interea temporis*,[27] noting this manner of expression, "the midst of the years," for a Hebraism),[28] during which space he intercedes for mercy for them. Or whether "the midst of the years," do not denote some certain point of times, as the season of their return from captivity, about the midst of the years between their first king, and the coming of the Messiah, putting a period to their church and state. Whether of these is more probable, is not needful to insist upon; this is certain, that a certain time is pointed at; which will yield us,

Observation 6. *The church's mercies and deliverance, have their appointed season*: "in the midst of the years" it shall be accomplished. As there is a decree bringing forth the wicked's destruction (Zeph. 2:2), so there is a decree goes forth in its appointed season for the church's deliverance, which cannot be gainsaid (Dan. 9:23). Every vision is for its appointed season and time (Hab. 2:3), then "it will surely come, it will not tarry." There is a determination upon the weeks and days of the church's sufferings and expectations, "Seventy weeks are determined upon thy people" (Dan. 9:24). As there are "three transgressions," and a "four," of rebels, for which God "will not turn away their punishment" (Amos 1:3), so a three afflictions, and a four, of the people of God, after which he will not shut out their supplications.

Hence that confidence of the prophet, "Thou shalt arise, and have mercy upon Zion for," (says he), "the time to favour her, yea the set time is come" (Ps. 102:13–14). There is a time, yea a set time, for favor to be showed unto Zion. As a time to break down, so a time to build up:[29] an acceptable time, a day of salvation.[30] "It came to pass, at the end of 430 years, even the self-same day it came to pass, that all the hosts of the Lord went out of Egypt" (Ex. 12:41). As a woman with child goes not beyond her appointed months, but is pained to be delivered, no more can the fruitful decree cease from bringing forth the church's deliverance in the season thereof.

---

26 The numbering is added for clarity and consistency.
27 This is a reference to the translation found in the Tremellius-Junius Bible, the *Testamenta Veteris Biblia sacra* (Frankfurt, 1579).
28 In the margin: בְּקֶרֶב שָׁנִים, in the inward of years.—Owen.
29 Eccl. 3:3.
30 Isa. 49:8.

Two Reasons Why God Will Act in His Appointed Season

Reason 1. Because there is an appointed period of the church's humiliation, and bearing of her iniquities. Israel shall bear their iniquities in the wilderness, but this is exactly limited to the space of forty years. When their iniquity is pardoned, their warfare is accomplished (Isa. 40:2). They say some men will give poison that shall work insensibly, and kill at seven years' end. The great physician of his church, knows how to give his sin-sick people potions, that shall work by degrees, and at such an appointed season take away all their iniquity. Then they can no longer be detained in trouble. God will not continue his course of physic, unto them one day beyond health recovered. This is "all the fruit of" their afflictions, "to take away" their iniquities (Isa. 27:9), and when that is done, who shall keep bound what God will loose? When sin is taken away from within, trouble must depart from without.

Reason 2. Because the church's sorrows are commensurate unto, and do contemporize with, the joys and prosperity of God's enemies, and hers. Now wicked men's prosperity has assured bounds. The wickedness of the wicked shall come to an end.[31] There is a time when the iniquity of the Amorites comes to the full (Gen. 15:16): it comes up to the brim in the appointed day of slaughter. When their wickedness has filled the ephah, a talent of lead is laid upon the mouth thereof, and it is carried away on wings (Zech. 5:6–8), swiftly, certainly, irrecoverably. If then the church's troubles, contemporize, rise and fall, with their prosperity, and her deliverance, with their destruction! If the fall of Babylon be the rise of Zion; if they be the buckets, which must go down, when the church comes up;[32] if they be the rod of the church's chastisement, their ruin being set and appointed, so also must be the church's mercies.

Since Deliverance Will Come in God's Time, the Godly Should Wait in Faith

Use. In every distress, learn to wait with patience for this appointed time, "He that believeth will not make haste."[33] "Though it tarry, wait for it, it will surely come."[34] He that is infinitely good has appointed the time, and therefore it is best. He that is infinitely wise, has determined the season, and therefore it is most suitable. He who is infinitely powerful, has set it down, and therefore

---

31 Ps. 7:9.
32 An allusion to the proverbial expression "like two buckets of a well, if one goes up the other must go down." See Morris Palmer Tilley, *A Dictionary of the Proverbs in England in the Sixteenth and Seventeenth Centuries: A Collection of the Proverbs Found in English Literature and the Dictionaries of the Period* (Ann Arbor, MI: University of Michigan Press, 1966), B695.
33 Isa. 28:16.
34 Hab. 2:3.

it shall be accomplished. Wait for it believing, wait for it praying, wait for it contending. Waiting is not a lazy hope, a sluggish expectation. When Daniel knew the time was come, he prayed the more earnestly (Dan. 9:2–3). You will say perhaps, "What need he pray for it when he knew the time was accomplished!" I answer; the more need. Prayer helps the promise to bring forth. Because a woman's time is come, therefore shall she have no midwife? Nay therefore give her one. He that appointed their return, appointed that it should be a fruit of prayer. Wait contending also, in all ways wherein you shall be called out.[35] And be not discouraged, that you know not the direct season of deliverance. "In the morning sow thy seed, and in the evening, withhold not thine hand, for thou knowest not whether shall prosper, this or that, or whether they both shall be alike good" (Eccl. 11:6).

PART 3: THE ARGUMENTS IN HABAKKUK'S PRAYER THAT SUPPORT FAITH (3:3–17)

But proceed we with the prophet's prayer.

From verse 3 to 17, he lays down several arguments, taken from the majesty, power, providence, and former works of God, for the supporting of his faith, to the obtaining of those good things, and works of mercy, which he was now praying for. We shall look on them, as they lie in our way.

Exposition of Habakkuk Remembering the Former Works of God (3:3)

Verse 3. "God came from Teman, the Holy One from mount Paran: Selah: his glory covered the heavens, the earth was full of his praise."

Teman was a city of the Edomites, whose land the people of Israel compassed in the wilderness, when they were stung with fiery serpents, and healed with looking on a brazen serpent, set up to be a type of Christ.[36] Teman is put up for the whole land of Edom: and the prophet makes mention of it, for the great deliverance and mercy granted there to the people, when they were

---

35 In the margin: *Bonum Agonem subituri estis in quo. Agonothetes Deus vivus est: Christarchos Spiritus Sanctus, corone aeternitatis brabium, Epithetes Jesus Christus.* Tertul ad Mar.—Owen. This is a slightly adapted quotation from Tertullian's *Ad martyras* (To the martyrs) 3: "You are about to enter a noble contest in which the living God acts the part of superintendent and the Holy Spirit is your trainer, a contest whose crown is eternity . . . your Master, Jesus Christ." For the Latin text, see Tertullian, *Ad martyres*, in *Opera omnia*, ed. J.-P. Migne, Patrologia Latina 1 (Paris: Migne, 1844), 624. For the English translation, see Tertullian, *Disciplinary, Moral and Ascetical Works*, trans. Rudolph Arbesmann, Emily Joseph Daly, and Edwin A. Quain, Fathers of the Church 40 (Washington, DC: Catholic University of America Press, 1959), 23.

36 In the margin: Gen. 36:15; Jer. 49:7; Obad. 1:9.—Owen.

almost consumed. That's God's coming from Teman. See Numbers 21:5–9. When they were destroyed by fiery serpents, he heals them by a type of Christ, giving them corporeal, and raising them to a faith of spiritual salvation.

Paran, the next place mentioned, was a mountain in the land of Ishmael, near which Moses repeated the law, and from thence God carried the people immediately to Canaan: another eminent act of mercy.[37]

Unto these he adds the word "Selah": as it is a song a note of elevation in singing: as it respects the matter, not the form, a note of admiration and special observation: Selah, consider them well for they were great works indeed.

The Saints Anticipate Future Blessing by Remembering Former Mercies
Special mercies, must have special observation.

Now by reason of these actions, the prophet affirms that the glory of God covered the heavens, and the earth was full of his praise. Lofty expressions of the advancement of God's glory, and the fullness of his praise among his people of the earth, which attended that merciful deliverance, and gracious assistance. Nothing is higher or greater than that which covers heaven, and fills earth.

God's glory is exceedingly exalted, and his praise increased everywhere, by acts of favor and kindness to his people.[38]

That which I shall choose from among many others that present themselves a little to insist upon, is that—

Observation 7. *Former mercies with their times and places are to be had in thankful remembrance unto them who wait for future blessings.* Faith is to this end separated by them. "Awake, awake, put on strength, O arm of the Lord, awake as in the ancient days, in the generations of old: art not thou it that hath cut Rahab, and wounded the dragon? Art not thou it that dried the sea, the waters of the great deep, that hath made the depths of the sea a way for the ransomed to pass over?" (Isa. 51:9–10). The breaking of Rahab, that

---

37 In the margin: Deut. 1.—Owen.
38 In the margin: *Gloria est frequens de aliquo fama cum laude.* Ci. lib. 2. de. inv. *Consentiens laus bonorum, incorrupta vox bene judicantium de excellente virtute.* Idem Tusc., l. 4.—Owen. The first of these two quotations from Cicero is from *De inventione* 2.166: "Glory consists in a person's having a widespread reputation accompanied by praise." For the Latin text and English translation, see Cicero, *On Invention. The Best Kind of Orator. Topics*, trans. H. M. Hubbell, Loeb Classical Library 386 (Cambridge, MA: Harvard University Press, 1949), 332–33. The second quotation is from his *Tusculanarum disputationum* 3.2.3: "The agreeing approval of good men, the unbiased verdict of judges deciding honestly the question of pre-eminent merit." For the Latin text and English translation, see Cicero, *Tusculan Disputations*, trans. J. E. King, Loeb Classical Library 141 (Cambridge, MA: Harvard University Press, 1927), 228–29.

is Egypt, so called here, and Psalms 87:4, 89:10, for her great strength which the word signifies, and the wounding of the dragon, that great and crooked afflicter Pharaoh is remembered, and urged for a motive to a new needed deliverance. "Thou brakest the heads of leviathan in pieces, and gavest him to be meat to the people in the wilderness" (Ps. 74:13–14). Leviathan, the same dragon, oppressing, persecuting Pharaoh; thou brakest his heads, his counsels, armies, power, and gavest him for meat, that the people for forty years together might be fed, sustained and nourished, with that wonderful mercy. "Out of the eater came forth meat; out of the strong came forth sweetness."[39]

In this reciprocation God walks with his people. Of free grace he bestows mercies and blessings on them: by grace works the returns of remembrance and thankfulness unto himself for them: then showers that down again in new mercies. The countries which send up no vapors, receive down no showers.[40] Remembrance with thankfulness of former mercies, is the matter as it were, which by God's goodness, is condensed into following blessings. For—

Two Reasons Why the Saints Should Anticipate Future
Blessing by Remembering Former Mercies

Reason 1. Mercies have their proper end when thankfully remembered. What more powerful motive to the obtaining of new, than to hold out, that the old were not abused. We are encouraged to cast seed again into that ground, whose last crop witnesses that it was not altogether barren: that sad spot of good Hezekiah, that he rendered not again according to the benefit done unto him, is set down as the opening a door of wrath against himself, Judah and Jerusalem (2 Chron. 32:25). On the other side suitable returns, are a door of hope for further mercies.

Reason 2. The remembrance of them strengthens faith, and keeps our hands from hanging down in the time of waiting for blessings. When faith is supported the promise is engaged, and a mercy at any time more than half obtained, "Faith is the substance of things hoped for" (Heb. 11:1). "God" (says the apostle) "hath delivered us from so great a death, and doth deliver," now what conclusion makes he of this experience? "In whom we trust, that he will

---

39 Judg. 14:14.
40 This trope was employed by preachers to illustrate the importance of thankfulness. See, e.g., Lancelot Andrewes, *Apospasmatia Sacra: Or A Collection of Posthumous and Orphan Lectures* [...] (London, 1657), 56. Or Daniel Featley, *Clavis Mystica: A Key Opening Divers Difficult and Mysterious Texts* [...] (London, 1636), 570. Featley explained, "We reade of small or no raine that falls at any time on divers parts of Africa; and the cause is supposed to bee the sandy nature of the soyle, from whence the Sun can draw no vapours ... which ... resolve themselves into kinde showers refreshing the earth."

yet deliver us" (2 Cor. 1:10). It was a particular mercy, with its circumstances, as you may see verse 9, which he made the bottom of his dependence. In the favors of men, we cannot do so: they may be weary of helping, or be drawn dry, and grow helpless. Ponds may be exhausted, but the ocean never. The infinite fountains of the Deity, cannot be sunk one hair's breadth by everlasting flowing blessings. Now circumstances of actions, time, place, and the like, ofttimes take deep impressions: mercies should be remembered with them. So does the apostle again, "He did deliver me from the mouth of the lion": (Nero, that lion-like tyrant) and what then? "He shall deliver me from every evil work" (2 Tim. 4:17–18). David esteemed it very good logic, to argue from the victory God gave him over the lion, and the bear, to a confidence of victory over Goliath (1 Sam. 17:37).

Remember the Great Recent Works of God in the First Civil War

Use. The use of this, we are led unto. "Thus saith the Lord, which maketh a way in the sea, and a path in the mighty waters: which bringeth forth the chariot and horse, the army and the power, they shall lie down together, they shall not rise, they are extinct, they are quenched as tow."[41] "Remember ye not the former things, neither consider the things of old" (Isa. 43:16–18). Let former mercies be an anchor of hope in time of present distresses. "Where is the God of Marston Moor, and the God of Naseby,"[42] is an acceptable expostulation in a gloomy day. O what a catalog of mercies, has this nation to plead by in a time of trouble? God came from Naseby, and the Holy One from the West: Selah: his glory covered the heavens, and the earth was full of his praise. He went forth in the north, and in the east he did not withhold his hand.[43] I hope the poor town wherein I live is more enriched with a store-mercy[44]

---

41 I.e., coarse and broken pieces of flax or hemp.
42 The Battles of Marston Moor (July 2, 1644) and Naseby (June 14, 1645) were notable parliamentary victories during the civil war. Marston Moor was the largest battle of the civil war, and Parliament's stunning victory under Fairfax broke Newcastle's northern army and led to the surrender of York. At Naseby the New Model Army secured total victory in its first major battle. According to Scott, Naseby "confirmed the Independents and their army as the most powerful force in British Politics." See David Scott, *Politics and War in the Three Stuart Kingdoms, 1637–49* (Basingstoke, UK: Palgrave Macmillan, 2004), 97. Gentles describes how at Naseby, "Fairfax had struck the king a mortal blow." See Ian Gentles, *The New Model Army: Agent of Revolution* (New Haven: Yale University Press, 2022), 35–43.
43 Owen adapts his text from Hab. 3:3 by inserting geographic references that almost certainly refer to the parliamentary victories seen in the surrender of Pembroke Castle to the west (July 1648), the victories to the north in Lancashire at Preston and Winwick Pass (August 1648), and to the east with the fall of Colchester in Essex (August 1648).
44 I.e., a precious and treasured mercy.

of a few months, than with a full trade of many years.[45] "The snares of death compassed us, and the floods of ungodly men made us afraid" (Ps. 18:4): but "the Lord thundered in the heavens, the highest gave his voice, hailstones and coals of fire: yea he sent out his arrows, and scattered them, and he shot out lightnings, and discomfited them: he sent from above, he took us, he drew us out of many waters, he delivered us from our strong enemy, and from them which hated us, for they were too strong for us" (Ps.18:13–14, 16–17).[46] How may we say with the same psalmist in any other distress, "O my God my soul is cast down within me, therefore will I remember thee from the land of Jordan, and of the Hermonites, from the hill Mizar" (Ps. 42:6). "Where is the God of Elijah," divides anew the waters of Jordan (2 Kings 2:14).

Exposition of the Glory Manifest in God's Former Works (3:4)

Verse 4. The following verses set forth the glory and power of God, in the accomplishment of that great work of bringing his people into the promised land: with those mighty things he performed in the wilderness. Verse 4 if I mistake not sets out his glorious appearance on Mount Sinai: of which the prophet affirms two things:

1. That "his brightness was as the light":
2. That, "he had horns coming out of his hand, and there was the hiding of his power."

1. For the first: is it not that brightness which appeared, when the mountain burned with fire to the midst of heaven (Deut. 4:11): a glorious fire in the midst of clouds and thick darkness. The like description you have of God's presence, "He made darkness his secret place," and "brightness was before him" (Ps. 18:11–12). As the light, the sun, the fountain and cause of it: called "light" (Job 31:26). Now this glorious appearance holds out the kingly power and majesty of God in governing the world, which appears but unto few. "The

---

45 In the margin: No place in the county so threatened. No place in the county so preserved. Small undertakings there blessed: Great opposition blasted. *Non nobis, Domine, non nobis.*—Owen. Owen is speaking of his hometown, Coggeshall, in County Essex. The Latin quotation is translated "not unto us, O Lord, not unto us," which is from Psalm 115 and continues, "but unto thy name give glory, for thy mercy, and for thy truth's sake" (Ps. 115:1 KJV). Fairclough preached on this text at the official thanksgiving on Thursday, September 7. See Natalie Mears et al., eds., *National Prayers: Special Worship Since the Reformation*, vol. 1, *Special Prayers, Fasts and Thanksgivings in the British Isles, 1533–1688* (Woodbridge, UK: Boydell, 2013), 491.
46 In this quotation from Psalm 18, Owen has glossed the first-person singular with the first-person plural.

Lord reigneth, let the earth rejoice, clouds and darkness are round about him a fire goeth before him, his lightnings enlightened the world" (Ps. 97:1–[4]).

2. Secondly, "He had horns coming out of his hand." So the words most properly, though by some otherwise rendered. That "horns" in Scripture are taken for strength and power, needs no proving.[47] The mighty power of God which he made appear to his people, in that glorious representation of his majesty on Mount Sinai, is by this phrase expressed. There his chariots were seen to be "twenty thousands, even many thousands of angels, and the Lord among them [. . .] in that holy place" (Ps. 68:[17]). There they perceived that "he had horns in his hand": an almighty power to do what he pleased. Whence it is added, "And there was the hiding of his power." Though the appearance of it was very great and glorious, yet it was but small to the everlasting hidden depths of his omnipotency:

(The most glorious appearance of God comes infinitely short of his own eternal majesty as he is in himself: it is but a discovery, that there is the hiding of infinite perfection). Or, there his power appeared to us, which was hidden from the rest of the world.

God Reveals His Great Purposes to the Saints

Observation 8. *When God is doing great things, he gives glorious manifestations of his excellencies to his secret ones.* The appearance on Sinai, goes before his passage into Canaan. "Surely the Lord God will do nothing, but he revealeth his secret unto his servants the prophets" (Amos 3:7). When he is to send Moses for the deliverance of his people, he appears to him in a burning unconsumed bush (Ex. 3:2), a sign manifesting the presence of his power, to preserve his church unconsumed in the midst of burning fiery afflictions. Unto this very end, were all the visions, that are recorded in the Scripture; all of them accommodated to the things which God was presently doing. And this he does:

Two Reasons Why God Makes Such Revelations

Reason 1. That they may thereby be prepared to follow him, and serve him in the great works he has for them to do. Great works are not to be done without great encouragements. If God appears not in light, who can expect he should appear in operation? He that is called to serve providence in high things, without some especial discovery of God, works in the dark, and knows not whither he goes, nor what he does.[48] Such a one travels in the wilderness,

---

47 In the margin: Deut. 33:17; Psal. 75:10; Zech. 1:18.—Owen.
48 In the margin: John 12:35; Revel. 16:10.—Owen.

without a directing cloud. Clear shining from God, must be at the bottom of deep laboring with God. What is the reason, that so many in our days, set their hands to the plough, and look back again?[49] Begin to serve providence in great things, but cannot finish? Give over in the heat of the day! They never had any such revelation of the mind of God upon their spirits, such a discovery of his excellencies, as might serve for a bottom of such undertakings. Men must know that if God has not appeared to them in brightness, and showed them "the horns in his hand," hid from others, though they think highly of themselves, they'll deny God twice and thrice before the close of the work of this age. If you have no great discoveries, you will wax vain in great undertakings. New workings on old bottoms, are like new wine in old bottles, both are spoiled and lost.[50] The day is the time of work, and that because of the light thereof: those who have not light may be spared to go to bed.

Reason 2. That they may be the better enabled to give him glory, when they shall see the sweet harmony that is between his manifestations and his operations. When they can say with the psalmist, "As we have heard, so have we seen" (Ps. 48:8), as he reveals himself, so he works. When his power and mercy answer his appearance in the bush, it is a foundation to a prayer, "The good-will of him that dwelt in the bush" bless thee.[51] When a soul shall find God calling him forth to employments, perhaps great and high, yet every way suiting that light and gracious discovery which he has given of himself, one thing answering another, it sets him in a frame of honoring God aright.

Seriously Consider the New Light That Had Been Revealed

Use. This might be of rich consideration could we attend it: for hence—

1. As I said before, is apostasy from God's work. He appears not unto men, how can they go upon his employment? Men that have no vision of God, are in the dark, and know not what to do. I speak not of visions beyond the word, answers of prayers, gracious applications of providences, with wise consideration of times and seasons. Some drop off every day, some hang by the eyelids,[52] and know not what to do; the light of God is not sent forth to lead and guide them (Ps. 43:3): wonder not at the strange backslidings of our days, many acted upon by engagements,[53] and for want of light, know not to the last what they were a-doing.

---

49 Luke 9:62.
50 Matt. 9:17.
51 Deut. 33:16.
52 I.e., hang by a slight hold.
53 This could well be a reference to those who supported the Treaty of Engagement that King Charles I had entered into with some of the moderate Scottish Covenanters in December 1647. It was

2. Hence also is the suiting of great light, and great work, in our days. Let new light be derided while men please, he will never serve the will of God in this generation, who sees not beyond the line of foregoing ages.

3. And this thirdly, may put all those, whom God is pleased to employ in his service, upon a diligent inquiry into his mind. Can a servant do his master's work, without knowing his pleasure? We live for the most part from hand to mouth, and do what comes next: few are acquainted with the designs of God.

Exposition of the Fearful Harbingers of a Great Work of God (3:5)

Verse 5. The going forth of the Lord with his people toward their rest, with reference to his harbingers, is described. "Before him went the pestilence, and burning coals went forth at his feet."

"Before him," at his face. The "pestilence," this is often reckoned among the weapons wherewith God fights with any people to consume them:[54] and as speeding an instrument of destruction it is, as any the Lord ever used toward the children of men.

"At his feet went forth burning coals." A redoubling say some of the same stroke: burning coals, for burning diseases.

When one blow will not do the work appointed, God redoubles the stroke of his hand (Lev. 26:22–25):

Or burning coals, dreadful judgments, mortal weapons, as fire and flames are often taken in other descriptions of God's dealing with his enemies (Pss. 11:6; 18:8): prevailing fire is the most dreadful means of destruction (Heb. 12:29; Isa. 33:14).[55]

[In] Exodus 23:28 God threatens to send the hornet upon the Canaanites, before the children of Israel: some stinging judgments, either on their consciences, or bodies, or both. Something of the same kind is doubtless here held out: he sent plagues and diseases among them to weaken and consume

---

an undertaking to invade England on the king's behalf in return for the establishment of a trial period of Presbyterianism in England. The Westminster Assembly would have been augmented and would have agreed to the future church settlement. See S. R. Gardiner, ed., *Constitutional Documents of the Puritan Revolution, 1625–1660*, 3d ed. (Oxford: Oxford University Press, 1906), 328–32. The Duke of Hamilton led an "Engager" army of ten thousand Scots across the border only to be defeated by the Parliamentarians at the Battle of Preston on August 17, 1648. For Owen, the Covenanter army, who had played such a vital role in the Battle of Marston Moor, had now apostatized from God's work.

54 In the margin: Exod. 9:15; Levit. 26:25; 2 Sam. 24:13; Ezek. 14:19; Mat. 24:7.—Owen.

55 Donagan comments that what set the destruction of Colchester apart, at least in the popular imagination, was fire, particularly the burning of the suburbs, with over three hundred houses being destroyed. See Barbara Donagan, *War in England, 1642–1649* (Oxford: Oxford University Press, 2010), 330, 333.

them, before his people's entrance. His presence was with Israel, and the pestilence consuming the Canaanites before their entrance is said to be לְפָנָיו "at his faces," or "appearances," before him, before the entrance of the presence of his holiness. And the following judgments that quite devoured them, were "the coals going out at his feet," which he sent abroad when he entered their land, with his own inheritance, into theirs, to cast out those *malae fidei possessores*.[56]

1. Sicknesses, diseases, and all sorts of judgments, are wholly at God's disposal.[57] "Affliction cometh not forth of the dust, neither doth trouble spring out of the ground, yet man is born to trouble, as the sons of the burning coal lift up in flying" (Job 5:6–7).

2. When God intends the total destruction of a people, he commonly weakens them by some previous judgments. Let the truth of this, be found upon them that hate us, and the interpretation thereof, be to the enemies, of this nation: but the Lord knows, all our hearts may well tremble, at what will be the issue of the visitations of the last years.

God Has All Means at His Disposal to Bring Judgment on His Enemies

Observation 9. *God never wants instruments to execute his anger, and ruin his enemies.* His treasury of judgments, can never be exhausted. If Israel be too weak for the Amorites, he will call in the pestilence and burning diseases to their assistance. What creature has not this mighty God used against his enemies? An angel destroys Sennacherib's host (Isa. 37:36), and smites Herod with worms (Acts 12:23). Heaven above sends down a hell of fire and brimstone on Sodom and Gomorrah (Gen. 19:24). The stars in their courses fought against Sisera (Judg. 5:20). Devils do his will herein, he sent evil angels among the Egyptians (Ps. 78:49). Fire consumes persecuting Ahaziah's companies (2 Kings 1:10–11). The water drowns Pharaoh and his chariots (Ex. 14:28). Earth swallows up Korah, with his fellow rebels (Num. 16:32). Bears rend the children that mocked Elisha (2 Kings 2:24). Lions destroy the strange nations in Samaria (2 Kings 17:25). Frogs, lice, boils, hail, rain, thunder, lightning, destroy the land of Egypt (Ex. 8–10). Locusts are his mighty army to punish Israel (Joel 2:25). Hailstones destroy the Canaanites (Josh. 10:11). Stones of the wall slay the Syrians (1 Kings 20:30). Pestilence and burning diseases are his ordinary messengers. In a word, all creatures, serve his providence, and wait his commands, for the execution of his righteous judgments. Neither

---

56 Lat. "possessors in bad faith."
57 Dysentery spread through Colchester during the eleven-week siege. See Donagan, *War in England*, 338.

the beasts of the field, nor the stones of the earth, will be any longer quiet than he causes them to hold a league with the sons of men.

Two Uses Arising from This Observation
Fear Such a Mighty God

Use 1. To teach us all to tremble before this mighty God. Who can stand before him, who commands so many legions?[58] If he will strike he wants no weapons: if he will fight, he wants no armies. All things serve his will. He says to one, "come," and it comes, to another, "go," and it goes, to a third, "do this," and it does it.[59] He can make use of ourselves, our friends, our enemies, heaven, earth, fire, water, etc., anything, for what end he pleases.[60] There is no standing before his armies; for they are all things, and himself to make them effectual. There is no flying from his armies, for they are everywhere, and himself with them. Who would not fear this King of nations? He that contends with him, shall find it "as if a man did flee from a lion, and a bear met him: or went into the house and leaned his hand on the wall, and a serpent bit him" (Amos 5:19): no flying, no hiding, no contending. Worms kill Herod;[61] a fly choked Adrian,[62] etc.

Be Confident That No Enemy Can Stand against Him

Use 2. To be a bottom of confidence and dependence in an evil day. He that has God on his side, has also all things, that are seen and that are not seen. The mountain is full of fiery chariots for Elisha's defense, when outwardly there was no appearance (2 Kings 6:17). All things wait their Master's beck, to do him service, as for the destruction of enemies, so for the deliverance of his. What though we had no army in the time of war? God has millions, many thousands of angels (Ps. 68:17), one whereof can destroy so many thousands of men in a night (Isa. 37:36): he can choose (when few others will appear with him against the mighty, as in our late troubles) "foolish things to confound the wise, and weak things to confound the strong."[63] Sennacherib's angel is

---

58 In the text: *qui tot imperat legionibus*.—Owen.
59 Matt. 8:9.
60 The Scottish invasion had been hampered by the wettest summer in living memory. See Ian Gentles, *The English Revolution and the Wars of the Three Kingdoms, 1638–1652* (Harlow, UK: Pearson, 2007), 343; John Wellens, "The Siege of Colchester," *East Anglian* Magazine 7, no. 9 (1948): 464–65.
61 Acts 12:23.
62 Foxe records how Pope Adrian IV (1100–1159) "chanced to be choked with a fly getting into his throat." See John Foxe, *The Acts and Monuments of John Foxe: A New and Complete Edition* [. . .], ed. Stephen Reed Cattley, 8 vols. (London: Seeley and Burnside, 1837–1841), 2:195.
63 1 Cor. 1:27.

yet alive, and the destroyer of Sodom is not dead. And all those things are at our command, if their help may be for our good: "Judah ruleth with God" (Hos. 11:12), has a rule by faithful supplications over all those mighty hosts. Make God our friend, and we are not only of the best, but also the strongest side. You that would be on the safest side, be sure to choose that which God is on. Had not this mighty all-commanding God been with us, where had we been in the late tumults? So many thousands in Kent,[64] so many in Wales,[65] so many in the north,[66] so many in Essex, shall they not speed? Shall they not divide the prey? "Is not the day of those factious Independents come?" was the language of our very neighbors:[67] the snare is broken, and we are delivered.[68]

Exposition of God Surveying the Land Before Driving Out the Nations (3:6)

Verse 6. The Lord having sent messengers before him into Canaan, stands himself as it were upon the borders, and takes a view of the land.

"He stood and measured the earth, he beheld and drove asunder the nations, and the everlasting mountains were scattered, the perpetual hills did bow: his ways are everlasting."

Two things are here considerable,

1. The Lord's exact foreview of the promised land: "He stood, and measured the earth, and beheld the nations."
2. His operation at that time, "He drove asunder the nations, and the" etc.

God Carefully Surveys the Promised Inheritance of His People

1. "He stood and measured." The prophet here represents the Lord on the frontier of Canaan, as one taking view of a piece of land, and exactly measuring it out, as intending it for his own, weighing and considering the bounds and limits of it, to see if it will answer the end for which he purposes it. God's

---

64 A reference to the royalist rising that broke out in Kent in May 1648, in which some eleven thousand men threatened London. See Gentles, *English Revolution*, 335–37.
65 In the spring, parliamentary troops mutinied and declared for the king, occupying Pembroke, Chepstow, and Tenby Castles in south Wales. See Gentles, *English Revolution*, 334–35.
66 In April, the royalists took control of Berwick and Carlisle in order to secure the road south of the Duke of Hamilton's Engager army of nine thousand men.
67 The Scots employed this description of the Independents. See David Buchanan, *Truth Its Manifest, Or A Short and True Relation* [. . .] (London, 1645), 121–27; James Fraser, *Chronicler of the Frasers*, ed. William MacKay (Edinburgh: Scottish History Society, 1905), 393.
68 Ps. 124:7.

exact notice and knowledge of his people's possession is in those words held out. He views where the lines of every tribe shall run.

Nothing happens or is made out to any of God's people, without his own careful providential predisposition.

He views the circuit of the whole, where, and how, divided, and separated from the dwellings of the unclean, and habitations of the uncircumcised.

Fixed bounds, measured limits of habitation is a necessary ingredient, to the making up of a national church.

2. What he did: which is two ways expressed, (1) In reference to the inhabitants, (2) to the land itself:

(1) For the inhabitants, he drove them asunder: וַיַּתֵּר and he made to leap out of their old channels. Those nations knit and linked together among themselves, by leagues and civil society, he separated, disturbed, divided in counsels and arms (as in the case of the Gibeonites),[69] persecuted by the sword, that they suddenly leaped out of their habitations, the residue wandering as no people.

God's justly nation-disturbing purposes are the bottom of their deserved ruin.

(2) For the land, "The everlasting mountains," etc. Those strong firm lasting mountains of Canaan, not like the mountains of sand in the desert where the people were, but to continue firm to the world's end, as both the words here used עַד and עוֹלָם, "perpetuity," and "everlasting," do in the Scripture frequently signify. Now these are said to be scattered and to bow, because of the destruction of the inhabitants of those lasting hills, being many of them high and mighty ones like perpetual mountains:[70] they being given in possession to the sons of Israel, even "the chief things of the ancient mountains, and the precious things of the lasting hills" (Deut. 33:15).

Observation 10. *God takes an exact foreview of his people's portion and inheritance.* Like a careful father, he knows beforehand, what he intends to bestow upon them. He views it, measures it, prepares it to the utmost bounds. They shall not have a hair's breadth which he has not allotted them: nor want the least jot of their designed portion.

Be Content Knowing That God Has Carefully
Measured Out His People's Lot and Inheritance

Use. Learn to be contented with your lot. He is wise also, who took a view of it, and measured it, and found it just commensurate to your good: had he

---

69 In the margin: Josh. 9:3.—Owen.
70 In the margin: Numb. 13:33.—Owen.

known that a foot's breadth more had been needful, you would have had it. Had he seen it good, you had had no thorns in your lands, no afflictions in your lives. O how careful, how solicitous are many of God's people! How full of desires! Oh that it were with me thus or thus! Possess your souls in patience: as you cannot add to, no more shall any take from your proportion. He took the measure of your wants, and his own supplies long since. That which he has measured out, he will cut off for you. He knows how to suit all his children.

Do Not Attempt to Rob the Saints of Their Liberties and Privileges

Observation 11. *It is dangerous encroaching, for any of the sons of men upon God's people's portion, lot, privileges or inheritance.* God has measured it out for them, and he will look that they enjoy it. Shall men remove his bounds, and landmarks, and be free?[71] Will it be safe trespassing upon the lands of the Almighty? Will it be easy and cheap? Will he not plead his action with power? Especially seeing he has given them their portion. If he has given Seir to Edom, what does he vexing and wasting Jacob? Shall they not possess what the Lord their God gives them to possess? (Judg. 11:24). He has cautioned all the world; kings and others, in this kind, "Touch not mine anointed, do my prophets no harm" (Ps. 105:14–15). Touch them not, nor anything that is theirs: harm them not in anything I bestow on them. They have nothing but what their Father gives them, and Christ has bought for them. Will a tender father think you, contentedly look on, and see a slave snatch away his children's bread? If a man has engaged himself to give a jewel to a dear friend, will he take it patiently to have an enemy come and snatch it away before his face? God is engaged to his people for all their enjoyments, and will he quietly suffer himself to be robbed, and his people spoiled? Shall others dwell quietly in the land which he has measured for his own?

Two Uses Arising from This Observation

Understand the Relevant Lessons of History

Use 1. See whence the great destructions of people and nations in these latter ages have come. Is it not for touching these forbidden things? The holy

---

71 In the margin: Vid. Tertul. *Ad Scalulam de persecutione.*—Owen. Owen is referencing Tertullian's *Ad Scapulam* (To Scapula) and, possibly, his *De fuga in persecutione* (On flight in persecution). In *Ad Scapula*, Tertullian tells the proconsul of Africa that Christians submit to those in lawful authority but also warns that "no city will go unpunished for the shedding of our blood," pointing to "the rains of the past year," the failed harvest, and various other omens (3.3–5). See Tertullian, *Apologetical Works*, trans. Rudolph Arbesmann, Emily Joseph Daly, Edwin A. Quain, Fathers of the Church 10 (Washington, DC: Catholic University of America, 1950), 154–56.

vessels of the temple at Jerusalem ruined Babylon.[72] Is not the wasting of the Western nations, at this day from hence, that they have served the whore to deck herself, with the spoils of the spouse? Helped to trim her with the portion of God's people: taking away their liberties, ordinances, privileges, lives, to lay at her feet. Doubtless God is pleading with all these kingdoms for their encroaching. They who will not let him be at peace with his, shall have little quiet of their own. The eagle that stole a coal from the altar, fired her nest.[73] I know how this has been abused to countenance the holding of Babylonish wedges.[74] God will preserve to his people his own allowance, not Rome's supplement. This nation has yet itching fingers, and a hankering mind after the inheritance of God's people: let them take heed, he has knocked off their hands a hundred times, and sent them away with bloody fingers.[75] O that we were wise, that we be not quite consumed. Of you I hope better things, and such as accompany salvation,[76] yet give me leave to cautionate you a little.

[72] Dan. 5:2, 23–30.
[73] The title page of Ephraim Udall's anonymous work *Noli Me Tangere: Or a Thing to Be Thought On* [. . .] (London, 1642) featured an image, drawn from Aesop's Fables, of an eagle carrying sacrificial flesh from an altar to its chicks that inadvertently destroyed the nest because a live coal was still attached to the meat. Udall was arguing against an attack upon episcopal land, claiming that those who bought and sold such land brought divine curses upon themselves. Udall wished to see cathedral lands and tithes maintained indefinitely and his opposition to the parliamentary cause saw him ejected as a malignant in 1643. See Arnold Hunt, "Udall, Ephraim (*bap.* 1587, *d.* 1647)," in *Oxford Dictionary of National Biography* (Oxford: Oxford University Press, 2004), accessed October 18, 2023, https://doi.org/10.1093/ref:odnb/27972. Owen is inverting the typical use of the trope of sacrilege. See Cowan, *John Owen and the Civil War Apocalypse: Preaching, Prophecy, and Politics* (London: Routledge, 2017), 101.
[74] One abuse that Owen likely has in mind is that exemplified by some from his own county, Essex, who were arguing that Parliament had reneged on its commitments to the Solemn League and Covenant and was too closely aligned with the army. The issues that are highlighted at length are Parliament's willingness to countenance religious toleration, its attempt to include "two dissenting forms of Church-Government, in one, and the same Policy," and being "too ready" to sell bishops' and church lands. See *The Humble Petitions, Serious Suggestions and Dutifull Expostulations of Some Moderate and Loyall Gentlemen, Yeomen and Freeholders of the Eastern Association* (London, [April] 1648), 4–5, 15. This strongly Presbyterian work, coordinated by Nathaniel Ward, included an attack on Parliament's County Committees and was drawn up in Chelmsford on April 12. Owen's allusion to "Babylonish wedges" is drawn from the account of the sin of Achan (Josh. 7:21). The implication of Owen's use of this motif is that if the "Jericho" of episcopacy has fallen, then the bishops' lands ought now to be devoted to destruction, with the sale of those lands representing the perpetual abolition of episcopacy. Accordingly, for Owen, those unwilling to see church lands sold had, like Achan, been seduced by something "Babylonian." For the sale of church lands, see Ian Gentles, "The Sales of Bishops' Lands in the English Revolution," *English Historical Review* 95, no. 376 (1980): 573–96.
[75] In an aggressive Restoration attack on nonconformity, Samuel Parker claimed that Owen was specifically referring to the "hands of the Cavaliers." See Parker, *A Defence and Continuation*, 588.
[76] Heb. 6:9.

(1) As to privileges and liberties of this life. Their liberties and estates, are not as other men's: but more exactly measured for their good, and sanctified to them in the blood of Christ. If in these things God has called you to the defense and protection of his, he will expect a real account. You had better give away a kingdom that belongs to others, than the least of that which God has made for his saints.[77] Think not anything small which God accounts worthy to bestow on his. If he has meted out liberty for them, and you give them slavery, you will have a sad reckoning.

(2) In point of ordinances, and Christ-purchased privileges: here it is dangerous encroaching indeed.[78] God exactly measured Canaan, because it was to be the seat of a national church. If you love your lives, if you love your souls, be tender on this point. Here if you meddle with that which belongs not unto you, were you kings, all your glory would be laid in the dust (2 Chron. 26:18). Woe to them who cut short the saints of God in the least jot, of what he has allotted to them in spirituals. Is it for any of you, O you sons of men, to measure out God's children's portion, long since bequeathed them by Christ? Let them alone with what is given them. If God call Israel out of Egypt to serve him, shall Pharaoh assign who, and how they shall go, first men only, then all without their cattle? "Nay," says Moses, "we will go as God calls" (Ex. 10:26).

Was not one main end of the late tumults, to rob God's people of their privileges, to bring them again under the yoke of superstition? What God brake in war, do not think he will prosper in peace. If you desire to thrive, do not the same, nor anything like it. Take they anything of yours that belongs to Caesar,[79] the civil magistrate, restrain them, keep them within bounds. But if they take only what Christ has given them, O touch them not, harm them not.[80] The heap is provided for them, let them take for themselves.[81] Think it not strange, that

---

77 The authors of *Humble Petitions* were outraged by the rift that had opened between Parliament and its former Scottish allies. Owen's response is that it would be better to give away the hope of being allied to Scotland than fail to tolerate the godly in England who could not submit to a Presbyterian settlement.

78 In a marginal note: *Nero primus in Christianos ferociit: tali dedicatore damnationis nostrae etiam gloriamur, qui enim scit illum intelligere potest, non nisi aliquod bonum grande à Nerone damnatum.* Tertul. Apol.—Owen. This is a reference to Tertullian, *Apologeticus* 5.3. "[Nero was the first in ferocity against Christians,] we glory—nothing less than glory—to have had such a man to inaugurate our condemnation. One who knows Nero can understand that, unless a thing were good—and very good—it was not condemned by Nero." For the Latin text and English translation, see Tertullian, *Apology*, 28–31.

79 Matt. 22:21.

80 Ps. 105:15. Owen would make the same point in *The Shaking and Translating of Heaven and Earth* (1649) and *Branch of the Lord* (1650).

81 Ex. 16:16–17.

everyone should gather his own manna. The Lord forbid that I should [ever] see the magistrates of England, taking away liberties, privileges, ordinances or ways of worship, from them to whom the Almighty has made a free grant of them.

(3) If in taking what God has measured out for them, they should not all comply with you, in the manner and measure of what they take, do them no harm, impoverish not their families, banish them not, slay them not. Alas! Your judgments, were you kings, and emperors, is not a rule to them.[82] They must be tried by their own faith. Are their souls think you more precious to you than themselves? You say they take amiss: they say, "No," and appeal to the word.[83] Should you now smite them? Speak blood, is that the way of Jesus Christ? Should it be as you affirm, you would be puzzled for your warrant. To run when you are not sent,[84] surely in this case is not safe. But what if it should prove in the close, that they have followed divine directions? Do you not then fight against God, wound Jesus Christ, and prosecute him as an evildoer? I know the usual colors, the common pleas, that are used for the instigation of authority to the contrary. They are the very same and no other, that have slain the saints of God, this twelve hundred years. Arguments for persecution are dyed in the blood of Christians, for a long season, ever since the dragon gave his power to the false prophet,[85] they have all died as heretics and schismatics.[86] Suppose you saw in one view all the blood of the witnesses of Christ, which had been let out of their veins, by vain pretenses, that you heard in one noise the doleful cry of all pastorless churches, dying martyrs,

---

82 In the margin: *Nova et inaudita est ista praedicatio, quae verberibus exigit fidem.* Grego. Ep. 52.—Owen. This is a reference to Gregory the Great's letter to John, Patriarch of Constantinople, *Epistola ad Iohannem Episcopum Constantinopolitanum*, Register of Letters III, 52: "But new and unheard of is this preaching, which exacts faith by blows." For the Latin text, see Gregory the Great, *Epistolarum*, in *Opera omnia*, ed. J.-P. Migne, Patrologia Latina 77 (Paris: Migne-Garnier, 1862), 649. For the English translation, see "Epistle LII," in *Epistles of St. Gregory the Great*, in *Nicene and Post-Nicene Fathers*, Second Series, 12:136. Owen would use this quotation again in *Of Toleration* (1649).

83 In the margin: *Magistrum neminem habemus nisi solum Deum; hic ante te est, nec abscondi potest, sed cui nihil facere possis.* This is a quotation from Tertullian's *Ad Scapulam* 5: "We have no master but God alone. He, to whom you can do nothing, is before you and cannot be hidden." For the Latin text, see *Ad Scapulam*, 704. For the English translation, see Tertullian, *Apologetical Works*, 160.

84 Jer. 23:21.

85 Rev. 16:13–14.

86 Marshall summarizes how "late patristic and late medieval anti-heretical literature increasingly focused not only on the conversion of the heretics and schismatics themselves, but also on the fate of those others whom they might persuade to become heretics or schismatics, and to stress that the duties of justice (preventing harm) and charity (saving these potential converts' souls) required punishment, silencing, and even execution of heretics and schismatics." See John Marshall, *John Locke, Toleration and Early Enlightenment Culture* (Cambridge: Cambridge University Press, 2006), 212–13.

harborless children of parents inheriting the promise, wilderness-wandering saints, dungeoned believers, wrested out by pretended zeal to peace and truth, and perhaps it may make your spirits tender as to this point.

Understand God's Purposes in Recent Events

Use 2. See the warrantableness of our contests for God's people's rights. It was Jephthah's only argument against the encroaching Ammonites (Judg. 11). By God's assistance they would possess what the Lord their God should give them.[87] If a grant from heaven will not make a firm title, I know not what will. Being called by lawful authority, certainly, there is not a more glorious employment, than to serve the Lord, in helping to uphold the portion he has given his people. If your hearts be upright, and it is the liberties, the privileges of God's saints, conveyed from the Father, purchased by Christ, you contend for, go on and prosper, the Lord is with you.

God Does the Work of Driving Out the Nations

2. From what God did.[88]

Observation 12.[89] *The works and labors of God's people are transacted for them in heaven, before they once undertake them.* The Israelites were now going to Canaan, God does their work for them beforehand.[90] They did but go up and take possession; Joshua and Caleb tell the people not only that their enemies' defense was departed from them, but that they were but bread for them (Num. 14:9): not corn that might be prepared, but bread, ground, made up, baked, ready to eat.[91] Their work was done in heaven. "Known unto God are all his works from the beginning of the world" (Acts 15:18). All that is done here below, is but the writing of a visible copy, for the sons of men to read, out of the eternal lines of his own purpose.

Continue to Play Your Part in God's Work

Use. Up and be doing, you that are about the work of the Lord. Your enemies are bread ready to be eaten, and yield you refreshment. Do you think if our

---

[87] Judg. 11:23–24.
[88] Goold omitted this line. It refers to his earlier analysis of God's "operation at that time."
[89] Following Goold, the numbering is corrected from the original, which mistakenly marked this as a second "Obser. 11." This renumbering applies to all subsequent observations in this work.
[90] In the margin: Isa. 26:12.—Owen.
[91] This is striking given the consequences of the eleven-week siege in which a contemporary report summed up the situation with respect to corn: "How eminent are their granaries of corn, (which before the enemies came, exceeded all parts of England) . . . where there was plenty before, are empty now." See *A True and Exact Relation of the Taking of Colchester* (London, 1648), 4.

armies had not walked in a trodden path they could have made such journeys as they have done of late? Had not God marched before them, and traced out their way from Kent to Essex,⁹² from Wales to the north,⁹³ their carcasses had long ere this, been cast into the field. Their work was done in heaven before they began it. God was gone over the mulberry trees;⁹⁴ the work might have been done by children, though he was pleased to employ such worthy instruments. They see I doubt not their own nothingness, in his all-sufficiency. Go on then, but with this caution, search by all ways and means to find the footsteps of the mighty God, going before you.

Exposition of the State of the Surrounding Oppressive Nations (3:7)

Verse 7. The trembling condition of the oppressing nations round about when God appeared so gloriously for his people, is held out [in] verse 7.

"I saw the tents of Cushan in affliction: the curtains of the land of Midian did tremble."

You have here three things considerable.

1. The mention of two nations, enemies of the church, Cushan and Midian.
2. The state and condition of those nations, the tents of the one in affliction, and the curtains of the other in trembling.
3. The view the prophet had of this, I saw it says he, "I saw, &c."

1. For the first, these two nations, Cushan and Midian, were the neighboring people to the Israelites, being in the wilderness when God did such great things for them. First, Cushan, that is the tent-dwelling Arabians on the south side, toward Ethiopia, being as the Ethiopians of the posterity of Cush (thence called Cushan), the eldest son of scoffing Ham (Gen. 10:6),⁹⁵ enemies and opposers of the church (doubtless) all the way down from their profane ancestors.⁹⁶ These now beheld the Israelites, going to root out their allies, and kindred the Amorites of Canaan, the posterity of Canaan, the younger brother of their progenitor Cush (Gen. 10:6). Midian [was] a people inhabiting the eastside Jordan, on the borders of Moab: so called from their

---

92 A reference to Fairfax leading his troops from Maidstone to Colchester.
93 A reference to Cromwell leading his troops from Pembroke to Preston.
94 In the margin: 2 Sam. 5:24.—Owen.
95 In the margin: Joseph Antiq. Chap. 1.—Owen. This is a reference to Flavius Josephus, *Antiquities* 1.6 and its description of the descendants of Ham. See Josephus, *Jewish Antiquities*, vol. 1, Books 1–3, trans. H. St. J. Thackeray, Loeb Classical Library 242 (Cambridge, MA: Harvard University Press, 1930), 62–65.
96 In the margin: 2 Kings 19:9; Jer. 13:23; Isa. 37:9.—Owen.

forefather, Midian the son of Abraham by Keturah (Gen. 25:3–4). These obtained a temporal blessing for a season, from the love borne to their faithful progenitor. In the days of Jacob, they were great merchants (Gen. 37:28). At this time, in less than four hundred years, they were so multiplied, that they had five kings of their nation (Num. 31:8): some knowledge of the true God, was retained as it should seem until now among some of them, being received by tradition from their fathers. Moses' father-in-law, was a priest of this country (Ex. 2:15–16), not altogether unacquainted with Jehovah (Ex. 18), and was himself, or his son persuaded to take up his portion in Canaan (Num. 10:29–30). But for the generality of the nation, being not heirs of the promise, they were fallen off to superstition and idolatry. Exceeding enemies they were to the people in the wilderness, vexing them with their wiles, and provoking them to abominations, that the Lord might consume them (Num. 25:17).

None so vile enemies to the church as superstitious apostates.

These two nations then set out all manner of opposers, gross idolaters as Cushan, and superstitious envious apostates as Midian.

2. Their state and condition severally: (1) "The tents of Cushan" were in affliction: the tents, the Arabian Ethiopians of Cush, dwelling in tents: the habitation for the inhabitant, by a hypallage.[97] They were "in affliction," under vanity, under iniquity, the place of vanity, so variously are the words rendered: תַּחַת אָוֶן, "under affliction, vanity, or iniquity." Sin, and the punishment of it, are frequently in the Scripture of the same name: so near is the relation. *Aven* is properly and most usually "iniquity," but that it is here taken for the consequent of it, a consuming, perplexed, vexed condition can be no doubt. The Cushanites then were in affliction, full of anguish, fear, dread, vexation to see what would be the issue of those great and mighty things which God was doing in their borders for his people. Afflicted with Israel's happiness and their own fears, as is the condition of all wicked oppressors.[98]

(2) "The curtains of the land of Midian," for the Midianites dwelling in curtained tabernacles, by the same figure as before. They trembled, יִרְגְּזוּן "moved themselves, were moved," that is shaken with fear and trembling,

---

97 I.e., a figure of speech in which the natural relations of elements in a proposition are inverted.
98 In the margin: *Tantos invidus habet poena justa tortores, quantos invidiosus habuerit laudatores.* Propser, dr Vita contemp.—Owen. This is a quotation from Julianus Pomerius's *De vita Contemplativa* 3.5, whose authorship was, in Owen's time, mistakenly attributed to Prosper of Aquitaine: "The envious man has by just punishment as many tormentors as the envied man had praisers." For the Latin text, see Julianus Pomerius, *De vita Contemplativa*, in *Opera omnia*, ed. J.-P. Migne, Patrologia Latina 59 (Paris: Migne-Garnier, 1862), 480. For the English translation, see Julianus Pomerius, *The Contemplative Life*, trans. Mary Josephine Suelzer, Ancient Christian Writers 4 (Westminster, MD: Newman, 1947), 112.

as though they were ready to run from the appearance of the mighty God with his people. The story of it, you have in the book of Numbers:[99] as it was prophetically foretold by Moses concerning other nations, "The people shall hear, and be afraid, sorrow shall take hold on the inhabitants of Palestina: then the dukes of Edom shall be amazed, the mighty men of Moab, &c." (Ex. 15:14–16). God filled those nations with anguish sorrow and amazement, at the protection he granted his people.

3. The prophet's view of all this: "I saw it," or "I see it": though it were 870 years before, supposing him to prophesy about the end of Josiah or beginning of Jehoiakim, yet taking it under the consideration of faith he makes it present to his view.

Faith looks backward and forward, to what God has done, and to what he has promised to do: Abraham saw the day of Christ, so many ages after, because he found it by faith in the promise:[100] Habakkuk saw the terrors of Cushan and Midian so many days before, because faith found it recorded among the works of God to support itself in seeking the like mercies to be renewed: so that this is the sum of this verse.

"O Lord, faith makes it evident, and presents it before my view, how in former days, when thou wast doing great things for thy people, thou filledst all thine, and their enemies, with fear, vexation, trembling, and astonishment."

Summary of Four Observations to Be Raised from the Exposition of 3:7

1. *Faith gives a present subsistence, to forepast[101] works as recorded, and future mercies as promised, to support the soul in an evil day*: "I saw." I have made the doctrine by analogy look both ways, though the words of the text look but one.[102]

2. God's dealing with his enemies, in the time of his church's deliverance is of special consideration: "I saw, &c."[103]

3. The measuring out of God's people's portion fills Cushan with affliction and Midian with trembling. Their terrors follow God's measuring, v. 6.[104]

4. The season of the church's deliverance being come, Cushan and Midian, opposing enemies, and superstitious revolters shall surely wax vain and perish.[105]

---

99 In the margin: Num. 25. ch. 27. & 31.—Owen. This is a reference to the Midianites in the book of Numbers.
100 John 8:56.
101 I.e., bygone.
102 This will be observation 13.
103 This will be observation 14.
104 This will be observation 15.
105 This will be observation 16.

Faith Makes Both Past and Future Mercies Present to the Soul

For the first, Observation 13, that *"Faith gives a present subsistence, to forepast works as recorded, and future mercies as promised, to support the soul in an evil day."*[106] the apostle tells us, that "faith is the substance of things hoped for, the evidence of things not seen" (Heb. 11:1).

1. "Of things hoped for": it looks forward to the promises, and so gives the substance of them in present possession, so confirming our minds and hearts, that they may have a subsistence as it were within us, though not actually made out unto us.¶[107]

2. It is "the evidence of things not seen": it extends itself not only to things promised, but taking for its object the whole word of God, it makes evident, and present, things that are past also.¶

The faith commended, is of things long since done, even the making of the "things that are seen" of the "things that do not appear" (Heb. 11:3). "Abraham saw my day," says our Savior (John 8:56). He saw it as Habakkuk saw the tents of Cushan in affliction. Faith made it present to him: all the ages between him and his promised seed were as nothing to his keen-sighted faith. Hence the apostle puts the mercies of the promise, all in one form and rank as already wrought, though some of them were enjoyed and some of them in this life cannot be. "Whom he hath justified, them he hath glorified" (Rom. 8:30): he has done it for them already, because he has made them believe it, and that gives it a present subsistence in their spirits. And for forepast works, they are still mentioned by the saints, as if they had been done in their days, before their eyes. Elisha calls up to remembrance a former miracle, to the effecting the like (2 Kings 2:14).

There be three things, in the past, or future mercies, which faith makes present to the soul, giving in the substance of them, (1) their love, (2) their consolation, (3) their use and benefit.

(1) The love of them: the love that was in former works, and the love that is in promised mercies, that faith draws out, and really makes ours. The love of every recorded deliverance, is given to us by faith. It looks into the good-will, the free grace, the loving-kindness of God, in every work that ever he did for his, and cries, "Yet this is mine: this is the kernel of that blessing, and this is mine: for the same good-will, the same kindness he has towards me also. Were the same outward actings needful, I should have them also." The free love of every mercy is faith's proper object. It makes all Joshua's great

---

106 In the text: faith gives a present, &c.—Owen.
107 The ¶ symbol indicates that a paragraph break has been added to Owen's original text.

victories, present to every one of us. The promise that had the love and grace in it which ran through them all, is given him: "I will be with thee, I will not fail thee, nor forsake thee" (Josh. 1:5). Now the apostle tells us, that the truth and love of this promise is ours (Heb. 13:5). Faith may, does assure itself, that what goodwill soever, was in all the great mercies which Joshua received upon that promise, is all ours. All the goodwill and choice love of, "I will never leave thee nor forsake thee," is mine and thine, if we are believers. He that has this present, has all Joshua's victories present. The very glory of the saints in heaven is ours in the love of it. We enjoy that love, which gave them glory, and will crown us also in due time.

(2) In their comforts and refreshments. "Thou gavest leviathan to be meat to the people in the wilderness" (Ps. 14).[108] They fed their souls full of the sweetness of that mercy, the destruction of their oppressing tyrant: we chew the cud upon the blessings of former ages. Who has not with joy, delight, and raised affections, gone over the old preservations of the church in former years? How does David run them over with admiration, closing every stop with, "His mercy endureth for ever"? Psalm 136. And for things to come, as yet in the promise only, whether general to the whole church, as the calling of the Jews, the coming in of the fullness of the Gentiles, the breaking out of light, beauty and glory upon the churches and saints, the confusion of nations not subjecting themselves to the standard of the gospel, etc. or in particular, farther assurance of love than presently enjoyed, nearer communion with Father and Son, being with Christ, freed from misery and corruption, dwelling with God for ever, how does faith act over these and the like things in the heart, leaving a savor and relish of their sweetness continually upon the soul? O how sweet also are the things of the world to come unto poor believers! Christ leads the soul by faith, not only into the chambers of presently enjoyed loves, but also into the foreprepared everlasting mansions in his Father's house.[109] Thus it gives poor mortal creatures, a sweet relish of eternal joys: brings heaven into a dungeon, glory into a prison, a crown into a cottage, Christ into a slaughterhouse.

Two Reasons for This Observation

Reason 1. From the nature of faith: though it do not make the thing believed to be (the act cannot create its own object), yet applying it, it makes it the believer's. It is the bond of union between the soul and the thing promised. He that believes in Christ, by that believing receives Christ (John 1:12), he

---

108 The correct reference is Ps. 74:14
109 John 14:2.

becomes his. It is a grace uniting its subject and object, the person believing, and the thing believed. There needs no ascending into heaven or descending, the word of faith makes all things nigh, even within us (Rom. 10:6–7). Some glasses will present things at a great distance very near: faith looking through the glass of the gospel, makes the most remote mercies to be not only in a close distance, but in union. It "is the subsistence of things hoped for," that which they have not in themselves, it gives them in the full-assured minds of believers.

Reason 2. From the intendment of all mercies: they are for every believer. All things are theirs, world, life, death, things present, things to come (1 Cor. 2:22).[110] All promises being made to every believer, and all mercies being the fruit of these promises, they must all belong to every believer. Now if all these should be kept from us at that distance wherein they fail in their accomplishment in respect of time, what would they avail us? God therefore has appointed that they shall have a real, though not a natural presence and subsistence at all times, to all believers.

Two Uses from This Observation

Use the Past to Transform the Present

Use 1. See hence what use you make of past mercies, deliverances, blessings, with promised incomings: carry them about you, by faith, that you may use them at need: "Where is the God of Elijah":[111] "Awake, awake, O arm of the Lord,"[112] etc. "I saw the tents of Cushan": take store mercies along with you in every trial. Use them, or they'll grow rusty, and not pass in heaven. Learn to eat leviathan many years after his death. Forget not your pearls, scatter not away your treasure, be rich in a heap of mercies, faith will make you so. The love, the comfort, the benefit of all former and future blessings are yours, if you know how to use them. Oh how have we lost our mercies in every hedge and ditch! Have none of us skill to lay up the last eminent deliverance against a rainy day?

Use the Future to Transform the Present

[Use] 2. Learn how to make the poorest and most afflicted condition, comfortable and full of joy. Store your cottage, your sickbed, by faith, with all sorts of mercies. They are the richest furniture in the world. Gather up what is already cast out, and fetch the rest from heaven. Bring the firstfruits of glory into your bosom. See the Jews called, the residue of opposers subdued, the gospel

---

[110] The correct reference is 1 Cor. 3:22.
[111] 2 Kings 2:14.
[112] Isa. 51:9.

exalted, Christ enthroned, all your sins pardoned, corruption conquered, glory enjoyed: roll yourself in those golden streams every day. Let faith fetch in new and old: ancient mercies, for your supportment, everlasting mercies, for your consolation. He that has faith, has all things.

Special Consideration Should Be Given to How God Treats His Enemies in the Season of the Church's Deliverance

Observation. 14. *God's dealing with his enemies, in the season of his church's deliverance is of especial consideration*; "I saw the tents, &c.," so did the Israelites, behold the Egyptians dead on the shore (Ex. 14:30–31).

"The heathen raged, the kingdoms were moved, he uttered his voice, the earth melted, the Lord of hosts is with us, the God of Jacob is our refuge, selah: come, behold the works of the Lord, what desolations he hath made in the earth" (Ps. 46:6–8). The enemies' undertaking, verse 6, God's protection to his people, verse 7, a view of the adversaries' desolation, verse 8, are all orderly held out.

The Lord tells Moses, that he will harden the heart of Pharaoh, that he might show his power, to this very end, that it might be considered, and told to one another (Ex. 10:2–3).

How many psalms have we that are taken up in setting forth God's breaking, yoking, befooling, terrifying his adversaries at such a season?

The remembrance of the slaughter of the firstborn of Egypt, was an ingredient in the chiefest ordinance the ancient church enjoyed (Ex. 14).[113]

Two Reasons to Engage in Such Serious Consideration

Reason 1. Much of the greatness and intenseness of God's love to his own, is seen in his enemies' ruin. "I gave Egypt for thy ransom, Ethiopia and Seba for Thee. Since thou wast precious in my sight, thou hast been honourable, and I have loved thee, therefore will I give men for thee, and people for thy life" (Isa. 43:3–4). When God gives such mighty kingdoms for a small handful, it appears they are precious to him. "Whosoever shall gather together against thee shall fall for thy sake" (Isa. 54:15). When God will maintain a quarrel with all the world, swear that he will never have peace with Amalek, until he be consumed, break nations, kings and kingdoms, stretch out his hand in judgment round about, and all to save, preserve, prosper, protect, a small handful, surely he has endeared affections for them. In the days wherein we live, can we look, and see, wise men befooled, mighty warriors vanquished,

---

[113] Following Goold, the reference should be corrected to Ex. 12.

men of might become as children, their persons slain, and trodden down in the field, can we but cry, "Lord, what are we, and what is our house that thou shouldst do such things for us?"[114] A serious view of what God has done in this nation of late, what armies he has destroyed, what strongholds demolished, what proud haughty spirits defeated, what consultations made vain, is enough to make us admire the riches of his love all our days. We may know what esteem a man sets upon a jewel by the price he gives for it. Surely God values them, for whom he has given the honors, the parts, the polities, the lives of so many tall cedars, as of late he has done.[115] The loving-kindness of God to his church is seen, as in a glass, in the blood of their persecutors.

Reason 2. The manifestation of God's sovereignty, power, and justice, is as dear to him as the manifestation of his mercy. The properties he lays out in destruction, are equally glorious, with those he lays out in preservation. In the proclamation of his glorious name he omits them not (Ex. 34:6–7). In these he triumphs gloriously when he has overthrown the horse and his rider in the sea (Ex. 15).

Seriously Consider How God Dealt with His Enemies in the Second Civil War

Use. Let not our eyes in the late deliverance be always on the light side of the work, our own mercies: the dark side of terror and judgment is not without its glory. The folly that was in their counsels, the amazement that was in their armies, the trembling that accompanied all their undertakings, the tympanous[116] products of all their endeavors, do all cry out, *Digitus Dei est hic*.[117] Had not God showed infinite wisdom, they had not been so abundantly foolish; had not he been infinite in power, the many thousands of enemies had not been so weak.

In the late engagement in this country, when God stirred us up, with some others in these parts, to make some opposition to the enemy gathering at Chelmsford,[118] what were think you the workings of God's providences against them?[119] How came it to pass that we were not swallowed up by them? For—

1. They were desirous to ruin us: if we may judge their desires to answer their interest, or their expressions, with the language of their friends round about us, to answer their desires.

---

114 See 2 Sam. 7:18.
115 Isa. 2:13.
116 I.e., swollen or puffed out; pompous.
117 Lat. "The finger of God is here."
118 The Essex royalists under Sir Charles Lucas had gathered at Chelmsford on June 4.
119 Donagan notes that the siege was "in a sense accidental." Donagan, *War in England*, 317.

2. They were able to do it. They had from the beginning and so all along, near as many thousands, as we had hundreds, of them very many old experienced soldiers,[120] with us not three men, that had ever seen any fighting.[121]

3. They were resolved to do it. Witness their own confessions, and frequent declarations of their purposes, while the business was in agitation.[122]

4. They were provoked to it. For the first and only considerable opposition was made to them in this place, and thereby first their assistance from Colchester hindered, which how much they valued, witness the senseless letter they would have forced the committee to subscribe, to persuade us not to disturb their levies there.[123] Secondly, suppressing and discouraging all those affected to them and their designs in these parts of the county, restraining some, disarming others, awing all. Thirdly, hastening the coming of the army, lest their friends should suffer. Fourthly, encouraging their coming, by declaring that they had friends here,[124] by which and the like they were abundantly provoked.

5. That they were also invited to it, though by persons somewhat inconsiderable, with promises of a full party of friends to assist them, which they might have had, and a rich booty from their enemies to support them, which they might have found, is too apparent.

Now being thus advantaged, thus encouraged, thus provoked, and resolved, why did they not attempt it, why did they not accomplish their desires? Is it not worth the while to consider how they were restrained?[125] Was not much of God's wisdom seen in mixing a spirit of giddiness and error in the midst of them, that they knew not well how to determine, nor at all to execute their determinations? Was not his power seen in causing experienced soldiers, as they were, with their multitudes, to be afraid of a poor handful of unskillful men, running together because they were afraid to abide in their houses? Was

---

120 At least twenty-four of the officers in the insurgency had seen active service during the first civil war—e.g., Lord Capel and Lord Loughborough, as well as several former parliamentary colonels.

121 Lucas found the road blocked at Coggeshall by Sir Thomas Honywood, who had assembled a force of volunteers. John Rushworth, *Historical Collections of Private Passages of State*, 8 vols. (London, 1721), 7:1150–53.

122 By the end of April, the Essex country petition of March 1648 had reportedly attracted some twenty thousand signatures. At the beginning of May, some two thousand marched on Westminster in protest against the level of taxation and demanding that negotiations with the king be reopened. See Robert Ashton, *Counter-Revolution: The Second Civil War and Its Origins, 1646–8* (New Haven, CT: Yale University Press, 1994), 142–43.

123 The petitioners were concerned about the burden of the levies which had been imposed by the parliamentary country committees.

124 The royalists had gone to Colchester in the hope of recuring more troops in Lucas's hometown.

125 In the margin: Gen. 20:6; Psal. 76:10.—Owen.

not his justice exalted in keeping them only for the pit which they had digged for others?[126] Doubtless the hand of God was lifted up. O that we could all learn righteousness, peculiarly among ourselves of this place: is there nothing of God to be discerned, in the vexations, birthless consultations, and devices of our observers? Nothing of power in their restraint? Nothing of wisdom in the self-punishment of their anxious thoughts? Nothing of goodness that after so long waiting for advantage, they begin themselves to think, that neither divination nor enchantment will prevail?

The Enemies of the Saints Are Motivated by Envy and Fear

Observation 15. *The measuring out of God's people's portion fills Cushan with affliction, and Midian with trembling.* Their eye is evil, because God is good. Israel's increase is Pharaoh's trouble (Ex. 1:10). When Nehemiah comes to build the walls of Jerusalem, it grieved the enemy exceedingly "that one was come a man to seek the welfare of the children of Israel" (Neh. 4:10).[127] This is the season of that dispensation which you have mentioned, "Thus saith the Lord, behold my servants shall eat, but ye shall be hungry, behold my servants shall drink but ye shall be thirsty, behold my servants shall rejoice, but ye shall be ashamed: behold my servants shall sing for joy of heart, but ye shall cry for sorrow of heart, and shall howl for vexation of spirit. And ye shall &c." (Isa. 65:13–15).

The reasons of this are taken, (1) from their envy, (2) from their carnal fear, the two principles whereby they are acted in reference to the saints of God.

Two Reasons for This Observation

Reason 1. Their envy:[128] they have a devouring envy at them, which at length shall shame them and consume them (Isa. 26:11). They are of their father

---

126 Ps. 7:15.
127 The correct reference is Neh. 2:10.
128 In the margin: *Quis facile potest quale sit hoc malum verbis exprimere, quo invidus odio hominis, persequitur divinum munus in homine*: Pros. vit. cont. *Invidia est tristitia de bono proximi* [. . .] *prout proprium malum aestimatur et est diminutivum proprii boni.* Aqu. 22ae. q. 36. A.1.c.—Owen. The first is another quotation from Pseudo Prosper, *The Contemplative Life* 3.5: "Who can easily express in words what an evil this is whereby the envious through hatred of a man attacks the divine good in him." For the Latin text, see Julianus Pomerius, *De vita Contemplativa*, 480. For the English translation, see Julianus Pomerius, *Contemplative Life*, 112. The second reference is a summary of Aquinas, *Summa theologiae* 2a2ae, q. 36, a. 1: "Envy is a sorrow over another's good fortune . . . as it considers it an evil fortune lessening one's own good fortune." For the Latin text and English translation, see Thomas Aquinas, *Summa Theologiae*, vol. 35, *Consequences of Charity (2a2ae 334–46)*, trans. Thomas R. Heath (Cambridge: Cambridge University Press, 2006), 36–37.

the devil, and he (through envy) was a "murderer from the beginning" (John 8:44). The portion God measures out unto his people is in distinguishing mercies, differencing blessings: in such things as the world has not, gives not. Now this is that, which envy takes for its proper object. That others should have enjoyments above them, beyond them, this envious men cannot bear. God accepts Abel, not Cain; presently Cain is wroth, and his countenance falls (Gen. 4:[6]). Jacob gets the blessing, and this fills the heart of Esau, with murderous revenge (Gen. 27:41). Upon all God's appearances with the apostles, how were the Jews cut to the heart, vexed, perplexed? God gives distinguishing mercies to his people, such protections, such deliverances, this Cushan and Midian cannot bear.

2. Their carnal fear: they have all of them that conclusion in their breasts, which Haman's wise men and wife made to him (Est. 6:13). If they begin to fall before the seed of the Jews, utter ruin will follow. When God begins to own his people as them in the Acts, chapter 5:24, "they doubt whereunto this will grow." Their hearts tell them secretly they are usurpers of all they have, and when God owns any, they instantly fear lest for their sakes they should be called to account. When a distinction begins to be made in ordinances, privileges, deliverances, protections, evidently given to some peculiar ones, they tremble within that they are set apart for no good. This picking and choosing of men by the Lord (Ps. 4:3), they cannot bear with. Such mighty works attend the Israelites, what thinks Midian will be the end of this? It is true their pride calls on them to act openly more of their malice than their fear: but yet this lies at the bottom: like a boasting atheist's nightly thoughts.[129] The chief priests and Pharisees, having gotten the apostles before them, what big words they use to countenance the business? "Who gave you this power?" (Acts 4:7). But when they are by themselves they cry, "What shall we do?" and, "Whereunto will this grow?" This lies at the bottom with many at this day, though they boast and lift up their mouths to heaven, their hearts do tremble as an aspen leaf.

The Church's Deliverance Provokes Both Oppressors and the Superstitious

Use. Learn not to be troubled, at the great tumultuating, which is among many against the ways of God at this day. God is measuring out his children's portion, giving them their bread in season, viewing for them the lot of their inheritance. Men of the world, profane Cushanites, superstitious apostatical Midianites, will not, cannot be quiet. Vexed they are, envious and afraid,

---

129 In the margin: *Noctu dubitant.*—Owen. Lat. "They doubt at night." This is an allusion to a quotation about atheists, which is often attributed to Seneca.

and will act according to those principles. Cushanites see religion owned, Midianites theirs disclaimed, and both are alike provoked. The Lord convert them, or rebuke them, or the one will have the armies, the other their wiles. Only judge not their hearts by the outward appearance always: they seem gallant to you, indeed they are frighted, galled, vexed. I have seen a galled horse under dressing, leap and curvet,[130] as though it had been out of mettle[131] and spirit, when indeed it was pain and smart that made him do it. They pretend to despise us when they envy us. They look like contemners, but are tremblers: be not troubled at their outward appearance, they have inward anguish; they bite others, but are lashed themselves.

The Enemies of the Church Rise Only to Be Destroyed

Observation 16. *The season of the church's deliverance being come, Cushan and Midian must wax vain and perish.* That there is such a season, I told you before. When four hundred thirty years are expired, Egypt must be destroyed, the Amorites rooted out, and all the nations round made to tremble. When seventy years of captivity expire, Babylon must be ruined, and the Chaldean monarchy quite wasted, that the Jews may return. The church being to be delivered, Haman must be hanged. This you have fully set out, [in] Revelation 6:12–17.[132] It is the fall of heathenish tyranny, by the prevailing of the gospel, which you have there described. Rome and Constantinople, pope and Turk, are preserved, for a day and an hour, wherein they shall fall and be no more. If the season of enjoying ordinances and privileges, be come to this nation, that the tabernacle of God, will be here among men, woe be to Cushanites, woe be to Midianites, open opposers, and secret apostates. They shall not be able to be quiet, nor to prevail. God will not let them rest, nor obtain their purposes: the story of Haman must be acted over again; their hearts shall be stirred up to their own ruin (Rev. 20:8). This is the frame of perishing Babylonians in the day of Zion's restoration.

Three Reasons for This Observation

The reasons are, Reason 1. Because at the deliverance of his people God will plead with their enemies for their oppressions. "It is the day of the Lord's vengeance, the year of recompenses for the controversy of Zion" (Isa. 34:8). It is "the vengeance of the Lord" and "his temple" that lights upon them in

---

130 I.e., to leap or jump.

131 I.e., eagerness.

132 Owen would make the same point about the judgment of pagan Rome in both *The Shaking and Translating of Heaven and Earth* (1649) and *Branch of the Lord* (1650).

that day (Jer. 50:28). "The violence done to me and my flesh, be upon Babylon shall the inhabitant of Zion say, and my blood upon the inhabitants of Chaldea shall Jerusalem say" (Jer. 51:35), in this day great Babylon must come into remembrance (Rev. 16:19–20).

[Reason] 2. The discerning trial, that shall, and does come along with the church's vindication, will cut off all superfluous false professors, so that they also shall perish (Mal. 3:2–3). Christ comes with a fan to send away the chaff in the wings of the wind. Have we not seen this end of many zealots?

[Reason] 3. The Amorites live in Canaan, and must be removed. Oppressors, and hypocrites enjoy many rites of the church, which must be taken from them: Rome and her adherents, shall not have so much left, as the name or title, appearance or show of a church. The outward court [which] they have trodden down and defiled, shall be quite left out, in the measuring of the temple (Rev. 11).

Faith Makes the Promises of Future Deliverance Present to the Soul

Use. Bring this observation home to the first from this verse, and it will give you the use of it:[133] proceed we to the next verse.

Exposition of the Mighty Works of God for His People (3:8)

Verse 8. "Was the Lord displeased against the rivers? Was thine anger against the rivers? Was thy wrath against the sea, that thou didst ride upon thine horses and thy chariots of salvation?"

"Was the Lord displeased" חָרָה "kindled," did he burn? That is in wrath: heat is a great ingredient in the commotion of anger, in us, here alluded to, or because the effects of anger are so often compared to fire. Against the rivers or floods? Again, "Was thine anger?" אַפֶּךָ "thy nose or face," or "thine anger," אַף signifies both: the face is the seat of anger's appearance: fury comes up into the face.[134] "Was thine anger, thy troubling anger" (so the word) "against the sea?" the Red Sea, through which your people passed. "That thou didst ride upon thy horses, thy chariots of salvation" or, "thy chariots were salvation," *currus salutares*, "thy safety-bringing chariots."

---

133 The uses of the first observation from Hab. 3:7 involved faith making these promises of future deliverance present to the soul, even in the place of great trial.

134 In the margin: *Caetera licet abscondere, & in abdito alere; ira se profert, et in faciem exit.* Senec. de ira.—Owen. This is a reference to Seneca, *De ira* (*On Anger*) 1.1.5: "Other vices may be concealed and cherished in secret; anger shows itself openly and appears in the countenance." For the Latin text and English translation, see Seneca, *Moral Essays*, vol. 1, *De Providentia. De Constantia. De Ira. De Clementia*, trans. John W. Basore, Loeb Classical Library 214 (Cambridge, MA: Harvard University Press, 1928), 108–9.

The words are an admiring expostulation, about the mighty works of the Lord, for his people, upon the sea, rivers, and inanimate creatures.

1. The rivers: Jordan and its driving back is doubtless especially intended. The Lord showed his power, in disturbing that ancient river in his course, and making his streams run backward. The story of it you have [in] Joshua 3:15–16. The people being to enter into Canaan, the Lord divides the waters of that river, making them beneath to sink away, and those above to stand on a heap. This the prophet magnifies, "What ailed thee O Jordan that thou wast driven back?" (Ps. 114:5). What marvelous, powerful disturbing thing is happened to you, that contrary to your ancient natural course, your streams should be frighted, and run back to the springs from whence they came?

2. The sea: that is the Red Sea, which in like manner was divided (Ex. 14:21), which the prophet also admires in the forecited psalm: "The sea saw it and fled: what ailed thee, O thou sea, that thou fleddst?" What strong mighty impression of power was on you, that the multitudes of your waters should be parted, and your channel discovered dry to the bottom?

3. "That thou didst ride upon thine horses and thy chariots of salvation." This you have again, "Thou didst walk through the sea with thine horses," verse 15. These were those clouds and winds which the Lord sent before the Israelites, to the sea and Jordan, to drive them back. "He maketh the clouds his chariot, and walketh upon the wings of the wind" (Ps. 104:3). So Psalm 18:10, "He did fly upon the wings of the wind."

After the manner of men, God is represented as a mighty conqueror, riding before his armies and making way for them. The power and majesty of God, was with, and upon those clouds and winds, which went before his people, to part those mighty waters, that they might pass dry: and therefore they are called his saving chariots, because by them his people were delivered.

Or by horses and chariots here, you may understand the angels, who are the host of God. "The chariots of God are twenty thousand, even thousands of angels" (Ps. 68:17), they have appeared as horses and chariots of fire (2 Kings 6:17). And their ministry no doubt the Lord used in these mighty works of drying rivers, and dividing seas. Either way, the glorious power and majesty of God, in his delivering instruments, is set forth.

Thus the words severally, now jointly:

This admiring interrogation includes a negation. "Was the Lord kindled against the rivers, was thy face against the rivers, &c." Was it that the deep had offended the Most High, that by thine angels, winds and clouds, you did so disturb the floods in their ancient course, and make naked their hidden channels, until the hoary deep cried out for fear, and lifted up his aged hands to the Almighty as it were for pity, verse 10? No surely, no such thing; all those keep the order by you unto them appointed; it was all for the salvation and deliverance of your people. God was not angry with Jordan when he drove it back, nor with the sea when he divided it, but all was effected for Israel's deliverance.

In His Mighty Works, God Shakes the Heaven and the Earth

Observation 17. *The very senseless creatures are, as it were sensible of the wrath and power of the Almighty.* Effects of anger being in and upon the deep, "he utters his voice, and lifts up his hands on high," verse 10.

God often in the Scripture sets forth his power and majesty, by the trembling of heaven, and the shaking of the earth, the vanishing of mountains, and the bowing of perpetual hills, the professed humble subjection of the most eminent parts of the creation. The sea shall fly as afraid, the rocks as weak rend and crumble, the heavens be darkened, "the mountains skip like rams, and the little hills like young sheep" (Ps. 114:4).

> The mountains tremble, and the earth, the vast
> Abyss of sea, and towering height of hills,
> When on them looks the Sovereign's awful eye.[135]

"The heavens shook, the earth dropped at the presence of God" (Ps. 68:8). The almighty Creator, holds the whole frame of the building in his own hand, and makes what portion he pleases, and when he pleases, to tremble, consume, and vanish before him. Though many things are not capable of sense and reason, yet he will make them do such things as sense and reason should prompt the whole subjected creation unto, to teach that part their duty who were endued therewith. A servant is beat, to make a child learn his duty.

Proud Hearts Should Tremble

Use. See hence the stoutness of sinful hearts. More stubborn than the mountains, more flinty than the rocks, more senseless than the great deep. Friend

---

135 In the text: Τρέμει δ' ὄρη, καὶ γαῖα, καὶ πελώριος / Βυθὸς θαλάσσης, κωρέων ὕψος μέγα, / Ὅταν ἐπιβλέψῃ / γοργὸν ὄμμα δεσπότου./ Aeschilus Justin. in apol.—Owen. These words are found in Pseudo-Justin Martyr's *On the Sole Government of God* 2. For the Greek text, see Justin Martyr, *De monarchia*, ed. J.-P. Migne, Patrologia Graeca 6 (Paris: Migne-Garnier, 1857), 316. For the English translation of wider context, see *Justin on the Sole Government of the Church*, in *Ante-Nicene Fathers*, 1:290. Eusebius cites it in *Praeparatio evangelica* 13.13 as a fragment said to be composed by the Athenian dramatist Aeschylus. Eusebius, *Praeparatio evangelica (Preparation for the Gospel)*, trans. E. H. Gifford (Oxford: Clarendon, 1903), 689.

are you stronger than Horeb, yet that trembled at the presence of this mighty God, whom it never had provoked? Are your lusts like the streams of Jordan, yet they ran back from his chariots of salvation? Are your corruptions more firmly seated on your soul, than the mountains on their bases, yet they leaped like frighted sheep, before that God against whom they had not sinned: and will you, a small handful of sinful dust, that have ten thousand times provoked the eyes of his glory, not tremble before him, coming on his horses and chariots of salvation, his mighty works and powerful word? Shall a lion tremble and you not be afraid, who are ready to tremble with a thought of that poor creature? Shall the heavens bow, the deep beg for mercy, and you be senseless? Shall all creatures quake for the sin of man, and sinful man be secure? Know you not that the time is coming wherein such men will desire the trembling rocks, to be a covert to their more affrighted souls?[136]

No People or Nation Can Thwart the Deliverance of the Saints

Observation 18. *No creatures, seas nor floods, greater or lesser waters, shall be able to obstruct or hinder God's people's deliverance, when he has undertaken it.* Is the sea against them? It shall be parted; is Jordan in the way? It shall be driven back; both sea and Jordan shall tremble before him: Euphrates shall be dried up to give the kings of the east a passage (Rev. 16:12).

Waters in the Scriptures are sometimes afflictions, sometimes people and nations. Be they seas, kings and princes, or be they rivers, inferior persons, they shall not be able to oppose. God has decked his house and made it glorious with the spoils of all opposers. There you have the spoils of Pharaoh, gathered up on the shore of the Red Sea, and dedicated in the house of God (Ex. 15). There you have all the armor of Sennacherib's mighty host with the rest of their spoils, hung up to show (2 Chron. 32:21). There you have the glory and throne and dominion of Nebuchadnezzar, himself being turned into a beast (Dan. 4:33). There you shall have the carcasses of Gog and Magog with all their mighty hosts, for coming to encamp against the city of God (Ezek. 39). There you have the imperial robes of Diocletian and his companion, abdicating themselves from the empire for very madness that they could not prevail against the church.[137] Kings of armies shall fly apace; and she that

---

136 Rev. 6:16.
137 In the margin: Euseb. *vit. Con. Const. Orat.*—Owen. Owen is referencing two works that recount the abdication of Diocletian and Maximian: first Eusebius's *Vita Constantini* 1.18, and then Constantine's *Oratio ad sanctorum coetum* 25. For the former, see *Life of Constantine*, trans. Averil Cameron and Stuart G. Hall (Oxford: Clarendon, 1999), 76. For the latter see his *Constantine's Oration to the Assembly of the Saints* and the chapter titled "Of Diocletian,

tarries at home shall divide the spoil (Ps. 68:12). All opposers, though nations and kingdoms, shall perish and be utterly destroyed (Isa. 60:12;[138] Rev. 19:18).

The Reason for This Observation

Reason. God will not exalt any creature unto a pitch of opposition to himself, or to stand in the way of his workings. The very end of all things in their several stations, is to be serviceable to his purposes toward his own. Obedience in senseless creatures, is natural, even against the course of nature in the season of deliverance. "Sun stand thou still upon Gibeon, and thou moon in the valley of Ajalon" (Josh. 10:12). "Who art thou, O great mountain? Before Zerubbabel, thou shalt become a plain" (Zech. 4:7). The most mountainous opposers shall be levelled, when the Spirit of God sets in for that purpose. There is a strength in every promise and engagement of God unto his people, that is able to carry the whole frame of heaven and earth before it. If they can believe, all things are possible to them that believe. When the decree is to bring forth, the fruit of the promise, it will overturn empires, destroy nations, divide seas, ruin armies, open prisons, break chains and fetters, and bear down all before it. As the wind shut up in the earth, will shake the pillars as it were of its mighty body, but it will find or make a passage. The least promise of deliverance, if the season thereof be come, though it were shut up under strong and mighty powers, crafty counsels, dungeons and prisons, like the doors and lasting bars of the earth, the truth and power of God shall make them all to tremble, and give birth to his people's deliverance.

The Events of the Second Civil War Show That Nothing Can Hinder God's Purposes

Use 1. Have we seen nothing of this in our days? No seas divided? No Jordans driven back? No mountains levelled? No hills made to tremble? Whence then was the late confusion of armies? Casting down of mighty ones, reviving of dead bones, opening of prison doors, bringing out the captives appointed to be slain? Is it not from hence, that nothing can stand against the breaking out of a promise, in its appointed season? "Was the Lord displeased with the

---

who ignobly abdicated the Imperial Throne, and was terrified by the Dread of Lightning for his Persecution of the Church." For the English translation, see *The Oration of Constantine*, in *Nicene and Post-Nicene Fathers*, Second Series, 1:579–80. Owen also referred to Diocletian in *A Semron Preached* [. . .] *January 31*, which is included in this volume, and *Branch of the Lord* (1650), which is in *Complete Works of John Owen*, vol. 19.

138 Owen would make a similar point from this text from Isaiah in *Of Toleration* (1649), *The Shaking and Translating of Heaven and Earth* (1649), and *Branch of the Lord* (1650).

rivers?" Was his anger against the walls and houses, "that he rode upon his horses, and chariots of salvation?"

Use 2. Let faith be strengthened in an evil time. Poor distressed soul all the difficulty of your deliverance lies in thine own bosom. If the streams of your unbelief within, be not stronger than all seas of opposition without, all will be easy. O learn to stand still with quietness, between a host of Egyptians and a raging sea, to see the salvation of God.[139] Be quiet in prison, between your friends' bullets,[140] and your enemies' swords, God can, God will make a way. If it were not more hard with us to believe wonders, than it is to the promise to effect wonders for us, they would be no wonders, so daily, so continually would they be wrought.

God Has All Means at His Disposal to Deliver His People

Observation 19. *God can make use of any of his creatures to be chariots of salvation.* This is the other side of that doctrine which we gathered from verse 5, "Winds and clouds shall obey him." Ravens shall feed Elijah that will not feed their own young.[141] The sea shall open for Israel, and return upon the Egyptians. And this both in an ordinary way as Hosea 2:21–22, and in an extraordinary way as before. So many creatures as God has made so many instruments of good has he for his people: this is farther confirmed, verse 9.

SECOND PART OF THE SERMON EXPOUNDING 3:9[142]

Verse 9. "Thy bow was made quite naked, according to the oaths of the tribes, even thy word: sela[h]: thou didst cleave the earth with rivers."

With nakedness thy bow was made naked. The rest is elliptical, and well supplied in the translation.

---

139 Ex. 14:13.
140 The issue of bullets had been a contentious issue during the siege of Colchester, with both sides accusing the other of using "chewed or poisoned bullets" designed to cause more damage and gangrenous wounds. See Donagan, *War in England*, 342.
141 In the margin: Ἐκβάλλει τοὺς νιοττοὺς ὁ κόραξ Arist. Hist. Anima. 6. *Pellunt nidis pullos sicut & Corvi.* Plin. Nat. Hist.—Owen. The first quotation is of Aristotle's *Historia animalium* 6: "The raven ejects the chicks." For the Greek text and English translation, see Aristotle, *History of the Animals*, vol. 2, *Books 4–6*, trans. A. L. Peck, Loeb Classical Library 438 (Cambridge, MA: Harvard University Press, 1970), 248–49. The second quotation is from Pliny the Elder, *Natural History* 10.15: "Ravens also drive their chicks out of the nests and compel them to fly." For the Latin text and English translation, see Pliny, *Natural History*, vol. 3, *Books 8–11*, trans. H. Rackham, Loeb Classical Library 353 (Cambridge, MA: Harvard University Press, 1940), 312–13.
142 In the margin: SERM. 2.—Owen.

The verse has two parts—

1. A general proposition, "Thy bow was made naked, &c."
2. A particular confirmation of that proposition by instance, "Thou didst cleave the earth with rivers."

Exposition of God Manifesting His Almighty Power according to His Promise (3:9a)

1. The proposition holds out two things:

   (1) What God did, "He made his bow quite naked."
   (2) The rule he proceeded by herein, "According to the oaths of the tribes, even his word."

The assertion of this verse, is not of some particular act, or work, as the former, but a general head or fountain of those particular works, which are enumerated in the following verses.

(1) A bow is a weapon of war, an instrument of death, and being ascribed to God after the manner of men, holds out, his strength, power, might, and efficacy to do whatever he pleases. And this is said to be "quite naked": when a man goes about to use his bow, he pulls it out of his quiver, and so makes it "naked." The exercising of God's power, is the making naked of his bow. This he did in all those wonders, wherein he stretched out his hand, in bringing his people into the promised land, here pointed at. And it is said that with nakedness it was made naked, because of those very high dispensations and manifestations of his almighty power. This is the making naked of his bow.

(2) For the rule of this, it is "the oaths of the tribes," or as afterward "his word." The oaths of the tribes, that is the oaths made to them: the word he stood engaged to them in. The promise God made by oath unto Abraham, that he would give him the land of Canaan, for an inheritance, even to him, and his posterity (Gen. 12:7; 13:14–15), is here intimated. This promise was often renewed to him and the following patriarchs. Hence it is called "oaths," though but the same promise often renewed: and it had the nature of an oath, because it was made a covenant. Now it was all for the benefit of the several tribes, in respect of actual possession, and was lastly renewed to them (Ex. 3:17). Hence called "the oaths of the tribes": not which they sware to the Lord, but that which the Lord sware to them. So afterward it is called his word. "Thy word." This then is the purport of this general proposition.

"O Lord according as thou promisedst, and engagedst yourself by covenant to Abraham, Isaac, and Jacob, with their posterity, that thou would give them the land of Canaan to be theirs for an inheritance, so by the dispensation of thy mighty power, thou hast fully accomplished it": and this he lays down for the supportment of faith in a time of trouble.

The words would afford many observations, I shall insist only on one.

In His Mighty Power, God Will Keep All His Promises

Observation 20.[143] *The Lord will certainly make good all his promises, and engagements to his people, though it cost him the making of his bow quite naked, the manifestation of his power in the utmost dispensations thereof.* God's workings, are squared to his engagements. This is still the close of all gracious issues of providence, God has done all according "as he promised" (Josh. 22:4; 2 Sam. 7:21). He brought out his people of old, with a mighty hand, with temptations, signs and wonders, and a stretched-out arm, and all, because he would keep the oath which he had sworn, and the engagement which he had made to their fathers (Deut. 7:8). What obstacles soever may lie in the way he has done it, he will do it. Take one instance, particular places are too many to be insisted on. It was the purpose of his heart, to bring his elect home to himself, from their forlorn lost condition. This he engages himself to do (Gen 3:15), assuring Adam of a recovery from the misery he was involved in by Satan's prevalency. This surely is no easy work. If the Lord will have it done, he must lay out all his attributes in the demonstration of them to the uttermost. His wisdom and power must bow their shoulders (as it were) in Christ unto it: he was "the power of God and the wisdom of God."[144] His engaged love must be carried along through so many secret, mysterious marvels, as the angels themselves "desire to look into," and shall forever adore.[145] Though the effecting of it, required that which man could not do, and God could not suffer, yet his wisdom will find out a way, that he shall both do it, and suffer it, who is both God and man. To make good his engagement to his elect, he spared not his only Son:[146] and in him were hid, and by him laid out, "all the treasures of wisdom and knowledge."[147]

Now this is a precedent, of God's proceeding in all other engagements whatsoever. Whatever it cost him, he will spare nothing to make them good

---

[143] Here there is a further error in the numbering with the occurrence of a second observation numbered "19." This has been corrected to observation 20.
[144] In the margin: 1 Cor. 1:24.—Owen.
[145] In the margin: 1 Pet. 1:12.—Owen.
[146] Rom. 8:32.
[147] In the margin: Col. 2:3.—Owen.

to the uttermost. He is our rock and his work is perfect.[148] A good man, if he want not power, will go through with his serious promises though he be engaged "to his own hurt" (Ps. 15:4). The power of the mighty God is serviceable to his will to the uttermost. He cannot will, what he cannot do. His will and power are essentially the same. And his power shall not he wanting to execute what his goodness has moved him to engage unto, for his own glory.

Two Reasons for This Observation

Reason 1. "He is the Rock, his work is perfect, all his ways are judgment, a God of truth, and without iniquity" (Deut. 32:4). Here are many attributes of God to make good this one thing, that his work is perfect. His αὐτάρκεια,[149] self-sufficiency, perfection, righteousness. I will pitch on one, He is a God of truth. So he is again called [in] Psalm 31:5, and in other places. The truth of God in his promises and engagements, requires an accomplishment of them whatever it cost, what power soever is required thereunto. This the saints make their bottom to seek it. Remember "thy loving-kindnesses, which thou swarest in thy truth" (Ps. 89:49). It is impossible but that should come to pass which you have sworn in your truth. No stronger plea, than, "Remember the word wherein thou hast caused thy servants to put their trust." Jacob says, he is less than all the mercy and all the truth of God (Gen. 32:10). He sees God's truth in all his mercy, by causing all things to come to pass, which he has promised him. It is true, some particular promises have their conditions, whose truth consists not in the relation between the word, and the thing, unless the condition intercede. But the great condition under the gospel, being only the good of them, to whom any engagement is made, we may positively lay down, that God's truth requires the accomplishment of every engagement for his people's good.[150] It is neither mountain nor hill, king, kingdom, nor nation, hell nor mortality, nor all combined, that can stand in the way to hinder it.[151]

Reason 2. His people stand in need of all, that God has engaged himself to them for. God's promises are the just measure of his people's wants. Whatever he has promised, that his people do absolutely want. And whatsoever they want, that he has promised. Our wants, and his promises are every way commensurate. If you know not, what you stand in need of, search the promises and see. Whatever God has said he will do for you, that you

---

148 Deut. 32:4.
149 *Autárkeia*: self-sufficiency.
150 In the margin: Rom. 8:28.—Owen.
151 In the margin: Mat. 16:18.—Owen.

have absolute need should be done. Or if you are not so well acquainted with the promises, search thine own wants, what you stand absolutely in need of for your good, that assuredly God has promised. If then this be the case of engagements, they shall all be made good. Think you, will God let his people want that which they have absolute necessity of? By absolute necessity I mean such as is indispensable, as to their present estate and occasions. That may be of necessity in one generation, which is not in another: according to the several employments we are called to. Does God call forth his saints "to execute vengeance upon the heathen, and punishments upon the people, to bind their kings with chains, and their nobles with fetters of iron, to execute upon them the judgment written," as Psalm 149:7–9?[152] Does he bring them forth to burn the whore, to fight with the beast, and overcome him and his followers?[153] It is of indispensable necessity, that he give them glorious assistance in their undertakings. They shall be assisted, protected, carried on, though it cost him the making of his bow quite naked. According to the several conditions he calls them to, the several issues of providence, which he will have them serve in, so want they his appearance, in them, with them, for them, and it shall be present. Let them be assured they are in his way, and then though some prove false and treacherous, some base and cowardly, though many combine and associate themselves against them, in many places, in all places, though whole kingdoms and mighty armies appear for their ruin, be they reviled and clamored, by all round about them, all is one, help they need, and help they shall have, or God will make his bow quite naked.

Four Uses of This Observation

In the Events of the Siege, God Manifested His Power to Keep His Promises

Use. 1. This day is this doctrine fulfilled before us. God's bow is made quite naked, according to his word. We are less than all the truth he has showed unto us. Though great working and mighty power has been required, such as he has not shown in our days, nor in the days of our fathers, yet the Lord has not stood at it, for his word's sake, wherein he has made us to put our trust. I speak of the general mercies we have received. The surrender of Colchester, the particular celebrated this day, though marching in the rear for time, is

---

152 Samuel Fairclough had expounded this text as he preached alongside Owen at the post-Colchester thanksgiving. For Fairclough, the chains with which he wished the king to be bound were "our solemn league and covenant." See Samuel Fairclough, *The Prisoners Praises for Their Deliverance from the Long Imprisonment in Colchester* [. . .] (London, 1650), 40.
153 In the margin: Revel. 17:14.—Owen.

for the weight in the van,[154] a mercy of the first magnitude. Essex has seen more power, in a three months' recovery, than in the protection of six years.[155]

That the mouths of men are stopped, and their faces filled with shame, who made it their trade to revile and threaten the saints of God, that the adverse strength, which has lain hid these seven years, should be drawn forth united and broken to pieces; that the people of God, divided, and mutually exasperated through their abuse of peace, should by the sword of a common enemy, and the help of a common friend, have their wrath abated, their counsels united, and their persons set in a hopeful way, of closing or forbearance: that God by their own counsels should shut up men collected from sundry parts to ruin others, in a city with gates and walls for their own ruin; that they should deny peace tendered upon such conditions, because of the exigencies of the time, as might have left them power, as well as will for a farther mischief; that such salvation should go forth in other parts, as that the proceedings here, should not be interrupted; that the bitter service which men here underwent, should ever and anon be sweetened with refreshing tidings from other places, to keep up their spirits in wet,[156] watching, cold and loss of blood; all these I say, and sundry other, suchlike things as these, are "the Lord's doing," and "marvellous in our eyes."[157] Especially let us remember how in three things the Lord made his bow quite naked in his late deliverance.

(1) In leavening the counsels of the enemy with their own folly.
(2) In ordering all events to his own praise.
(3) By controlling with his mighty power the issue of all undertakings.

(1) In leavening their counsels with their own folly. God's power and the efficacy of his providence, is not more clearly manifested in anything than in his effectual working in the debates, advices, consultations and reasonings of his enemies: compassing his ends by their inventions.[158] When God is in none

---

154 I.e., the abbreviation for vanguard, the foremost part of an advancing army.
155 Essex had been largely spared from the conflict during the First Civil War, only to become a center of royalist rebellion in 1648. See Charles Carlton, *Going to the Wars: The Experience of the British Civil Wars, 1638-1651* (London: Routledge, 1992), 204–6.
156 It was "a miserably wet summer" that resulted in "a sodden siege, in which rain exacerbated the discomforts of besieged and besiegers alike." Donagan, *War in England*, 319.
157 Ps. 118:23.
158 In the margin: *Quod homines peccant eorum est: quod peccando hoc vel illud agant ex virtute Dei est, tenebras prout visum est dividentis.* August. *de praed.* *Oportet haereses esse, sed tamen non ideo bonum, haereses, quia eas esse oportebat: quasi non et malum oportuerit esse, nam et dominum tradi oportebat, sed vae traditori.* Tertul., Praef. ad Haer. The first quotation is drawn

of the thoughts of men by his fear, he is in them all by his providence. The sun is operative with his heat, where he reaches not with his light, and has an influence on precious minerals, in the depths and dark bottoms of rocks and mountains. The all-piercing providence of God, dives into the deep counsels of the hearts of the sons of men, and brings out precious gold from thence, where the gracious light of his countenance, shines not at all. Men freely advise, debate, use and improve their own reasons, wisdom, interests, not once casting an eye to the Almighty, and yet all this while do his work, more than their own. All the counselings, plottings, of Joseph's brethren,[159] all the transactions of the Jews, Herod, and Pilate, about the death of Christ,[160] with other the like instances, abundantly prove it. Take a few instances, wherein God "made his bow quite naked" in the counsels of his and our enemies.

In general they consult to take arms, wherein God had fully appeared against them, wherein all probability their work would have been done without them. Had they not fought, by this time they had been conquerors. One half-year's peace more, which we desired on any terms, and they would on no terms bear, in all likelihood had set them where they would be. Their work went on, as if they had hired the kingdom, to serve them in catching weather.[161] What with some men's folly, others' treachery,[162] all our divisions, had not their own counsels set them on fighting, I think we should suddenly have chosen them, and theirs, to be umpires of our quarrels. God saw when it was time to deal with them. In their undertaking in our own county,[163] I could give sundry instances, how God mixed a perverse spirit of folly and error

---

from Augustine's *On the Predestination of the Saints* 16: "That men sin is their own doing: that in sinning they do this or that, is owing to the mighty power of God, who divides the darkness as he pleases." For the Latin text, see *De praedestinatione sanctum*, in *Opera omnia*, ed. J.-P. Migne, Patrologia Latina 44 (Paris: Migne-Garnier, 1865), 984. For the full English text, see "The Predestination of the Saints," in *Answer to the Pelagians IV: To the Monks of Hadrumetum and Provence*, trans. Roland J. Teske, *The Works of Augustine: A Translation for the 21st Century* I/26 (Hyde Park, NY: New City Press, 1999), 176. The second quotation is from Tertullian, *The Prescription Against Heretics* 30: "For it must needs be that there should *be heresies*: and yet heresies are not on that account a good, because it was necessary that they should exist. As if it were not necessary that evil also should not exist! For it was necessary even that the Lord should be betrayed, but woe to the betrayer!" For the Latin text, see Tertullian, *De praescriptionibus*, in *Opera omnia*, ed. J.-P. Migne, Patrologia Latina 2 (Paris: Migne, 1844), 42. For the English translation, see Tertullian, *Apologetic and Practical Treatises*, vol. 1, trans. C. Dodgson (Oxford: Parker, 1842), 463.

159 Gen. 45:7; 50:20.
160 Acts 4:27–28.
161 I.e., unsettled weather.
162 The royalist forces were augmented with former parliamentarians.
163 The English county of Essex.

in all their counsels. A part of the magistracy of the county is seized on:[164] therein their intention toward the residue is clearly discovered, yet not any attempt made to secure them, which they might easily have accomplished, although they could not but suppose, that there were some gentlemen of public and active spirits left, that would be industrious in opposition unto them. Was not the Lord in their counsels also, when they suffered a small inconsiderable party, in a little village within a few miles of them,[165] to grow into such a body as at length they durst[166] not attempt, when they might have broken their whole endeavor with half a hundred of men? Doubtless of innumerable such things as these, we may say with the prophet, "The princes of Zoan are become fools, the princes of Noph are deceived, they have also seduced the people, even they that are the stay of the tribes, the Lord hath mingled a perverse spirit in the midst of them, they have caused the people to err in every work, as a drunken man staggereth in his vomit" (Isa. 19:13–14). Doubtless the wrath of man shall praise the Lord,[167] and the remainder of it will he restrain.

(2) In ordering all events to his own praise. The timing of the enemies' eruptions in several places, is that which fills all hearts with wonder and all mouths with discourse in these days. From the first to the last, they had their season. Had they come together, to the eyes of flesh, the whole nation had been swallowed up in that deluge. In particular, let Essex take notice of the goodness of God; the high thoughts and threats of men, which made us for divers weeks fear a massacre, were not suffered to break out into open hostility, until the very next day after their strength was broken, in the neighbor county of Kent.[168] As if the Lord should have said, "I have had you in a chain all this while: though you have showed your teeth, you have not devoured: now go out of my chain, I have a net ready for you." For the armies coming to our assistance, I cannot see how we needed them many days sooner, or could have wanted them one day longer. Further these homebred eruptions were timely seasoned, to rouse the discontented soldiery and divided nation, to be ready to resist the Scottish invasion.[169] God also being magnified in this, that in this sweet disposal of events, unto his glory, the counsels of many of those,

---

164 The Parliamentary County Committee being taken hostage in Chelmsford.
165 Coggeshall.
166 I.e., dare.
167 Ps. 76:10.
168 Fairfax suppressed the rebellion at Maidstone, Kent, on June 1, and the surviving royalists reached London on June 3 but were dispersed. The rebellion broke out in Essex on June 4.
169 The Scottish Engager army crossed on the border on July 8.

in whom we thought we might confide, ran totally cross to the appearance of God in his providence.

What shall we say to these things? If the Lord be for us, who shall be against us?[170] All these things came forth from the Lord of hosts, who is wonderful in counsel, and excellent in operation (Isa. 28:29). Whoso is wise will ponder them, and they shall understand the loving-kindness of the Lord.[171]

(3) In controlling mighty actions. I mean, giving success to his people in all their undertakings. The commander-in-chief of all the forces in this kingdom,[172] since his sitting down before Colchester, was proffered a pass to go beyond the seas for his security.[173] Whence is it, that he has now the necks of his enemies, and has given any of them their lives at their entreaty? Greater armies than this, have been buried under lesser walls; did not the number of the besieged at first, exceed the number of the besiegers? Were not their advantages great? Their skill in war, among men of their own persuasion, famous and renowned?[174] So that the sitting down before it, was judged an action, meet only for them, who could believe they should see the bow of God, made quite naked. It had been possible doubtless to reason's eye, that many of those fictions, wherewith a faction in the great city fed themselves of the many routings, slaughters, and destructions of the army, might have been true.[175] Some of them I say, for some were as childish as hellish. In brief, they associated themselves and were broken in pieces. High walls, towering imaginations, lofty threats all brought down. "So let all thine enemies perish O Lord, but let them that love him, be as the sun when he goeth forth in his might," and let the land have rest for many years (Judg. 5:31).

Such Deliverances Are Gracious and Undeserved

Use 2. This will discover unto us the bottom and rise of all God's appearances for his people: even the engaging of his own free grace. He does not "make his bow quite naked," according to their deservings, but his own word. Not because they of themselves are better than others, but because he loves them

---

170 Rom. 8:31.
171 Ps. 107:43.
172 Fairfax had been appointed commander-in-chief of the parliamentary army in July 1647.
173 For negotiations during the siege over the issue of passes, see Donagan, *War in England*, 349–55. Initially, Fairfax offered generous terms of surrender that would have allowed the "Gentlemen and Officers to go beyond sea, and the souldiers to go home, without prejudice" (351).
174 There were experienced officers such as Lord Capel, Lord Loughborough, and a number of ex-parliamentary colonels.
175 A reference to the thoughts of some royalists in the City of London.

more than others.¹⁷⁶ Were God's assistances, suited to our walkings, they would be very uneven: but his goodwill is constant so are our deliverances.

Thankful Obedience Is the Appropriate Response

Use 3. Be exhorted to thankfulness, not verbal but real: not the exultation of carnal affections, but the savory obedience of a sound mind.¹⁷⁷ There are many ingredients in thanksgiving: suitable and seasonable obedience to answer the will of God in his mercies, is doubtless the crown of all. Look, then, under the enjoyment of blessings, in general, to close walking with God in the duties of the covenant, and in particular, to the especial work of this your generation, and you are in the way to be thankful.

Learn the Lessons Taught by This Providential Judgment

Use 4. Be sedulously¹⁷⁸ careful to prevent that, which God has mightily decried by our late mercies: viz. mutual animosities, strife, contention, and violence, against one another, I mean of those that fear his name.¹⁷⁹ God has interposed in our quarrels from heaven. The language of our late deliverance is, be quiet, lest a worse thing happen unto you.¹⁸⁰ Our poor brethren of Scotland, would not see the hatefulness of their animosities toward their friends, until God suffered that very thing, to be the means to deliver them up to the power of their enemies. The weapons they had formed, were used

---

176 In the margin: Deut. 7:7–8.—Owen.
177 In the margin: *In beneficio referendo plus animus quam census operatur*, Ambr. *Offi.*, li. 1. cap. 32.—Owen. This is a reference to Ambrose's *De officiis* (On the office of ministers), 1.32, sec. 166: "When it comes to returning a kindness, the attitude of the heart counts for more than the amount of money a person has." For the Latin text and English translation, see *De officiis*, vol. 1, *Introduction, Text and Translation* (New York: Oxford University Press, 2001), 214–15.
178 I.e., diligently.
179 In the margin: Ἡ διαφωνία τῆς νηστείας, τὴν ὁμόνοιαν τῆς πίστεως συνίστησιν. Irenae. Epist. ad Vict. apud Euseb. lib. 5. cap. 2[4]. Φιλόνικοί ἐστε ἀδελφοὶ καὶ ζηλωταὶ περὶ μὴ ἀνηκόντων εἰς σωτηρίαν. Clem. Ep. ad Cor.—Owen. The first quotation is from a letter in which Irenaeus, true to his name, sought to make peace between Victor of Rome and Polycrates of Ephesus in a dispute over the date of Easter: "And the disagreement in the fast confirms our agreement in the faith." For the Greek text and English translation, see Eusebius, *Ecclesiastical History*, vol. 1, *Books 1–5*, Loeb Classical Library 153 (Cambridge, MA: Harvard University Press, 1926), 510–11. The second quotation is from Clement's *First Epistle* 45.1: "Be competitive and zealous, brothers, but about the things that relate to salvation." Clement's appeal is made in the immediate aftermath of his condemnation of the Corinthians for removing some blameless ministers from office (44.6). For the Greek text and English translation, see Michael W. Holmes, ed. and trans., *The Apostolic Fathers: Greek Texts and English Translations*, 3rd ed. (Grand Rapids, MI: Baker, 1992), 104–5.
180 John 5:14.

against themselves. Let us learn betimes to agree about our pasture, lest the wolves of the wilderness devour us. Persecution and idolatry have ruined all the states of the Christian world.

Exposition of God's Mighty Work (3:9b)

2. Of the assertion we have spoken hitherto. Come we now to the particular confirmation of it by instance.

"Thou didst cleave the earth with rivers."[181] "Cleave the earth," or make channels in the earth, for waters to flow in.

Another most eminent work of almighty power is here set forth. Eminent in itself, and eminent in its typical signification. And the same thing being twice done, has a plural expression; "rivers."

Bringing Great Rivers from Flinty Rocks

(1) The bringing of streams of waters, from the rock, for the thirsty people in the wilderness, is that which is here celebrated. Now this the Lord did twice.

When the people were in Rephidim, in the first year after their coming from Egypt, they fainted in their journeys for want of water, and (according to the wonted custom of that rebellious people) complained with murmuring (Ex. 17:6). So they extorted all their mercies, and therefore they were attended with such sore judgments. While the meat was in their mouths,[182] the plague was on their bones.

Mercies extorted by murmurings, unseasoned with loving-kindness, though they may be quails in the mouth, will be plagues in the belly. Let us take heed lest we repine the Almighty into a full harvest, and lean souls.[183] Get and keep mercies in God's way, or there is death in the pot.[184]

Forty years after this, when the first whole evil generation was consumed, the children, who were risen up in their fathers' stead, fall a murmuring for water in the wilderness of Zin: and with a profligacy[185] of rebellion wish they had been consumed with others in the former plagues (Num. 20:4). Here also the Lord gives them water, and that in abundance, verse 11. Now, of this observe.

[1] The places from whence this water marvelously issued: they were rocks that, in all probability, never had spring from the creation of the world: further they are observed to be rocks "of flint." "Which turned the rock into a stand-

---

[181] Hab. 3:9.
[182] Num. 11:33.
[183] In the margin: Psl. 106:15.—Owen.
[184] 2 Kings 4:40.
[185] I.e., licentiousness; dissoluteness.

ing water, the flint into a fountain of waters" (Ps. 114:8). So Deuteronomy 8:15. A rock into a pool, and a flint into a stream, is much beyond Samson's riddle of sweetness from the eater.[186]

[2] The abundance of waters that gushed out; waters to satisfy that whole congregation, with all their cattle, consisting of some millions. Yea and not only they, but all the beasts of that wilderness were refreshed thereby also. "The beast of the field shall honour me, the dragon and the owl, because I give waters in the wilderness, rivers in the desert, to give drink to my people, my chosen" (Isa. 43:20).

(The very worst of the sons of men, dragons and owls fare the better for God's protecting providence toward his own.)[187]

And all this was in such abundance, that it was as plentiful as a sea. "He clave the rocks in the wilderness, and gave them drink as out of the great depths, he brought streams also out of the rock, and caused waters to run down like rivers" (Ps. 78:15–16). So also it is celebrated [in] Isaiah 41:18; 48:21; Hosea 13:5, and in many other places.

Great deliverances call for frequent remembrances.

Thus were rivers brought out of the rocks: and with, or for these rivers, God did cleave the earth, that is, either he provided channels for those streams to run in, that they might not be wasted on the surface of that sandy wilderness, but preserved for the use of his people; or else the streams were so great and strong, that they pierced the earth, and parted channels for themselves.

Great rivers of water, brought out of flinty rocks, running into prepared channels, to refresh a sinful thirsty people, in a barren wilderness, I think, is a remarkable mercy.

This Is a Type of God's Unexpected Deliverance of His Church

(2) As it was eminent in itself, so likewise is it exalted in its typical concernment. Is there nothing but flints in this rock? Nothing but water in these streams? Nothing but the rod of Moses in the blows given to it? Did the people receive no other refreshment, but only in respect of their bodily thirst? Yes says the apostle, "They drank of that spiritual rock which followed them, and that rock was Christ" (1 Cor. 10:4). Was not this rock, a sign of that Rock of Ages on which the church is built? (Matt. 16:18). Did not Moses' smiting, hold out his being smitten with the rod of God (Isa. 53:4–5)? Was not the pouring out of these plentiful streams, as the pouring out of his precious blood, in a sea of mercy, abundantly sufficient to refresh the whole fainting church in the wilderness?

---

186 Judg. 14:14.
187 In the margin: *Vir bonus Commune bonum.* Gen. 39:3.—Owen. "A good man is a good to all"—i.e., a good man is a common good. The reference is to Joseph in Potiphar's house.

Latet Christus in petra, "Here is Christ in this rock." Had Rome had wisdom to build on this Rock, though she had not had an infallibility, as she vainly now pretends, she might have had an infallibility (if I may so speak) yea she had never quite failed. Give me leave to take a few observations from hence: as—

[1] Sinners must be brought to great extremities, to make them desire the blood of Jesus. Weary and thirsty, before rock water come. Thirst is a continually galling pressure. When a soul gasps like a parched land, and is as far from self-refreshment, as a man from drawing waters out of a flint, then shall the side of Christ be opened to him.[188] You that are full of your lusts, drunk with the world, here is not a drop for you. If you never come into the wilderness, you shall never have rock water.

[2] Mercy to a convinced sinner seems ofttimes as remote, as rivers from a rock of flint. The truth is, he never came near mercy, who thought not himself far from it. When the Israelites cried, "We are ready to die for thirst," then stood they on the ground, where rivers were to run.

[3] Thirsty souls shall want no water, though it be fetched for them out of a rock. Panters after the blood of Jesus, shall assuredly have refreshment and pardon, through the most unconquerable difficulties. Though grace and mercy seem to be locked up from them, like water in a flint, whence fire is more natural than water, yet God will not strike the rock of his justice and their flinty hearts together, to make hell-fire sparkle about their ears, but with a rod of mercy on Christ, that abundance of water may be drawn out for their refreshment.

[4] The most eminent temporal blessings, and suitable refreshment (water from a rock for them that are ready to perish), is but an obscure representation of that love of God, and refreshment of souls, which is in the blood of Jesus. Carnal things are exceeding short of spiritual, temporal things of eternal.

[5] The blood of Christ is abundantly sufficient for his whole church, to refresh themselves; streams, rivers, a whole sea.

These, and the like observations flowing from the typical relation of the blessing intimated, shall not further be insisted on, one only I shall take from the historical truth.

God Continues to Bring about Unexpected Deliverances

Observation 21. *God sometimes brings plentiful deliverances and mercies for his people from beyond the ken*[189] *of sense and reason, yea from above the ordinary reach of much precious faith.* I mean not what it ought to reach, which is all

---

[188] John 19:34.
[189] I.e., range of knowledge or understanding.

the omnipotency of God; but what ordinarily it does, as in this very business it was with Moses.

I say "plentiful deliverances," mercies like the waters that gushed out in abundant streams, until the earth was cloven with rivers: that the people should not only have a taste and away, but drink abundantly, and leave for the beasts of the field.

From beyond the ken of sense and reason, by events which a rationally wise man, is no more able to look into, than an eye of flesh is able to see water in a flint: or a man probably suppose that divers millions of creatures should be refreshed with waters out of a rock, where there was never any spring from the foundation of the world.

Now concerning this observe,

1. That God has done it.
2. That he has promised he will yet do it.
3. Why he will so do?

The Divine Deliverance of Colchester

1. First he has done it. I might here tire you with precedents. I could lead you from that mother deliverance, the womb of all others, the redemption that is in the blood of Jesus, down through many dispensations of old, and of late, holding out this proposition to the full. One shall suffice me, and if some of you cannot help yourselves with another, you are very senseless.

Look upon Peter's deliverance (Acts 12).[190] The night before he was to be slain, he was kept safe in a prison. "A prison," he had neither will, nor power to break. He was "bound with two chains," beyond his skill to unloose or force asunder;[191] kept he was by sixteen soldiers, doubtless men of blood and vigilancy; having this to keep them waking, that if Peter escaped with his head, they were to lose theirs. Now that his deliverance was above sense and reason, himself intimates, verse 11, "He hath delivered me from the expectation of the Jews." The wise subtle Jews, concluded the matter so secure, that without any doubts or fears, they were in expectation of his execution the next day. That it was also beyond the ready reach of much precious faith, you have an example in those believers, who were gathered together in the house of Mary, verse 12, calling her "mad," who first affirmed it, verse 15, and

---

[190] In the margin: Preached at the Committee at Rumford.—Owen. In this sermon, delivered in the market town of Romford, Essex, Owen makes an explicit analogy between the miraculous release of Peter from imprisonment and the deliverance of the Parliamentary County Committee.
[191] Acts 12:6.

being "astonished" when their eyes beheld it, verse 16. The whole seeming so impossible to carnal Herod, after its accomplishment, that he slays the keepers as false in their hellish trust. A just recompense for trusty villains.

The time would fail me to speak of Isaac and Joseph, Gideon, Noah, Daniel, and Job, all precedents worthy your consideration.[192] View them at your leisure, and you will have leisure, if you intend to live by faith.

God's Promise to Bring About Such Unexpected Deliverances

2. He has said it. It is a truth abounding in promises and performances. I shall hold out one or two, it will be worth your while to search for others yourselves. He that digs for a mine, finds many a piece of gold by the way.

"Fear not thou worm Jacob, and ye few men of Israel, behold, I will make thee, a new sharp thrashing instrument having teeth, thou shalt thresh the mountains, and beat them small, and shalt make the hills as chaff, thou shalt fan them &c." (Isa. 41:14–16).

To make a worm a thrashing instrument with teeth, to cause that instrument to beat mountains and hills into chaff, that chaff to be blown away with the wind, that, that worm may rejoice in God, to advance a small handful of despised ones to the ruin of mountainous empires, and kingdoms, until they be broken and scattered to nothing, is a mercy that comes from beyond the ken of an ordinary eye.

The prophet professes that the deliverance promised was beyond his apprehension: "Son of man can these bones live? And I answered, O Lord God, thou knowest" (Ezek. 37:3). The Lord intimates in the following verses, that he will provide a means for his church's recovery, when it seems as remote therefrom, as dry bones scattered upon the face of the earth are from a mighty living army. This he calls opening their graves, verse 12–13.[193]

Two Reasons Why God Delivers Weak Saints in Such Seemingly Dire Straits

Reason (1). Because he would have his people wholly wrapt up in his all-sufficiency. Not to straiten themselves, with what their faith can ken in a promise: much less to what their reason can perceive in appearance. In the application of promises to particular trials and extremities, faith oftentimes is exceedingly disturbed, either in respect of persons, or things, or seasons. But when it will wholly swallow up itself in all-sufficiency, the fountain of all promises, there is no place for fear or disputing. Have your souls in spiritual

---

[192] In the margin: Gen. 22:14; 39 etc.—Owen.
[193] Ezek. 37:12–13.

trials never been driven from all your outworks,[194] unto this main fort?[195] Has not all hold of promises in time of trial given place to temptations, until you have fallen down in all-sufficiency, and there found peace? God accounts a flight to the strong tower of his name to be the most excellent valor. This is faith's first, proper, and most immediate object: to particular promises it is drawn out, on particular occasions: here is, or should be, its constant abode (Gen. 17:1): and indeed the soul will never be prepared to all the will of God, until its whole complacency be taken up in this sufficiency of the Almighty. Here God delights to have the soul give up itself to a contented losing of all its reasonings, even in the infinite unsearchableness of his goodness and power. Therefore will he sometimes send forth such streams of blessings, as can flow from no other fountain, that his may know where to lie down in peace. Here he would have us secure our shallow bottoms in this quiet sea, this infinite ocean, whither neither wind, nor storm, do once approach. Those blustering temptations which rage at the shore, when we were half at land, and half at sea, half upon the bottom of our own reason, and half upon the ocean of providence, reach not at all unto this deep. Oh if we could in all trials, lay ourselves down in these arms of the Almighty, his all-sufficiency in power and goodness, oh how much of the haven should we have in our voyage, how much of home, in our pilgrimage, how much of heaven in this wretched earth! Friends, throw away your staves, break the arm of flesh, lie down here quietly in every dispensation, and you shall see the salvation of God. I could lose myself in setting out of this, wherein I could desire you would lose yourselves in every time of trouble.

"Hast thou not known? Hast thou not heard that the everlasting God, the Lord, the Creator of the ends of the earth, fainteth not, neither is weary? There is no searching of his understanding. He giveth power to the faint and to them that have no might, he increaseth strength. Even the youths shall faint and be weary, and the young men shall utterly fall. But they that wait upon the Lord shall renew their strength, they shall mount up with wings as eagles, they shall run and not be weary, they shall walk and not be faint" (Isa. 40:28–31).

Reason (2). To convince the unbelieving world itself of his power, providence, and love to them that put their trust in him: that they may be found to cry, "Verily there is a reward for the righteous, verily he is a God that judgeth

---

194 I.e., outward fortifications.
195 This is a striking illustration given the context of the sermon. A broadsheet engraving of the siege was produced by Thomas Witham titled *The Siege of Colchester by the Lord Fairfax, As It Was with the Line and Outworks* [. . .] (London, 1648). It provides a panoramic view of the forts and positions of the parliamentary army.

in the earth."[196] When the Egyptian magicians see real miracles, beyond all their juggling pretenses, they cry out, "This is the finger of God" (Ex. 8:19). Profane Nebuchadnezzar beholding the deliverance of those three worthies, from the fiery furnace, owns them for the "servants of the most high God" (Dan. 3:26). Daniel being preserved in the lions' den, Darius acknowledges the power and kingdom of "the living God" (Dan. 6:26). Glorious appearances of God for his people beyond the reach of reason, wrest from the world amazement, or acknowledgment, and in both God is exalted. He will appear in such distresses, as that he will be seen of his very enemies: they shall not be able, with the Philistines to question whether it be his hand, or a chance happened to them,[197] but conclude, with the Egyptians, that fly they must for God fights for his people (Ex. 14:25). If God should never give blessings but in such a way, as reason might discover their dependence on secondary causes, men would not see his goings, nor acknowledge his operations. But when he mightily makes bare his arm, in events beyond their imaginations, they must vail[198] before him.

Four Uses

Consider Colchester to Be Such an Unexpected Deliverance

Use 1. Consider whether the mercy celebrated this day, ought not to be placed in this series of deliverances, brought from beyond the ken of sense and reason, from above the reach of much precious faith. For the latter, I leave it to your own experience, to the former let me for the present desire your consideration of these five things.

(1) By whom you were surprised and put under restraint. Now these were of two sorts: [1] the heads and leaders, [2] the tumultuous multitude.

[1] For the first, some of them being dead,[199] and some under durance,[200] I shall not say anything. "There can be no quarrel with vanquished men, bereft of the light of heaven."[201] I leave the stream from the flint to your own thoughts.[202]

---

196 In the margin: Psal. 58:11.—Owen.
197 In the margin: 1 Sam. 6:9.—Owen.
198 I.e., lower (often weapons) in submission or respect.
199 Sir Charles Lucas and Sir George Lisle had been executed by firing squad on the surrender of Colchester.
200 E.g., Lords Goring and Capel were held and awaiting trial by the House of Lords.
201 In the text: *Nullum cum victis certamen, et aethere cassis.*—Owen. This is a quotation from the Latin ambassadors who come seeking permission of Aeneas to bury the dead in Virgil's *Aeneid* 11.104. For the Latin text and English translation, see Virgil, *Aeneid: Books 7–12. Appendix Vergilliana*, trans. H. Rushton Fairclough, rev. G. P. Goold, Loeb Classical Library 64 (Cambridge, MA: Harvard University Press, 1918), 242–43.
202 An allusion to the smoke rising from the firing squad of *flintlock* muskets.

[2] For the multitude, an enraged, headless, lawless, godless multitude, gathered out of inns, taverns, alehouses, stables, highways, and the like nurseries of piety and pity. Such as these having got their superiors under their power, governors under their disposal, their restrainers under their restraint, their oppressors, as they thought, under their fury, what was it that kept in their fury and their revenge, which upon the like occasions and advantages, has almost always been executed? Search your stories, you will not find many that speak of such a deliverance. For a few governors prevailed on, unto durance, by a godless rout,[203] in an insurrection, and yet come off in peace and safety, is surely a work of more than ordinary providence.

(2) Consider the season of your surprisal,[204] when all the kingdom was in an uproar, and the arm of flesh almost quite withered as to supply. The north invaded,[205] the south full of insurrections,[206] Wales unsubdued,[207] the great city at least suffering men to lift up their hands against us;[208] so that to the eye of reason the issue of the whole, was if not lost, yet exceedingly hazardous:[209] and so to the eye of reason your captivity endless. Had they gone on as was probable they would, whether you had this day been brought out to execution, or thrust into a dungeon, or carried up and down as a pageant, I know not, but much better condition, I am sure rationally you could not expect.

(3) The end of your surprisal. Among others, this was apparently one, to be a reserve for their safety, who went on, in all ways of ruin. You were kept to preserve them in those ways, wherein they perished. Whether could reason reach this or no; that you being in their power, kept on purpose for their rescue, if brought to any great strait, with the price of your heads, to redeem their own, that they should be brought to greater distress, than ever

---

203 I.e., an unruly and disreputable group.
204 I.e., surprise.
205 At the end of April, Berwick and Carlisle had been seized in preparation for the Engager Army's invasion. The Duke of Hamilton subsequently crossed the border into the north of England on July 8.
206 Particularly the revolts in Kent and Essex, and the Downs Mutiny.
207 The royalist insurgents in south Wales held the fortified castles of Chepstow, Tenby, and Pembroke.
208 In the summer of 1648, London was "a powder keg, waiting for the flame" with the royalists busy recruiting men and gathering supplies with the intent of coming to the aid of the forces in Colchester. See Gentles, "The Struggle for London," 298–99.
209 In the margin: *Idem huic urbi dominandi finis erit, qui parendi fuerit.* Senec. de Ro.—Owen. This is a quotation from Seneca the Younger's *De clementia* (On mercy) 1.3, which described the importance of Rome for the emperor and the empire: "The end of this city's rule will be one with the end of her obedience." For the Latin text and English translation, see Seneca, *Moral Essays*, 368–69.

any before in this kingdom, and you be delivered, without the least help to them in their need, it was beyond your friends' reason, who could not hope it, it was beyond our enemies' reason who never feared it, if you believed it, you have the comfort of it.

(4) The refusal of granting an exchange, for such persons, as they accounted more considerable than yourselves, and whose enlargement might have advantaged the cause they professed to maintain, exceedingly more than your restraint, what does it but proclaim your intended ruin?[210] This was the way of deliverance, which for a long season, reason chiefly rested on, the main pillar of all its building, which when it was cut in two, what could be seen in it but desolation.

(5) The straits you were at length reduced to, between your enemies' swords and your friends' bullets,[211] which intended for your deliverance, without the safeguard of providence, might have been your ruin, piercing more than once, the house wherein you were. Surely it was then an eminent work of faith to stand still, and see the salvation of God.[212]

The many passages of providence evidently working for your preservation, which I have received from some of yourselves, I willingly pass over. What I have already said is sufficient to declare that to reason's eye you were as dead bones upon the earth. For our parts who were endangered spectators, at the best, we were but in the prophet's frame, and to any question about your enlargement, could answer only, "The Lord alone knows."[213] And now behold the Lord has chosen you out, to be examples of his loving-kindness, in fetching mercy for you, from beyond the ken of reason, yea from above the reach of much precious faith. He has brought water for you out of the flint. Reckon your deliverance under this head of operations, and I hope you will not be unthankful.

Learn to Live by Faith

Use 2. You that have received so great mercy, we that have seen it, and all who have heard the doctrine confirmed, let us learn to live by faith. Live above all things that are seen. Subject them to the cross of Christ. Measure your

---

210 During the negotiations for a prisoner exchange, Norwich "refused point blank to negotiate, or negotiations foundered on a technicality or drifted to inconclusion." See Donagan, *War in England*, 349.
211 It was said that the hostages were deliberately housed in a vulnerable position. Donagan, *War in England*, 348.
212 Ex. 14:13.
213 Ezek. 37:3.

condition, by your interest in God's all-sufficiency. Do not in distress calculate what such, and such things can effect, but what God has promised. Reckon upon that, for it shall come to pass. If you could get but this one thing, by all your sufferings and dangers, to trust the Lord to the utmost extent of his promises, it would prove a blessed captivity. All carnal fears would then be conquered, all sinful compliances with wicked men removed, etc.

Respond with Gratitude to Such a Mighty Deliverance

Use 3. Be exhorted to great thankfulness, you that have been made partakers of great deliverances.[214] In great distresses, very nature prompts the sons of men to great promises. You have heard the ridiculous story of him, who in a storm at sea, promised to dedicate a wax candle to the blessed Virgin, as big as the mast of his ship, which he was resolved when he came on shore to pay with one of twelve in the pound.[215] Let not the moral of that fable be found in any of you. Come not short of any of your engagements. No greater discovery of a hypocritical frame, than to flatter the Lord in trouble, and to decline upon deliverance in cold blood. The Lord of heaven give you strength to make good all your resolutions: as private persons, in all godliness and honesty, following hard after God in every known way of his; as magistrates, in justice equity and faithful serving the kingdom of Christ: especially let them never beg in vain for help at your hands, who did not beg help in vain, for you at the hands of God.

Learn Spiritual Lessons from This Temporal Deliverance

Use 4. Consider, if there be so much sweetness in a temporal deliverance, oh what excellency is there in that eternal redemption, which we have in the

---

214 In the margin: *Erunt homicidae, tyranni, fulteri, raptores, Sacrilegi proditores, infra ista omnia, ingratus est.* Senec. Benef. L. 1. *Gratiarum cessat decursus, ubi recursus non fuerit.* Bern. Serm. 50.—Owen. The first quotation is from Seneca, *De beneficiis* (On benefits) 1.10, which suggests that ingratitude is the worst of vices. "Homicides, tyrants, thieves, adulterers, robbers, sacrilegious men, and traitors there always will be; but worse than all these is the crime of ingratitude." For the Latin text and English translation, see Seneca, *Moral Essays*, vol. 3, *De beneficiis*, trans. John W. Basore, Loeb Classical Library 310 (Cambridge, MA: Harvard University Press, 1935), 32–33. The second quotation is from Bernard of Clairvaux's Lenten sermon, *In capite jejunii* (*The Head of the Fast*) 1.4: "If there is no reciprocity the descent of grace stops." For the Latin text, see Bernard, *Sermones de tempore*, in *Opera omnia*, ed. J.-P. Migne, Patrologia Latina 183 (Paris: Migne-Garnier, 1862), 170. For the English translation, see *Sermons for Lent and the Easter Season*, trans. Irene Edmonds, ed. Mark A. Scott, Cistercian Fathers 52 (Collegeville, MN: Liturgical Press, 2013), 27.

215 This is a reference to a story of the captain on an Italian ship in the Gulf of Venice who determined to discharge his debt at twelve, rather than twenty, shillings to the pound. It is recounted in William Biddulph, *The Travels of Certaine Englishmen into Africa, Asia, Troy, Bythnia, Thracia, and to the Blacke Sea, &c* (London, 1609), 8.

blood of Jesus?[216] If we rejoice for being delivered from them, who could have killed the body, what unspeakable rejoicing is there in that mercy whereby we are freed from the wrath to come. Let this possess your thoughts, let this fill your souls, let this be your haven from all former storms, and here strike I sail, in this, to abide with you, and all the saints of God for ever.

FINIS.[217]

---

[216] In the margin: *Si tanti vitrum, quanti Margaritum?* Tertul.—Owen. This is a quotation from Tertullian's *To the Martyrs* 4: "If the bead made of glass is rated so highly, how much must the true pearl be worth?" For the Latin text, see Tertullian, *Ad martyres*, 626. For the English translation, see Tertullian, *Disciplinary, Moral and Ascetical Works*, 28. In other words, if human suffering is so valuable, then what must be the value of suffering for Christ?

[217] Lat. "The End."

A SERMON PREACHED TO THE HONORABLE HOUSE OF COMMONS, IN PARLIAMENT ASSEMBLED: ON JANUARY 31. A DAY OF SOLEMN HUMILIATION.

With a Discourse about Toleration, and the Duty of the Civil Magistrate about Religion, Thereunto Annexed. Humbly Presented to Them, and All Peace-Loving Men of This Nation.

By John Owen, pastor of the church of Christ, which is at Coggeshall in Essex

---

London, printed by Matthew Simmons, in Aldersgate Street, 1649

[Parliamentary Order]

Die Mercuriie, 31 Januarii 1648.[1]

Ordered by the Commons assembled in Parliament, that Master Allen,[2] do give the thanks of this House, to Master Owen, for the great pains he took in his sermon, preached before the House this day at Margaret's, Westminster; and that he be desired to print his sermon at large, wherein he is to have the like privilege of printing it, as others in the like kind usually have had.[3]

Hen: Scobell Cler:[4]
Parl. Dom. Com.[5]

---

1 Lat. 'Wednesday, 31 January, 1649.
2 Alderman Francis Allein (1605–1658), a recruiter member of Parliament for Cockermouth in Cumberland, was a wealthy goldsmith and member of the London Common Council. Although he did not sign the king's death warrant, he did take a hard line in the High Court of Justice and broadly supported the revolution as an active member of the Rump Parliament. See David Underdown, *Pride's Purge: Politics in the Puritan Revolution* (Oxford: Clarendon, 1971), 214, 242. Of relevance to the tract appended to the published version of Owen's sermon is the fact that Allein was willing to see toleration given to gathered congregations within the parochial structures of the English Church. See Keith Lindley, *Popular Politics and Religion in Civil War London* (Aldershot, UK: Scholar Press, 1997), 278, 390.
3 *Journals of the House of Commons*, 13 vols. (London: HMSO, 1802–1803), 6:126.
4 I.e., Henry Scobell Clerk. Henry Scobell (1610–1660) had been appointed Clerk of the House of Commons earlier in the month.
5 I.e., Clerk of Parliament.

[Dedication]

To the Right Honorable the Commons of England, Assembled in Parliament

Sirs,

It has always suited the wisdom of God, to do great things in difficult seasons. He sets up walls in troublous times (Dan. 9:25). His builders must hold swords and spears, as well as instruments of labor (Neh. 4:16). Yea while sin continued in its course here (which began in heaven, and having contemporized with the earth, shall live forever in hell). Great works for God, will cause great troubles among men. The holy, harmless Reconciler of heaven and earth,[1] bids us expect the sword, to attend his undertakings for, and way of making peace (Matt. 10:34). All the waves in the world; arise to their height and roaring, from the confronting of the breath of God's Spirit, and the vapors of men's corruptions. Hence seasons receive their degrees of difficulty, according to the greatness and weight of the works which in them God will accomplish. To their worth and excellency is man's opposition proportioned. This, the instruments of his glory in this generation, shall continually find true to their present trouble, and future comfort.

As the days approach for the delivery of the decree,[2] to the shaking of heaven and earth,[3] and all the powers of the world, to make way for the establishment of that kingdom which shall not be given to another people (the

---

1 Col. 1:20.
2 Zeph. 2:1.
3 In the margin: Heb. 12:26–27.—Owen. Owen would offer an extended discussion of this in his parliamentary sermon from April 1649, *The Shaking and Translating of Heaven and Earth*, which is included in this volume.

great expectation of the saints of the Most High before the consummation of all)[4] so tumults, troubles, vexations and disquietness, must certainly grow and increase among the sons of men.[5]

A dead woman (says the proverb) will not be carried out of her house under four men.[6] Much less will living men, of wisdom and power, be easily and quietly dispossessed of that share and interest in the things of Christ, which long-continued usurpation, has deluded them into an imagination of being their own inheritance. This then being shortly to be effected, and the scale being ready to turn against the man of sin,[7] notwithstanding his balancing it in opposition to the witness of Jesus, with the weight and poise of earthly power, no wonder if heaven, earth, sea, and dry land, be shaken in their giving place to the things that cannot be moved.[8] God Almighty having called you forth (right honorable) at his entrance to the rolling up of the nation's heavens like a scroll,[9] to serve him in your generation in the high places of Armageddon,[10] you shall be sure not to want experience of that opposition which is raised against the great work of the Lord, which generally swells most, against the visible instruments thereof.

And would to God, you had only the devoted sons of Babel to contend withal, that the men of this shaking earth were your only antagonists: that the malignity of the dragon's tail, had had no influence on the stars of heaven, to prevail with them to fight in their courses against you.[11] But *iacta est alea*,[12] the providence of God must be served, according to the discovery made of his

---

4 In the margin: Dan. 7:27.—Owen.
5 In the margin: *Ego nisi istos tumultus viderem, verbum Dei in mundo non esse dicerem.* Luth. de s. A.—Owen. This is a reference to Martin Luther, *De servo arbitrio* (*On the Bondage of the Will*) (1525): "Personally, did I not see these upheavals, I should say that the Word of God was not in the world." For the Latin text, see *D. Martin Luthers Werke, Kritische Gesamtausgabe* (Weimar: Hermann Böhlau und Nachfolger, 1883–2009), 18.625-26. For the English translation, see *The Bondage of the Will: A New Translation of "De servo arbitrio" (1525); Martin Luther's Reply to Erasmus of Rotterdam*, trans. J. I. Packer and O. R. Johnston (Cambridge: James Clarke, 1957), 92.
6 John Ray, *A Collection of English Proverbs Digested into a Convenient Method for the Speedy Finding any one upon Occasion* (Cambridge, 1678), 354. "A dead woman will have four to carry her forth." The inference is that the move might be more difficult than at first imagined.
7 2 Thess. 2:3.
8 Heb. 12:28.
9 In the margin: Isa. 34:4–5.—Owen.
10 In the margin: Revel. 16:16.—Owen.
11 In the margin: Revel. 12:4.—Owen.
12 Lat. "The die is cast." This quotation is attributed by Suetonius to Julius Caesar as he led his army across the Rubicon. For the Latin text and English translation, see Suetonius, *The Lives of the Caesars*, vol. 1, Julius. Augustus. Tiberius. Gaius. Caligula, trans. J. C. Rolfe, Loeb Classical Library 31 (London: Heinemann, 1914), 76–77.

own unchangeable will, and not the mutable interests and passions of the sons of men. For verily "the Lord of hosts hath purposed to pollute the pride of all glory, and to bring into contempt all the honourable of the earth" (Isa. 23:9).

The contradictions of sinners against all that walk in the paths of righteousness and peace, with the supportment which their spirits may receive (as being promised) who pursue those ways, notwithstanding those contradictions, are in part discovered in the ensuing sermon: the foundation of that whole transaction of things, which is therein held out, in reference to the present dispensations of providence (being nothing but an entrance into the unraveling of the whole web of iniquity, interwoven of civil and ecclesiastical tyranny, in opposition to the kingdom of the Lord Jesus) I chose not to mention. Neither shall I at present add anything thereabout, but only my desire that it may be eyed as the granted basis of the following discourse. Only by your very favorable acceptation of the making out those thoughts, which were the hasty conception, and like Jonah's gourd,[13] the child of a night or two (which with prayer for a rooting in the hearts of them to whom they were delivered, had certainly withered, in their own leaves, had they not received warmth and moisture from your commands in general, and the particular desires of many of you, to give them a life of a few days longer). I am encouraged to the annexing of a few lines, as a freewill offering to attend the following product of obedience.

Now this shall not be as to the opposition which you do and shall yet farther meet withal, but as to the causes, real, or pretended, which are held forth as the bottom of that contradiction wherewith on every side you are encompassed.

The things in reference whereunto, your procedence[14] is laden with such criminations,[15] as these sad days of recompense, have found to be comets portending no less than blood, are first civil, then religious.

For the first, as their being beyond the bounds of my calling, gives them sanctuary from being called forth to my consideration, so neither have I the least thoughts with Absalom of a more orderly carrying on of affairs,[16] might my desires have any influence into their disposal. Waiting at the throne of grace,[17] that those whom God has entrusted with, and enabled for, the transaction of these things, may be directed and supported in their employment, is the utmost of my undertaking herein.

---

13 Jonah 4:6.
14 I.e., course of action, particularly in the business of Parliament.
15 I.e., severe accusations of a crime or offence.
16 2 Sam. 15:4.
17 Heb. 4:16.

For the other, or religious things, the general interest I have in them as a Christian, being improved by the superadded title of a minister of the gospel (though unworthy the one name, and the other), gives me not only such boldness as accrues from enjoyed favor, but also such a right as will support me to plead concerning them, before the most impartial judicature.[18]

And this I shall do (as I said before) merely in reference to those criminations, which are laid by conjectural presumptions on your honorable assembly, and made a cause of much of that opposition and contradiction you meet withal. Now in particular, it is the toleration of all religions or invented ways of worship, wherein your constitutions are confidently antedated in many places of the nation, the thing itself withal, being held out, as the most enormous apprehension, and desperate endeavor for the destruction of truth and godliness that ever entered the thoughts of men, professing the one and the other. The contest hereabout, being *adhuc sub judice*,[19] and there being no doubt, but that the whole matter, commonly phrased as above, has (like other things) sinful and dangerous extremes. I deemed it not amiss, to endeavor the pouring a little cold water upon the common flames, which are kindled in the breasts of men about this thing. And who knows, whether the words of a weak nothing, may not by the power of the fountain of beings, give some light into the determination and establishment of a thing of so great concernment and consequence, as this is generally conceived to be. What is in this my weak undertaking, of the Lord, I shall beg of him, that it may be received, what is of myself I beg of you that it may be pardoned. That God Almighty would give you to "prove all things" that come unto you in his way, and to "hold fast that which is good",[20] granting you unconquerable assistance, in constant perseverance, is the prayer of,

Coggeshall, Feb. 28.

Your devoted servant in our dearest Lord:
John Owen.

---

18 I.e., the judiciary.
19 Lat. "as yet before the judge."
20 1 Thess. 5:21.

A Sermon Preached to the Honorable House of Commons, Jan. 31. 1648.[1]

> *Let them return to thee, but return not thou unto them. And I will make thee unto this people a fenced brazen wall, and they shall fight against thee, but they shall not prevail against thee: for I am with thee to save thee, and to deliver thee, saith the Lord.*
>
> JEREMIAH 15:19–20

INTRODUCTION AND INITIAL OBSERVATIONS FROM THE CHAPTER AS WHOLE

The words of my text having a full dependence upon, and flowing out from, the main subject matter of the whole chapter; I must of necessity take a view thereof, and hold out unto you the mind of God contained therein, before I enter upon the part thereof chiefly intended: and this I shall do with very brief observations, that I may not anticipate myself, from a full opening and application of the words of my text.

And this the rather are my thoughts led unto, because the whole transaction of things between the Lord and a stubbornly sinful nation, exceedingly accommodated to the carrying on of the controversy, he is now pleading with that wherein we live, is set out (as we say) to the life therein.

Of the whole chapter there be these five parts:

---

[1] The year should be corrected from 1648 to 1649. At the time, the new year was taken to begin on Lady Day, March 25.

1. The denunciation of fearful wasting, destroying, judgments; against Judah and Jerusalem, verse 3 and so on to the 10.
2. The procuring, deserving cause of these overwhelming calamities, verses 4 and 6.
3. The inevitableness of these judgments, and the inexorableness[2] of the Lord as to the accomplishment of all the evils denounced, verse 1.
4. The state and condition of the prophet, with the frame and deportment of his spirit, under those bitter dispensations of providence, verses 10, 15–18.
5. The answer and appearance of God unto him upon the making out of his complaint, verses 11–14 and 19–21.

My text lies in the last part, but yet with such dependence on the former as enforces to a consideration of them.

PART 1: GOD THREATENS A RANGE OF JUDGMENTS AGAINST A SINFUL PEOPLE (15:3–10)

1. There is the denunciation of fearful wasting, destroying judgments, to sinful Jerusalem, verse 2, and so onward, with some interposed ejaculations, concerning her inevitable ruin, as verses 5–6.

Here's death, sword, famine, captivity, verse 2, banishment, verse 4, unpitied desolation, verse 5, redoubled destruction, bereaving, fanning, spoiling, etc., verses 6–9.

That universal devastation of the whole people, which came upon them in the Babylonish captivity, is the thing here intended; the means of its accomplishment by particular plagues and judgments, in their several kinds (for the greater dread and terror), being at large enumerated: the faithfulness of God, also, being made hereby to shine more clear, in the dispersion of that people; doing, not only for the main, what before he had threatened, but in particular, executing the judgments recorded (Luke 21:24 etc.; Deut. 28:15 etc.); fulfilling hereby what he had devised, accomplishing the word he had commanded in the days of old (Lam. 2:17).

That which hence I shall observe is only from the variety of these particulars, which are held out as the means of the intended desolation.

Observation 1. *God's treasures of wrath against a sinful people, have sundry and various issues for the accomplishment of the appointed end.*

---

2 I.e., the unalterable nature.

When God walks contrary to a people, it is not always in one path, he has seven ways to do it, and will do it seven times (Lev. 26:24). He strikes not always with one weapon, nor in one place. As there is with him ποικίλη χάρις, "manifold and various grace" (1 Pet. 4:10), love and compassion making out itself in choice variety, suited to our manifold indigencies:[3] so there is, ὀργὴ τεθησαυρισμένη, "stored, treasured wrath," (Rom. 2:5), suiting itself in its flowings out, to the provocations of stubborn sinners.

The first emblem of God's wrath against man, was a "flaming sword turning itself every way" (Gen. 3 last):[4] not only in one, or two, but in all their paths, he meets them with his "flaming sword."

As a wild beast in a net, so are sinners under inexorable judgments;[5] the more they strive, the more they are enwrapped, and entangled. They shuffle themselves from under one calamity, and fall into another; "As if a man did flee from a lion, and a bear met him; or went into the house and leaned his hand on the wall, and a serpent bit him" (Amos 5:19). Oh remove this one plague, says Pharaoh;[6] if he can escape from under this pressure, he thinks he shall be free: but, when he fled from the lion, still the bear met him, and when he went into the house, the serpent bit him.

And as the flaming sword turns every way, so God can put it into everything: to those that cry, "Give me a king,"[7] God can give him in his anger; and from those that cry, "Take him away," he can take him away in his wrath (Hos. 13:10–11).[8]

Oh, that this might seal up instruction to our own souls; what variety of calamities have we been exercised withal, for sundry years? What Pharaoh-like spirits have we had under them? Oh that we were delivered this once, and then all were well! How do we spend all our thoughts to extricate ourselves from our present pressures? If this hedge, this pit were passed, we should have smooth ground to walk in! Not considering that God can fill our safest paths with snares and serpents: "Give us peace, give us wealth, give us, as we were, with our own, in quietness." Poor creatures! Suppose all these desires were in sincerity, and not as with the most they are, fair colors of foul and bloody

---

3   I.e., wants or deficiencies.
4   Gen. 3:24.
5   In the margin: Isa. 51:20.—Owen.
6   In the margin: Exod. 10:17.—Owen.
7   1 Sam. 8:5.
8   The idea that God granted the people of Judah a king in his wrath was used at the time by apologists for the Commonwealth to argue that kingship was not endowed with inviolable sanctity that many claimed for it. See Nicole Greenspan, *Selling Cromwell's Wars: Media, Empire and Godly Warfare, 1650–1658* (London: Routledge, 2016), 21.

designs; yet if peace were, and wealth were, and former things were, and God were not, what would it avail you? Cannot he poison your peace, and canker[9] your wealth? And when you were escaped out of the field from the lion and the bear, appoint a serpent to bite you, leaning upon the walls of your own house? In vain do you seek to stop the streams, while the fountains are open; turn yourselves whither you will, bring yourselves into what condition you can, nothing but peace and reconciliation with the God of all these judgments, can give you rest in the day of visitation: you see what variety of plagues are in his hand: changing of condition will do no more to the avoiding of them, than a sick man's turning himself from one side of the bed to another; during his turning, he forgets his pain by striving to move, being laid down again, he finds his condition the same as before; this is the first thing, we are under various judgments, from which by ourselves there is no deliverance.

PART 2: DIVINE JUDGMENT COMES AGAINST IDOLATROUS AND TYRANNICAL NATIONS (15:4, 6)

2. The second thing here expressed is, the procuring cause of these various judgments, set down, verse 4—"Because of Manasseh son of Hezekiah king of Judah, for that which he did in Jerusalem."

The sins of Manasseh filled the ephah of Judah's wickedness, and caused the talent of lead to be laid on the mouth thereof.[10] Oftentimes in the relation of his story, does the Holy Ghost emphatically express this; that, "For his sin Judah should be destroyed" (2 Kings 21:11). Yea when they had a little reviving under Josiah, and the bowels of the Lord began to work in compassion toward them; yet as it were, remembering the provocation of this Manasseh, he recalls his thoughts of mercy (2 Kings 23:26–27). The deposing of divine and human things is oftentimes very opposite.[11] God himself proceeds with them in a diverse dispensation: in the spiritual body the members offend and the head is punished: "The iniquity of us all did meet on him" (Isa. 53:[6]). In the civil politic body, the head offends and the members rue it; Manasseh sins, and Judah must go captive.

---

9 I.e., to cause to become infected with a corrupting disease or influence.
10 In the margin: Zech. 5:7.—Owen.
11 In the margin: *Est quaedam aemulatio divinae rei, & humanae*, Tertul. Ap.—Owen. This is a quotation from Tertullian's *Apologeticus* 50.16: "There is a rivalry between God's ways and man's." For the Latin text and English translation, see Tertullian, *Apology*, in Tertullian, Minucius Felix, *Apology. De Spectaculis. Minucius Felix: Octavius*, trans. T. R. Glover and Gerald H. Rendall, Loeb Classical Library 250 (Cambridge, MA: Harvard University Press, 1931), 226–27.

God Justly Punishes the Nation for the Sins of the King

Three things present themselves for the vindication of the equity of God's righteous judgments, in the recompensing the sins of the king upon the people.

1. The concurrence and influence of the people's power into their rule and government: they that set him up, may justly be called to answer for his miscarriage. The Lord himself had before made the sole bottom of that political administration to be their own wills. "If thou wilt have a king, after the manner of the nations" (Deut. 17:14; 1 Sam. 8:7), though for particulars, himself (according to his supreme sovereignty) placed in many, by peculiar exemption, otherwise his providence was served by their plenary consent, or by such dispensation of things as you have related. "Then were the people of Israel divided into two parts, half of the people followed Tibni the son of Ginath to make him king, and half followed Omri: but the people that followed Omri prevailed against the people that followed Tibni; so Tibni died, and Omri reigned" (1 Kings 16:21–22). Now they, who place men in authority to be God's vicegerents do undertake to God for their deportment in that authority, and therefore may justly bear the sad effects of their sinful miscarriages.

2. Because for fear of Manasseh's cruelty, or to flatter him in his tyranny for their own advantage, the greatest part of the people had apostatized from the ways and worship of Hezekiah, to comply with him in his sin. As at another time "they willingly walked after the commandment" (Hos. 5:11). And this is plainly expressed, Manasseh "seduced" the people "to do more evil than the nations" (2 Kings 21:9). When kings turn seducers, they seldom want good store of followers: now if the blind lead the blind, both will, and both justly may fall into the ditch.[12] When kings command unrighteous things, and people suit them with willing compliance, none doubts, but the destruction of them both is just and righteous.[13] See verse 6 of this chapter.

3. Because the people by virtue of their retained sovereignty, did not restrain him in his provoking ways. So Zuinglius, Artic. 42,[14] "One who does

---

12 Matt. 15:14.
13 Roger L'Estrange included this sentence in his section of what Dissenters had said to encourage and justify the regicide. See Roger L'Estrange, *The Dissenters Sayings* [. . .] (London, 1681), 44.
14 This is a reference to Zwingli's Sixty-Seven Articles of 1523. Article 42 states of kings, "Should they become unfaithful and not act according to the precepts of Christ, they may be deposed in the name of God." See James T. Dennison Jr., *Reformed Confessions of the 16th and 17th Centuries in English Translation*, vol. 1, *1523–1552* (Grand Rapids, MI: Reformation Heritage Books, 2008), 6. In his exposition of those articles, Zwingli argues that if unfaithful kings were not deposed, then "the entire people will be penalized on their account." Owen follows Zwingli in using Manasseh as an example of how a people who will not depose a king "will be punished

not forbid wrongdoing, when he has the power, commands it":[15] when Saul would have put Jonathan to death, the people would not suffer him so to do, but delivered Jonathan that he died not (1 Sam. 14[:45]). When David proposed the reducing of the ark, his speech to the people was, "If it please you, let us send abroad to our brethren everywhere, that they may gather themselves to us, and all the congregation said that they would do so, because the thing was right in the eyes of all the people" (1 Chron. 13:2).[16] So they bargain with Rehoboam about their subjection, upon condition of a moderate rule (1 Kings 12). By virtue of which power also they delivered Jeremiah from the prophets and priests that would have put him to death (Jer. 26:16). And on this ground might they justly feed on the fruit of their own neglected duty.[17]

The People Are "Wrapped Up" in the Sins of Their King

Be it thus, or otherwise, by what way soever the people had their interest therein; certain it is, that for the sins of Manasseh, one way or other, made their own, they were destroyed: and therefore these things being written for our example,[18] it cannot but be of great concernment to us, to know what were those sins which wrapped up the people of God in irrevocable destruction: now these the Holy Ghost fully manifests in the story of the life and reign of this Manasseh, and they may all be reduced unto two chief heads.

(1) False worship or superstition: "He built high places, made altars for Baal, and a grove as did Ahab" (2 Kings [21:3]).

(2) Cruelty: "He shed innocent blood very much, till he had filled Jerusalem with blood from one end of it to another," verse 16.

Whether this cruelty be to be ascribed to his tyranny in civil affairs, and so the bloodshed, is called "innocent," because not of malefactors, or to his persecution, in subordination to his false worship instituted as before

---

with him." See Zwingli, *Huldrych Zwingli Writings*, vol. 1, *The Defense of the Reformed Faith*, ed. and trans. E. J. Furcha (Allison Park, PA: Pickwick, 1984), 278–79.

15 In the text: *Qui non vetat, cum potest, jubet*.—Owen. This is a quotation from Seneca the Younger's *Trojan Women* 291. For the Latin text and English translation, see Seneca, *Tragedies*, vol. 1, *Hercules. Trojan Women. Phoenician Women. Medea. Phaedra*, ed. and trans. John G. Fitch, Loeb Classical Library 62 (Cambridge, MA: Harvard University Press), 166–67.

16 1 Chron. 13:2–4.

17 In the text: See Bilson on Obed., part 3. page 271.—Owen. Bishop of Winchester Thomas Bilson (ca. 1547–1616) and his *The True Difference between Christian Subjection and Unchristian Rebellion* [. . .] (London, 1586), 270–71. In this paragraph Owen is appealing to the exact texts used by Bilson in order to argue that subjects should not consent to the wickedness of a tyrannical king.

18 1 Cor. 10:11.

(as the pope and his adherents have devoured whole nations in *ordine ad spiritualia*),[19] is not apparent: but this is from hence and other places most evident; that superstition and persecution, will-worship and tyranny, are inseparable concomitants.[20]

Nebuchadnezzar sets up his great image, and the next news you hear, the saints are in the furnace (Dan. 3:20). You seldom see a fabric of human-invented worship, but either the foundation or topstone is laid in the blood of God's people. "The wisdom" (religion, or way of worship) "that is from above is first pure, then peaceable, gentle, easy to be entreated, full of mercy and good fruits, without partiality, [and] without hypocrisy" (James 3:17) when the other is "earthly, sensual, devilish, bringing along envying, strife, confusion, and every evil work," verse 16. Persecution and blood is the genuine product of all invented worship. I might from hence name, and pursue other observations, but I shall only name one, and proceed.

Observation. *When false worship with injustice by cruelty have possessed the governors of a nation, and wrapped in the consent of the greatest part of the people; who have been acquainted with the mind of God, that people and nation without unprecedented mercy is obnoxious*[21] *to remediless ruin.*

Those two are the Bel and Dragon,[22] that what by their actings, what by their deservings, have swallowed that ocean of blood which has flowed from the veins of millions slain upon the face of the earth. Give me the number of the witnesses of Jesus, whose souls under the altar cry for revenge against their false worshiping murderers,[23] and the tale of them, whose lives have been sacrificed to the insatiable ambition and tyranny of bloodthirsty potentates, with the issues of God's just vengeance on the sons of men, for compliance in these two things, and you will have gathered in the whole harvest of blood, leaving but a few straggling gleanings upon other occasions. And if these things have been found in England, and the present administration with

---

19 Lat. "in relation to the spiritual." Jesuit theologians such as Robert Bellarmine asserted the right of the pope to depose kings and to absolve subjects from oaths of allegiance by right of the Papacy's indirect and secondary power to judge temporal matters in relation to the spiritual. See, e.g., Robert Bellarmine, *Tractatus de potestate Summi Pontificis in rebus temporalibus* (Cologne, 1611), 15. For the English translation, see John Courtney Murray, "St Robert Bellarmine on the Indirect Power," *Theological Studies* 9, no. 4 (1948): 497.
20 In the margin: See the Appendix at the end of this Sermon.—Owen. This is a reference to his tract *Of Toleration*.
21 I.e., liable to.
22 The story of Bel and the Dragon is found in the apocryphal additions to the book of Daniel. It told of thieving priests, a false idol, and the worship of a dragon who would soon be destroyed.
23 In the margin: Rev. 6:9–10.—Owen.

sincere humiliation, do not run across to unravel this close-woven web of destruction, all thoughts of recovery will quickly be too late. And thus far, sin and providence drive on a parallel.

PART 3: RUIN IS INEVITABLE UNLESS THERE IS SPIRITUAL RENEWAL (15:1)

3. The inevitableness of the desolation threatened, and the inexorableness of God in the execution of it, verse 1, is the third thing considerable: "Though Moses and Samuel stood before me, yet my mind could not be toward this people."[24]

Should I insist upon this, it would draw me out unto Scripture evidences, of a nation's traveling in sin, beyond the line of God's patience, and so not to be exempted from ruin: but instead thereof I shall make it a part of my daily supplications, that they may be to our enemies, if God's enemies, and the interpretation of them to those that hate us.

In brief, the words contain an impossible supposition, and yet a negation of the thing for whose sake it is supposed: Moses and Samuel were men, who in the days of their flesh offered up strong supplications,[25] and averted many imminent judgments from a sinful people; as if the Lord should say, "All that I can do in such a case as this, I would grant at the intercession of Moses and Samuel, or others interceding in their spirit and zeal; but now the state of things is come to that pass, the time of treaty being expired, the black flag hung out, and the "decree having brought forth" (Zeph. 2:2), that upon their utmost entreaty, it cannot, it shall not be reversed."

Observation. *There is a time when sin grows ripe for ruin;* "For three transgressions, and for four the Lord will not turn away the iniquity of a people" (Amos 1:9). When the sin of the Amorites has filled the cup of vengeance, they must drink it (Gen. 15:16). England under several administrations of civil government, has fallen twice, yea thrice, into nation-destroying sins; providence has once more given it another bottom; if you should stumble (which the Lord avert) at the same block of impiety and cruelty, there is not another sifting to be made to reserve any grains from the ground;[26] I doubt not but our "three transgressions and four" will end in total desolation, the Lord be your guide, poor England lies at stake.

Observation. *The greatest difficulty that lies in bringing of total destruction upon a sinful people, is in the interposition of Moses and Samuel;* if Moses would

---

[24] Jer. 15:1.
[25] See Heb. 5:7.
[26] Amos 9:9.

but have stood out of the gap, and let the Almighty go, he had broken in upon the whole host of Israel (Ex. 32:9–10). And let it by the way be observed of the spirit of Samuel, that when the people of God were most exorbitant, he cries, "As for me, God forbid that I should sin against the Lord in ceasing to pray for you" (1 Sam. 12:23). Scarce answered by those, who if their interest be not served, or at best, their reason satisfied, will scarce yield a prayer for, yea pour out curses against, their choicest deliverers: the Lord lay it not to their charge; for us seeing that praying deliverers are more prevalent than fighting deliverers (it is though Moses and Samuel, not Gideon and Samson, stood before me), as some decay, let us gather strength in the Lord, that he may have never the more rest for their giving over, until he establish mount Zion a praise in the earth.[27]

PART 4: GOD'S INSTRUMENTS OFTEN ENDURE SUCH HARD PROVIDENCES AND OPPOSITION THAT THEY FEEL READY TO GIVE UP (15:10, 15–18)

4. Come we now to the fourth thing in this chapter; the prophet's state and condition, with the frame and deportment of his heart and spirit under these dispensations. And here we find him expressing two things of himself.

1. What he found from others, verse 10.
2. What he wrestled withal in his own spirit, verses 15–18.

God's Instruments Often Face Severe Opposition from the People

1. What he found from others, he tells you it was cursing and reproach, etc.: "I have neither lent on usury, nor have men lent to me on usury, yet every one of them doth curse me," verse 10.

Now this return may be considered two ways.

(1) In itself, "Every one" (saith he) of this people "doth curse me."
(2) In reference to his deportment: "I have neither borrowed nor lent on usury, yet they curse me."

(1) From the first, observe:

Observation. *Instruments of God's greatest works and glory, are oftentimes the chiefest objects of a professing people's cursings and revenges.*¶[28]

---

27 Isa. 62:7.
28 The ¶ symbol indicates that a paragraph break has been added to Owen's original text.

The return which God's laborers meet withal in this generation, is in the number of those things, whereof there is "none new under the sun."[29] Men, that under God, deliver a kingdom, may have the kingdom's curses for their pains.

When Moses had brought the people of Israel out of bondage, by that wonderful and unparalleled deliverance, being forced to appear with the Lord for the destruction of Korah and his associates, who would have seduced the congregation to its utter ruin, he receives at length this reward of all his travail, labor, and pains, "All the congregation gathered themselves against him and Aaron, laying murder and sedition to their charge, telling them they had killed the people of the Lord" (Num. 16:41–42). A goodly reward for all their travails: if God's works do not suit with the lusts, prejudices, and interests of men, they will labor to give his instruments the devil's wages. Let not upright hearts sink, because they meet with thankless men, "to do good and suffer is a Christian thing."[30] A man may have the blessing of God, and the curse of a professing people at the same time. "Behold, I and the children whom God hath given me, are for signs and for wonders in Israel" (Isa. 8:[18]). "Though we are condemned by men, we are acquitted by God":[31] man's condemnation and God's absolution, do not seldom meet upon the same persons, for the same things: if you labor to do the work of the Lord, pray think it not strange, if among men, curses be your reward and detestation your wages.

God's Instruments Often Feel at a Loss and Ready to Abandon the Cause

(2) In reference to the prophet's deportment, "He had neither lent nor had any lent to him upon usury";[32] he was free from blame among them, had no dealings with them, in those things which are usually attended with reproaches, as he shows by an instance in usury,[33] a thing that a long time has heard very ill.

Observation. *Men every way blameless and to be embraced in their own ways are oftentimes abhorred and laden with curses, for following the Lord in his ways.*

---

29 Eccl. 1:9.
30 In the text: *Bona agere, et mala pati, Christianorum est.*—Owen. Owen thus adapts the language used on the title page of the purported spiritual autobiography of the late king *Eikon Basilike* that bore the sentence *Bona agere et mala pati, Regium est* ("to do good and suffer evil it is a kingly thing"). See *Eikon Basilike: The Pourtraicture of His Sacred Majestie in His Solitudes and Sufferings* (London, 1649).
31 In the text: *Cum ab hominibus damnamur, à Deo absolvimur.*—Owen. In the margin: Tert. Apol.—Owen. This is a paraphrase of a quotation from the end of Tertullian's *Apologeticus* 50.16. For the Latin text and English translation, see Tertullian, *Apology*, 226–27.
32 Ezek. 18:8.
33 I.e., lending money at unreasonably high rates of interest.

"Caius Seius is a good man, but a bad one because he is a Christian";[34] what precious men should many be, would they let go the work of God in this generation? No advantage against them, but in the matter of their God, and that is enough to have them to the lions (Dan. 6:5). He that might be honored for compassing the ends suiting his own worldly interest, and will cheerfully undergo dishonor for going beyond, to suit the design of God, has surely some impression upon his spirit, that is from above.

2. You have the prophet's deportment, and the frame of his spirit during those transactions between the Lord and that sinful people: and this he holds out in many pathetical complaints, to be fainting, decaying, perplexed, weary of his burden, not knowing how to ease himself, as you may see at large, verses 15–18.

Observation. *In dark and difficult dispensations of providence, God's choicest servants are oftentimes ready to faint under the burden of them.*¶

How weary was David when he cried out in such a condition, "O that I had wings like a dove, for then would I fly away and be at rest" (Ps. 55:6). Long had he waited for a desired issue of his perplexed state, and had perhaps oftentimes been frustrated of his hope of drawing to a period of his miseries, and now finding one disappointment to follow on the neck of another, he is weary and cries, "What nothing but this trouble and confusion still? 'Oh that I had wings like a dove,' a ship to sail to a foreign nation (or the like), there to be at peace." In the like strait another time, see what a miserable conclusion he draws, of all his being exercised under the hand of God, "Verily I have cleansed my heart in vain, and washed my hands in innocency" (Ps. 73:13); and again, he says in the perturbation[35] of his mind, "All men are liars" (Ps. 116:11): that all the promises, all the encouragements, which in his way he had received from God, should fail of their accomplishment.

It is not with them, as it was with that wicked king of Israel, who being disappointed of peace and deliverance in his own time, cries out, "This evil is of the Lord, why should I wait upon him any longer?" (2 Kings 6:33). The season of deliverance suited not his expectation; therefore he quite throws off the Lord and his protection. Not unlike many among ourselves, whose desires and expectations being not satisfied in the closing of our distractions, according to the way, which themselves had framed for the Lord to walk in, are ready to cast off his cause, his protection to comply with the enemies of his

---

34 In the text: *Bonus vir Caius Sejus, sed malus quia Christianus.*—Owen. This is a quotation adapted from Tertullian's *Apologeticus* 3.1. For original text and translation, see Tertullian, *Apology*, 18–19.
35 I.e., the state of being worried or upset.

name, "But if a god does not please man, he shall not be a god at all":[36] but it may be observed, that deliverance came not to that people until Jehoram was weary of waiting, and then instantly God gives it in;[37] when God has tired the patience of corrupted men, he will speak peace to them that wait for him.[38]

Thus it is not with the saints of God, only being perplexed in their spirits, dark in their apprehensions, and fainting in their strength, they break out ofttimes into passionate complaints (as Jeremy for a cottage in the wilderness),[39] but yet for the main holding firm to the Lord: and the reasons of this quailing[40] are:

(1) The weakness of faith, when the methods of God's proceedings are unfathomable to our apprehensions; while men see the paths wherein the Lord walks, they can follow him through some difficulties; but when that is hid from them, though providence so shut up all other ways, that it is impossible God should be in them, yet if they cannot discern (so proud are they) how he goes in that wherein he is, they are ready to faint and give over. God is pleased sometimes to make darkness his pavilion and his secret place, "A fire devours before him, and it is very tempestuous round about him" (Ps. 50:3). When once God is attended with fire, darkness, and tempest, because we cannot so easily see him, we are ready to leave him: now this the Lord usually does in the execution of his judgments, "Thy righteousness is like the great mountains, thy judgments are a great deep" (Ps. 36:6). His righteousness, his kindness, is like a great mountain, that is easy to be seen, a man cannot overlook it, unless he willfully shut his eyes; but his judgments are like the great deep; who can look into the bottom of the sea, or know what is done in the depths thereof? God's works in their accomplishment are oftentimes so unsuited to the reasons and apprehensions of men, that very many who have been strong in their desires, and great in expectation of them, upon their bringing forth to light, have quite rejected and opposed them as none of his, because distant from what they had framed to themselves. It is evident from the gospel, that the people of the Jews were full of expectation and longing for the great work of the coming of the Messiah, just at the season wherein he came, yet being come, because not accommodated to their preimagina-

---

36 In the text: *Si Deus homini non placuerit, Deus non erit.*—Owen. This is a paraphrase of Tertullian's *Apologeticus* 5.1. For the Latin text and English translation, see Tertullian, *Apology*, 28–29.
37 2 Kings 6:33.
38 Perhaps a reference to those members of Parliament who were purged from the House of Commons in December 1648.
39 Jer. 9:2. The Geneva Bible speaks of the "cottage of wayfaring men."
40 I.e., losing heart or giving way to fear.

tions, they rejected him, as having neither form nor comeliness in him to be desired (Isa. 53:2). And the prophet Amos tells many, who desired the day of the Lord, that that day should be darkness to them and not light (Amos 5:18, 20). So in every generation many desirous of the accomplishment of God's work, are shaken off from any share therein, by finding it unsuited to their reasons and expectations.

Now when the Lord is pleased thus to walk in darkness, many not being able to trace him in his dispensations, are ready to lie down and sink under the burden: David seems to profess, that he had nothing at such a time to uphold him but this, that God must be there, or nowhere; "I had said" (says he) "that it was in vain to walk as I do, but that I should have condemned the generation of your children" (Ps. 73:15). And truly God never leaves us without so much light, but that we may see clearly where he is not, and so by recounting particulars we may be rolled where he is, though his goings there be not so clear. Ask if God be in the counsels of men, who seek themselves, and in the ways of those who make it their design to ruin the generation of the just. If you find him there, seek no farther; if not, let that give you light, to discern, where he makes his abode, that you turn not aside to the flocks of others.

(2) A reducing the works of providence to inbred rules of their own. But this I cannot pursue.

A Call for Patience and Tenderness toward Those Who Are Faltering

Use. Be tender toward fainters in difficult seasons; if they leave waiting on the Lord, because the evil is of him, if they cast in their lot with the portion of the ungodly, they will in the end perish in their gainsaying: but as for such, as what for want of light, what for want of faith, sit down and sigh in darkness, be not too hasty in laying further burdens on them: when first the confederacy was entered into by the Protestant princes in Germany against Charles the Fifth, Luther himself for a season was bewildered, and knew not what to do, until being instructed in the fundamental laws of the empire, he sat down fully in that undertaking, though the Lord gave it not the desired issue.[41] Our Savior Christ asks, if when he comes, he shall find faith on the

---

41 In the text: Sleid. *Com.* Lib. 8.—Owen. This is a reference to the historian Johann Sleidan (1506–1556) and his *Commentarii* (Strasbourg, 1555) translated as *A Famous Chronicle of Oure Time* [. . .] (London, 1560), bk. 8, fol. sig. 100v. This records Luther's initial doubts and subsequent change of mind about the legitimacy of taking up arms in self-defense because, as the translator added in a marginal note, the "inferior magistrate may in some cases resist the superior." For the significance of Sleidan's work, see Alexandra Kess, *Johann Sleidan and the Protestant Vision of History* (Aldershot, UK: Ashgate, 2008), 89–117.

earth (Luke 18:8). It is his coming with the spirit of judgment and burning,[42] a day of trial and visitation, he there speaks of: now what faith shall he want, which will not be found in that day? Not the faith of adherence to himself for spiritual life and justification, but of actual closing with him in the things he then does; that shall be rare, many shall be staggered, and faint in that day.

SUMMARY OF PARTS 1–4

And thus by the several heads of this chapter, have I led you through the very state and condition of this nation at this time.

First, variety of judgments are threatened to us, and incumbent on us, as in the first part. Secondly, of these, false worship, superstition, tyranny, and cruelty, lie in the bottom, as their procuring causes, which is the second. Thirdly, these if renewed under your hand, will certainly bring inevitable ruin upon the whole nation, which is the third. Fourthly, all which, make many precious hearts, what for want of light, what for want of faith, to fail, and cry out for "the wings of a dove," which is the fourth. I come in the fifth place to God's direction to you for the future, in this state and condition, which being spread in divers verses as the Lord gives it to the prophet, I shall meddle with no more of it, than is contained in the words, which at our entrance I read unto you: "Let them return," etc.

PART 5: GOD'S WORD TO THE NATION IN SUCH A CONDITION (15:11–14, 19–21)

Summary of the Four Observations Relevant to the Nation

In the words observe four things,

1. God's direction to the prophet, and in him, to all, that do his work in such a season, as this described: "Let them return to thee, return not thou to them."[43]
2. Their assistance and supportment in pursuance of that direction: "I will make thee, to this people, a brasen fenced wall."[44]
3. The opposition, with its success and issue, which in that way, they should meet withal: "They shall fight against thee, but shall not prevail."[45]

---

42 Isa. 4:4.
43 Jer. 15:19.
44 Jer. 15:20.
45 Jer. 15:19.

4. Their consolation and success from the presence of the Lord: "For I am with thee to deliver thee, etc."[46]

Direction to Those Engaged in God's Work about the Dangers of Compromise and Backsliding

1. There is God's direction,

Many difficulties in this troublesome season, was the prophet intricated withal: the people would not be prevailed with, to come up to the mind of God, they continuing in then stubbornness, the Lord would not be prevailed with, to avert the threatened desolation; what now shall he do? To stand out against the bulk of the people suits not his earthly interest; to couple with them, answers not the discharge of his office; to wait upon them any longer, is fruitless; to give up himself to their ways, comfortless: hence his complaints, hence his moanings. Better lie down and sink under the burden, than always to swim against the stream of an unreformable multitude: in this strait the Lord comes in with his direction, "Let them return unto thee, etc." "Keep your station, perform your duty, comply not with the 'children of backsliding.' "[47] But whatever be the issue, if there be any closing wrought, let it be, by working them off from their ways of folly. All condescension on your part, where the work of God is to be done, is in opposition to him; if they return, embrace them freely; if not, do your duty constantly.

That which is spoken immediately to the prophet, I shall hold out to all, acting in the name and authority of God, in this general proposition.

Observation. *Plausible compliances of men in authority, with those against whom they are employed, are treacherous contrivances against the God of heaven, by whom they are employed.*[48]

If God be so provoked, that he curses him, who "doth his work negligently,"[49] what is he by them that do it treacherously? When he gives a sword into the hands of men, and they thrust it into his own bowels, his glory and honor, those things so dear to him? He that is entrusted with it, and dares not do justice on everyone, that dares do injustice, is afraid of the creature, but makes very bold with the Creator.

---

46 Jer. 15:20.
47 Jer. 3:14, 22.
48 Samuel Parker claimed that this was Owen's response when, postregicide, "some of the old Souldiers and Officers begin to whisper Cavalierism and Loyalty." See Parker, *A Defence and Continuation of the Ecclesiastical Politie* [. . .] (London, 1671), 503.
49 Jer. 48:10. Owen is quoting the alternative marginal reading from the Authorized Version (KJV).

"It is the glory of God to conceal a thing, but it is the glory of a king to find out a matter" (Prov. 25:2): that which God aims to be glorious in, to manifest his attributes by, is the concealing and covering our iniquities in Christ; but if the magistrate will have glory, if he will not bring upon himself dishonor by dishonoring God, he is to search and find out the transgressions, with whose cognizance he is entrusted, and to give unto them condign retribution. If the Lord curse them, who come not forth "to his help against the mighty" (Judg. 5:23), what is their due who, being called forth by him, do yet help the mighty against him? For a man to take part with the kingdom's enemies, is no small crime; but for a commission officer to run from them by whom he is commissionated, to take part with the adversary, is death without mercy: yet have not some in our days arrived at that stupendous impudence, that when as private persons they have declaimed against the enemies of the nation, and by that means got themselves into authority, they have made use of that authority to comply with, and uphold those, by an opposition to whom, they got into their authority? Which is no less than an atheistical attempt to personate the Almighty, unto such iniquities as without his appearance, they dare not own: but "he that justifieth the wicked, and he that condemneth the just, are both are abomination to the Lord" (Prov. 17:15) and not only to the Lord, but to good men also; "He that saith to the wicked, thou art righteous, him shall the people curse, nations shall abhor him" (Prov. 24:24).

I speak only as to the general (for me let all particulars find mercy), with a sad remembrance of the late workings of things among us, with those vile sordid compliances which grew upon the spirits of magistrates and ministers with those, whose garments were dyed with the blood of God's saints and precious ones (as formerly they were called, for now these names are become terms of reproach) and would this complying went alone, but pretenses and accusations must be found out against such as follow with them, when they begin to call darkness light, they will ere long call light darkness:[50] by which means, our eyes have seen, men of their own accord laying down the weapons wherewith at first they fought against opposers, and taking up them, which were used against themselves, as has happened more than once, to penmen both in our own, and our neighbor nation.[51] Now this revolting from prin-

---

50 Isa. 5:20.
51 Owen will address this at length in *Of Toleration*. One possible example of those authors that Owen has in mind might be Samuel Rutherford, who, having penned *Lex, Rex: The Law and the Prince* [. . .] (London, 1644) in defense of armed resistance, wrote *A Survey of the Spirituall Antichrist* [. . .] (London, 1648), and in the summer of 1649 he would produce his four-hundred-page *A Free Disputation against Pretended Liberty of Conscience* [. . .] (London,

ciples of religion and righteousness, to a compliance with any sinful way or person, is a treacherous opposition to the God of heaven; for,

It cannot be done but by preferring the creature before the Creator, especially in those things which are the proximate causes of deviation.

Compromise and Backsliding Are Often Caused by Fear and a Desire for Perishing Things

Two principal causes I have observed of this crooked walking.

(1) Fear.
(2) That desire of perishing things, which has a mixture of covetousness and ambition. The first makes men wary what they do against men, the other makes them weary of doing anything for God, as whereby their sordid ends are not like to be accomplished.

(1) Fear: when once magistrates begin to listen after *quid sequiturs*,[52] and so to withdraw from doing good, for fear of suffering evil, paths of wickedness are quickly returned unto, and the authority of God despised. "Let this man go, and take heed of Caesar" (John 19:12), did more prevail on Pilate's treacherous heart, than all the other clamors of the Jews; yea, was not the whole Sanhedrim swayed to desperate villainy, for fear the Romans should come and take away their kingdom? (John 11:48). When men begin once to distrust that God will leave them in the briers, to wrestle it out themselves (for unbelief lies at the bottom of carnal fear), they quickly turn themselves to contrivances of their own, for their own safety, their own prosperity, which commonly is by obliging those unto them by compliances, in an opposition to whom they might oblige the Almighty to their assistance: surely they conclude he wants either truth or power to support them in his employment.

If a prince should send an ambassador to a foreign state to treat about peace, or to denounce war; who, when he comes there, distrusting his master's power to make good his undertaking, should comply and wind up his interest with them to whom he was sent, suffering his sovereign's errand to fall to the ground, would he not be esteemed as arrant[53] a traitor as ever

---

1649). Chadwick described it as "the ablest defence of persecution in the seventeenth-century." See Owen Chadwick, *The Reformation* (Harmondsworth, UK: Penguin, 1964), 403.

52 Lat. "what follows." In other words, Owen is cautioning magistrates about the dangers of allowing their decisions to be unduly determined by pragmatic considerations.

53 I.e., notorious.

lived? And yet though this be clipped coin among men, it is put upon the Lord every day as current.[54]

From this principle of carnal fear and unbelief, trembling for a man that shall die, and the son of man that shall be as grass, forgetting the Lord our maker (Isa. 51:12), are all those prudential follies which exercise the minds of most men in authority, making them, especially in times of difficulties, to regulate and square all their proceedings, by what suits their own safety and particular interests, counseling, advising, working for themselves, quite forgetting by whom they are entrusted, and whose business they should do.

(2) A desire of perishing things tempered with covetousness and ambition: hence was the sparing of the fat cattle, and of Agag by Saul (1 Sam. 15).[55] When those two qualifications close on any, they are diametrically opposed to that frame which of God is required in them, viz. that they should be men fearing God, and hating covetousness:[56] the first will go far, being only a contrivance for safety; but if this latter take hold of any, being a consultation to exalt themselves, it quickly carries them beyond all bounds whatsoever. The Lord grant, that hereafter there may be no such complaints in this nation, or may be causeless, as have been heretofore, viz. that we have poured out our prayers, jeoparded[57] our lives, wasted our estates, spent our blood, to serve the lusts and compass the designs of ambitious ungodly men.

The many ways whereby these things entrench upon the spirits of men, to bias them from the paths of the Lord, I shall not insist upon, it is enough that I have touched upon the obvious causes of deviation, and manifested them to be treacheries against the God of all authority.

---

54 Clipping of the rims of coins made from precious metals was a regular occurrence in the seventeenth century and led to the debasement of currency. This was a timely illustration because in July 1649 the Commons extended the penalties of high treason to those who would counterfeit or clip any coins "current" within the Commonwealth. See "July 1649: An Act declaring what Offences shall be Adjudged Treason," in *Acts and Ordinances of the Interregnum 1642–1660*, ed. C. H. Firth and R. S. Rait, 3 vols. (London: HMSO, 1911), 2:193–94.

55 The sinfulness of sparing a tyrannical king from death is significant in the context of the regicide. In November 1648, some of the opposition to the Newport Treaty likened Charles to Agag. When Saul disobeyed, he incurred God's displeasure and was rejected. This necessitated Samuel stepping in to bring justice by means of the sword. See *Two Petitions Presented to His Excellency the Lord Fairfax* [...] (London, November 25, 1648) and *The Peoples Eccho to the Parliaments Declarations, concerning a Personall Treaty with the King* [...] (London, 1648), 12. Cardell also referenced how Saul had been "*deceiv'd*" in sparing Agag, and it took Samuel to come and act as the "Executioner." John Cardell, *Gods Wisdom Justified, and Mans Folly Condemned, Touching All Maner of Outward Providential Administrations, in a Sermon* (London, 1649), 17.

56 Ex. 18:21.

57 I.e., jeopardized.

Several Specific Applications to Those in Government

Use. Be exhorted to beware of relapses, with all their causes and inducements, and to be constant to the way of righteousness, and this I shall hold out unto you in two particulars.

Many Have Backslidden in Recent Years

1. Labor to recover others, even all that were ever distinguished and called by the name of the Lord, from their late fearful returning to sinful compliances with the enemies of God and the nation: I speak not of men's persons, but of their ways. For three years this people have been eminently sick of the folly of backsliding,[58] and without some special cordial are like to perish in it, as far as I know.

Look upon the estate of this people as they were differenced seven years ago,[59] so for some continuance, and as they are now, and you shall find in how many things we have returned to others, and not one instance to be given of their return to us; that this may be clear take some particulars.

(1) In words and expressions, those are *index animi*;[60] turn them over and you may find what is in the whole heart. "Out of the abundance of the heart the mouth speaketh."[61] Now is not that language, are not those very expressions, which filled the mouths of the common adversaries only, grown also terms of reproach upon the tongues of men, that suffered sometimes under them, and counted it their honor so to do? Hence that common exprobration,[62] a parliament of saints, an army of saints, and such like derisions of God's ways, now plentiful with them, who sat sometimes and took sweet counsel with us?[63] Ah! Had it not been more for the honor of God, that we had kept our station, until others had come to us, so to have exalted the name and profession of the gospel, than that we should so return to them, as to join with them in making the paths of Christ a reproach? Had it not been better for us with Judah to continue ruling with God, and to be faithful with the saints (Hos. 11:12), than to stand in the congregation of the mockers, and to sit in the seat of the scornful?[64] What shall we say when the saints of God are as signs and wonders to be spoken against in Israel? (Isa. 8:18). O that men would remember how

---

58 Since the end of the First Civil War in 1646.
59 In 1642 at the beginning of the First Civil War.
60 Lat. "index of the heart."
61 Luke 6:45.
62 I.e., an instance of upbraiding and severe criticism.
63 Owen was addressing the Rump of the purged Parliament, where many seats were empty.
64 Ps. 1:1.

they have left their first station; when themselves use those reproaches unto others, which for the same cause themselves formerly bare with comfort! It is bitterness to consider how the gospel is scandalized by this woeful return of ministers and people, by casting scriptural expressions by way of scorn, on those with whom they were sometimes in the like kind companions of contempt. Surely in this we are returned to them, and not they to us.

(2) In actions and those,

[1] Of religion, not only in opinion, but practice also, are we here under a vile return. We are become the lions, and the very same thoughts entertained by us, against others, as were exercised toward ourselves. Are not others as unworthy to live upon their native soil in our judgments, as we ourselves in the judgments of them formerly over us?[65] Are not groans for liberty, by the warmth of favor, in a few years hatched into attempts for tyranny? And for practice, what hold has former superstition, in observing days and times, laid upon the many of the people again, witness the late solemn superstition,[66] and many things of the like nature.

[2] For civil things, the closing of so many formerly otherwise engaged, with the adverse party in the late rebellion,[67] with the lukewarm deportment of others at the same time, is a sufficient demonstration of it;[68] and may not the Lord justly complain of all this, "What iniquity have you seen in me, or my ways, that you are gone far from me, and have walked after vanity, and are become vain?" (Jer. 2:5), "Why have you changed your glory for that which doth not profit," verse 11. "Have I been a dry heath, or a barren wilderness to you?"[69] Oh that men should find no more sweetness in following the Lamb under wonderful protections, but that they should thus turn aside into every wilderness: what indignity is this to the ways of God? I could give you many reasons of it; but I have done, what I intended, a little hinted, that we are a returning people, that so you might be exhorted to help for a recovery: and how shall that be?

---

65 A number of the godly had been forced to leave England in the 1630s, often traveling to the Netherlands or New England.
66 Presumably a reference to the celebration of advent and Christmas.
67 The Second Civil War (1648).
68 There were mass defections during the Second Civil War. For example, Colonels Poyer, Powell, and Laugharne led thousands into the royalist cause in south Wales, and Lieutenant Colonel Henry Farr led "the most spectacular, but certainly not the only, example of defections from the county militia." See Robert Ashton, *Counter-Revolution: The Second Civil War and Its Origins, 1646-8* (New Haven, CT: Yale University Press, 1994), 465–66. See also Andrew Hopper, *Turncoats and Renegadoes: Changing Sides during the English Civil Wars* (Oxford: Oxford University Press, 2012), 96.
69 Jer. 17:6.

Backsliders Restored by a Commitment to Righteous Zeal

2. By your own keeping close to the paths of righteousness; if you return not, others will look about again: this breach, this evil is of you, within your own walls, was the fountain of our backsliding. Would you be the repairers of breaches, the restorers of paths for men to walk in,[70] do these two things.

(1) Turn not to the ways of such, as the Lord has blasted under your eyes, and these may be referred to three heads.

[1] Oppression.
[2] Self-seeking.
[3] Contrivances for persecution.

[1] Oppression, how detestable a crime it is in the eyes of the Almighty, what effects it has upon men, making wise men mad (Eccl. 7:7). How frequently it closes in the calamitous ruin of the oppressors themselves, are things known to all. Whether it has not been exercised in this nation, both in general by unnecessary impositions, and in particular by unwarrantable pressures, let the mournful cries of all sorts of people testify. Should you now return to such ways as these, would not the anger of the Lord smoke against you? Make it I beseech you your design to relieve the whole, by all means possible, and to relieve particulars, yea even of the adverse party where too much overborne. Oh let it be considered by you, that it be not considered upon you. I know the things you are necessitated to, are not to be supported by the air. It is only what is unnecessary as to you, or insupportable as to others, that requires your speedy reforming; that so it may be said of you as of Nehemiah 5:14–15.[71] And for particulars (pray pardon my folly and boldness), I heartily desire a committee of your honorable House might sit once a week, to relieve poor men that have been oppressed by men, sometimes enjoying parliamentary authority.[72]

[2] Self-seeking, when men can be content to lay a nation low, that they may set up themselves upon the heaps and ruins thereof. Have not some sought to advance themselves under that power, which with the lives and blood of the people they have opposed? Seeming to be troubled at former things,

---

[70] Isa. 58:12.
[71] Nehemiah was a "frequently invoked biblical figure" in parliamentary fast sermons. See Achsah Guibbory, "'Fast Sermons' during the English Revolution," in *Early Modern Nationalism and Milton's England*, ed. David Loewenstein and Paul Stevens (Toronto: University of Toronto Press, 2008), 124.
[72] It was suggested in one contemporary newssheet that "a third part of the people of most parishes" were in need of aid. See *Moderate Intelligencer* 210 (March 22–29, 1649), 1957.

not because they were done, but because they were not done by them. But innocent blood will be found a tottering foundation for men to build their honors, greatness, and preferments[73] upon. O return not in this unto any. If men serve themselves of the nation, they must expect that the nation will serve itself upon them. The best security you can possibly have that the people will perform their duty in obedience, is the witness of your own consciences, that you have discharged your duty toward them, in seeking their good by your own trouble, and not your own advantages in their trouble. I doubt not but that in this, your practice makes the admonition a commendation, otherwise the word spoken, will certainly witness against you.

[3] Contrivances for persecution, how were the hearts of all men hardened like the nether millstone,[74] and their thoughts did grind blood and revenge against their brethren! What colors, what pretenses had men invented to prepare a way for the rolling of their garments in the tears: yea, blood of Christians. The Lord so keep your spirits from a compliance herein, that withal the bow be not too much bent on the other side, which is not impossible.

Be there a backsliding upon your spirit to these, or suchlike things as these, the Lord will walk contrary to you, and were you as the signet upon his hand, he would pluck you off.[75]

(2) Return not to the open enemies of our peace: I could here enlarge myself to support your spirits in the work mentioned (Job 29:14–15), but I must go on to the following parts of my text, and pass from the direction given to the supportment, and assistance promised: "I will make thee to this people a brasen and a fenced wall."[76]

The Promise of Divine Guidance and Protection to God's Chosen Instruments

An implied objection, which the prophet might put in, upon his charge to keep so close to the rule of righteousness, is here removed. If I must thus abide by it, to execute whatsoever the Lord calls me out unto, not shrinking, nor staggering at the greatest undertakings, what will become of me in the issue? Will it not be destructive to stand out against a confirmed people? No, says the Lord, it shall not be: "I will make thee, etc."

Observation. *God will certainly give prevailing strength, and unconquerable defense unto persons constantly discharging the duties of righteousness,*

---

73 I.e., promotion in office or station.
74 Job 41:24.
75 Jer. 22:24.
76 Jer. 15:20.

especially when undertaken in times of difficulty and opposition. "I will make thee, etc."¶

The like engagement to this you have, made to Ezekiel, chapter 3:8–9. Neither was it so to the prophets alone, but to magistrates also when Joshua undertook the regency of Israel in a difficult time, he takes off his fear and diffidence with this very encouragement (Josh. 1:5). He says, he will make them a wall, the best defense against opposition, and that not a weak tottering wall, that might easily be cast down, but a "brazen" wall, that must needs be impregnable: what engines can possibly prevail against a wall of brass?

And to make it more secure, this brazen wall shall be "fenced" with all manner of fortifications and ammunition; so that the veriest coward in the world, being behind such a wall, may without dread or terror apply himself to that, which he finds to do. God will so secure the instruments of his glory against a backsliding people, in holding up the ways of his truth and righteousness, that all attempts against them shall be vain, and the most timorous spirit may be secure, provided he go not out of the Lord's way; for if they be found beyond the line, the brazen wall, they may easily be surprised. And indeed, who but a fool would run from the shelter of a brazen wall, to hide himself in a little stubble? And yet so do all who run to their own wisdom, from the most hazardous engagement that any of the ways of God can possibly lead them unto.¶

It is a sure word, and for ever to be rested upon, which the Lord gives in to Asa, "The Lord is with you, while ye be with him" (2 Chron. 15:2): an unbiassed magistracy, shall never want God's continued presence: very Jeroboam himself receives a promise upon condition of close walking with God in righteous administrations, of having a house built him like the house of David (1 Kings 11:38).¶

What a wall was God to Moses in that great undertaking of being instrumental for the delivery of Israel from a bondage and slavery of four hundred years' continuance: Pharaoh was against him whom he had deprived of his sovereignty and dominion over the people: and what a provocation the depriving of sovereignty is unto potentates, needs no demonstration: to the corruption of nature which inclines to heights and exaltations, in imitation of the fountain whence it flows; they have also the corruption of state and condition, which has always inclined to absoluteness and tyranny: all Egypt was against him, as being by him visibly destroyed, wasted, spoiled, robbed, and at length smitten in the apple of the eye, by the loss of their firstborn;[77]

---

[77] Ex. 11:5.

and if this be not enough, that the king and people, whom he opposed were his enemies, the very people, for whose sakes he set himself to oppose the others, they also rise up against him, yea seek to destroy him; one time they appeal to God for justice against him, "The Lord look upon you and judge" (Ex. 5:21). They appeal to the righteous God to witness, that he had not fulfilled what he promised them, to wit, liberty, safety, and freedom from oppression, but that rather by his means their burdens were increased: and in this they were so confident (like some among us), that they appealed unto God for the equity of their complaints. Afterward being reduced to a strait, such as they could not see how possibly they should be extricated from, without utter ruin (like our present condition in the apprehension of some), they cry out upon him for the whole design of bringing them into the wilderness, and affirm positively, that though they had perished in their former slavery, it had been better for them, than to have followed him in this new and dangerous engagement (Ex. 14:11–13). That generation being (as Calvin observes) so inured to bondage, that they were altogether unfit to bear with the workings and pangs of their approaching liberty.[78] Afterward, do they want drink? Moses is the cause; did they want meat? This Moses would starve them (Ex. 15:24; 16:7). He could not let them alone by the fleshpots of Egypt, for this they are ready to stone him (Ex. 17:3). At this day, have we too much rain, or too short a harvest, it is laid on the shoulders of the present government. It was no otherwise of old.¶

At length this people came to that height, as being frightened by the opposition, they heard of, and framed to themselves in that place whither Moses would carry them, they presently enter into a conspiracy and revolt, consulting to cast off his government, and choose new commanders, and with a violent hand to return to their former condition (Num. 14:4), an attempt as frequent as fruitless among ourselves. When this would not do, at length upon the occasion of taking off Korah and his company, they assemble themselves together, and lay (not imprisonment but) murder to his charge, and that of "the people of the Lord" (Num. 16:41). Now what was the issue of all those oppositions? What effect had they? How did the power of Pharaoh, the revenge of Egypt, the backsliding of Israel prevail? Why God made this one Moses "a fenced brasen wall" to them all, he was never in the least measure prevailed against; so long as he was with God, God was with him, no matter who was against him.

[78] In the margin: Calv. in Num. Cap. 4.—Owen. It is unclear what passage Owen has in mind. Perhaps Calvin's treatment of Num. 14 in *Commentaries on the Four Last Books of Moses*, vol. 4, trans. Charles William Bingham (Edinburgh: Calvin Translation Society, 1843), 71–85.

One thing only would I commend to your consideration, viz. that this Moses, thus preserved, thus delivered, thus protected, falling into one deviation, in one thing, from close following the Lord, was taken off from enjoying the closure and fruit of all his labor (Num. 20:12). Otherwise he followed the Lord in a difficult season, and did not want unconquerable supportment: take heed of the smallest turning aside from God: Oh lose not the fruit of all your labor for self; for a lust, or anything that may turn you aside.

Now, the Lord will do this,

1. Because of his own engagement.
2. For our encouragement.

1. Because of his own engagement, and that is twofold,

(1) Of truth and fidelity.
(2) Of honor and glory.

(1) His truth and veracity is engaged in it. "Those that honour him, he will honour" (1 Sam. 2:30). If men honor him with obedience, he will honor them with preservation: "He will be with them, while they are with him" (2 Chron. 15:2). While they are with him in constancy of duty, he will be with them to keep them in safety, "He will never leave them, nor forsake them" (Josh. 1:5), "No weapon that is formed against them shall prosper" (Isa. 54:17). Now God is never as the waters that fail to any that upon his engagements wait for him; he will not shame the faces of them that put their trust in him. Why should our unbelieving spirits charge that upon the God of truth, which we dare not impute to a man that is a worm, a liar? Will a man fail in his engagement unto him, who upon that engagement undertakes a difficult employment for his sake? The truth is, it is either want of sincerity in our working, or want of faith in dependence, that makes us at any time come short of the utmost tittle, that is in any of the Lord's engagements.

[1] We want sincerity, and do the Lord's work, but with our own aims and ends, like Jehu;[79] no wonder, if we be left to ourselves for our wages and defense.

[2] We want faith also in the Lord's work, turn to our own counsels for supportment; no marvel if we come short of assistance; "If we will not believe, we shall not be established."[80]

---

79 2 Kings 10:16, 29–31.
80 Isa. 7:9.

Look to sincerity in working, and faith in dependence, God's truth and fidelity will carry him out to give you unconquerable supportment: deflection from these, will be your destruction: you that are working on a new bottom, work also on new principles, put not new wine into old bottles,[81] new designs into old hearts.

(2) Secondly, he is engaged in point of honor, if they miscarry in his way, what will he do for his great name? Yea so tender is the Lord herein of his glory, that when he has been exceedingly provoked to remove men out of his presence yet because they have been called by his name, and have visibly held forth a following after him, he would not suffer them to be trodden down, lest the enemy should exalt themselves, and say, "Where is now their God?"[82] They shall not take from him the honor of former deliverances and protections: in such a nation as this, if the Lord now upon manifold provocations should give up parliament, people, army, to calamity, and ruin, would not the glory of former counsels, successes, deliverances, be utterly lost? Would not men say it was not the Lord, but chance that happened to them?

2. For our encouragement, the ways of God are oftentimes attended with so many difficulties, so much opposition, that they must be embraced merely because his; no other motive in the world can suit them to us. I mean for such as keep them immixed from their own carnal and corrupt interests: now because the Lord will not take off the hardship and difficulty of them, lest he should not have the honor of carrying on his work, against tumultuating opposition, he secures poor weaklings of comfortable assistance, and answerable success, lest his work should be wholly neglected. It is true, the Lord as our sovereign master may justly require a close laboring in all his ways, without the least sweetening endearments put upon them, only as they are his whose we are, who has a dominion over us: but yet as a tender father, in which relation he delights to exercise his will toward his own in Christ, he pities our infirmities, knowing that we are but dust:[83] and therefore to invite us into the dark, into ways laborsome and toilsome to flesh and blood, he gives us in this security, that we shall be as "a fenced brasen wall"[84] to the opposing sons of men.

Three Applications of This Principle to Those in Government
The Folly of Opposition to God's Chosen Instruments

Use 1. To discover the vanity and folly of all opposition to men called forth of God to his work, and walking in his ways; would you not think

---

81 Matt. 9:17.
82 Ps. 115:2.
83 Ps. 103:13–14.
84 Jer. 15:20.

him mad, that should strike with his fist, and run with his head against "a fenced brasen wall," to cast it down? Is he like to have any success, but the battering of his flesh, and the beating out of his brains? What do the waves obtain by dashing themselves with noise and dread against a rock, but their own beating to pieces? What prevails a man by shooting his arrows against the sky, but a return upon his own head? Nor is the most powerful opposition to the ways of God like to meet with better success: God looks no otherwise upon opposers than you would do upon a man attempting to thrust down "a fenced brasen wall" with his fingers. Therefore it is said, that in their proudest attempts, strongest assaults, deepest counsels, combinations, and associations, "he laughs them to scorn," derides their folly, contemns their fury, lets them sweat in vain, until their day be come (Ps. 2). How birthless in our own, as well as other generations have been their swelling conceptions? What then is it that prevails upon men to break through so many disappointments against the Lord, as they do? Doubtless that of Isaiah 23:9, surely "the Lord of hosts" hath a purpose "to stain the pride of all glory, and to bring into contempt all the honourable of the earth." God gives up men unto it, that he may leave no earthly glory or honor without pollution or contempt: and therefore has opposition in our days, been turned upon so many hands, that God might leave no glory without contempt: yet with this difference, that if the Lord will own them, he will recover them from their opposition, as has happened of late to the ministry of one, and will happen ere long to the ministry of another nation;[85] when the Lord has a little "stained the pride of their glory"; they shall be brought home again by the spirit of judgment and burning:[86] but if he own them not, they shall perish under the opposition. And when it has been wheeled about on all sorts of men, the end will be.

85 Presumably a reference to the anti-Engager ministers in Scotland who supported the Marquis of Argyll's faction and the suggestion of the hope of a similar turn of events in Ireland. The "recovered" Scottish ministry included the likes of Robert Blair, Patrick Gillespie, Samuel Rutherford, James Guthrie, and James Durham. The prospects of a similar response from the Presbyterians in Ulster looked increasingly unlikely since a fortnight later the Belfast Presbytery condemned the actions of the English Parliament in "A Necessary Representation of the Present Evills," a document of significant enough importance for Milton to be commissioned to answer it. See Toby C. Barnard, *Cromwellian Ireland: English Government and Reform in Ireland, 1649–1660* (Oxford: Oxford University Press, 2000), 122; Barbara K. Lewalski, *The Life of John Milton: A Critical Biography* (Oxford: Blackwell, 2000), 240; Joad Raymond, "Complications of Interest: Milton, Scotland, Ireland, and National Identity in 1649," *Review of English Studies* 55, no. 220 (2004): 315–45.
86 Isa. 4:4.

The Wisdom of Recognizing That Parliament's Victories Come from God

Use 2. "Be wise now therefore, O ye rulers, be instructed, ye that are judges of the earth, serve the Lord with fear, and rejoice with trembling" (Ps. 2:10–11).[87] See whence your assistance comes; see where lie the hills of your salvation, and say, "Asshur shall not save us, we will not ride upon horses, neither will we say any more to the work of our hands, Ye are our gods, for in thee the fatherless findeth mercy" (Hos. 14:3). It is God alone who is "a sun and shield:"[88] "his ways do good to the upright in heart."[89] Behold, here is a way to encompass England with "a brasen wall": let the rulers of it walk in right ways, with upright hearts. Others have been careful to preserve the people to them, and the city to them, oh be you careful to preserve your God unto you; he alone can make you a fenced wall; if he departs, your wall departs, your shade departs. Give me leave to insist a little on one particular, which I choose out among many others: when God leads out his people to any great things, the angel of his presence is still among them: see at large, Exodus 23:20–22. The angel of the covenant, in whom is the name of God, that has power of pardoning or retaining transgressions, Jesus Christ, the angel that redeems his out of all their troubles (Gen. 48:16), he is in the midst of them, and among them; and God gives this special caution if we would have his assistance, that we should beware of him, and obey him, and provoke him not: would you then have God's assistance continued, take heed of provoking the angel of his presence: provoke him not by slighting of his ways, provoke him not by contemning his ordinances;[90] if you leave him to deal for himself, he will leave you to shift for yourselves: what though his followers are at some difference (the best knowing but in part) about the administration of some things in his kingdom; the envious one having also sown some bitter seeds of persecution, strife, envy, and contention among them? What though some poor creatures are captivated by Satan, the prince of pride, to a contempt of all his ordinances, whose souls I hope the Lord will one day free from the snare of the devil? Yet I pray give me leave (it is no time to contest, or dispute it) to bear witness in the behalf of my Master to this one truth, that if by your own personal practice and observance, your protection, countenance,

---

87 A text amended to remove the reference to "kings," thus reflecting the new postregicide reality.
88 Ps. 84:11.
89 Ps. 125:4.
90 In the margin: See the Appendix about Toleration.—Owen. For Owen, it was not toleration but the persecution of the godly that called forth divine wrath. Parliament, he opined, should be more concerned about the danger of provoking "the angel of the covenant" rather than offending advocates of the Solemn League and Covenant in the City of London.

authority, laws, you do not assert, maintain, uphold the order of the gospel, and administration of the ordinances of Christ, notwithstanding the noise and clamors of novel fancies, which like Jonah's gourd, have sprung up in a night, and will wither in a day,[91] you will be forsaken by the angel of God's presence, and you will become an astonishment to all the inhabitants of the earth: and herein I do not speak as one hesitating or dubious, but positively assert it, as the known mind of God, and whereof he will not suffer any long to doubt (Ps. 2 ult.).[92]

God Will Be with Parliament So Long As It Does God's Work in God's Way

Use 3. "Strengthen the weak hands, and confirm the feeble knees, say to them that are of a fearful heart, be strong, fear not, behold your God will come with vengeance, even God with a recompense, he will come and save you" (Isa. 35:3–4). Let the most weak and fearful, the fainting heart, the trembling spirit, and the doubting mind know, that full and plenary security, perfect peace, attends the upright in the ways of God. You that are in God's way, do God's work, and take this cordial for all your distempers,[93] return not to former provoking ways, and he will make you "a fenced brasen wall."

And so I come to the third thing which I proposed to consider,

Judicial Hardening Stands Behind the Self-Defeating Opposition to God's Instruments

The opposition, which men cleaving to the Lord in all his ways shall find, with the issue and success of it, "They shall fight against thee, but shall not prevail."[94]

The words may be considered either as a prediction depending on God's prescience, of what will be, or a commination[95] from his just judgment, of what shall be.

In the first sense the Lord tells the prophet, from the corruption, apostasy, stubbornness of that people, what would come to pass. In the second, what for their sins and provocations, by his just judgment, should come to pass. Time will not allow me to handle the words in both acceptations: wherefore I shall take up the latter only, viz. that it is a commination of what shall be for the farther misery of that wretched people, they shall judicially be given up to a fighting against him.

---

91 Jonah 4:10.
92 I.e., last, referring to Ps. 2:12.
93 I.e., illnesses.
94 Jer. 15:20.
95 I.e., the recital of a threat of divine judgment.

Observation. *God oftentimes gives up a sinful people to a fruitless contention, and fighting with their only supporters and means of deliverance.*[96] "They shall, etc."¶

Jeremiah had labored with God for them, and with them for God, that, if possible peace being made they might be delivered, and to consummate their sins, they are given up to fight against him.

I cannot now insist upon particular instances, consult the history of the church in all ages, you shall find it continually upon all occasions verified. From the Israelites opposing Moses, to the Ephraimites' contest with Jephthah,[97] the rejecting of Samuel,[98] and so on to the kings of the earth, giving their power to the beast to wage war with the Lamb,[99] with the inhabitants of the world combining against the witnesses of Christ, is this assertion held out. In [the] following story, no sooner did any plague or judgment break out against the Roman Empire, but instantly, *Christianos ad leones*,[100] their fury must be spent upon them, who were the only supporters of it from irrecoverable ruin. Now the Lord does this,

1. To seal up a sinful people's destruction. Eli's sons hearkened not, "because the Lord would slay them" (1 Sam. 2:25). When God intends ruin to a people, they shall walk in ways, that tend thereunto: now is there a readier way for a man to have a house on his head, than by pulling away the pillars whereby it is supported? If by Moses standing in the gap, the fury of the Lord be turned away, certainly if the people contend to remove him, their desolation sleeps not. When therefore the Lord intends to lay "cities waste without inhabitants, and houses without men, to make a land utterly desolate," the way of its accomplishment is by making "the hearts of the people fat, and their ears heavy, and shutting their eyes that they should not see," and attend to the means of their recovery (Isa. 6:10–11), so gathering in his "peace and mercies" from a provoking people (Jer. 16:[5]).

2. To manifest his own power and sovereignty in maintaining a small handful, ofttimes a few single persons, a Moses, a Samuel, two witnesses[101] against the opposing rage of a hardened multitude. If those who undertake his work and business in their several generations, should have withal, the concurrent obedi-

---

96 Parker claimed that this was Owen's response when "Presbyterians and Royalists begin to make head against those bold and bloody Usurpers." Parker, *Defence and Continuation*, 504.
97 Judg. 12:4–5.
98 1 Sam. 8:5–7.
99 Rev. 17:12–14.
100 Lat. "The Christians to the lions." This is a quotation from Tertullian's *Apologeticus* 39.2. For the Latin text and English translation, see Tertullian, *Apology*, 182–83.
101 Rev. 11:3.

ence and assistance of others, whose good is intended, neither would his name be so seen, nor his ways so honored, as now, when he bears them up against all opposition. Had not the people of this land been given up (many of them) to fight against the deliverers of the nation, and were it not so with them even at this time, how dark would have been the workings of providence, which now by wrestling through all opposition are so conspicuous and clear. When then a people, or any part of a people, have made themselves unworthy of the good things intended to be accomplished by the instruments of righteousness and peace, the Lord will blow upon then waves, that with rage and fury, they shall dash themselves against them, whom he will strengthen with the munition of rocks, not to be prevailed against. So that God's glory and their own ruin, lie at the bottom of this close working of providence, in giving up a sinful people to a fruitless contending, with their own deliverers, if ever they be delivered.

Four Reasons Why God Remains Both Just and Good in Giving Up His Enemies

Obj[ection]. But is not a people's contending with the instruments, by whom God works among them, and for them, a sin and provocation to the eyes of his glory? How then can the Lord be said to give them up unto it?

Ans[wer]. Avoiding all scholastical discourses, as unsuited to the work of this day; I shall briefly give in, unto you, how this is a sinful thing, yet sinners are given up unto it, without the least extenuation of their guilt, or color for charge on the justice and goodness of God.

(1) Then to give up men unto a thing in itself sinful, is no more, but so to dispose and order things, that sinners may exercise and draw out their sinful principles, in such a way. This then the Lord does, the Scripture is full of examples, and has testimonies innumerable: that herein the Holy One of Israel is no ways copartner with the guilt of the sons of men, will appear by observing the difference of these several agents in these four things.

[1] The principle, by which they work.
[2] The rule, by which they proceed.
[3] The means, which they use.
[4] The end at which they aim.

The Nature of God's Sovereignty

[1] The principle of operation in God is his own sovereign will and good pleasure. He does whatsoever he pleases (Ps. 115:3). He says his purpose shall stand,

and he will do all his *pleasure* (Isa. 46:10). He has mercy on whom he *will* have mercy, and whom he *will* he hardens (Rom. 9:18); giving no account *of his matters* (Job 33:13).[102] This our Savior renders the only principle and reason of his hidden operations: "O Father so it seemed good in thy sight" (Matt. 11:26). His sovereignty in doing what he will with his own, as the potter with his clay, is the rise of his operations: so that whatever he does, "who will say unto him, 'What doest thou?'" (Job 9:12). "Shall the thing formed say unto him that formed it, why hast thou made me thus?" (Rom. 9:20). And hence two things will follow.

{1} That what he does, is just, and righteous, for so must all acts of supreme and absolute dominion be.

{2} That he can be author of nothing, but what has existence and being itself, for he works as the fountain of beings. This sin has not. So that though every action, whether good or bad, receives its specification from the working of providence, and to that, is their existence in their several kinds to be ascribed, yet an evil action, in the evilness of it, depends not upon divine concourse and influence, for good and evil make not sundry kinds of actions, but only a distinction of a subject in respect of its adjuncts and accidents.

But now the principle of operation in man, is nature vitiated[103] and corrupted: I say "nature," not that he works naturally, being a free agent, but that these faculties, will and understanding, which are the principles of operation, are in nature corrupted, and from thence can nothing flow but evil: "An evil tree bringeth forth evil fruit": "Men do not gather figs from thistles":[104] "A bitter fountain sends not forth sweet waters":[105] "Who can bring a clean thing out of an unclean?"[106] If the fountain be poisoned, can the streams be wholesome? What can you expect of light and truth from a mind possessed with vanity and darkness? What from a will averted from the chiefest good, and fixed upon present appearances? What from a heart, the figment of whose imagination is only evil?

The Distinction between Primary and Secondary Causation

[2]. Consider the difference in the rule of operation: everything that works has a rule to work by, this is called a law. In that thing which to man is sinful, God works as it is a thing only, man as it is a sinful thing. And how so? Why everyone's sin is his aberration from his rule of operation or working.

---

102 In the original, the italicized text in this paragraph is set in all caps for emphasis.
103 I.e., defective and impaired.
104 Matt. 7:16–18.
105 James 3:11.
106 Job 14:4.

Ἁμαρτάνειν,[107] is *aberrare a scopo*.[108] To sin, is, not to collime[109] aright at the end proposed; ἡ ἁμαρτία ἐστὶν ἡ ἀνομία[110] is a most exact definition of it: irregularity is its form, if it may be said to have a form: a privation's form, is deformity. Look then in any action wherein an agent exorbitates[111] from its rule, that is sin: now what is God's rule in operation? His own infinite wise will alone; he takes neither motive, rise, nor occasion for any internal acts, from anything without himself; he does whatever he pleases (Ps. 115:3). He "worketh all things according to the counsel of his own will" (Eph. 1:11). That is his own law of operation, and the rule of righteousness unto others: working them agreeably to his own will, which he always must do, he is free from the obliquity[112] of any action. What now is the rule of the sons of men? Why the revealed will of God; "Revealed things belong to us that we may do them" (Deut. 29:29). God's revealed will is the rule of our walking; our working; whatever suits not, answers not this, is evil. "Sin is the transgression of the law" (1 John 3:4). Here then comes in the deformity, the obliquity, the ataxy[113] of anything. God works, and man works; those agents have several rules. God works according to his rule, hence the action is good, as an action: man deviates from his rule, hence it is sinful in respect of its qualifications and adjuncts. Man writes fair letters, upon a wet paper, and they run all into one blot, not the skill of the scribe, but the defect in the paper is the cause of the deformity: he that makes a lame horse go, is the cause of his going, but the defect in his joints, is the cause of his going lame: the sun exhales a steam from the dunghill, the sun is the cause of the exhalation, but the dunghill of the unwholesome savor. The first cause is the proper cause of a thing's being, but the second of its being evil.

God's Use of Means

[3] Consider the several operations and actings of God and man: for instance in a rebellious people's fighting against their helpers under him.

Now the acts of God herein may be referred to six heads.

{1} A continuance of the creature's being and life; "upholding him by the word of his power" (Heb. 1:3). When he might take him off in a moment:

---

107 Gk. "sin."
108 Lat. "to stray from one's mark."
109 I.e., aim.
110 Gk. "sin is lawlessness." This is a quotation from 1 John 3:4.
111 I.e., deviates from the path.
112 I.e., deviation or perversity.
113 I.e., disorder; irregularity.

"enduring them with much long-suffering" (Rom. 9:22). When he might cut them off as he did the opposers of Elijah, with "fire from heaven" (2 Kings 1:12).

{2} A continuance of power of operation to them, when he could make their hands to wither like Jeroboam's, when they go about to strike (1 Kings 13:4). Or their hearts, to die within them, like Nabal's, when they intend to be churlish[114] (1 Sam. 25:37), but he raises them up, or makes them to stand, that they may oppose (Rom. 9:1[7]).

{3} Laying before them a suitable object for the drawing forth their corruption unto opposition, giving them such helpers as shall in many things cross their lusts, and exasperate them, thereunto; as Elijah a man of a fiery zeal, for a lukewarm Ahab.[115]

{4} Withholding from them that effectual grace, by which alone that sin might be avoided; a not actually keeping them from that sin by the might of his Spirit and grace; that alone is effectual grace, which is actual; "He suffers them to walk in their own ways."[116]

And this the Lord may do,

First, in respect of them, judicially, they deserve to be forsaken: Ahab is left to fill up the measure of his iniquities, "Add iniquity to iniquity" (Ps. 69:27).

Secondly, in respect of himself, by way of sovereignty, doing what he will with his own, hardening whom he will (Rom. 9:[18]).

{5} He positively sends upon their understandings that, which the Scripture sets out under the terms of blindness, darkness, folly, delusion, slumber, a spirit of giddiness, and the like; the places are too many to rehearse. What secret actings in, and upon the minds of men, what disturbing of their advices, what mingling of corrupt affections with false carnal reasonings, what givings up to the power of darkness, in Satan the prince thereof, this judicial act does contain, I cannot insist upon: let it suffice, God will not help them, to discern, yea he will cause that they shall not discern but hide from their eyes the things that concern their peace,[117] and so give them up to contend with their only helpers.

{6} Suitably, upon the will and affections he has several acts; obfirming[118] the one, in corruption, and giving up the other to vileness (Rom. 1:24, 26), until the heart become thoroughly hardened, and the conscience seared: not forc-

---

[114] I.e., grudging or ungracious.
[115] 1 Kings 18.
[116] Acts 14:16.
[117] Luke 19:42.
[118] I.e., making stubborn or obdurate.

ing the one, but leaving it to follow the judgment of practical reason, which being a blind, yea a blinded guide, whither can it lead a blind follower, but into the ditch? Not defiling the other with infused sensuality, but provoking them to act according to inbred, native corruption, and by suffering frequent vile actings to confirm them in ways of vileness.

Take an instance of the whole; God gives helpers and deliverers to a sinful people, because of their provocations, some or all of them shall not taste of the deliverance, by them to be procured; wherefore though he sustains their lives in being, whereby they might have opportunity to know his mind, and their own peace, yet he gives them a power to contend with their helpers, causing their helpers to act such things, as under consideration of circumstances, shall exceedingly provoke these sinners: being so exasperated and provoked, the Lord who is free in all his dispensations, refuses to make out to them that healing grace, whereby they might be kept from a sinful opposition: yea being justly provoked, and resolved that they should not taste of the plenty to come, he makes them foolish and giddy in their reasonings and counsels, blinds them in their understandings, that they shall not be able to discern plain and evident things, tending to their own good, but in all their ways, shall err like a drunken man in his vomit; whence that they may not be recovered, because he will destroy them, he gives in hardness and obstinacy upon their hearts and spirits, leaving them to suitable affections, to contend for their own ruin.

Now what are the ways and methods of sinful man's working in such opposition, would be too long for me to declare; what prejudices are erected, what lusts pursued, what corrupt interests acted and followed; how self is honored, what false pretenses coined, how God is slighted, if I should go about to lay open, I must look into the hell of these times, than which nothing can be more loathsome and abominable: let it suffice, that sinful self, sinful lusts, sinful prejudices, sinful blindness, sinful carnal fears, sinful corrupt interests, sinful fleshly reasonings, sinful passions, and vile affections do all concur in such a work, are all woven up together in such a web.

The Difference between Divine and Human Purposes

[4] See the distance of their aims. God's aim is only the manifestation of his own glory (than which nothing but himself is so infinitely good, nothing so righteous that it should be) and this by the way of goodness and severity (Rom. 11:22), goodness in faithfulness and mercy, preserving his, who are opposed, whereby his glory is exceedingly advanced: severity toward the opposers, that by a sinful cursed opposition, they may fill up the measure of

their iniquities, and receive this at the hand of the Lord, that they "lie down in sorrow,"[119] wherein also he is glorious.

God forbid, that I should speak this, of all, that for any time, or under any temptation may be carried to an opposition, in any kind, or degree to the instruments of God's glory among them: many for a season may do it, and yet belong to God, who shall be recovered in due time:[120] it is only of men given up, forsaken, opposing all the appearances of God with his saints and people in all his ways, of whom I speak.

Now what are the ends of this generation of fighters against this "brasen wall," and how distant from those of the Lord's? "They consult to cast him down from his excellency," whom God will exalt (Ps. 62:4). They think not as the Lord, neither does their heart mean so, but it is in their heart to destroy and to cut off (Isa. 10:7). To satisfy their own corrupt lusts, ambition, avarice,[121] revenge, superstition, contempt of God's people because his, hatred of the yoke of the Lord, fleshly interests; even for these, and such like ends as these, is their undertaking.

Thus though there be a concurrence of God and man in the same thing, yet considering the distance of their principles, rules, actings, and ends; it is apparent that man does sinfully, what the Lord does judicially; which being an answer to the former objection, I return to give in some uses to the point.

Three Applications to Those in Government and Those Who Oppose Them
Those Who Follow God in Difficult Days Should Expect Opposition
Use 1. Let men, constant, sincere, upright in the ways of God, especially in difficult times know, what they are to expect from many, yea the most of the generation, whose good they intend, and among whom they live; opposition and fighting are like to be their lot, and that not only it will be so because of men's lusts, corruptions, prejudices, but also it shall be so from God's righteous judgments against a stubborn people: they harden their hearts that it may be so, to compass their ends, and God hardens their hearts that it shall be so to bring about his aims: they will do it to execute their revenge upon others, they shall do it to execute God's vengeance upon themselves. This may be for consolation, that in their contending there is nothing but the wrath of man against them, whom they oppose (which God will restrain, or cause it to turn to his praise) but there is the wrath of God against themselves, which

---

[119] Isa. 50:11.
[120] Presumably an expression of the desire to see members of Parliament who were presently hostile to the regime being won over.
[121] I.e., insatiable desire for wealth or gain.

who can bear? This then let all expect, who engage their hearts to God, and "follow the Lamb whithersoever he goes."[122]

Men walking in the sincerity of their hearts are very apt to conceive that all sheaves should bow to theirs,[123] that all men should cry, "Grace, grace,"[124] to their proceedings. Why should any oppose? *Quid meruere?*[125] Alas! The more upright they are, the fitter for the Lord by them to break a gainsaying people: let men keep close to those ways of God whereto protection is annexed, and let not their hearts fail them because of the people of the land; the storm of their fury will be like the plague of hail in Egypt; it smote only the cattle that were in the field; those, who upon the word of Moses drove them into the houses, preserved them alive.[126] If men wander in the field of their own ways, of self-seeking, oppression, ambition, and the like, doubtless the storm will carry them away; but for those, who keep house, who keep close to the Lord, though it may have much noise, terror, and dread with it, it shall not come nigh them. And if the Lord for causes best known, known only to his infinite wisdom, should take off any Josiahs in the opposition, he will certainly effect two things by it.[127]

(1) To give them rest and peace.

(2) To further his cause and truth, by drawing out the prayers and appeals of the residue, and this living they valued above their lives.

All you then that are the Lord's workmen be always prepared for a storm, wonder not, that men see not the ways of the Lord, nor the judgments of our God, many are blinded. Admire not, that they will so endlessly engage themselves into fruitless oppositions, they are hardened. Be not amazed, that evidence of truth and righteousness will not affect them, they are corrupted. But this do, come and enter into the chambers of God, and you shall be safe until this whole indignation be overpast.[128]

I speak of all them, and only them, who follow the Lord in all his ways with upright hearts, and single minds, if the Lord will have you to be a rock and "a brasen wall" for men to dash themselves against, and to break in pieces,

---

[122] Rev. 14:4.
[123] Gen. 37:7.
[124] Zech. 4:7.
[125] Lat. "What have they done?" This is a quotation from Ovid, *Metamorphoses* 15.120. For the Latin text and English translation, see Ovid, *Metamorphoses*, vol. 2, *Books 9–15*, trans. Frank Justus Miller, rev. G. P. Goold, Loeb Classical Library 43 (Cambridge, MA: Harvard University Press, 1916), 372–73.
[126] Ex. 9:19–21.
[127] 2 Kings 22:19–20.
[128] Isa. 26:20.

though the service be grievous to flesh and blood, yet it is his, whose you are, be prepared, the wind blows, a storm may come.

Those Opposed to the Cause Should Engage in Self-Examination

Use 2. Let men set upon opposition make a diligent inquiry, whether there be no hand in the business but their own? Whether their counsels be not leavened with the wrath of God? And their thoughts mixed with a spirit of giddiness, and themselves carried on to their own destruction? Let me see the opposer of the present ways of God, who upon his opposition is made more humble, more self-denying, more empty of self-wisdom, more fervent in supplications and waiting upon God, than formerly: and I will certainly blot him out of the roll of men judicially hardened. But if therewith men become also proud, selfish, carnally wise, revengeful, furious upon earthly interests, full, impatient, doubtless God is departed, and an evil spirit from the Lord prevails on them.[129] O that men would look about them before it be too late, see the Lord disturbing them, before the waves return upon them; know that they may pull down some antics that make a great show of supporting the church,[130] and yet indeed are pargeted posts supported by it;[131] the foundation is on a rock, that shall not be prevailed against.

All Should See the Sovereign Hand of God at Work

Use 3. See the infinite wisdom and sovereignty of Almighty God, that is able to bring light out of darkness, and to compass his own righteous judgments by the sinful advisings and undertakings of men. Indeed the Lord's sovereignty and dominion over the creature does not in anything more exalt itself, than in working in all the reasonings, debates, consultations of men, to bring about his own counsels through their free workings. That men should use, improve their wisdom, freedom, choice, yea lusts, not once thinking of God, yet all that while do his work more than their own: "This is the Lord's doing, and it is marvellous in our eyes."[132]

Of the last part of my text I shall not speak at all, neither indeed did I intend.[133]

---

[129] See 1 Sam. 16:14.
[130] In medieval architecture, "antics" were decorative wall features.
[131] Pargetted posts were frequently covered in lime plaster or mortar. One of the English counties with which decorative pargework was particularly associated was Essex, where Owen ministered. See George Bankart, *The Art of the Plasterer* (1908; repr., London: Routledge, 2002), 77. Owen employed the same illustration in *The Branch of the Lord* (1650), which is included in volume 19.
[132] Ps. 118:23.
[133] This point was about the consolation and success that God's instruments of deliverance would enjoy.

[The Discourse on Toleration Appended to
the Published Version of the Sermon]

Of Toleration

And the Duty of the Magistrate, about Religion

PREFACE

The times are busy, and we must be brief. Prefaces for the most part are at all times needless, in these, troublesome. Mine shall only be, that ἄνευ προοιμίων καὶ παθῶν,[1] "without either preface or passion," I will fall to the business in hand. The thing about which I am to deal, is commonly called "toleration in religion," or "toleration of several religions."[2] The way wherein I shall proceed, is not by contest, thereby to give occasion for the reciprocation of a saw of debate with any, but by the laying down of such positive observations, as being either not apprehended, or not rightly improved, by the most, yet lie at the bottom of the whole difference between men about this business, and tend in themselves to give light unto a righteous and equitable determination of the main thing contended about: and lastly herein, for method, I shall first, consider the grounds upon which that nontoleration, whereunto I cannot consent, has been and is still endeavored to be supported, which I shall be necessitated to remove, and then in order assert the positive truth, as to the substance of the business under contest: all in these ensuing observations.

1   In Athens, the orator who was to speak at the Areopagus was instructed to do so without preamble or any emotional appeal. The phrase was often attributed to Lucian in *Anacharis* 19. For the Greek text and an English translation, see *Lucian Anacharsis or Athletics. Menippus or The Descent into Hades. On Funerals. A Professor of Public Speaking. Alexander the False Prophet. Essays in Portraiture. Essays in Portraiture Defended. The Goddesse of Surrye*, trans. A.M. Harmon, Loeb Classical Library 162 (Cambridge, MA: Harvard University Press, 1925), 28–29.
2   For example, Richard Holdsworth, *An Answer without a Question, or, The Late Schismatical Petition for a Diabolicall Toleration of Severall Religions Expounded* [. . .] (London, 1649).

PART 1: CONSIDERATION OF THE GROUNDS FOR NONTOLERATION

Eight Problems with the Arguments Used to Support Religious Coercion

Those Opposed to Toleration Have Yet to Provide a Compelling Case for the Civil Punishment of Those in Error

1. Although the expressions of "toleration," and "nontoleration," wherewith the thing in controversy is vested, do seem to cast the affirmative upon them who plead for a forbearance in things of religion toward dissenting persons, yet the truth is, they are purely upon the negation, and the affirmative lies fully on the other part: and so the weight of proving (which ofttimes is heavy) lies on their shoulders. Though nontoleration sound like a negation, yet punishment (which terms in this matter are ἰσοδυναμοῦντα),[3] is a deep affirmation. And therefore it suffices not men to say, that they have consulted the mind of God, and cannot find that he ever spoke to any of his saints or people to establish a toleration of error: and yet this is the first argument to oppose it, produced in the late testimony of the reverend and learned Assembly of the Church of Scotland.[4] Affirmative precepts must be produced, for a nontoleration, that is the punishing of erring persons. For actings, of such high concernment, men do generally desire a better warrant than this, "There is nothing in the word against them." Clear light is needful for men, who walk in paths, which lead directly to houses of blood. God has not spoken of nontoleration, is a certain rule of forbearance. But God has not spoken of toleration, is no rule of acting in opposition thereunto. (What he has spoken, one way or other, shall be afterward considered.) Positive actings must have positive precepts, and rules for them, as conscience is its own guide. If then you will have persons deviating in their apprehensions from the truth of the gospel, civilly punished, you must bring better warrant than this, that God has not spoken against it, or I shall not walk in your ways, but refrain my foot from your path.[5]

---

3   Gk. "terms having the same meaning."
4   In January 1649, the Commissioners of the General Assembly of the Church of Scotland issued *A Solemn Testimony against Toleration, and the Present Proceedings of Sectaries and Their Abettors in England, in Reference to Religion and Government* (Edinburgh, 1649). This tract declared that "we have searched after the minde of Christ ... and no where can we finde in the Scriptures of truth, either precept or precedent allowed of God for Toleration of any Errour, much lesse did it ever come into his minde, or did he speak to any of his servants concerning a Toleration of all Errour." They targeted "a cursed toleration" that would "bring forth many blasphemies and abominations." See *Solemn Testimony*, 3, 8.
5   Prov. 1:15.

*Those Opposed to Toleration Should Recognize That
Not All Things Fall under Human Cognizance*

2. That undoubtedly there are very many things under the command of the Lord, so becoming our duty, and within his promise, so made our privilege, which yet if not performed, or not enjoyed, are not of human cognizance, as faith itself. Yet because the knowledge of the truth is in that rank of things, this also is urged as of weight, by the same learned persons, to the business at hand.

*It Is Wrong to Say That Those in Favor of Toleration Do Not Allow
for the Punishment of Those in Error Who Disturb the Peace*

3. Errors, though never so impious, are yet distinguished from peace-disturbing enormities. If opinions in their own nature tend to the disturbance of the public peace, either that public tranquility is not of God, or God allows a penal[6] restraint of those opinions. It is a mistake, to affirm, that those who plead for toleration, do allow of punishment for offenses against the second table, not against the first.[7] The case is the same both in respect of the one, and the other. What offenses against the second table are punishable? Doubtless not all: but only such as by a disorderly eruption pervert the course of public quiet and society. Yea none but such, fall under human cognizance. The warrant of exercising vindictive power among men, is from the reference of offences to their common tranquility. "It is in the public interest that crimes do not go unpunished."[8] Where punishment is the debt, *Bonum totius*,[9] is the creditor to exact it. And this is allowed, as to the offenses against the first table. If any of them in their own nature (not some men's apprehensions) are disturbances of public peace, they also are punishable. Only let not this be measured by disputable consequences, no more than the other are. Let the evidence be in the things themselves, and *Actum est*,[10] let who will plead for them. Hence,

Popish religion, warming in its very bowels, a fatal engine against all magistracy among us, cannot upon our concessions plead for forbearance: it

---

6 I.e., punitive.
7 As the Commissioners had done. See *Solemn Testimony*, 3. According to Coffey, in their parliamentary preaching, "the English Westminster Divines . . . constantly reiterated the teaching that magistrates were keepers of both tables of the law." See Coffey, *Persecution and Toleration in Protestant England*, 32.
8 In the text: *Delicta puniri, publice interest*.—Owen. Cf. Hugo Grotius, *Defensio fidei catholicae de satisfaction Christi* (Leiden, 1617), 43.
9 Lat. "for the good of the whole."
10 Lat. "it has been done."

being a known and received maxim, that the gospel of Christ, clashes against no righteous ordinance of man.

And let this be spoken to the third argument of the forenamed reverend persons, from the analogy of delinquencies against the first and second table.[11]

It Is Problematic to Apply the Law against Idolatry to Those in Error

4. The plea for the punishment of erring persons, from the penal constitution under the Old Testament against idolaters (which in the next place is urged), seems not very firm and convincing.[12] The vast distance that is between idolatry, and any errors whatsoever, as merely such, however propagated or maintained with obstinacy, much impairs the strength of this argumentation.

Idolatry is the yielding unto a creature the service and worship due to the Creator.[13] *Idololatria est circa omne idolum famulatus et servitus*,[14] "The attendance and service of any idol." *Idololatrae dicuntur qui simulacris eam servitutem exhibent quae debetur Deo*, "They are idolaters who give that service to idols which is due unto God."[15] To render glory to the creature as to God, is idolatry,[16] say the Papists.[17] Suitable to the description of it given

---

11 See *Solemn Testimony*, 3.
12 See *Solemn Testimony*, 5–6.
13 In the text: Reinold. de Idol., li. 2. cap. 1, s. 1.—Owen. This is a reference to the Oxford divine and moderate Puritan controversialist John Rainolds (1549–1607) and his *De Romanae ecclesiae idolatria* [On the idolatry of the Roman church] (Oxford, 1596), 327–28.
14 In the text: (Tertul. de [Id]ol).—Owen. This is a quotation from Tertullian, *De idolatria* (*On Idolatry*) 3.4: "Every attendance upon any idol, every service rendered to one, is idolatry." For the Latin text, see Tertullian, *De idolatria*, in *Opera omnia*, ed. J.-P. Migne, Patrologia Latina 1 (Paris: Migne, 1844), 665. For the English translation, see *Early Latin Theology: Selections from Tertullian, Cyprian, Ambrose and Jerome*, ed. S. L. Greenslade, Library of Christian Classics (Louisville: Westminster, 1956), 85.
15 In the text: (August. Lib. i. de Trinit cap. 6).—Owen. This is a quotation from Augustine, *De Trinitate* 1.1.13. For the Latin text, see Augustine, *De Trinitate*, in *Opera omnia*, ed. J.-P. Migne, Patrologia Latina 42 (Paris: Migne-Garnier, 1865), 827. For an English translation, see Augustine, *The Trinity*, ed. John E. Rotelle, trans. Edmund Hill, *The Works of Saint Augustine: A Translation for the 21st Century* (Hyde Park, NY: New City Press, 1991), 75.
16 Reformed theologians thought the Roman Catholic definition of idolatry was too narrow in holding idolatry to consist only in giving divine worship to the creature as though it was divine.
17 In the text: Bell., de Eccles. Triumph., lib. ii. cap. 24; Greg, de Valen. de Idol., lib. i. cap. 1.—Owen. The first reference is to Robert Bellarmine (1542–1621), *Controversiarum de ecclesia triumphante, sive de gloria & cultu sanctorum* [*Controversies on the Church Triumphant, or the Glory and Veneration of the Saints*] (Ingolstadt, 1586–1589), bk. 2, chap. 24. This chapter deals with the sign of the cross. For the Latin text, see Bellarmine, *Opera omnia*, ed. Justinus Fèvre, vol. 3 (Paris: Lucovicum Vivès, 1870). The second reference is to Gregory of Valencia (ca. 1550–1603), who authored a Jesuit defense of the veneration of the saints and the Mass in response to the Lutheran professor of theology in Tübingen Jakob Heerbrand (1521–1600), titled *Apologeticus de idolatria, adversus impium libellum Jacobi Herbrandi etc.* (Ingolstadt, 1579).

by the apostle (Rom. 1:25), plainly, that whereunto the sanction under debate was added, as the bond of the law against it (which was the bottom of the commendable proceedings of divers kings of Judah against such), was a voluntary relinquishment of Jehovah revealed unto them, to give the honor due unto him to dunghill idols. Now though error and ignorance ofttimes lie at the bottom of this abomination, yet error properly so called, and which under the name of heresy is opposed, is sufficiently differenced therefrom. That common definition of heresy, that it is an error, or errors, in or about the fundamentals of religion, maintained with stubbornness and pertinacy after conviction (for the main received by most Protestant divines) will be no way suited unto that which was before given of idolatry, and is as commonly received;[18] being indeed much more clear, as shall be afterward declared. That this latter is proper and suitable to those scriptural descriptions, which we have of heresy, I dare not assert: but being received by them who urge the punishment thereof, it may be a sufficient ground of affirming, that those things whose definitions are so extremely different, are also very distant and discrepant in themselves, and therefore constitutions for the disposal of things concerning the one, cannot *eo nomine*,[19] include the other. Neither is the inference any stronger, than, that a man may be hanged for coveting, because he may be so for murdering.

The penal constitutions of the Judaical polity (for so they were which yet I urge not) concerning idolaters, must be stretched beyond their limits, if you intend to enwrap heretics within their verge. If heretics be also idolaters, as the Papists (the poor Indians who worship a piece of red cloth,[20] the Egyptians who adored the deities, which grew in their own gardens,[21] being not more besotted with this abomination than they who prostrate their souls unto, and lavish their devotion upon, a piece of bread, a little before they prepare it for the draught, so casting the stumbling block of their iniquities before the

---

18 On the concept of "fundamental" articles, see Richard A. Muller, *Post-Reformation Reformed Dogmatics: The Rise and Development of Reformed Orthodoxy, ca. 1520 to ca. 1725*, 4 vols. (Grand Rapids, MI: Baker, 2003), 1:406–30. Defining heresy was, as Coffey has shown, a "ticklish business." See John Coffey, "A Ticklish Business: Defining Heresy and Orthodoxy in the Puritan Revolution," in *Heresy, Literature and Politics in Early Modern English Culture*, ed. David Loewenstein and John Marshall (Cambridge: Cambridge University Press, 2006), 108–31.
19 Lat. "by that name."
20 The Flemish Jesuit François de Coster (1532–1619) reported that the people of Lapland worshiped a red cloth hung upon the top of a spear. See, François de Coster, *Enchiridion Controversiarum* [. . .] (Cologne, 1585), 192.
21 For the idea that the Egyptians worshiped onions grown in their own gardens, see Tashiro, "English Poets, Egyptians Onions, and the Protestant View of the Eucharist," *Journal of the History of Ideas* 30, no. 4 (1969): 563–78.

faces of poor heathens and Jews, causing Averroes[22] to breathe out his soul in this expression of that scandal, "Since the Christians eat the God whom they worship, let my soul be with Philosophers."[23]) I say then, the case seems to me, to have received so considerable an alteration, that the plea of forbearance is extremely weakened; as to my present apprehension: however for the present, I remove such from this debate.

Similar Challenges in Applying the Law against Blasphemy

5. The like to this also, may be said concerning blasphemy, the law whereof is likewise commonly urged in this cause.[24] The establishment for the punishment of a blasphemer is in Leviticus 24:16. Given it was upon the occasion of the blaspheming and cursing of the son of an Egyptian, upon his striving and contending with an Israelite.[25] Being (probably) in his own apprehension, wronged by his adversary, he fell to reviling his God. The word here used to express his sin, is נָקַב,[26] signifying also to pierce, and is twice so rendered (Isa. 36:6; Hab. 3:14). Desperate expressions piercing the honor and glory of the Most High, willingly and willfully, were doubtless his death-deserving crime. It is the same word that Balak used to Balaam, when he would have persuaded him to a deliberate cursing and pouring out of imprecations on the people of God (Num. 23:13–14). A resolved piercing of the name and glory of God, with cursed reproaches, is the crime here sentenced to death. The schoolmen[27] tell us, that to complete blasphemy of the perverse affection of the heart in detestation of the goodness of God, joined with the reproaches of his name, is required.[28] Which how remote it is from error of any sort (I mean within the compass of them whereof we speak), being a pure misapprehension of the understanding,

---

22 The Muslim polymath Ibn Rushd (1126–1198).
23 In the text: *Quoniam Christiani manducant Deum quem adorant, sit anima mea cum Philosophis*. French Protestants had utilized this saying (which had been attributed to Averroes) to suggest that the doctrine of transubstantiation damaged the cause of the gospel because it was so easily ridiculed by unbelievers. See, e.g., the 1636 work of Pierre Du Moulin (1568–1658), *The Anatomy of the Mass*, trans. Robert Shanks (Glasgow: Collins, 1833), 172.
24 See *Solemn Testimony*, 5.
25 Lev. 24:10.
26 Heb. "to curse" or "to pierce."
27 I.e., medieval philosophers and theologians employing the scholastic method.
28 In the text: Thom. 22ae. q. 13, a. 1, ad 1um.—Owen. This is a reference to Thomas Aquinas, *Summa theologiae* 2ae, q. 13, which concerns the sin of blasphemy. Art. 1 asks, "Is blasphemy opposed to the profession of faith?" and responds by saying that blasphemy is more than unbelief and involves "disparaging some excellent goodness, especially that of God." For the Latin text, see Aquinas, *Summa Theologiae*, vol. 32, *(2a2ae: 8–16): Consequences of Faith*, trans. Thomas Gilby (Cambridge: Cambridge University Press, 2006), 104–7.

embraced (though falsely) for the honor of God, I suppose is easily conceived: and so consequently that the argument for the death of a person erring, because he came off no easier, of old who blasphemed, is *a baculo ad angulum*.[29]

If any shall say that blasphemy is of a larger extent, and more general acceptation in the Scripture, I shall not deny it. But yet that, that kind of blasphemy which was punishable with violent death, was comprehensive of any inferior crime, I suppose cannot be proved. However, blasphemy in the Scripture is never taken in any place, that I can remember, for a man's maintaining his own error, but for his reviling and speaking evil of the truth which he receives not, and so Paul before his conversion was a blasphemer.[30]

Now if men to whom forbearance is indulged in bypaths of their own, shall make it their work to cast dirt on the better ways of truth, it is to me very questionable whether they do not offend against that prime dictate of nature, for the preservation of human society,[31] "Do not do unto others what you do not want done to yourself";[32] and for such I will be no advocate.

Neither can indeed the law of blasphemy, be impartially urged by us in any case of heresy whatsoever. For,

(1) The penal sanctions of the laws of God are not in England esteemed of moral equity, and perpetually indispensable; for if so, why do adulterers unmolested, behold the violent death of stealers?

(2) The blasphemer by that law was not allowed his clergy. Die he must without mercy, no room being left for the intervention of repentance, as to the removal of his temporal punishment. When once the witnesses' garments were rent, he was anathema: but in case of any heresy, repentance, yea, recantation, is a sure antidote (at least for once, so it is among the Papists) against all corporeal sufferings.

Further Problems in Applying the Punishment of False Prophets

6. Neither does that place in Zachary,[33] chapter 13:3,[34] concerning the running through of the false prophet, more prove or approve of the punishment of

---

[29] Lat. "from the staff to the corner." This phrase is used to describe the type of logical fallacy exemplified by the claim that because a stick stands in the corner today, therefore tomorrow it will rain.
[30] In the margin: Acts 26:11; Acts 18:6; 1 Tim. 1:13.—Owen.
[31] In the Whitehall debates, Henry Ireton had defended the magistrate's role in matters of religion, arguing that one purpose of government was "the preserving of humane society in peace." See William Clarke, *The Clarke Papers* [. . .], ed. C. H. Firth, 4 vols. (London: Camden Society, 1891–1901), 2:79.
[32] In the text: *Quod tibi fieri non vis, alteri ne feccris.*—Owen. This is a version of the Golden Rule.
[33] I.e., Zechariah.
[34] For the importance of this text, particularly in the context of the Blasphemy Ordinance, see John Coffey, *John Goodwin and the Puritan Revolution: Religion and Intellectual Change in Seventeenth-*

death to be inflicted for misapprehensions in the matters of religion (and if it proves not that, it proves nothing, for slaying is the thing expressed, and certainly if proofs be taken from the letter, the letter must be obeyed, or we force the word to serve our hypothesis) than that place of John 10, "He that entereth not by the door is a thief and a robber";[35] which Bellarmine strongly urges to this very purpose, because thieves and robbers, are so dealt withal righteously.[36] If such deductions may be allowed it will be easy to prove, *quidlibet, ex quolibet*,[37] at any time.

If the letter be urged, and the sense of the letter as it lies (indeed the figurative sense of such places is the proper literal sense of them),[38] let that

---

Century England (Woodbridge, UK: Boydell, 2006), 146–47. Samuel Rutherford devoted an entire chapter to "Prophecies in the Old Testament Especially, Zach. 13. 1, 2, 3, 4, 5, 6. For Punishing False Prophets Vindicated," arguing that the passage referred to "the Church of Christ" and taught that "false teachers under the New Testament ought to be punished with the sword." See Rutherford, *A Free Disputation against Pretended Liberty of Conscience* [. . .] (London, 1649), 209–10. Similarly, William Prynne (1600–1669) used the text on the title page of *The Sword of Christian Magistracy Supported* [. . .] (London, 1647). Prynne argued that it was a prophecy "of the times of the Gospel" and used it to support his call for the punishment of heresy and blasphemy "with Pecuniary, Corporall, and in some Cases with Banishment, and Capitall Punishments." See Prynne, *Sword of Christian Magistracy*, title page and 149. The importance of Prynne's work may be seen in Wolfgang Meyer's translation of it into Latin in 1649 and a second edition that appeared in 1653. In contrast to Prynne, John Goodwin advanced a different interpretation in *A Postscript or Appendix to* [. . .] *Hagiomastix* [. . .] (London, 1647), arguing that the passage "respecteth onely the Nation, and Church of the Jews." See Goodwin, *Postscript or Appendix to Hagiomastix*, 2. See also Lawrence Rabone, "John Goodwin on Zechariah 13:3: Toleration, Supersessionism and Judeo-Centric Eschatology," *Bulletin of the John Rylands Library* 96, no. 2 (2020): 47–68.

35 John 10:1.
36 In the text: Bell. lib. *de Laicis* cap. 21.—Owen. This is a reference to Robert Bellarmine's treatise on civil government *De laicis* (*The Laity*) (1603). Chapter 21 is titled "Heretics Condemned by the Church Can Be Punished with Temporal Punishments and Even Death." Here Bellarmine argues that in John 10:1 the thief and murderer are heretics, seducers, and the founders of sects. For an English translation, see Bellarmine, *On Temporal and Spiritual Authority: On Laymen or Secular People; On the Temporal Power of the Pope, against William Barclay; On the Primary Duty of the Supreme Pontiff: Political Writings of Robert Bellarmine*, ed. and trans. Stefania Tutino (Indianapolis, IN: Liberty Fund, 2012), 104.
37 Lat. "anything of anything." This is a reference to manipulative and dishonest interpretation.
38 In the margin: August. de Util. Creden., cap. 3. Thom. pp. q. 1, a. 10. Zanch. de SS. q. 12, cap. 2, reg. 10. Tilen. Syntag. Theol. de Interpret. S. Thes. 8. Whitak. de SS., qu. 5, cap. 2. Armin. Disput. Pri. Thes. 9, 1. Ames. Med. Theol. cap. 34. Thes. 22.—Owen. In this long series of references, Owen refers to the following: Augustine, *De utilitatecredendi* (*On the Advantage of Believing*) 3.5–9. For the Latin text, see S. Aureli Augustini, *De utilitatecredendi liber*, ed. Joseph Zycha, *Corpus Scriptorum Ecclesiasticorum Latinorum* 25.1 (Vienna: Tempsky, 1891), 7–8. For an English translation, see *On Christian Belief*, trans. Ray Kearney, *The Works of Saint Augustine: A Translation for the 21st Century* (Hyde Park, NY: New City Press, 2005), 119–23. Thomas Aquinas, *Summa theologica* 1a, q. 1, a. 10: "Whether in Holy Scripture a Word May Have Several Senses?" For the text, see Aquinas, *Summa Theologiae*, vol. 1, *Christian Theology*

sense alone be kept to: let parents then pass sentence, condemn, and execute their children, when they turn seducers. And that in any kind whatsoever, into what seduction soever they shall be engaged; be it most pernicious, or in things of less concernment; the letter allows of none of our distinctions; be they convinced or not convinced, obstinate or not obstinate, all is one, so it must be, "thrust through" and slain by their parents, must they fall to the ground; only observe, "his father and his mother that begat him" must be made magistrates, prophets with unclean spirits be turned into heretics, only "thrusting through," that must be as it is in the letter; yea though plainly the party of whom it is said, "Thou shalt not live," verse 3, is found alive, verse 6.[39] Surely such an Orleans gloss[40] is scarce sufficient to secure a conscience in slaying heretics. But when men please, this whole place shall directly point at the discipline of the churches, and their spiritual censures under the gospel, curing deceivers and bringing them home to confession and acknowledgment of their folly. See the late *Annot. of the Bible*.[41]

Take More Care in the Interpretation of Romans 13

7. From the asserting of the authority, and description of the duty of the magistrate (Rom. 13), the argument is very easy, that is produced, for the

---

(1a. 1), trans. Thomas Gilby (Cambridge: Cambridge University Press, 2006), 36–41. Jerome Zanchi, *De sacra Scriptura tractatus* (Heidelberg, 1593), 420–26. Daniel Tilenus, *Syntagmatis disputationum theologicarum* (Sedan, 1611), thesis 8. William Whitaker, *Disputatio de sacra Scriptura* (1588), q. 5, chap. 2. For an English translation, See William Whitaker, *A Disputation on Holy Scripture*, trans. and ed. William Fitzgerald (Cambridge: Cambridge University Press, 1849), 403–10. Jacob Arminius, *Disputationes Privatae*, in *Opera theologica* (Leiden, 1629), 346. For an English translation, see James Arminius, "The Private Disputation of James Arminius on the Principal Articles of the Christian Religion," in *The Works of James Arminius*, trans. James Nichols, 3 vols. (London, 1828), 2:328–29. William Ames, *Medulla s. s. theologiae*, 2nd ed. (London, 1629), chap. 34, thesis 22. For an English translation, see William Ames, *The Marrow of Theology*, trans. John D. Eusden (Grand Rapids, MI: Baker, 1997), 188.

39 Thus, for Owen, this passage ought not to be taken literally.
40 An allusion to the schools of Orléans, (in)famous for interpretive glosses, giving rise to the proverb "The Orleans gloss destroys the text." See Le Roux de Lincy, *Le livre desproverbes Français* [. . .], 2 vols., 2nd ed. (Paris: A. Delahaye, 1859), 1:375. Thus, a *glose d'Orléans* refers to an obscure commentary, one proverbial for destroying the text.
41 Meric Casaubon et al., *Annotations upon All the Books of the Old and New Testament* [. . .] (London, 1645). According to the *Annotations*, Zechariah 13:3 provides "a representation of the Spirit of knowledge, discretion, and zeale in Christs true Church, to discerne false doctrines, and to oppose them. Figurative terms, taken from that which was commanded against false Prophets." Then, in the commentary on verse 6 it states, "If it appears that he hath passed through the Churches discipline, because he hath been a seducer, he shall confesse it, and give God the glory, approving of the Churches severitie, used for his correction. A representation of the wonderfull power of the Spirit and light of God, in convincing and correcting the Ministers of errour."

suppressing, by external force of erroneous persons:[42] the paralogism is so foul and notorious, in this arguing, "He is to suppress evil deeds, heresy is an evil deed, therefore that also," that it needs no confutation. That he is to punish all evil deeds was never yet affirmed. Unbelief is a work of the flesh; so is coveting: one the root sin, against the first, the other against the second table: yet in themselves, both exempted from the magistrate's cognizance and jurisdiction. The evildoers doubtless for whose terror and punishment he is appointed, are such as by their deeds, disturb that human society, the defense and protection whereof, is to him committed. That among the number of these, are errors, the depravations of men's understandings, has not yet been proved.

The Law concerning the Death of the Seducer Is Difficult to Apply

8. The case of the seducer, from Deuteronomy 13, is urged with more show of reason than any of the others, to the business in hand;[43] but yet the extreme discrepancies between the proof, and the thing intended to be proved, makes any argumentation from this place, as to the matter in hand, very intricate, obscure, and difficult. For,

(1) The person here spoken of, pretends an immediate revelation from heaven: he pretends dreams, and gives signs and wonders, verses 1, and so exempts his spirit from any regular trial: heretics for the most part, offer to be tried by the rule that is *in medio*,[44] acknowledged of all; a few distempered enthusiasts[45] excepted.

(2) His business is, to entice from the worship of Jehovah, not in respect of the manner but the object, verse 5. All heretics pretend the fear of that great name.

---

42 This argument was advanced by Prynne, *Sword of Christian Magistracy*, 2–3, 23, 26–27, 98, 104, 109–12, 148–50.

43 George Gillespie appealed to this text in his *Wholesome Severity Reconciled with Christian Liberty, or The True Resolution of a Present Controversie concerning Liberty of Conscience* [. . .] *And in Conclusion a Paraenetick to the Five Apologists for Choosing Accommodation Rather Than Toleration* (London, 1645), 5, 9. Samuel Rutherford said that this example was "no temporary law" for the Jews only but demonstrated that "the Law teacheth that false teachers and hereticks are to be punished with the sword." See Rutherford, *Free Disputation*, 185, 205–6. Rutherford had also appealed to this passage in support of the right of the magistrates to punish idolaters and apostates in *The Due Right of Presbyteries* [. . .] (London, 1644), 356, and would do so in *Free Disputation*, 70–71. Prynne made this argument in *Sword of Christian Magistracy*, 4, 20, 61, 105, 111–12, 115, 124. This text was also appealed to in *Solemn Testimony against Toleration*, 7.

44 Lat. "in the mean."

45 I.e., those who claim to receive direct inspiration outside of Scripture. See Michael Heyd, *"Be Sober and Reasonable:" The Critique of Enthusiasm in the Seventeenth and early Eighteenth Centuries* (Leiden: Brill, 1995), 11–23.

(3) The accepting and owning idol dunghill gods[46] in his room, is the thing persuaded to, verse 2 (and those were only stocks and stones),[47] and this in opposition to Jehovah, who had revealed himself by Moses. Heretics, worship him, own him, and abhor all thoughts of turning away from following after him, according to their erroneous apprehensions. Manichees, Marcionites, Valentinians,[48] and such like names of infidels, I reckon not among heretics, neither will their brainsick, paganish follies, be possibly comprehended under that definition of heresy which is now generally received. Mohammedans are far more rightly termed heretics, than they.[49]

(4) This seducer was to die without mercy: and Aynsworth[50] observes from the rabbines,[51] that this offender alone, had traps laid to catch him; and were he but once overheard to whisper his seduction, though never so secretly, there was no expiation of his transgression, without his own blood: but now this place is urged for all kind of restraint and punishment whatsoever. (Now where God requires blood, is it allowed to man, to commute at an inferior rate?) So I confess, it is urged. But yet what lies at the bottom, in the chambers of their bellies who plead for the power of the magistrate to punish erring persons, from those and such like places as these, is too apparent. Blood is there: swiftly, or slowly, they walk to the chambers of death.

(5) Obstinacy after conviction, turbulency, etc., which are now laid down, as the main weights that turn the scale[52] on the side of severity, are here not once mentioned, nor by anything in the least intimated. If he have done it, yea but once, openly, or secretly, whether he have been convinced of the sinfulness of it, or no, be he obstinate or otherwise, it is not once inquired, die he must, as if he had committed murder, or the like indispensable death-procuring crime. If the punishment then of erring persons be urged from this place, all consideration of their conviction, obstinacy, pertinacy, must be laid aside: the text allows them no more plea in this business, than our law does in the case of willful murder:

---

46 The Junius-Tremellius Old Testament rendered the Hebrew word *gillulim* in Deut. 29:17 as *stercoreos deos*, and in the Authorized Version translation of that verse the marginal alternative is "donguie gods."
47 I.e., idols of wood or stone (Jer. 3:9).
48 Three dualistic belief systems that Owen regarded as pagan.
49 Owen, like many early modern Protestants, categorized Islam as a Christian heresy. See Emanuele Colombo, "Western Theologies and Islam in the Early Modern World," in *The Oxford Handbook of Early Modern Theology, 1600–1800*, ed. Ulrich L. Lehner, Richard A. Muller, and A. G. Roeber (New York: Oxford University Press, 2016), 485.
50 Henry Ainsworth (1571–1622), *Annotations upon the Five Bookes of Moses, the Booke of Psalmes and the Song of Songs or Canticles* (London, 1639), 49.
51 I.e., rabbis.
52 I.e., shift the balance.

(6) Repentance and recantation will in the judgment of all, reprieve an erring person from any sentence of any punishment corporeal whatsoever; and many reasons may be given, why they should so do. Here is no such allowance. Repent or not repent, recant or not recant, he has no sacrifice of expiation provided for him, die he must.

(7) The law contains the sanction of the third commandment as the whole,[53] was a rule of the Jewish polity in the land of Canaan: this among us is generally conceived not binding, as such.

(8) The formal reason of this law by some insisted on, because he sought to "turn" a man from Jehovah:

[1] Is of force only in this case of the object whereunto seduction tends; viz. strange gods, and no other.

[2] Turning from Jehovah respects not any manner of backsliding in respect of the way of worship, but a falling away from him as the object of worship.

Now there being these and many other discrepancies hindering the cases proposed from running parallel, I profess for my part, I cannot see how any such evident deductions can possibly be drawn from hence, as to be made a bottom of practice and acting in things of so high concernment. What may be allowed from the equity of those and the like constitutions, and deduced by analogy and proportion to the business in hand, I shall afterward declare.

PART 2: ASSERTION OF THE TRUTH ABOUT TOLERATION

General Presuppositions

The sum of what is usually drawn from Holy Writ, against such forbearance as I suppose may be asserted, and for the punishing heretics with capital punishments being briefly discussed, I proceed in the next place to such other general observations, as may serve to the farther clearing of the business in hand, and they are these that follow.

The Church Should Oppose Error with Gospel Means

1. The forbearance of, or opposition unto errors, may be considered, with respect either unto civil or spiritual judicature.¶[54]

For the latter, it is either personal or ecclesiastical, properly so called. Personal forbearance of errors in a spiritual sense, is a moral toleration or

---

53 Ex. 20:7.
54 The ¶ symbol indicates that a paragraph break has been added to Owen's original text.

approbation of them. So also is ecclesiastical. The warrant for procedence against them, on that hand is plain and evident. Certainly this way, no error is to be forborne. All persons who have any interest and share in truth, are obliged, in their several ways and stations, to an opposition unto every error. An opposition to be carried on by gospel mediums, and spiritual weapons. Let them according as they are called or opportuned, disprove them from the word, "contending earnestly for the faith once delivered unto the saints."[55] Erring persons are usually ("*bono animo*,"[56] says Salvian) very zealous to propagate their false conceptions; and shall the children of truth be backward in her defense? Precepts unto this as a duty, commendations of it, encouragements unto it, are very frequent in the gospel. Alike is this duty incumbent on all churches walking to the rule. The spiritual sword of discipline, may be lawfully sheathed in the blood of heresies. No spiritual remedy, can be too sharp for a spiritual disease. When the cure is suited to the malady, there is no danger of the application. And this is not denied by any. He that submits himself to any church society, does it *ea lege*,[57] of being obedient to the authority of Christ; in that church in all its censures. "To a willing person, injury is not done."[58] Error is offensive, and must be proceeded against. Examples and precepts of this, abound in the Scriptures. The blood of many erring persons (I doubt not) will one day have a *quo warranto*[59] granted them against their (as to the particulars in debate) orthodox slayers, who did it to promote the service of God. Let them not fear an afterreckoning, who use the discipline of Christ, according to his appointment.

This being considered, the occasion of a most frequent paralogism[60] is removed. If errors must be tolerated, say some, then men may do what they please, without control? No means it seems must be used to reclaim them? But! is gospel conviction no means? Has the sword of discipline no edge? Is there

---

55 Jude 3.
56 The fifth-century writer Salvian of Marseilles described those in Gaul who embraced Arianism as having erred "with a good heart," not out of hatred for God but believing that they were honoring God. See Salvian, *On the Government of God* 5.2. For the Latin text, see Salvian, *De gubernatione Dei*, in *Opera omnia*, ed. J.-P. Migne, Patrologia Latina 53 (Paris: Migne-Garnier, 1865), 95–96. For the English translation, see *The Governance of God*, in *The Writings of Salvian, the Presbyter*, trans. Jeremiah F. O'Sullivan, Fathers of the Church 3 (Washington, DC: Catholic University of America Press, 1962), 130.
57 Lat. "on the condition of."
58 In the text: *Volenti non fit injuria*.—Owen. This is a reference to a common-law doctrine concerning situations in which an individual has voluntarily assumed the risk.
59 Lat. "by what warrant?" This refers to writ requiring an individual to show the authority they had for exercising a certain power.
60 I.e., a logical fallacy, particularly one that the reasoner is unaware of or believes to be true.

no means of instruction in the New Testament established, but a prison and a halter?[61] Are the hammer of the word,[62] and the sword of the Spirit,[63] which in days of old, broke the stubbornest mountains, and overcame the proudest nations, now quite useless? God forbid. Were the churches of Christ, established according to his appointment, and the professors of the truth, so knit up "in the unity of the Spirit and bond of peace,"[64] as they ought to be, and were in the primitive times; I am persuaded those despised instruments would quickly make the proudest heretic to tremble. When the churches walked in sweet communion, giving each other continual account of their affairs, and warning each other of all, or any such persons, as either in practice, or doctrine, walked not with a right foot (as we have examples in Clem. Epist. ad Corinth,[65] the churches of Vienne and Lyons, to those of Asia: Euseb.[66] of Ignatius to several persons and churches,[67] of Irenaeus to Victor. Euseb.[68] Dionysius to Stephen, ibid.,[69] and the like), heretics found such cold entertainment, as made them ashamed if not weary of their chosen wanderings; but this is not my present business.

The Main Question in the Toleration Debate

2. There is an opposition, or forbearance, in reference to a civil judicature, and precedence of things, which respects errors, in a real sense, as to the inflicting, or not inflicting of punishment, on religious delinquents. And this is the sole thing under debate, viz.

61 I.e., a rope with a noose.
62 Jer. 23:29.
63 Eph. 6:17.
64 Eph. 4:3.
65 *The First Epistle of Clement to the Corinthians* (ca. 96). For an English translation, see *The First Epistle of Clement*, in *Ante-Nicene Fathers: The Writings of the Fathers Down to A.D. 325*, 10 vols., ed. Alexander Roberts and James Donaldson (1886; repr. Peabody, MA: Hendrickson, 1995), 1:1–23.
66 *The Letter of the Churches of Vienne and Lyons to the Churches of Asia and Phrygia* (ca. 178), preserved by Eusebius, *Ecclesiastical History* 5.1–2. For the Greek text and English translation, see *Ecclesiastical History*, vol. 1, *Books 1–5*, trans. Kirsopp Lake, Loeb Classical Library 153 (Cambridge, MA: Harvard University Press, 1926), 404–41.
67 The epistles of Ignatius of Antioch (ca. 105–115): To Polycarp; to the Smyrnaeans; to the Philadelphians; to the Romans; to the Trallians; to the Magnesians; and to the Ephesians. For these various texts, see *Ante-Nicene Fathers*, 1:49–96.
68 Passages from a letter sent by Irenaeus of Lyons to Victor bishop of Rome (ca. 189–198) are preserved in Eusebius, *Ecclesiastical History* 5.24. For the text, see Eusebius, *Ecclesiastical History*, 1:504–9.
69 Dionysius of Alexandria to Stephen, bishop of Rome, (ca. 257–258) preserved in Eusebius, *Ecclesiastical History* 7.5. For the Greek text and English, see Eusebius, *Ecclesiastical History*, vol. 2, *Books 6–10*, trans. J. E. L. Oulton, Loeb Classical Library 265 (Cambridge, MA: Harvard University Press, 1932), 138–41.

Whether persons enjoying civil authority over others, being entrusted therewithal, according to the constitutions of the place and nation where the lot of them both, by providence is fallen, are invested with power from above, and commanded in the word of God, to coerce, restrain, punish, confine, imprison, banish, hang, or burn, such of those persons under their jurisdiction, as shall not embrace, profess, believe, and practice, that truth and way of worship, which is revealed unto them of God, or how far, into what degrees, by what means, in any of these ways, may they proceed.[70]

The general propositions and considerations of the penal laws of God, which were before laid down, have, as I suppose, left this business to a naked debate from the word of truth, without any such prejudices on either part, as many take from a misapprehension of the mind of God in them; and therefore by the reader's patience, I shall venture upon the whole anew, as if no such arguments had ever been proposed, for the affirmative of the question in hand, not declining the utmost weight, that is in any of them, according to equity and due proportion. And here, first, I shall give in a few things.

(1) To the question itself.
(2) To the manner of handling it.

Defining the Question

(1) To the question itself, for herein, I suppose,

[1] That the persons enjoying authority, do also enjoy the truth, which is to the advantage of the affirmative.

[2]. That their power in civil things is just and unquestionable, which also looks favorably on that side.

[3] That nontoleration makes out itself in positive infliction of punishment, which is so, or is nothing. Casting men out of protection, exposing them to vulgar violence, is confessedly unworthy of men representing the authority of God, and contrary to the whole end of their trust.

The Manner in Which the Debate Has Been Carried Out

(2) To the manner of handling this question among persons at variance; and here, I cannot but observe.

[1] That if I have taken my aim aright, there is no one thing under debate among Christians, that is agitated with more confidence and mutual animosity

---

70 In the original, this paragraph is set in italics for emphasis.

of the parties litigant: each charging other with dreadful inferences, streams of blood, and dishonor to God, flowing out from their several persuasions. So that ofttimes, instead of a fair dispute, you meet on this subject with a pathetical outcry, as though all religion were utterly contaminated and trampled underfoot, if both these contradictory assertions be not embraced. Now seeing that in itself, it is a thing wherein the gospel is exceedingly sparing, if not altogether silent, certainly there must be a farther interest, than of judgment alone, or else that, very much prejudicated with corrupt affections, or men could not possibly be carried out with so much violence, upon supposed self-created consequences, wherewith in this cause they urge one another.

[2] That generally, thus much of private interest appears in the several contesters that nontoleration is the opinion of the many, and these enjoying the countenance of authority: toleration of the oppressed, who always go under the name of the faction or factions, the unavoidable livery of the smaller number professing a way of worship by themselves, be it right or wrong. I do not desire to lay forth the usual deportment, of men seeking the suppressing of others differing from them, toward those in authority. It is but too clearly made out, by daily experience: if they close with them, they are *custodes utriusque tabulae*,[71] the church's nursing fathers,[72] etc., what they please. But if they draw back, for want of light or truth to serve them, logs and storks find not worse entertainment from frogs, than they from some of them.[73] Such things as these, may (nay ought to) be especially heeded by everyone, that knows what influence corrupt affections have upon the judgments of men, and would willingly take the pains to wipe his eyes for the discerning of the truth

These things premised, I assert, that—

71 Lat. "custodians of both tables" (of the Decalogue). For instance, Edmund Calamy told members of the House of Lords that God had empowered them "to suppress these divisions and differences in Religion by your Civill Authoritie, as farre as you are able, lest you be accessary unto them. For God hath made you *Custodes utriusque tabulae*, Keepers not of the second Table onely, (as some fondly imagine) but of the first Table also, and not onely Keepers, but *Vindices utrius (que) Tabulae*, Punishers also of those that transgresse against either of them." See Calamy, *An Indictment Against England Because of her Selfe-Murdering Divisions: Together with an Exhortation to an England-Preserving Unity and Concord* [. . .] (London, 1645), 37.

72 This trope is from Isa. 49:23.

73 Owen alludes to Aesop's Fable of the frogs choosing a king. First a log was chosen, which they thought too benign, and then a stork, who made them its prey. The moral of the fable is that the multitude is never satisfied. See "The Frogs Chuse a King" in Roger L'Estrange, *Fables of Aesop and Other Eminent Mythologists: With Morals and Reflexions* (London, 1694), 19–20. For the political use of Aesop's *Fables*, see Kisklansky, "Turning Frogs into Princes: Aesop's *Fables* and the Political Culture of Early Modern England," in *Political Culture and Cultural Politics in Early Modern England*, ed. Susan D. Amussen and Mark A. Kishlansky (Manchester: Manchester University Press, 1995), 338–60.

No Warrant for the Magistrate to Punish Those Simply in Error

Nontoleration in the latitude, which is for persons in authority, enjoying the truth (or supposing they do enjoy it) to punish in an arbitrary way (according to what they shall conceive to be condign),[74] men, who will not forsake their own convictions, about any head, or heads, of Christian religion whatsoever; to join with what they hold out, either for belief or worship (after the using of such ways of persuasion as they shall think fit) is no way warranted in the gospel, nor can any sound proof for such a course be taken from the Old Testament.

The testimonies out of the law which I can apprehend to have any color or appearance of strength in them, with the examples approved of God that seem to look this way: I considered at our entrance into this discourse.

I speak of punishing in an arbitrary way, for all instances produced to the purpose in hand, that speak of any punishment, mention nothing under death itself; which yet (at least in the first place) is not aimed at by those that use them in our days, as I suppose. Now some divines of no small name, maintain, that God has not left the imposition of punishment in any measure, to the wills of men.

Some arguments for the proof of the former assertion as laid down, I shall in due place make use of; for the present, I desire to commend to the serious pondering of all Christians in general, especially of those in authority, these ensuing considerations.

Relevant Considerations

Religious Coercion Has Frequently Been Used to Suppress the Truth

1. That it is no privilege of truth, to furnish its assertors, with this persuasion, that the Dissenters from it ought forcibly to be opposed, restrained, punished: no false religion ever yet in the world, did enthrone itself in the minds of men, enjoying a civil sovereignty over the persons of others, but it therewithal commanded them, under pain of neglect and contempt of itself, to crush any underling worship, that would perk up in inferior consciences.

The old heathens carried their gods into the war (as did the Philistines, 1 Chronicles 14:12, and the Israelites the ark, with heathenish superstition 1 Samuel 4:3), to whom they ascribed the success they obtained, and in requital of their kindness, they forced the dunghill deities of the conquered nations, to attend the triumph of their victorious idols; and unless they adopted them into the number of their own gods, all farther worship to them was forbidden. Hence were these inventions among the old Romans, by spells and enchantments to entice away a deity from any city they besieged (they being as expert

---

[74] I.e., deserved; appropriate.

at the getting of a devil as Tobias's Raphael,[75] or the present Romanists at his fumigation),[76] by which means they shrived[77] into the honor of having thirty thousand unconquered idols (as Varro in Augustine *De civit. Dei.*)[78] and deserved worthily, that change of their city's epithet from Ἐπιτομὴ οἰκουμένης to Ἐπιτομὴ δεισιδαιμονίας,[79] which it justly inherits to this very day. Rabshakeh's provocation to the example of the gods of the nations (2 Kings 18:33–34), and the Roman senate's consultation concerning the admitting of Christ to a place among their idols, that he might have been freely worshiped (their consent being prevented, by his almighty providence, who will not be enrolled among the vilest works of his most corrupted creatures), do both declare this thing.[80]

Now not to speak of Cain,[81] who seems to me, to have laid the foundation of that cruelty, which was afterward inserted into the church's orthodoxies, by the name of *Haereticidium*,[82] we find the four famous empires of the world[83] to have drunk in this persuasion to the utmost, of suppressing all by force and violence, that consented not to them, in their way of worship.

Nebuchadnezzar, the crown of the golden head,[84] set up a furnace with an image, and a negative answer to that query, "Do you not serve my gods, nor

---

75 In the book of Tobit, the angel Raphael advises Tobias to burn a fish's entrails in the bridal chamber in order to drive away the demon Asmodeus (Tob. 6:16–17; 8:2–5).

76 I.e., censing with incense. The Laudian ceremonialism of the 1630s saw a reintroduction of the use of incense. See, e.g., Graham Parry, *Glory, Laud and Honour: The Arts of the Anglican Counter-Revolution* (Woodbridge, UK: Boydell, 2006), 78.

77 I.e., to be granted absolution after confession and penance.

78 Marcus Terentius Varro (116–27 BC), a friend of Cicero and a prolific writer of more than seventy-four books, was Augustine's principal source of information on traditional Roman religion and had diligently cataloged the names the Roman deities. Varro's *Divine Antiquities* has been lost, but its description of the number of Roman gods is known largely due to Augustine's reference to it. See Augustine, *De civitate Dei* 4.22, 7.17. For the Latin text and English translation, see Augustine, *The City of God*, vol. 2, Books 4–7, trans William M. Green, Loeb Classical Library 412 (Cambridge, MA: Harvard University Press, 1963), 78–81, 434–37. The figure of thirty thousand demigods comes from the eighth-century BC Greek poet Hesiod. See Hesiod, *Works and Days*, 252–67. For text and translation, see Hesiod, *Theogony. Works and Days. Testimonia*, ed. and trans. Glenn W. Most, Loeb Classical Library 57 (Cambridge, MA: Harvard University Press, 2018), 106–7.

79 The notion of Rome as "the epitome of the world" (a city that stands for the world) was attributed to the Sophist Antonius Polemo by Galen. See Simon Swain, *Hellenism and Empire: Language, Classicism, and Power in the Greek World, AD 50–250* (Oxford: Clarendon, 1996), 364. Owen is inferring that Rome is better described as the "epitome of superstition."

80 Eusebius appeals to a nonextant Greek translation of Tertullian's *Apology* in support of his claim that Tiberius consulted with the Senate over the possibility of admitting Christ into the Roman Pantheon (*Ecclesiastical History* 2.2). For text, see Eusebius, *Ecclesiastical History*, 1:112–13.

81 Gen. 4:8.

82 I.e., the act of killing heretics.

83 The four famous empires are Babylonia, Medo-Persia, Greece, and Rome.

84 Dan. 2:38.

worship my image?"⁸⁵ served to cast the servants of the living God, into the midst of the fire, Daniel 3[:24].

Daniel's casting into the lions' den, chapter 6, shows that the Persian silver breast and arms, did not want iron hands,⁸⁶ to crush or break the opposers of, or dissenters from, their religious edicts.

And though we find not much, of the short-lived founder of the Grecian dominion,⁸⁷ yet what was the practice of the branches of that empire, especially in the Syrian and Egyptian sprouts,⁸⁸ the three books of the Maccabees, Josephus,⁸⁹ and others, do abundantly manifest.

For the Romans, though their judgment and practice (which fully and wholly, are given over from the dragon to the beast and false prophet)⁹⁰ be written in the blood of thousands of Christians, and so not to be questioned, yet that it may appear, that we are not the only men in this generation, that this wisdom of punishing dissenters was not born with us, I shall briefly give in what grounds they proceeded on, and the motives they had to proceed as they did.

(1) First, then, they enacted it as a law, that no religious worship should be admitted or practiced, without the consent, decree, and establishment of the senate. Mention is made of a formal law to this purpose in Tertullian,⁹¹ though now we find it not. The foundation of it was doubtless in that of the twelve tables:⁹² ("Let none have gods to himself, neither let any privately worship new or strange deities, unless they be publicly owned and enrolled.")⁹³ And that it was their practice and in the counsels of the wisest among them, appears in that advice given by Maecenas to Augustus in Dio Cassius: "Worship (he says) the divine power thy self, according to the constitutions of your country, always and at all time, and compel others so to honour it; not only for God's

---

85 Dan. 3:14.
86 Dan. 2:32.
87 Alexander the Great, who defeated the Persians and conquered most of the then-known world.
88 Dan 8:8, 22.
89 Josephus, *Jewish Antiquities*.
90 Rev. 13:11.
91 In the text: Apol., cap. v.—Owen. This is a reference to Tertullian, *Apologeticus* 5.1. For the Latin text and an English translation, see Tertullian, *Apology*, in Tertullian, Minucius Felix, *Apology. De Spectaculis. Minucius Felix: Octavius*, trans. T. R. Glover and Gerald H. Rendall, Loeb Classical Library 250 (Cambridge, MA: Harvard University Press, 1931), 28–29.
92 The legislation that stood as the foundation of Roman law dating to the fifth century BC.
93 In the text: *Separatim nemo habessit Deos, neve novos, sed ne Advenas, nisi publicèascitos, privatim colunto.*—Owen. This is a quotation from Cicero, *De legibus* 2.19, the second law in Cicero's draft constitution. For the Latin text and English translation, see Cicero, *On the Republic. On the Laws*, trans. Clinton W. Keyes, Loeb Classical Library 213 (Cambridge, MA: Harvard University Press, 1928), 392–93.

sake, whom yet whoso contemneth, he will never do any honorable thing, but because, these (not so worshiping) introducing new deities, do persuade many to transgress (or to change affairs) whence are conjurations, seditions, private societies; things no way conducing to monarchies."[94]

Hence doubtless was that opposition which Paul met withal in divers of the Roman territories; thus at Athens (though as I suppose they enjoyed there, their own laws and customs, very suitable as it should seem to those of the Romans), preaching Jesus, he was accused to be "a setter forth of strange gods" (Acts 14).[95] For although as Strabo observes of the Athenians, that publicly by the authority of the magistrates, "they received many things of foreign worships,"[96] yet that none might attempt any such things of themselves, is notorious from the case of Socrates, who as Laertius witnesses, was condemned, as "one who thought not those to be gods, whom the city thought so to be, but brought in certain new deities."[97] Hence I say was Paul's opposition, and his haling[98] to Mars Hill: without doubt also, this was the bottom of that stir and trouble he met withal about Philippi.[99] It is true, private interest lay in the bottom with the chief opposers, but this legal constitution was that which was plausibly pretended. "They

---

[94] In the text: Τὸ μὲν θεῖον πάντη πάντως αὐτός τε σέβου, κατὰ τὰ πάτρια, καὶ τοὺς ἄλλους τιμᾶν ἀνάγκαζε· τοὺς δὲ δὴ ξενίζοντάς τι περὶ αὐτὸ, καὶ μίσει καὶ κόλαζε, μὴ μόνον τῶν θεῶν ἕνεκα, ὧν καταφρονήσας οὐδ' ἄλλου ἄν τινος προτιμήσειεν, ἀλλ' ὅτι καινά τινα δαιμόνια οἱ τιοῦτοι ἀντεισφέρουσιν ἀναπείθουσιν ἀλλοτριονομεῖν· κἀκ τούτου καὶ συνωμοσίαι καὶ συστάσεις, ἑταιρεῖαι τε γίγνονται, ἅπερ ἥκιστα μοναρχίᾳ συμφέρει.—Owen. The translation in the text is Owen's. The Roman historian Dio Cassius (ca. 150–235) reports a long speech by Maecenas to Augustus offering advice on how to consolidate his power at the end of Rome's long civil wars. See his *History of Rome* 52.36. For the Greek text and English translation, see Dio Cassius, *Roman History*, vol. 6, *Books 51–55*, trans. Earnerst Cary and Herbert B. Foster, Loeb Classical Library 83 (Cambridge, MA: Harvard University Press, 1917), 172–75.

[95] The correct reference is Acts 17:18.

[96] In the text: πολλὰ τῶν ξενικῶν ἱερῶν παρεδέξαντο.—Owen. This is a quotation from Strabo, *Geography*, bk. 10, 3.18. Strabo (64/63 BC–ca. AD 24) was a Greek historian, and in this work he provided an account of all the peoples and countries known during the reign of the emperor Augustus. Here he notes that the Athenians were famous for incorporating various deities into their pantheon. For the Greek text and English translation, see Strabo, *Geography*, vol. 5, *Books 10–12*, trans. Horace Leonard Jones, Loeb Classical Library 211 (Cambridge, MA: Harvard University Press, 1928), 108–9.

[97] In the text: *Separatim nemo habessit Deos, neve novos, sed ne Advenas, nisi publicèascitos, privatim colunto.*—Owen. This is a quotation from Diogenes Laërtius, the third-century biographer of the Greek philosophers, recording the charges brought against Socrates in his *Lives of Eminent Philosophers* 2.40. In particular, Socrates was condemned for failing to recognize the traditional Greek gods. See Diogenes Laertius, *Lives of Eminent Philosophers*, vol. 1, *Books 1–5*, trans. R. D. Hicks, Loeb Classical Library 184 (Cambridge, MA: Harvard University Press, 1925), 170–71.

[98] I.e., dragging forcibly.

[99] Acts 16:19–20.

teach customs, which are not lawful for us to receive, neither to observe being Romans" (Acts 16:21), οὐκ ἔξεστι Ῥωμαίοις, "it is not lawful for us Romans" to receive the religion they hold out, because statutes are made among us against all religious worship not allowed by public authority. Let Calvin's short annotation on that place be seen.[100] Gallio's refusing to judge between Jews (as he thought) in a Jewish controversy,[101] is no impeachment of this truth: had it been about any Roman establishment, he would quickly have interposed. Now this law among them was doubtless, "Christians are the ruination of the estate."[102]

This then in the first place was enacted, that no worship should be admitted, no religion exercised, but what received establishment and approbation from them, who supposed themselves, to be entrusted with authority over men in such things. And this power of the dragon was given over to the beast and false prophet. The anti-Christian power succeeding in the room of the paganish, the pope and councils of the emperors and senate, it was quickly confirmed that none should be suffered to live in peace, who received not his mark and name (Rev. 13:16–17). Whereunto for my part, I cannot but refer, very many of those following imperial constitutions, which were made at first against the opposers of the church's orthodoxism, but were turned against the witnesses of Jesus in the close.

(2) This being done, they held out the reasons of this establishment. I shall touch only one, or two, of them, which are still common to them, who walk in the same paths with them.

[1] Now the first was, that toleration of sundry ways of worship, and several religions, tends to the disturbance of the commonwealth, and that civil society, which men under the same government do, and ought to enjoy. So Cicero tells us, in *On the Laws*, "The worship of private gods, whether new or alien, brings confusion," etc.[103] It brings in confusion of religion, and civil

---

100 Calvin notes that the reliance on a precedent can be used to exclude proper argument and reasons that "the Papists also deal with us today, saying 'This has been decreed by a General Council'; 'An opinion is too well accepted for it to be right to question it'; 'Long usage has given approval to this'; 'This has been established by consent for more than a thousand years (*saeculorum*).'" Calvin concludes that such an approach serves only "to leave no authority to the Word of God." See John Calvin, *Calvin's New Testament Commentaries: The Acts of the Apostles*, vol. 2, trans. John W. Fraser, ed. David W. Torrance and Thomas F. Torrance (Grand Rapids, MI: Eerdmans, 1966), 80.

101 Acts 18:15.

102 In the text: *fundi Christiani calamitas*.—Owen. This is adapted from Terence's *Eunuchus* 1.1.34. For the text, see *Terence's Comedies, Translated into English Prose [. . .] Together with the Original Latin*, trans. S. Patrick (Dublin, 1810), 141.

103 In the text: lib. 2, De Legibus: *Suos deos, aut novos, aut alienigenas coli, coufusionem habet*.—Owen. This is a quotation from Cicero, *De legibus* 2.26. For text and translation, see Cicero, *On the Republic. On the Laws*, 400–01.

society. The same is clearly held out, in that counsel of Maecenas to Augustus before mentioned. "They" (says he) "who introduce new deities, draw many into innovations; whence are conspiracies, seditions, conventicles, no way profitable for the commonwealth."[104]

[2] The other main reason was, that hereby the gods, whom they owned and worshiped, were dishonored and provoked to plague them. That this was continually in their mouths and clamors, all the acts at the slaying of the martyrs, the rescripts of emperors, the apologies of the Christians, as Tertullian, Justin Martyr,[105] Arnobius,[106] Minucius Felix,[107] do abundantly testify. All trouble was still ascribed to their impiety, upon the first breaking out of any judgment, as though the cause of it had been the toleration of Christians, presently the vulgar cry was, "*Christianos ad leones.*"[108] Now that those causes and reasons, have been traduced to all those, who have since acted the same things, especially to the emperors' successor at Rome, needs not to be proved: with the power of the Dragon, the wisdom also is derived; see that great champion Cardinal Bellarmine, fighting with these very weapons.[109] And indeed, however illustrated, improved, adorned, supported, flourished, and sweetened they are the sum of all that to this day has been said in the same case.

(3) Having made a law, and supported it with such reasons as these, in proceeding to the execution of the penalty of that law, as to particular persons (which penalty being as now, arbitrary was inflicted, unto banishment, imprisonment, mine digging, torturing in sundry kinds, maiming, death, according to the pleasure of the judges), they always charged upon those persons, not only the denying and opposing their own deities, religion, and worship, but also, that, that which they embraced, was foolish, absurd, detestable, pernicious, sinful, wicked, ruinous to commonwealths, cities, society, families, honesty, order, and the like. If a man should go about to delineate the Christian religion by the lines and features drawn thereof, in the invectives and accusations of

---

104 Dio Cassius, *History of Rome* 52.3. For the English text, see Dio Casius, *Roman History*, 174–75.
105 Dennis Minns and Paul Purvis, *Justin, Philosopher and Martyr: Apologies*, Oxford Early Christian Texts (Oxford: Oxford University Press, 2009, 200–01.
106 Arnobius of Sicca, *The Case Against the Pagans*, trans. George E. McCracken, 2 vols, Ancient Christian Writers 7–8 (New York: Newman, 1949).
107 Minucius Felix, *Octavius*, 326–35.
108 Lat. "The Christians to the lions." This is a quotation from Tertullian's *Apologeticus* 39.2. For the Latin text and English translation see Tertullian, *Apology*, 182–83.
109 In the text: Lib. de Laicis, cap. 21.—Owen. Owen, once again, appeals to Bellarmine's treatise on civil government, this to chapter 21, "Heretics Condemned by the Church Can Be Punished with Temporal Punishments and Even Death."

their adversaries, he might justly suppose, that indeed, that was their god, which was set up at Rome with this inscription, "The ass-hoofed God of the Christians."[110] Being an image with ass's ears, in a gown, claws or talons upon one foot, with a book in his hand.[111] Charged they were, that they worshiped an ass's head, which impious folly, first fastened on the Jews by Tacitus, (in these words,[112] "They dedicated, in a shrine, a statue of that creature whose guidance enabled them to put an end to their wandering and thirst,"[113] having before set out a feigned direction received by a company of asses),[114] which he had borrowed from Apion, a railing Egyptian of Alexandria was so engrafted in their minds,[115] that no defensative could be allowed.[116] The sun, the cross,

[110] In the text: *DEUS CHRISTIANORUM ONONYCHITES.*—Owen. Owen presents the quotation in all caps for emphasis. This is a quotation from Tertullian's *To the Nations* 1.14. For the Latin text, see Tertullian, *Ad nationes*, in *Opera omnia*, ed. J.-P. Migne Patrologia Latina 1 (Paris: Migne, 1844), 579–80. See also the similar reference in Tertullian, *Apologeticus* 16. For the text and English translation, see Tertullian, *Apology*, 80–81.

[111] Similar to the cartoon from ca. AD 200 carved in a room on the Palatine Hill in Rome with the inscription "Alexamenos worships his God." See Felicity Harley-McGowan, "The Alexamenos Graffito," in *The Reception of Jesus in the First Three Centuries*, vol. 3, *From Celsus to the Catacombs: Visual, Liturgical, and Non-Christian Receptions of Jesus in the Second and Third Centuries CE*, ed. Chris Keith (London: T&T Clark, 2002), 105–40.

[112] In the text: Histor., lib. 5 cap. [4].—Owen. Owen extends the quotation in two marginal notes. In the margin: *Moses [. . .] novos ritus contrariosque cæteris mortalibus indidit. Profana illic omnia, quae apud nos sacra; rursum concessa apud illos, quae nobis incesta. [Effigiem animalis, quo monstrante errorem sitimque depulerant, penetrali sacravere] [. . .] Provectissima ad libidinem gens alienarum concubitum abstinent, inter se nihil illicitum.* Tacitus de Judaeis. Hist. l. 5.—Owen. This is a reference to two passages from Tacitus's *Histories* 5.4–5: "Moses introduced new religious practices, quite opposed to those of all other religions. The Jews regard as profane all that we hold sacred; on the other hand, they permit all that we abhor. They dedicated, in a shrine, a statue of that creature whose guidance enabled them to put an end to their wandering and thirst . . . although as a race, they are prone to lust, they abstain from intercourse with foreign women; yet among themselves nothing is unlawful." For the Latin text and English translation, see Tacitus, *Histories: Books 4–5. Annals Books: 1–3*, trans. Clifford H. Moore, Loeb Classical Library 249 (Cambridge, MA: Harvard University Press, 1931), 178–79, 182–83.

[113] In the text: *Effigiem animalis quo monstrante, errorem sitimque depulerant penetrali sacravere.*—Owen.

[114] This is the myth of the "golden ass" set up in remembrance of the wild asses that had led them to water during their wilderness wandering.

[115] In the text: (Joseph. ad. App. lib. 1).—Owen. This is a reference to Flavius Josephus, *Contra Apionem* 2.79–80. Owen erroneously cites bk. 1. Josephus addresses, Apion, a Hellenized Egyptian from Alexandria, who had been told that when the Selucid king, Antiochus IV Epiphanes (ca. 215–164 BC), entered the temple in Jerusalem during the Maccabean crisis he found "the head [of an ass] made of gold and worth a high price." See Josephus, *The Life. Against Apion*, trans. H. St. J. Thackeray, Loeb Classical Library 186 (Cambridge, MA: Harvard University Press, 1926), 324–25.

[116] In margin: *Judaeos, impulsore Chresto quotidie tumultuantes Roma expulit*: falsely and foolishly, Suet. Claud., cap. 25. *Quaesitissimis poenis afficiebat, quos per flagitia invisos vulgus Christianos apellabat.* Plu. Tac. An., lib. 15. *afflicti suppliciis Christiani, genus hominum superstitionis novae*

"*sacerdotis genitalia*,"[117] were either really supposed, or impiously imposed on them, as the objects of their worship. The blood and flesh of infants, at Thyestean banquets,[118] was said to be their food and provision: promiscuous lust, with incest, their chiefest refreshment.[119] Such as these it concerned them, to have them thought to be, being resolved to use them, as if they were so indeed: hence I am not sometimes without some suspicion, that many of the impure abominations, follies, villainies, which are ascribed unto the primitive heretics, yea, the very Gnostics themselves (upon whom the filth that lies is beyond all possible belief),[120] might be feigned, and imposed, as to a great part thereof. For though not the very same, yet things as foolish and opposite to the light of nature, were at the same time, charged on the most orthodox.

But you will say, they who charged these things upon the Catholics, were Pagans, enemies of God and Christ; but these, who so charged heretics were Christians themselves: and so, say I also, and therefore for reverence of the name (though perhaps I could), I say no more. But yet this I say, that story which you have in Minucius Felix, or Arnobius, eighth book apologetical, of the meeting of Christians, the drawing away of the light by a dog tied to the

---

ac maleficae: Sueton. in Nerone: cap. 16.—Owen. The first reference is to Suetonius, *Claudio* 25: "Since the Jews constantly made disturbances at the instigation of Chrestus [emperor Claudius], expelled them from Rome." For the Latin text and English translation, see Suetonius, *Lives of the Caesars*, vol. 2, trans. J. C. Rolfe, Loeb Classical Library 38 (Cambridge, MA: Harvard University Press, 1914), 50–51. The second reference is to Tacitus, *The Annals of Imperial Rome* 15.44. Tacitus records Nero's attempt to blame the fire of Rome (AD 64) on the Christians in which he "and punished with the utmost refinement of cruelty, a class of men, loathed for their vices, whom the crowd styled Christians." For the Latin text and English translation, see Tacitus, *Annals: Books 13–16*, trans. John Jackson, Loeb Classical Library 322 (Cambridge, MA: Harvard University Press, 1937), 282–83. The final reference is to Suetonius, *Nero* 16.2, who describes how "punishment was inflicted on the Christians, a class of men given to new and mischievous superstition." For the Latin text and English translation, see Suetonius, *Lives of the Caesars*, 2:106–7.

[117] Minucius Felix records in *Octavius* 9.4 the rumors spread about the early Christians including the accusation that they worshiped "the priest's genitals." For the Latin text and English translation, see Minucius Felix, *Octavius*, 337, 405.

[118] In Greek mythology, Thyestes had an affair with the wife of his brother, Atreus. In revenge, Atreus killed the sons of Thyestes, cooked their flesh, and served it to their unsuspecting father.

[119] This charge of cannibalism at "Thyestean banquets" and incest was stated by the second-century apologist Athenagoras in his *Plea for Christians* 3.1–2. For the Latin text see Athenagoras, *Legatio pro Christianis*, ed. Miroslav Marcovich, Patristische Texte und Studien 31 (Berlin: De Gruyter, 2015), 26. Similar rumors were reported by Justin Martyr in *Apology* 26.7. For the Greek text and English translation, see Minns and Purvis, *Justin, Philosopher and Martyr: Apologies*, 150–51.

[120] In the text: Epiphan. Tom. 2. lib. 1, Har. 26.—Owen. This is a reference to Epiphanius, the fourth-century bishop of Salamis on Cyprus, who authored the *Panarion* (*Medicine Chest*), a work conceived as the "antidote" to the "venom" of some eighty heresies. *Panarion* 26.1–9 deals with the grotesque sexual excess of the notorious libertine gnostic sect of the Phibionites. See *The Panarion of Epiphanius of Salamis*, trans. Frank Williams, 2 vols. (Leiden: Brill, 2009–2012), 1:82–99.

candlestick, so to make way for adulteries and incests:[121] I have heard more than once told with no small confidence, of Brownists[122] and Puritans. Has not this very same course been taken in latter ages? Consult the writings of Waldensis, and the rest of his companions, about Wickliffe and his followers,[123] see the occasion of his falling off from Rome, in our own chronicles, in Fabian of old,[124] yea, and Daniel of late[125] to gratify a Popish court; of Eckius,[126] Hosius,[127] Staphylus,[128] Bolsec,[129] Bellarmine,[130] and the rest who have undertaken to portray out unto us, Luther and Calvin with their followers; and you will quickly see that their great design was to put (as they did upon the head of John Huss at the Council of Constance, when he was led to the stake) the

---

121 The incident with the dog and the candlestick is recorded in Minucius Felix, *Octavius* 9.6. For the Latin text and English translation, see Minucius Felix, *Octavius*, 338–39. Arnobius of Sicca (d. ca. 330) wrote seven books *Adversus gentes* (*Against the Heathen*). *Adversus* 1.2–6 records some of the accusations against the early Christians. Tertullian refutes this in *Apologeticus* 8.3. For the text and translation, see Tertullian, *Apology*, 42–43.

122 I.e., a term to describe Elizabethan and early Stuart separatists, named after Robert Brown of Norwich (ca. 1550–1633).

123 Thomas Netter of Walden (ca. 1375–1430) was an English scholastic theologian and controversialist who participated in a number of Lollard trials. His main work, *Doctrinale antiquitatum fidei ecclesiae catholicae* (Paris, 1521–1532) was designed to refute the doctrines of Wycliffe and the Hussites.

124 Robert Fabyan (d. 1513), *The New Chronicles of England and France* (London, 1516). In Fabyan's work, Wycliffe (d. 1384) and the Lollards are presented as heretics: "In this yere also or about this tyme began ye heresy of John Wycelyffe to sprynge in Englande the which was greatly auauncid by meane of Scysme in the Church." Cited in David Womersley, "Fabyan's *Chronicle*: Reading and Religion Reformed," in his *Divinity and State* (Oxford: Oxford University Press, 2010), 33.

125 The Jacobean poet Samuel Daniel (1562–1619) cast Wycliffe as someone discontent and ambitious, motivated by jealousy, hatred, and revenge. See Samuel Daniel, *The Collection of the Historie of England* (London, 1618), 217–18. For the ambiguous reception of Wycliffe, see Vaclav Murdoch, *The Wyclif Tradition* (Athens, OH: Ohio University Press, 1978).

126 Johann Eck (1486–1543), a German scholastic theologian and chancellor of Ingolstadt University. He was a notorious opponent of Martin Luther.

127 Stanisław Hozjusz (1504–1579), a Polish theologian and preacher, was the prince-bishop of Warmia, promoted to cardinal in 1561, and participated in the final sessions of the Council of Trent. His seminal work was the *Confessio catholicae fidei Christianae* (Confession of the catholic Christian faith), which first appeared in 1551.

128 Friedrich Staphylus (1512–1564), professor in Kaliningrad (Königsberg), was initially influenced by Luther and Philip Melanchthon but later converted to Roman Catholicism. He was an advisor to Ferdinand of Habsburg, king of Bohemia. See, e.g., his pamphlet *Theologiae Martini Lutheri trimembris epitome* [Abridgement of the Tripartite doctrine of Martin Luther] (Dillingen, 1558).

129 Jérôme-Hermès Bolsec (d. ca. 1584) was a former Carmelite monk who settled in Geneva and came into conflict with Calvin over the doctrine of predestination in the 1550s. He returned to the Roman Catholic Church and settled in France, writing polemical works such as *Histoire de la vie, moeurs, actes, doctrines et mort de Jean Calvin* [History of the life, mores, deeds, doctrines, and death of John Calvin] (Lyon, 1577).

130 The Jesuit theologian Cardinal Robert Bellarmine (1542–1621).

ugly vizard of some devilish appearance,[131] that under that form, they might fit them for fire and fagot.

And herein also is the polity of the dragon, derived to the false prophet, and a color tempered, for persecutors to imbrue[132] their hands in the blood of martyrs.

This was the old Roman way, and I thought it not amiss to cautionate those, enjoying truth and authority, that if it be possible, they may not walk in their steps and method: the course accounted so sovereign, for the extirpation[133] of error, was as you see, first invented for the extirpation of truth.

Religious Coercion Has Either Harmed the Church or Done Little for Truth

2.[134] Secondly, I desire it may be observed, that the general issue and tendence of unlimited arbitrary persecution or punishing for conscience' sake, because in all ages "The greater part of mankind are bad,"[135] and the worst of men have sat at the upper end of the world, for the most part, more false worshipers, having hitherto enjoyed authority over others, than followers of the Lamb,[136] has been pernicious, fatal, and dreadful to the profession and professors of the gospel, little, or not at all, serviceable to the truth.

I have heard it averred, by a reverend and learned personage, that more blood of heretics has been shed by wholesome severity,[137] in the maintenance of the truth and opposition unto errors, than has been shed of the witnesses of Jesus, by the sword of persecution, in the hands of heretics and false worshipers. An assertion, I conceive, under favor, so exceedingly

---

131 According to Petr Mladoňovic, as Jan Hus was led out to be burned on July 6, 1415, a "vizard" in the form of a tall paper heretic's hat was placed on his head, decorated with demons and bearing the inscription "*Haeresiarcha*" (leader of a heretical movement). See Milena Kubíková, "The Heretic's Cap of Hus," *The Bohemian Reformation and Religious Practice* 4 (2002): 143–50.
132 I.e., stain.
133 I.e., to destroy completely.
134 In the text: Secondly.—Owen. Following Goold, this is changed to the number 2 for the sake of consistency.
135 In the text: οἱ πλείονες κακοί.—Owen. This is a saying attributed to Bias, one of the seven sages of Greece. For the Greek text and English translation, see D. E. Macdonnel, ed., *A Dictionary of Quotations, in Most Frequent Use* [. . .] (London, 1811), s.v.
136 Rev. 14:4.
137 This phrase was used in the title of an important work by George Gillespie, written "to vindicate the lawful, yea necessary use of the coercive power of the Christian Magistrate in suppressing and punishing heretics and sectaries." Gillespie warned Congregationalists, like Owen, "O doe not involve your selves in the plea of Toleration with the Separatists and Anabaptists. Do not partake in their Separation, lest you partake in their suppression. Let us hear no more Paraeneticks for Toleration, or liberty of Conscience." See Gillespie, *Wholesome Severity*, preface, 38.

distant from the reality of the thing itself, that I dare take upon me, against any man breathing, that in sundry Christian provinces, almost in every one of the west, more lives have been sacrificed to the one idol *Haereticidium*, of those that bear witness to the truth, in the belief, for which they suffered, than all the heretics properly so called, that ever were slain in all the provinces of the world, by men professing the gospel: and I shall give that worthy divine, or any other of his persuasion, his option, among all the chiefest provinces of Europe, to tie me up unto which they please. He that shall consider that above sixty thousand persons, were in six years or little more, cut off in a judicial way, by Duke D'Alva[138] in the Netherlands, in pursuit of the sentence of the inquisition, will conclude, that there is *causa facilis*[139] in my hand.

The ancient contest, between the Homoousians and the Arians, the first controversy the churches were agitated withal, after they enjoyed a Christian magistrate (and may justly be supposed to be carried on to the advantage of error, beyond all that went before it,[140] because of the civil magistrates interesting themselves in the quarrel) was not carried out to violence and blood, before the several persuasions, lighted on several dominions, and state interests: as between the Goths, Vandals, and the rest of their companions on one side, who were Arians,[141] and the Romans on the other. In all whose bickerings notwithstanding, the honor of severity, did still attend the Arians, especially in Affricke,[142] where they persecuted the Catholics with horrible outrage and fury. Five thousand at one time were barbarously exposed to all manner of

---

[138] In the wake of the iconoclastic riots that took place in 1566 across the provinces of the Netherlands, Margaret of Parma reluctantly conceded toleration of Lutheran and Reformed practice. This, however, quickly came to an abrupt halt with the arrival of the Spanish soldier Fernando Álvarez de Toledo (1507–1582), the third Duke of Alva, who was notorious for his tyrannical rule as governor-general of the Netherlands (1567–1573). The escalation of the Inquisition in the extraordinary tribunal the *Raad van Beroerten* (the so-called Council of Troubles that was dubbed by Protestants the Council of Blood) condemned thousands to death or imprisonment for heresy or rebellion (often *in absentia*). It is estimated that around eleven hundred people were executed and around sixty thousand fled, many of them to England (notably to Norwich). See Jonathan I. Israel, *The Dutch Republic: Its Rise, Greatness, and Fall, 1477–1806* (Oxford: Clarendon, 1998), 152–69; William Maltby, *Alba: A Biography of Fernando Alvarez de Toledo, Third Duke of Alba, 1507–1582* (Berkley: University of California Press, 1983), 140.

[139] Lat. "an easy cause to argue."

[140] For Constantine's role in the Trinitarian debates at the Council of Nicaea (325), see Lewis Ayres, *Nicaea and Its Legacy: An Approach to Fourth-Century Trinitarian Theology* (Oxford: Oxford University Press, 2004), 89–90.

[141] The Barbarian kingdoms of the Vandals and the Goths, who were established within the former Roman Empire, took Arianism as their creed.

[142] I.e., Africa, specifically North Africa in this context.

cruel villainy.[143] Some eruptions of passion had been before among emperors themselves, but still with this difference, that they who Arianized, carried the bell[144] for zeal against dissenters. Witness Valens,[145] who gave place in persecution to none of his pagan predecessors; killing, burning, slaying, making havoc of all orthodox professors: yea perhaps, that which he did, at least was done by the countenance of his authority, at Alexandria, upon the placing in, of Lucius an Arian in the room of Athanasius, thrusting Peter beside the chair, who was rightly placed according to the custom of those times,[146] perhaps I say, the tumults, rapes, murders, then, and there acted, did outgo what before had been done by the pagans.[147] It were tedious to pursue the lying, slandering, invectives, banishments, deaths, tumults, murders, which attend this council all along, after once they began to invoke the help of the emperors one against another: yet in this space some magistrates, weary with persecuting ways, did not only abstain practically from force and violence, as most of the orthodox emperors did, but also enacted laws, for the freedom of such as dissented from them. Jovianus a pious man, grants all peace, that will be peaceable; offended only with them, who would offer violence to others.[148]

---

143 Following the Vandal invasion of Roman North Africa under Geiseric (d. 477) in the fifth century, the Arian Vandals persecuted the Nicene church. With the legitimization of the Vandal kingdom, Arianism became official state policy. According to Victor of Vita's *History* 2.26–32, Geiseric's son, Huneric, engaged in systematic persecution of the Catholics, seizing church property and sending nearly five thousand deacons, priests, and bishops into exile in the desert. See Victor of Vita, *History of the Vandal Persecution*, ed. and trans. John Moorhead (Liverpool: Liverpool University Press, 1992), 33.

144 I.e., won the race.

145 Valens (328–378), the Roman emperor of the East, converted to Arianism and persecuted the orthodox. After the death of Athanasius in 373, Valens's "obstinate insistence on a Homoian state church and his consequent attempts to struggle against Nicene opponents turned him into the ferocious persecutor our sources love to hate." Noel Lenski, *Failure of Empire: Valens and the Roman State in the Fourth Century A.D.* (Berkeley: University of California, 2014), 243.

146 In what Owen describes as "the custom of those times," Athanasius had named Peter as his successor as bishop of Alexandria (one of the most important religious positions in the East). Valens, however, imposed a Homoian bishop, Lucius, and sent an army with him to ensure his consecration. Peter, having been temporarily imprisoned, fled to Rome. See Lenski, *Failure of Empire*, 255.

147 In the text: see *Theodorit, Eccles. Hist.*, lib. 4. cap. 22.—Owen. This a reference to Theodoret, *History of the Church* 4.19 (according to the numbering from modern versions), which contains bishop Peter of Alexandria's remarkably detailed description of the "most shocking" atrocities committed as the governor sent troops to clear the churches of those loyal to Peter in preparation for the arrival of Lucius, the Homoian bishop, "a vast body of troops." For the English translation, see *The Ecclesiastical History of Theodoret*, in *Nicene and Post-Nicene Fathers*, Second Series, ed. Philip Schaff, and Henry Wace, 14 vols. (1890–1900; repr. Peabody: Hendrickson, 2004), 3:121–22.

148 In the text: *Socrates Eccles. Hist.*, lib. 4. cap. 21.—Owen. This is a reference to Socrates Scholasticus, *Ecclesiastical History* 3.22–25. Jovian, the Roman emperor of the East (363–364), annulled the anti-Christian legislation of his predecessor, Julian "the Apostate." He proclaimed

Gratianus makes a law, whereby he granted liberty to all sects, but Manichees, Photinians, and Eunomians.[149] Many more the like examples might be produced.

The next difference about the worship of God (to the Arian and its branches) that was controverted in letters of blood, was about images, and their worship;[150] in which, though some furious princes, in opposition to that growing idolatry, which by popes, bishops, priests, and especially monks, was in those days violently urged,[151] did mingle some of their blood with their sacrifices;[152] yet not to the tithe almost, of what the *Iconolatrae* getting uppermost,[153] returned upon them and their adherents.[154]

This if occasion were, might be easily demonstrated from Paulus Diaconus,[155] and others. After this, about the year 850, about which time the *Iconolatrae*,

---

Christianity the religion of the empire, recalled Christians who had been banished, closed pagan temples, and stopped pagan sacrifice. Jovian stated that he "would not molest any one on account of his religious sentiments." Although Jovian reigned for only a number of months, Socrates presented him as having brought peace to the empire. See *The Ecclesiastical History, by Socrates Scholasticus*, in *Nicene and Post-Nicene Fathers*, Second Series, 2:95.

149 In the text: *Zozo. Eccles. Hist.*, lib. 7. cap. 1.—Owen. This is a reference to an edict, referenced in Sozomen, *Ecclesiastical History* 7.1, which brought to an end the persecution under Valens. It records how the Western emperor Gratian (375–383) assured freedom of worship to many of the sects except the Manichees, who were suspect because of their Persian origins, and sects of the Photinians (followers of a form of Monarchianism) and the Eunomians (heterousian Anomoeans). For the text, see *The Ecclesiastical History of Sozomen*, in *Nicene and Post-Nicene Fathers*, Second Series, 2:377.

150 The iconoclasm controversy of the eighth and ninth centuries.

151 In 726, the Byzantine Emperor Leo III (r. 717–741) ordered the destruction of religious icons. This was accompanied by the persecution of those who supported the veneration of images, and was particularly severe under the reign of Leo's successor, Constantine V (740–775), who was, according to the histories, associated with acts of violence, especially directed toward monks. The outbreak of the second iconoclasm (814–842) took place when Leo V removed icons from churches and public buildings. See Patricia Karlin-Hayter, "Iconoclasm," in *The Oxford History of Byzantium*, ed. Cyril Mango (New York: Oxford University Press, 2002), 153–69.

152 Luke 13:1.

153 The *Iconolatrae*, also known as the *Iconodules*, were image worshipers. Owen makes the same point about the cruelty of those who restored the use of images in *Country Essay* (1646).

154 Relationships between the Latin West and the Greek East deteriorated and eventually culminated in the brutal sack of Constantinople, the capital of the Byzantine Empire, by Latin Crusaders in 1204. This was "an episode coloured by brutality and determination, depravity and avarice, political intrigue and religious zeal." Jonathan Phillips, *The Fourth Crusade and the Sack of Constantinople* (New York: Penguin, 2004), xiii.

155 The eight-century Benedictine monk Paul Warnefrid (ca. 725–800) authored *Historia Langobardorum* (*History of the Lombards*). It records the Carolingian conquest of the Lombard kingdom of Italy. The Papacy had gone to great efforts to persuade the Frankish court of the legitimacy of the invasion by presenting the Lombards as pagans. Paul wrote in order to rehabilitate the Christian reputation of the Lombards and their kings. Eduardo Fabbro, "Charlemagne and

having ensnared the West by polity, the posterity of Charles the Great,[156] who had stoutly opposed the worship of images, complying with the popes, the fathers of that worship, for their own ends, and wearied the east by cruelty, that contest growing toward an end, the whole power of punishing for religion, became subservient to the dictates of the pope, the kings of the earth giving their power to the beast,[157] (unto which point things had been working all along) from thence I say, until the death of Servetus in Geneva,[158] the pursuit of Gentilis,[159] Blandeata,[160] and some other madmen in Helvetia,[161] for the space well-nigh of seven hundred years, the chiefest season of the reign of Satan and Antichrist, all punishing for religion, was managed by the authority of Rome, and against the poor witnesses of Jesus, prophesying in sackcloth,[162] in the several regions of the West. And what streams of blood were poured out, what millions of martyrs slain in that space, is known to all. Hence Bellarmine boasts that the Albigenses[163] were extinguished by the sword.[164] It is true there were laws enacted of old by Theodosius,[165] Valentinian, Martian,[166] as *C. de*

---

the Lombard Kingdom That Was: The Lombard Past in Post-Conquest Italian Historiography," *Journal of the Canadian Historical Association* 25, no. 2 (2014): 1–26.

156 Charlemagne (r. 747–814).

157 Rev. 17:12–13.

158 Miguel Servet (ca. 1510–1553), a Spanish physician whose anti-Trinitarianism led to his condemnation as a heretic by Roman Catholics and to his execution in Geneva.

159 Giovanni Valentino Gentile (d. 1566) was an Italian humanist who had fled Italy in 1557 and found refuge in the Italian congregation in Geneva, where he was condemned to death for advancing anti-Trinitarian ideas. He recanted and escaped only to continue propagating anti-Trinitarian ideas in Poland until he was forced to leave following the Edict of Parczów in 1564. He was eventually arrested and executed by the sword in Berne.

160 Giorgio Biandrata (ca. 1516–1588), an Italian physician and anti-Trinitarian who clashed with Calvin in debate and was exiled to Eastern Europe. See Wulfert de Greef, *The Writings of John Calvin: An Introductory Guide*, trans. Lyle D. Bierma (Louisville, KY: Westminster John Knox, 2008), 165–67.

161 I.e., the Swiss Cantons.

162 Rev. 11:3.

163 I.e., a sect in southern France in the twelfth and thirteenth centuries, suppressed by Pope Innocent III.

164 In the text: *De laicis* 22.—Owen. Bellarmine answers an objection to the burning of heretics, arguing that experience proves the utility of such terrors because "the Donatists, Manicheans, and Albigenses were overthrown and destroyed by weapons." For the English translation, see Bellarmine, *On Temporal and Spiritual Authority*, 111.

165 The fifth-century Theodosian Code was compiled by Theodosius II (ca. 401–450) and collects together the various imperial laws that saw heretics excluded from privilege, forbidden to assemble, deprived of property, banished, or put to death.

166 The imperial constitutions of the emperors Valentinian III (419–455) and Marcian (emperor of the East, 450–457), allowed for a range of punishment against heretics ranging from financial penalties, exile, lashes, or even death.

haereticis,[167] *L. Manichaeis*,[168] *L. Arianis*,[169] *L. Unicuique*; which last provides for the death of seducers;[170] but yet truly, though they were made by Catholics, and in the favor of Catholics, considering to what end they were used, I can look upon them no otherwise, but as very bottom stones of the tower of Babel.

This, then in its latitude proving so pernicious to the profession of the gospel, having for so long driven the woman into the wilderness,[171] and truth into corners, being the main engine whereby the tower of Babel was built, and that which at this day they cry grace unto,[172] as the foundation stone of the whole anti-Christian fabric (see Becanus *de fide haeresicis servanda*,[173] *Bell. De Laicis*, etc.)[174] we had need be cautious, what use we make (as one terms it well) of the broom of Antichrist, to sweep the church of Christ.[175] Whether that we are in the truth, and they blinded with error, of whom we have spoken, be a sufficient plea, we shall see anon. In the meantime, we may do well to remember what Lewes the twelfth of France said, yea, swore, concerning the inhabitants of Mirindol,[176] whom by the instigation of his

---

167 This is a reference to law 62, title 5, bk. 16 of the Theodosian Code, which saw heretics punished by exile. For the text, see *The Theodosian Code and Novels, and the Sirmondian Constitutions*, trans. Clyde Pharr (Princeton, NJ: Princeton University Press, 1952), 462.

168 This is a reference to law 64, title 5, bk. 16 of the Theodosian Code. For the text, see *Theodosian Code*, 462.

169 Arianism was another heresy named in law 12, title 5, bk. 16. For the text, see *Theodosian Code*, 452.

170 This probably refers to *Quicumque* and law 8, title 5, bk. 1, from 455, which is found in the Justinian Code. It allowed for the execution of those who attempted to spread heresy and fines for those who listened to them. For text, see *Corpus iuris civilis: Volumen secundum*, ed. Paulus Krueger (Berlin: Weidmannos, 1892), 52.

171 Rev. 12:6.

172 Zech. 4:7.

173 This is a reference to the Jesuit controversialist Martin Becan (1563–1624), who in *Disputatio theologica de fide haereticis de fide servanda* (Mainz, 1607) was hostile to religious freedom even if it did allow the Roman Catholic prince some latitude to grant toleration under exceptional circumstances. For the Latin text, see Becanus, *Opuscula theologica*, vol. 2 (Mainz, 1610), 1–82, where this is reprinted under the title provided by Owen. For an English translation of the work, see Martinus Becanus, *On the Duty to Keep Faith with Heretics*, ed. Wim Decock, trans. Isabelle Buhre (Grand Rapids, MI: CLP Academic, 2019).

174 This is a further reference to Bellarmine's *De laicis* (Concerning the laity), which argued that heretics ought not to be allowed religious freedom and could, legitimately, be punished with temporal punishments and even death.

175 Joseph Caryl had used this phrase in his parliamentary sermon *Englands Plus Ultra, Both of Hoped Mercies, and of Required Duties: Shewed in a Sermon Preached to the Honourable Houses of Parliament, the Lord Major, Court of Aldermen, and Common-Councell of London; Together with the Assembly of Divines, at Christ-Church, April 20 1646* [. . .] (London, 1646), 24.

176 Louis XII (1498–1515) said of the Waldenses, "These worthy people are better Christians than we." See William Hazlitt, *The Israel of the Alps: A History of the Persecutions of the Waldenses* (London: Ingram, Cooke, 1852), 22.

prelates[177] he had ordered to be slain, when news was brought him, what was their conversation and way of life, "Let them be heretics if you please" (says he) "but assuredly they are better than me, and my Catholics." Take heed lest the punished be better than the punishers.

Let me add to this observation only this, that the attempt to suppress any opinions whatsoever by force, has been for the most part fruitless; for either some few particular persons, are proceeded against, or else greater multitudes: if some particulars only, the ashes of one, has always proved the seed of many opinionatists: examples are innumerable, take one, which is boasted of as a pattern of severity taken from antiquity. About the year 390, Priscillianus, a Manichee, and a Gnostic, by the procurement of Ithacius and Idacius, two bishops, was put to death by Maximus, a usurping emperor, who ruled for a season, having slain Gratianus; (as that kind of men would always close with any authority that might serve their own ends). Now what was the issue thereof;[178] Martinus a Catholic bishop renounces their communion who did it:[179] the historian, that reports it, giving this censure of the whole, "So as a terrible example, men who were most unworthy of the light of day, were removed,"[180] though the men (Priscillian and his companions) were most unworthy to live, yet their sentence of death, was most unjust. But no matter for this, was not the heresy suppressed thereby? See what the same historian,[181] who wrote not long after, and was able to testify the event, says of it,[182] "The heresy was so far from being suppressed hereby, that it was confirmed, and

177 I.e., clergymen of high status, usually bishops or archbishops.
178 Priscillian was a fourth-century Spanish convert who taught ascetic doctrines that were said to be gnostic or Manichaean. Henry Chadwick dates the rise of Priscillianism to the 370s. See Henry Chadwick, *Priscillian of Avila: The Occult and Charismatic in the Early Church* (Oxford: Clarendon, 1976), 8. In 381 Ithacius, bishop of Ossonoba (modern Faro), and Idacius, bishop of Mérida and Metropolitan of Lusitania, denounced the movement to Gratian, the Western emperor (367–383). Gratian was usurped by Magnus Maximus, under whose authority Priscillian was charged with sorcery and executed. After the death of Priscillian, the movement acquired strength and spread geographically.
179 Bishop Martin of Tours and others were involved in the excommunication of Ithacius and his associates. See Sulpicius Severus, *Chronicles* 2.49. For an English translation, see Sulpicius Severus, *The Complete Works*, trans. Richard J. Goodrich, Ancient Christian Writers 70 (New York: Newman, 2015), 177–78.
180 In the text: *Sic pessimo exemplo, sublati sunt homines luce indignissimi*—Owen. The quotation is adapted from Sulpicius Severus, *Chronicles* 2.51.3. For the Latin text, see Sulpicius Severus, *Chronicorum libri duo*, in *Opera omnia*, ed. J.-P. Migne, Patrologia Latina 20 (Paris: Migne-Garnier, 1845), 158. Owen supplies his own translation. For a translation of the wider context, see Sulpicius Severus, *Complete Works*, 180.
181 This is a reference to the historian and hagiographer Sulpicius Severus (ca. 355–ca. 420).
182 In the text: (it is Severus Sulpitius, lib. 2. *Eccles. Hist.*)—Owen.

propagated":[183] his followers who before honored him as a saint, now adore him as a martyr: the like in all ages has been the issue, of the like endeavors.

But now, if this course be undertaken against multitudes, what is or has been the usual end of such undertakings? Take some examples of late days: Charles the fifth,[184] the most mighty emperor of Germany, undertakes by violence to extirpate the Lutherans and Calvinists out of the empire. After a tedious war, the death of many thousands, the wasting of the nation, in the close of all, himself is driven out of Germany; and the business left much where it began.[185] Philip of Spain, will needs force the inquisition upon the Netherlands?[186] What is the issue? After the expense of an ocean of blood, and more coin than would have purchased the country twice over,[187] his posterity is totally deprived of all sovereignty over those parts.

Patrick Hamilton, and George Wishart are put to death in Scotland by the procurement of a cardinal;[188] the cardinal is instantly murdered by some desperate young men,[189] and a war raised there about religion, which was never

---

183 In the text: "*Non solum non repressa est haeresis,*" (says he) "*sed confirmata, et Latius propagata est, &c.*"—Owen. For the Latin text, see Sulpicius Severus, *Chronicorum libri duo*, 158. Owen again supplies his own translation of 2.51.4. For a translation of the wider context, see Sulpicius Severus, *Complete Works*, 181.

184 The Holy Roman emperor, Charles V (1519–1556), was defeated by the German Lutheran princes who represented the remnants of the Schmalkaldic League at the battle of Innsbruck and in the Peace of Augsburg (1555) acknowledged that each prince could chose the religion of his own state (*cuius regio, eius religio*). In the 1540s, Charles V intensified his campaign against Calvinists in the Netherlands by means of exile and execution. See Andrew Pettegree, "Religion and Revolt," in *The Origins and Development of the Dutch Revolt*, ed. Graham Darby (London: Routledge, 2001), 69.

185 In the text: Sleid. Com.—Owen. This is a reference to the Lutheran historian Johann Sleidan (1506–1556), *De statu religionis et reipublicae, Carolo Quinto, Caesare, commentarii* [Commentaries on the state of religion and the empire under Charles V] (Strasbourg, 1555).

186 This extension of the "Spanish inquisition" into the Hapsburg Netherlands began under the reign of Charles V and increased in its scope during the early years of the reign of Philip II, who was insistent on rigorous enforcement of Tridentine orthodoxy on the people of the Netherlands. The resultant popular unrest was one of the causes that forced Philip to dispatch the army of the Duke of Alba to the Netherlands in 1567. This in turn led to the Dutch Revolt and the extraordinary cruelty and brutality of the Eighty Years' War (1568–1648).

187 Philip's campaign in the Low Countries became an unsustainable financial drain: by 1575, he was bankrupt and his authority in the Netherlands collapsed the following year. Geoffrey Parker, *The Army of Flanders and the Spanish Road, 1567–1659: The Logistics of Spanish Victory and Defeat in the Low Countries' Wars* (Cambridge: Cambridge University Press, 2004), 116.

188 Patrick Hamilton (1504–1528), an early Scottish Reformer influenced by Martin Luther, was tried as a heretic by Archbishop James Beaton (ca. 1473–1539) and, found guilty, was burned at the stake. David, Cardinal Beaton (nephew of James), arranged for the trial and execution of the Protestant preacher George Wishart (ca. 1513–1546).

189 In reprisal, Cardinal Beaton was murdered at St Andrews Castle in May 1546.

well quieted until, having hunted their queen out of her native kingdom, she had her head chopped off in England:[190] *History of Reformation in Scotland*.[191] The wars, seditions, tumults, murders, massacres, rapes, burnings, etc., that followed the same attempt in France, cannot be thought of without horror and detestation.[192] Neither knew those things any end, until the present forbearance was granted.[193] Instances might be multiplied, but these things are known to all. If any shall say, "All these evils followed the attempting to suppress truth, not error," I shall answer him another time, being loath to do it, unless compelled: only for the present I shall say, that error has as much right, to a forcible defense, as truth.

Grounds and Reasons Offered in Favor of Lawful Coercion Resemble Those Employed by Unjust Persecutors

3.[194] To stir us up yet farther, to a serious consideration of the grounds and reasons which are laid down, for the inflicting of punishment upon any, for exorbitancies in things of religion (upon what has been said) the perpetual coincidence of the causes by them held forth, who pretend to plead for just severity, with their pretenses who have acted unjust persecution, should be well heeded.

The position is laid down in general on both sides, that "Erring persons are so, and so, to be dealt withal." That such is the power and duty of the magistrate in such cases. The definition of heresy is agreed on for the main; only the Papists place the church's determination where others thrust in the heretic's conviction (a thing much more obscure to bystanders and judges also). The appellations wherewith truth persecuted, and error pursued, are clothed, still the same.

---

190 Mary Queen of Scots abdicated the throne in 1567 and escaped to England the following year. After eighteen years of being held in custody, she was beheaded in 1586. This is a striking comment given that the regicide had taken place on the day before the sermon was preached, to which this tract was appended.

191 This is a reference to John Knox's *History of the Reformation in Scotland*, a five-volume history written by the Scottish Reformer between 1559 and 1566.

192 The French Wars of Religion (1562–1598) began with the Massacre of Huguenots at Vassy. During this civil and religious war there were atrocities on both sides and rampaging armies engaged in murder, rape, pillaging and burning. Penny Roberts, "Peace, Ritual, and Sexual Violence During the Religious Wars," in *Ritual and Violence: Natalie Zemon Davis and Early Modern France*, ed. Graeme Murdock, Penny Roberts, and Andrew Spicer (Oxford: Oxford University Press, 2012), 75–99. The most notorious massacre took place on the streets of Paris on St Bartholomew's Day in August 1572. See Natalie Zemon Davis, "The Rites of Violence: Religious Riot in Sixteenth-Century France," *Past and Present* 59 (1973): 51–91.

193 The Edict of Nantes (1598) granted substantial rights to Huguenots and brought to an end the French Wars of Religion.

194 In the original, this is numbered 6. Following Goold, this has been corrected to 3.

The consequences urged on all sides, of dishonor to God, trouble to the state, and the like not at all discrepant. The arguments for the one, and other, for the most part the same. Look what reasons one sect gives for the punishing of another, the names being changed are retorted. He blasphemes to the heretic, who charges blasphemy upon him. We use no other arguments, cite no other texts, press no other consequences for the punishing of other heretics, than the Papists the wisest heretics breathing, do for the punishment of us.

No color, no pretense, but has been equally used in all hands: none can say, "This is mine," to Luther's objection, that the church of Christ never burned a heretic, for Husse and Hierome were none;[195] Bellarmine answers, they were heretics to them Catholics, which did suffice.[196] And indeed this vicissitude of things is very pernicious. All Christians almost are heretics to some enjoying authority (as Salvian said the case was between the Homoousians and Arians in his time):[197] and most of those enjoying authority, are persuaded it is their duty, to suppress them whom they account heretics; and answerably have more or less acted, according to this persuasion, until by blood, wars, and horrid devastations of nations, some of them have been wearied: from the first Ceraysado[198] against the Albigenses,[199] through the war of the Hussites under Zisca

---

195 This is from Luther's *Defense and Explanation of All the Articles of Dr. Martin Luther Which Were Unjustly Condemned by the Roman Bull* (1521). For the text in English, see *Luther's Works*, vol. 32, *Career of the Reformer II*, ed. George W. Forell (Philadelphia: Muhlenberg, 1958), 87. Luther said, "From the beginning until now the church has never yet burned a heretic, and never will, though in ancient times there were many heretics of various sorts. . . . If they say that John Huss and Jerome of Prague were burned at Constance, I reply that I was speaking of heretics. John Hus and Jerome of Prague were good Christians, who were burned by heretics and apostates and antichristians, namely, the papists, for the sake of the holy gospel." For further discussion, see Tom Schwanda, "The Protestant Reception of Jan Hus in Great Britain and the American Colonies," *Journal of Moravian History* 16, no. 2 (2016): 65–89.

196 In the text: *de Laic.* cap. 21.—Owen. This appears to be a reference to *De laicis* 22, where Bellarmine is refuting an argument, which he attributed to Luther, whereby it was said that "the Church from the beginning until now burned no heretic; therefore, it does not seem to be the will of the spirit that they be burned." For the text, see Bellarmine, *On Laymen*, 110.

197 In *De gubernatione Dei* (The government of God) 5.2, Salvian of Marseille wrote the following about the Arians of Vandal Africa: "Indeed, with us they are heretics, but in their own opinion they are not. So much do they judge themselves Catholics that they defame us with the title of heresy. What they are to us, therefore, we are to them." See *The Governance of God*, in *The Writings of Salvian, the Presbyter*, 130.

198 I.e., crusade. A war instigated by the Church against infidels or heretics.

199 Pope Innocent III launched a campaign against the Albigensian Cathars in the Languedoc region of southern France (1209–1229). This was followed by a period of persecution in which the Inquisition, established in 1233, succeeded in eradicating Catharism by 1350. See Jonathan Sumption, *The Albigensian Crusade* (London: Faber, 1999). In English Protestant works such as John Bale's *Image of Both Churches* (London, 1550) and John Foxe's *Acts and Monuments*, the Albigenses are

and the Procopii,²⁰⁰ those dreadful massacres, before recounted, what a stage of blood, has Europe been made on this account? I desire that to this point the declaration of the Netherlands, at the beginning of their troubles (whom Bellarmine affirms to have petitioned for liberty of conscience, as he was writing *de Haereticidio*,²⁰¹ the thing being long before granted at Spira,²⁰² at the convention of the States of the Empire, in the year 1526),²⁰³ may be seriously considered.²⁰⁴

The Pre-Constantinian Church Received No Support from the Magistrate, and Yet There Were No Long-Lasting Heresies

4.²⁰⁵ For the necessity of courses of extremity, against erroneous persons, for the upholding "the faith once delivered to the saints,"²⁰⁶ and the keeping the churches in peace, it does not appear to me to be so urgent as is pretended; for three hundred years, the church had no assistance from any magistrate against heretics; and yet in all that space, there was not one long-lived, or far-spreading heresy in comparison of those that followed. As the disease is spiritual, so was the remedy which in those days was applied; and the Lord Jesus Christ, made it effectual. The Christians also of those days, disclaimed all thoughts of such proceedings. The expressions of the most ancient, as Polycarpus, Ignatius, Irenaeus, concerning heretics, are sharp and cutting: their avoiding of them being admonished, precise and severe; their confutations of them, laborious²⁰⁷ and diligent; their church censures and ejections, piercing and sharp; communion among the churches, close, exact, and carefully preserved; so that a stubborn heretic was thrust out of Christian society. But for corporeal punishment to be inflicted on them, in their writings, not a

---

presented as important Protestant forerunners, particularly because of their resistance to the rise of the papal monarchy. See Henry Christmas, ed., *Select Works of John Bale* [. . .] (Cambridge: Cambridge University Press, 1849), 563; John Foxe, *Acts and Monuments* [. . .] (London, 1570), 295.

200 The persecution of the Bohemian Hussites led to the Hussite Wars (1419–1436) in which Johann Žižka (ca. 1360–1424), Prokop Holý (Prokop the Shaven, d. 1434), and Prokůpek (Prokop the Lesser, d. 1434) were the key leaders of the Hussite forces. See Thomas A. Fudge, *The Magnificent Ride: The First Reformation in Hussite Bohemia* (Aldershot, UK: Ashgate, 1998).

201 This is a reference to Bellarmine's *De laicis*, and in particular to chap. 18. See Bellarmine, *On Laymen*, 81–82.

202 I.e., Speyer, a city in the Palatinate.

203 The Second Diet of Speyer (1526) had (as a temporary measure) allowed the princes and free cities of the empire the liberty to choose their own confession. The failure of this compromise led to the ongoing "troubles" in the form of the Eighty Years' War (1568–1648).

204 This is a call for serious consideration to be given to something akin to the Dutch model of toleration.

205 In the original this is misnumbered 7.

206 Jude 3.

207 I.e., hardworking.

syllable. Until Augustine was changed from his first resolution and persuasion, by the madness of Donatistical Circumcellions,[208] this doctrine had but poor footing in antiquity. And whether his reasons as to this point be convincing, let any impartial man read his Epistle 50, and determine.[209] What some say, "The Christians would have been of another mind had they enjoyed Christian magistrates," is so suited to our present frame and temper, but so unworthy of them, that I should wrong them by a defensative. What was their sense of them in a spiritual way is clear. John they say would not abide in a bath, where Cerinthus the heretic, infected with Judaism and Paganism, was; saying, "Let us depart, lest the building fall on us where Cerinthus is."[210] Marcion meeting Polycarpus, and asking him whether he knew him or acknowledged him, his answer was, "Yea, to be the first-born of the devil."[211] Ignatius his epistles are full of the like expressions. Irenaeus says, he "would have no words with them."[212] Tertullian's books testify for him at large, with what keenness of spirit he pursued the heretics of his days (though before the end of them; he had the unhappiness to be almost one himself). Cyprian cries out,[213] "Neither eat, nor talk, nor deal with them."[214] Antonius the hermit leaves testimony

---

208 I.e., a group of the Donatists composed of runaway slaves and ruined peasants who, courting martyrdom, engaged in social and ecclesiastical revolt only to be suppressed by the government.

209 This is a reference to Augustine's letter-treatise to Boniface (ca. 417), tribune of North Africa (commonly now numbered as Epistle 185). In response to queries raised by Boniface, Augustine seeks, under certain circumstances, to justify the state exercising coercive power against heretics and schismatics. He argues that the Donatists must submit to the laws that Christian emperors have established in defense of the truth. Enacting penalties against them is not, he claims, persecution but rather an act of justice as Christian emperors use their power in service of the church. See Augustine, *Part II—Letters*, vol. 3, *Letters 156–210*, ed. Boniface Ramsey, trans. Roland Teske, *The Works of Saint Augustine: A Translation for the 21st Century* (Hyde Park, NY: New City Press, 2004), 184–86, 190–93.

210 In the text: Iren., lib. 3. cap. 3; Euseb. Eccles. Hist., lib. 3. cap. 25.—Owen. This is a reference to Irenaeus's description of Polycarp's account of the apostle John meeting Cerinthus, "the enemy of the truth," in a bathhouse in Ephesus. Cerinthus led a sect of Jewish Christians with gnostic tendencies, and he denied the divinity of Christ. See Irenaeus, *Against Heresies*, 3.3.4. See, *St Irenaeus of Lyons against the Heresies*, trans. Dominic J. Unger, vol. 1, Ancient Christian Writers 55 (New York: Newman, 1992), 243. The incident is also described by Eusebius in *Ecclesiastical History* 3.28. See Eusebius, *Ecclesiastical History*, 1:264–65.

211 In the text: Euseb., lib. 4. cap. 14.—Owen. This is a reference to Polycarp meeting Marcion as recorded by Eusebius, *Ecclesiastical History* 4.14. See Eusebius, *Ecclesiastical History*, 1:338–39.

212 In the text: lib. 3. cap. 3.—Owen. This is a reference to Irenaeus, *Against Heresies*, 3.3.4, who, having recounted these incidents with John and Polycarp, writes about not engaging in any verbal communication with heretics.

213 In the text: "*Nulla cum talibus convivia, nulla colloquia, nulla commercia misceantur:*"—Owen.

214 In the text: Epist. 3. *ad Cornel.*—Owen. This is a reference to Cyprian, Epistle 59 to Cornelius. For the English translation, see St. Cyprian, *Letters 1–81*, trans. Rose Bernard Donna, Fathers of the Church 51 (Washington, DC: Catholic University of America Press, 1964), 192.

when he was dying, that "he never had peaceable conference with them all his days," *Vita Anton, inter Oper. Athan.*[215] Surely, had these men perceived the mind of God for their bodily punishment, they would not have failed to signify their minds therein; but truly their expressions hold out rather the quite contrary.[216] Ignatius, [in his] *Epist. ad Philad.* [says,][217] "Count them enemies and separate from them, but for beating or persecuting them, that is proper to the heathen who know not God, nor our Saviour, do not you so." Tertullian in very many places, lays down general maxims tending to more liberty than is now pleaded for; one or two places may be pointed at. "Look to it, whether this also may form part of the accusation of irreligion—to do away with freedom of religion, to forbid a man choice of deity, so that I may not worship whom I would, but am forced to worship whom I would not. No one, not even a man, will wish to receive reluctant worship."[218] And again to Scapula the governor of Carthage to dissuade him from the persecution he intended. "However, it is a fundamental human right, a privilege of nature, that every man should worship according to his own convictions: one man's religion neither harms nor helps another man. It is assuredly no part of religion to compel religion—to which free-will and not force should lead us—the sacrificial victims even being required of a willing mind. You will render no real service to your gods by compelling us to sacrifice. For they can have no desire of offerings from the unwilling."[219] And I desire to know, whether

215 This is a reference to Athanasius's account of the life of Antony of Egypt (251–356). As Antony spoke to the monks about his death, he exhorted them to be "zealous in protecting the soul from foul thoughts . . . do not approach the Meletian schismatics. . . . Nor are you to have any fellowship with the Arian." See Athanasius, *The Life of Antony; and, The Letter to Marcellinus*; trans. Robert C. Gregg (New York: Paulist, 1980), 95.

216 In the text: Τοὺς μισοῦντας τὸν Θεὸν, μισεῖν χρὴ καὶ ὑμᾶς, καὶ ἐπὶ τοῖς ἐχθροῖς αὐτοῦ ἐκτήκεσθαι· οὐ μὴν καὶ τύπτειν αὐτοὺς ἢ διώκειν, καθὼς τὰ ἔθνη τὰ μὴ εἰδότα τὸν Κύριον καὶ Θεὸν, ἀλλ' ἐχθροὺς μὲν ἡγεῖσθαι καὶ χωρίζεσθαι ἀπ' αὐτῶν: says.—Owen. This is from the long recension of Ignatius's *Epistle to the Philadelphians* 3, 9–10. For the Greek text, see Ignatius, *Epistolae*, ed. J.-P. Migne, Patrologia Graeca 5 (Paris: Migne-Garnier, 1857), 281. For an English translation of wider context, see *Epistle of Ignatius to the Philadelphians: Shorter and Longer Versions*, in *Ante-Nicene Fathers*, 1:80.

217 This is a reference to Ignatius's epistle to the Philadelphians.

218 In the text: *Videte ne et hoc ad irreligiositatis elogium concurrat, adimere libertatem religionis, et interdicere optionem divinitatis, ut non liceat mihi colere quem velim, sed cogar colere quem nolim. Nemo se ab invito coli vellet, ne homo quidem. Apol., cap. 23.*—Owen. This is a reference to Tertullian, *Apologeticus* 24.6. For the Latin text and English translation, see Tertullian, *Apology*, 132–33.

219 In the text: *Tamen humani juris et naturalis potestatis est unicuique quod putaverit colere: nec alii obest, aut prodest alterius religio: sed nec religionis est, cogere religionem, quae sponte, suscipi debeat, non vi; cum et hostiae ab animo libenti expostulentur: ita et si nos compuleritis ad sacrificandum, nihil præstabitis diis vestris, ab invitis enim sacrificia non desiderabunt.*—Owen. This

that which he makes to be the plea of Christians, may not also be used by all erring persons: "As if all your power against us were not in our control! I am a Christian certainly,—but I wish to be. Then only can you condemn me, if I wish to be condemned. When then your power against me is useless I so will, no power at all, your power depends on my will, not on power in you."[220] Hence was that query of Lactantius: "Who can force me to believe what I will not, or not to believe what I will?"[221] And long after these Gregory of Rome, lib. 2. Ep. 52, tells us, "new and unheard of is this preaching, which exacts faith by blows":[222] to beat in faith with stripes, was then, a new kind of preaching. These and the like were their expressions.

It is true, in the three first centuries many fond, foolish, corrupt opinions were broached by sundry brainsick men; but they laid little hold of the churches, kept themselves in the breasts of some few disorderly wanderers, and did very little promote the mystery of iniquity:[223] but afterward, when the Roman emperors, and the great men of the earth, under, and with them, began to interpose in the things of religion, and were mutually wooed, instigated, and provoked by the parties at variance (as indeed it is a shame to consider upon all meetings, assemblies, disputes, councils, what running, what flattering, what insinuation at court were used on all hands), what root did divers heresies take (how far were they propagated? Witness Arianism, which had almost invaded the whole world).

---

is a quotation from Tertullian, *Ad Scapula* 2.2, a text cited by Owen on a number of occasions. For the Latin text, see *Ad Scapula*, 699. For the English translation, see Tertullian, *To Scapula*, in *Ante-Nicene Fathers*, 3:105.

220 In the text: *Totum quod in nos potestis, nostrum sit arbitrium. Certe si velim, Christianus sum, tunc ergo me damnabis si damnari velim. Cum vero quod in me potes, nisi velim, non potes, jam meae voluntatis est quod potes, non tuae potestatis.* Apol. cap. ult.—Owen. This is a reference to Tertullian, *Apologeticus* 49.6. For the text and the translation, see Tertullian, *Apology*, 220–21.

221 In the text: *Quis imponet mihi necessitatem aut credendi quod nolim, aut quod velim non credenda.*—Owen. This is an adapted form of the question asked by the North African convert Lactantius in his early fourth-century work, *Divine Institutes* 5.13. Owen had already cited this passage in *A Vision of Unchangeable Free Mercy* (1646). For the Latin text, see *Divinarum institutionum*, in *Opera omnia*, ed. J.-P. Migne, Patrologia Latina 6 (Paris: Migne, 1844), 594. For English text, see Lactantius, *The Divine Institutes, Books I–VII*, trans. Mary Francis McDonald, Fathers of the Church 49 (Washington, DC: Catholic University of America Press, 1964), 361.

222 In the text: *Nova et inaudita est ista praedicatio, quae verberibus exigit fidem.*—Owen. This is a reference to Gregory the Great's *Epistola ad Iohannem Episcopum Constantinopolitanum* III, 52/53. For the Latin text, see Gregory the Great, *Epistolarum, Opera omnia*, ed. J.-P. Migne, Patrologia Latina 77 (Paris: Migne-Garnier, 1862), 649. For the English translation, see *Register of the Epistles of Saint Gregory the Great*, in *Nicene and Post-Nicene Fathers*, Second Series, 12:136. Owen had included this quotation in *Ebenezer* (1648), which is included in this volume.

223 2 Thess. 2:7.

Furthermore, by the ways which were invented, oft from the rule, for the extirpation of errors; when by the instigation of prelates, the emperors were (to their own ruin), persuaded to them, the man of sin walked to his throne.[224] Those very laws, edicts, and declarations, which were obtained against erring persons, did the bishops of Rome invert and use against all the witnesses of Jesus. The devil durst not be so bold, as to employ that his grand agent in his apprenticeship against the saints: but he first suffers him, to exercise his hand against heretics, intending to make use of him afterward to another purpose. In most of those contests, which the Roman pontiffs had with their fellow bishops, by which they insensibly advanced their own supremacy, it was the defense of Catholics they undertook, as in the case of Athanasius and others.

Neither did the Christians of old, at once step into the persuasion of punishing corporeally in case of religion: Constantine makes a decree at first, Τὴν ἐλευθερίαν θρησκείας οὐκ ἀρνητέαν εἶναι, "that liberty of worship is not to be denied," and therefore the Christians, as others, should have liberty to keep the faith of their religion and heresy.[225] And in the same edict he says (how truly I know not, but yet great Constantine said it), "That it is most certain, that this is conducing to the peace of the empire, that free option and choice of religion be left to all."[226] Afterward when he began a little farther to engage himself in the business of religion, being indeed wearied with the petitions of bishops and their associates,[227] for the persecution of one another, what troubles in a few years did he intricate himself withal, perplexed he was in his spirit to see the untoward revengefulness of that sort of people; insomuch that he writes expressly to them, being assembled in council at Tyre, "That they had neither care of the truth, nor love to peace, nor conscience of scandal, nor would by any means be prevailed on to lay down their malice and animosities."[228] At length an Arian priest curries favor with his sister Constantia: she gets him into the esteem of her brother; after some insinuations of his, new edicts,

---

224 2 Thess. 2:3.

225 In the text: Euseb., *Eccles. Hist.*, lib. 10. cap. 5.—Owen. This is a quotation from the so-called Edict of Milan. For the Greek text and an English translation, see Eusebius, *Ecclesiastical History*, 2:444–45.

226 Eusebius, *Ecclesiastical History* 10.5. The English translation in the text is Owen's. For the Greek text and an English translation, see Eusebius, *Ecclesiastical History*, 2:447.

227 This may be an oblique reference to proliferation of petitions about matters of religion in the 1640s.

228 In the text: Socrat. *Hist.*, lib. 1. cap. 22.—Owen. This is a reference to Socrates Scholasticus, *Ecclesiastical History* 1.34 and to the letter that Constantine wrote to the Council of Tyre (335). Constantine had lost patience with the contentious Eastern bishops and threatened to act in order to bring peace to the church. See *Ecclesiastical History, by Socrates Scholasticus*, in *Nicene and Post-Nicene Fathers*, Second Series, 2:32–33.

new synods, new recallings, new banishments of other persons, follow one upon the neck of another.[229] And when this knack was once found out, of promoting a sect by imperial favor, it is admirable to consider how those good princes, Constantine and his sons, were abused, misled, enraged, engaged into mutual dissensions, by the lies, flatteries, equivocations of such as called themselves bishops.[230] As also how soon with the many, the whole business of religion was hereupon turned into a matter, of external pomp and dominion. But it is beside my purpose to rake into that hell of confusion, which by this means, brake in upon the churches in succeeding ages. Only, for the following imperial edicts and constitutions in the behalf of the catholic faith, and for the punishing of erring persons, I desire to observe,

(1) That the emperors were stirred up to them, by turbulent priests, and aspiring prelates; let the pope's letters to them witness this.[231]

(2) That they were still bottomed, upon such, and such councils, that were not to be opposed or spoken against, when all of them were spent for the most part, about things quite beside and beyond the Scripture (as feastings, and fastings, and bishops' jurisdictions) and some of them, were the very ulcers, and imposthumations[232] of Christian religion, as those of Nice and Ephesus, both the second;[233] and in general all of them the sea, upon which the whore exalted her seat and throne;[234] and these things did those good men, either deceived by the craft of heretics, or wearied by the importunity of the orthodox.

---

229 In the text: Rufin. *Eccles. Hist.*, lib. 1. cap. 11.—Owen. This is a reference to Rufinus's *Ecclesiastical History* 10.12, which records how Constantia, Constantine's sister, introduced an unnamed presbyter who covertly supported the Arian party to her brother, thus setting in motion the events that led to the restoration of Arius. See Rufinus, *History of the Church*, trans. Philip R. Amidon, Fathers of the Church 133 (Washington, DC: Catholic University of America, 2016), 400–02.

230 In the text: Rufin., lib. 1. cap. 15, 16, &c.—Owen. A further reference to Rufinus's *Ecclesiastical History* 10.16–17, which outlines how "depraved priests," fearing that Athanasius might gain access to emperor Constantius in order to "instruct him fully, according to the scriptures, in the truth of the faith, which they were distorting," accused Athanasius of every sort of wrong—that is, of murdering Arsenius and cutting off his arm in order to practice magic with it. See Rufinus, *History of the Church*, 407–8.

231 In the text: Leo, *Epist.* 75. &c.—Owen. This is a reference to Pope Leo the Great's (d. 461) Epistle 156 to his namesake, Emperor Leo, dated 457. It told the emperor that he had been given authority to protect the peace of the church and urged him to defend the faith by expelling anti-Chalcedonians from Constantinople. For the Latin text, see Leo the Great, *Epistolae*, in *Opera omnia*, ed. J.-P. Migne, Patrologia Latina 54 (Paris: Migne, 1846), 1127–32.

232 I.e., abscesses and swellings.

233 The Second Council of Nicaea (787) and the Second Council of Ephesus (449). Owen would likely be thinking about the canons of Nicaea II, which allowed for the veneration of images and how before it Ephesus II (dubbed the "Robber Council") endorsed Monophysitism.

234 Rev. 17:15.

And yet, notwithstanding all this (as I shall afterward declare), I cannot close with that counsel which Themistius a philosopher gave to Valens the emperor,[235] and am most abhorrent from the reason of his counsel, viz. "That he should let all sects alone, because it was for the glory of God, to be honoured with diversities of opinions, and ways of worship": yet though this reason be false and impious, the advice itself was well conducing at that time, to the peace of the churches, something qualifying the spirit of that heretical emperor, who before had cruelly raged, against all orthodox professors of the deity of Christ.[236]

Providential Judgments Have Frequently Fallen on Persecutors

5.[237] Lastly, add unto all that has been said (*vice coronidis*)[238] for the use of such as enjoying authority, may have misapprehensions of some truths of Christ, a sad consideration concerning the end and issue, which the Lord in his righteous judgment has in all ages given to persecutors and persecution. Nero (of whom says Tertullian, "He gloried and rejoiced in the blood of Christians"),[239] who was the first that employed the sword against our religion, being condemned by the senate to be punished *more majorum*,[240] slew himself with this exprobration[241] of his own sordid villainy, "I have lived in shame and I will die with more shame."[242] Domitian, the inheritor of his rage and folly, was murdered in his own house, by his servants.[243] Trajan by a resolution of his joints, numbedness of body, and a choking water, perished miserably.[244]

235 Themistius (ca. 317–ca. 388) was a statesman and rhetorician who served as an advisor to a number of emperors, including Valens (328–378).
236 In the text: Socrat., lib. 4. cap 27.—Owen. This is a reference to Socrates Scholasticus, *Ecclesiastical History*, 4.32, and provided a record of a speech in which Themistius urged emperor Valens to end the persecution of Nicene Christians on the basis that disagreements among Christians were trivial and that God willed there to be a diversity of religions. See *Ecclesiastical History, by Socrates Scholasticus*, in *Nicene and Post-Nicene Fathers*, Second Series, 2:115.
237 In the original, this is numbered 8. Following Goold, it has been corrected to 5.
238 Lat. "in place of a crown."
239 In the text: *Tali dedicatore gaudet sanguis Christianus*. This is an allusion to Tertullian's *Apologeticus* 5.3. For text, see Tertullian, *Apology*, 28.
240 Lat. "in the traditional way." In Suetonius' account (*Nero* 49.2), Nero received word that the Senate would punish him according to "the ancient fashion,"—that is, stripped naked and beaten to death with rods. See Suetonius, *Lives of the Caesars*, 2:170–71.
241 I.e., upbraiding utterance.
242 In the text: *Turpiter vixi, turpius morior*. Sueton. *in Nero*.—Owen. This is adapted from Suetonius, *Nero* 49.3. For the text, see Suetonius, *Lives of the Caesars*, 2:172.
243 In the text: *Idem* in Domit. This is a reference to the detailed account of the assassination of emperor Domitian (81–96) by his domestic staff provided by Suetonius in *Domitian* 17.1–3. See Suetonius, *Lives of the Caesars*, 2:358–61.
244 In the text: Dio Cassius *de Tra*.—Owen. This is a reference to Cassius Dio's account of the death of emperor Trajan (98–117) in *Roman History* 68.33. Trajan had been partially paralyzed by a

OF TOLERATION 381

This is he whose order not to seek out Christians to punishment, but yet to punish them appearing, you have in his epistle to Pliny a provincial governor under him,[245] which though commended by Eusebius,[246] yet is canvassed by Tertullian, as a foolish, impious, wicked constitution.[247] Hadrian perishing, with a flux[248] and casting of blood, paid some part of the price of the innocent blood which he had shed.[249] Severus poisoned himself, to put an end to his tormenting pains.[250] Maximinus, with his son yet a child, was torn in pieces of the soldiers, all crying out, "That not a whelp was to be left of so cursed a stock."[251] Decius having reigned scarce two years, was slain with his children.[252] Valerian being taken by Sapores king of Persia, was carried about in a cage, and being seventy years old, was at length flayed alive.[253] Another

---

stroke and was plagued by dropsy and other ailments. For the Greek text and an English translation, see Dio Cassius, *Roman History*, vol. 8, *Books 61–70*, trans. Earnest Cary with Herbert B. Foster, Loeb Classical Library 176 (Cambridge, MA: Harvard University Press, 1925), 423.

245 In the text: Plin. *Epist.* 97.—Owen. This is a reference to Trajan's letter to Pliny. For text, see Pliny the Younger, *Letters*, vol. 2, *Books 8–10. Panegyricus*, trans. Betty Radice, Loeb Classical Library 59 (Cambridge, MA: Harvard University Press, 1969), 291.

246 In the text: *Eccles. Hist.*, lib. 3. cap. 30.—Owen. This is a reference to Eusebius, *Ecclesiastical History* 3.33. For the text, see Eusebius, *Ecclesiastical History*, 1:277.

247 In the text: Apol. cap. 2.—Owen. This is a reference to Tertullian, *Apologeticus* 2.6–8. For the text, see Tertullian, *Apology*, 11.

248 I.e., an abnormal flow of blood.

249 In the text: Aelius Spart. *in Had.*—Owen. This is a reference to *Life of Hadrian* 24–25, attributed to Aelius Spartianus. Emperor Hadrian (117–138) suffered a hemorrhage and was in such pain through prolonged illness that he asked slaves and doctors to kill him. For the Latin text and an English translation, see *Historia Augusta*, vol. 1, trans. David Magie, Loeb Classical Library 139 (Cambridge, MA: Harvard University Press, 1921), 73–79.

250 In the text: Jul. *Capitol.*—Owen. This is a reference to Julius Capitolinus, one of the *scriptores* of *Historia Augusta*. His *Life of Severus* 19 records the death of Septimius Severus (193–211). For the text, see *Historia Augusta*, 1:415. Severus endured great pain from gout, and it is difficult to determine the exact circumstances of his death.

251 Emperor Maximus Thrax was murdered by his troops at the Siege of Aquileia in 238. See Julius Capitolinus, *The Two Maximini* 23. For the Latin text and an English translation, see *Historia Augusta*, vol. 2, trans. David Magie, in Loeb Classical Library 140 (Cambridge, MA: Harvard University Press, 1924), 359. Owen's quotation is from Pseudo-Aurelius Victor, *Epitome de Caesaribus* 25. For the Latin text, see *Sexti Aurelii Victoris liber de Caesaribus*, ed. Franz Pichlymayr (Leipzig: Tuebneri, 1911), 135.

252 In the text: Euseb., lib. 7. cap. 1.—Owen. This is a reference to the death of Emperor Decius (249–251), who was killed in a battle against the Goths along with his son. His other son died shortly afterward from the plague. See Eusebius, *Ecclesiastical History* 7.1. For the text, see Eusebius, *Ecclesiastical History*, 2:137.

253 In the text: Euseb., lib. 7. cap. 9.—Owen. This is a reference to Eusebius, *Ecclesiastical History* 7.13. For the text, see Eusebius, *Ecclesiastical History*, 2:168–69. Emperor Valerian (253–260) was taken captive by the Persian Emperor, Sapor I (240–272), and he died in 264. According to Lactantius in *On the Deaths of Persecutors*, he was flayed, and his skin was displayed in a

Valerian, of the same stamp, with his brother and kindred, was murdered at Milan.[254] Diocletian being smitten with madness, had his palace consumed with fire from heaven, and perished miserably.[255] The city of Alexandria in the time of Gallienus,[256] was for its persecution, so wasted with variety of destroying plagues and judgments, that the whole number of its inhabitants, answered not the gray-headed old men that were in it before.[257] What was the end of Julian, is known to all.[258] Now truly of many of these, we might well say (as one of old did) *Quales imperatores?*[259] As Trajan, Hadrian, Severus, Julian, what excellent emperors had they been, had they not been persecutors. And all this says Tertullian is come to pass, that men might learn μὴ θεομαχεῖν.[260] He that desires to see more of this, let him consult, *Tertul. Apol.*

Persian temple. See Lactantius, *De mortibus persecutorum*, ed. and trans. J. L. Creed, Oxford Early Christian Texts (Oxford: Clarendon, 1984), 10–11. Lactantius believed that providence had vindicated the early martyrs through the painful deaths endured by the emperors who had instigated the persecution.

254 Valerian's son and coemperor, Gallienus (253–268), was murdered in his camp near Milan as he faced a rebellion by the Danubian generals.

255 Lactantius portrayed Diocletian (284–305) as the most despicable and violent of the persecuting emperors. See Lactantius, *De mortibus persecutorum*, 60–63. The reference to "fire from heaven" alludes to the destruction of his bedchamber and palace that left Diocletian in a state of perpetual "fear of the thunderbolt." See Constantine, *Oration to the Assembly of the Saints* 25. For the text, see Eusebius, "Constantine's Oration," in *The Life of the Blessed Emperor Constantine: From 306 to 337 A.D.; In Four Books* (London: Samuel Bagster, 1845), 288.

256 Emperor Gallienus (253–268).

257 In the text: Dionys. apud Euseb., lib. 7. cap. 20.—Owen. This is a reference to Dionysius of Alexandria's account of the plague that broke out in the city ca. 252 as it is recounted by Eusebius, *Ecclesiastical History* 7.20–22. For the text, see Eusebius, *Ecclesiastical History*, 2:183–89. Eusebius reports the details of the register of citizens entitled to the public distribution of corn as evidence of the dramatic decline in the population. After the plague, the total number of people aged between 14 to 80 years was less than those aged between 40 to 70 years beforehand.

258 Flavius Claudius Julianus (331–363), better known as Julian "the Apostate," whose dying words, according to Theodoret, were "*Vicisti Galilaee*" (Thou hast won, O Galilean). See Theodoret, *Ecclesiastical History* 3.20. For the English text, see *The Ecclesiastical History of Theodoret*, in *Nicene and Post-Nicene Fathers*, Second Series, 3:106.

259 Lat. "What kind of emperors?" This might be an allusion to a quotation, attributed to Emperor Trajan, by John of Salisbury (1115–1180) in *The Statesman's Book* 4.8: "*Se talem velle imperatorem esse privatis, quales imperatores sibi esse privatus optasset.*" For the Latin text, see *Policraticus: sive, De nugis curialium, et vestigiis philosophorum* (Leiden, 1595), 199. "For he wished to be an emperor to private persons of such a kind as he had wanted the emperors to be when he was a private person." For the translation, see John of Salisbury, *Policraticus: Of the Frivolities of Courtiers and the Footprints of Philosophers*, ed. and trans. Cary J. Nederman, Cambridge Texts in the History of Political Thought (Cambridge: Cambridge University Press, 1990), 50–51.

260 Gk. "not to fight against God."

et ad Scap.,²⁶¹ *Euseb. Eccles. Hist.*, lib. 7. cap. 21,²⁶² *August. de civit. Dei*, lib. 18. cap. 52,²⁶³ *Eutrop.*, lib. 8.²⁶⁴ It would be tedious to descend to examples of latter ages, our own and the neighbor nations, do so much, too much, abound with them; let this that has been spoken suffice, to cautionate mortal men, how they meddle with the vessels of the sanctuary.²⁶⁵

Ob[servation]. But now may some say, "What will be the issue of this discourse; do you then leave everyone at liberty in the things of God? Has the magistrate nothing to do, in, or about religion? Is he to depose the care thereof? Shall men exasperated in their spirits by different persuasions, be suffered to devour one another as they please etc.?"

Ans[wer]. I have only showed the weakness of those grounds, which some men make the bottom of their testimonies, against the toleration of anything but what themselves conceive to be truth; as also taken away the chief of those arguments, upon which, such a proceeding against erring persons is bottomed, as tends to blood and death: what positively the civil magistrate, may, nay, ought to do, in the whole business of religion, comes in the next place to be considered, being the third and last part of our discourse: now my thoughts unto this I shall hold out under these, three heads.

PART 3: THE ROLE OF THE MAGISTRATE IN MATTERS OF RELIGION

Summary of the Three Questions to Be Addressed

1. What, is the magistrate's duty, as to the truth, and persons professing it.
2. What, in reference to the opposers and revilers of it.
3. What, in respect of Dissenters from it.

---

261 This is a reference to Tertullian's *Apologeticus* (*Apology*) and *Ad Scapula* from which the Greek phrase above is drawn (4.1). For the Greek text cited, see *Ad Scapula*, in *Opera omnia*, ed. J.-P. Migne, Patrologia Latina 1 (Paris: Migne, 1844), 702. For the English translation, see Tertullian, *To Scapula*, in *Ante-Nicene Fathers*, 3:106.

262 This is an account of the plague spreading through Alexandria in Eusebius, *Ecclesiastical History* 7.21. For the text, see Eusebius, *Ecclesiastical History*, 2:179–83.

263 This is Augustine's treatment of the suffering of the church after the completion of the ten persecutions in *De civitate Dei* bk. 18, chap. 52. For text, see Augustine, *City of God*, vol. 6, trans. William Chase Greene, Loeb Classical Library 416 (Cambridge, MA: Harvard University Press, 1960), 73–79.

264 This is a reference to book 8 of the *Breviarium historiae Romanae* (Abbreviated history of Rome) by the fourth-century Roman historian Eutropius. Book 8 begins with the death of the "destructive tyrant" Domitian and provides an account of Roman history from the time of Trajan to the death of Alexander Severus. For the text, see Eutropius, *Breviarium*, trans. H.W. Bird (Liverpool: Liverpool University Press, 1993), 48–55.

265 Dan. 1:2; 5:3, 23.

First Head: The Duty of the Magistrate in Settling and Establishing the Profession of the Gospel Set Out in Five Propositions

Ensure That the Gospel Is Declared to the Nation

And I shall begin with the first, which to me, is, much of chiefest importance.

His power, or rather his duty herein, I shall hold out in these ensuing propositions.

(1) As all men in general, so magistrates, even as such, are bound to know the mind and will of God, in the things which concern his honor and worship. They are bound, I say, to know it. This obligation lies upon all creatures, capable of knowing the Creator, answerably to that light, which of him they have, and the means of revelation which they do enjoy. He of whom we speak, is supposed to have that most sovereign and supreme of all outward teachings, the word of God, with such other helps, as are thereby revealed, and therein appointed. So as he is bound to know the will of God, in everything him concerning; wherein he fails, and comes short of the truth, it is his sin; the defect being not in the manner of the revelation, but in the corruption of his darkened mind. Now that he is to make this inquiry, in reference to his calling, is evident from that of David, "He that ruleth over men must be just, ruling in the fear of the Lord" (2 Sam. 23:3):[266] this fear is only taught by the word. Without a right knowledge of God and his mind, there can be no true fear of him. That command also, for the Jewish magistrate, to study it day and night, and to have the book of the law continually before him, because it was the rule of that civil polity, whereof he was under God the head and preserver, by analogy confirms this truth (Deut. 18).[267]

(2) If he desire this wisdom sincerely, and the Lord intend him as a light of the morning, as a rising sun, a morning without clouds, to his people,[268] doubtless he will reveal himself to him, and teach him his mind, as he did David and Solomon, and other holy men of old. And as to this, I shall only with due reverence, cautionate the sons of men, that are exalted in government over their brethren, that they take heed of a lifted-up spirit, the greatest closer of the heart against the truth of God. He has promised, to teach the humble and the lowly in mind; the proud he beholds afar off.[269] Is not this

---

[266] This text was used in support of the army's *Remonstrance*. See *An Abridgment of the Late Remonstrance of the Army* (London, 1648), 6.

[267] The correct reference is 17:18–19. Again, Deut. 17 was used in *Abridgment of the Late Remonstrance of the Army*, 6.

[268] 2 Sam. 23:4.

[269] Ps. 138:6.

the great reason, that the rulers believe not on him, and the nobles lay not their necks to the yoke of the Lord,[270] even because their hearts are lifted up within them, and so lie in an unteachable frame before the Lord?

(3) The truth being revealed to them, and their own hearts made acquainted therewith, after their personal engagements, to the practice of the power of godliness, according to the "revelation of God in the face of Jesus Christ,"[271] three things are incumbent on him in reference thereunto.

1. That according to the measure of its revelation unto him, he declare, or take care that it be declared unto others, even all committed to his governing charge. The general equity, that is in the obligation of, strengthening others, when we are confirmed, desiring them to be like ourselves, in all participation of grace from God, the nature of true zeal for the glory and name of the Lord, are a sufficient warrant for this, yea demand the performance of this duty. So Jehoshaphat, being instructed in the ways of God, sent princes and priests to teach it in all the cities and towns of Judah (2 Chron. 17:8–10).[272] As also did Hezekiah (2 Chron. 30:6–8).[273] Let this then be our first position.

[First Position]. *It belongs to the duty of the supreme magistrate, the governor, or shepherd of the people in any nation, being acquainted with the mind of God, to take care that the truth of the gospel be preached to all the people of that nation, according to the way appointed, either ordinary or extraordinary.*

I make no doubt but God will quickly reject them from their power who, knowing their Master's will, are negligent herein.

Protect the Propagation of the Gospel from Those Who Oppose It

2. As he is to declare it, so he is to protect it from all violence, whatever. Jesus Christ, is the great king of nations, as well as the holy king of saints. His gospel has a right to be preached in every nation, and to every creature under heaven. Whoever forbids or hinders the free passage of it, is not only sinful and impious toward God, but also injurious toward men. Certainly the magistrate is to protect everyone, and everything, in their own right, from the violence and injury of unruly men. In the preaching and receiving the gospel, there is a right acted, superior to all earthly privileges whatever. In this then the magistrate is to protect it, that under him the professors thereof "may lead a quiet and peaceable life, in all godliness and honesty."[274] And for this

---

[270] Neh. 3:5.
[271] 2 Cor. 4:6.
[272] 2 Chron. 17:7–9.
[273] 2 Chron. 30:6–9.
[274] 1 Tim. 2:2.

cause, they to whom the sword is committed,[275] may with the sword lawfully defend the truth, as the undoubted right, and privilege of those who do enjoy it, and of which they cannot be deprived without the greatest injury. Jephthah laid it down as the ground of the equity of the wars he waged against the Ammonites, that they would possess what the Lord their God gave them to possess; the defense whereof, he pursued to the subversion of their (at first) invading enemies (Judg. 11:24, 33). (It is no new thing to begin in defense, and end in offence.) Now, if the truth be given us of the Lord our God, to possess, certainly it may be contended for, by those who owe protection thereunto; and if this were not so, we may pray, and prevail for the prosperity of those in authority; and yet when we have done, not have a right to a quiet and peaceable life; let this then be the second assertion.

[Second Position] *The gospel being preached, and declared as of right it ought to be, it is the duty of the magistrate, by the power wherewith he is entrusted, to protect and defend it against all or any persons, that by force, or violence shall seek to hinder the progress, or stop the passage of it under what pretense soever.*

And that a neglect of this also, will be attended with the anger of the Lord, and the kindling of his wrath, shall not long be doubted of any.

Introduction to Further Responsibilities

3. Thirdly, the protecting, assisting, and supporting of all the professors of it, in that profession, and in ways of truth's appointment, for the practice of that which is embraced, and the furtherance of it, toward them who as yet embrace it not, is also required, and of this there are sundry parts.

(1) That seeing Christ Jesus has appointed his disciples to walk in such societies, and requires of them such kind of worship, as cannot be performed without their meeting together ὁμοθυμαδὸν,[276] "in one place," that he either provide, or grant being provided, the use of such places under his protection, as may in all, or any kind be suited, and fitted for that end and purpose. And the ground of this is:

[1] From the right which the gospel of Christ has to be received among men, according to his own appointment; whether that be the appointment of Christ, or no[t], among us is no question.

[2] Because the magistrate has the sole power of all public places, and the protection of them, is committed to him alone, by virtue of that consent unto government which is among any people. This proved as above.

---

275 Rom. 13:4.
276 With one accord. See Acts 1:14; 2:46; Rom. 15:6.

(2) A protection in the use of those places, and all things exercised in them, answerable to that which he does and is bound to grant unto men in their own private dwellings, and families. The reason why I am protected from all hurt or violence in my family, is because I have a right to dispose of all things in my family being my own, and so has not another; it was asserted before, that Christians have a right to the ordinances of Christ, and truth a right to be at liberty. And therefore, if any shall invade, disturb, or trouble them in their rights, and liberties, he is bound, *ex officio*,[277] to give them a protection, "not bearing the sword in vain."[278]

Now being in my family, in my private house, the assistance of those in authority is due:

[1] In respect of them without.
[2] In respect of them within.

[1] For them without, if anyone will against my consent, intrude himself upon my family enjoyments, to share with me, or violently come to take away that is mine, or disturb me in the quiet possession of it, the magistrate takes cognizance of such disturbances, and punishes them according to equity. Suitably, if any person or persons whatsoever, shall with violence put themselves upon the enjoyment of such ordinances as those enjoying the rights of the gospel have obtained to themselves, or shall come in their celebration of them, to cause disturbance, certainly, that magistrate protects not everyone in his undoubted rights, who does not accommodate the wronged parties, with the assistance of his power to the punishment of the transgressors.

[2] For house dwellers, servants, or any others, who may break out into such offenses, and incorrigibleness, as the amendment thereof, may be beyond what I am entrusted to do, to any, by law of God or man, shall not the magistrate here also interpose? Is not his assistance here abundantly required and always granted?

From parity of reason, is it not as due for their protection, who in the enjoyment of their public religious rights may receive disturbance, and be under force, from some, incorrigible by any rule among themselves. For instance, suppose, a person justly excommunicated, and ejected [from] any society of Christians as to any spiritual communion, yet will with outward force and

---

[277] Lat. "from the office"—i.e., by virtue of that office.
[278] Rom. 13:4.

violence, put himself upon them in their closest acts of communion, doubtless their rights, are here to be by power preserved.

[3] That whereas the preachers of the gospel are now to be maintained in an ordinary way, and to expect their supportment in a usual course of providence, and seeing that many to whom we have proved that the gospel is to be declared, by the care of the magistrate, will not, or cannot make such provisions for them as is needful, in these last evil days of the world, it is incumbent on those nursing fathers,[279] to provide for them, who because of their continual labors in the work of the Lord, are disenabled, to make provision for themselves. Where churches are settled according to the rule of the gospel, and not too much straitened by reason of want, there may be an alteration as to this proposal. That this engagement lies first upon the churches, was seen of old; hence that caution or canon of the Council of Chalcedon, cap. 6, Μηδεὶς χειροτονείσθω ἀπολελυμένος,[280] "Let none be ordained at large": "*Ne dicatur, mendicat in palaestra infelix clericus,*" says the scholiast:[281] "lest he should be driven to beg for want of maintenance."[282]

This being the sum of what as to this head, I have to assert, I shall give in the proofs of it, and then draw some farther positions.

Four Proofs That the Magistrate Has Such Responsibilities

1. The bottom of the whole, arises from that right which the gospel has to be preached to all nations and people, and that right paramount to all civil sanctions and constitutions, which every soul has to receive it in the profession thereof. And all this flows from the donation of the Father unto Jesus Christ, whereby he is made "heir of all things" (Heb. 1:[2]), having the "nations given him for his inheritance, the uttermost parts of the earth for his possession" (Ps. 2:8). Being also "Lord of lords, and King of king,"[283] acting nothing in taking possession of his own, but what his sovereignty bears him out in.

---

279 Isa. 49:23.

280 Canon 6 of the Council of Chalcedon (451) states, "Neither presbyter, deacon, nor any of the ecclesiastical order shall be ordained at large." In other words, no one was to be ordained to a ministerial office without reference to service in a particular community—i.e., ordained for a specific title. For the Greek text, see *The Canons of the First Four General Councils*, ed. William Bright (Oxford: Clarendon, 1892), xli. For an English translation, see *The XXX Canons of the Holy and Fourth Synods, of Chalcedon*, in *Nicene and Post-Nicene Fathers*, Second Series, 14:271.

281 I.e., an ancient commentator.

282 Gloss in Gratian's *Decretum*, pt. 1., dist. 70. The commentary by the Castilian canonist and Dominican theologian Cardinal Juan de Torquemada (1388–1468) on the text that had become the first part of canon law as codified by Pope Gregory IX in 1234. See *Gratiani decretorum primam doctissimi commentarii*, 5 vols. (Venice, 1578), 1:498.

283 Rev. 17:14.

2. All this tends to the apparent good, of those committed to his charge, that they may lead their lives in godliness and honesty, which is the very chief end of magistracy committed unto men. This is directly intended, all other things come in by accident, and upon suppositions.

3. No person living can pretend to the least injury by this, none is deprived, none wronged.

4. The precepts given unto them, and the promises made concerning them, do abundantly confirm all that has been asserted. They are commanded as kings and judges to serve the Lord, in promoting the kingdom of the Lord Jesus Christ (Ps. 2:10–11). And it is promised, that "they shall be nursing-fathers and nursing-mothers to the church" of Christ (Isa. 49:23), even then, when she shall "suck the breasts of kings" (earthly things are the milk of kingly breasts), "when her officers shall be peace, and her exactors righteousness" (Isa. 60:16–17). This at least, reaches to all we have ascribed to them. All is but bowing the knee of magistracy at the name of Jesus.

Hence are these positions.

Provide Places for Gospel Worship
[Third Position] *The providing or granting of places requisite for the performance of that worship which in the gospel is instituted, is the duty of the Christian magistrate.*

Protect the Church from Violent Disturbances
[Fourth Position] *Protection as to peace and quietness, in the use of the ordinances, of the Lord Jesus Christ, from violent disturbers, either from without, or within, is also incumbent on him.*

Maintain and Support as Required
[Fifth Position] *Supportment and provision as to earthly things, where regularly failing, is of him required.*

Implications Arising from These Five Position Statements on the Duty of the Magistrate

And in the neglect of any of these, that takes place, which is threatened [in] Isaiah 60:12.[284] Two or three consectaries,[285] added hereunto, shall close this part of the magistrate's power, or rather duty about the things of religion. As,

---

[284] A warning of destruction to nations and kingdoms that will not serve God.
[285] I.e., consequences or deductions.

Three Consequences
These Positive Responsibilities Do Not Extend to Those in Error

Con[sectory] 1. Positive actings by way of supportment and assistance, maintenance, allowance of public places, and the like, in the behalf of persons deviating from the truth, in those things wherein they deviate, [are] contrary to the rule of the word, and duty of them in authority. For,

Error has neither right, nor promise, nor is any precept given in the behalf thereof.

All People, Including Those Who Err, Are to Be Protected from Violence

Con[sectory] 2. The defense and protection of erring persons, from violence and injury, in those things wherein they have a right, is no acting of his duty about religious things; but a mere dealing for the preservation of human society, by the defense of persons, not acting against the rules thereof.

Minor Differences Do Not Fall under the Magistrate's Purview

Con[sectory] 3. Every particular minute difference, among the professors of the truth, cannot be proved to come under the cognizance of the magistrate, he being to attend the worship which for the main is acceptable to God in Christ, neither do any testimonies extend his duty any farther:[286] Hence—

Two Corollaries concerning Dissent

Corol[lary] 1. The present differences about church society, and the subject or seat of discipline, which are between those Dissenters, who are known by the names of Presbyterians, and Independents, as they are in themselves

---

286 In a margin: For this cause the Emperors of old still allowed the Novatians the liberty of worship.—Owen. This is a reference to the followers of Novatian (d. 258), a presbyter in Rome who refused to extend peace to those who had lapsed under the persecutions of the mid-third century. Constantine initially granted the Novatians toleration but shortly afterward withdrew it. See Eusebius, *Vita Constantini* 3.63–65. For an English translation, see *Life of Constantine*, trans. Averil Cameron and Stuart G. Hall (Oxford: Clarendon, 1999), 151–53, 306–7. The Western emperor Gratian (375–383) and the Eastern emperor Theodosius I (379–395) granted the Novatians a degree more toleration than other heretical groups. In 383 Theodosius held a synod in Constantinople at which the creeds of alleged heretical groups were examined. The Novatians, though schismatic, were deemed to be orthodox in Nicene fundamentals and therefore were permitted to gather for worship. See Socrates Scholasticus, *Ecclesiastical History* 5.10. For text, see *The Ecclesiastical History*, by Socrates Scholasticus, in *Nicene and Post-Nicene Fathers*, Second Series, 2:122–23.

(not heightened by the prejudices, lusts, corruptions, and interests of men), hinder not at all, but that the magistrate is bound to the performance of the duties before mentioned unto both parties. And the reasons of this are, because—

(1) The things wherein they are agreed, are clearly as broad, as the magistrate's duty can be stretched to cover them.

(2) Neither party (I am persuaded) in their retired thoughts, dare avow the main of the worship by their Dissenters embraced, to be as such, rejected of the Lord.

(3) No example in the world, can be produced out of the Old Testament, or New, or ecclesiastical history, of a forcible decision of such minute differences.[287]

Corol[lary] 2. All the plea of persons erring in doctrine or worship, is not from what the magistrate must do, but from what he may not do.

And this for the first part shall suffice.

Second Head: The Duty of the Magistrate to Support, Maintain, and Defend the Profession of the Gospel from Opposition, Disturbance, and Blasphemy

Secondly, there is another part of the magistrate's power, the other side of his sword to be exercised toward the opposition of that truth which he has embraced: and this has a twofold object.

1. Things.
2. Persons.

1. Things are of two sorts:

(1) Ways of worship.
(2) Outward appearances, monuments, accommodations and declarations of those ways.

Of the first I shall speak afterward.

---

[287] In the text: See Socrat: *Eccles. Hist.*, lib. 6. cap. 20.—Owen. This is a reference to Socrates Scholasticus's *Ecclesiastical History*, but the citation should probably be corrected to 5.20, which gives an account of how the Novatians of Constantinople enjoyed imperial tolerance under Emperor Theodosius and how "he allowed them all to assemble in their own conventicles." For the text, see *The Ecclesiastical History, by Socrates Scholasticus*, in *Nicene and Post-Nicene Fathers*, Second Series, 2:128–29.

Ensure That No Public Places Are Used for False Worship

(2) By the second, I mean all the outward attendances of any false or erroneous worship, which are either helps to, or declarations of the superstition, idolatry, error, or falseness of it; as temples for idolatrous service, crosses, pictures, and the like abused relics of old, unwarranted zeal.

Now, concerning these, I affirm.

[1] That the magistrate ought not to make provision of any public places for the practice of any such worship as he is convinced to be an abomination unto the Lord. When I say he ought not to make provision, I understand, not only a not actual caring that such be, but also a caring that such may not be. He should not have a negation of acting as to anything of public concernment. His not opposing, here is providing. For instance; he must not allow, that is, it is his duty to oppose, the setting apart of public places, under his protection for the service of the Mass (as of late in Somerset House),[288] or for any kind of worship in itself disallowed, because not required, and so, not accepted. This were to be bound to help forward sin, and that such sin whereof he is convinced, which is repugnant to the whole revealed will of God. A magistrate, I told you before, is not to act according to what he may do, but what he must do: now it cannot be his duty to further sin.

[2] Outward monuments, ways of declaring and holding out false and idolatrous worship, he is to remove: as the Papists' images, altars, pictures, and the like, Turks' mosques, prelates' service book. Now these are of two sorts.

{1} Such things as in their whole use and nature, serve only for the carrying on of worship, in itself wholly false, and merely invented. As altars, images, crosses.

{2} Such as are used for the carrying on of worship true in itself, though vilely corrupted, as praying, and preaching; such are those places commonly called, churches.

The first are to be abolished, the latter aright used. (I speak as to public appearances, for private disquisitions after such things, I may be otherwise minded.) The reason of this difference, is evident to all.

---

288 One of the stipulations of Queen Henrietta Maria's marriage treaty was that a chapel was to be built for her private use. This was constructed by Inigo Jones at Somerset House, and its opening was marked by a high Mass. In this chapel, the queen was served by French Capuchin friars, and it became a notoriously potent symbol of Roman Catholicism in the center of London. In the 1640s, the chapel was sacked, and the Capuchins were deported. See Caroline M. Hibbard, "The Somerset House Chapel and the Topography of London Catholicism," in *The Politics of Space: European Courts, ca. 1500–1750*, ed. Marcello Fantoni, George Gorse and Malcolm Smuts (Rome: Bulzoni, 2009), 317–37.

Thus in days of old, Constantine shut up pagans' temples,[289] and demolished some of the most filthy of them.[290] Theodosius utterly cast them to the ground, though not without some blows and bloodshed.[291] The command of God for the abolishing all monuments of idolatry (Deut. 12:1–3), with the commendation of those kings of Judah who accordingly performed this duty (2 Chron. 17:6; 30:14), are enough to confirm it, and to bottom this position.

[Sixth position]. *It is the duty of the magistrate not to allow any public places for (in his judgment) false and abominable worship, as also to demolish all outward appearances and demonstrations of such superstitious, idolatrous, and unacceptable service.*

Let Papists, who are idolaters, and Socinians, who are anthropolatrae,[292] plead for themselves.

Five Rules Regarding the More Difficult Issue of Restraining People Who Publicly Oppose the Truth

2. Now secondly for persons, there seems something more of difficulty, yet certain clear rules may be proposed concerning them also, to hold out when they and their proceedings come under the cognizance of the civil magistrate, and are obnoxious to the sword which he bears. And they are these.

Those Who Disturb the Peace Should Be Restrained

(1) Such persons, as having embraced any false principles and persuasion in, or about things concerning God and his worship, do pursue the upholding or propagating of such principles, in a disorderly manner to the disturbance of civil society, are doubtless under his restraining power, to be acted and put forth in such ways as to other persons, running out into the same, or

---

289 In the text: Euseb. *de Vita Constant*, lib. 4. cap. 23–24.—Owen. This is a reference to Eusebius's *Vita Constantini* 4.23–24, which outlines how the emperor promoted Christianity and suppressed idolatry. For the text, see Eusebius, *Life of Constantine*, 161.

290 In the text: lib. 3. cap. 52.—Owen. This is a further reference to Eusebius's *Vita Constantini* 3.52, which refers to the destruction of the pagan statues and worship at the site of the oak of Mamre near Hebron so that a church could be built. For the text and commentary, see Eusebius, *Life of Constantine*, 141, 299–300.

291 In the text: Socrat. *Eccles. Hist.*, lib. 5. ca. 16.—Owen. This is a reference of Socrates Scholasticus's *Historia Ecclesiastica* 5.16, which gives an account of the actions of Theodosius I at the end of the fourth century, in particular the destruction of the Temple of Serapis (the Serapeum built by Ptolemy III Euergetes) in Alexandria (ca. 391). From 381 the emperor had issued a series of decrees against paganism, and in 391 he legislated to close pagan temples. For the text, see *The Ecclesiastical History, by Socrates Scholasticus*, in *Nicene and Post-Nicene Fathers*, Second Series, 2:126.

292 I.e., man worshipers.

the like compass of disorder, upon other grounds, and from the instigation of other lusts. The pretense of disturbance and confusion upon the bearing with differences in opinion about things commanded in religion, we before rejected as a color[293] fitted chiefly for the wearing of persecution. But actual disturbances indeed, must have actual restraints. For instance, if a man, being persuaded that the power of the magistrate, is in Christian religion, groundless, unwarrantable, unlawful,[294] should thereupon stir up the people to the abolishing, and removal of that power, such stirrings up, and such actings upon that instigation, are, as opposite to the gospel of Christ (which opposes no lawful regimen among the sons of men), so also prejudicial to human society, and therefore to be proceeded against by them who bear not the sword in vain. This case we know happened once in Germany,[295] and may do so again in other places. If such as these suffer, it is "as murderers, or thieves, or evil-doers, or busy-bodies in other men's matters," which is a shameful thing, no way commendable or praiseworthy (1 Pet. 4:15).

The Golden Rule Should Always Be Applied

(2) If any persons whatsoever, under any pretense whatsoever, shall offer violence or disturbance to the professors of the true worship of God, so owned, established, and confirmed as above said, in, and for the profession of that true, so owned worship, service, and declaration of the mind of God, such persons are to fear that power, which is the minister of God, and a revenger to them that do evil. Let us suppose of them, what they suppose, and for their own justification and support in irregular ways, bear out of themselves, that they enjoy the truth, others walking in paths of their own; yet then this practice is contrary to that prime dictate of nature which none can pretend ignorance of, viz.: "Do not that to another that you would not have done to yourself";[296] if men that would not think it equitable to be so dealt with, as they deal with others, supposing themselves in their condition, do yet so deal with them, they are αὐτοκατάκριτοι,[297] and do pronounce sentence against themselves out of their own mouths. This then deserves punishment, and breaking out to the disturbance of public order, ought to be punished. We before proved the protection of public places to

---

293 I.e., pretext.
294 This is what some of the radical tolerationists had argued for in the Whitehall debates of December 1648.
295 The establishment of the Anabaptist kingdom in the Westphalian city of Münster in 1534–1535.
296 Owen had cited this negative version of the Golden Rule in the *Country Essay* of 1646.
297 Gk. "self-condemned"; see Titus 3:11.

belong to the magistrate: so that he not only may, but, if he will not be false to him by whom he is entrusted, he must put forth his authority for the safeguarding and revenging of them. Yea also and this rule may pass, when some things in the way publicly established, are truly offensive. What the ancient Christians thought of the zeal of Audas,[298] a Christian bishop, who would needs demolish a pagan temple in Persia, I know not, but I am sure his discretion is not much extolled who, by that one fiery act of destroying πυρεῖον,[299] or "temple of slain," occasioned a cruel persecution of thirty years' continuance.[300]

With Blasphemy There Is a Case for a Degree of Corporal Restraint

(3) When any have entertained any singular opinion, in matters of great weight and importance, such as nearly concern the glory of God, and the minds of Christians, in reverence of his holy name, are most tenderly affected withal, so that without much horror of mind, they can scarce hear those errors, whereby those grand truths are opposed, yet those persons, who have entertained such uncouth opinions, shall not be content, so to have done, and also in all lawful ways (as to civil society) endeavored to propagate the said opinions to others, but in the pursuit of this their design of opposing truth, shall publicly use such expressions, or perform such acts, as are fit to pour contempt and scorn upon the truth which they do oppose, reviling it also, or God himself so represented, as he is in the truth they abominate, with odious and execrable appellations (as for instance, the calling the Holy Trinity, *Tricipitem Cerberum*),[301] if the question be put, whether in this case the magistrate be not obliged to vindicate the honor of God, by corporeal restraints, in some degrees at least upon the persons of those men, truly for my part, I incline to the affirmative. And the reason hereof is this; though men, through the incurable blindness of

---

298 Abdā, bishop of Hormizd-Ardashir, was executed by the Sasanian shah for refusing to rebuild the Pyraeum, a Zoroastrian fire temple that he had destroyed in Khuzistan. See J. P. Asmussen, "Christians in Iran," in *The Cambridge History of Iran*, vol. 3(2), *The Seleucid, Parthian and Sasanian Periods*, ed. Ehsan Yarshater (Cambridge: Cambridge University Press, 1983), 940–41.

299 Gk. "pyree"—i.e., a temple devoted to fire.

300 In the text: Theod. *Eccles. Hist.*, lib. 5. cap. 139.—Owen. This is a reference to Theodoret, *Ecclesiastical History* 5.38. For the text, see *The Ecclesiastical History of Theodoret*, in *Nicene and Post-Nicene Fathers*, Second Series, 3:157. This persecution began near the end of the reign of Yazdgard I (399–420) and continued under Bahrām V (421–438).

301 I.e., the mythological three-headed dog Cerberus. Miguel Servet (ca. 1510–1553) used this scandalous anti-Trinitarian language to describe the Trinity as "a diabolical monster with three heads," which led to his burning in Geneva (1553). Bruce Gordon, *The Swiss Reformation* (Manchester: Manchester University Press, 2002), 219.

their minds, falling into error of judgment, and misinterpretation of the word, may disbelieve the deity of Christ, and the Holy Spirit, yet that any pretense from the word, persuasion of conscience, or dictate of religion, should carry them out to reviling opprobrious[302] speeches of that, which of God, is held out contrary to their apprehensions, is false and remote from reason itself. For this cause Paul says he was a blasphemer,[303] not because being a Jew, he disbelieved the gospel, but because so disbelieving it, he moreover loaded the truths thereof, with contumelious[304] reproaches. Such expressions, indeed, differ not from those piercing words of the holy name of God which he censured to death (Lev. 24:15), but only in this, that there seems in that to be a plain opposition unto light, in this not so. The like may be said of a Jew's crucifying a dog.[305]

Problematic Itinerant Preachers Can Be Dealt With by Existing Legislation

(4) There are a sort of persons termed in Scripture ἄτακτοι[306] (1 Thess. 5:14), ἀγοραῖοι[307] (Acts 17:5); ἄτοποι[308] (2 Thess. 3:2); ἀνυπότακτοι[309] (1 Tim. 1:9), and the like, disorderly,[310] vagabond, wandering,[311] irregular persons, fixed to no calling, abiding in no place, taking no care of their families,[312] that under a pretense of teaching the truth,[313] without mission, without call, without warrant, uncommanded, undesired, do go up and down, from place to place, creeping into houses, etc.[314] Now that such ways as these, and persons in these ways, may be judicially inquired into, I no way doubt. The story is famous of Sesostris, king of Egypt,[315] who made a law, that all

---

302 I.e., reproachful words expressing scorn.
303 1 Tim. 1:13.
304 I.e., words designed to disgrace.
305 Owen appears to be referencing an allegation of Jews engaging in the ritual killing of dogs in a mock parody of Christ's crucifixion. This tale of ritual slaughter was an example of the revival of anti-Semitic medieval stories. See, e.g., William Prynne, *A Short Demurrer to the Jewes* [...], 2nd ed. (London, 1656).
306 Gk. "disorderly or idle persons."
307 Gk. "rabble or people of the baser sort."
308 Gk. "those who are wicked."
309 Gk. "those who are insubordinate or disobedient."
310 2 Thess. 3:7, 11.
311 1 Tim. 5:13.
312 See 1 Tim. 5:8.
313 See Phil. 1:18.
314 2 Tim. 3:6.
315 Sesostris was a legendary ancient pharaoh of Egypt, really a composite of several Middle Kingdom rulers. See Gae Callender, "The Middle Kingdom Renaissance (ca. 2055–1650 BC)," in *The Oxford History of Ancient Egypt*, ed. Ian Shaw (Oxford: Oxford University Press, 2000), 154.

the subjects of his kingdom, should once a year give an account of their way and manner of living, and if anyone were found to spend his time idly, he was certainly punished;[316] and the laws of most nations have provided that their people shall not be wanderers, and whosoever has not a place of abode, and employment, is by them a punishable vagabond.[317] And in this by much experience of the ways, walking, and converse of such persons, I am exceedingly confirmed in. I did as yet never observe any other issue upon such undertakings, but scandal to religion, and trouble to men in their civil relations.

The Magistrate Should Act against the Worst Excesses of the Sects

(5) When men, by the practice of any vice or sin, draw others to a pretended religion, or by pretense of religion, draw men to any vice or known sin, let them be twice punished, for their real vice, and pretended religion. The truth is, I have been taught exceedingly to disbelieve all the strange imputations of wickedness and uncleanness, that are imposed upon many, to be either the end or the medium of the practice of that communion in religion which they do profess and embrace: I remember that when I was a boy, all those stories were told me of Brownists and Puritans, which afterward, I found to have been long before the forgeries of pagans, and imposed on the primitive Christians. I dare boldly say I have heard stories of them a hundred times, holding out that very thing, and those deeds of darkness, which Minutius Felix holds out in the tongue of an infidel concerning the Christians of those days;[318] but yet because sundry venerable persons to whom antiquity has given sanctuary from being arraigned on the point of false testimony, have left it

---

316 Herodotus in *Histories* 2.109 records how Sesostris divided the land into plots and ordered every plot holder to pay an annual tax. See Herodotus, *The Histories*, trans. Tom Holland (London: Penguin, 2014), 151.

317 The Rump Parliament would pass legislation to deal with "rogues, vagabonds, and beggars" shortly after this tract was published. See "May 1649: An Act for the Relief and Imployment of the Poor, and the Punishment of Vagrants, and other disorderly Persons, within the City of London, and the Liberties thereof," *Acts and Ordinances of the Interregnum 1642–1660*, ed. C. H. Firth and R. S. Rait, 3 vols. (London: HMSO, 1911), 2:104–10. Itinerants were often depicted as idle. See David Underdown, *Revel, Riot, and Rebellion: Popular Politics and Culture in England, 1603–1660* (Oxford: Oxford University Press, 1985), 250; and Hitchcock, *Vagrancy in English Culture and Society, 1650–1750* (London: Bloomsbury, 2016), 21–26.

318 Minucius Felix dealt with the fable of the incestuous banquet in *Octavius* 9.5–6. For the text, see Minucius Felix, *Octavius*, 337–39. Tertullian replied to allegations of Christians being involved in shameful acts such as murder, cannibalism and incest as part of their secret societies. See *Apologeticus* 2.5, 7.1. For the text, see Tertullian, *Apology*, 11, 37. Similar sensationalist allegations of immorality had been made against the Brownists; see, e.g., Christopher Lawne, *The Prophane Schisme of the Brownists or Separatists* [. . .] (London, 1612), 15–16, 32–41.

upon record of sundry heretics in their days, as the (Gnostics and others) that they were conjoined into *societates tessera pollutionis*,[319] and some assert that the like iniquities are not wholly buried, I made the supposition, and hope that if they depose themselves from common sense and reason, the magistrate will never exalt them to the privilege and exemption of religion.

In these, and such like cases as these, when men shall break forth into disturbance of common order and enormities against the light of nature, beyond all positive command of any pretended religion whatsoever, that the magistrate ought to set hedges of thorns in their ways, sharpened according to their several delinquencies; I suppose no man not abhorred of common sense, can once hesitate or doubt. And I am the more inclined to assert a restraint to all such as these, because it may be established to the height, without the least prejudice unto the truth, though persons erring should enjoy the place of authority.

The Remaining Issue of How to Respond to Peaceable Error

That which now remains in this head, to be considered, is concerning persons maintaining and upholding any great and pernicious errors, but in such ways, as are not by any of the former disorders to be brought under the cognizance of the civil magistrate, but good, honest, allowable, and peaceable in themselves, not at all to be questioned, but in reference to the things that are carried on, in an[d] by those ways; as communication by discourse, and private preaching, and the like. Now concerning these, it is generally affirmed, that persons maintaining any error in or against any fundamental article of faith,[320] or religion, and that with obstinacy or pertinacy, after conviction, ought to be proceeded against, by the authority of the civil magistrate, whether unto death or banishment, imprisonment or confiscation of goods.[321]

Now unto this, supposing what I have written heretofore, concerning the incompetency of all, and the nonconstitution of any judge in this case, with the answers—given at the beginning of this treatise, to most of the places, produced usually for the affirmative, reserving the consideration of pressing conformity to the next head, to be handled:[322] I shall briefly give in my thoughts: and,

---

[319] Lat. "secret and shameful societies."
[320] Owen, once again, makes the distinction between fundamental and nonfundamental articles of faith.
[321] Ezra 7:26.
[322] A reference to the third and final head that addressed what the magistrate is to do with various sorts of Dissenters.

Three Things That Cannot Be Assumed

That I cannot but observe, that in the question itself, there are sundry things, gratis assumed: as,

1. That it is known and confessed, what articles in religion are fundamental; and this also to the magistrate: when no one thing among Christians is more questionable; most accounting them so (be they what they will), wherein they differ from others. So that one way or other, all Dissenters shall be hooked in, directly or indirectly to clash upon fundamentals. In this, Papists are secure, who make the church's propositions sufficient to make an article fundamental.

2. That the persons holding the error are convinced, when perhaps they have been only confuted:[323] between which two there is a wide difference; he that holds the truth may be confuted, but a man cannot be convinced but by the truth. That a man should be said to be convinced of a truth, and yet that truth not shine in upon his understanding, to the expelling of the contrary error, to me is strange. To be convinced, is to be overpowered by the evidence of that, which before a man knew not; I myself, once knew a scholar invited to a dispute with another man, about something in controversy in religion; in his own, and in the judgment of all the bystanders, the opposing person was utterly confuted: and yet the scholar within a few months, was taught of God, and clearly convinced, that it was an error which he had maintained, and the truth which he opposed. And then, and not till then, did he cease to wonder that the other person was not convinced by his strong arguments, as before he had thought. May not a Protestant be really worsted[324] in a dispute by a Papist? Has it not so ere now fallen out? If not, the Jesuits are egregious liars. To say a man is convinced, when either for want of skill, and ability, or the like, he cannot maintain his opinion, to, and against, all men, is a mere conceit. The truth is, I am so far from this morose severity of looking upon all erring persons as convinced, that have been confuted, that I rather in charity incline to believe, that no erring person, while he continues in his error, is convinced. It will not easily enter into my dull apprehension, how a man can be convinced of an error (that is enlightened with a contrary truth) and yet hold that error still: I am loath to charge more corrupt and vile affections upon any, than do openly appear; that of Paul affirming that some men are self-condemned,[325] is quite of another nature: I think a person is said to be convinced, not when there

---

323 I.e., to overcome or silence in argument.
324 I.e., to defeat in an argument.
325 Titus 3:11.

is sufficiency in the means of conviction, but when there is such an efficacy in them, as to lay hold upon his understanding.

3.[326] That they are obstinate and pertinacious is also a cheap supposal, taken up without the price of a proof. What we call obstinacy, they call constancy: and what we condemn them for, as pertinacy,[327] they embrace as perseverance: as the conviction is imposed, not owned, so is this obstinacy, if we may be judges of other men's obstinacy, all will be plain: but if ever they get uppermost, they will be judges of ours: besides, I know not what good it will do us, or how it will advantage our cause, to suppose men obstinate and convinced before we punish them: no such qualifications being anywhere in the book of God urged in persons deserving punishment: if they have committed the crime, whereunto the penalty is annexed, be they obstinate or not, they shall be punished.

Legal Arguments against Corporal Restraint and
Punishment of Those in Peaceable Error

But now supposing all this, that we are clear in all fundamentals that we are convinced, that they are convinced, and doubt not but that they are obstinate, if they keep themselves in the former bounds, what is to be done? I say, besides what we spoke at the entrance of this discourse,[328] I shall as to any ways of corporeal coaction[329] and restraint, oppose some few things.

1. The nonconstitution of a judge in case of heresy, is a thing civilly criminal. As to spiritual censures and an ecclesiastical judgment of errors, and false doctrines, we find them appointed, and a lawful judge as to the determining concerning them, divinely instituted: so that in such ways they may be warrantably proceeded against (Rev. 21:3). But now, for any judge that should make disquisition concerning them, or proceed against them as things criminal, to be punished with civil censures, I conceive the Scripture is silent: and indeed, who should it be? The custom of former ages was, that some persons of one sort, should determine of it as to right, viz.: that such or such a thing, was heresy, and such or such a one, a heretic (which was the work of priests and prelates) and persons of another sort, should de facto punish, and determine to be punished, those, so adjudged by the former: and these were as they called them the secular magistrates, officers of this world. And indeed, had not "the god of this world

---

326 In the original, this was numbered 5, but, following Goold, it is corrected to 3.
327 I.e., perverse obstinacy.
328 Part 1 of the discourse was Owen's rejection of the arguments typically used to support nontoleration.
329 I.e., constraint or coercion.

blinded their eyes,"[330] and "the God of the spirits of all flesh"[331] hardened their hearts, they would not have so given up their power, to the man of sin as to be made so sordidly instrumental to his bloody cruelty: we read that the priests and prophets assemble themselves in judgment, and so pronounce sentence upon the prophet Jeremy that he should die for a false prophet (Jer. 26:10–11). Jeremy makes his appeal to the secular magistrate and all the people, who taking cognizance of the cause, pronounce sentence in the behalf of the condemned person, against the priests and prophets, and deliver him whether they will or not, verse 16. I spare the application of the story: but that princes and magistrates should without cognizance of the thing, or cause, proceed to punishment or censure of it, upon the judgment of the priests, condemning such or such a man for a heretic, or a false prophet, blessed be the Lord, we have no warrant: had this proceeding been regular, Jeremy had died without mercy for a false prophet, as thousands since, standing before the Lord in his spirit have done. This course then, that the civil magistrate should proceed to sentence of corporeal punishment, upon others judging of the fault, is vile, sordid, unwarrantable, and exceedingly unworthy of any rational man, much more such as are set over the people of the land: that the same persons must determine of the cause, and appoint the punishment is clear: now, who must these be?

(1)[332] Are they the ministers of the gospel? Of all others, they are the most likely to be the most competent judges in spiritual causes: let it be so; but then also, they must be the determiners and inflicters of the punishment upon default: now let them pour out upon obstinately erring persons, all the vengeance, that God has betrusted them withal, "The weapons of our warfare are not carnal, but mighty through God, etc."[333] By this course, admonition, avoiding, rejection, excommunication, will be the utmost that can be inflicted on them: which for my part I desire may be exercised to the utmost extent of the rule.¶

(2) Shall the magistrate be made judge of the cause as well as of the person?[334] Is he entrusted to determine, what is error, what not; what heresy, what not; who is a heretic, who not; and so what punishment is due to such, and such errors, according to the degrees, wherein they are?¶

[1] Why first, I desire an institution of this ordinance in the church? Where is the magistrate entrusted with such a power? Where are rules prescribed to him, in his proceedings?¶

---

330 2 Cor. 4:4.
331 Num. 16:22; 27:16.
332 Following Goold, this numbering is added for the sake of clarity.
333 2 Cor. 10:4.
334 In the margin: Of Iudgements.—Owen.

[2] Is not a judiciary determination concerning truth and error (I mean truths of the gospel) a mere church act? And that church power, whereby it is effected? Must not then the magistrate, *quâ talis*,[335] be a church officer? Will men of this mind, tolerate Erastianism?[336]

(3) If there be a twofold judicature appointed for the same person, for the same crime, is it not because one crime may in divers respects fall under several considerations? And must not these considerations be preserved immixed, that the formal reason of proceeding in one court, may not be of any weight in the other? We proved before, and it is granted of all, that the church is judge in case of heresy and error, as such, to proceed against them, as contrary to the gospel; their opposition to the faith delivered to the saints, is the formal reason upon which that proceeds to censure: if now this be afterward, brought under another sentence, of another judicature, must it not be under another consideration? Now what can this be, but its disturbance of civil society, which, when it does so, not in pretense, but really and actually, none denies it to be the magistrate's duty to interpose with his power.

(4) If the magistrate be judge of spiritual offences, and it be left to him to determine and execute judgment in such proportion, as he shall think meet according to the quality and degrees thereof; it is a very strange and unlimited arbitrariness over the lives and estates of men: and surely they ought to produce very clear testimonies, that they are entrusted from the Lord herewith, or they can have no great quiet in acting.

(5) It seems strange to me, that the Lord Jesus Christ should commit this architectonical power in his house, unto magistrates, foreseeing of what sort the greatest number of them would be, yea determining that they should be such, for the trial and affliction of his own. View the times that are past, consult the stories of former ages, take a catalog of the kings and rulers that have been, since first magistrates outwardly embraced Christian religion in this, and other nations, where the gospel has been planted, and ask your own consciences whether these be the men, to whom this high trust in the house of God is committed. The truth is, they no sooner left serving the dragon in the persecution of the pagans, but presently in a very few years, they gave up their power to the beast,[337] to set up another state in opposition to the Lord Jesus Christ and his gospel: in the supportment whereof, the most of them

---

335 Lat. "as such."
336 I.e., the idea that ecclesiastical power is subordinate to the state and that the state may exercise jurisdiction over the church, often associated with the thought of Thomas Erastus (1524–1583).
337 Rev. 13:4; 17:13.

continue laboring till this very day. "Shall these hands raise up Troy?"[338] What may be added in this case, I refer to another opportunity.

Arguments from the Nature of the Gospel against Corporal Restraint and Punishment in Such Cases

Gospel constitutions in the case of heresy or error, seem not to favor any course of violence; I mean of civil penalties. Foretold it is, that heresies must be (1 Cor. 11:19), but this, for the manifesting of those that are approved, not the destroying of those that are not; I say destroying, I mean with temporal punishment, that I may add this by the way; for all the arguments produced for the punishment of heretics, holding out capital censures, and these being the tendence of all beginnings in this kind, I mention only the greatest, including all other arbitrary penalties, being but steps of walking to the utmost censures. Admonitions, and excommunication upon rejection of admonition,[339] are the highest constitutions (I suppose) against such persons: "Waiting with all patience upon them that oppose themselves, if at any time God will give them repentance to the acknowledgment of the truth":[340] imprisoning, banishing, slaying, is scarcely a patient waiting; God does not so wait upon unbelievers. Perhaps those, who call for the sword on earth are as unacquainted with their own spirits, as those that called for fire from heaven (Luke [9:54]). And perhaps the parable of the tares gives in a positive rule as to this whole business:[341] occasion may be given of handling it at large: for the present I shall not fear to assert, that the answers unto it, borrowed by our divines from Bellarmine, will not endure the trial:[342] we hope that spiritual quiet, and inoffensiveness in the whole mountain of the Lord, which is wrapped up in the womb of many promises, will at length be brought forth to the joy of all the children of Zion.

---

338 In the text: *Hae manus Trojam exigent?*—Owen. This is a quotation from Seneca the Younger's *Troades* (*Trojan Women*) 740. The words of Andromache are used to deny that such hopes were never realistic. For the Latin text and English translation, see Seneca, *Tragedies*, vol. 1, *Hercules. Trojan Women. Phoenician Women. Medea. Phaedra*, ed. and trans. John G. Fitch, Loeb Classical Library 62 (Cambridge, MA: Harvard University Press), 206–7.

339 Titus 3:10.

340 2 Tim. 2:25.

341 Matt. 13:24–30.

342 Robert Bellarmine dealt with the objection based on the parable's lesson that both wheat and weeds should grow together until harvest time in his *De laicis* and *On the Temporal Power of the Pope*. See Bellarmine, *On Temporal and Spiritual Authority*, 115–16, 221–24. George Gillespie provided five answers to objections against the coercive power of the magistrate in matters of religion based on this parable. See *Wholesome Severity*, 15–18. William Prynne provided a detailed exposition of the parable in response to its use by those who argue that it means that heretics should "not be pulled up nor rooted out by the Magistrate" in *Sword of Christian Magistracy Supported*, 77–81.

Examples of the Other Arguments That Could Be Advanced against Corporal Restraint and Punishment in Such Cases

Sundry other arguments taken from the nature of faith, heresy, liberty of conscience, the way of illumination, means of communication of truth, nature of spiritual things, pravitious[343] tendence of the doctrine opposed, if it should be actually embraced by all enjoying authority, and the like; I thought at present to have added, but I am gone already beyond my purposed resting place.

Third Head: How the Magistrate Might Deal with Various Sorts of Dissent

Come we in a few words to the last thing proposed (wherein I shall be very brief, the main of what I intended being already set down) the power of the magistrate to compel others, to the embracing of that religion and way of worship, which he shall establish and set up, which for the greater advantage we shall suppose to be the very same, both for the things proposed to be believed, and also practiced, which God himself has revealed, and requires all men everywhere to embrace. What is to be done, for the settling and establishing of the profession of the gospel, and the right apprehension of the mind of God therein, contradistinct from all those false and erroneous persuasions, which in these, or former days are, or have been held forth in opposition thereunto, was before declared;[344] how it is to be supported, maintained, protected, defended, safeguarded, from all oppositions, disturbances, blasphemings, was then, and there set down.[345]

Now supposing, that sundry persons living under the power and owning civil obedience to the magistrate, will not consent to sound doctrine, nor receive, in some things (fewer or more, less, or greater) that form of wholesome words,[346] which he holds forth, and owns as the mind of Christ in the gospel, nor communicate with him, in the worship, which by the authority of those words, or that truth, he has as before established, it is inquired what is the duty of the magistrate in reference to the bringing of them into that subjection which is due unto, and an acknowledgment of, the truth; and to this I shall briefly give in my answer in these following positions.

The Provisional Nature of This Response

1. In reference unto us, in this nation, the greatest difficulty in giving a full return to this question, arises from the great disorder of the churches of God

---

343 I.e., characterized by pravity and wickedness.
344 The first head of part 3.
345 The second head of part 3.
346 1 Tim. 6:3.

among us: were the precious distinguished from the vile,[347] churches rightly established, and church discipline exercised, that Christians were under some orderly view, and men might be considered, in their several capacities wherein they stand, an easy finger would untie the knot of this *quaere*;[348] but being in that confusion, wherein we are, gathering into any order being the great work in hand, I suppose under favor, that the time is scarce come, for the proposal of this question: but yet something may be given in unto it though not so clear, as the former supposal being effected, would cause it to be.

The Apostles' Creed as a Starting Point for Defining Fundamentals, Given the Controversy over Confessions

2. The constant practice of the churches in former ages, in all their meetings for advice and counsel, to consent unto some form of wholesome words, that might be a discriminating *tessera*[349] of their communion in doctrine, being used in prime antiquity, as is manifest in that ancient symbol commonly esteemed apostolical,[350] (of the chief heads whereof mention in the like summary is made in the very first writers among them, having also warrant from the word of God, and being of singular use to hold out unto all other churches of the world, our apprehensions of the mind of God, in the chief heads of religion) may be considered: if this be done by the authority of the magistrate, I mean if such a declaration of the truth, wherein the churches by him owned and protected, do consent, be held out as the confession of that truth which he embraces, it will be of singular use unto, yea indeed must necessarily precede any determination of the former question: of the nature and use of confessions, etc., so much has of late been learnedly disputed, that I shall not pour out any of mine own conceptions for the present about them, in that hasty tumultuary manner, wherein I am enforced to expose this essay.

The Importance of Distinguishing Dissent in Lesser Matters from Dissent in Fundamentals

3. Those who dissent from the truth so owned, so established, so decreed, do so, either in less matters of small consequence, and about things, generally confessed not fundamental, or in great and more weighty heads of doctrine, acts of worship, and the like: both agreeing in this, that they will not hold

---

[347] Jer. 15:19.
[348] Lat. "question" or "subject of enquiry."
[349] Lat. "sign" or "watchword."
[350] The Apostles' Creed.

communion as either to all, or some parts and duties thereof, [with] those churches and persons who do embrace the truth, so owned, as before, and act accordingly.

For the first of these, or such as Dissent about things of no great concernment in comparison of those other things wherein they do agree, with them, from whom they do dissent, I am bold positively to assert, that, saving and preserving the rules and qualifications set down under the second head, the magistrate has no warrant from the word of God, nor command, rule, or precept, to enable him, to force such persons to submit unto the truth as by him established, in those things, wherein they express a conscientious Dissent, or to molest them with any civil penalty in case of refusal or nonsubmission: nor yet did I ever in my life meet with anything in the shape of reason to prove it, although the great present clamor of this nation, is punctually as to this head: whatever be pretended, this is the Helena about which is the great contest.[351]

Spiritual Means Should Be Employed, and the Magistrate Should Act against Only Those Dissenters Who Disturb the Peace

What I pray will warrant him then to proceed?

Will the laws against idolatry and blasphemy,[352] with their sanctions toward the persons of blasphemers and idolaters? (For I must ingenuously confess, all that which in my poor judgment looks with any appearance of pressing toward *Haereticidium*, is the everlasting equity of those judicial laws: and the arbitrariness of magistrates, from a divine rule in things of the greatest concernment, to the glory of God, if free from them, and that these laws, I doubt, will scarcely be accommodated unto anything under contest now in this age of the world among Christians). But shall I say, a warrant taken from hence for the compelling of men, sound in so many fundamentals, as were it not for the contest with them, we would acknowledge sufficient for the entertainment of the Lord Jesus in their bosoms, to subject to, and close with, the things contrary to their present light and apprehension (though under a promise of being taught of God), or to inflict penalties upon a refusal so to do? *Credat Apella*.[353]

---

351 In Greek mythology suitors came from around the world to compete for the hand in marriage of the beautiful Spartan princess Helen of Troy. This contest was an indirect cause of the destruction of the Trojan War.

352 For example, Parliament's Blasphemy Ordinance of May 1648 would have potentially punished Congregationalists and Baptists.

353 Lat. "Apella may believe." The implication of this proverbial phrase is that Apella (the Jew) may believe this, but that others would not be so credulous. The Romans regarded the Jews to be very superstitious. See Horace, *Satires* 1.5. For the Latin text and an English translation, see

Shall the examples of extraordinary judgments upon idolaters, false prophets, by sword and fire from heaven, (on magicians, apostates, and the like) be here produced? Though such arguments as these have made thousands weep tears of blood, yet the consequence, in reason, cannot but provoke laughter to all men not wholly forsaken of directing principles.

True Uniformity Requires a Work of the Spirit

Qu[estion]. "What then shall be done" they will say? They have been admonished, rebuked, convinced, must they now be let alone?

Ans[wer]. Something as to this I shall add, in the close of this discourse; for the present let learned Whitaker[354] answer for me: and first, to the first, of their being confuted:[355] "Let controversies (says he) be determined how you please, until the conscience be quieted by the Holy Spirit, there will be little peace." Unto which I shall not add anything, considering what I said before of conviction: and to the latter of letting them alone, to then own ways, "It is certainly more desirable for the church that it should be troubled for a time with some trifling disagreements than that it should slumber in a faithless peace; hence it is not enough simply to preserve the peace by whatever means necessary, if a truly holy peace is not thus secured."[356] Better some trouble, than a perfidious, compelled peace. See him handle this more at large, with some excellent conclusions to this purpose.[357]

For these then (and under this head I compare all such persons as keeping in practice within the bounds before laid forth, do so far hold the foundation, as that neither by believing what is not, or disbelieving what indeed is, they do take in, or keep off, any such thing as wherewithal being embraced, or without which, being rejected, the life of Christ cannot in any case possibly consist, nor salvation by him be obtained), as the magistrate is not bound by any rule or precept to assist and maintain them, in the practice of those things

---

Horace, *Satires. Epistles. The Art of Poetry*, trans. H. Rushton Fairclough, Loeb Classical Library 194 (Cambridge, MA: Harvard University Press, 1926), 72–73.

354 William Whitaker (1548–1595), Regius Professor of Divinity at the University of Cambridge.

355 In the text: *Possunt quidem controversiae ad externum forum deferri, et ibi definiri: sed conscientia in eo foro non acquiescit, non enim potest conscientia sedari sine Spiritu sancto.*—Owen. For the Latin text, see William Whitaker, *Praelectiones in controversiam de Romano Pontifice* [. . .] (Hanau, 1608), 17. The English translation in the text is Owen's.

356 In the text: *Ecclesiae quidem optatius est levibus quibusdam dissensionibus ad tempus agitari, quam in perfida pace acquiescere; non ergo sufficit aliquo modo pacem conservari nisi illam esse sanctam pacem constiterit* Whit., Con. 4 de Rom. Pont. qu. 1, cap. 1, sect. 2.—Owen. For the text, see Whitaker, *Praelectiones*, 19.

357 In the text: Con. 4 de Rom. Pont. q. 1, cap. 1, s. 19, pa. 48 et 50.—Owen. For text, see Whitaker, *Praelectiones*, 48, 50.

wherein they dissent from the truth, so he is bound, to protect them in peace and quietness in the enjoyment of all civil rights and liberties; nor has he either warrant, or allowance to proceed against them, as to the least penalty for their Dissent in those things, they cannot receive. Attempts for uniformity among saints, or such as for ought we can conclude, either from their opinions or practices may be so, by external force are purely anti-Christian.

Now for those that stand at a greater distance from the publicly owned and declared truths, such as before we spoke of, the orderly way of dealing with such, is in the first place, to bring them off from the error of the way, which they have embraced: and until that be done, all thoughts of drawing in their assent to that, from which at such a distance they stand, is vain and bootless.[358] Now what course is to be taken for the effecting of this? Spiritual ways of healing are known to all, let them be used, and in case they prove fruitless, for ought that yet I can perceive, the person of men so erring must be left in the state and condition we described under the second head.

And now to drive on this business any farther by way of contest, I will not; my intention at the beginning, was only positively to assert, and to give in briefly the scriptural and rational bottoms, and proofs of those assertions; wherein I have gone aside, to pull, or thrust a line of debate, I have transgressed against my own purpose; I hope it will be pardoned: though I am heartily desirous anything which passes my pen, may be brought to the test, and myself reduced where I have gone amiss, yet my spirit faints within me, to think of that way of handling things in controversy, which some men, by reciprocation of answers, and replies have wound themselves into Bolsecte,[359] and Staphylus,[360] and Stapleton,[361] seem to live again, and much gall from beneath to be poured into men's ink. O the deep wounds, the gospel has received by the mutual keen invectives of learned men: I hope the Lord will preserve me, from being engaged with any man of such a frame of spirit: what has been asserted may easily be cast up in a few positions, the intelligent reader will quickly discern what is aimed at, and what I have stood to avow.

---

[358] I.e., ineffectual.

[359] Jérôme-Hermès Bolsec (d. ca. 1584), a Protestant controversialist who became a bitter opponent of Calvin and who was eventually banished from Geneva.

[360] Friedrich Staphylus (1512–1564), a onetime Lutheran well known as a counter-Reformation apologist and polemicist. See, e.g., *Theologiae Martini Lutherani trimembris epitome* [*An Abridgement of the Tripartite Theology of Martin Luther*] (Antwerp, 1558).

[361] Thomas Stapleton (1535–1598) an English Roman Catholic Controversialist at Louvain who authored rejoinders to Protestants such as *A Returne of Untruthes upon M. Jewelles Replie* (Antwerp, 1566); and *A Counterblast to M. Hornes Vayne Blaste against M. Frekenham* (Louvain, 1567).

Two Assumptions for Any Further Debate about Toleration

If what is proposed, be not satisfactory, I humbly offer to the honorable Parliament, that a certain number of learned men, who are differently minded as to this business of toleration, which almost everywhere is spoken against, may be desired and required to a fair debate of the matter in difference, before their own assembly, that so, if it be possible, some light may be given to the determination of this thing of so great concernment, in the judgments of all men, both on the one side and on the other, that so they may "try all things, and hold fast that which is good."[362]

Corol[lary 1.] That magistrates have nothing to do, in matters of religion (as some unadvisedly affirm), is exceedingly wide from the truth of the thing itself.

[Corollary] 2. Corporal punishments for simple error, were found out to help to build the tower of Babel:

> "If you can better these principles, tell me; if not, join me in following them."[363]

FINIS.[364]

---

[362] 1 Thess. 5:21.

[363] In the text: *Si quid novisti rectius istis, Candidus imperti; si non, his utere mecum.*—Owen. This quotation is from Horace, *Epistulae* (*Epistles*) 1.6.67–68. For the Latin text and English translation, see Horace, *Satires. Epistles. The Art of Poetry*, 290–91.

[364] Lat. "The End."

ΟΥΡΑΝΩΝ ΟΥΡΑΝΙΑ

The Shaking and Translating
of Heaven and Earth.
A Sermon Preached to the Honorable House
of Commons in Parliament Assembled:
On April 19. A Day Set Apart for
Extraordinary Humiliation.

———

By John Owen

———

Isaiah 66:14, 16

And when ye see this, your heart shall rejoice, and your bones shall flourish like an herb: and the hand of the Lord shall be known towards his servants, and his indignation towards his enemies.

For by fire and by his sword, will the Lord plead with all flesh: and the slain of the Lord shall be many.

———

London:
Printed by M. Simmons, and are to be sold by John Cleaver, at his Shop at Paul's Churchyard near the school. 1649.

Where also are to be sold the author's former sermon, preached the 31 January 1649. And likewise his 2 sermons for a memorial of the deliverance of Essex County and Committee.

[Parliamentary Order][1]

Die Veneris,[2] 20 April 1649.

Ordered by the Commons assembled in Parliament, that Sir William Masham[3] do give hearty thanks from this House to Mr. Owen for his great pains in his sermon preached before the House yesterday at Margaret's Westminster; and that he be desired to print his sermon at large, as he intended to have delivered it (if time had not prevented him) wherein he is to have the like liberty of printing thereof, as others in like kind usually have had.

Hen: Scobell[4]
Cler. Parl.[5]

---

1 In the original publication, this parliamentary order appears without any introduction on the opening page before the title page.
2 Lat. "Friday."
3 Sir William Masham (1591–1656), a well-established member of the Essex gentry and the most prominent prisoner during the siege of Colchester. He was one of those to whom Owen dedicated *Ebenezer* (1648). In February 1649, he had been readmitted to the House of Commons and elected to the new Council of State. See *The History of Parliament: The House of Commons 1640–1660*, ed. Stephen K. Roberts, 9 vols. (Woodbridge, UK: Boydell and Brewer, 2023), s.v.
4 I.e., Henry Scobell.
5 I.e., Clerk of Parliament.

[Dedication]

To the Right Honorable the Commons of England Assembled in Parliament

SIRS,

All that I shall preface to the ensuing discourse, is, that seeing the nation's welfare and your own actings are therein concerned; the welfare of the nation, and your own prosperity in your present actings, being so nearly related as they are to the things of the ensuing discourse, I should be bold to press you to a serious consideration of them as now presented unto you, were I not assured by your ready attention unto, and favorable acceptation of their delivery, that being now published by your command, such a request would be altogether needless. The subject matter of this sermon being of so great weight and importance as it is, it had been very desirable that it had fallen on an abler hand, as also that more space and leisure had been allotted to the preparing of it, first for so great, judicious, and honorable an audience; and secondly, for public view, than possibly I could beg from my daily troubles, pressures and temptations, in the midst of a poor, numerous, provoking people. As the Lord has brought it forth, that it may be useful to your Honorable Assembly, and the residue of men that wait for the appearance of the Lord Jesus, shall be the sincere endeavor at the throne of grace of

Your most unworthy servant

In the work of the Lord,
Coggeshall: May 1 1649.

John Owen.

A Sermon Preached to the Honorable House of Commons, upon Thursday the 19th of April 1649

Being by Order of That House Especially Appointed for a Day of Humiliation.

And this word, yet once more, signifieth the removing of those things that are shaken, as of things that are made, that those things which cannot be shaken may remain.

HEB. 12:27

INTRODUCTION: THE GRACE AND DUTY OF PERSEVERANCE

The main design of the apostle in this scripture to the Hebrews, is to prevail with his countrymen who had undertaken the profession of the gospel, to abide constant and faithful therein, without any apostasy unto or mixture with Judaism, which God and themselves had forsaken, fully manifesting, that in such backsliders the soul of the Lord has no pleasure, chapter 10:38.

A task, which whoso undertakes in any age, shall find exceeding weighty and difficult, even to persuade professors to hold out, and continue in the glory of their profession unto the end, that with patience doing the will of God, they "might receive the promise";[1] especially if there be "lions in the way,"[2] if opposition or persecution do attend them in their professed subjection to the Lord Jesus.

---

1 In the margin: Chap. 10:36.—Owen. I.e., Heb. 10:36.
2 In the margin: Prov. 22:13; 26:13.—Owen.

Of all that deformity and dissimilitude to the divine nature which is come upon us by the fall, there is no one part more eminent, or rather no one defect more evident, than inconstancy and unstableness of mind, in embracing that which is spiritually good. Man being turned from his unchangeable rest, seeks to quiet and satiate his soul with restless movings toward changeable things.[3]

Now he who works all our works for us and in us (Isa. 26:12), works them also by us: and therefore that which he will give, he persuades us to have, that at once his bounty, and our duty, may receive a manifestation in the same thing.[4] Of this nature is perseverance in the faith of Christ, which as by him it is promised, and therefore is a grace, so to us it is prescribed, and thereby is a duty. "Let us ask him to bestow, what he requires us to enjoy."[5] Yea, "Give what thou command, and command what you please."[6]

As a duty it is by the apostle here considered, and therefore pressed on them, who by nature were capable, and by grace enabled for the performance thereof. Pathetical exhortations, then unto perseverance in the profession of the gospel, bottomed on prevalent scriptural arguments and holy reasonings, are the sum of this epistle.

The arguments the apostle handles unto the end proposed are of two sorts:

1. Principal.
2. Deductive, or emergencies from the first.

1. His principal arguments are drawn from two chief fountains:

(1) The author, and,
(2) The nature and end of the gospel.

---

[3] In the margin: Psal. 116:7.—Owen.
[4] In the margin: 1 Thes. 1:3; 2 Thes. 1:11; Deut. 10:16; Chap. 30:6; Ezek. 18:31; Chap. 36:26; Acts 11:18.—Owen.
[5] In the text: *Petamus ut det, quod ut habeamus jubet*: August.—Owen. This is a reference to Augustine's *On the Good of Widowhood* 21, an epistolary treatise written ca. 414. For the Latin text, see Augustine, *Do bono viduitatis*, Corpus Scriptorum Ecclesiasticorum Latinorum 41 (Vienna: Hoelder-Pichler-Tempsky, 1900), 329. The English translation is Owen's. For an English translation of the wider context, see Augustine, *Marriage and Virginity: The Excellence of Marriage, Holy Virginity, The Excellence of Widowhood, Adulterous Marriages, Continence*, ed. David G. Hunter, trans. Ray Kearney, vol. 9 of *The Works of Saint Augustine: A Translation for the 21st Century* (Hyde Park, NY: New City, 1999), 127.
[6] In the text: *Da, Domine, quod jubes, et jube quod vis.*—Owen. This is a reference to Augustine's *Confessions* 10.29.40. For the Latin text, see Augustine, *Confessionum*, trans. P. Knöll, Corpus Scriptorum Ecclesiasticorum Latinorum 33.1 (Vienna: Tempsky, 1896), 256. The English translation is Owen's. For an English translation of the wider context, see Augustine, *Confessions*, trans. Henry Chadwick (Oxford: Oxford University Press, 1992), 202.

(1) The author of the gospel is either—

[1] Principal and immediate, which is God the Father, who having at sundry times and in divers manners formerly spoken by the prophets, herein speaks by his Son, chapter 1:1.

[2] Concurrent and immediate, Jesus Christ, this great salvation, being begun to be spoken to us by the Lord, chapter 2:3.

This latter he chiefly considers, as in and by whom the gospel is differenced from all other dispensations of the mind of God.

Concerning him to the end intended, he proposes—

{1} His person,

{2} His employment.

{1} For his person, that thence he may argue to the thing aimed at, he holds out,

1st. The infinite glory of his deity: being "the brightness of the Father's glory, and the express image of his person": chapter 1:3.

2nd. The infinite condescension of his love, in assuming humanity, for "because the children were partakers of flesh and blood, he also himself took part of the same," chapter 2:14.

And from the consideration of both these, he presses the main exhortation which he has in hand, as you may see, chapter 2:1–2, chapter 3:12–13, etc.

{2} The employment of Christ he describes in his offices, which he handles—

1st. Positively, and very briefly, chapter 1–3.

2nd. Comparatively, insisting chiefly on his priesthood, exalting it in sundry weighty particulars, above that of Aaron, which yet was the glory of the Jewish worship, and this at large, chapter 6–10.

And this being variously advanced and asserted, he lays as the main foundation, upon which he places the weight and stress of the main end pursued, as in the whole epistle is everywhere obvious.

(2) The second head of principal arguments he takes from the gospel itself, which considering as a covenant he holds out two ways:

[1] Absolutely, in its efficacy in respect of—

{1} Justification, in it God is merciful to unrighteousness, and sins, and iniquities he remembers no more, chapter 8:12. Bringing in perfect remission, that there shall need no more offering for sin: chapter 10:[18].

{2} Sanctification, he puts his laws in our hearts, and writes them in our minds, chap. 10:16, in it purging our consciences by the blood of Christ, chapter 9:14.

{3} Perseverance, I will be to them a God, and they shall be to me a people: chapter 8:10. All three are also held out in sundry other places.

[2] Respectively to the covenant of works, and in this regard assigns unto it principal qualifications, with many peculiar eminences them attending, too many now to be named: now these are,

{1} That it is new, he saith, "A new covenant, and he hath made the first old," chapter 8:13.

{2} Better; it is "a better covenant," and built upon "better promises": chapter 8:6, 7:22.

{3} Surer, the priest thereof being ordained, "not after the law of a carnal commandment, but after the power of an endless life": chapter 7:16.

{4} Unalterable, so in all the places before named, and sundry others.

All which are made eminent in its peculiar mediator Jesus Christ, which is the sum of chapter 7.

And still in the holding out of these things, that they might not forget the end for which they were now drawn forth, and so exactly handled, he interweaves many pathetical entreaties, and pressing arguments by way of application, for the confirming and establishing his countrymen in the faith of this glorious gospel, as you may see almost in every chapter.

2. His arguments less principal, deduced from the former, being very many, may be referred to these three heads.

(1) The benefits by them enjoyed under the gospel.

(2) The example of others, who by faith and patience obtained the promises: chapter 11.

(3) From the dangerous and pernicious consequence of backsliding, of which only, I shall speak. Now this he sets out three ways.

[1] From the nature of that sin, it is a "crucifying to themselves the Son of God afresh, and putting him to open shame," chap. 6:6, a "treading under foot the Son of God, counting the blood of the covenant an unholy thing, and doing despite to the Spirit of grace": chapter 10:29.

[2] The remediless punishment which attends that sin: "There remaineth no more sacrifice for it, but a certain fearful looking for of judgment, and fiery indignation, which shall devour the adversaries": chapter 10:26–27.

[3] The person against whom peculiarly it is committed, and that is he who is the author, subject, and mediator of the gospel, the Lord Jesus Christ; concerning whom, for the aggravation of this sin, he proposes two things.

{1} His goodness and love, and that in his great undertaking to be a Savior, being "made like unto his brethren in all things, that he might be a merciful and faithful high priest in things pertaining to God, to make reconciliation for the sins of the people": chapter 2:17. And of this, there is a sweet and choice line, running through the whole discourse, making the sin of backsliding, against so much love and condescension appear exceeding sinful.

{2} His greatness or power, which he sets out two ways:

1st. Absolutely, as he is God, to be "blessed for ever":[7] chapter 1[8] and "It is a fearful thing to fall into the hands of the living God": chapter 10:31.

2nd. Comparatively, as he is the mediator of the new covenant in reference to Moses. And this he sets forth as by many and sundry reasonings in other places of the epistle, so by a double testimony in this twelfth chapter, making that inference from them both, which you have, verse 25, "See that you refuse not him that speaketh, for if they escaped not who refused him who spake on earth, how much more shall not we escape if we turn away from him who speaketh from heaven."

Now the first testimony of his power, is taken from a record of what he did heretofore; the other, from a prediction of what he will do hereafter. The first you have, verse 26, in the first part of it: "His voice then shook the earth": "then,"[9] that is, when the law was delivered by him, as it is described verse 18–20 foregoing. When the mountain, upon which it was delivered, the mediator Moses, into whose hand it was delivered, and the people for whose use it was delivered, did all shake and tremble at the voice, power, and presence of Christ, who, as it hence appears, is that Jehovah who gave the law (Ex. 20:2).[10]

The other in the same verse is taken from a prediction, out of Haggai 2:6, of what he will do hereafter, even demonstrate and make evident his power beyond whatever he before effected, "He hath promised, saying, 'Yet once more I shake not the earth only, but also heaven.'"

And if any one shall ask, wherein this effect of the mighty power of the Lord Jesus consists, and how from thence professors may be prevailed upon to keep close to the obedience of him in his kingdom, the apostle answers, verse 27, "And this word, yet once more, signifies the removing of those things that are shaken, as of things that are made, that those things which cannot be shaken may remain."[11] And thus am I stepped down upon the words of my text, finding them in the close of the arguments drawn from the power of Christ, to persuade professors to constancy in the paths of the gospel; and having passed through their coherence, and held out their aim and tendence, their opening and application come now to be considered: and herein these three things.

---

7 Rom. 9:5.
8 I.e., Heb. 1:1–14.
9 In the original, "then" is set in all caps for emphasis.
10 In the margin: Exod. 19:18–19; Chap. 20:18.—Owen.
11 Heb. 12:27.

OPENING OF THE TEXT

1. The apostle's assertion, "The things that are shaken shall be removed, as things that are made";
2. The proof of this assertion: "This word, once more, signifieth no less."
3. His inference from this assertion, thus proved: "The things that cannot be shaken must remain."

The Assertion: "The Things That Are Shaken Shall Be Removed"

1. In the first I shall consider,

(1) What are the things that are shaken.
(2) What is their shaking.
(3) What their removal being shaken.

Defining the Things That Are Shaken

(1) For the first, there is a great variety of judgment among interpreters; the foregoing verse tells us it is not only the earth, but the heaven also; but now what heaven and earth this should be is dubious, is not apparent. So many different apprehensions of the mind of God in these words, as have any likeness of truth, I must needs recount and remove, that no prejudice may remain from other conceptions, against that which from them we shall assert.[12]

[1] The earth (say some) is the men of the earth, living thereon: and the heavens are the angels, their blessed inhabitants: both shaken, or stricken with amazement upon the nativity of Christ, and preaching of the gospel. The heavens were shaken, when so great things were accomplished, as that "the angels themselves desired to look into them" (1 Pet. 1:12). And the earth was filled with amazement, when, the Holy Ghost being poured out upon the apostles for the preaching of the gospel, men of every nation under heaven were amazed, and marveled at it (Acts 2:5–7). Thus Rollocus, Piscator, and sundry other famous divines.[13] But,

{1} The shaking here intimated by the apostle, was then when he wrote, under the promise, not actually accomplished as were the things by them

---

12 In the margin: *Nescio an facilior hic locus fuisset, si nemo eum exposuisset.* Mald: *ad Luc.* 2 v. 34.—Owen. This is a reference to Juan de Maldonado SJ (ca. 1534–1583), who in his comments on Luke 2:34 wrote that "this text had been plainer unexplained." See his *Commentarii in quatuor evangelistas* (Paris, 1668), 946.
13 Owen is rejecting the interpretation offered by Robert Rollock (ca. 1555–1599), *Analysis logica in epistolam ad Hebraeos* (Edinburgh, 1605), 214–15, and Johann Piscator (1546–1625), *Analysis logica quinque postremarum epistolarum Pauli* (Herborn, 1603), 375.

recounted: for he holds it forth as an issue of that great power of Christ which he would one day exercise for the farther establishment of his kingdom.

{2} This, that now is to be done, must excel that which formerly was done at the giving of the law, as is clearly intimated in the inference, "Then he shook the earth, but now the heavens also," (it is a gradation to a higher demonstration of the power of Christ) which that the things of this interpretation are is not apparent.

{3} It is marvelous these learned men observed not, that the heavens and the earth shaken, verse 26, are the things to be removed, verse 27. Now how are angels and men removed by Christ? are they not rather gathered up into one spiritual body and communion?[14] Hence, verse 27, they interpret the shaken things to be Judaical ceremonies, which, verse 26, they had said to be men and angels.

[2] Others by heaven and earth understand the material parts of the world's fabric, commonly so called: and by their shaking, those portentous signs and prodigies, with earthquakes, which appeared in them, at the birth, and death of the Lord Jesus. A new star,[15] preternatural darkness,[16] shaking of the earth, opening of graves, rending of rocks, and the like,[17] are to them this shaking of heaven and earth. So Junius,[18] and after him most of ours.

But this interpretation is obnoxious to the same exceptions with the former, and also others: for,

{1} These things being past before, how can they be held out under a promise?[19]

{2} How are these shaken things removed, which with their shaking they must certainly be, as in my text.

---

14 In the margin: Ephes. 1.10. ἀνακεφαλαιώσασθαι, i.e. μίαν κεφαλὴν παρασχεῖν ἀγγέλοις καὶ ἀνθρώποις τὸν Χριστόν· ἀπεσχισμένοι γὰρ ἦσαν οἱ ἄγγελοι καὶ ἄνθρωποι: Ocumen. in loc.—Owen. The first part of this reference is to the word *anakephalaiōsasthai*, which speaks of the all things being "united" or "gathered together in one" in Christ (Eph. 1:10). It is followed by a quotation from a commentary on Ephesians, attributed to "Oecumenius" of Trikka, which may be translated as "to present one head to angels and men—for angels and men were divided and he united them." For the text, see Pseudo-Oecumenius, *Commentaria*, in *Opera Omnia*, ed. J.-P. Migne, Patrologia Graeca 118 (Paris: Migne-Garnier, 1857), 1176.
15 In the margin: Matth. 2:2.—Owen.
16 In the margin: Matt. 27:45; Luk. 23:44-45.—Owen.
17 In the margin: Mat. 27:51-52.—Owen.
18 Francis Junius (1545–1602), a student of Beza, best known for his Latin translation of the Old Testament.
19 In the margin: "Ὁ γὰρ βλέπει τις, τί καὶ ἐλπίζει Rom. 8:28.—Owen. This is actually a quotation from Rom. 8:24: "For what a man seeth, why doth he yet hope for?" (KJV).

{3} This shaking of heaven and earth is ascribed to the power of Christ as mediator, whereunto these signs and prodigies cannot rationally be assigned, but rather to the sovereignty of the Father, bearing witness to the nativity and death of his Son: so that neither can this conception be fastened on the words.

[3] The fabric of heaven and earth is by others also intended, not in respect of the signs and prodigies formerly wrought in them; but of that dissolution, or as they suppose, alteration, which they shall receive at the last day: so Pareus,[20] Grotius,[21] and many more. Now though these avoid the rock of holding out as accomplished what is only promised, yet this gloss also is a dress disfiguring the mind of God in the text. For,

{1} The things here said to be shaken, do stand in a plain opposition to the things that cannot be shaken, nor removed; and therefore they are to be removed, that these may be brought in. Now the things to be brought in are the things of the kingdom of the Lord Jesus: what opposition, I pray, does the material fabric of heaven and earth stand in to the kingdom of the Lord Jesus? Doubtless none at all, being the proper seat of that kingdom.

{2} There will on this ground, be no bringing in of the kingdom of the Lord Jesus, until indeed that kingdom in the sense here insisted on is to cease, that is after the day of judgment, when the kingdom of grace shall have place no more.

Those are the most material and likely mistakes about the words; I could easily give out, and pluck in again three or four other warping senses, but I hope few in these days of accomplishing will once stumble at them; the true mind of the Spirit, by the help of that Spirit of truth comes next to be unfolded.¶[22]

(1) And first what are the things that are shaken?

As the apostle here applies a part of the prophecy of Haggai, so that prophecy even in the next words gives light into the meaning of the apostle. Look what heaven and earth the prophet speaks of, of those and no other speaks the apostle. The Spirit of God in the Scripture is his own best interpreter. See then the order of the words as they lie in the prophet. "I will shake heaven and earth: I will shake all nations" (Hag. 2:6-7). God then shakes heaven and earth, when he shakes all nations: that is, he shakes the heaven and earth of the nations. "I will shake heaven and earth, and I will shake all nations," is a

---

20 The German Reformed theologian David Pareus (1548–1622).
21 Dutch jurist, philosopher, and theologian Hugo Grotius (1583–1645).
22 The ¶ symbol indicates that a paragraph break has been added to Owen's original text.

pleonasm[23] for "I will shake the heaven and earth of all nations." These are the things shaken in my text.[24]

The heavens of the nations, what are they? Even their political heights and glory, those forms of government which they have framed for themselves and their own interest: with the grandeur and luster of their dominions.

The nations' earth is the multitudes of their people, their strength and power, whereby their heavens, or political heights, are supported.

It is then neither the material heavens and earth, nor yet Mosaical ordinances, but the political heights and splendor, the popular multitudes and strength of the nations of the earth, that are thus to be shaken, as shall be proved.

That the earth in prophetical descriptions or predictions of things, is frequently, yea almost always taken for the people and multitudes of the earth, needs not much proving. One or two instances shall suffice.[25] The earth helped the woman against the flood of the dragon (Rev. 12:16), which that it was the multitudes of earthly people, none doubts. That an earthquake or shaking of the earth, are popular commotions, is no less evident from Revelation 11:13, where by an earthquake great Babylon receives a fatal blow.

And for the heavens, whether they be the political heights of the nations, or the grandeur of potentates, let the Scripture be judge; I mean, when used in this sense of shaking, or establishment,

---

23 I.e., a rhetorical figure that uses more words than strictly necessary for the sake of emphasis or clarity.

24 In the margin: *Nunquam Pauli sensum ingredieris, nisi Pauli Spiritum imbiberis*: Ber: fer. De Monte. Τὸ χρίσμα διδάσκει ὑμᾶς περὶ πάντων: 1 John 2:27. Ἐν πνεύματι ἁγίῳ νοούμεναι καὶ ἀνοιγόμεναι αἱ γραφαὶ δεικνύουσιν ἡμῖν τὸν Χριστὸν, εἰκότως θυρωρὸς τὸ πνεῦμα τὸ ἅγιον. Theophilac. In Joh. 10.—Owen. This marginal note begins with a quotation from the *Golden Letter* to the Carthusian brethren of Mont-Dieu, often attributed to Bernard of Clairvaux (d. 1153), but authored by his friend William of Saint-Thierry (d. 1148): "You will never enter into Paul's meaning until by constant application to reading him and by giving yourself to constant meditation you have imbibed his spirit." For Latin text, see Bernard of Clairvaux, *Epistolae*, in *Opera omnia*, ed. J.-P. Migne, Patrologia Latina 184 (Paris: Migne-Garnier, 1862), 327. For the English translation, see *The Golden Epistle: A Letter to the Brethren at Mont Dieu*, trans. Theodore Berkely (Kalamazoo, MI: Cistercian Publications, 1980), 51. This is followed by a portion of the Greek text of 1 John 2:27: "This anointing teaches you all things." Finally, there is a quotation from the Byzantine archbishop and exegete Theophylact of Ohrid (ca. 1055–ca. 1125), commenting on John 10:1–5: "The Scriptures, being understood and laid open by the Holy Spirit, reveal Christ to us, the Holy Spirit being like a doorkeeper." For the Greek text, see Theophylact, *Commentarius in Joannis Evangelium (continuatio)*, ed. J.-P. Migne, Patrologia Graeca 124 (Paris: Migne-Garnier, 1857), 65.

25 In the margin: Psal. 68:9; Hab. 2:20; Matth. 24:7; 1 Sam. 14:25.—Owen. Owen may be referencing the Hebrew text of Ps. 68 because the relevant verse in English translations is 68:8. It is also likely that the final reference in this note should be to 1 Sam. 14:15.

I am the Lord thy God, who divided the sea, whose waves roared: the Lord of hosts is his name And I have put my words in thy mouth, and have covered thee in the shadow of mine hand, that I may plant the heavens, and lay the foundations of the earth, and say unto Zion, Thou art my people. (Isa. 51:15–16)

By a repetition of what he has done, he establishes his people in expectation of what, [1] he will do. And first he minds them of that wonderful deliverance from an army behind them, and an ocean before them, by his miraculous preparing dry paths for them in the deep: "I am the Lord who divided the sea, whose waves roared."

[2] Of his gracious acquainting them with his mind, his law and ordinances at Horeb, "I have put," (says he) "my words in thy mouth."

[3] Of that favorable and singular protection afforded them in the wilderness; when they were encompassed with enemies round about: "I covered thee in the shadow of mine hand."

Now to what end was all this, why, says he, "That I might plant the heavens, and lay the foundations of the earth." What! Of these material visible heavens and earth? Two thousand four hundred sixty years before at least, were they planted and established: it is all but making of "Zion a people," which before was scattered in distinct families. And how is this done? Why the heavens are planted, or a glorious frame of government and polity is erected among them, and the multitudes of their people are disposed into an orderly commonwealth, to be a firm foundation and bottom, for the government among them. This is the heavens and earth of the nations which is to be shaken, in my text.

"All the host of heaven shall be dissolved, and the heavens shall be rolled together as a scroll, and all their host shall fall down as the leaf falleth from the vine" (Isa 34:4). Now these dissolved, rolled heavens, are no other, but the power and heights of the opposing nations, their government and tyranny, especially that of Idumea,[26] as both the foregoing and following verses do declare. "The indignation of the Lord," (says he) "is upon the nations, and his fury upon all their armies, he hath delivered them to the slaughter, their slain," etc.[27]

"I beheld the earth, and lo, it was without form and void: and the heavens, and they had no light. I beheld the mountains, and lo, they trembled, and all

---

26 I.e., Idumaea or Edom.
27 Isa. 34:2.

the hills moved lightly" (Jer. 4:23–25). Here's heaven and earth shaken; and all in the razing of the political state and commonwealth of the Jews by the Babylonians, as is at large described in the verses following.

"I will cover the heaven, and make the stars thereof dark: I will cover the sun with a cloud, and the moon shall not give her light. All the bright lights of heaven will I make dark over thee, and set darkness upon thy land, saith the Lord God" (Ezek. 32:7).[28] Behold heaven and earth, sun, moon, and stars, all shaken and confounded, in the destruction of Egypt, the thing the prophet treats of, their kingdom and nation being to be ruined.

Not to hold you too long, upon what is so plain and evident, you may take it for a rule, that in the denunciations of the judgments of God, through all the prophets, heaven, sun, moon, stars, and the like appearing beauties and glories of the aspectable heavens, are taken for governments, governors, dominions in political states, as Isaiah 14:12–15; Jeremiah 15:9, chapter 51:25.[29]

Furthermore, to confirm this exposition, St. John, in the Revelation, holds constantly to the same manner of expression. Heaven and earth in that book are commonly those which we have described. In particular, this is eminently apparent, "And I beheld when he had opened the sixth seal, and, lo, there was a great earthquake; and the sun became black as sackcloth of hair, and the moon became as blood; and the stars of heaven fell unto the earth: and the heaven departed as a scroll when it is rolled together; and every mountain and island were moved out of their places &c" (chap. 6:12–15). The destruction and wasting of the pagan-Romish state, the plagues and commotions of her people, the dethroning her idol worship, and destruction of persecuting emperors and captains, with the transition of power and sovereignty from one sort to another, is here held out under this grandeur of words, being part of the shaking of heaven and earth in my text.[30]

---

28 The reference should be expanded to include Ezek. 32:7–8.
29 In the margin: Isa. 13:13; Psal. 68:8; Joel 2:10; Revel. 8:12; Matth. 24:29; Luk. 21:25; Isa. 60:20; Obad. 4; Rev. 8:13, Chap. 11:12, Chap. 20:11.—Owen.
30 In the margin: Euseb. Eccles. Hist. lib. 9, c. 8, 10; li. 8, ca. [17]. De vita Constan. Li. 1. Ca. 50, 51, 52.—Owen. These refer to sections from the writings of Eusebius. First, his *Ecclesiastical History* and its descriptions of the following: plagues and a time of great persecution (9.8); Maximinus's ordinance of 313, which allowed Christians to construct church buildings (9.10); and the Galerius' edict of toleration of 311 (8.17). For the text, see Eusebius, *Ecclesiastical History*, vol. 2, *Books 6–10*, trans. J. E. L. Oulton, Loeb Classical Library 265 (Cambridge, MA: Harvard University Press, 1932), 351, 375, 317. Second, his *Vita Constantini* 1.50–52 deals with plots being devised against Licinius as a providential judgment for his crimes against the Christians of the east. See Eusebius, *Life of Constantine*, trans. Averil Cameron and Stuart G. Hall (Oxford: Clarendon, 1999), 89–91.

Add lastly hereunto, that the promises of the restoration of God's people into a glorious condition after all their sufferings, is perpetually in the Scripture, held out under the same terms; and you have a plentiful demonstration of this point.

"Behold, I create new heavens and a new earth: and the former shall not be remembered, nor come into mind. Be you glad and rejoice for ever in that which I create," etc. (Isa 60:17–18).[31]

"Nevertheless we according to his promise, look for new heavens and a new earth, wherein dwelleth righteousness" (2 Pet. 3:13).

"I saw a new heaven and a new earth, for the first heaven and the first earth were passed away, and there was no more sea" (Rev. 21:1). The heaven and earth are restored, but the sea, that shall be no more.

Those gatherings together of many waters, rivers from all places,[32] or pretended clergymen from all nations into general councils, which were the sea or many waters on which the whore sat,[33] shall have no place at all, in the church's restored condition.

I hope it is now fully cleared, what is meant by the things that are shaken: even the political heights, the splendor and strength of the nations of the earth, the foundation of the whole is laid, and our heap (or building, if your favor will so accept it) will go on apace; for to the analogy hereof, shall the residue of the words be interpreted.[34]

The Shaking of These Things Involves a Shaking of Governments

(2) The second thing considerable is, what is the shaking of these things?[35] To this the answer is now made brief and facile. Such as are the things shaken, such must their shaking be. Spiritual, if spiritual; natural, if natural; civil, if civil.[36] Now they being declared and proved to be civil things, such also is their shaking. Now, what is a civil shaking of civil constitutions? How are such things done in the world? What are these earthquakes? Truly the accomplishment hereof is in all nations so under our eyes, as that I need not speak one word thereunto.

---

31 In the margin: Isa. 66:22–24.—Owen.
32 In the margin: Gen. 1:10.—Owen.
33 In the margin: Revel. 17:1.—Owen.
34 In the margin: Dimidium facti, etc.—Owen. This is a reference to a line from Horace, *Epistulae* (Epistles) 1.40, which reads "*Dimidium facti qui coepit habet: sapere aude*." That is, "He who has begun is half done: dare to know!" For the Latin text and English translation see Horace, *Satires. Epistles. The Art of Poetry*, trans. H. Rushton Fairclough, Loeb Classical Library 194 (Cambridge, MA: Harvard University Press, 1926), 265–65.
35 In the margin: Part II.—Owen.
36 In the margin: Mat. 24:6–7; Jer. 4:19; Isa. 9:5.—Owen.

This Shaking Will Take Place Prior to This New Era

(3) Neither shall I insist upon the third inquiry, viz.: when this shaking shall be?[37] The text is plain, that it must be previous to the bringing in of those things that cannot be moved: that is the prosperous estate of the kingdom of Christ.[38] Only we may observe, that besides other shakings in particular nations of less general concernment and importance, this prophecy has and shall receive a twofold eminent accomplishment, with reference unto a twofold eminent opposition, which the kingdom of Christ has met withal in the world.

(1) First, from the pagan-Roman state, which, at the gospel's first entrance held in subjection most of the chief provinces of the then known world. What were the bloody endeavors of the heaven and earth of that state for the suppression thereof is known to our children:[39] the issue of the whole in the accomplishment of this promise, shaking those heavens and earth to pieces, I before pointed at from Revelation 6:12–15, beginning in the plagues of the persecuting emperors,[40] and ending in the ruin of the empire itself. But,

(2) The immovable things were not yet in their glory to be brought in. More seed of blood must be sown, that the end of the gospel's year may yield a plentiful harvest. That shaking was only for vengeance upon an old cursed, and not for the bringing in of a new blessed state. The vials of God's wrath having crumbled the heavens and earth of pagan Rome into several pieces, and that empire being removed as to its old form, by the craft of Satan it became molded up again into a papal sovereignty, to exercise all the power of the first beast in persecution of the saints (Rev. 13:12).[41] This second pressure though long and sore must have an end; the new-molded heaven and earth of papal anti-Christian Rome, running by a mysterious thread, through all the nations of the West, must be shaken also: which when it is accomplished, there shall be no more sea.[42] There is not another beast to arise, nor another state to be formed; let endeavors be what they will, the Lord Jesus shall reign.

---

37 In the margin: Part 3.—Owen.
38 In the margin: Χρόνους ἢ καιροὺς, οὓς ὁ πατὴρ ἔθετο ἐν τῇ ἰδίᾳ ἐξουσίᾳ, Acts 1:7. Σεισμοὶ κατὰ τόπους, Matt. 24:7.—Owen. The first speaks of "the times or the seasons, which the Father hath put in his own power" (Acts 1:7 KJV) and the second "earthquakes, in divers places" (Matt. 24:7 KJV).
39 In the margin: Ἐξῆλθε δόγμα παρὰ Καίσαρος Αὐγούστου, ἀπογράφεσθαι πᾶσαν τὴν οἰκουμένην, Luk. 2:1.—Owen. This is translated, "And it came to pass in those days, that there went out a decree from Caesar Augustus that all the world should be taxed" (KJV).
40 Owen discussed the plagues that befell the persecuting emperors in *Of Toleration* (1649), included in this volume, utilizing Lactantius, *De mortibus persecutorum*.
41 In the margin: Τὸ κατέχον, 2 Thes. 2:6.—Owen. "What holdeth."
42 In the margin: Revel. 18:2; Isa. 60:12; Psal. 2:6.—Owen.

The Removal Involves a Transformation

[Thirdly],[43] what is the removal of heaven and earth, being shaken: the word here translated "removal" is μετάθεσις, whence that is come to pass I dare not positively say. This doubtless is a common fault among translators, that they will accommodate the words of a text to their own apprehension of the sense and matter thereof. Understanding, as I suppose, that the things here said to be shaken, were the Jewish ordinances, they translated their disposition a "removal"; as the truth is they were removed. But the word signifies no such thing.[44] As its natural import, from its rise and composition is otherwise, so neither in the Scripture nor any profane author, does it ever signify properly a "removal." Translation, or changing, is the only native, genuine import of it: and why it should in this place be haled[45] out of its own sphere, and tortured into a new signification, I know not.[46] Removal is of the matter, translation of the form only. It is not then a destruction and total amotion,[47] of the great things of the nations, but a change, translation and a new molding of them, that is here intimated. They shall be shuffled together almost into their primitive confusion, and come out new molded for the interest of the Lord Jesus. All the present states of the world, are cemented together by anti-Christian lime, as I shall show afterward: unless they be so shaken as to have every cranny searched and brushed, they will be no quiet habitation for the Lord Christ, and his people. This then is the μετάθεσις of the "heaven and earth" of the nations.

Now this is evident from that full prediction which you have of the accomplishment hereof, Revelation 17:12–13, [14] 16.

Verse 12 the kingdoms of the West "receive power one hour with the beast."

Verse 13 in their constitution and government at first received, "they give their power to the beast," and fight against the Lamb.

---

43 In the margin: II Generall Head.—Owen. In the text "Secondly"—Owen. Following Goold, and for consistency with Owen's threefold scheme for the treatment of the assertion, this has been corrected to "Thirdly."
44 In the margin: Heb. 11:5; Iude 4; Gal. 1:6; Heb. 6:18, 7:12.—Owen.
45 I.e., forced or dragged.
46 In the margin: Mutationem: Trem: Translationem Erasm. Ar: Mont.—Owen. This is a reference to the following: Immanuel Tremellius (ca. 1510–1580), who, with Francis Junius (1545–1602), produced the Protestant Latin Bible, the *Testamenti Veteris Biblia sacra* (Frankfurt, 1579); Desiderius Erasmus (1469–1536) and his Greek and Latin *Novum instrumentum* [New instrument] (Basel, 1516); and Benito Arias Montano (1527–1598), who edited the Antwerp Polyglot, *Biblia regia* [The royal Bible] (Antwerp, 1569–1572).
47 I.e., removal of a person from office or removal of property from its owner.

Verse 14 the Lamb with his faithful and chosen ones overcomes them. There, their heaven and earth is shaken.

Verse 16 their power is translated, new molded, and becomes a power against the beast, in the hand of Jesus Christ.

This then is the shaking and removal, in my text: which is said to be, "as of things that are made": that is, by men, through the concurrence of divine providence for a season (which making you have, Revelation 17:12–17) not like the kingdom of Christ, which being of a purely divine constitution, shall by no human power receive an end.

The other parts of the text follow briefly.

The Proof of This Assertion: "This Word, Once More, Signifies No Less"

2. The next thing is the apostle's proof of this assertion. And he tells you, this, "Once more," the beginning of this sentence he urged from the prophet, signifies no less.

The words in the prophet are, עוֹד אַחַת מְעַט הִיא,[48] "Yet once, it is a little," *meghat hi*, "It is a little," is left out by the apostle, as not conducing to the business in hand. Ἔτι ἅπαξ,[49] (as he renders *hod achath*)[50] are a sufficient demonstration of the assertion. In themselves they hold out a commutation of things, and as they stand in conjunction in that place of the prophet, declare that that shaking and commutation must be for the bringing in of the kingdom of the Lord Christ. In brief, being interpreted, by the same Spirit whereby they were indited, we know the exposition is true.

The Inference from The Assertion: "The Things That Cannot Be Shaken Must Remain"

3. The last head remains under two particulars.

(1) What are "the things that cannot be shaken."
(2) What is their remaining.

The Dawn of a New Golden Era for the Church

(1) For the first, "the things that cannot be shaken," verse [27], are called "a kingdom that cannot be moved," verse 28. A kingdom subject to none of those

---

48 Hag. 2:6.
49 "Yet once more" (Heb. 12:26).
50 It is unusual in Owen's texts for the Hebrew to appear in the transliterated form as it does in this sentence.

shakings and alterations, which other dominions have been tossed to and fro withal.[51] Daniel calls it, a not giving of the kingdom to another people (Dan. 2:44), not that oecumenical[52] kingdom which he has with his Father, as king of nations, but that oeconomical kingdom which he has by dispensation from his Father, as king of saints. Now this may be considered two ways:

[1] As purely internal and spiritual, which is the rule of his Spirit in the hearts of all his saints; this "cometh not with observation," it is "within" us (Luke 17:20–21).[53] Consisting in "righteousness, peace, and joy in the Holy Ghost" (Rom. 14:17).

[2] As external, and appearing in gospel administrations; so is Christ described as a king in the midst of their kingdom (Rev. 1:14–17), as also chapter 4 as also chapter 11:15.[54] And both these may be again considered two ways.

{1} In respect of their essence and being, and so they have been, are, and shall be continued in all ages: he has built his church upon a rock, "and the gates of hell shall not prevail against it" (Matt. 16:18).

{2} In reference to their extent in respect of subjects, with their visible glorious appearance, which is under innumerable promises to be very great in the latter days. "And it shall come to pass in the last days, that the mountain of the Lord's house shall be established in the top of the mountains, and shall be exalted above the hills, and all nations shall flow unto it" (Isa. 2:2).[55]

These then are the things which cannot be shaken, which we may reduce to three heads.

[1] The growth of righteousness, peace, and joy in the saints, being filled with light and love from the special presence of Christ, with a wonderful increase of the number of them, multitudes of the elect being to be born in those days: the residue of the Jews and fullness of the Gentiles meeting in onefold, and there "dwelleth righteousness" (2 Pet. 3:13).[56]

[2] The administration of gospel ordinances, in power and purity, according to the appointment and unto the acceptation of the Lord Jesus. The temple of God and the altar being measured anew, the outward court, defiled with Gentile worship, is left out (Rev. 11:1–2).[57]

---

51 In the margin: Psal. 2:6; Psal. 110:2; Acts 2:36; Rev. 1:18; 1 Cor. 15:24–27.—Owen.
52 I.e., belonging to the whole world.
53 In the margin: Luk. 6:20; Mark 12:34 etc.—Owen.
54 In the margin: Psal. 45:6, Psal. 145:13; Isa. 9:7; Obad. 21.—Owen.
55 In the margin: Isa. 11. 5, 6, 7, 8, 9, 10, Chap. 18.18, 19, Chap. 30:18–19; Micah 4:1.—Owen. The Isa. 1:18–19 reference should be 19:18–19.
56 In the margin: Isa. 49:18–22, Chap 54:1–3, etc., v. 11–12, Chap. 60:16–17; Ezek. 48:35; Amos 9:11; Rom. 11:15, etc.—Owen. The third scripture reference is likely an appeal to Isa. 54:11–12.
57 In the margin: Isa. 49:22–23, Chap 66:21; Mal. 3:3; Ezek. 43:9–11; Revel. 21:3.—Owen.

[3] The glorious and visible manifestation of those administrations, in the eyes of all the world, in peace and quietness, none making afraid or hurting in the whole mountain of the Lord (Isa. 65:25).[58]

For the personal reign of the Lord Jesus on earth, I leave it to them, with whose discoveries I am not, and curiosities I would not be acquainted.[59]

But as for such who from hence do, (or for sinister ends pretend to) fancy to themselves a terrene kingly state, unto each private particular saint, so making it a bottom "Live as you will,"[60] for everyone to do that which is good in his own eyes, to the disturbance of all order and authority, civil and spiritual, as they expressly clash against innumerable promises, so they directly introduce such confusion and disorder, as the soul of the Lord Jesus does exceedingly abhor.

It is only the three things named, with their necessary dependencies, that I do assert.

These Things Will Remain and Be Firmly Established

(2) And lastly, of these it is said they must remain, that is, continue, and be firmly established, as the word is often used (Rom. 9:11).

The words of the text being unfolded, and the mind of the Holy Ghost in them discovered, I shall from them commend to your Christian consideration this following position.

DOCTRINE ARISING FROM THE OPENING OF THE TEXT

Observation. *The Lord Jesus Christ by his mighty power, in these latter days, as anti-Christian tyranny draws to its period, will so far shake and translate the political heights, governments, and strength of the nations, as shall serve for the full bringing in of his own peaceable kingdom; the nations so shaken, becoming thereby a quiet habitation for the people of the Most High.*

Proof of the Doctrine

Though the doctrine be clear from the text, yet it shall receive farther scriptural confirmation, being of great weight and concernment.

---

58 In the margin: Chap. 54:11–13, etc.; Zech. 14:9–11.—Owen. The first scripture reference is very likely a further appeal to Isa. 54:11–13.

59 In the margin: Acts 3:21.—Owen.

60 In the text: *vivendi ut velis*.—Owen. This is a quotation from Cicero's *Paradoxa Stoicorum* 5.34. For text and translation, see Cicero, *Stoic Paradoxes*, in *On the Orator: Book 3. On Fate. Stoic Paradoxes. Divisions of Oratory*, trans. H. Rackham, Loeb Classical Library 349 (Cambridge, MA: Harvard University Press, 1942), 284–85.

Confirmation from Daniel 2:44

"And in the days of these kings shall the God of heaven set up a kingdom, which shall never be destroyed: and the kingdom shall not be left to other people, but it shall break in pieces and consume all these kingdoms, and it shall stand for ever" (Dan. 2:44).

That this is affirmed of the kingdom of Christ under the gospel, none ever doubted.

Three things are here remarkably intimated of it:

1. The time wherein it shall most eminently be established: and that is "In the days of these kings," of which Daniel was speaking.
2. The efficacy of its being set up, "It shall break in pieces all these kingdoms."
3. Its own stability, "It shall never be destroyed."

1. For the first, there is great debate, about the principal season of the accomplishing of this prediction: much hesitation who those kings are in whose days the kingdom of Christ is eminently to be established. In the days when the two legs of the Roman Empire shall be divided into ten kingdoms, and those kingdoms have opposed themselves to the power of Christ, that is in the days wherein we live, say some. Yea most of the ancients took this for the Roman Empire: and to these the bringing in of the kingdom of Christ, is the establishment of it in these days:[61] others understand the Syrian and Egyptian branches of the Grecian monarchy,[62] and the bringing in of Christ's kingdom to be in his birth, death, and preaching of the gospel, wherein certainly the foundations of it were laid: I will not contend with any mortal hereabout. Only I shall oppose one or two things to this latter interpretation: as,

(1) The kingdom of Syria was totally destroyed and reduced into a Roman province sixty years before the nativity of Christ;[63] and the Egyptian thirty.[64]

---

61 Until the sixteenth century, the dominant interpretation was that the fourth monarchy was that of Rome. See Kirsten Macfarlane, *Biblical Scholarship in an Age of Controversy: The Polemical World of Hugh Broughton (1549–1612)* (Oxford: Oxford University Press, 2021), 61.
62 Two of the leading Hellenistic states formed when the Macedonian Empire of Alexander the Great divided the Seleucid Empire in Syria and the Ptolemaic Kingdom of Egypt. This view was popularized in the annotations to the Latin Bible produced by Tremellius and Junius.
63 The Roman general Pompey the Great deposed the last Seleucid king, Antiochus XIII Asiaticus, in 64 BC and annexed Syria to the Roman Republic.
64 In the naval battle of Actium, Octavian defeated the combined fleets of Mark Antony and the last Ptolemaic ruler, Queen Cleopatra VII. Following this, Egypt became a province of the Roman Empire (30 BC).

So that it is impossible that the kingdom of Christ by his birth should be set up in their days.

(2) It is ascribed to the efficacy of this kingdom that being established, it shall break in pieces all those kingdoms: which how can it be, when at the first setting of it up, they had neither place, nor name, nor scarce remembrance.

So that it must needs be the declining divided Roman Empire,[65] shared among sundry nations, that is here intimated: and so consequently the kingdom of Christ to be established, is that glorious administration thereof, which in these days, their days, he will bring in. Be it so, or otherwise, this from hence cannot be denied, that the kingdom of Christ will assuredly shake and translate all opposing dominions, until itself be established in and over them all, ὅπερ ἔδει δεῖξαι,[66] which is all I intend to prove from this place. The ten-partite empire of the West, must give place to the stone cut out of the mountain without hands.[67]

"The kingdom and dominion, and the greatness of the kingdom under the whole heaven, shall be given to the people of the saints of the Most High: whose kingdom is an everlasting kingdom, and all dominions shall serve and obey him" (Dan. 7:27). Hitherto is the end of the matter.

Either Antichrist is described in the close of this chapter,[68] or one very like him, St. John painting him in the Revelation with all this man's colors.[69] Plainly intimating, that though, in the first place, that mad raging tyrant, Antiochus the Illustrious was pointed at,[70] yet that another was to rise in his likeness, with his craft and cruelty, that, with the assistance of the ten horns,[71] should plague the saints of the Christians, no less than the others had done those of the Jews. Now what shall be the issue thereof? Verse 26, his dominion with his adherents shall be taken away, and consumed:[72] and then shall it be given to the people of the Most High, as before.[73] Or they shall enjoy the kingdom of Christ in a peaceable manner; their officers being made peace, and their exactors righteousness.[74]

---

65 The Western and Eastern divisions of the Roman Empire.
66 The Greek phrase in Latin translation is *quod erat demonstrandum*, or QED—i.e., conclusive demonstration or proof of something.
67 Dan. 2:34–35.
68 Dan. 7:25.
69 Rev. 13:1–7; 17:3–16.
70 The Seleucid king, Antiochus IV Epiphanes (ca. 215–164 BC).
71 Dan. 7:24.
72 Dan. 7:26.
73 Dan. 7:25.
74 Isa. 60:17.

It is clearly evident from these and other places in that prophecy, that he who is the only potentate, will sooner or later shake all the monarchies of the earth, where he will have his name known, that all nations may be suited to the interest of his kingdom, which alone is to endure.

Confirmation from Other Old Testament Texts
Isaiah 60 in many places, indeed throughout, holds out the same.

Verse 12, The nation and kingdom that will not serve thee, shall be broken in pieces: that is, all the nations of the earth, not a known nation, but the blood of the saints of Christ is found in the skirts thereof. Now what shall be the issue when they are so broken:

Verses 17–18, "I will make thy officers peace, and thine exactors righteousness: violence shall no more be heard in thy land, wasting nor destruction within thy borders, but thou shalt call thy walls salvation, and thy gates praise."

See at your leisure to this purpose: Amos 9:11–15; Jeremiah 31:23–25; Isaiah 33:20–24.

I shall only add that punctual description which you have of this whole "matter" as Daniel calls it in the Revelation,[75] with respect unto its accomplishment. [In] chapter 17 the Roman harlot, having procured the ten kings or kingdoms, into which the last head of the Roman Empire sprouted, about the year 450, by the inundation of the northern nations,[76] to join with her, they together make war against the Lamb, verses 12–14.[77]

[Verse] 12. "The ten horns which thou sawest" (upon the last head of the great beast the Roman monarchy) "are ten kings, which have received no kingdom as yet,"[78] (to wit, when John saw the vision) "but receive power as kings one hour with the beast" (about four hundred years after this, the pope ascended to his sovereignty, and these Western nations growing into distinct dominions about the same time.)

[Verse] 13. "These have one mind" (that is, as to the business in hand, for otherwise they did and do vex one another with perpetual broils[79] and wars) "and shall give their power and strength unto the beast" (or swear to

---

75 Dan. 7:28.
76 The invasions of Germanic peoples from beyond the frontiers of the Roman Empire.
77 Rev. 17:12–14.
78 Lists of the ten kings varied but always included England and France, and usually Sweden. See Joseph Mede, *The Apostasy of the Latter Times* [. . .] (London, 1644), 82; Thomas Brightman, "A Revelation of the Apocalyps," in *The Workes of that Famous, Reverend, and Learn Divine, Mr. Tho: Brightman* [. . .] (London, 1644), 394–95; John Cotton, *An Exposition upon the Thirteenth Chapter of the Revelation* (London, 1656), 81.
79 I.e., disturbance or quarrel.

defend the rights of holy church, which is no other than Babylon, and act accordingly).

[Verse] 14. "These shall make war with the Lamb," (having sworn and undertaken the defense of holy church, or Babylon, they persecuted the poor heretics with fire and sword, that is the witnesses of the Lamb, and in them the Lamb himself, striving to keep his kingdom out of the world) "and the Lamb shall overcome them," (shaking and translating them into a new mold and frame) "for he is Lord of lords, and King of kings, and they that are with him" (whose help and endeavors he will use) "are called, and chosen, and faithful."

[Verse] 16. "The ten horns which thou sawest upon the beast," (being now shaken, changed and translated in mind, interest, and perhaps government) "these shall hate the whore, and shall make her desolate," (are instrumental in the hand of Christ for the ruin of that anti-Christian state which before they served) "and naked, and shall eat her flesh, and burn her with fire."

Hence, chapter 18:2, Babylon, and that whole anti-Christian state, which was supported upon their power and greatness, having lost its props, comes toppling down to the ground; "Babylon the great is fallen, is fallen": verse 2. And the saints take vengeance on the whore for all her former rage and cruelty. "Double unto her double according to her works," verse 6.

Verse 9. "And the kings of the earth" (being some of them shaken out of their dominion for refusing to close with the Lamb) "who have committed fornication, and lived deliciously with her" (learning and practicing false worship of her institution) "shall bewail her, and lament for her," (as having received succor from her, her monasteries and shavelings,[80] in their distress, whereunto indeed they were brought for her sake) "when they shall see the smoke of her burning,"[81] (beholding her darkness, stink and confusion, in her final desolation.)

Now all this shall be transacted with so much obscurity and darkness, Christ not openly appearing unto carnal eyes, that, though "many shall be purified, and made white, yet the wicked shall do wickedly, and none of the wicked shall understand, but the wise shall understand" (Dan. 12:10). There shall be no such demonstration of the presence of Christ, as to open the eyes of hardened men: but at length having suffered the poor, deceived wretches to drink of the cup prepared for them,[82] he appears himself gloriously, chapter 19:13, in a more eminent manner than ever before, to the total destruction

---

80 I.e., a term of contempt for tonsured clerics.
81 Rev. 18:9.
82 Rev. 18:6.

of the residue of opposers.⁸³ And that this will be the utmost close of that dispensation wherein now he walks, I no way doubt.

Four Reasons for the Doctrine

The assertion being cleared and proved, the reasons of it come next to be considered: and the first is, that—

To Bring Justice against the Persecutors of the Saints

Reason 1. It shall be done by the way of recompense and vengeance. It is the great day of the wrath of the Lamb (Rev. 6:17): "The land shall be soaked with blood, and the dust made fat with fatness. For it is the day of the Lord's vengeance, and the year of recompense for the controversy of Zion" (Isa. 34:7–8). The day of vengeance is in his heart, when the year of his redeemed is come (Isa. 63:4).⁸⁴

The kings of the earth have given their power to Antichrist, endeavoring to the utmost to keep the kingdom of Christ out of the world. What, I pray, has been their main business for seven hundred years and upward, even almost ever since the man of sin was enthroned?⁸⁵ How have they earned the titles, Eldest Son of the Church, The Catholic and Most Christian King,⁸⁶ Defender of the Faith,⁸⁷ and the like?⁸⁸ Has it not been by the blood of saints? Are there not in every one of these kingdoms, the slain, and the banished ones of Christ to answer for? In particular;

Has not the blood of the saints of Jesus, eclipsed by Antichrist and his adherents, Wickliffites⁸⁹ and Lollards,⁹⁰ cried from the ground for vengeance upon the English "heaven and earth" for a long season?⁹¹ Did not their bodies lie in the

---

83 Rev. 19:13.
84 In the margin: Psal. 2:4, 5, Psal. 137:8–9; Isa. 47:1–3, Isa. 49:26; Ier. 50:33–34, Chap. 51:24–25, 34–35; Zech. 12:2–4, Chap. 14:12; Rev. 18:6 etc.—Owen.
85 In other words, Owen is identifying the tenth century as the time when the Roman Catholic Church began to oppose and persecute the true church.
86 These titles were initially granted by the bishop of Rome to the Merovingian kings who ruled the Franks, and the honors were frequently accorded to the French kings indicating the special relationship between the French monarchy and the Papacy.
87 *Defensor Fidei* was a title granted to King Henry VIII by Pope Leo X in 1521.
88 Roger L'Estrange included this sentence in his section of what Dissenters had said about the nature of civil government. See his *The Dissenters Sayings* [. . .] (London, 1681), 16.
89 I.e., followers of John Wycliffe (ca. 1328–1384) or his doctrines. Wycliffe was posthumously pronounced a heretic by the Council of Constance in 1415.
90 I.e., a name of contempt given to followers of Wycliffe or those who held opinions similar to his. By the end of the fourteenth century, they had spread across England.
91 In the margin: Acts & Mon: Histor. Pap.—Owen. This is a reference to John Foxe (ca.1516–1587) and his Protestant martyrology, *Acts and Monuments* (1562, 1570, 1576, 1583), which contained a history of the papacy.

streets of France, under the names of Waldenses, Albigenses,[92] and poor men of Lyons?[93] Has not Germany, and the annexed territories, her Huss and Hussites,[94] Hierome[95] and Subutraquians,[96] to answer for? Is not Spain's inquisition enough to ruin a world, much more a kingdom?[97] Have not all these, and all the kingdoms round about, washed their hands and garments in the blood of thousands of Protestants? And do not the kings of all these nations as yet stand up in the room of their progenitors with the same implacable enmity to the power of the gospel? Show me seven kings that ever yet labored sincerely to enhance the kingdom of the Lord Jesus, and I dare boldly say, "It is not yet agreed who was the eighth."[98] And is there not a cry for all this, "How long, Lord, holy and true, doest thou not avenge our blood on them that live on the earth?" (Rev. 6:10). Does not Zion cry, "The violence done to me and my flesh be upon Babylon," and, "My blood upon those heavens of the nations?"[99] And will not the Lord avenge his elect, that cry unto him day and night,[100] will he not do it speedily? Will he not call the fowls of heaven to eat the flesh of kings, and captains, and great men of the earth? (Rev. 19:18). Will he not make these heavens like the wood of the vine, not a pin to be taken off them to hang a garment on,[101] in his whole tabernacle?

92 Also known as the Cathars, "the pure ones," a medieval religious movement in Provence and Languedoc, with a particular center in the French town of Albi. The movement was declared heretical, and in 1208 Pope Innocent III launched the Albigensian Crusade (1209–1229), in which it was violently suppressed. In 1233, Pope Gregory IX commissioned the Dominican Inquisition to act against the heresy. See Mark Gregory Pegg, *A Most Holy War: The Albigensian Crusade and the Battle for Christendom* (Oxford: Oxford University Press, 2009).

93 The Waldensians originated in the late twelfth century as the *Pauperes* (Poor Men), who followed Pierre Vaudès (often known as Peter Waldo), a rich merchant from Lyons who embraced a life of poverty. They were found in parts of southern France, Piedmont, and Germany. The Waldensians were declared heretical by Pope Lucius III in 1184 and were subject to episodes of violent persecution. Euan Cameron, "Medieval Heretics as Protestant Martyrs," in *Martyrs and Martyrologies: Papers Read at the 1992 Summer Meeting and the 1993 Winter Meeting of the Ecclesiastical History Society*, ed. Diana Wood (Oxford: Blackwell, 1993), 185–207.

94 Jan Hus (ca. 1372–1415), the Czech theologian and preacher who was condemned to be burned at the stake by the Council of Constance.

95 Jerome of Prague (1379–1416) was a follower of Hus who was also burned for heresy.

96 I.e., those followers of Hus who maintained that the cup as well as the bread should be administered to the laity—i.e., communion should be "in both kinds."

97 The Spanish Inquisition, reorganized 1478–1483, when Pope Sixtus IV (who became pope in 1471) granted Ferdinand and Isabella authority to establish a state-run inquisition that became notorious for its severity, especially in the sixteenth century. It was extended into the Hapsburg Netherlands, and Philip II's enforcement of it was one of the factors that led to his bankruptcy.

98 In the text: *Octavus quis fuerit, nondum constat.*—Owen.

99 See Jer. 51:35.

100 Luke 18:7.

101 Ezek. 15:2–3.

The time shall come, wherein the earth shall disclose her slain, and not the simplest heretic as they were counted, shall have his blood unrevenged: neither shall any atonement be made for this blood, or expiation be allowed, while a toe of the image,[102] or a bone of the beast is left unbroken.[103]

To Establish Government That Will Advance the Kingdom of Christ

Reason 2. That by his own wisdom he may frame such a power, as may best conduce to the carrying on of his own kingdom among the sons of men.[104]

He has promised his church, that he will give unto it, holy priests and Levites (Isa. 66:20–21), which shall serve at the great feast of tabernacles (Zech. 14:16). A sufficient demonstration that he will dwell still in his churches by his ordinances, whatsoever some conceive; so also, that he will make her civil "officers peace, and her exactors righteousness" (Isa. 60:17–18):[105] they shall be so established, that the nations, as nations, may serve it; and the kingdoms of the world shall become the kingdoms of our Lord (Rev. 11:15).

For the present, the government of the nations (as many of them as are concerned therein), is purely framed for the interest of Antichrist. No kind of government in Europe, or line of governors so ancient, but that the beast is as old as they, and had a great influence into their constitution or establishment, to provide that it might be for his own interest.

I believe it will be found a difficult task, to name any of the kingdoms of Europe (excepting only that remotest northward) in the setting up, and establishment whereof, either as to persons or government, the pope has not expressly bargained for his own interest, and provided, that should have the chiefest place in all the oaths and bonds that were between princes and people.

Bellarmine, to prove that the pope had a temporal power indirectly over all kings and nations (if he mean by indirectly, gotten by indirect means, it is actually true as to too many of them), gives sundry instances,[106] in most of the most eminent nations in Europe, how he has actually exercised such a power for his own interest.[107]

---

102 Dan. 2:42.
103 Rev. 17:16.
104 In the margin: Psal. 2:9–12; Rev. 17:14; Matt. 28:20; 1 Cor. 11:26; Ephes. 4:11–13; 1 Tim. 6:13–14.—Owen.
105 In the margin: Ps. 45:16; Isa. 49:7, 23.—Owen.
106 In the margin: Revel. 18:3, Οἱ βασιλεῖς τῆς γῆς μετ' αὐτῆς ἐπόρνευσαν.—Owen. This is translated, "And the kings of the earth have committed fornication with her" (KJV).
107 In the margin: Bell. de Rom. Pon., li. 5. cap. 8.—Owen. This is a reference to Robert Bellarmine's *De controversiis Christianae fidei* (On the controversies of the Christian faith) and the

There have been two most famous and remarkable changes of the government of these nations, and into both of them what an influence the pope had, is easily discernible.

The first was between the years 4 and 500 after Christ,[108] when the Roman Empire of the West, that which withheld the man of sin from acting his part to the life,[109] was shivered[110] to pieces by many barbarous nations: who settling themselves in the fruitful soils of Europe,[111] began to plant their "heavens," and lay the foundations of their "earth," growing up into civil states: for the most part appointing them to be their kings in peace, who had been their leaders in war.[112]

This furious inundation settled the Franks in Gaul,[113] the Saxons in England,[114] the West Goths in Spain, the East Goths and Longobards into Italy,[115] and set up the Allemanns in Germany;[116] from some whereof though for divers years the papal world was exceedingly tormented, and Rome itself sacked,[117] yet in the close and making up of their governments, their manners and religion, they all submitted to the usurpation of the man of sin, so that in all their windings up there was a salve for him and his authority.[118]

The second great alteration took up a long space, and was in action about three hundred years,[119] reckoning it from the translation of the

---

volume dealing with *De Romano pontifice* (*On the Roman Pontiff*), book 5 of which deals with the temporal power of the pope, with chapter 8 providing examples of how the pope claims to exercise indirect power. The examples offered by Bellarmine that are most relevant to Owen's subsequent argument include the following: Pope Zachary (741–752) deposing Childeric III (ca. 717–775) and replacing him with Pepin the Short (714–768), the father of Charlemagne; Pope Leo III (795–816) translating the empire from the Greeks to the Germans with Leo crowning Charlemagne as emperor on Christmas Day 800. For the Latin text, see Roberti Bellarmini, *Opera Omnia*, 12 vols. (Paris: Vives, 1870–1874), 2:160–62.

108 A reference to the events of the fifth century.
109 In the margin: 2 Thes. 2:6–7.—Owen.
110 I.e., split into fragments.
111 Primarily the Germanic peoples who settled in territory of the former Western Roman Empire.
112 In the margin: Dan. 2:41.—Owen.
113 The Franks conquered Gaul in the sixth century.
114 The Saxons conquered parts of southern Britain in the fifth and sixth centuries.
115 The Goths founded kingdoms in Italy, France, and Spain in the fourth and fifth centuries.
116 The Alemanni were a confederation of German peoples who occupied southwest Germany in the third to fifth centuries.
117 Rome was sacked in the early fifth century by the Visigoths.
118 In the margin: Οὗτοι μίαν γνώμην ἔχουσι, καὶ τὴν δύναμιν καὶ τὴν ἐξουσίαν ἑαυτῶν τῷ θηρίῳ διαδιδώσουσιν, Rev. 17:13.—Owen. This is translated, "These have one mind, and shall give their power and strength unto the beast" (KJV).
119 The period from the middle of the eighth century to the middle of the eleventh century.

French crown from Childeric the fourth[120] unto Pepin[121] and his son Charles,[122] by papal authority,[123] unto the conquest of England by the Normans,[124] in which space the line of Charles in France was again by the same authority and the power of Hugh Capet cut off:[125] no state in Europe, the choice patrimony of the beast, that did not receive a signal alteration, in this space, nor was there any alteration, but that the pope had a hand in every one of them, and either by pretended collations of right, to pacify the consciences of bloodthirsty potentates, in the undertaking and pursuing their unjust conquests, or foolish mitered confirmations of sword purchases, he got them all framed to his own end and purpose, which was to bring all these nations into subjection to his Babylonish usurpations, which their kings finding no way inconsistent with their own designs did willingly promote, laboring to enforce all consciences into subjection to the Roman see.

Hence it is, as I observed before,[126] that such an interposition was made of the rights of holy church, that is Babylon the mother of fornications,[127] in all the ties, oaths, and bonds between princes and people. And for the advancement of the righteous judgments of God, that the sons of men may learn to fear and tremble before him, it may be observed, that that which does, and shall stick upon potentates to their ruin, is not so much their own or any other interest, as the very dregs of this papal anti-Christian interest,

---

120 Childeric III (ca. 717–754) was the last of the Merovingian kings who had ruled the Franks for over two hundred fifty years. In 751, Pope Zachary sanctioned the usurpation of the throne by Pepin the Short (714–768), which led the way to the creation of the Carolingian dynasty.

121 Pepin the Short, king of the Franks, was anointed *patricius Romanorum* (protector of the Romans) by Pope Stephen II in 754. Pepin had led an army of Franks into Italy to assist the cause of the papacy against its old enemy the Germanic Lombards, and on the basis of the Donation of Constantine (now known to be a forgery), Pepin granted a large portion of central Italy to the papacy.

122 Charlemagne (742–814).

123 Charlemagne came to power in 768 and donated even more lands to the pope, thus strengthening the relationship between the Frankish kings and the papacy. In 800, Pope Leo III crowned Charlemagne *imperator Romanorum* (Holy Roman emperor).

124 Pope Alexander II (1061–1073) excommunicated King Harold, the last Anglo-Saxon king of England, and granted his throne to William, Duke of Normandy, who invaded under a papal banner in 1066. John Warren, in his fast sermon that day, concurred as to the significance of this moment as he recalled the translation of government which took place in England "five or six hundred yeers" ago. See John Warren, *The Potent Potter* (London, 1649), 13.

125 Hugh Capet (ca. 938–996) succeeded the last Carolingian king and founded the Capetian line of Frankish kings in 987.

126 In the margin: Rev. 13:15–16.—Owen.

127 Rev. 17:6.

thrust into their oaths and obligations, for no end in the world, but to keep the Lord Jesus out of his throne.[128]

This is a second reason why the Lord Jesus by his mighty power at the bringing in of his immovable kingdom, "will shake the heavens and the earth of the nations"; even because in their present constitution they are directly framed to the interest of Antichrist, which by notable advantages at their first molding, and continued insinuations ever since, has so riveted itself into the very fundamentals of them, that no digging or mining, but an earthquake, will cast up the foundation stones thereof.[129] The Lord Jesus then, having promised the service of the nations to his church, will so far open their whole frame to the roots, as to pluck out all the cursed seeds of the mystery of iniquity,[130] which by the craft of Satan and exigencies of state, or methods of advancing the pride and power of some sons of blood, have been sown among them.

To Fulfill God's Promise for an Ingathering of the Jews

Reason 3. Because as is their interest, so is their acting. The present power of the nations stands in direct opposition to the bringing in of the kingdom of Christ. Two things there are which confessedly are incumbent on him in this day of his advancement.

[1] The bringing home of his ancient people,[131] to be onefold with the fullness of the Gentiles;[132] raising up the tabernacle of David, and building it as in days of old:[133] in the accomplishment of innumerable promises, and in answer to millions of prayers, put up at the throne of grace, for this very glory in all generations. Now there be two main hinderances of this work that must be removed: the first whereof is,

{1} Real, the great river Euphrates, the strength and fullness of whose streams does yet rage so high, that there is no passage for the kings of the

---

128 In the margin: Πέμψει αὐτοῖς ὁ Θεὸς ἐνέργειαν πλάνης, 2 Thes. 2:11.—Owen. This is translated, "God shall send them strong delusion" (KJV).

129 In the margin: *Roma sedes Petri, quae Pastoralis honoris Facta caput mundo, quidquid non possidet armis Religione tenet.* Prosp. de Ingrat.—Owen. "Rome, the See of Peter. This has become the chief pastoral office of the whole world; and what she does not hold by force of arms she rules over by her religious authority." For the Latin text and English translation, see Prosper of Aquitaine, *Carmen de Ingratis: A Translation with an Introduction and Commentary*, trans Charles Huegelmeyer, Patristic Studies 95 (Washington, DC: Catholic University of America Press, 1962), 46–47.

130 2 Thess. 2:7.

131 A reference to the calling and conversion of the Jews.

132 In the margin: Joh. 10:16; Isa. 37:31.—Owen.

133 In the margin: Jer. 30:9; Ezek. 34:23; Chap. 37:24–25; Hos. 3:5; Amos 9:11.—Owen.

East to come over.¹³⁴ Wherefore this must be dried up, as other waters were for their forefathers in the days of old (Rev. 16:12).¹³⁵ Doubtless this is spoken in allusion to Abraham's coming over that river into Canaan when the church of God in his family was there to be erected; whence he was called the Hebrew, that is, the passenger, to wit, over that river (Gen. 14:13), and then it may well enough denote the Turkish power,¹³⁶ which proud as it is at this day, possessing in peace all those regions of the East, yet God can quickly make it wither, and be dried up: or the deliverance of the Jews from Babylon, when it was taken and destroyed by the drying up of the streams of that river, and so the yoke of her tyranny broken from the church's neck,¹³⁷ and so it can be no other but the power of the Romish Babylon supported by the kings of the nations, which must therefore be shaken and dried up.¹³⁸

{2} Moral: or the idolatry of the Gentile worshipers.¹³⁹ The Jews stick hard as yet at this, that God should abolish any kind of worship, which himself had once instituted: but that he should ever accept any false worship, which he had once strictly prohibited, and nowhere to this day appointed, to this they will never be reconciled.¹⁴⁰ Now such is all the invented idolatrous worship which the kings of the earth have sucked in from the cup of fornication

---

134 The "kings of the East" was taken as a reference to the Jews. See Cotton, *The Powring Out of the Seven Vials* (London, 1642), 93.
135 In the margin: Exod. 14:21; Josh. 3:15–16; Hab. 3:8.—Owen.
136 A reference to the Ottoman Empire, which, according to Owen's scheme, would fall prior to the restoration of Israel.
137 In the margin: Ier. 51:31–32.
138 Like John Cotton, Owen believed that the drying up of the Euphrates primarily involved the withering of the Roman Catholic Church since he viewed its idolatry as the most significant obstacle to Jewish conversion. See Cotton, on the "Sixth Vial," in *Powring Out*, 22–24.
139 In the margin: Revel. 11:2.—Owen.
140 Early modern Jews invoked the rhetoric of "idolatry" and "superstition" against Christianity, even styling some Christian nations as "lands of idolatry." Owen is arguing that the idolatrous worship of professing Christian nations discredited the gospel in the eyes of many Jews. This point is captured well by Thomas Calvert (1606–1679) in his translation of the testimony of "Samuel of Morocco," a late-medieval Jew who converted to Christianity, *The Blessed Jew of Marocco, or, A Blackmoor Made White: Being a Demonstration of the True Messias out of the Law and Prophets* (London, 1648), 45–46: "The Idolatry of some corrupt Christians, as they of the Romish faith, doth much keep them back, who hate all kinds of Idolatry." Edward Spencer wrote, "For wee hate Idolatry as much as you." Spencer, *A Brief Epistle to the Learned Manasseh Ben Israel* (London, 1650), 2. All that being said, even though the Reformed churches had removed external forms of idolatry, those (like the Jews in Amsterdam) who were able to compare the differences between Protestants and Roman Catholics claimed that the Reformed had failed to remove the idolatrous foundation of Christianity in the doctrines of the Holy Trinity and the incarnation. See Miriam Bodian, *Hebrews of the Portuguese Nation: Conversos and Community in Early Modern Amsterdam* (Indianapolis: Indiana University Press, 1997), 68–73.

held out to them in the hand, and by the authority of the Roman whore; this still they cleave close unto, and will not hearken to the angel preaching "the everlasting gospel," that men should "worship him who made the heavens, and the earth, and the sea, and the fountains of waters" (Rev. 14:6–7), that is, the God of heaven in Jesus Christ, in opposition to all their iconolatry,[141] artolatry,[142] hagiolatry,[143] staurolatry,[144] and mass abominations. This then must also be removed; and because, as you saw before, it is so riveted and cemented into and with all the orbs of the nations, heaven and earth, they must be shaken, and brought εἰς μετάθεσιν,[145] before it can be effected.

[2] The second thing he has to accomplish, is the tremendous, total destruction of Babylon, the man of sin,[146] and all his adherents that are not obedient to the heavenly call (Rev. 18:4).[147] Now as Samson, intending the destruction of the princes, lords, and residue of the Philistines, who were gathered together in their idol temple, effected it by pulling away the pillars whereby the building was supported; whereupon the whole frame toppled to the ground:[148] so the Lord, intending the ruin of that mighty power, whose top seems to reach to heaven,[149] will do it by pulling away the pillars and supporters of it, after which it cannot stand one moment. Now what are the pillars of that fatal building? Are they not the powers of the world as presently stated and framed? Pull them away, and, alas, what is Antichrist? It is the glory of the kings put upon her, that makes men's eyes so dazzle on the Roman harlot. Otherwise she is but like the Egyptian deities, whose silly worshipers through many glorious portals and frontispieces,[150] were led to adore the image of an ugly ape.[151]

---

141 I.e., the worship of images or icons.
142 I.e., the adoration of the host consecrated in the Eucharist.
143 I.e., the worship of saints.
144 I.e., the worship of the cross or crucifix.
145 Gk. "to removal or translation."
146 2 Thess. 2:3.
147 In the margin: Psal. 137:8, 9; Isa. 47:7–9; Ier. 51:25–26; Reval. 17:1–2; Zach. 2:7; Ier. 51:6.—Owen.
148 In the margin: Iudg. 16:28–29.—Owen. As Crawford Gribben notes, Samson became "increasingly popular among radical voices in and after the revolutionary decade, most famously in Milton's *Samson Agonistes* (1671)." Crawford Gribben, *John Owen and English Puritanism: Experiences of Defeat* (New York: Oxford University Press, 2016), 107. Elizabeth Harvey comments on how "Many revolutionaries cited Samson as the illustrious example of one who destroyed the idolaters in his time." See Elizabeth D. Harvey, "Samson Agonistes and Milton's Sensible Ethics," in *The Oxford Handbook of Milton*, ed. Nicholas McDowell and Nigel Smith (Oxford: Oxford University Press, 2009), 647.
149 Gen. 11:4.
150 I.e., an elaborate doorway.
151 The second-century satirist Lucian of Samosata mocked Egyptian temples decorated with gold even though the "god" found inside was an animal like an ape. Lucian, *Jupiter Tragoedus* (*Zeus*

Add hereunto, that in this mighty work, the Lord Jesus Christ will make use of the power of the nations, the horns of them, that is, their strength (Rev. 17:16), they must hate the whore, and make her desolate and naked, and eat her flesh, and burn her with fire: now whether this can be accomplished or no, in their present posture, is easily discernible.[152] Does not the papal interest lie at the bottom of all or the most ruling lines of Christendom? Can that be ejected without unbottoming their own dominion? Do they not use the efficacy of the Roman jurisdiction to balance the powers of their adversaries abroad, and to awe their subjects at home? Has he not a considerable strength in every one of their own bosoms? Are not the locusts of their religious orders,[153] all sworn slaves to the pope, for number sufficient to make an army to fight the greatest emperor in the world? Are not most potentates tied by oath, or other compact, to maintain either the whole, or some part of the old tower,[154] under the name of rites of holy church, prelates, and the like? And can any expect that such as these, should take up the despised quarrel of the saints, against that flourishing queen? Doubtless no such fruit will grow on these trees before they are thoroughly shaken.

To Stir Up the Saints to Lay Hold of the Kingdom of Christ

Reason 4. That his own people seeing all earthly things shaken, and removing, may be raised up to the laying hold of that durable kingdom that shall not be removed.[155] All carnal interests will doubtless be shaken with that of Babylon. Many of God's people are not yet weaned from the things that are seen:[156] no sooner is one carnal form shaken out, but they are ready to cleave to another: yea to warm themselves in the feathered nests of unclean birds.[157] All fleshly

---

Rants) 42. For the text, see Lucian, *Zeus Rants*, in *The Downward Journey or The Tyrant. Zeus Catechized. Zeus Rants. The Dream or The Cock. Prometheus. Icaromenippus or The Sky-Man. Timon or The Misanthrope. Charon or The Inspectors. Philosophies for Sale*, trans. A. M. Harmon, Loeb Classical Library 54 (Cambridge, MA: Harvard University Press, 1915), 155.

152 In the margin: *Petra dedit Petro, Petrus diadema Rudolfo.*—Owen. "The Rock gave the crown to Peter and Peter gives it to Rudolf." This was the alleged inscription on a crown that it was said Pope Gregory VII gave to Duke Rudolf of Swabia. See H. E. J. Cowdrey, *Pope Gregory VII, 1073–1085* (Oxford: Clarendon, 1998), 171.

153 Rev. 9:7–11.

154 See Gen. 11:4.

155 In the margin: Heb. 12:28.—Owen.

156 In the margin: 2 Cor. 4:18.—Owen.

157 Lev. 11:13–19; Deut. 14:11–18. In Revelation, fallen Babylon becomes "a cage of every unclean and hateful bird" (Rev. 18:2). For a discussion of how his may be a reference to the political ideas of classical republicanism and Renaissance humanism, see Martyn C. Cowan, *John Owen and the Civil War Apocalypse: Preaching, Prophecy, and Politics* (London: Routledge, 2017), 109.

dominion within doors, and all civil dominion that opposes without doors, shall be shaken. Now these things are so glued also to men's earthly possessions, the talons of the birds of prey, having firmly seized on them, that they also must be shaken with them. And therefore from them also will he have us to be loosed (2 Pet. 3:12–13).

And these are some of the reasons of the position laid down, which is so bottomed, so proved, as you have heard: of the speedy accomplishment of all this I no way doubt. "I believe, and therefore I have spoken."[158] Whether I shall see any further perfection of this work while I am here below, I am no way solicitous; being assured that if I fail of it here, I shall through the grace of him who loved us, and gave himself for us,[159] meet with the treasures of it otherwhere.

Six Uses of the Doctrine

Come we to the uses.

Be Acquainted With the Special Work That God Is Doing in These Days in Order to Be Able to Follow Hard After God

Use 1. The rise of our first use I shall take from that of the prophet: "Who is wise, and he shall understand these things? Prudent, and he shall know them? For the ways of the Lord are right, and the just shall walk in them: but the transgressors shall fall therein" (Hos. 14:9). Labor for this heavenly wisdom and prudence, that we may know these things, and be acquainted with the mind and will of God, in the season and generation wherein we live. His way is not so in the dark, nor his footsteps in the deep,[160] but that we may perceive what he is about.

Our Savior gives it in as a sure testimony of the Pharisees' hypocrisy, notwithstanding all their pretenses, and possession of Moses' chair,[161] that they were wise in earthly things, and had drawn out experiences by long observation, of what was like to come to pass as to the weather, by considering the ordinary signs of the alterations thereof; but notwithstanding that mighty effectual concurrence of signs in heaven and earth, with the accomplishment of prophecies, all pointing to the instant establishment of the kingdom of God in the coming of the Messiah, not discerning them at all, they come and cry, "If thou be the Christ, give us a sign"; when without satisfying their sinful curiosity, heaven and earth were full of signs round about them (Luke 12:54–56).

---

158 2 Cor. 4:13.
159 Eph. 5:2.
160 See Ps. 77:19.
161 Matt. 23:2.

Men who will not receive God's signs, suppose they should be wonderful proficients in credulity, might they have signs of their own fancying. The rich glutton thought, that if his way of teaching might have been set up, by men rising from the dead, there would have been a world of converts, more than were made by preaching the word of God.[162] Men suppose, that if God from heaven should give in some discriminating prodigy, oh how abundantly should they be satisfied: the truth is, the same lust and corruption that makes them disbelieve God's signs, moves them to look after signs of their own.

For this very thing then, were the Pharisees branded as hypocrites,[163] that having wisdom in natural things, to calculate and prognosticate from necessary signs, yet in the works of the Lord, though the signs which in his wisdom he was pleased to give, were plentiful round about them, they must have some of their own choosing. I pray God none such be found in our day.

It is said of the men of Issachar, that they "had understanding of the times to know what Israel ought to do" (1 Chron. 12:32). Israel is in the dark, and knows not what to do, if the times and seasons be not discovered to them.[164] If the mind and will of the Lord in their generation, be not made out unto a people, it will be their ruin.

Hence it is, that the Lord encourages us to make inquiry after these things, to find out the seasons wherein he will do any great work for his people, knowing that without this, we shall be altogether useless in the generation wherein we live,

"Ask me of things to come concerning my sons, and concerning the work of my hands command you me" (Isa. 45:11).[165]

And what is this that the Lord will have his people to inquire of him about? Even the great work of the ruin of Babylon, and restoration of his church, which yet was not to be accomplished for two hundred forty years. And this he tells you plainly in the following verses.

"I have raised him up" (Cyrus) "in righteousness, and I will direct all his ways, he shall build my cities, and he shall let go my captives, not for price nor reward, saith the Lord of hosts," verse 13.[166]

---

162 In the margin: "Ἔχουσι Μωσέα καὶ τοὺς προφήτας. Οὐχὶ πάτερ Ἀζραάμ· ἀλλ' ἐάν τις ἀπὸ νεκρῶν πορευθῇ, Luk. 16:29–30.—Owen. This quotation from the Greek New Testament reads, "They have Moses and the prophets, [. . .] Nay, father Abraham, but if one went unto them from the dead" (KJV).

163 Luke 12:56.

164 In the margin: Esther 1:13.—Owen.

165 In the original, "things to come" and "command" are set in all caps for emphasis.

166 Isa. 45:13.

The Lord is earnest with his people to inquire into the season of the accomplishment of his great intendments for the good of his church, when as yet they are afar off, how much more when they are nigh at hand, even at the doors. "Whoso is wise, and will observe these things, they shall understand the loving-kindness of the Lord" (Ps. 107 ult.).[167]

The prophet tells you (Dan. 9:2) that this was his great study, and at length he understood by books, the approach of the time, wherein God would deliver his church from Babylonish captivity and pollution: now this discovery has two or three notable products.

(1) It puts him upon earnest supplications for the accomplishment of their promised deliverance in the appointed season. Wide from that atheistical frame of spirit, which would have a predetermination of events and successes, to eradicate all care and endeavor to serve that providence, which will produce their accomplishment. A discovery of the approach of any promised, and before-fixed work of God, should settle our minds to the utmost endeavor of helping the decree to bring forth.

(2) He finds great acceptation in this his address to the Lord by supplications, for the establishing of that work which he had discovered was nigh at hand: for,

[1] An answer is returned him fully to his whole desire in the midst of his supplications: verse 21. "Whiles I was praying, the man Gabriel came," etc.[168]

[2] The work which he had discovered to be approaching, was instantly hastened and gone in hand withal: verse 23. "At the beginning of thy supplications the commandment came forth."[169] Oh that God would stir up his saints, in the spirit of Daniel, to consider and understand by books, the time that he has appointed for the deliverance of his people, that fixing their supplications for the speeding thereof, the commandment may come forth for its full accomplishment.

[3] Having attained this, the Lord gives him fresh discoveries, new light of the time for the birth of the Messiah, which he thought not of, prayed not for: "Seventy weeks are determined," etc., [verse] 24.[170] So delighted is the Lord

---

167 Ps. 107:43. The *Declaration of the English Army Now in Scotland* [. . .] (London, 1650), written when Owen was with the troops, stated that the end of this psalm explains how "the Lord speaks to his people by his Providence, as well as by his Word; and he is angry with his people that do not take notice thereof, and promiseth blessing to those that do." See, *Declaration of the Army*, sig. B3r.
168 Dan. 9:21.
169 Dan. 9:23.
170 Dan. 9:24.

with his people's diligent inquiry into his ways, and walkings toward them, that thereupon he appears unto them, in the revelation of his mind, beyond all that they did expect or desire.

Four Sins That Would Hinder Gaining Such Wise Understanding

Now all this have I spoken to stir you up unto that, whereunto at the entrance of this use, you were exhorted: that you would labor for that spiritual wisdom and prudence, which may acquaint your hearts, at least in some measure, with the mind and will of God, concerning his work in the generation wherein you live. And farther to provoke you hereunto, know that you cannot but wander, as in many other, so especially in four sinful things:

1. Sinful cares.
2. Sinful fears.
3. Sinful follies.
4. Sinful negligence.

1st. Sinful cares. Anxious and dubious thoughts about such things as, perhaps the Lord intends utterly to destroy, or at least render useless. Had it not been the greatest folly in the world, for Noah and his sons, when the flood was approaching to sweep away the creatures from the face of the earth, to have been solicitous about flocks and herds, that were speedily to be destroyed.[171] Many men's thoughts, at this day do even devour them, about such things, as if they knew the season, would be contemptible unto them. Would you labor for honor, if you knew that God at this time, were laboring to lay all the "honour of the earth in the dust?"[172] Could you set your heart upon the increase of riches, wert you acquainted, that God intends instantly to make "silver as stones, and cedars as sycamores,"[173] though not for plenty, yet for value? Would men be so exceedingly solicitous about this or that form of religion, this or that power to suppress such or such a persuasion, if they knew that the Lord would suddenly fill the earth with his knowledge, "as the waters cover the sea"?[174] Should our spirits sink for fear of this or that persecutor or oppressor, were it discovered unto us that in a short time nothing shall "hurt or destroy" in

---

171 In the margin: Gen. 6:13.—Owen.
172 In the margin: Isa. 23:9.—Owen.
173 In the margin: 1 Kin. 10:27.—Owen.
174 In the margin: Hab. 2:14.—Owen. Here Owen dismisses the arguments that were being made for a uniform liturgy and polity as nothing more than "sinful cares."

the whole mountain of the Lord?[175] Should we tremble at the force and power of this or that growing monarchy,[176] giving its power to the beast, had God revealed unto us, that he is going to shake it until it be translated? Certain it is, that the root of all the sinful cares which sometimes are ready to devour the hearts of God's people, is this unacquaintedness with the work and mind of the Lord.

2nd. Sinful fears; our Savior having told his disciples of wars, tumults, seditions, famines, earthquakes, etc., which were to come upon the earth, bids them, when they see these things, to "lift up their heads for joy."[177] But how should this be? Rejoice in the midst of so many evils and troubles, in the most whereof they were to have a Benjamin's mess, a double portion![178] "Yea," says our Savior, "Rejoice, for I have told you before, that then it is that your deliverance and redemption draws nigh.[179] It is for them to shake and tremble, who are in the dark, who know not what the Lord is doing. They may be at their wits' end, who know no other end of these things: but for you who know the mind of the Lord, what he intends and will effect by these things, cast off all sinful fears, and rejoice in him who comes."

Among us in these days new troubles arise, wars, and rumors of wars, appearances of famine, invasions, conspiracies, revolts, treacheries, sword, blood, oh how do men's faces wax pale, and their hearts die within them? Sometimes with David they could fly to the Philistines,[180] and wind up their interest with them whom God will destroy: every new appearance of danger shuffles them off from all their comforts, all their confidence. Hence poor souls are put upon doubling and shifting in the ways of God, in such a frame as God exceedingly abhors. They know not why any mercy is given, nor to what end, and therefore are afraid to own it, lest some sudden alteration should follow, and make it too hot for them to hold it: and all this because they know not the mind of the Lord, nor the judgment of their God; were they

---

175 In the margin: Isa. 65:25.—Owen.
176 Perhaps Owen may have had in mind William II (1626–1650), Prince of Orange, Stadtholer of the United Provinces, who was married to Princess Mary (1631–1660), daughter of the late Charles I and sister of Charles II. It was feared that William was seeking to become the absolute monarch of the United Provinces, and it looked as if he might seek to intervene on behalf of his brother-in-law, Charles II. This did not come to pass because William II died suddenly of smallpox in 1650. Steven C. A. Pincus, *Protestantism and Patriotism: Ideologies and the Making of English Foreign Policy, 1650–1668* (Cambridge: Cambridge University Press, 1996), 15–16.
177 Luke 21:28a.
178 Gen. 43:34.
179 Luke 21:28b.
180 1 Sam. 27:1–2.

but acquainted with it, so far as it is evidently revealed, they would quickly see all things working together to the appointed end.

3rd. Sinful follies. Toil and labor in vain is, of all follies the greatest folly, like the Jews under Julian, building of their temple in the day, God casting it to the ground in the night.[181] When a man labors, toils, wearies and spends himself, for the accomplishing of that which shall never come to pass, and that, which if he would but inquire, he might know shall never come to pass, he cannot well want the livery of a brutish man. How many poor creatures, that think themselves wiser than those of Charchan, and Dedan, and all the children of the East,[182] do spend and consume their days and time in such ways as this, laboring night and day to set up what God will pull down, and what he has said shall fall. "Come on, let us deal wisely," says Pharaoh to his Egyptians (Ex. 1:10), to root out and destroy these Israelites: poor fool! Is there any wisdom or counsel against the Most High? I could give instances plenty in these days of men laboring in the dark, not knowing what they are doing, endeavoring with all their strength to accomplish that whereof the Lord has said, "It shall not prosper":[183] and all because they discern not the season.

4th. Sinful negligence. You are no way able to do the work of God in your generation. It is the commendation of many saints of God, that they were "upright, and served the will of God in their generation."[184] Besides the general duties of the covenant, incumbent on all the saints at all seasons, there are special works of providence which, in sundry generations the Lord effects, concerning which, he expects his people should know his mind, and serve him in them. Now, can a servant do his master's work, if he know not his will? The Lord requires that, in the great things which he has to accomplish in this generation, all his should close with him. What is the reason that some stand in the marketplace idle all the day?[185] Some work for a season,

---

181 Under the Roman emperor Flavius Claudius Julianus (331–363), better known as Julian "the Apostate," there was an effort to rebuild the temple in Jerusalem in 363. The program was unsuccessful because of fire, earthquake, and Julian's death later that year. See G. W. Bowersock, *Julian the Apostate* (Cambridge, MA: Harvard University Press, 1978), 89–90.
182 The children of the East (1 Kings 4:30) were proverbial for their wisdom. Goold took the editorial decision to gloss "Charchan" as "Teman" to stand alongside the inhabitants of Dedan (Jer. 49:7–8). See John Owen, *The Works of John Owen*, ed. William H. Goold, 24 vols. (Edinburgh: Johnstone and Hunter, 1850–1855), 8:273. Charchan, or in Chinese *Qiemo*, was an ancient city kingdom located on the Southern Silk Route.
183 Dan. 11:27.
184 Acts 13:36.
185 Matt. 20:3.

and then give over, they know not how to go a step farther, but after a day, a week, a month, or year, are at a stand? Worse than all this, some counterwork the Lord with all their strength? The most neglect the duty which of them is required: what is the reason of all this? They know in no measure what the Lord is doing, and what he would have them apply themselves unto. The best almost live from hand to mouth, following present appearances, to the great neglect of the work which the Lord would have hastened among us: all this comes from the same root.

Four Ways to Gain This Understanding of the Work of God

Qu[estion]. But now, if all these sad and sinful consequences attend this nescience[186] of the mind of God, as to the things which he is doing, in the days wherein we live, so far as he has revealed himself, and requires us to observe his walkings, by what ways and means may we come to the knowledge thereof, that we be not sinfully bewildered in our own cares, fears, and follies, but that we may follow hard after God,[187] and be upright in our generation?

Ans[wer]. There be four things whereby we may come to have an insight into the work which the Lord will do, and accomplish in our days:

1. The light which he gives.
2. The previous works which he does.
3. The expectation of his saints.
4. The fear of his adversaries.

1. The light which he gives. God does not use to set his people to work in the dark; they are the "children of light," and they are no "deeds of darkness" which they have to do.[188] However others are blinded, they shall see. Yea he always suits their light to their labor, and gives them a clear discerning of what he is about. "The Lord God doth nothing, but he reveals his secrets to his servants."[189] The light of every age, is the forerunner of the work of every age.

When Christ was to come in the flesh, John Baptist comes a little before.[190] A new light, a new preacher. And what does he discover and reveal? Why he calls them off from resting on legal ceremonies, to the doctrine of

---

[186] I.e., ignorance or lack of knowledge.
[187] Ps. 63:8.
[188] Eph. 5:8, 11; 1 Thess. 5:5.
[189] Amos 3:7.
[190] Mark 1:2–3.

faith, repentance, and gospel ordinances: tells them "the kingdom of God is at hand": instructs them in the knowledge of him who was coming:[191] to what end was all this? Only that the minds of men being enlightened by his preaching, who was a "burning and a shining lamp,"[192] they might see what the Lord was doing.

Every age has its peculiar work, has its peculiar light. Now what is the light which God manifestly gives in our days? Surely not new doctrines (as some pretend), indeed old errors, and long since exploded fancies. Plainly the peculiar light of this generation, is that discovery which the Lord has made to his people, of the mystery of civil and ecclesiastical tyranny. The opening, unraveling, and revealing the anti-Christian interest, interwoven, and coupled together, in civil, and spiritual things, into a state opposite to the kingdom of the Lord Jesus, is the great discovery of these days.[193] Who almost is there among us now, who does not evidently see, that for many generations the Western nations have been juggled[194] into spiritual and civil slavery, by the legerdemain[195] of the whore, and the potentates of the earth, made drunk with the cup of her abominations?[196] How the whole earth has been rolled in confusion, and the saints hurried out of the world, to give way to their combined interest? Has not God unveiled that harlot, made her naked, and discovered her abominable filthiness?[197] Is it not evident to him that has but half an eye, that the whole present constitution of the government of the nations, is so cemented with anti-Christian mortar, from the very top to the bottom, that without a thorough shaking they cannot be cleansed? This then plainly discovers that the work which the Lord is doing, relates to the untwining of this close combination against himself, and the kingdom of his dear Son, and he will not leave until he have done it.

---

191 Matt. 3:1–8.
192 John 5:35.
193 Two months later, in his June 1649 sermon *Human Power Defeated*, which is included in this volume, Owen would describe the "interest of Christ" as "the ordering, framing, carrying on of affairs, as is most conducible to the unraveling and destruction of the mystery of iniquity." Samuel Parker claimed that Owen, preaching "before his Masters of the Rump," sought to prove that "the Lord Jesus Christ is resolved to embroil all the ancient Kingdoms, and subvert all the setled Governments of the West, to restore the purity of his Gospel-worship: *i.e.* in plainer and less Canting English, to carry on the great work of a Thorough Reformation by Civil Wars and Rebellions." Parker, *A Defence and Continuation of the Ecclesiastical Politie* [. . .] (London, 1671), 68.
194 I.e., deceived or tricked.
195 I.e., skillful deception and trickery.
196 Rev. 17:4; Jer. 51:7.
197 Rev. 17:16.

To what degree in the several nations this shaking shall proceed, I have nothing to determine in particular, the Scripture having not expressed it. This only is certain, it shall not stop, nor receive its period, before the interest of anti-Christianity be wholly separated from the power of those nations.

(2nd). The previous works he does. How many of these does our Savior give, as signs of the destruction of Jerusalem, and so consequently of propagating the gospel more and more to the nations (Matt. 24; Luke 21). How fearful and dreadful they were in their accomplishment, Josephus the Jewish historian relates:[198] and how by them the Christians were forewarned, and did by them understand what the Lord was doing, Eusebius and others declare.[199]

"When," (says he) "you shall see the abomination of desolation" (the Roman eagles and ensigns) "standing in the holy place" (Matt. 24:15), or, "Jerusalem compassed with armies," as Luke 21:20, then know by that, that "the end thereof is come, and your deliverance at hand."[200]

The works of God are to be sought out of them that have pleasure in them.[201] They are vocal-speaking works; the mind of God is in them. They may be heard, read, and understood: the "rod may be heard, and who hath appointed it."[202] Now generally he begins with lesser works, to point out to the sons of men, what he is about to accomplish. By these may his will be known, that he may be met in righteousness.

Now what, I pray, are the works that the Lord is bringing forth upon the earth? What is he doing in our own and the neighbor nations? Show me the potentate upon the earth, that has a peaceable molehill, to build himself a habitation upon? Are not all the controversies, or the most of them, that at this day are disputed in letters of blood, among the nations, somewhat of a distinct constitution from those formerly under debate? Those tending merely to the power and splendor of single persons, these to the interest of

---

198 Josephus's *Jewish War*, containing his description of the fall of Jerusalem in AD 70, was "one of the most popular historical texts of the European Renaissance" and was "immensely popular among the wider reading public." See Beatrice Groves, *The Destruction of Jerusalem in Early Modern English Literature* (Cambridge: Cambridge University Press, 2015), 35.
199 Eusebius recounts the flight of the Christians to Pella in the Transjordan before the war. For text, see Eusebius, *Ecclesiastical History*, vol. 1, *Books 1–5*, trans. Kirsopp Lake, Loeb Classical Library 153 (Cambridge, MA: Harvard University Press, 1926), 200. The other accounts that are referred to may include that of Epiphanius of Salamis in his *Panarion* 29.7.7–8. For the text, see *The Panarion of Epiphanius of Salamis*, trans. Frank Williams, 2 vols. (Leiden: Brill, 2009–2012), 1:129.
200 Matt. 24:14; Luke 21:28.
201 Ps. 111:2.
202 Mic. 6:9.

the many.[203] Is not the hand of the Lord in all this? Are not the shaking of these "heavens" of the nations from him? Is not the voice of Christ in the midst of all this tumult? And is not the genuine tendence of these things, open and visible unto all?

What speedy issue all this will be driven to, I know not: so much is to be done as requires a long space. Though a tower may be pulled down faster than it was set up, yet that which has been building a thousand years, is not like to go down in a thousand days.

(3rd). The expectation of the saints, is another thing, from whence a discovery of the will of God, and the work of our generation, may be concluded. The secret ways of God's communicating his mind unto his saints, by a fresh favor of accomplishing prophecies, and strong workings of the Spirit of supplications, I cannot now insist upon. This I know, they shall not be "led into temptation,"[204] but kept from "the hour" thereof, when it comes upon the whole earth.[205] When God raises up the expectation of his people to anything, he is not unto them as waters that fail.[206] Nay he will assuredly fulfill the desires of the poor.

Just about the time that our Savior Christ was to be born of a woman, how were all that waited for salvation in Israel raised up to a high expectation of the kingdom of God;[207] such as that people never had before, and assuredly shall never have again: yea famous was the waiting of that season through the whole Roman Empire. And the Lord, whom they sought, came to his temple.[208] Eminent was their hope, and excellent was the accomplishment.

Whether this will be made a rule to others or no, I know not: this I am assured, that being bottomed on promises, and built up with supplications, it is a ground for them to rest upon. And here I dare appeal to all, who with any diligence have inquired into the things of the kingdom of Christ, that have any savor upon their spirits of the accomplishment of prophecies, and promises, in the latter days, who count themselves concerned in the glory of the gospel, whether this thing of consuming the mystery of iniquity, and

---

203 Examples of what Owen may have had in mind include the internal crisis that France was experiencing in the Fronde (1648–1653), the secessionist revolts against the absolutism of the Spanish Habsburgs, and opposition to William II in the Netherlands. Donald H. Pennington, *Europe in the Seventeenth Century*, 2nd ed. (Abingdon, UK: Routledge, 2014), 326–31, 388–97, 469–75.

204 Matt. 6:13.

205 Rev. 3:10.

206 Jer. 15:18.

207 In the margin: Luk. 3:15.—Owen.

208 Mal. 3:1.

vindicating the churches of Christ into the liberties purchased for them by the Lord Jesus, by the shaking and translating all opposing heights and heavens, be not fully in their expectations. Only the time is in the hand of God, and the rule of our actings with him, is his revealed will.

(4th). Whether the fears of his adversaries, have not their lines meeting in the same point, themselves can best determine. The whole world was more or less dreaded at the coming of Christ in the flesh. When, also, the signs of his vengeance did first appear to the Pagan world, in calling to an account for the blood of his saints, the kings and captains presently cry out, "The great day of his wrath is come, and who shall be able to stand?" (Rev. 6:17).

I am not of counsel to any of the adherents to the man of sin, or any of those who have given their power unto the beast,[209] I have not a key to the bosoms of the enemies of Christ; I am neither their interpreter, nor do they allow me to speak in their behalf, yet truly upon very many probable grounds, I am fully persuaded, that were the thoughts of their hearts disclosed, notwithstanding all their glittering shows, dreadful words, threatening expressions, you shall see them tremble, and dread this very thing, that the whole world as now established will be wrapped up in darkness, at least until that cursed interest which is set up against the Lord Jesus, be fully and wholly shaken out from the heavens and earth of the nations.

And thus without leading you about by chronologies and computations, which yet have their use, (well to count a number[210] being wisdom indeed),[211] I have a little discovered unto you some rules, whereby you may come to be acquainted with the work of God in the days wherein we live, and also what that work is; which is our first use: the next shall be for direction to guide you what you ought to do, when you know what is the work of your generation.

Enthrone Christ as King

Use 2. Be exhorted to prepare to meet the Lord, to make his way straight:[212] and this I would press distinctly.

(1) As to your persons.
(2) As to your employments.

---

209 Rev. 17:13.
210 The number of the beast, 666. See David Brady, "The Number of the Beast in Seventeenth- and Eighteenth-Century England," *Evangelical Quarterly* 45 (1973): 220–21.
211 Rev. 13:18.
212 See Isa. 40:3; Mark 1:3.

The Priority of a Personal Commitment to Christ as King

(1) As to your persons: give the Lord Jesus a throne in your hearts, or it will not at all be to your advantage, that he has a throne and kingdom in the world. Perhaps you will see the plenty of it, but not taste one morsel.[213] Take first that which comes not by observation, that which "is within you,"[214] which is "righteousness, and peace, and joy in the Holy Ghost."[215] Take it in its power, and you will be the better enabled to observe it coming in its glory. "Seek first this kingdom of God, and the righteousness thereof, and all these things shall be added unto you."[216] Oh that it were the will of God, to put an end to all that pretended holiness, hypocritical humiliation, self-interested religion, that have been among us,[217] whereby we have flattered God with our lips, while our hearts have been far from him.[218] Oh that it might be the glory of this assembly, above all the assemblies of the world, that every ruler in it, might be a sincere subject in the kingdom of the Lord Jesus. Oh that it might suffice that we have had in our Parliament, and among our ministers, so much of the "form," and so little of the "power" of godliness;[219] that we have called [the] world Christ, and lusts Christ, and self Christ, working indeed for them, when we pretended all for Christ. Oh that I could nourish this one contention in your honorable assembly, that you might strive who should excel in setting up the Lord Jesus in your hearts.

You may be apt to think, that if you can carry on and compass your purposes, then all your enemies will be assuredly disappointed: do but embrace the Lord Jesus in his kingly power in your bosoms, and *ipso facto*[220] all your enemies are everlastingly disappointed: you are the grains, which in the sifting of the nation, have been kept from falling to the ground.[221] Are you not the residue of all the chariots of England? Oh that in you might appear the reality of the kingdom of the Lord Jesus, which has been so long pretended

---

213 See 2 Kings 7:2, 19.
214 Luke 17:21.
215 Rom. 14:17.
216 Matt. 6:33.
217 The regular monthly parliamentary fasts had now come to an end. Hughes explains that one of the reasons they came to an end was anxieties that the fasts had become merely "formal observance." Ann Hughes, "Preachers and Hearers in Revolutionary London: Contextualising Parliamentary Fast Sermons," *Transactions of the Royal Historical Society* 24 (2014): 59.
218 Isa. 29:13.
219 2 Tim. 3:5.
220 Lat. "by that very fact."
221 Amos 9:9.

by others: that sound righteousness, not a pharisaical rigid supercilious affectation, not a careless belief and comportment, the issue of novel fancies, might be found upon your spirits; that you may be thought meet to rejoice with the Lord in his kingdom: otherwise this "day of the Lord" which we have described, however desired and longed after, will be "darkness to you, and not light."[222]

Two Particular Responsibilities of the Magistrate in These Days
(2) In reference to your great employments, whereunto the Lord has called you, and here I shall briefly hold out unto you one or two things.

[1] That you would seriously consider, why it is that the Lord shakes the heavens and the earth of the nations, to what end this tends, and what is the cause thereof. Is it not from hence, that he may revenge their opposition to the kingdom of his dear Son? That he may shake out of the midst of them, all that anti-Christian mortar wherewith, from their first chaos they have been cemented? That so the kingdoms of the earth, may become the kingdoms of the Lord Jesus:[223] Is not the controversy of Zion pleaded with them?[224] Are not they called to an account for the transgression of that charge given to all potentates, "Touch not mine anointed?"[225] And what is the aim of the Lord Jesus herein, whose mighty voice shakes them? Is it not to frame and form them for the interest of his own kingdom? That he may fulfill the word he has spoken to Zion, "I will make thy officers peace, and thine exactors righteousness?"[226]

Consider then (I pray) what you have in hand: wait upon your King the Lord Christ, to know his mind. If you lay any stone in the whole building, that advances itself against his scepter, he will shake all again: dig you never so deep, build you never so high, it shall be shaken.[227] Nay, that there be no opposition will not suffice; he has given light enough to have all things framed for his own advantage. The time is come, yea the full time is come, that it should be so, and he expects it from you. Say not in the first place, this, or that, suits the interest of England, but look what suits the interest of Christ; and assure yourselves that the true interest of any nation, is

---

222 Amos 5:18.
223 Rev. 11:15.
224 Isa. 34:8.
225 Ps. 105:15.
226 Isa. 60:17.
227 This may be suggestive of the Diggers and the activity of the lead miners in the Peak District. See Cowan, *John Owen and the Civil War Apocalypse*, 102–3.

wrapped up therein.[228] More of this in the treatise annexed to my sermon of January 31.[229]

[2] Be encouraged under all those perplexities and troubles, which you are, or may be wrapped in: lift up the hands that hang down, and let the feeble knees be strengthened:[230] "It is but yet a little while, and he that shall come, will come, and will not tarry."[231] The more you are for Christ, the more enemies you shall be sure to have; but the Lamb shall overcome.[232] He is come to revenge the blood of his slain upon this generation, and to free the residue from the jaws of the terrible. "He is our rock," and "his work is perfect":[233] What he has begun, faster, or slower, he will surely accomplish.

It is a thing of the utmost imaginable indifferency, whether any of our particular persons behold these things here below or no: if otherwise, we shall for the present have "rest with him, and stand in our lot at the end of the days":[234] but for the work itself, "the decree is gone forth,"[235] and it shall not be recalled; receive strength and refreshment in the Lord.

Expect This Shaking to Continue

Use 3. Wonder not when the heaven is shaken; if you see the stars fall to the ground;[236] we had some who pretended to be church stars, that were merely fixed to all men's view, and by their own confession, in the political heavens.[237]

---

228 This should be understood in the context of the development of the political theory of "interest." This was derived from the French Huguenot leader Henri, Duke of Rohan, and it influenced a number of important theorists such as Marchamont Nedham, James Harrington, and Algernon Sidney. Jonathan Scott has demonstrated that by 1648 interest theory had become "the political language of the new model army." See Jonathan Scott, "The Rapture of Motion: James Harrington's Republicanism," in *Political Discourse in Early Modern Britain*, ed. Nicholas Phillipson and Quentin Skinner (Cambridge: Cambridge University Press, 1993), 144; Scott, *Algernon Sidney and the English Republic, 1623–1677* (Cambridge: Cambridge University Press, 1988), 53, 76, 207; Blair Worden, *Literature and Politics in Cromwellian England: John Milton, Andrew Marvell, Marchamont Nedham* (Oxford: Oxford University Press, 2009), 14–30.
229 Owen's *Of Toleration* (1649).
230 Heb. 12:12.
231 Heb. 10:37.
232 Rev. 17:14.
233 Deut. 32:4.
234 Dan. 12:13.
235 Dan. 9:25.
236 Rev. 6:13.
237 The is probably a reference to the clericalism of Laudian era that saw clergy appointed to secular offices and jurisdictions: e.g., Archbishop Laud, who served on the privy council, masterminded the appointment of Bishop Juxon as Lord Treasurer in 1636, the first cleric to hold the position since the Reformation. See Andrew Foster, "The Clerical Estate Revitalised," in *The Early Stuart Church 1603–42*, ed. Kenneth Fincham (London: Macmillan, 1993), 139–60.

The first shaking of this nation, shook them utterly to the ground.[238] If others also tremble like an aspen leaf, and know not which wind to yield unto, or sail backward and forward by the same gale, wonder not at that neither; when men lay any other foundation than the immovable cornerstone,[239] at one time or other, sooner or later, assuredly they will be shaken.

Prepare for a Time of Purging and Purification

Use 4. Let the professing people that are among us look well to themselves: "The day is coming that will burn like an oven."[240] Dross will not endure this day; we have many a hypocrite as yet to be uncased. Take heed you that act high, if a false heart, a defiled heart be among you, there shall be no place for it in the mountain of the Lord's house.[241] "The inhabitants of Zion shall be all righteous" (Isa. 60:21). Many that make a great show now upon the stage, shall be turned off with shame enough; try and search your hearts, force not the Lord to lay you open to all. The "spirit of judgment and burning" will try you.[242] Tremble, I pray, for you are entering the most purging trying furnace, that ever the Lord set up on the earth.

Look to Heavenly Things

Use 5. Be loose from all shaken things: you see the clouds return after the rain: one storm in the neck of another.[243] Thus it must be, until Christ has finished his whole work. "Seeing that all these things must be dissolved, what manner of persons ought we to be in all manner of holy conversation."[244] Let your eyes be upward, and your hearts be upward, and your hands be upward, that you be not moved at the passing away of shaken things. I could here encourage you by the glorious issue of all these shakings, whose foretaste might be as marrow to your bones, though they should be appointed to consumption before the accomplishment of it: but I must close.

---

238 For the abolition of episcopacy, see "October 1646: An Ordinance for the Abolishing of Archbishops and Bishops within the Kingdom of England, and Dominion of Wales, and for setling of their Lands and Possessions upon Trustees, for the use of the Commonwealth," in *Acts and Ordinances of the Interregnum 1642–1660*, ed. C. H. Firth and R. S. Rait, 3 vols. (London: HMSO, 1911), 1:879–83.
239 1 Cor. 3:11.
240 Mal. 4:1.
241 Isa. 2:2.
242 Isa. 4:4.
243 The illustration of the rain in uses 5 and 6 would have been evocative, given that 1648 had been an "extremely wet year," something Owen's neighboring clergyman was careful to detail in his diary. See Joyce Macadam, "English Weather: The Seventeenth-Century Diary of Ralph Josselin," *The Journal of Interdisciplinary History* 43, no. 2 (2012): 230.
244 2 Pet. 3:11.

Be Confident That All Opposition Will End

Use 6. See the vanity, folly, madness of such as labor to oppose the bringing in the kingdom of the Lord Jesus. Can you hinder the rain from descending upon the earth when it is falling? Can you stop the sun from rising at its appointed hour? Will the conception for you dwell quietly in the womb beyond its month? Surely you may with far more ease turn and stop the current and course of nature, than obstruct the bringing in of the kingdom of Christ, in righteousness and peace. Whence comes it to pass, that so many nations are wasted, destroyed, spoiled, in the days wherein we live? That God has taken quietness and peace from the earth? Doubtless from hence, that they will smite themselves against the "stone cut out of the mountain without hands."[245] Shall not "the decree bring forth?"[246] Is it not in vain to fight against the Lord? Some are angry, some troubled, some in the dark, some full of revenge, but the truth is, whether they will hear or forbear, Babylon shall fall, and all the glory of the earth be stained,[247] and the kingdoms become the kingdoms of our Lord Jesus Christ.[248]

FINIS.[249]

---

[245] Dan. 2:34.
[246] Zeph. 2:2.
[247] Isa. 23:9.
[248] Rev. 11:15.
[249] Lat. "The End."

[Sermon]

Human Power Defeated

*The stout-hearted are spoiled, they have slept their sleep:
and none of the men of might have found their hands.*

PS. 76:5.

THE OCCASION AND STRUCTURE OF PSALM 76

The common circumstances of this psalm, concerning the penman, title, and the like, I shall not at all inquire after.[1] The time of its being given to the church is alone to us considerable; and yet all the knowledge thereof also is but conjectural. What particular time it was wherein it was given, we know not; but that it was given for the use of all times, that we know. Probable it is, from verse 3, that it was established as a monument of praise in the days of Hezekiah, when by the immediate hand of God, Jerusalem was delivered from the army of Sennacherib.[2] For a return of which mercy, though good Hezekiah came short of the obligation laid on him, rendering not again according to the benefit done unto him;[3] yet the Lord himself takes care for his own glory, setting forth this psalm as a monument of the praise due to his name unto all generations.

The deliverance of Jerusalem then from so great ruin, as that impending over it from the threatening army of Sennacherib under their walls, being the

---

1 This sermon does not have a title page like the others in this volume because it was included as "Sermon XII" in *A Complete Collection of the Sermons of the Reverend and Learned John Owen* [. . .], ed. John Asty (London: John Clark, 1721), 79–91. There the editorial note records the occasion as "*Upon the defeat of the levellers at* Burford, 19. May 1649. *This Sermon was preached before Parliament 7 June following: as appears by* Whitlock's *Memoirs, fol. 391. col. 2*" (79; italics original).
2 2 Kings 19:35.
3 2 Chron. 32:25.

occasion of penning this psalm, it cannot but yield us a meet foundation of making mention of the name of the Lord in a suitable work this day.

In general, the whole is eucharistical,[4] and has two parts: first narratory,[5] concerning the work of God for his people: secondly laudatory, or the praise of his people for those works.

The first part has three particulars:

1. An exordium,[6] by way of exultation and rejoicing, verses 1–2.
2. A special narration of the work of God, for which the praise of the whole is intended verses 3, 5–6.
3. An apostrophe[7] to the Lord concerning the one, and the other, verse 4.

The latter contains:

1. A doctrinal observation for the use of the church, from the whole, verse 7.
2. The reasons and confirmation of the doctrine so laid down, taken from the power and righteousness of God in the actions recounted, verses 8–9.
3. A threefold use of the doctrine so confirmed. Of instruction, verse 10. Of exhortation, verse 11. Of establishment and consolation, verse 12.

The particulars preceding my text I shall a little touch upon, that the mind of the Holy Ghost therein may be the more clear unto you, and the doctrine from thence appear with the greater evidence.

The Exordium (76:1–2)

1. In the exordium, verses 1–2, you have two things: (1) The names of the place wherein the work mentioned was wrought, and the praise returned held forth; and these are, Judah, Israel, Salem, Zion. (2) The relation of God unto this place, which lies at the bottom of the work he did for them, and the praise they returned unto him. He was known; his name was great among them; there was his tabernacle and his dwelling place; which may be referred to two heads: the knowledge of his will, verse 1 and the establishment of his worship, verse 2.

---

4 I.e., for giving thanks in a religious context.
5 I.e., of the nature of narrative.
6 I.e., the introductory part of the discourse.
7 I.e., a figure of speech in which the speaker or writer turns to address a person or thing.

(1) For the description of the place, by its several names and titles, I shall not insist upon it: they are all but various expressions of the same thing. It is the church of God that is adorned with all these titles and names of singular endearment. Judah, that single tribe of which the Messiah was to come:[8] Israel, a prevailing people, the posterity of him that prevailed with God:[9] Salem, the place he chose above all the places of the earth to settle his name therein:[10] and Zion, the choice ornament of that Salem, a model wherein the beauty and excellency of all the other are contracted, whose gates were then so dear unto the Lord.[11] Or perhaps, you have the distribution of the whole into its several parts: Judah, the governing tribe: Israel, the body of the people: Salem, the chief place of their residence and glory: and Zion, the presence of God in his worship among them all. Now the mention of these titles of the church, so dear to the Lord, does front the following narration, to afford us this observation.

Observation. The care of Salem, of Zion, lies at the bottom of all God's powerful actings and workings among the sons of men. Every mighty work of God throughout the world, may be prefaced with these two verses. The whole course of affairs in the world, is steered by providence in reference to the good of Salem: Zion has been the rise and downfall of all the powers of the world: it is her deliverance or trial that is intended in their raising, and her recompense and vengeance in their ruin. God works not among the nations for their own sakes. When they are sifted with a sieve, they are but the chaff, Israel is the corn, for whose sake it is done, whereof "not the least grain shall fall" to the ground (Amos 9:9). She is "precious" in God's sight and "honorable"; he loves her: therefore he gives men for her, and people for her life (Isa. 43:4). The men of the world are very apt to pride themselves in their thoughts, as though great were their share and interest in the glorious things that God is accomplishing: like a fly that sat on the chariot wheel, and cried, "What a dust have I raised round about?"[12] The truth is, their names are written in the dust,[13] and they are of no account in the eyes of the Lord in all he is accomplishing, but only to exalt his name in their miscarriage and destruction. Was it not in the thoughts of some

---

8 Gen. 49:10.
9 Gen. 32:28.
10 2 Chron. 33:4.
11 Ps. 87:2.
12 This fable of the fly on the chariot wheel appeared in the *Hecatomythium* (1490) of the Italian writer Laurentius Abstemius (Lorenzo Astemio). Francis Bacon included the fable at the start of essay 54, titled "Of Vaine-Glory." For the text, see Francis Bacon, *Bacon's Essays*, ed. Alfred S. West (Cambridge: Cambridge University Press, 1931), 159. Owen also used this illustration in *A Vision of Unchangeable Free Mercy* (1646), which is included in this volume.
13 Jer. 17:13.

lately among us, that their right hand had accomplished the work of the Lord, and that the end of it must be the satisfaction of their lusts? And has not the Lord declared, that they have neither part nor lot in this matter? It was Salem, not self; Zion, not Babylon, or confusion, that lay at the bottom of the whole.

(2) There is a relation of God unto this place. His will was known there, verse 1; and his worship was established, verse 2. And these also have their particular mention.

Observation. In the deliverance of his people, God has a special regard to the honor of his ordinances. Why so great things for Salem? Why there his word is preached, whereby his will is known, and his name made great: there his tabernacle is fixed, and his dwelling place established: there he gives his presence in his worship and ordinances, wherein he is delighted. "Because of thy temple at Jerusalem shall kings bring presents unto thee" (Ps. 68:29). Here is the temple, Christ; and then the worship of Christ: for their sake it shall be done. When vengeance is recompensed upon an opposing people, it is the vengeance of the temple (Jer. 50:28). And it is a voice from thence that renders recompense to his enemies (Isa. 66:6). The great work which the Lord at this day is accomplishing in the world, looks fully on this one thing. Wherefore is it that God shakes the powers of this world, and causes the towers to totter which they uphold?[14] Is it not that the way of his worship may be vindicated from all their abominations, and vengeance taken upon them for their opposition thereunto? And there is no greater sign of God's care for a people, than when he shows a regard to his ordinances among that people. The defense he gives, is of the glory of the assemblies of mount Zion (Isa. 4:5). When the ark departs, you may call the children, "Ichabod."[15] The taking away of his candlestick,[16] the removal of his glory from the temple,[17] is an assured prologue to the utter ruin of a people.

And has not the Lord had a special eye this way in the late deliverance? It is his promise, that he will purge the rebels from among his people.[18] And he has done it. Were there not children of Edom among them, who cried, "Down with them, down with them even to the ground"?[19] Has not God magnified his despised word above all his name? Was it not as an offscouring[20] to many particular persons among them in the late murmuring for preeminence, against those whom the

---

14 A trope that Owen developed at length in his parliamentary sermon from April 1649, *The Shaking and Translating of Heaven and Earth*, which is included in this volume.
15 An expression of regret for the departed glory (1 Sam. 4:21).
16 Rev. 2:5.
17 Ezek. 10:15–19.
18 Ezek. 20:38.
19 Ps. 137:7.
20 I.e., someone or something rejected and cast aside. See 1 Cor. 4:13.

Lord has chosen? Who I suppose have no other joy in their employment, than Moses had in his; who once desired the Lord to slay him, that he might be freed from his burden;[21] only the will of the Lord, and the good of a poor thankless people swayed their hearts unto it.[22] And were there here any more discriminating rods cast in before the Lord, to have that bud and spring which he owned, as Numbers 17, than this one: Scripture, or no Scripture; solemn worship, or none at all? I speak only as to some particulars, and that I can upon my own experience. The Lord give their hearts a free discovery of his thoughts in this business. Doubtless he has had respect to his tabernacle and dwelling place. For my part, they are to me as the Theban shield;[23] and notwithstanding all my pressures, I would labor to say as Mephibosheth, "Let all go, since I see the king in peace."[24]

I might farther observe from both these things together, that among the people of God alone is the residence of his glorious presence. This song is held out from Zion. "In his temple doth every one speak of his glory" (Ps. 29:9). "Bless ye God in the congregations, the Lord, from the fountain of Israel" (Ps. 68:26). "Praise waiteth for thee, O God, in Zion" (Ps. 65:1). As a "lame leg," and as "a thorn in the hand," ungraceful, painful, "so is a parable in the mouth of fools" (Prov. 26:7, 9). It is "the saints" who are bid to "be joyful" in the Lord, and "the high praises of God" must be in their mouths (Ps. 149:5–6). They are high things, that beseem only those whom God does magnify. If the Lord give us matter of praise, pray know from whom it will be acceptable, whose praises they are he delights to inhabit.[25] If you have some defiling lust, the sunshine of mercies will exhale nothing but the offensive steam of carnal affections. The sacrifices of wicked hearts are "an abomination to the Lord."[26] If your fleshly

---

21 Num. 11:14–15.
22 In Henry Denne's renunciation of his involvement in the rising, he wrote that "*Moses* was the meekest man in his time upon the earth, yet did the Conspirators charge him as fiercely and hainously as any Officer of the present Army is charged this day, in taking too much upon him, lifting up himself, making himself a Prince over the people." See Henry Denne, *The Levellers Designe Discovered: Or the Anatomie of the Late Unhappie Mutinie* (London, 1649), 5 (italics original).
23 Epaminondas, a Greek general of Thebes, was fatally wounded by a Spartan javelin, and when he regained consciousness his first question was whether his shield was safe. Only then did he ask whether his army had won the battle. This incident is recorded in Diodorus of Sicily, *Library of History* 15.87.6. For the Greek text, see Diodorus Siculus, *Library of History*, vol. 7, *Books 15.20–16.65*, trans. Charles L. Sherman, Loeb Classical Library 389 (Cambridge, MA: Harvard University Press, 1952), 197. For the significance of the shield, see Adam Schwartz, *Reinstating the Hoplite: Arms, Armour and Phalanx Fighting in Archaic and Classical Greece* (Stuttgart: Franz Steiner Verlag, 2009), 153. Thus, in this engagement with the Levellers, Owen believed that the "Theban shield" was the ordinances of Christian worship.
24 2 Sam. 19:30.
25 Ps. 22:3.
26 Prov. 15:8.

affections work this day without the beatings of a pure heart, and the language of a pure lip, the Lord will reject your oblations. Would you have your praise as sweet to the Lord, as a mercy is to you; be assured that in Christ you are the Israel of God,[27] and your prayers shall prevail, your praise shall be accepted.

A Narrative of the Great Work That God Did for His People (76:3, 5–6)

2. The second particular, as I observed, is a special narration of the works of God, for which the whole is intended, verses 3–6. And therein you have these two things: (1) The place where these acts were wrought, and are remembered, "there" verse 3. (2) The acts themselves related, which refer, [1] To God the worker, "He brake," verse 3. [2] To the persons on whom they were wrought, verses 5–6.

Remembering the Place Where God Did This Great Work

(1) The place where these things were acted, and the monuments of them erected, that is, "there"; there in Salem and Zion, Judah and Israel; there, not so much in those places, as with reference unto them.

Observation. All the mighty actings of God regard his church, and there are the monuments and trophies of his victories against his enemies erected. To the first part of this, I spoke before. A word for the latter. God decks and makes Zion glorious with the spoils of his adversaries. There the glory of Pharaoh and all his host, drowned in the Red Sea, is dedicated (Ex. 15). There are the shields of all the mighty men in the host of Sennacherib, slain by an angel, hung up (Isa. 37:35–36). There is the honor, the robes, the crown, and the reason of Nebuchadnezzar laid up, for the glory of Zion (Dan. 4:33–34), himself being changed into a beast. There is all the pomp and glory of Herod deposited (Acts 12:23), when, as a reward of his pride and persecution, he was devoured of worms. There is the glory of all persecutors, with the blood of Julian in a special manner, who threw it into the air, and cried, "You have won, Galilean."[28] There Haman is visibly exalted upon the gallows by himself erected for the ruin of a prince of the people (Est. 7:10). There the peace and the joy of the church, their choice frame under the bloody massacres of the inhabitants of Zion, is set to show, for the glory of it. There all the rochets[29] of popish prelates, the crowns, and glory,

---

27 Gal. 6:16.
28 In the text: *Vicisti Galillaee*.—Owen. According to Theodoret, these were the dying words of Flavius Claudius Julianus (331–363), better known as Julian "the Apostate." See Theodoret, *Ecclesiastical History* 3.20. For an English translation, see *The Ecclesiastical History of Theodoret*, in *Nicene and Post-Nicene Fathers*, Second Series, ed. Philip Schaff, and Henry Wace, 14 vols. (1890–1900; repr., Peabody: Hendrickson, 2004), 3:106.
29 I.e., vestments, typically of white linen, often worn by bishops.

and thrones of the kings of the earth, all set apart, as monuments and trophies of God's victories in Zion. There is a place reserved for the man of sin,[30] and all the kings of the earth who have committed fornication with the mother of harlots,[31] whose destruction sleeps not.[32] God will at length certainly glorify Salem with the arrow of the bow, the shield, the sword, and all spoils of its oppressors.

Remembering the Great Work That God Did in This Day of Distress
(2) There is what he did describe, both immediately in the actions themselves, verse 3, and with reference to the persons toward whom he so acted, verse 5. Now because the former is fully contained in the latter, I shall not handle it apart, but descend immediately to the consideration of the words of my text, being a declaration of what the Lord has done for his people in the day of their distress, with particular reference to the cause of that distress.

And here we shall look a little—

1. To the reading of the words: and
2. To their explication.

1. To the reading: The "stout-hearted"; or, the "strong in heart," the "mighty in heart": so in the original. Men of stout, stubborn, unpersuadable hearts and courage, whose epithet is, that they are "far from righteousness" (Isa. 46:12). The Septuagint have rendered it, ἀσύνετοι τῇ χαρδίᾳ, "the foolish in heart." Stubborn-hearted men are foolish-hearted men: not to yield unto, is worse than not to understand, what is good. They "are spoiled," אֶשְׁתּוֹלְלוּ, "have yielded themselves to the spoil"; so properly, and so rendered by most interpreters; which sense I shall follow. "They have slept their sleep," נָמוּ, *dormitarunt*,[33] "they have slumbered their sleep." What it is "to slumber a sleep" we shall see afterward. The residue of the words are literally rendered, save only in the placing of the negation; for whereas we set it on the persons, "none of the men"; in the original it is upon the act, "have not found," affirming concerning the persons, "all the men of might have not," that is, "none of the men of might have"; a very frequent Hebraism, imitated by John [in] 1 John 3:15, Πᾶς ἀνθρωποκτόνος οὐκ ἔχει ζωὴν, "Every man-slayer hath not life,"[34] i.e. "none hath." And so you have the words: "The stout of heart have

---

30 2 Thess. 2:3.
31 Rev. 17:5.
32 2 Pet. 2:3.
33 In the Latin Vulgate *dormierunt*.
34 "Manslayer" is the translation followed by Tyndale and the Geneva Bible.

yielded themselves to the spoils, they have slumbered their sleep; and none of the men of might have found their hands."

2. The words thus read contain three general heads.

(1) A twofold description of the enemies of Salem.

[1] In respect of their internal affections: they were "stout of heart," men of high spirit and haughty courage, *cedere nescientes*,[35] not knowing how to yield to anything but the dictates of their own proud spirits.

[2] In respect of their power for outward acting, "Men of might," strong of hand, as well as stout of heart. Courage without strength will but betray its possessor, and strength without courage is but *inutile pondus*,[36] a burdensome nothing; but when both meet, a stout heart and strong hands, who shall stand before them? Thus you have the enemies set out like Goliath, with his spear and helmet, defying the host of the living God.[37]

(2) You have a twofold issue of God's providence, in dealing with them suitably to this their double qualification.

[1] He opposes himself to the stoutness of their hearts, and they "yield themselves to the spoil."[38] Where observe, first, the act itself: they "yield themselves." Nothing in the world so contrary to a stout heart, as to yield itself. To yield, is a thing of the greatest distance and contrariety[39] to the principle of a stout heart in the world. It is far more reconcilable to death, than yielding. But this God will effect. Secondly, the extent of this yielding: it was "to the spoil." This exceedingly heightens the mighty working of the Lord against them. Should they be brought to yield to reason, persuasion, and union, it were well; but that they should be so prevailed on as to yield to the spoil, that is, to the mercy of those against whom they rose and opposed themselves, this is *digitus Dei*.[40]

[2] He opposes himself to their actual might: they "found not their hands."[41] Hands are the instruments of acting the heart's resolution. The strength and power of a man is in his hands; if they be gone, all his hope is gone. If a man's sword be taken from him, he will do what he can with his hands; but if his hands be gone, he may go to sleep, for any disturbance he will work. For men not to find their hands, is not to have that power for the execution of their designs which formerly they had. In former days they had hands, power for

---

35 Lat. "not knowing how to yield."
36 Lat. "an unprofitable lump" or "a useless burden."
37 1 Sam. 17:7–10.
38 Ps. 76:5.
39 I.e., the quality or state of opposition.
40 Lat. "the finger of God." See Ex. 8:19.
41 Ps. 76:5.

doing great things; but now when they would use them against Salem, they could not find them. And why so? God had taken them away; God took away their power, their strength departed from them. Samson found not his strength, when his locks were cut; though he thought to do as at other times, yet he was deceived and taken.[42] When God takes away men's power, they go forth, and think to do as in former days; but when they come to exercise it, all is gone; their hands are laid out of the way, in allusion to one that seeks.

(3) There is the total issue of this whole dispensation, placed in the midst of both, as arising from both: "They have slumbered their sleep." When their hearts yielded, and their hands were lost, courage and power both taken away, what else should they do? Some take this for an expression of death, as it is sometimes used, "Lighten mine eyes, lest I sleep the sleep of death" (Ps. 13:3). I rather conceive it to hold out that condition, which God threatens to bring upon the enemies of his people, when he sends them a "spirit of slumber" (Rom. 11:8). Now in such a condition two things are eminent:

[1] Its weakness. A condition of slumber and sleep is a weak condition. A sleeping man is able to do nothing. Jael can destroy a drowsy Sisera.[43]

[2] Its vanity. Men in their sleep are apt to have foolish, vain fancies. This then is that which the Lord holds out concerning the enemies of his church, his people, his ways, when their hearts are gone, and their hands gone. They shall be brought to a condition of weakness in respect of others; they shall not be able to beat them: and of vanity in themselves, they shall feed themselves with vain thoughts, like the dream of a hungry man, "He dreameth, and behold he eateth; he waketh, and behold he is empty" (Isa. 29:8). They please themselves for a little season with strong apprehensions of the accomplishment of their hearts' lusts, and cobweb fancies; but the issue is shame and disappointment.

THREE MAIN DOCTRINAL OBSERVATIONS

The words, being opened, will yield us these three observations:

1. Men of stout hearts and strong hands, of courage and power, are often engaged against the Lord.
2. God suits the workings of providence for deliverance to the qualifications and actings of his opposers; their stout hearts shall yield, their strong hands be lost.

---

42 Judg. 16:19–20.
43 Judg. 4:21.

3. Though men have courage, might, and success; yet when they engage themselves against the Lord, weakness and vanity shall be the issue thereof.

In the brief handling whereof I hope you shall find the word of God, and the works of God exceedingly suited.

Strong and Courageous Men Often Oppose the Ways of God

[Observation] 1. Men of courage, power, and success, of eminent qualifications, are oftentimes engaged against the Lord, and the ways of the Lord.

I shall multiply neither testimonies nor instances of this truth; for that were but to set up a candle in the sun: the experience of all ages has made it good. One or two places may suffice. "Rebuke the company of spearmen, the multitude of the bulls, with the calves of the people" (Ps. 68:30). There are not only "calves of the people," easily deluded, sottish[44] men, but also multitudes of "bulls," heady, high-minded, bearing down all before them, throwing up all bounds and fences, laying all common to their lusts, not easily to be resisted;[45] these also are among the adversaries of the ways of the Lord. The first open opposers of the ways of God, were "giants," "mighty men," and "men of renown" (Gen. 6:4). At once "two hundred and fifty princes of the assembly, famous in the congregation, and men of renown," joined themselves in rebellion against the Lord (Num. 16:2). And that—

(1) Because these very qualifications of a stout heart, strong hands, and former success are apt of themselves, if destitute of directing light and humbling grace, to puff up the spirits of men, and to engage them in ways of their own, contrary to the mind of the Lord. When men take advice of their stout hearts, strong hands, and former success, they are very evil counselors. When Jeremiah advised the Jews from the Lord for their good, the proud men answered, they would not obey (Jer. 43:2). When Pharaoh is made stout for his ruin, he cries, "Who is the Lord, that I should obey his voice?" (Ex. 5:2). And for success, God makes the Assyrian the rod of his anger, sends him against the people of his wrath, with charge "to take the spoil, and to take the

---

44 I.e., foolish.
45 The appellation "Leveller" was derived from the Midland Revolt of 1607 when fences and hedges were pulled down and levelled to protest the enclosure of previously common land. See Steve Hindle, "Imagining Insurrection in Seventeenth-Century England: Representations of the Midland Rising of 1607," *History Workshop Journal* 66 (2008): 21–61. Thus, the language of removing bounds and fences and laying all in common was striking in the context of the Leveller uprising.

prey, and to tread them down like the mire of the streets" (Isa. 10:6). He goes accordingly and prospers; but when he has so done, see what a conclusion he makes. He goes against Jerusalem, and cries, "Let not your God deceive you. Have the gods of the nations delivered them; and do you think so to be?" (Isa. 37:10, 12). From the success he had from God, he concluded the success he should have against him. Like those of late among ourselves, who having been partners with others in former successes, while they went upon the command of God, doubtless received in their stout hearts establishment, and strengthening to other undertakings, as if the God of the Parliament could not help.¶[46]

Amaziah, king of Judah, wages war with Edom, and they are destroyed before him (2 Kings 14:7). The war was of the Lord. Upon this he is lifted up, and causelessly provokes Jehoash, king of Israel, verse 8, against the mind and will of God. Jehoash sends him word, that if "the thistle" pride itself against "the cedar," the "wild beast" will tread it down, verse 9. But he had former success, and on he will go to his ruin. The stout-hearted men (for a delivery from whose fury and folly, we desire this day to lift up the name of the Lord) having received help and assistance against Edom, will needs lift up the "thistle" against the "cedar," act out of their own sphere, turn subjection into dominion, to their shame and sorrow. But it were better, their hearts should be filled with sorrow than the nation, and especially the people of God in the nation, with blood and confusion, ending in bondage and tyranny. And this is the first account of it, why men of such qualifications are engaged against the Lord. The qualifications themselves do set up for it, if destitute of divine light, and humbling grace. Such men will run upon God, and the thick bosses of his buckler.[47]

(2) God will have it so, that the greater may be his glory in the powerful protection and defense of his own, with the destruction, disappointment, and ruin of their enemies. If his enemies were all sottish, weak, foolish, childish, until he makes them so, where would be the praise of his great name? When would there be "A knot worthy of God to unloose,"[48] work worthy of the appearance of the Most High? But when there is a great mountain before Zerubbabel (Zech. 4:7), a high, haughty, oppressing empire, to level that to a

---

46 The ¶ symbol indicates that a paragraph break has been added to Owen's original text.
47 Job 15:26.
48 In the text: *Nodus Deo vindice dignus.*—Owen. In other words, a great dilemma. Adapted from Horace, *Ars Poetica* 191. For the Latin text and English translation, see Horace, *Satires. Epistles. The Art of Poetry*, trans. H. Rushton Fairclough, Loeb Classical Library 194 (Cambridge, MA: Harvard University Press, 1926), 466.

plain is glorious. When God will get himself a name, he raises up, not a poor, effeminate Sardanapalus,[49] a poor, sensual, hypocritical wretch, as some have been;[50] the Lord will not make an open contest by such a one, (such as some of our sore oppressors have been) but he will raise up a Pharaoh, a crooked leviathan,[51] a stout-hearted, cunning-headed, strong-handed oppressor; and he tells him, such a one as he, "For this cause have I raised thee up, for to show in thee my power, and that my name may be declared throughout all the earth" (Ex. 9:16). "Thou ail a fit subject" (says he) "for me to exalt my glory in thy ruin." The beast is to make war with the Lamb; and he shall not do it alone, God will give him in assistance.[52] And who shall these be? Women, and children, and weak ones? No; he will put it into the heart of the kings of the earth "to give their power and strength to the beast" (Rev. 17:17), to break them in pieces. This will be glory indeed. All the opposers which formerly have risen, or at least most of them, have had the power to that height, as they have been exceedingly above all outwardly appearing means of being resisted. The breaking of the old monarchies, and of papal power, is a work meet for the Lord. And in this shall mainly consist the promised glory of the church of Christ in after days, whose morning star[53] I doubt not, is now upon us; the Lord will more immediately and visibly break the high, stout, haughty ones of the earth for the sake of his people, than in former times. Look upon all the glorious things that are spoken concerning Zion in the latter days, and you shall find them all interwoven with this still, the shaking of heaven,[54] the casting down of thrones,[55] and dominions, and mighty ones. I mention this, because indeed I look upon this late mercy, as the after-drops of a former refreshing shower, as an appendix of goodwill, for the confirming the former work which God had wrought. "Though," says he, "'ye have lien among the pots,' have been in a poor, defiled condition, a condition of bondage; 'yet shall ye be as the wings of a dove covered with silver, and her feathers with yellow gold,' ye shall be made exceeding glorious." But how, or when shall this be? Why, "when the Almighty scatters kings" for her sake, then shall she be as "white as snow in Salmon" (Ps. 68:13–14). When God by his almighty power takes away so great opposers, then glory and beauty

---

49 I.e., the legendary last emperor of the Assyrian monarchy in the seventh-century BC. For a further description, see Thomas Beard, *Theatre of Gods Judgments* [...] (London, 1642), 280.
50 Presumably a reference to the late king, Charles I.
51 Isa. 27:1.
52 Rev. 17:14.
53 I.e., the precursor and herald of a new dawn. See Rev. 22:16.
54 Heb. 12:27.
55 Dan. 7:9.

shall arise upon you. And this in some degree lies also at the bottom of the late dispensation of providence. Men's hearts were full of fear of a storm; yea, a storm was necessary, that some evidence might be given of the Lord's continuing his presence among you; that if hereafter we be forsaken, it may appear that it was for our own unbelief, unthankfulness, and folly, and not for doing the work of the Lord. Now how was this expected? "Why, this poor people, or that, unacquainted with the things of their peace, will rise and make opposition." "No," says the Lord, "you shall not have so easy a trial; you shall have men of stout hearts, and strong hands, with many former successes on their shoulders; that when deliverance is given in, my name may be glorious indeed."

Two Uses of the First Observation
Faith Delivers the Saints from Fear

Use 1. Be not moved at the most formidable enemies, that may arise against you in the ways of God. "It was told the house of David, saying, Syria is confederate with Ephraim: and his heart was moved, and the heart of his people, as the trees of the wood are moved with the wind" (Isa. 7:2). When strong combinations arise, how apt are we to shake and tremble before them, especially when they have some strangeness, as well as strength? That Syria should come against Judah, is no wonder. But what, I pray, makes Ephraim too, their brother, and fellow in former afflictions? Besides, Syria and Ephraim were always at a mortal difference among themselves. But they who agree in nothing else, usually consent in opposition to the ways of God. Then you shall have Edom, Ammon, Amalek, and Ashur altogether of one mind (Ps. 83:6–8). And the kings of the West, that perpetually devour one another, yet have one mind in exalting the Beast, and opposing the Lamb (Rev. 17:14). As in our late troubles, there was a concurrence not only in the main of Syria and Ephraim, the two grand extremes, but also of innumerable particular fancies and designs; so that if a man should have met them, like him in the fable, the lion, the ass, and the fox, he could not but wonder where they were going together,[56] whither they were traveling together. But I say, when such combinations are made, how apt are we to shake and tremble? They are

---

56 In the text: *Quò iter unà facerent.*—Owen. This an allusion to the fable of the lion, the ass, and the fox who went hunting together, agreeing to divide the spoil equally among themselves. The ass divided the large fat stag into three equal measures, but then the lion killed the ass and asked the fox to divide the spoil. For this version of the fable, see Geffrey Whitney, *A Choice of Emblemes* [...] (Leiden, 1586), 154. Owen would, once again, use this quotation and illustration in his sermon to Parliament on February 28, 1650.

stout men, valiant men and perhaps Ahithophel is with them.[57] Why, if they were not such, I pray how should the Lord have any praise in the close of the dispensation? We would be delivered, but we care not that God should be glorified. If God's glory were dear to us, we should not care how high opposition did arise. Precious faith, where are you fled? Had we but some few grains of it, we might see the rising of the greatest mountains to be but a means to make the name of God glorious, by removing them into the midst of the sea.[58] Has it not been thus in the days of old? The Lord humble us for our unbelief.

The Strong and Mighty Must Be Watchful

Use 2. Let men to whom the Lord has given stout hearts, strong hands, and great success, watch carefully over their own spirits, lest they be led aside into any way against the mind of God. Great endowments are ofttimes great temptations. "The pride of thy heart hath deceived thee, thou that dwellest in the rock, whose habitation is high, that saith in his heart, 'Who shall bring me down to the ground?'" (Obad. 3). Was it not the ruin of Amaziah, of whom notwithstanding it was said, "He did that which was right in the sight of the Lord" (2 Chron. 25:2)? He who is heightened against the king of terrors,[59] if he has not humility, one of the chief of graces, will quickly choose himself paths of his own. Alas! Poor creatures, if hearts and hands be, and God be not, what will it avail? But of this afterward. I now proceed to the second observation.

In God's Works of Providence, The Nature of Divine Deliverance Is Fittingly Tailored

[Observation] 2. God suits the workings and actings of providence for deliverance to the qualifications of the opposers.

Are they stout hearts? They shall be made to yield themselves. Are they men of might? They shall lose their power; they shall not find their hands. To this I shall speak very little. This is the cutting off of Adonibezek's toes and thumbs.[60] God countermines them in their actings, and blows them up in their own mine.[61] "In the thing wherein they deal proudly, he is above them"

---

57 2 Sam. 15:31.
58 Matt. 21:21.
59 Job 18:14.
60 Judg. 1:7.
61 Mining was an established part of siege warfare in the British Civil Wars and involved digging a shaft below a defensive wall, filling a chamber with gunpowder, and then exploding the bomb. Peter Harrington, *English Civil War Archaeology* (Princes Risborough, UK: Shire, 1992), 94–96. It was first used by Prince Rupert in 1643 to mine the walls of parliamentarian Lichfield. See Barbara Donagan, *War in England 1642–1649* (Oxford: Oxford University Press, 2010), 90.

(Ex. 18:11). They shall not soar so high on the wings of their pride, but that still they shall find God uppermost. When they take counsel, and think to carry it by their advices, God says; "I am wise also, and will bring evil" (Isa. 31:2). When they think to carry it by a high hand, his strength shall appear against them. When Herod owns the blasphemy of being called a god, he shall rot and be eaten of worms (Acts 12:23). Pharaoh cries: "Come on, let us deal wisely against Israel" (Ex. 1:10). He of all men shall play the fool, for his own ruin, and the ruin of his people (Ex. 14:27–28). If Sennacherib boasts of his mighty host, be sure he shall not find his hands.[62] How evidently has the Lord thus carried on his providence in the late dispensation? Were not many of the headless, heady undertakers, *robusti animo*,[63] mighty of heart? And were they not forced to yield themselves? Yea, to "yield themselves to the spoil?" Were they not deep in their plotting? Doubtless they, or their seducers, had dug deep to lay their design; though of the generality of them it cannot be said, as was of Caesar and his companions, "They undertook to destroy the Republic whilst sober."[64] They were brought to act things in very folly and confusion. They were great men of might: whence is it, they made no more opposition? The Lord laid their hands out of the way. Many reasons might be given of this, but I must pass to the last point,

God Turns the Courage and Strength of Those Who Engage against Him into Weakness and Folly

[Observation] 3. Though men have courage, might, and former successes to accompany them, yet when they engage themselves against the Lord, or any way of his, vanity, weakness, and disappointment will be the issue thereof.

"Can your heart endure, or can your hands be strong, in the days that I shall deal with you?" says the Lord (Ezek. 22:14). "Let the potsherds strive with the potsherds of the earth; woe unto him that contendeth with his maker" (Isa. 45:9). "He is wise in heart, and mighty in strength: who hath hardened himself against him, and prospered?" (Job 9:4). "The Lord bringeth

---

62 Isa. 37:35–36.
63 Lat. "stout hearts," from the Latin rendering of Ps. 76:6 in the Tremellius-Junius Bible, the *Testamenta Veteris Biblia sacra* (Frankfurt, 1579).
64 In the text: *Accessere sobrii ad perdendum rem publicam.*—Owen. This is adapted from the words of Cato as found in Quintilian, *The Orator's Education* 8.2.9. For the Latin text and English Translation, see Quintilian, *The Orator's Education*, vol. 3, *Books 6–8*, ed. and trans. Donald A. Russell, Loeb Classical Library 126 (Cambridge, MA: Harvard University Press, 2002), 330–31. See also Suetonius, *Julius Caesar* 53.1. For the Latin text and English translation, see Suetonius, *The Lives of the Caesars*, vol. 1, *Julius. Augustus. Tiberius. Gaius. Caligula*, trans. J. C. Rolfe, Loeb Classical Library 31 (London: Heinemann, 1914), 102–3.

the counsel of the heathen to nought, but the counsel of the Lord standeth for ever; he maketh the devices of the people of none effect" (Ps. 33:10–11). Whoever rises up without him, or against him, shall fall and come to nothing. This is a plain point, that we suppose ourselves exceedingly well-versed in. But he who searches our spirits, and is acquainted with, our inward parts, knows how great is our unbelief in this very thing. And therefore in tender condescension, he has carefully provided for our support herein. A man would think one word once spoken were enough to convince and persuade the whole world of this truth; but the Lord knows, there must be line upon line, here a little and there a little, to give his own people any establishment herein. And therefore it is, that in so many places in his word he has asserted and affirmed this one thing, viz, let men be never so strong, powerful, and successful, if once they engage against him, they are utterly destroyed, unless he pluck them out of the snare. "Associate yourselves, etc." (Isa. 8:9).[65]

Six Ways That Those in Power Can Know They Are Truly Engaged in God's Cause and Therefore Be Confident of Divine Protection

But you will say: "Engage against the Lord? That is true; whoever engageth against him, shall surely fall. But who is so mad as to do so? Very Rabshakeh himself affirms that he came not up to Jerusalem without the Lord, but that the Lord sent him to go up against the land to destroy it" (Isa. 36:10). It is true he said so: and by this observation you have an answer to the Scripture. For though he said so, he lied before the Lord, and belied the Lord; his undertaking was against the Lord, and against his mind, as the sequel fully manifested.[66] Many suppose they engage for God, when they engage against him. To engage against the Lord, is to engage against his mind and will. To undertake without the will of God, is enough to be the ruin of the best and stoutest, as we see in the case of Josiah.[67] But to engage against him, who can do it, and stand when he is provoked? This then is that which neither stout hearts, nor strong hands shall ever be able to go through withal. For instance; to engage against that authority which God will own and defend, is successlessly to engage against the Lord. Now because these are the days wherein the Lord will shake heaven and earth,[68] beat the nations with a rod

---

65 The verse continues with a warning that those who "gird" themselves for battle against God would "be broken in pieces" (KJV).
66 Isa. 37:36.
67 2 Chron. 35:21–22.
68 Heb. 12:26–27, the text on which Owen had addressed Parliament just two months prior to the occasion of this sermon.

of iron,[69] breaking much of the power of the world; it may be asked by some: how it shall be known, that any authority is such as the Lord will not destroy and overturn, but own it as a way of his own? I answer; to omit the rule of reason, law, and common established principles among men, all which give a great light unto the rule of walking in this case; I shall give you six scriptural significations, *à posteriori*[70] of such an authority, as the Lord will make as a brazen wall,[71] or a rock in the sea, against which the waves dash with noise and fury, but are themselves broken to pieces.

(1) If it be such as the Lord has honored with success and protection in great, hazardous, and difficult undertakings for himself. Thus was it with Moses. Never had a leader of a people more murmurings, revilings, and rebellions against him. The story is obvious unto all. He was envied, hated, reproached of all sorts, from the princes of the congregation[72] to the mixed multitude.[73] But Moses had traveled through the sea and the desert with the Lord, and was encompassed with success and protection; and therefore all attempts against him shall be birthless and fruitless. This is one; but it will never do alone, unless conjoined with those that follow.

(2) If the persons enjoying that authority abide to act for God, and not for themselves, after such success and protection. Saul began to act for God, and he "vexed" all his enemies, which way soever "he turned himself."[74] But afterward turning to himself, God left him to himself.[75] Cyrus, how honored, how anointed was he for his great undertaking against Babylon?[76] But afterward pursuing his own ambition, he was requited with blood, for the blood he sought.[77] The Lord is with them that are with him, and while

---

69 Ps. 2:9; Rev. 2:27.
70 Lat. "from the later," an argument based on evidence (effects) in contrast to reasoning from theoretical principles.
71 Jer. 15:20. The text of Owen's postregicide *A Sermon Preached* [...] *January 31* (1649), which is included in this volume, and one that Cromwell had employed in his speech to the General Council of the Army at Whitehall on March 23, 1649. See Oliver Cromwell, *The Letters, Writings, and Speeches of Oliver Cromwell*, ed. John Morrill, 3 vols. (Oxford: Oxford University Press, 2022), 2:27.
72 Num. 16:2.
73 Num. 11:4.
74 1 Sam. 14:47.
75 1 Sam. 16:14.
76 Isa. 45:1, 13.
77 In *A Vision of Unchangeable Free Mercy* (1646), Owen commented how a short time after issuing the decree Cyrus was "cut off." In the sixth-century BC, the Persians invaded the kingdom of Massagetae, ruled by Queen Tomyris, but were eventually defeated, and Cyrus himself was killed. According to Herodotus, Tomyris ordered that Cyrus's head be cut off and placed in blood, retorting that this might finally quench his thirst for blood. See Herodotus, *The Histories*, 1.205–14, in *The Histories*, trans. Tom Holland (London: Penguin, 2014), 101–5.

they are so.⁷⁸ The establishment of the house of Saul is far from the Lord: for "those that honour him, he will honour; and they that despise him shall be lightly esteemed" (1 Sam. 2:30). There is no more certain sign in the world of persons devoted to ruin, or at least of their being divested of their authority, than that having followed God for a season in their enjoyment of success and protection, they turn aside to pursue their own ends, like Jehu.⁷⁹ I could give you an example of this, as yet not much above half a year old.⁸⁰ But when men undertake with the Lord, and for him, and having known his assistance therein, shall continue to lay out themselves in his ways; the Lord will then build them a house like David, which shall not be prevailed against.

Here I must give one caution by the way; that I am very far from countenancing any to move against just and righteous authority, who discern not these things: the Lord forbid. Let men look to the rule of their obedience, which I have nothing to do withal at this time. I only describe such, as unto whom, if any dare to make opposition in an ordinary dispensation of providence, it will prove fruitless and vain.

3. The third thing is, that they subject their power to the power of the Lord Christ, who is Lord of lords, and King of kings.⁸¹ The psalmist tells the rulers of the earth, that the reason of their spoiling is, that they do not "kiss the Son" (Ps. 2:12), or yield unfeigned obedience to the mighty King, whom God has set on his holy hill. God has promised that he will give in the service of kings and nations to Christ in his kingdom, and therein shall be their security.⁸² When God puts it into the heart of rulers, to rule according to the interest of Christ and his gospel, and to seek the advancement of his scepter, they shall surely be as a fenced wall.⁸³ I cannot stay to show, what this interest of Christ is. In a word, it is the ordering, framing, carrying on of affairs, as is most conducible to the unraveling and destruction of the mystery of iniquity.⁸⁴

4. If they are supported by the prayer of a chosen people who seek their welfare, not for their own interest and advantage, but for the advantage of the gospel, and the ways of Christ by them asserted. If God's own people pray for them in authority, that under them they may enjoy some share of their own,

---

78 See 2 Chron. 15:2.
79 2 Kings 10:29–31.
80 This is probably a reference to those in Parliament who wished to continue to negotiate for a Presbyterian-royalist settlement at Newport.
81 Rev. 17:14.
82 See Ps. 72:11; Isa. 60:12.
83 Jer. 15:20.
84 Owen made a similar point in *A Sermon Preached* [...] *January 31* and *The Shaking and Translating of Heaven and Earth*, both of which are included in this volume.

and obtain some ends suited to any carnal interest of theirs, God will reject those prayers. But when they seek their welfare, because it is discovered to them, that in their peace the gospel shall have peace and prosperity; surely the Lord will not cast out their prayers, nor shame the face of his poor supplicants.

5. If in sincerity, and with courage and zeal, they fulfill the work of their magistracy, in the administration of righteous judgment; especially in those great and unusual acts of justice, in breaking the jaws of the wicked and terrible, and delivering the spoil out of the teeth of the mighty (Job 29:17). Innumerable are the demonstrations of God's owning such persons.

6. If they have not the qualifications of that power, which in these latter days God has promised to destroy. Now these are two; I will but name them unto you. First, drinking the cup of fornication that is in the hand of the harlot,[85] i.e. practicing any false worship and forms invented besides the word. Secondly, giving their power to the beast,[86] or engaging in any ways of persecution against any of the ways of God, or his saints in those ways. That the Lord is about to shake, break, and destroy all such powers as these, I did not long since, by his assistance, here demonstrate.[87]

And so have I completed my instances that they who engage against such an authority as is attended with these qualifications, engage against the Lord. I could also give other instances in other ways and institutions of God; but I chose these as most accommodated to the season.

If now I should tell you, that notwithstanding all clamors to the contrary, these things for the main are found in your assemblies,[88] thousands in the world would, yet I hope your own consciences would not, return the lie for so saying. But yet, though the Lord seems to bear witness to some integrity in his late dispensations, I shall only pray, that what is wanting may be supplied; that you may never want the like protection in the like distress.

Two Reasons Why Even the Strongest Opposition Will Not Succeed

Come we now briefly to the reasons why those who oppose such authority shall not succeed. And it were an easy labor to multiply reasons hereof. The sovereignty, the power, all the attributes of God would furnish us with arguments: I shall omit them all; [and] only touch upon two, that are couched in the text.

---

85 Rev. 17:4.
86 Rev. 17:13.
87 This is a reference to Owen's parliamentary sermon, delivered two months beforehand on April 19, published as *The Shaking and Translating of Heaven and Earth* (1649).
88 Owen was addressing members of the House of Commons and the London Common Council.

They shall have no better issue, because (1) The Lord will take away their stout hearts, whereby they are supported. (2) He will take away their strong hands, whereby they are confirmed: and when hearts and hands are gone, they also are gone.

God Has a Host of Ways to Take Away the Courage of His Enemies

(1) He will take away their stout hearts, that they shall no more be able to carry them out to any success in their great undertakings. He will break that wheel at the very fountain,[89] that it shall no more be the spring of their proceedings.

Now this the Lord usually does one, or more of these four ways. [1] He fills them with fury and madness; so taking away their order. [2] He fills them with folly and giddiness; so taking away their counsel. [3] He fills them with terror and amazement; so depriving them of their courage. Or, [4] with contrition and humility; so changing their spirits.

[1] He fills them with fury and madness, taking away their order, which is the tie and cement of all societies, in all undertakings. "Though all the people of the earth," saith the Lord, "be gathered together against Jerusalem, they shall not prosper."[90] And why so? "I will smite every horse with astonishment, and his rider with madness" (Zech. 12:4). Madmen have often great strength, and with it great fury; but know not how to use it, except to their own ruin. When they think to do the greatest mischief, they cut and gash themselves. Thus the Lord threatens those, who in outward profession are his own people, when they walk contrary to him: "The Lord shall smite thee with madness of heart, and thou shalt not prosper in thy ways" (Deut. 28:28–29). Because smitten with madness, therefore they shall not prosper. This is that untamable fury, whereby men are carried out to sinful, destructive enterprises, as the horse rushes into the battle. A judgment which some men vocally, as well as actually at this day proclaim to be upon their spirits. They cry their blood boils, and their hearts rage for revenge; reviling those in authority, whereby to foment (Acts 19).[91] Hence they stir up men for the engaging in such designs, as if accomplished, in the judgment of all men not mad like themselves, would certainly prove ruinous to themselves and others. And in this frame they delight, of it they boast, not once considering that it is a badge and character of men, whom God will disappoint and destroy in their proceedings; it being nothing but the working of that evil spirit, which came

---

89 See Eccl. 12:6.
90 Zech. 12:3.
91 Esp. Acts 19:29–34, 40.

upon Saul, stirring him up to rage and fury, when once the meek, calming Spirit of the Lord departed from him.[92]

[2] He will fill them with folly and giddiness; so taking away their counsel. Foolish and giddy undertakers do but "conceive chaff," and "bring forth stubble."[93] "The princes of Zoan are become fools, the princes of Noph are deceived, they have also seduced Egypt; the Lord hath mingled a perverse spirit in the midst thereof, and they have caused Egypt to err in every work thereof, as a drunken man staggereth in his vomit" (Isa. 19:13–14). This he calls taking away the spirit of Egypt, and destroying the counsel thereof ([Isa. 19]:3). There is no means of ruin, destruction, and disappointment that God does more frequently threaten than this: he will take wisdom from the wise, and then pour contempt upon the spirit of princes:[94] when to their madness, he adds blindness, to their fury, folly, to their rage, giddiness, what can be the issue but such as is expressed: "They shall stagger like a drunken man in his vomit?" Stand before him, and he'll pour his filth upon you; let him alone, and he and it will quickly tumble to the ground. What, I pray, can be expected from mad, blind, furious, foolish, raging, giddy men? Should a man use these expressions of any, it would be visible he railed; yet God has spoken it that all undertakers against him shall be so, and no otherwise. Now hence arises upon the spirits of such men a twofold effect: first, they shall not be able to advise rationally against others: nor, secondly, shall they be able to receive suitable advice from others: they shall be able neither to make out counsel to support them in the way wherein they are, nor to take in counsel for their reducing to better paths. If this were not evident in the late dispensation of the Lord toward poor creatures, setting up themselves against the Lord, then never did any providence speak plain in any latter age.

[3] He will fill them with fear and amazement; so taking away their courage. This God caused to fall upon a whole host at one time; that without seeing an enemy, they ran and fled, and lost all they had, and the spoil (2 Kings 7:6–7).[95] And he threatens that in such a condition, he will make men like women, they shall "be afraid and fear" (Isa. 19:16). Yea, this is the way of God's usual dealing; first, he overcomes the spirit of his enemies, and then their armies or force; and the Lord is magnified therein, as is fully set out [in] Exodus 15:14–16. The hearts and spirits of men are all in the hand of God; he can pluck them in, or let them out, as seems good unto him; make him that was mighty one day, the

---

92 1 Sam. 16:14–16.
93 Isa. 33:11.
94 Ps. 107:40.
95 The army of the Syrians fled after the Lord caused them to hear the sound of a great army.

next day to be of no power: what is left of fury, folly shall devour; and what is left of folly, fear shall consume; and the purpose of the Lord shall be established.

[4] If he has any favor for them, and so will not proceed in these ways of revenge against them, which would end in their speedy ruin: he will give them contrition and humility, so changing them. What a clear testimony of this did he give in the business of Jacob and Esau: Esau resolves and threatens his death upon the first opportunity (Gen. 27:41), an opportunity is put into his hands by Jacob's return into Canaan (Gen. 32), means of revenge he is ready, furnished withal, and comes out accordingly with a band of cutthroats for the purpose, in the same chapter.[96] What should any man now rationally expect, but that poor Jacob must certainly be ruined, and the mother slain with the children?[97] In an instant the Lord touches the heart of Esau, and all his menaces of revenge issue in tears and expressions of love and joy (Gen. 33:4). It is to be rejoiced in that the stout hearts of some men are changed upon their disappointment, and the issue of the mercy is no loss to you, to the nation, and themselves therein; though truly to them it had been an argument of greater love, had the Lord graciously bent their spirits unto it before. But by his infinite wisdom he has accomplished his holy will.

Now in one, more, or all of these ways, will the Lord proceed with the mighty of heart, that set up themselves against him, until he takes away their hearts, and makes them useless; that either willingly or unwillingly, "they shall yield themselves" even "to the spoil."

God Can Simply Take Away the Strength of His Enemies
(2) He will not only take away their hearts, but also their hands; he will not only dispirit them, but he will also disarm them; he will take not only wisdom from their hearts, but the wheels from their chariots.[98] He is the God of the power of men, as well as of the spirits of men. Will he continue power and strength unto men to use it against him that gives it?

Four Uses of This Doctrine
At Burford God Defeated the Levellers, Turning Their Strength into
Weakness and Thwarting Their Evil Designs against Church and State
Use 1. To discover the ground of God's late dispensation, in taking away the hearts from the stout, and hands from the mighty, bringing them into a

---

[96] Gen. 32:6.
[97] Gen. 32:11.
[98] Ex. 14:25.

condition of weakness and vanity. Their undertakings were against the Lord, and their hearts could not endure, neither could their hands be strong.

I shall give some instances in their undertaking against the Lord.

(1) In their declared enmity to the ministry of the gospel: not to the persons of ministers, because engaged in some faction in the state, wherein perhaps many may be opposed, and that from the Lord: nor yet because of their persuasion for the administration of ordinances, after this or that form; which often arises to very great animosities: the Lord pardon them unto his people: but because in general they do administer ordinances. Now certainly there is so much of God in that administration, that if they be opposed, not for other causes, or upon other pretenses, but *eo nomine*,[99] as administrators of ordinances, that opposition is made to God himself. It was part of the end of Christ's ascension, that he might bestow those gifts upon them, which they do enjoy (Eph. 4:8). And shall the fury of men, make the work of God, the purchase of Christ, of none effect? Doubtless in this respect, God will make as many as are sincere "a fenced brasen wall" (Jer. 15:20). Men may batter their hands, and beat out their brains against them; but they shall not prevail. It is true, as many of them are pleased in these days to engage themselves in several parties; so if they do close and act with them that are pernicious to the commonwealth, all inconvenience that lights upon them, is from themselves; their profession gives them no sanctuary from opposition: but when they are envied, *eo nomine*, as administrators of ordinances, not in such or such a way, but as ordinances; shall not the Lord plead for this thing? Now that this was aimed at by some, I suppose none can doubt. The Lord open the eyes of them who in this deliverance have received deliverance, but will not see it. I fear some men had almost rather perish, than be delivered not in their own way. Envy in some men will outbalance safety. Alas! We are proud beggars, when we will refuse the mercy of God, if we may not appoint the hand whereby it shall be bestowed.

(2) Against the spiritual ordinances of God themselves. These are the carved work which they aimed to break down with their axes and hammers. Christ has said, "I will build my church."[100] Their voice was, "Down with it! Down with it even to the ground!"[101] Poor creatures! They dashed themselves against the rock. Is this a time, think you, to engage against all ordinances, when the Lord Jesus is joining battle with all the world for their

---

[99] Lat. "by that name."
[100] Matt. 16:18.
[101] From Coverdale's translation of Psalm 137 as opposed to the Authorized Verion's (KJV) "rase it, rase it."

abuse of them? And is vindicating them in order to more purity, beauty, luster, power, efficacy, and peace, than ever yet he adorned them withal? You were not wise, poor souls, to discern the seasons! What! No time to pluck down, but when Christ himself is building? Ah! Turn your weapons against Babylon; it will prove far the more thriving warfare. Let Zion alone, if but for your own sakes. Jerusalem will prove a "burdensome stone" to all that take her up.[102] You have received more loss in a week of days from Christ in this nation, than you would have done in a week of years from Antichrist in another. God will make them that shall go for Ireland, sensible of this truth (Ps. 48:12–14).[103]

(3) Principally and immediately against magistracy; if not in the abstract, yet openly as established in the hands of those, whom the Lord has owned in the darkest day that ever this nation saw.[104] It is the hope of my soul, that the Lord has borne witness, that they have the sixfold qualification before mentioned. And why would they have at once destroyed the Parliament, and their own commander? Look upon the end of their common workmen: was it not that everyone might have enjoyed their lust for a season? Of the more crafty: was it not to get themselves power, to attempt their folly, and execute their fury? Look upon the end of the work: was it not to have wrapped us in confusion for a few months, and then to have given us up to the revengeful will of enraged enemies? So that truly there is but one thing wonderful to me in all this business, that God should take away the hearts and hands of these men in this enterprise, and that is, that he should do it in mercy for such an unthankful, unworthy, unbelieving people, as we are. In this is he forever to be admired and blessed. "At thy rebuke, O God of Jacob, both the chariot and the horses" have failed.[105]

Providence Reassures Those in Power of Divine Protection,
So Long As They Are Walking in God's Ways

Use 2. If this be the cause why "they have slumbered their sleep";[106] be instructed, ye that are rulers of this nation, in the ways of peace, protection, and safety: be in the ways of God, and do the things of God, and no weapon that

---

[102] Zech. 12:3.
[103] A description of Zion as a well-fortified garrison, able to withstand a strong enemy. Owen's sermon *The Branch of the Lord* (Edinburgh, 1650), which is included in volume 19, had this text printed on the title page.
[104] The Levellers were not opposed to magistracy "in the abstract," but they had sought to implement the *Agreement of the People* before the king would be brought to trial.
[105] Ps. 76:6.
[106] Ps. 76:5.

is formed against you shall ever prosper.[107] Many protections and deliverances you have had in your actings for him. Has he not deserved at your hands to be trusted and feared all your days, with all your power? As my heart has always been toward the governors in Israel,[108] who willingly offered themselves among the people; so truly my heart never more trembled over them, than now. Oh! Where shall we find hearts fit to receive so many mercies as have been given into our bosoms? Oh! Where shall we have hearts large enough to receive all these mercies? The oil ceased when the vessel would hold no more.[109] All my hope and confidence is, that God will work for his name's sake. I could exhort you to sundry particulars, and lay down several paths of God, walking wherein you shall be sure to find peace and safety; as especially that you would regard that which God has honored, whereunto the opposition which he had resolved to make void, was made.

Providence Calls Those Who Are Strong and Mighty to Watchful Self-Examination

Use 3. You that are men of courage, and might, and success, stout of heart and strong of hand, be watchful over yourselves, lest you should in anything be engaged against the Lord. The ways of the Lord are your locks, step but out of them, they will be cut, and you will become like other men, and be made a prey and a mocking to the uncircumcised that are round about.[110] These eminencies you have from God, are eminent temptations to undertakings against God, if not seasoned with grace and watchfulness. Ah! How many baits have Satan and the world suited to these qualifications. Samson shook himself, and went out, saying, "'I will do as at other times;' but he knew not that the Lord was departed from him."[111] You may think when you are walking in paths of your own, that you will do as at other times, but if your strength be departed away, what will be the end?

Providence Calls for Trust in God, Especially in the Context of the Forthcoming Irish Expedition

Use 4. Our last use should be of instruction in respect of God, that you may see, both what he can do, and trust him; and consider what he has done, and bless him. For the first; weapons of all sorts, men of all sorts, judgments of all

---

107 Isa. 54:17.
108 Judg. 5:9.
109 2 Kings 4:6.
110 Judg. 16:19–21.
111 Judg. 16:20.

sorts are at his command and disposal: see it in this psalm.[112] And for what he has done; if there be any virtue in the presence of Christ in his ordinances; if any worth in the gospel; if any sweetness in carrying on the work of Christ's revenge against Babylon; if any happiness in the establishment of the peace and liberty of a poor nation, purchased with so much blood, and so long a contest; if any content in the disappointment of the predictions and threats of God's enemies, and his people's; if any refreshment to our bowels,[113] that our necks are yet kept from the yoke of lawless lust, fury, and tyranny; if any sweetness in a hope that a poor, distressed handful in Ireland may yet be relieved; if any joy that God has given yet another testimony of his presence among us; if it be any way valuable, that the instruments of our deliverance be not made the scorned object of men's revengeful violence; if any happiness, that the authority under which we enjoy all these mercies, is not swallowed up: is it not all in the womb of this deliverance?[114] And who is he that has given it into our bosom?

---

[112] The weapons mentioned in Psalm 76 include arrows, shields, swords, horses, and chariots. The variety of men include the stouthearted, men of might, princes, and the kings of the earth. The judgments include the destruction of weapons, sending sleep, weakening the enemy, and audible judgment from heaven.

[113] Philem. 7, 20.

[114] See Phil. 2:1–2.

General Index

Abdā, 395n298
Abel, 122, 265
Abraham, 113, 120, 154
Abrahamic covenant, 273
Absalom, 149, 299
Abstemius, Laurentius, 122n77, 465n12
accommodation, 9–10, 35, 185
Achan, 251n74
Act of Settlement, 214n156
Adam, 25, 120, 154, 274
admonition, 189, 199, 202, 322, 401, 403
Adrian IV (Pope), 247n62
Aeneas, 148n226, 173n23, 194n41, 196n55, 288n201
Aeschylus, 269n135
Aesop's Fables, 129n113, 161n330, 251n73, 354n73
affections, 229, 231, 334
affliction, 246, 256
Agag, 56, 318
Ahab, 214, 334
Ainsworth, Henry, 349
Albigenses, 33, 62, 210n135, 368, 373–74, 439. *See also* Cathars
Albigensian Crusade, 439n92
Alemanni, 441n116
Alexander the Great, 434n62
Alexander II, 442n124
Ali ibn Abi Talib, 195n49
Allein, Francis, 86, 295n2
Álvarez de Toledo, Fernando, 62, 365n138
Amalek, 261, 475
amazement, 483
Amaziah, 473, 476
ambition, 56, 88, 203, 307, 317, 318, 336, 337, 479

Ambrose, 109n2, 171n12, 228n4, 231–32n15, 281n177
Ammonites, 254, 386
Amorites, 237, 267, 308
Amos, 313
Anabaptists, 32, 66, 200, 394n295
Andrewes, Lancelot, 180n55
angels, 423
An Humble Testimony (1681), 3
Ante-Nicene fathers, 64
anti-Arminianism, 25
antichrist, 13, 62, 77, 107, 138, 141, 435, 438, 440, 445
antiformalism, 58
Antiochus IV Epiphanes, 361n115, 435n70
Antiochus XIII Asiaticus, 434n63
anti-Pelagianism, 25, 125n96, 150n235
anti-Semitism, 396n305
antitoleration campaign, 13, 14, 15, 26, 34, 66, 173–81
anti-Trinitarianism, 35, 48n170, 63, 66, 368n158, 368n159, 368n160, 395n301
Antony of Egypt, 376n215
apostasy, 40, 73, 139n159, 143, 256, 305, 348n43, 417
Apostles' Creed, 67, 405
Appleby, David J., 51
Arians, 62, 64, 139n159, 180, 204n104, 208, 210n130, 211, 351n56, 365, 369n169, 373, 377
Aristotle, 118n47, 272n141
Arius, 379n229
Arminianism, 12, 35, 116, 143n191
Arnobius of Sicca, 212n145, 360
Asa, 323
Ascham, Anthony, 78

assurance, of salvation, 2
Astemio, Lorenzo, 465n12
Asty, John, 4, 70
Athanasius, 62, 210n130, 211n140, 376n215, 378
atheism, 63, 111, 265n129, 449
Athens, 79, 339n1, 358
Augustine of Hippo, 25, 111n20, 115n33, 117n44, 119n52, 123n84, 124n87, 125–26n96, 131n122, 134n134, 142n181, 150n235, 155n278, 169n3, 176n39, 193n36, 204n103, 278n158, 342n15, 346n38, 356n78, 375n209, 383n263, 418n5
Augustus, Octavian, 221n14, 429n39
authority, 193, 205, 315, 347–48, 481
Auxentius, 228n4

Babylon, 61, 75, 78, 80, 81, 90, 445, 446n157, 448
backsliding, 40, 56, 73, 142, 315–22, 420–21
Bacon, Francis, 122n77, 231n13, 465n12
Baillie, Robert, 19, 20, 146n214, 171n18, 174n29, 175n31, 178n45
Balaam, 344
Balak, 344
Bale, John, 210n135, 373n199
Baptists, 12
Baronio, Cesare, 142n181
barrenness, 153, 283
Bastwick, John, 137n147
Beaton, David, 371n188
Beaton, James, 371n188
Becan, Martin, 369n173
Belfast Presbytery, 327n85
Belgic Remonstrants, 197
Bellarmine, Robert, 159n315, 200n82, 307n19, 342n17, 346, 360, 363n130, 368n164, 369n174, 373, 403n342, 440, 441n107
Bernard of Clairvaux, 291n214, 425n24
Béroalde, Matthieu, 128n110
Best, Paul, 15, 33, 66
Beza, Theodore, 203, 423n18
Biandrata, Giorgio, 368n160
Biddulph, William, 291n215
Bilson, Thomas, 54, 306n17
Blair, Robert, 327n85
blasphemy, 15, 33, 48n170, 60, 65, 66, 207, 340n4, 344–45, 391, 395–96

blindness, 209, 334, 335, 395–96, 483
Bockelson, Jan, 200n84
Bolsec, Jérôme-Hermès, 363n129, 408n359
Bolton, Samuel, 24
Boniface I (Pope), 375n209
Bradwardine, Thomas, 119n51
Bramhall, John, 79
"brazen wall," 323, 336, 337
Bridge, William, 63
Brownists, 62, 363, 397
Browne, Robert, 363n122
Brutus, 114
Bucer, Martin, 211n138
Buckland, James, 5n21
bullets, 272, 290
Bullinger, Heinrich, 180n53
Burgess, Anthony, 174n30, 230n8
Burroughes, Jeremiah, 10–11, 63
Burton, Henry, 137n147, 200n80
Butler, James, 72

Cain, 122, 156, 265, 356
Calamy, Edmund, 354n71
Calgacus, 192n32, 192n33
Callistus, Nicephorus, 115n36, 142n181
Calvert, Thomas, 444n140
Calvinism, 180
Calvin, John, 115n33, 119n52, 180n52, 324, 359
cannibalism, 195n47, 397n318
Capel, Arthur, 36, 38, 51, 263n120, 280n174, 288n200
Capet, Hugh, 442n125
capital punishment, 60, 350. *See also* death penalty
Cardell, John, 51–52, 56, 318n55
Caryl, Joseph, 15–16, 24, 62, 369n175
Case, Thomas, 172n20, 178n46
Cathars, 76, 373n199, 439n92. *See also* Albigenses
Cerinthus, 375n210
Chadwick, Henry, 370n178
Chadwick, Owen, 317n51
chance, 45n154
charity, 173, 202–5
Charlemagne, 368n156, 441n107, 442n122
Charles I, 8, 40, 48, 54, 154n270, 244n53, 318n55
Charles II, 72, 77, 80, 451n176

GENERAL INDEX   491

Charles V, 160n325, 371n184
Childeric III, 441n107, 442n120
Christendom, 76, 181, 206, 446
church
    and coercion, 364–72
    deliverance of, 261, 265–66, 283–85
    golden era for, 431–33
    humiliation of, 237
    as opposing error, 350–52
church discipline, 17, 29, 58, 176, 178, 347n41
church government, 8, 27, 28–29, 182, 185
church members, 190
Church of Scotland, 340
Cicero, 155, 177n41, 195n44, 198n60, 239n38, 356n78, 357n93, 359, 433n60
Circumcellions, 194n38, 375
civil magistrate, 32, 65, 67, 148, 164, 187, 206, 353, 355, 383–409, 459–60
civil obedience, 404
Clarke, Samuel, 233n18
Clark, John, 4n20
classes, 17, 30
Cleaver, John, 70, 73
Clement of Rome, 281n179
clericalism, 460n237
Clopton, John, 69, 85
coercion, 62
Coffey, John, 20, 26, 31, 60, 67, 72, 188n19, 210n133, 341n7, 343n18
Colet, John, 73
Collins, Francis, 146n214
comfort, 259
Committee of Accommodation, 185n1
Committee for Plundered Ministers, 27n107, 30, 186n8
communication of properties, 140n164
Communion with God (1657), 4
Como, David R., 7n26, 175n34
compromise, 315–22
concurrence, 121, 336, 431, 447
confessions, 405
Congregationalism, 8, 10, 11, 13, 68, 177n43, 188n19, 364n137
conscience, 11, 12, 48, 322
Constantia, 379n229
Constantine, 136, 270n137, 378, 379, 393
Constantine V, 208n116, 208n118, 209n118, 211n138, 367n151
contingency, 45n154, 110, 111, 123
contradictions, 299

contrition, 484
conversion, 125
conviction, 125
Cooper, Tim, 22
Coppe, Abiezer, 58
corruption, 162, 334–35
Coster, François de, 343n20
Cotton, John, 148n228, 444n138
Council of Chalcedon (451), 203n100, 388
Council of Nicaea (325), 203n97, 365n140
councils, 203
Council of Trent, 146n213, 363n127
Council of Tyre (335), 378n228
Counter Reformation, 212n148
Country Essay (1646), 24, 30–34, 185–216, 367n153, 394n296
courage, 471, 477–78, 482–84
covenant, 419
covenant of works, 132, 137, 420
covetousness, 318
Cradock, Walter, 27n107
Cranford, James, 13, 175n31
creation, 135
Cromwell, Oliver, 12, 36, 43, 50, 53, 70, 82, 83, 90, 221n15, 255n93, 479n71
cruelty, 314
Cushan, 255–57
Cyprian, 64
Cyril of Jerusalem, 139n159
Cyrus, 127, 128, 448, 479

d'Anghiera, Pietro Martire, 130n117
Daniel, 238, 286, 288
Daniel, Samuel, 363n125
Darius, 45, 127, 128n110, 288
darkness, 130, 142, 154–55, 158, 313, 316, 332, 334
Davenport, Christopher, 146n213
David, 154, 241, 259, 306, 311, 313, 480
death penalty, 15, 33, 35, 60. *See also* capital punishment
Decius, 381
Dee, Francis, 146n214
defections, 320n68
defensative, 28, 182, 361, 375
delight, 231
deliverance, 130, 144, 237–38, 261, 265–66, 270–72, 280–85, 291–92, 311–12, 335, 466, 471, 476–77, 488

delusion, 334
demonology, 114
Denne, Henry, 467n22
Diaz, Juan, 213n150
Diet of Worms, 172n19
Dilly, Edward, 5n21
Dio Cassius, 357–58, 380n244
Diocletian, 270n137, 271n137, 382
Diodorus of Sicily, 467n23
Diogenes Laërtius, 358n97
Dionysius of Alexandria, 352n69, 382n257
disease, 246
Display of Arminianism (1643), 23, 121n76
Dissenters, 390–91, 399, 404–8
Dissenting Brethren, 8
distress, 154–55, 469–71
disturbance, 391
divine protection, 478–81, 486–87
divine right theory, 17, 21, 145n206
division, 182, 187
Domitian, 380, 383n264
Donagan, Barbara, 43, 245n55, 262n119
Donatists, 194n38, 375n208
Dow, Christopher, 146n214
Duke of Hamilton, 51, 245n53, 248n66
Du Moulin, Pierre, 68n246, 180n55
Durham, James, 327n85
Dury, John, 24
Dutch Arminians, 197n59
Dutch Reformed Church, 32, 63
Duty of Pastors and People Distinguished (1644), 23
dysentery, 246n57

Earl of Rutland, 78
Easter, 281n179
Ebenezer: A Memorial for the Deliverance of Essex, County, and Committee (1648), 1, 34–47, 50, 70, 217–92, 377n222, 413n3
ecclesiology, 29
Eck, Johann, 363n126
Edict of Milan (313), 378n225
Edict of Nantes (1598), 62, 372n193
Edomites, 238
Edwards, Thomas, 14–15, 16, 63, 85n317, 139n161, 143n192, 144n196, 171n18, 174–75n31
effectual grace, 334
Egyptians, 343

Eighty Years' War (1568–1648), 371n186, 374n203
Eikon Basilike, 310n30
elders, 177n43, 187, 189n22
election, 126, 432
Eleutherius, 142n181
Elijah, 214, 334
Elisha, 154, 247
emperors, 429
encouragement, 325, 326
enemies, 254–55, 257, 261, 262–64, 266–67, 278, 279, 322, 331, 470, 482–84
England, 142, 162
envy, 264–66
Epaminondas, 467n23
Ephraimites, 330
Epiphanius of Salamis, 176n39, 362n120, 455n199
Episcopius, Simon, 197n59
Erasmus, Desiderius, 170n7, 198n63, 430n46
Erastianism, 6, 19–20, 31, 402
Erastus, Thomas, 7n25, 20, 402n336
error, 16, 144, 191–94, 340, 341, 355, 398–403
Esau, 122, 130, 265, 484
eschatology, 6
Eunomians, 367n149
Eusebius of Caesarea, 65, 115n36, 128n110, 209n125, 269n135, 270n137, 352n66, 356n80, 378n226, 381, 383n262, 393n289, 393n290, 427n30, 455
Eusebius of Nicomedia, 210n129
Eustathius, 210n129
Eutropius, 383n264
Evelyn, John, 230n11
Everard, William, 58
evil, 333
excommunication, 19, 21, 31, 370n179, 401, 403
exile, 181n57, 208n115
exodus, as trope, 26–27, 57
Eyre, William, 84
Ezekiel, 118, 134

Fabyan, Robert, 363n124
Fagius, Paul, 211n138
Fairclough, Samuel, 42, 242n45, 276n152
Fairfax, Thomas, 36, 37, 38, 39, 43, 44, 46–47, 56, 70, 83, 221n19, 255n92, 279n168, 280n172, 280n173

faith, 206, 258–61, 267, 290–91, 312, 325, 475–76
false worship, 306–7, 314, 392–93, 437
families, 387
Farr, Henry, 36, 320n68
fasting, 69, 458n217
fear, 231, 264–66, 317, 451–52, 475–76, 483
fear of God, 234–35, 247, 384
Featley, Daniel, 240n40
fidelity, 325
First Civil War, 56, 131n119, 241–42, 263n120, 277n155, 319n58
Flacius Illyricus, Matthias, 192n31
Florus, 220n12
folly, 334, 452, 477–78, 483
fornication, 444–45
Foxe, John, 76, 121n74, 151n246, 204n102, 210n135, 373n199, 438n91
Francis I, 160n325
Franks, 438n86, 441n113, 442n120, 442n121
free will, 145
French Reformed Church, 180n55
French Wars of Religion (1562–1598), 372n192
fruits, 153
Fulgentius, 124n87
Funck, Johann, 128n110
fundamental articles of faith, 398, 399, 405
fury, 482
future blessing, 239–41, 260–61, 267

Galerius, 427n30
Gamaliel, 206
Gambe, Dafydd, 221n17
Gardiner, Stephen, 212n148
Gentile, Giovanni Valentino, 368n159
Gentles, Ian, 241n42
Gibeonites, 249
giddiness, 338, 483
Gideon, 286, 309
Giffard, William, 180n52
Gildas, 142n181, 151n246
Gillespie, George, 61, 327n85, 348n43, 364n137, 403n342
Gnosticism, 370
God
    attributes of, 481
    authority of, 317
    communion with, 157–58
    election of, 126
    fear of, 234–35, 247, 384
    glory of, 151, 242–45, 275, 331, 335
    goodness of, 149, 151
    good pleasure of, 131–37
    holiness of, 246
    instruments of, 309–13, 322–29
    justice of, 125
    mercy of, 144, 149, 262
    power of, 268, 269, 273, 274–80, 285, 287, 421
    promises of, 443–46
    purposes of, 129–31, 254, 271, 335–36
    revelation of, 243–44
    sovereignty of, 150, 331–32, 338
    will of, 116–20, 333, 384, 456, 478
    work of, 453–59, 468–69
    wrath of, 303, 328n90, 336, 429, 457
godliness, 137, 147, 175, 182, 216, 458
Golden Rule, 32–33, 66, 153, 193n36, 205–7, 345n32, 394–95
Goliath, 241, 470
Gomorrah, 246
Goodwin, John, 48, 49, 346n34
Goodwin, Thomas, 10, 63, 74, 84, 85, 86, 148n228
Goold, William, 5, 254n88
Goring, George, 36, 288n200
gospel
    author of, 419
    being without, 153–65
    danger of losing of, 150–53
    declared to the nation, 384–85
    enjoyment of, 152–53
    ministers of, 401
    nature of, 403
    opposition to, 385–86
    preachers of, 388
    propagation of, 118–20
    purity of, 144
    rejection of, 25, 139
    silence of, 354
Goths, 365n141, 441n115
government
    and kingdom of Christ, 440–43
    shaking of, 426, 428
Gratian, 367n149, 370n178, 388n282, 390n286
gratitude, 291

Gregory I (Pope), 253n82, 377
Gregory IX (Pope), 388n282, 439n92
Gregory Nazianzus, 203n99
Gregory of Valencia, 342n17
Grey, Zachary, 53
Gribben, Crawford, 4, 7, 37, 40, 51, 52, 89n334, 121n76, 164n351, 179n50, 445n148
Grotius, Hugo, 197n59, 424n21
Guibbory, Achsah, 174n29
guidance, 322–29
guilt by association, 173
Guthrie, James, 327n85

Habakkuk, 225
Hadrian, 381, 382
Hagar, 153
Haman, 161, 266, 468
Hamilton, Patrick, 371n188
happiness, 157, 159
hardening, 329–31, 337
hardship, 326
Harrington, James, 460n228
Hartopp, John, 4
Harvey, Elizabeth D., 89n334, 445n148
heart, as deceitful, 171
hearts, pride of, 269–70
heaven, 158
heavenly things, 461–62
Heerbrand, Jakob, 342n17
Henri, Duke of Rohan, 460n228
Henrician Reformation, 212n148
Henry V, 221n17
Henry VIII, 438n87
Hercules, 220n13
heresiographers, 16, 25, 139n161, 143n192
heresy, 9, 13–16, 21, 26–33, 60, 144, 176n39, 179n51, 191, 193, 200, 202, 207–14, 253, 343, 362, 364, 372, 400, 402
Herod, 246, 247, 286, 468
Herodotus, 397n316, 479n77
heterodoxy, 9, 13, 33, 61
Heylyn, Peter, 146n214, 147n220, 180n54
Hezekiah, 305, 385, 463
history, lessons of, 250–54
holiness, 246, 458
Holy Spirit
  and the conscience, 67, 407
  and preaching, 2
  revelation of, 425n24
  and uniformity, 407–8
holy war, 171n9
Homer, 196n51, 197n58
honor, 325, 326
Honywood, Thomas, 36, 37, 39, 46, 223, 263n121
Hooker, Richard, 20
hope, 231
Horace, 169n1, 170n4, 171n17, 181n60, 190n28, 409n363, 428n34, 473n48
Hozjusz, Stanisław, 363n127
Hughes, Ann, 458n217
human cognizance, 341
Human Power Defeated (1649), 81–90, 122n77, 454n193, 463–88
human purposes, 335–36
humility, 111, 231, 484
Huneric, 208n115
Hunnius, Aegidius, 180n52
Hus, Jan, 210n135, 363, 364n131, 373n195, 439n94
Hussites, 33, 76, 210n135, 363n123, 374n200, 439
hypocrisy, 31, 152, 191, 267, 447, 448, 458

Ibarhim I, 140n170
iconoclasm, 62, 209n118, 367n150
Idacius, 370n178
idolatry, 32, 54–55, 60, 79, 88, 200–201, 256, 304–8, 342–44, 393, 444
Ignatius of Antioch, 64, 117, 208n111, 352n67, 374, 375, 376
Ignatius of Loyola, 200n81
ignorance, 158–59
image worshipers, 208n118
immorality, 200–201
incest, 397n318
Independents, 9, 31, 189, 248
individualism, 6
inheritance, 133, 248–50, 251
injustice, 307
Innocent III (Pope), 373n199, 439n92
"Intrinsicall" power, 18
Ireland, 58, 72, 77, 87, 89, 90, 127n108, 138n156, 487–88
Irenaeus of Lyons, 64, 117, 281n179, 352n68, 374, 375n210
Irene, 136, 209n118

irenicism, 180n55
Ireton, Henry, 48, 49, 345n31
Irish Rebellion, 138n156
Isaac, 286
Ishmael, 153
Islam, 195n49, 349n49
Ithacius, 173n24, 370n178
itinerant preachers, 27n107, 66, 396–97

Jacob, 122, 130, 198n67, 484
Jael, 471
Jehiokim, 257
Jehoash, 473
Jehosaphat, 385
Jehu, 480
Jenkyn, William, 24, 174n29
Jenner, Robert, 23
Jephthah, 254, 330, 386
Jeremiah, 228, 330, 401
Jeroboam, 323, 334
Jerome, 220n11
Jerome of Prague, 373n195, 439n95
Jesuits, 114n32, 116n41, 135n139, 135n140, 164n352, 200, 307n19, 342n17, 343n20, 369n173, 399
Jesus Christ
  as angel of the covenant, 328
  ascension of, 485
  blood of, 132–33, 137, 284, 292
  gospel of, 155–57
  as king, 457–59
  person and work of, 419
  power of, 421, 424
  presence of, 437
Jewel, John, 212n149
Job, 154, 286
John the Baptist, 453–54
John Chrysostom, 161n334
John of Damascus, 123n83
Jones, Inigo, 392n288
Joseph, 149, 154, 230, 278, 283n187, 286
Joseph (husband of Mary), 113
Josephus, Flavius, 255n95, 361n115, 455
Joshua, 113
Josiah, 227n2, 257, 337, 478
Josselin, Ralph, 49, 56
Jovian, 62, 366–67n148
joy, 229–30, 231, 232, 432
Joyce, George, 56

Judaism, 75, 79, 259, 361, 396n305, 417, 443–46, 452
judgment, 3, 54, 160n320, 162, 233, 234, 246, 281–82, 302, 304–8, 329, 380–83
Julian "the Apostate," 139n159, 366–67n148, 382, 452, 468n28
Julius Caesar, 221n16, 298n12
Julius Capitolinus, 381n250
Junius, Francis, 74, 423n18, 430n46, 434n62
justice, 125, 126, 135, 262, 438, 481
justification, 145, 419
Justinian, 208n115
Justinian Code, 369n170
Justin Martyr, 136n144, 360
Juvenal, 26, 170n4, 170n6, 195n47
Juxon, Thomas, 22

Kalybites, Andrew, 208n116, 208–9n118
Killeen, Kevin, 3, 54
kingdom, growth of, 109–11
kingdom of Christ, 440–43
King, Henry, 44n154
kingship, 303n8, 305–8
Knox, John, 372n191
Korah, 310, 324

Lactantius, 193n37, 232n17, 377, 382n255
Lambert, John, 36
lamentation, 3
Lamont, William, 54
Landolfus Sagax, 208n116
Lapide, Cornelius à, 114n32, 116n41
Latimer, Hugh, 121n74, 212n148
Laudian Canons, 145n210
Laudianism, 12, 25, 27, 137n147, 145n205
Laud, William, 143n191, 147n225, 200n80, 460n237
law, 423
Lenthall, William, 47
Leo I (Pope), 379n231
Leo III (Pope), 208n118, 367n151, 441n107
Leo V (Pope), 367n151
Leo X (Pope), 438n87
lesser matters, 405–6
L'Estrange, Roger, 305n13, 438n88
Levellers, 81–82, 89, 486n104
Levi, 198n67
Lewis, John, 27n107
liberty, 141–50, 188, 195n44, 250, 320, 324

liberty of conscience, 11, 12, 48, 171n18
Licinius, 427n30
light, 130, 142, 244–45, 314, 316, 332, 453, 454
light of nature, 66, 132, 398
Lilburne, John, 49, 71, 81, 82
limbus patrum, 145, 146n214
Lim, Paul C. H., 171–72n18
Lisle, George, 36, 38, 44n154, 288n199
Lockyer, Robert, 71, 82
Lollards, 62, 76, 363n124, 438
Lombard, Peter, 117n44
Long Parliament, 5, 6, 8
Lord's Supper, 18, 114, 177n44, 180n53, 182n62
Loughborough, 263n120, 280n174
Louis XII, 369n176
Louis XIV, 72
love, 258–59
Lucan, 194n42
Lucas, Charles, 36, 38, 44n154, 262n118, 263n121, 288n199
Lucian of Samosata, 339n1, 445n151
Lucilius, 220n8
Lucius III (Pope), 439n93
Lucretius, 196n52
Ludlow, Edmund, 47
lusts, 159
Luther, Martin, 55, 156, 161, 172n19, 203, 213, 213n151, 298n5, 313n41, 363n126, 371n188, 373

madness, 482
Major, Georg, 114n29
Maldonado, Juan de, 422n12
Manasseh, 54, 304, 305, 306
Mandeville, John, 155n276
Mani, 204n103
Manichaeism, 204, 349, 370
manna, 164
man of sin, 457, 469
Maozim, 147
Marcellinus, Ammianus, 172n22
Marcian, 368n166
Marcion, 349, 375
Marquis of Argyll, 327n85
Marshall, John, 253n86
Marshall, Stephen, 52
Marston Moor, 40, 241, 245n53
Martin of Tours, 208n112, 370n179
martyrs, 207–11, 253, 360, 438–39

Mary Queen of Scots, 372n190
Masham, William, 39, 46, 50, 70, 222, 413n3
Matthijs, Jan, 200n84
Maximian, 270n137
Maximus, Magnus, 208n113, 370n178
Maximus Thrax, 381n251, 427n30
means, use of, 333–35
means of grace, 58, 117, 119, 120–22, 124, 134, 135, 149, 154
Mede, Joseph, 114n32, 208n116
Melanchthon, Philip, 156n285, 363n128
mercy, 149, 159–60, 233, 235–36, 239–40, 282
Messiah, 312, 447
methodology, 1
Meyer, Wolfgang, 346n34
Miciah, 154
Midian, 255–57
Midland Revolt, 472n45
Mildmay, Henry, 39, 45–46, 47, 49, 70, 222
Miller, George, 24
Milton, John, 52, 80, 89n334, 210n133, 220n13, 445n148
mining, 476n61
ministers, 164
minor differences, 390
Minucius Felix, 360, 362, 397n318
Mladoňovic, Petr, 364n131
modern preaching, 6
Monarchianism, 367n149
Monophysitism, 379n233
Montagu, Richard, 128n110, 146n214
Montano, Benito Arias, 430n46
Mordecai, 161
mortification, 4
Mortification of Sin in Believers (1656), 4
Moses, 55, 57, 133, 228, 230, 234, 243, 252, 308–9, 310, 323–25, 330, 421, 479
mosques, 65
Muhammad, 195n50
mulcts, 209n126
murder, 397n318
Murimuth, Adam, 138n151
Muslims, 11, 161, 207
mutineers, 87–89
mutiny, 82
Myslenta, Coelestin, 180n52

Nabal, 334
Nalton, James, 6, 22–23

names, 179
Naseby, 12, 40, 85n318, 220n10, 241
national judgment, 234
natural law, 88n332
nature, 332
Nebuchadnezzar, 45, 288, 307, 356, 468
Nedham, Marchamont, 78–79, 460n228
negligence, 452–53
Nehemiah, 24, 264, 321n71
Nero, 198, 252n78, 380
new covenant, 133, 420, 421
New Model Army, 12–13, 35, 36, 37, 38, 43, 71, 72, 220n10
Nicolaitanes, 199
Noah, 286, 450
nonconformity, 13
nonfundamental articles of faith, 202–5, 398n320
nontoleration, 59, 205, 339, 340–50
Novatian, 390n286, 391n287
Nye, Phillip, 48, 63

obedience, 137, 233, 271, 281, 299, 322
Oecumenius of Trikka, 423n14
Of Toleration: And the Duty of the Magistrate, about Religion (1649), 59–68, 81, 253n82, 271n138, 307n20, 316n51, 339–409
omnipotence, 285
Omri, 305
opposition, 129, 299, 309, 314, 326–27, 336–38, 391, 417, 462, 472–75, 481
oppression, 232, 267, 321
optimism, 87
ordinances, 58, 158, 328, 432, 466, 485
Origen, 117, 141n180
orthodoxy, 9, 14, 15, 26, 359
Ottoman Empire, 444n136
outward monuments, 392
Overton, Richard, 11, 12, 81, 82, 201n90
Ovid, 215n159, 337n125

pagans, 11, 161, 207, 362, 393, 395, 427, 429
Papacy, 31, 35, 77, 138, 144, 172n19, 192, 438n86
parable of the sower, 199n69
parable of the tares, 199n69, 403
Pareus, David, 424n20
parishes, 17, 30

Parker, Samuel, 1, 25n105, 52, 55n208, 220n7, 230n9, 251n75, 315n48, 330n96
Parliamentary County Committees, 187n10
parliamentary fasts, 458n217
past, 260
patience, 313
Paul
    at Athens, 358
    as blasphemer, 396
Paul the Deacon, 208n116, 367n155
peace, 200, 216, 306–7, 341, 432
peaceable error, 398–403
pecuniary mulcts, 209
paedobaptism, 67
Pelagianism, 169n3
Pepin the Short, 441n107
perishing things, 317, 318
persecution, 12, 41, 62, 64, 76, 181n58, 210n135, 214–15, 224n35, 253, 307, 321, 322, 328n90, 364, 372–74, 380–83, 417, 427n30, 429, 438–40
perseverance, 300, 417–21
Persius, 196n54
Peter, 285
Peter, Hugh, 16, 48
Pharaoh, 303, 323
Pharisees, 447, 448
Philip II, 439n97
Photinians, 367n149
Pico della Mirandola, Giovanni, 118n47
Pilate, Pontius, 317
Pindar, 183n64
Piscator, Johannes, 73, 123n83, 422n13
plagues, 427n30, 429
Plautus, 171n11
Pliny the Elder, 272n141
Plutarch, 114n32, 115n36, 174n28, 176n41, 220n6
Pneumatologia: Or, A Discourse concerning the Holy Spirit (1674), 2
Pocklington, John, 147n220
Pocock, J. G. A., 53
political events, 3
polity, 426
Polycarp, 64, 121n74, 374, 375n210
Polycrates of Ephesus, 281n179
Pomerius, Julianus, 256n98
Pompey the Great, 434n63
Powell, Vavasor, 27n107

power, 262, 471
praise, 464
prayer, 238, 480–81
preaching, 1–6, 58, 388, 396–97
pre-Constantinian church, 374–80
predestination, 125n96, 145
Presbyterianism, 17, 28, 67, 163n348, 165n362, 174n30, 189, 327n85
primary causation, 332
Prince, Thomas, 82
Priscillian, 173n24, 208n114, 370n178
prisoner exchange, 39n140, 45, 290n210
private house, 387
privileges, 160–61, 250
Prokop Holý, 374n200
Prokůpek, 374n200
promises, 135, 260, 267, 274–80, 286–88, 443–46
prophecy, 3
Prosper of Aquitaine, 25, 111n20, 124n91, 131–32n123, 134n135, 229n7, 231n12, 233n19
prosperity, 163, 237
protection, 322–29, 478–81, 486–87
Protestants, 180, 205, 207, 399, 444n140
providence, 43, 55, 111, 118, 129, 222, 223, 230n9, 244, 276, 277, 287, 298, 299, 309, 331, 380–83, 449, 470, 471, 475, 476–77, 486–87
providentialism, 6, 44n154
provinces, 17
Prynne, William, 21, 61, 137n147, 148n227, 200n80, 346n34, 348n43, 403n342
Pseudo-Justin Martyr, 269n135
Pseudo-Oecumenius, 116
Pseudo Prosper, 264n128
Pseudo-Tertullian, 176n39
public places, 392–93
punishment, 355, 400
purification, 461
Puritans, 62, 397
Putney Debates, 82

Quintilian, 477n64
Qur'an, 140

Rachel, 153
Rainolds, John, 342n13
Rainolds, William, 180n52

rebellion, 149, 150, 200, 279n168, 282, 320
recantation, 345, 350
Reformation, 127–29, 139
Reformed orthodoxy, 26
regicide, 51, 52, 55, 315n48, 328n87
Rehoboam, 306
religious anarchy, 200n84
religious coercion, 215–16, 355–72
religious persecution, 12
remnant, 186n9
Remonstrants, 32
repentance, 138, 231, 233, 345, 350
responsibilities, of civil magistrate, 388–89, 459–60
restoration, 428
revelation, 112, 243–44, 385
reverence, 231
Reynolds, Edwards, 233n18
Rich, Robert, 36
Ridley, Nicholas, 121n74, 212n148
righteousness, 264, 321, 432
rivers, 268, 282–83
Robinson, Robert, 2
Rollock, Robert, 73, 422n13
Roman Catholics, 11, 12, 25, 26, 32, 55, 63, 77, 79, 114n28, 116, 139, 145n197, 146, 202, 341, 342n16, 343, 345, 365, 392n288, 399, 438n85, 444n138
Roman Empire, 75, 76, 77, 220, 266n132, 289n209, 330, 434, 435, 436, 441, 456
Rowe, William, 39, 222
Rufinus of Aquileia, 210n128, 379n229, 379n230
ruin, 308–9
Rump Parliament, 397n317
Rupert (Prince), 72
Rushd, Ibn, 344n22
Rutherford, Samuel, 61, 171n18, 316n51, 327n85, 346n34, 348n43

Sabbatarianism, 147n225
sacramentarians, 180n53
sacraments, 58
Salem, 465–66
Saltmarsh, John, 11, 79
salvation, 2, 150, 158, 272, 277
Salvian of Marseilles, 204n104, 204n105, 204n106, 351n56

Samson, 89, 309, 445
Samuel, 56, 228, 308–9, 318n55, 330
Sánchez, Gaspar, 114n32, 116n41
sanctification, 419
Sapor I, 381n253
Sardanapalus, 87, 474
Satan, 75, 121, 274, 328
Saul, 318
Savoy Confession (1658), 68
Saxons, 142, 151, 441n114
Scaliger, Joseph Justus, 127n107
scandalous sins, 177n44
schism, 13
schismatics, 205, 253
Scobell, Henry, 295n4
Scotland, 252n77, 281, 327n85
Scott, David, 241n42
Scottish Covenanters, 9, 35, 40, 244n53
Scottish invasion, 247n60, 279
Scott, Jonathan, 460n228
seas, 270
secondary causes, 111, 332–33
Second Civil War, 37, 42, 43, 49, 51, 262–64, 320n67
Second Council of Ephesus (449), 203n100, 379n233
Second Council of Nicaea (787), 209n118, 379n233
Second Diet of Speyer (1526), 374n203
Sedgwick, Obadiah, 171n18
sedition, 33, 200, 211–14
Sedulius Scottus, 117
Seleucid Empire, 434n62
self-defense, 313n41
self-examination, 81, 338, 487
self-preservation, 88n332
self-seeking, 321–22
semi-Pelagianism, 111n20
Seneca, 265n129, 267n134, 291n214
Seneca the Younger, 289n209, 306n15, 403n338
Sennacherib, 86, 246, 463, 468
separation, 182
Sermon Preached [...] *January 31* (1649), 48–68, 86n328, 293–338
Servet, Miguel, 66, 368n158, 395n301
Sesostris, 396–97
Severus, Alexander, 383n264

Severus, Sulpicius, 173n24, 370n181, 381n250, 382
shaking, 422–28, 460–61
Shaking and Translating of Heaven and Earth (1649), 68–81, 252n80, 266n132, 297n3, 411–62, 466n14, 480n84, 481n87
Shelford, Robert, 146n214
Shelton, Ryan, 188n18
Short Defensative (1646), 24, 28–29, 169–83
sickness, 246
Sidney, Algernon, 460n228
siege warfare, 476n61
Simeon, 198n67
Simmons, Matthew, 52, 73
Simon the Zealot, 142n181
Simpson, Sidrach, 63
sin
  author of, 332
  of blasphemy, 344n28
  of kings, 305–8
  and liberty, 123
  of nations, 301
  as scandalous, 177n44
  as transgression of law, 333
sinful cares, 450–51
sinful people, 302–4
Sixtus IV (Pope), 439n97
Sixty-Seven Articles of (1523), 305n14
sleep, 471
Sleidanus, Johannes, 213n150, 313n41, 371n185
Socinianism, 35, 393
Socrates, 358
Socrates of Constantinople, 210n128
Socrates Scholasticus, 366n148, 378n228, 380n236, 391n287, 393n291
Sodom, 246
Solemn League and Covenant, 9, 22, 29, 42, 178n46, 251n74, 328n90
Somerset House, 55, 392
sorrow, 229–30, 232
sovereignty, 135, 262, 331–32, 338
Sozomen, 210n128
Spanish Inquisition, 439n97
Spencer, Edward, 444n140
spiritual means, 406
spiritual renewal, 308–9
Spittlehouse, John, 70
Staphylus, Friedrich, 363n128, 408n360

Stapleton, Thomas, 408n361
Stephens, Philemon, 23–24, 38, 52
strength, 477–78, 484
stubbornness, 315
Suárez, Franciscus, 135n139
Suetonius, 156n288, 298n12, 362n116, 380n240
suffering, 428
superstition, 137, 142, 143, 151, 162, 196, 256, 314, 355
Synod of Dordt, 32, 197

Tacitus, 192n33, 198n66, 215n157, 361, 362n116
Tedder, Richard, 146n214
Temple of Serapis, 393n291
temporal deliverance, 291–92
tenderness, 313
Tertullian, 64, 121n71, 128n110, 141n175, 144n193, 156n286, 179n48, 179n51, 191n30, 193n37, 228n4, 234–35n23, 238n35, 250n71, 252n78, 253n83, 278n158, 292n216, 304n11, 310n31, 311n34, 312n36, 330n100, 342n14, 357, 360, 377n219, 380, 381, 382, 383n261, 397n318
thankfulness, 240n40, 281, 291
Theban shield, 467
Themistus, 380n235
Theodoret, 65, 395n300, 468n28
Theodosian Code, 368n165, 369n167
Theodosius I, 390n286, 391n287, 393, 393n291
Theodosius II, 368n165
Theophanes the Confessor, 136n142, 208n116
Theophrastus, 118n47
Theophylact of Ohrid, 425n24
third commandment, 350
Third Punic War, 220n12
thirst, 284
Thirty-Nine Articles, 146n213
Thomas Aquinas, 113n27, 117n44, 135n140, 136, 264n128, 344n28, 346n38
Thomason, George, 13, 38
Thompson, James, 84
Thompson, William, 83, 84
Tibni, 305
toleration, 9–16, 26, 28, 31, 32, 59, 144n196, 171n18, 191–214, 350–83
Torquemada, Juan de, 388n282
tower of Babel, 409

Trajan, 380, 382
transformation, 260, 430–31
translation, 430
transubstantiation, 114
treason, 318n54
Tremellius, Immanuel, 430n46, 434n62
Tremellius-Junius Bible, 236n27, 477n63
Trevor-Roper, H. R., 22
Trinity, 35, 48n170, 395
Trojan horse, 28, 171
trust, 487–88
truth, 207–11, 216, 275, 325, 332, 355–72
Tweeddale, John, 73
Two Short Catechisms (1645), 23
tyranny, 54, 56, 57, 88, 143, 192, 206, 304–8, 314, 320, 454

Udall, Ephraim, 251n73
Ulster, 138n156, 327n85
Umar ibn al-Khattab, 195n49
unbelief, 318, 344n28, 348
"unction," 2
Underdown, David, 50
understanding, 453–59
uniformity, 407–8
unity of faith, 206
unworthiness, 134, 149
usury, 310
Uzziah, 41

vagabonds, 66, 156, 396–97
Valens, 62, 209n127, 210n128, 366n145, 380
Valentinian III, 368n166
Valerian, 381–82
Vandals, 62, 365n141, 366n143
Vane, Henry the Younger, 50
vanity, 332, 471, 472
Varro, Marcus Terentius, 356n78
Varthema, Ludovico di, 195n48
Varus, Publius Quinctilius, 221n14
Vásquez, Gabriel, 135n140
Vaudès, Pierre, 439n93
Venerable Bede, 116, 142n181
veneration of images, 379n233
vengeance, 457
victories, 328–29
Vincent of Lérins, 176n39
Vines, Richard, 24, 171n18
violence, 192, 354, 389, 390, 403

Virgil, 148n226, 172–73n23, 194n41, 196n55, 288n201
Visigoths, 441n117
vision, 112–14
Vision of Unchangeable Free Mercy (1646), 6–34, 103–65, 377n221, 465n12, 479n77
voluntary consent, 188n19

Waldensians, 62, 76, 210n135, 439, 439n93
Wales, 27n107, 163
Walwyn, William, 11, 58, 81, 82
Ward, Nathaniel, 251n74
Warren, John, 70, 442n124
waters, 270
weakness, 471, 472, 477–78
Webster, Tom, 52
Wentworth, Peter, 6–7, 23, 27n107
Westminster Assembly, 163n348, 177n44, 182n62, 186n8, 245n53
Westphal, Joachim, 180n53
Westrowe, Thomas, 6–7
Whalley, Edward, 82, 83
Whitaker, William, 407n354
White, Francis, 83
Whitelocke, Bulstrode, 50, 85, 86
wicked, 237, 317

wilderness, 162, 237, 283, 284
will, 334
William II, Prince of Orange, 80, 451n176, 456n203
William of Saint-Theirry, 425n24
Williams, Roger, 11, 31
Wilson, William, 38
Winstanley, Gerrard, 58, 77
wisdom, 156n285, 384
Wishart, George, 371n188
Witham, Thomas, 287n195
Wood, Anthony, 2, 54
Woodcock, Francis, 24
Worden, Blair, 50, 163n346
worship, 195, 306–7, 314, 389, 444, 467n23
worthiness, 134
wrath of God, 303, 328n90, 336, 386, 429, 457
Wyclif, John, 211n138, 363n124, 438

Zachary (Pope), 441n107, 442n120
Zerubbabel, 473
Zion, 465, 486n103
Žižka, Johann, 374n200
Zwingli, Huldrych, 113–14n28, 180n53, 305–6n14

Scripture Index

Genesis
1:10 . . . . 428n32
3 303
3:8 . . . . 154n271
3:15 . . . . 120n54, 274
3:24 . . . . 303n4
4:6 265
4:8 . . . . 122n79, 356n81
4:12 . . . . 156n291
4:26 . . . . 120n55
5:24 . . . . 120n58
5:25 . . . . 120n58
6:4 472
6:5 . . . . 120n57
6:12 . . . . 120n56
6:13 . . . . 450n171
6:18 . . . . 120n59
10:6 255
11:4 . . . . 445n149, 446n154
12:1 . . . . 120n60
12:7 273
13:14–15 273
14:13 444
15:2 . . . . 154n268
15:16 . . . . 237, 308
18:1–2 . . . . 113, 120n60
19:24 246
20:6 . . . . 263n125
21:16 . . . . 153n264
22:14 . . . . 286n192
22:39 . . . . 286n192
25:3–4 256
25:23 . . . . 131n120
25:29–34 . . . . 122n80
27:41 . . . . 265, 484
30:1 . . . . 153n262
32 484
32–33 . . . . 130n118
32:6 . . . . 484n96
32:10 275
32:11 . . . . 484n97
32:28 . . . . 465n9
33:4 484
35:18 . . . . 153n263
36:15 . . . . 238n36
37:3 . . . . 230n10
37:7 . . . . 149n230, 337n123
37:28 256
39:20–22 . . . . 154n265
43:34 . . . . 451n178
45:4–7 . . . . 123n85
45:7 . . . . 278n159
48:16 328
49:6–7 . . . . 198n67
49:10 . . . . 465n8
50:20 . . . . 278n159

Exodus
1:10 . . . . 264, 452, 477
2:15–16 256
3:2 243
3:17 273
5:2 472
5:21 324
8–10 246
8:19 . . . . 288, 470n40
9:15 . . . . 245n54
9:16 474
9:19–21 . . . . 337n126
10:2–3 261
10:17 . . . . 303n6
10:21–23 . . . . 155n273

SCRIPTURE INDEX 503

10:23	120n63, 163n347
11:5	323n77
12	261n113
12:11	114
12:41	236
14	261
14:11–13	324
14:13	272n139, 290n212
14:21	268, 444n135
14:25	127n105, 288, 484n98
14:27–28	477
14:28	246
14:30–31	261
15	262, 270, 468
15:14–16	257, 483
15:24	324
16:7	324
16:16–17	252n81
16:18	164n361
17:3	324
17:6	282
18	256
18:11	477
18:21	318n56
19:18–19	421n10
20:2	421
20:7	350n53
20:18	421n10
21:13	123
22:21	212n147
23:20–22	328
23:28	245
32:9–10	309
32:31	228
34:6–7	262

Leviticus

11:13–19	78, 446n157
19:34	212n147
24:10	344n25
24:15	396
24:16	344
26:22–25	245
26:24	303
26:25	245n54

Numbers

book of	257, 257n99
10:29–30	256
11:4	479n73
11:6–10	162n340
11:14–15	467n21
11:33	282n182
13:33	249n70
14	324n78
14:4	143n190, 324
14:9	254
16:2	472, 479n72
16:22	401n331
16:32	246
16:41	324
16:41–42	310
17	467
20:4	282
20:11	282
20:12	325
21:5	162n340
21:5–9	239
23:13–14	344
25	257n99
25:17	256
27	257n99
27:16	401n331
31	257n99
31:8	256

Deuteronomy

1	239n37
4:11	242
6:6	133
7:7	133
7:7–8	133, 281n176
7:8	133, 274
8:15	283
9:6	133n132
10:16	418n4
10:19	212n147
12:1–3	393
13	61, 348
13:1	348
13:2	349
13:5	348
14:11–18	78, 446n157
17:14	305
18	384
19:5	123
25:1–3	215n158
28:15	302

28:28–29	482
29:17	349n46
29:29	333
30:6	116n38, 418n4
32:4	275, 275n148, 460n233
32:14–15	232
32:32–33	160
33:15	249
33:16	244n51
33:17	243n47

Joshua

1:5	259, 323, 325
3:15–16	268, 444n135
5:13–15	113
7:21	251n74
9:3	249n69
10:11	246
10:12	271
10:18	159n314
22:4	274

Judges

1:7	476n60
4:21	471n43
5:9	487n108
5:20	246
5:23	316
5:31	280
6:36–40	143n185
6:37	120n64
8:16	149n231
11:23–24	254n87
11:24	250, 386
11:33	386
12:4–5	330n97
14:14	240n39, 283n186
16:19–20	471n42
16:19–21	487n110
16:20	487n111
16:28–29	445n148

1 Samuel

2:25	330
2:30	325, 480
4:3	355
4:21	466n15
6:9	288n197
8:5	303n7
8:5–7	330n98
8:7	305
12:23	228, 309
14:15	425n25
14:25	425n25
14:45	306
14:47	479n74
15	318
16:14	338n129, 479n75
16:14–16	483n92
17:7–10	470n37
17:37	241
17:39	174n26
25:37	334
27:1–2	451n180

2 Samuel

5:24	255n94
7:18	262n114
7:21	274
15:3–6	149n233
15:4	299n16
15:31	476n57
18:3	222n22
19:30	467n24
21:17	222n23
23:3	384
23:4	384n268
24:13	245n54
24:15	234n22

1 Kings

6:7	127n103
9:28	130n117
10:27	450n173
11:38	323
12	306
13:4	334
16:21–22	305
18	334n115
18:17	214n152
20:30	246
22:19–21	123n85
22:27–28	154n267

2 Kings

1:10–11	246
1:12	334
2:14	242, 258, 260n111

2:24	246
4:6	487n109
4:13–14	154n269
4:40	146n216, 282n184
5:18–19	123n85
6:17	247, 268
6:33	311, 312n37
7:2	458n213
7:6–7	483
7:19	458n213
10:16	325n79
10:29–31	325n79, 480n79
14:7	473
14:8	473
14:9	473
17:25	246
18:33–34	356
19:9	255n96
19:35	463n2
20–21	54
21:3	306
21:6	305
21:9	305
21:11	304
21:16	306
22:19–20	337n127
23:26–27	304

1 Chronicles
12:32	448
13:2	306
13:2–4	306n16
14:12	355

2 Chronicles
3:6	128n110
14:11	221n18
15:2	323, 325, 480n78
17:6	393
17:7–9	385n272
17:8–10	385
25:2	476
26:18	41
30:6–8	385
30:6–9	385n273
30:14	393
32:21	270
32:25	234n22, 240, 463n3
33	54

33:4	465n10
35:21–22	478n67

Ezra
book of	127
3:12–13	230
7:26	398n321

Nehemiah
book of	127
2	128n110
2:10	264n127
3:5	385n270
4:10	264
4:16	297
4:17	127n104
5:14–15	321

Esther
1:13	448n164
6:10	149n234
6:11	161n329
6:13	265
7:10	468

Job
1:18–21	154n266
5:6–7	246
7:12	122n81
9:4	477
9:12	332
14:4	234n21, 332n106
14:5	123n84
15:15–16	234n21
15:26	473n47
18:14	476n59
29:14–15	322
29:17	481
31:26	242
31:40	144n194
32:21	171n15
33:13	332
33:15	113
41:24	322n74

Psalms
book of	1
1:1	319n64
2	327, 329

2:4	438n84	65:1	467
2:5	438n84	65:5	230
2:6	429n42, 432n51	68	425n25
2:8	388	68:8	269, 427n29
2:9	479n69	68:9	425n25
2:9–12	440n104	68:12	271
2:10–11	328, 389	68:13–14	474
2:12	329n92, 480	68:17	243, 247, 268
4:3	265	68:26	467
4:6	157n300	68:29	466
7	229	68:30	472
7:9	237n31	69:27	334
7:15	264n126	72:11	480n82
11:6	245	73:13	311
13:3	471	73:15	313
14	259	73:25	157n303
15:4	275	74:13–14	240
16:11	157n304	74:14	259n108
18:4	242	74:19	110n16
18:8	245	75:10	243n47
18:10	268	76	86, 101, 463
18:11–12	242	76:1	464, 466
18:13–14	242	76:1–2	101, 120n60, 464
18:16–17	242	76:2	464, 466
22:3	219n4, 467n25	76:3	101, 463, 464, 468, 469
23:4	163n344	76:3–6	468
29:9	467	76:4	464
31:5	275	76:5	463, 469, 470n38, 470n41, 486n106
33:10–11	478		
33:11	123	76:5–6	101, 464, 468
36:6	126, 312	76:6	477n63, 486n105
42:1–2	158n306	76:7	464
42:6	242	76:8–9	464
43:3	244	76:10	123n85, 263n125, 279n167, 464
45:6	432n54		
45:16	440n105	76:11	464
46:6	261	76:12	464
46:6–8	261	77:9	232
46:7	261	77:19	447n160
46:8	261	78:15–16	283
48:8	244	78:49	246
48:12–14	89, 486	80:6	110
49:14	159, 159n316	80:6–9	110
50:3	312	80:7	110
55:6	311	80:8	110
58:11	288n196	80:10	110n5
61:2–3	228	83:6–8	475
62:4	336	84:1–4	158n306
63:8	453n187	84:11	328n88

87:2	465n11	5:20	229, 229n6
87:4	240	7:23	159
89:10	240	8:31	121n73, 157n302
89:49	275	11:8	219n1
97:1–4	243	11:18	217
99:8	230	15:8	467n26
102	228, 228n5	16:2	234n21
102:13–14	236	16:33	123n84
103:13–14	326n83	17:15	316
104:3	268	18:10	130n115, 228n3
105:14–15	250	19:21	123n84
105:15	252n80, 459n225	21:1	123n84
106:15	282n183	21:30	123n84
107	449	22:13	417n2
107:34	138n150	23:5	156n284
107:40	483n94	24:24	316
107:43	280n171, 449n167	25:2	316
108:13	110n9	25:18	171n16
110:2	432n51	26:7	467
111:2	455n201	26:9	467
114:4	269	26:13	417n2
114:5	268	30:9	232
114:8	283	30:33	171n13
115	242n45		
115:1	242n45	*Ecclesiastes*	
115:2	326n82	1:9	310n29
115:3	331, 333	3:3	236n29
116:7	418n3	3:11	232
116:11	311	7:7	321
118:23	277n157, 338n132	7:26	123n85
124:7	248n68	11:6	238
125:3	223n34	12:6	482n89
125:4	328n89		
136	259	*Song of Solomon*	
137:7	89, 466n19	2:2	110n14
137:8	445n147		
137:9	445n147	*Isaiah*	
138:6	384n269	1:1	112n24
145:13	432n54	1:18–19	432n55
147:19–20	120	2:2	161n332, 432, 461n241
149	42	2:13	262n115
149:5–6	467	4:4	141n177, 314n42, 327n86, 461n242
149:6–8	42	4:5	466
149:7–9	276	5:2–4	152n252
		5:2–6	162n337
Proverbs		5:5	144n195
1:15	340n5	5:20	316n50
1:26–27	231	6:1	113
5:19	229n6		

Reference	Page
6:9–10	126
6:9–11	123n85
6:10–11	330
6:13	152
7:2	475
7:9	325n80
8:9	478
8:18	310, 319
9:2	134n135
9:5	428n36
9:7	432n54
10:5–6	152n258
10:6	473
10:7	336
11:5	432n55
11:6	432n55
11:7	432n55
11:8	432n55
11:9	432n55
11:10	432n55
13:13	427n29
13:21	160n320
13:21–22	160n320
14:12–15	427
17:6	186n9
18:18	432n55
18:19	432n55
19:3	483
19:13–14	279, 483
19:16	483
19:18–19	432n55
23:9	299, 327, 450n172, 462n247
24:16	223n33
26:11	264
26:12	111, 254n90, 418
26:20	337n128
27:1	474n51
27:9	237
28:16	237n33
28:21	235
28:29	280
29:8	471
29:13	458n218
30:18–19	432n55
31:2	477
33:11	483n93
33:14	245
33:20–24	436
34:2	426n27
34:4	426
34:4–5	298n9
34:7–8	438
34:8	266, 459n224
34:13–14	160n320
34:14	160n320
35:3–4	329
36:6	344
36:10	478
37:9	255n96
37:10	473
37:12	473
37:31	443n132
37:35–36	468, 477n62
37:36	246, 247, 478n66
38:12	146n216
40:2	237
40:3	457n212
40:28–31	287
41:18	283
41:14–16	286
43:3–4	261
43:4	465
43:16–18	241
43:20	283
43:24	150n242
43:25	150n241
45:1	479n76
45:9	477
45:11	448
45:13	448, 448n166, 479n76
46:10	119, 119n52, 123, 332
46:12	469
47:1–3	438n84
47:7–9	445n147
48:21	283
49:7	440n105
49:8	236n30
49:15–16	235n25
49:16–17	235
49:18–22	432n56
49:22–23	432n57
49:23	354n72, 388n279, 389, 440n105
49:26	438n84
50:11	336n119
51	75
51:1	141n178

51:9	260n112	3:15	2
51:9–10	239	3:22	315n47
51:12	318	4:19	428n36
51:15–16	426	4:23–25	427
51:20	303n5	7:4	153n259
52:7	162n339	9:2	312n39
53:1	141n174	13:23	255n96
53:2	109n3, 110n4, 110n12, 313	14:17	228
53:3–5	110n9	15:1	97, 302, 308, 308n24
53:4–5	283	15:2	302
53:6	304	15:3–10	96, 302
54:1–3	432n56	15:4	96, 302, 304
54:11	110n9	15:5	302
54:11–12	432n56, 432n56	15:5–6	302
54:11–13	433n58	15:6	96, 302, 304
54:15	261	15:6–9	302
54:17	325, 487n107	15:9	427
58:11	143n186	15:10	97, 302, 309
58:12	321n70	15:11–14	97, 302, 314
60	436	15:15–18	97, 302, 309, 311
60:12	271, 389, 429n42, 436, 480n82	15:18	456n206
		15:19	314n43, 314n45, 405n347
60:16–17	389, 432n56	15:19–20	53, 301
60:17	435n74, 459n226	15:19–21	97, 302, 314
60:17–18	428, 436, 440	15:20	314n44, 315n46, 322n76, 326n84, 329n94, 479n71, 480n83, 485
60:20	427n29		
60:21	461		
62:7	309n27		
63:4	438	16:5	330
65:13–15	264	17:6	320n69
65:25	433, 451n175	17:9	171n14
66:6	466	17:13	465n13
66:14	411	17:16	228
66:16	411	22:24	322n75
66:20–21	440	23:21	253n84
66:21	432n57	23:28	115
66:22–24	428n31	23:29	352n62
66:24	158n311	26:10–11	401
68:8	425n25	26:16	306, 401
		30:9	443n133
Jeremiah		31:23–25	436
1:11	113n25	32:39	199n77
1:13	113n25	43:2	472
2:5	320	48:10	315n49
2:11	320	49:7	238n36
2:13	153n260	49:7–8	452n182
3:9	349n47	50:6	111
3:14	315n47	50:28	267, 466

Reference	Page
50:33–34	438n84
51:6	445n147
51:7	454n196
51:24–25	438n84
51:25	427
51:25–26	445n147
51:31–32	444n137
51:34–35	438n84
51:35	267, 439n99

Lamentations
Reference	Page
2:17	302

Ezekiel
Reference	Page
1	113, 118n49
1:5–7	113n25
1:20–21	125n92
2	235
2:5	126n101
2:10	235n24
3:5	134
3:8–9	323
4:16	149n232
6:3	128n110
7	128n110
10:15–19	466n17
10:18	151n245
14:14	190n26
14:19	245n54
14:20	190n26
15:2–3	439n101
16:3	141n179
16:6	150n237
18:8	310n32
18:31	418n4
20:38	466n18
22:14	477
31:8	126n98
32:7	427
32:7–8	427n28
34:23	443n133
36:26	116n38, 150n240, 418n4
36:32	111
37:3	286, 290n213
37:5	143n184, 150n238
37:12–13	286, 286n193
37:24–25	443n133
39	270
39:17–19	160n322
43:9–11	432n57
48:35	432n56

Daniel
Reference	Page
book of	210n134, 307n22
1:2	383n265
2	76
2:32	357n86
2:34	462n245
2:34–35	435n67
2:35	109
2:38	356n84
2:41	441n112
2:42	440n102
2:44	101, 432, 434
3:11	214n155
3:14	357n85
3:20	307
3:24	357
3:26	288
4:13–15	152n251
4:33	270
4:33–34	468
5:2	251n72
5:3	383n265
5:23	383n265
5:23–30	251n72
5:25–27	161n328
6	357
6:5	311
6:26	288
7:8–9	113n25
7:9	474n55
7:24	435n71
7:25	435n68, 435n73
7:26	435n72
7:27	298n4, 435
7:28	436n75
8:8	357n88
8:22	357n88
9	127, 127n107
9:2	148n229, 449
9:2–3	238
9:21	449, 449n168
9:23	127, 236, 449, 449n169
9:24	236, 449, 449n170

9:25 . . . . 127, 128n109, 148n229, 297, 460n235
10:5–6 113
11:10 223
11:27 . . . . 452n183
11:31 . . . . 147n218, 147n219
11:38 . . . . 147n219
12:10 . . . . 223n32, 437
12:13 . . . . 460n234

Hosea
2:5–9 . . . . 159n318
2:21–22 272
3:5 . . . . 443n133
5:11 305
5:15 . . . . 231n14
11:8 . . . . 142n183
11:8–9 . . . . 137n145
11:12 . . . . 248, 319
13:5 283
13:6 232
13:10–11 303
13:11 54
14:3 328
14:9 447

Joel
2:10 . . . . 427n29
2:25 246
2:28 . . . . 132n126

Amos
1:1 . . . . 112n24
1:3 236
1:9 308
3:2 . . . . 161, 161n333
3:7 . . . . 243, 453n189
3:8 235
5:18 . . . . 313, 459n222
5:19 . . . . 247, 303
5:20 313
9:9 . . . . 308n26, 458n221, 465
9:11 . . . . 432n56, 443n133
9:11–15 436

Obadiah
1 . . . . 112n24
3 476

4 . . . . 427n29
9 . . . . 238n36
21 . . . . 432n54

Jonah
4:6 . . . . 299n13
4:10 . . . . 329n91

Micah
4:1 . . . . 432n55
6:9 . . . . 455n202
7:18 235

Nahum
1:1 . . . . 112n24

Habakkuk
1:5–12 234
2:3 . . . . 236, 237n34
2:14 . . . . 450n174
2:20 . . . . 425n25
3 229
3:1 . . . . 93, 225n1, 227
3:1–9 225
3:1a 93
3:1b 93, 229
3:2 . . . . 94, 225n1, 227, 233, 234
3:2a 94, 234
3:2b 94, 235
3:3 . . . . 40, 94, 225n1, 238, 241n43
3:3–17 . . . . 94, 227, 238
3:4 . . . . 94, 225n1, 242
3:5 . . . . 94, 225n1, 272
3:6 . . . . 94, 225n1, 248
3:6–8 227
3:7 . . . . 95, 225n1, 255, 257, 267n133
3:8 . . . . 95, 225n1, 267, 444n135
3:9 . . . . 96, 220n9, 225n1, 272, 282n181
3:9a 96, 273
3:9b 96, 282
3:10 . . . . 268, 269
3:14 344
3:15 268
3:16 234

Zephaniah
2:1 .... 297n2
2:2 .... 236, 308, 462n246

Haggai
1:2 128
2:6 .... 421, 431n48
2:6–7 .... 74, 424

Zechariah
book of 345n33
1:8 .... 113n25
1:18 .... 243n47
2:1 .... 113n26
2:7 .... 445n147
3:9–10 .... 113n25
4:6 .... 143n188
4:7 .... 110n7, 110n9,
                          127n106, 271,
                          337n124, 369n172, 473
5:6–8 237
5:7 .... 304n10
12:2–4 .... 438n84
12:3 .... 482n90, 486n102
12:4 482
13:1 .... 346n34
13:2 .... 346n34
13:3 .... 345, 346n34, 347,
                          347n41
13:4 .... 346n34
13:5 .... 346n34
13:6 .... 61, 346n34, 347,
                          347n41
14:6–7 .... 40, 129, 232
14:9–11 .... 433n58
14:12 .... 438n84
14:16 440

Malachi
3:1 .... 456n208
3:1–4 138
3:2–3 267
3:3 .... 143n187, 432n57
3:4 .... 121n72
3:6 123
3:15 159
4:1 .... 461n240
4:2 .... 111n21, 121n72

Matthew
1:17 .... 120n62
2:2 .... 423n15
2:19 113
3:1–8 .... 454n191
4:16–17 154
5:13 .... 160n323
6:13 .... 456n204
6:23 .... 154n272
6:33 .... 458n216
7:16–18 .... 332n104
7:21 .... 161n334
7:21–22 .... 152n257
7:25–26 .... 157n297
7:26–27 .... 156n282
8:9 .... 247n59
8:34 .... 162n341
9:17 .... 244nn50, 326n81
9:37 .... 164n351
10:16 .... 110n15
10:25 .... 179n50
10:29 .... 123n84
10:34 297
11:21 .... 116, 126n100, 134
11:25–26 .... 124, 132, 133
11:26 .... 117n46, 140, 332
12:24–27 .... 179n50
13:7 .... 199n69
13:22 .... 199n69
13:24–30 .... 403n341
13:27–28 .... 199n69
13:30 .... 211n142
13:46 .... 158n307
15:14 .... 305n12
15:26–27 .... 155n274
15:27 .... 163n349
16:18 .... 157n297, 275n151,
                          283, 432, 485n100
17:9 113
21:13 .... 203nn101
21:21 .... 476n58
21:41 .... 138n153, 151n244
22:13 .... 158n309
22:21 .... 252n79
23:2 .... 447n161
23:4 .... 181n59
23:15 .... 164n353
23:23 .... 163n342
24 455

24:6–7 . . . . 428n36
24:7 . . . . 245n54, 425n25,
 429n38
24:14 . . . . 455n200
24:15 . . . . 126n101, 147n218, 455
24:24 . . . . 199n70
24:29 . . . . 427n29
24:40 . . . . 122n78
27:45 . . . . 423n16
27:51–52 . . . . 423n17
28:2 113
28:19 . . . . 133n129
28:20 . . . . 440n104

Mark
1:2–3 . . . . 453n190
1:3 . . . . 457n212
9:43–44 . . . . 158n311
12:34 . . . . 432n53
16:15 . . . . 121n70, 133

Luke
1:79 . . . . 135n138, 154n272,
 160n324
2:1 . . . . 429n39
2:2–3 . . . . 117n45
2:34 . . . . 126n101, 422n12
3:5 . . . . 110n8
3:15 . . . . 456n207
6:20 . . . . 432n53
6:45 . . . . 319n61
7:30 . . . . 162n335
8:37 . . . . 139n157
9:54 403
9:62 . . . . 244n49
10:42 . . . . 161n331
12:49 . . . . 139n158
12:54–56 447
12:56 . . . . 448n163
13:1 . . . . 367n152
13:7 . . . . 152n253
13:7–9 . . . . 162n336
13:19 . . . . 110n6
16:24 . . . . 158n310
16:29–30 . . . . 448n162
17:20–21 432
17:21 . . . . 175n33, 458n214
18:7 . . . . 439n100
19:42 . . . . 334n117

21 455
21:20 455
21:24 302
21:25 . . . . 427n29
21:28 . . . . 455n200
21:28a 451n177
21:28b 451n179
23:44–45 . . . . 423n16

John
1:3–5 . . . . 157n294
1:5 155
1:12 259
2:20 128
3:19 . . . . 138n154
4:14 . . . . 156n280
4:22 . . . . 120n61
4:34 . . . . 164n358
5:14 . . . . 281n180
5:35 . . . . 454n192
6:35 . . . . 163n345
6:50 . . . . 155n279
7:37–38 . . . . 156n280
8:44 . . . . 156n292, 265
8:56 . . . . 257n100, 258
10 . . . . 346, 425n24
10:1 . . . . 346n35
10:1–5 . . . . 425n24
10:16 . . . . 443n132
11:48 317
12:32 . . . . 121n68, 132n126,
 133n130
12:35 . . . . 243n48
12:37–42 . . . . 126n102
12:41 113
12:41–42 126
14:2 . . . . 259n109
14:5 . . . . 156n290
14:31 133
15:6 . . . . 157n296, 199n79
17:32 . . . . 132n126, 132n126
19:12 317
19:34 . . . . 284n188

Acts
1:7 . . . . 429n38
1:14 . . . . 386n276
2:5–7 422
2:36 . . . . 432n51

2:46	386n276
2:47	126
3:6	115n34
3:21	433n59
4	124n90, 156
4:7	265
4:12	124n90, 156n289
4:27–28	123, 278n160
5:5	209n123
5:24	265
5:38–39	206n110
8:9–24	126n99
10:43	133
11:18	418n4
12	285
12:6	285n191
12:7	113
12:11	285
12:12	285
12:15	285
12:16	286
12:23	246, 247n61, 468, 477
13:11	209n124
13:36	452n184
13:41	139
13:46	126n100, 139
13:48	126
13:51	139
14	358
14:16	124, 138n149, 334n116
14:16–17	132n125
15	203
15:18	111, 123, 254
16	115n33
16:9	109n1
16:10	112, 115
16:11	109
16:14	150n240
16:19–20	358n99
16:21	359
17:5	396
17:18	358n95
17:30	121n69
17:30–31	132n125
18:6	345n30
18:10	125
18:15	359n101
19	482
19:29–34	482n91
19:40	482n91
20:3	452n185
20:20	187n12
24:5	214n153
24:14	179n51
26:11	345n30
26:18	154n272
28:22	179n51
28:28	139

Romans

1:5	132n126
1:24	334
1:25	343
1:26	334
2:5	303
2:19	154n272
3	120
3:2	120n65
3:19	140n166
3:23	140n167
8:3	121n67
8:24	423n19
8:28	275n150, 423n19
8:28–29	125n93
8:30	258
8:31	280n170
8:32	132n126, 274n146
8:37	222n26
9	140
9:4	120
9:5	421n7
9:11	433
9:13	133n127
9:17	334
9:18	120n53, 134n133, 140n168, 332, 334
9:20	134n133, 332
9:22	124, 334
9:23	126n101
9:30–31	134
10:15	162n339
11:8	471
11:15	432n56
11:22	151n249, 335
11:33	134, 141n176
12:18	171n8
13	61, 98, 347

13:4................. 200n83, 386n275, 387n278
14:17 .... 432, 458n215
15:6.................. 386n276
16:26 .... 132n126

1 Corinthians
1:24.................. 274n144
1:25–26 .... 132n124
1:27.................. 247n63
1:29.................. 140n165
1:30.................. 156n281
2:22.................. 260
3:11.................. 461n239
3:12–15 .... 156n283
3:22.................. 260n110
4:7 .... 140, 150n236
4:12.................. 201n92
4:13.................. 466n20
6:9–10................ 135n137
6:9–11................ 116, 135
6:11.................. 135n137
10:4.................. 283
10:11 .... 306n18
11:19 403
11:26 .... 440n104
12:2.................. 124n88, 134
15:24–27 .... 432n51
15:33 .... 201n87

2 Corinthians
1:9 241
1:10.................. 241
4:4................... 110n11, 401n330
4:6................... 385n271
4:13.................. 447n158
4:18.................. 446n156
10:4.................. 199n78, 401n333
11:24 .... 215n158

Galatians
1:6 .... 430n44
4:4 .... 121n66
5 .... 202n93
5:19.................. 199n76, 201n85
5:19–21 153
5:22–23 153
6:16.................. 468n27

Ephesians
1:4................... 125n93
1:10.................. 423n14
1:11.................. 111, 122, 333
2:1................... 125n95, 150n239, 157n293
2:11.................. 125n95
2:12.................. 155
2:14–15 .... 133n128
4:3................... 352n64
4:8................... 485
4:11–13 .... 440n104
4:18.................. 157n294
5:2................... 447n159
5:8................... 154n272, 453n188
5:11.................. 453n188
6:17.................. 352n63

Philippians
1:18.................. 164n360, 396n313
1:29.................. 150n240
2:1–2 .... 488n114
2:5 .... 164n357
2:13.................. 150n240

Colossians
1:13.................. 154n272
1:20.................. 297n1
2:3 .... 274n147

1 Thessalonians
1:3 .... 418n4
2:16.................. 155n275
5:5................... 453n188
5:14.................. 396
5:21.................. 300n20, 409n362

2 Thessalonians
1:11.................. 418n4
2 .... 121, 124n89 137, 139, 139n159
2:3 .... 298n7, 378n224, 445n146, 469n30
2:3–4 .... 211n141
2:6................... 429n41
2:6–7 .... 441n109
2:7................... 209n122, 211n141, 377n223, 443n130
2:10–11 .... 139n160

2:11 .... 137n148, 443n128
2:12 .... 124n89
3:2 396
3:7 .... 396n310
3:11 .... 396n310

1 Timothy
1:9 396
1:13 .... 345n30, 396n303
2:2 .... 385n274
2:4 .... 111n20
3:16 .... 175n36
4:2 .... 201n86
4:7 .... 199n73
5:8 .... 396n311
5:13 .... 396n311
5:17 .... 201n91
6:3 .... 196n53, 199n68, 404n346
6:4 .... 199n73
6:13–14 .... 440n104

2 Timothy
2:17 .... 199n75
2:19 .... 125n94
2:25 .... 187n14, 403n340
3:5 .... 147n222, 175n36, 458n219
3:6 .... 396n314
4:2 .... 187n13
4:17–18 241

Titus
2:11–12 133
3:9 .... 163n343, 199n73
3:10 .... 198n61, 403n339
3:11 .... 202n94, 399n325

Philemon
7 .... 488n113
20 .... 488n113

Hebrews
1 421
1–3 419
1:1 .... 112, 419
1:1–14 .... 421n8
1:2 388
1:3 .... 333, 419

2:1–2 419
2:3 419
2:14 419
2:17 420
3:12–13 419
4:16 .... 299n17
5:7 .... 308n25
6 162
6–10 419
6:6 .... 211n136, 420
6:7–8 .... 153, 162n338
6:9 .... 251n76
6:18 .... 430n44
7 420
7:12 .... 430n44
7:16 420
7:22 420
7:25 .... 110n13
8:6 420
8:10 419
8:12 419
8:13 420
9:14 419
10:16 419
10:18 419
10:26–27 420
10:29 .... 137n146, 420
10:31 421
10:36 .... 417n1
10:37 .... 460n231
11 420
11:1 .... 240, 258
11:3 258
11:5 .... 430n44
11:34 .... 126n97
12:2 .... 157n299
12:10–11 .... 231n14
12:11 .... 130n116
12:12 .... 460n230
12:16 .... 122n80
12:18–20 421
12:21 234
12:25 421
12:26 .... 421, 423, 431n49
12:26–27 .... 224n36, 297n3, 478n68
12:27 .... 74, 140n162, 417, 421, 421n11, 423, 431, 474n54
12:28 .... 298n8, 431, 446n155

12:29 245
13:5 259

James
1:17 123
3:11 .... 332n105
3:16 307
3:17 .... 153, 307
5:5 .... 160n321

1 Peter
1:6 .... 231n14
1:12 .... 274n145, 422
2:7 .... 126n101
2:8 126
2:12 .... 224n38
3:16 .... 224n37
4:10 303
4:15 394
5:8 .... 116n37

2 Peter
2:1 .... 199n70
2:1–2 .... 199n74
2:3 .... 469n32
3:11 .... 461n244
3:12–13 447
3:13 .... 428, 432

1 John
2:11 .... 157n295
2:26 .... 199n72
2:27 .... 425n24
3:4 .... 119n51, 333, 333n110
3:13 .... 110n10
3:15 469
4:1 .... 199n71, 199n72

Jude
3 .... 351n55, 374n206
4 .... 126, 430n44
6 .... 155n277

Revelation
book of 427
1:8 .... 157n298
1:13–15 113
1:14–17 432
1:18 .... 432n51

2:4–5 137
2:5 .... 138n155, 150n243, 466n16
2:5–6 .... 199n72
2:6 .... 199n72
2:10 .... 110n10
2:15 .... 199n72
2:15–16 .... 199n72
2:17 .... 155n279
2:27 .... 479n69
3:10 .... 456n205
3:15–16 139
3:17 .... 158n312
3:18 .... 158n313
4 432
5:9 .... 133n131
6:9–10 .... 209n119, 307n23
6:10 439
6:12–15 .... 75, 427, 429
6:12–17 266
6:13 .... 460n236
6:16 .... 158n309, 270n136
6:17 .... 438, 457
8:12 .... 427n29
8:13 .... 427n29
9:3–11 .... 164n356
9:7–11 .... 446n153
9:10–19 .... 209n121
10:9 .... 159n317
11 267
11:1–2 432
11:2 .... 444n139
11:3 .... 330n101, 368n162
11:12 .... 427n29
11:13 425
11:15 .... 75, 81, 432, 440, 459n223, 462n248
12:4 .... 298n11
12:6 .... 369n171
12:16 425
13:1–7 .... 435n69
13:3 .... 176n40
13:4 .... 402n337
13:11 .... 357n90
13:12 429
13:15–16 .... 442n126
13:16–17 359
13:17 .... 140n163
13:18 .... 457n211

Reference	Pages
14:4	337n122, 364n136
14:6–7	445
16:10	121, 243n48
16:12	270, 444
16:13–14	253n85
16:16	298n10
16:19–20	267
17	76, 436
17:1	428n33
17:1–2	445n147
17:3–16	435n69
17:4	454n196, 481n85
17:5	469n31
17:6	442n107
17:12	436
17:12–13	368n157, 430
17:12–14	330n99, 436, 436n77
17:12–17	431
17:13	402n337, 436, 441n118, 457n209, 481n86
17:14	276n153, 388n283, 430, 431, 437, 440n104, 460n232, 474n52, 475, 480n81
17:15	379n234
17:16	430, 431, 437, 440n103, 446, 454n197
17:17	474
18:2	78, 429n42, 437, 446n157
18:3	440n106
18:4	445
18:6	437, 437n82, 438n84
18:9	437, 437n81
19:13	76, 437, 438n83
19:18	271, 439
20:4	209n120
20:11	427n29
21:1	428
21:3	400, 432n57
22:8	113
22:15	155n274
22:16	474n53